NORTH INDIA
HUMAN DEVELOPMENT REPORT

AF838643

NCAER PROJECT TEAM

Project Director
Abusaleh Shariff

Co-ordinator
Tarujyoti Buragohain

STUDY TEAM

Haryana
G. Chakrabarty
P. N. Magon
Tarujyoti Buragohain
Shanta Venkatram

Himachal Pradesh
G. Chakrabarty
D. K. Pant
A. C. Mallick
Tarujyoti Buragohain
B. L. Joshi

Punjab
G. Chakrabarty
Rajeshwari
Tarujyoti Buragohain
B. L. Joshi

Uttar Pradesh
G. Chakrabarty
P. K. Ghosh
Tarujyoti Buragohain
Rajesh Jaiswal

Assisted by S. K. Bathla, P. N. Magon, and Jaya Koti. Editorial help from Geeta Sant and Navratan Singh is grateful acknowledged.

NORTH INDIA
HUMAN DEVELOPMENT REPORT

National Council of Applied Economic Research

OXFORD
UNIVERSITY PRESS

OXFORD
UNIVERSITY PRESS
YMCA Library Building, Jai Singh Road, New Delhi 110001

Oxford University Press is a department of the University of Oxford. It furthers the University's objective of excellence in research, scholarship, and education by publishing worldwide in

Oxford New York

Athens Auckland Bangkok Bogota Buenos Aires Cape Town
Chennai Dar es Salaam Delhi Florence Hong Kong Istanbul Karachi
Kolkata Kuala Lumpur Madrid Melbourne Mexico City Mumbai Nairobi
Paris São Paulo Shanghai Taipei Tokyo Toronto Warsaw

with an associated company in Berlin

Oxford is a registered trade mark of Oxford University Press
in the UK and in certain other countries

Published in India
by Oxford University Press, New Delhi

© National Council of Applied Economic Research 2003

The moral rights of the author have been asserted
Database right Oxford University Press (maker)
First published in India 2003

All rights reserved. No part of this publication may be reproduced, stored in a retrieval system, or transmitted, in any form or by any means, without the prior permission in writing of Oxford University Press, or as expressly permitted by law, or under terms agreed with the appropriate reprographics rights organization. Enquiries concerning reproduction outside the scope of the above should be sent to the Rights Department, Oxford University Press, at the address above

You must not circulate this book in any other binding or cover and you must impose this same condition on any acquirer

ISBN 019 566194 X

Typeset in Garamond 10.5 on 12, by Excellent Laser Typesetters, Delhi 110 034
Printed at Roopak Printers, Delhi 110 032
Published by Manzar Khan, Oxford University Press
YMCA Library Building, Jai Singh Road, New Delhi 110 001

Foreword

The Human Development Report (HDR), published annually by the United Nations Development Programme (UNDP), defines 'development' as a process of widening people's choices. The HDRs propose a human development index (HDI) which combines the indicators corresponding to three critical choices: (i) to have access to income and assets needed for a decent standard of living, (ii) to acquire knowledge, and (iii) to enjoy a long and healthy life.

The National Council of Applied Economic Research (NCAER) has undertaken a major initiative, in collaboration with the Planning Commission, the United Nations Development Programme (UNDP), and other United Nations agencies to prepare the required database to develop a human development profile for the country. This book provides data on major indicators of human development in the north Indian states of Haryana, Himachal Pradesh, Punjab, and Uttar Pradesh. Each state profile consists of three chapters. The first chapter presents in a systematic manner various indicators of social concern, namely, education, health, and material well-being, disaggregated at the district level. The data gaps and deficiencies of secondary sources have been indicated. Some of the data gaps have been filled by NCAER surveyed data on population groups within the state. The NCAER survey discussed in the second chapter covers 'levels of living' which can be measured on the basis of household income, ownership of land and other durable assets, and other basic household amenities, such as literacy and enrolment pattern in different type of schools and household expenditure on education. The report also provides information on demographic characteristics, expenditure on short and long duration morbidity, and immunization patterns of both mother and child among different income groups. The third chapter for each state is a qualitative study of two villages and provides the grass root reality about the perception of education, health-seeking behaviour and social security.

I would like to express my deep appreciation of the dedicated work put in by G. Chakrabarty in coordinating secondary data collection and early collation of the reports; Shanta Venkataraman, B. L. Joshi, and Rajesh Jaishawal who managed the village studies for this report; and Tarujyoti Burgohain who brought the material together for publication in final form. The early part of the work was done under the dedicated overall supervision of S. P. Pal. It is only through the persistent efforts of Abusaleh Shariff that this work has reached its final publication stage.

SUMAN BERY

Preface

The measurement and analysis of socio-economic development is one of the major themes of development literature. The study of social indicators has contributed to a better understanding of the development process and the evolution of a framework for social indicator analysis. During the past four decades, attempts have been made at the macro level to improve the social statistical system, refine the concepts of development, identify social indicators for each area of concern, and select measures to construct indices of development. In the process, the general focus has shifted from economic growth to social development, equity, and social justice.

While economic parameters such as gross domestic product (GDP) and per capita and growth rate of GDP have not been unimpressive in the Indian context since independence, improvement in social indicators such as literacy, nutritional status, infant mortality rate, and incidence of poverty has been far from encouraging. The reasons identified for such low levels of social development are inadequacy of social infrastructure and lack of access to basic amenities especially by the socially and economically disadvantaged. Though the human development index (HDI) provides an insight into the level of development of human beings in a particular country, the aggregation conceals interregional and inter-group variations. To arrive at a region-specific and group-specific HDI and also to formulate strategies for human development, human development profiles (HDPs) at disaggregated levels are necessary.

The current study is an attempt in this direction. It presents the human development profile for four states in North India with the ultimate objective of facilitating the design of region-specific and group-specific policies. In this exercise of desegregation, the thrust is to assess existing levels of development and identify deficiencies with respect to select groups and categories. The social indicators considered for this purpose are key elements of the human development process, namely, education, health, and material well-being. The supply of social services and infrastructure at the local level determines the degree of access to and utilization of social services by various households and groups.

This volume studies the states of Haryana, Himachal Pradesh, Punjab, and Uttar Pradesh.

ABUSALEH SHARIFF

Contents

Tables and Illustrations

MAPS

FIGURES

Background Note

This report compiles human development data for the four north Indian states: Haryana, Himachal Pradesh, Punjab, and Uttar Pradesh. The first chapter of each section is a profile of the state based on district level secondary data, followed by a survey report based on primary data collected by the NCAER Household Survey, 1994. The third chapter makes detailed qualitative analysis of two villages in each state.

Survey Methodology

The units of observation and analysis for this study are rural households. The total number of rural households selected in the all-India sample is 33,230 spread over 1765 villages and 195 districts in all states in India. This report on four north Indian states is based on 8642 households spread over 442 villages in 50 districts. Each state has a specific sample size as follows: 1808 households from 90 villages in 11 districts of Haryana, 1210 households from 65 villages in 8 districts of Himachal Pradesh, 1373 households from 70 villages in 8 districts of Punjab, and 4251 households from 217 villages in 23 districts of Uttar Pradesh.[1] The allocation of sample households is shown in Table A.

TABLE A. Allocation of Sample Households in Various Strata for North Indian States

	Stratum	Selected sample households			
		Haryana	Himachal Pradesh	Punjab	Uttar Pradesh
1	Households containing at least one pregnant woman	301	113	251	290
2	Households containing at least one child aged less than 12 months but no pregnant women	305	116	360	594
3	Scheduled castes marginal farmer	51	88	8	244
4	Scheduled castes small farmer	46	25	14	155
5	Scheduled castes large farmer	40	0	20	30
6	Scheduled castes agricultural labourer	151	87	126	313
7	Scheduled castes others	154	81	116	253
8	Muslim marginal farmer	–	–	–	170
9	Muslim small farmer	–	–	–	114
10	Muslim large farmer	–	–	–	46
11	Muslim agricultural labourer	–	–	–	149
12	Muslim other	–	–	–	289
13	Others marginal farmer	151	251	76	382
14	Others small farmer	144	85	79	372
15	Others large farmer	94	44	115	249
16	Others agricultural labourer	108	104	98	295
17	Others other	263	216	110	306
	Total	1808	1210	1373	4251

[1] The survey methodology is elaborated in National Council of Applied Economic Research (2001), *South India Human Development Report*, Oxford University Press, New Delhi, pp. vii–x.

HARYANA

Haryana was carved out as a separate state in 1966, under the Punjab Reorganization Act. According to the 1991 Census, out of 164.6 lakh persons, 75.4 per cent live in rural areas. The economy of the state is basically agrarian. A successful green revolution has made the rural economy prosperous since the early 1970s. The state surplus in foodgrains is a major contributor to the central pool. However, in spite of higher per capita expenditure, the incidence of poverty is rising. Very wide inter-district variation is also observed in the size of landholding.

Haryana has a sound industrial base and the dairy industry is also well developed. At the end of the 1990s as many as 4843 registered factories in the state employed 2.7 lakh persons. The Indian army has 11.2 per cent of its soldiers from Haryana. In the 2001 Census, 68.59 per cent of the population has been enumerated as literate, 79.25 per cent among males and 56.31 per cent among females. Enrolment rates in primary schools are reported to be high.

Health care facilities in the state present a mixed scenario. There is only one hospital per 1.78 lakh persons in Sonipat district while in Bhiwani one hospital caters to only 22,000 persons. Life expectancy for both males and females is higher than the corresponding estimate for the whole country. Infant mortality rate is also much lower than the national rate. Overall, Haryana ranks very high among the major states in terms of composite indices, although separate composite indices for rural and urban areas exhibit rural–urban disparity.

1 Secondary Data Report for Haryana

1.1 General Characteristics

When India became independent, like Bengal, Punjab was partitioned between India and Pakistan. The eastern part came to India while the western part went to Pakistan. Eight princely states of east Punjab were grouped into a single state PEPSU, Patiala and East Punjab States Union, with Patiala as the capital. The PEPSU state was merged into Punjab in 1956. Under the Punjab Reorganization Act 1966, Haryana was carved out of Punjab as a separate state.

Haryana is a small state in the north-western part of the country where 164.6 lakh persons live in an area of 44,000 sq. km (1991). The population and area of the state account for 1.95 per cent of the Indian population and 1.44 per cent of the area of India, respectively. Thus, the state is more densely populated than the country as a whole.

The eastern Haryana plain is bordered by the low hills of the Shivalik system. The slope is generally from the north-east to the south-west and most of the rivers flow in this direction. A large number of rain-fed torrents flow down the outer slopes of the Siwalik. Of these streams, the most important ones are the Ghaggar, the Markanda, the Chautang, and the Saraswati. The state is devoid of any perennial river except the Yamuna, which flows along the extreme eastern side of the state and provides irrigation facilities.

The Haryana plain is a part of the Indo-Gangetic plain formed by alluvial deposits of the Himalayan rivers. The climate is semi-arid in the south-west and of the Gangetic type in the rest of the state. The weather is of a pronounced character, very hot in the summer and markedly cold in the winter.

There is no major railway station in Haryana. The rail routes connecting Delhi to Agra, Ajmer, Firozpur, and Chandigarh pass through Haryana. Ambala, Kurukshetra, and Panipat are the important railway stations. The state has about 22,000 km of motorable roads, including 655 km of the national highway. Of this 2000 km is unmetalled.

The neighbouring states are Himachal Pradesh in the north, Punjab in the west, Rajasthan in the south, and Uttar Pradesh in the east. The national capital region of Delhi juts into Haryana from the east. Haryana's capital, Chandigarh, is a union territory and is also the capital of Punjab.

Of the 164.6 lakh persons enumerated in Haryana during the 1991 Census, 53.62 per cent are males, 75.37 per cent live in rural areas, and 19.75 per cent belong to the Scheduled Caste (SC). There is no Scheduled Tribe (ST) population in Haryana. Among the religious communities, Hindus form an overwhelming majority, accounting for about 90 per cent of the state population, followed by Sikhs (6 per cent), who are largely concentrated in the districts of Kurukshetra, Karnal, and Sirsa. Muslims constitute about 4 per cent of the population and are concentrated in Faridabad and Gurgaon.

The growth rate of population in Haryana during 1991–2002 was 28.05 per cent which was higher than that for the country as a whole at 21.35 per cent. The sex ratio, estimated at 861 females per thousand males, is much lower than the national average of 933. The adjoining states of Punjab (874) and Uttar Pradesh (898) also have low sex ratios. The average density of population in the state works out to 477 persons per sq. km. It is lower in rural areas (288) but much higher in urban areas (3561).

In the 2001 Census, 68.59 per cent of the population has been enumerated as literate—79.25 per cent among males and 56.31 per cent among females. These proportions are higher than the corresponding national averages of 65.38 per cent, 75.85 per cent, and 54.16 per cent. Haryana ranks as high as ninth among major states as far as literacy is concerned (see Box 1.1).

The achieved health status of the people in Haryana presents a mixed scenario. The crude birth rate (CBR), estimated at 33.1 per thousand persons, is higher than the national average of 29.3. The crude death rate (CDR) of 8.2 per thousand is, however, lower than that for the country, estimated at 9.8. Estimates from the sample registration system (SRS) data indicate that the infant mortality rate (IMR), a fairly good indicator of the general health status of the population, is lower (68) than the national average (80 per thousand live births). Haryana has an edge over the rest of the country in terms of the expectation of life, for both males and females. The expectation of life for males in Haryana is 61.5 years, while that for females is 59.5 years; the corresponding estimates for the country are 55.9 and 55.9 years.

About 31 per cent of the population participates in various economic activities, 28.66 per cent as main workers and 2.34 per cent as marginal workers. About 48.26 per cent of the males and 6.01 per cent of the females are main workers. The Indian Army has 11.2 per cent of its soldiers from Haryana.

The economy of the state is basically agrarian. About 80 per cent of the population depends on agriculture. The successful green revolution has made the rural economy prosperous. The current yield rates of wheat and rice are around 3621 kg and 2659 kg per hectare respectively. The corresponding figures for Punjab are 3770 kg per hectare and 3391 kg per hectare while the averages for the country as a whole are 2323 kg per hectare and 1774 kg per hectare respectively. The state, with a surplus in foodgrains, is a major contributor of foodgrains to the central pool. Other crops grown in the state include oil seeds, cotton, sugarcane, potatoes, chillies, and tobacco. Haryana occupies second rank in per capita production of cereals, pulses, and milk (see Box 1.1).

The dairy industry is well developed in Haryana. Haryana is proverbially known as the 'milk pail' of India. The per capita per day availability of milk in Haryana is as high as 524 grams compared to the national average of only 218 grams.

Haryana also has a sound industrial base. A factory of Hindustan Machine Tools manufacturers tractors in Pinjore. Among the states, the largest numbers of tractors are manufactures in Haryana. The state of Haryana also manufacturers a third of the sanitary wares and a fourth of

BOX 1.1

Profile of Haryana

Item	Unit	Year	Haryana		Highest		Lowest		India
			Rank	Actual	State	Actual	State	Actual	Actual
CMIE index	No.	1993	3	136	Punjab	199	Bihar	43	100
HDI indicators (Pal & Pant)		1993	3	0.724	Punjab	0.793	Bihar	0.503	1
(Shiva Kumar)		1993	4	0.514	Kerala	0.651	UP	0.292	1
(Tilak)		1993	4	0.624	Kerala	0.775	UP	0.110	1
PCY (at 1980–1 prices)	Rs	1992–3	3	3411	Punjab	3730	Bihar	1142	2226
Urban population	%	1991	9	24.8	Maharashtra	38.7	HP	8.70	2739
Literacy	per '000	2001	9	686	Kerala	909	Bihar	475	654
Life expectancy	Years	1986–90	5	62.2	Kerala	69.5	MP	53.0	57.7
Electrified dwellings	%	1988–9	3	56.8	HP	83.9	Bihar	4.5	26.9
Annual PC consumption of electricity	KWh	1991	3	487	Punjab	703	Assam	96	299
Road length	per '000 sq. km	1991	10	601	Kerala	3567	MP	321	621
No. of beds in hospitals	'0000	1993	12	41.0	Kerala	255	MP	26.3	68.3
No. of dispensaries	'0000	1990	9	1.3	Gujarat	15.2	MP	0.4	3.4
Regd. med. practitioners	'0000	1992	–	–	Karnataka	77.7	UP	24.7	28.9
Agriculture									
Cereals (per capita)	kg	1993–4	2	571.3	Punjab	1016.3	Kerala	32.0	193.7
Pulses (per capita)	kg	1993–4	2	27.4	MP	48.8	Kerala	0.6	157.0
Total oil seeds (per capita)	kg	1993–4	3	50.8	MP	66.5	Kerala	0.4	24.6
Milk availability (per capita per day)	g	1991	2	524	Punjab	672	Assam	005	218
Manufacturing									
Share in net value added from manufacturing	%	1993	–	–	Maharashtra	22.8	Punjab	4.1	100.0
Regd. working factories	%	1993	13	2.6	Bihar	20.8	HP	0.6	100.0
Share in employment of regd. working factories	%	1993	13	3.1	Maharashtra	14.7	HP	0.6	100.0

Sources: CMIE Index 1993, District Profile, Centre for Monitoring Indian Economy; *Statistical Abstract*, 1992, CSO, Government of India.

the bicycles produced in the country. Panipat has acquired the name 'weavers' city of India'. At the end of 1990, as many as 4843 registered factories in Haryana employed 2.69 lakh persons.

Limestone and iron ore are among the minerals available in the state. The per capita state domestic product (SDP) at current prices, Rs 7502 in 1990–1, was higher than the corresponding figure (Rs 4964) for the country as a whole. Prosperity in rural Haryana, largely a result of the successful green revolution, has kept the incidence of poverty low. According to the estimates released by the Planning Commission, only 8.74 per cent of the state population was poor in 1999–2000, while about 26.10 per cent of the Indian popula-tion was poor in the same year. In terms of incidence of poverty, Haryana ranks fourth after Punjab (6.16 per cent), Chandigarh (5.75 per cent), and Himachal Pradesh (7.63 per cent).

Haryana is the first state to provide piped drinking water and electricity to all of its 6745 villages. The size of the districts in terms of area and population can be obtained from the Census of India, 1991.

1.2 Education

Education is an important dimension of the quality of life. Almost all the composite indices of development proposed in recent years take education as one of the component indicators. Education helps in understanding the various factors that affect the quality of life and enables one to derive the maximum benefit from the existing situation. Thus, it acts as a catalyst for improvement in other aspects of life. The union and state governments have taken up a number of programmes for improving the quality of education and universalization of elementary education. Article 45 of the Indian Constitution provides for free and compulsory education to all children up to the age of 14 years. The target initially set for 1960 has not yet been achieved because of various constraints.

The data on enrolment rates at the primary level for all districts for both boys and girls are given separately for urban and rural areas in Tables 1.E1 and 1.E2. Table 1.E3 gives the districtwise effective literacy rate.

1.2.1 Enrolment Rate

Enrolment in a school is the first step in the acquisition of knowledge through formal education. Low enrolment is a major hurdle in achieving a higher level of literacy. It is easier to acquire advanced technological knowledge and skill through systematic formal education than through informal process. Literacy is the first step in formal education.

The reported enrolment rate in primary schools in Haryana is quite high at 79.53 per cent—83.00 per cent among boys and 75.45 per cent among girls. This would mean that about 8 out of 10 children in the age group of 6–11 years are enrolled in some school.

Enrolment in rural areas is low at 45.45 per cent, while in urban areas it is as high as 200.63 per cent. Enrolment exceeds 100 per cent in urban Haryana as well as in the urban areas of all districts, except Faridabad. The reported enrolment rate in the urban areas of Mahendragarh and Rewari is as high as 503.5 per cent for boys. This raises doubts on the reliability of such estimates.

The method adopted to estimate enrolment rates is known to lead to gross overestimates. The numerator is obtained from the school records while the denominator is estimated from the Census data. There are reasons to believe that the denominator, the number of children in the age group 6–11 years, is underestimated; while the numerator, the number of children enrolled, is over-reported for various reasons. Moreover, children in the age group 6–11 years do not constitute a proper universe for enrolment in primary schools. Many children among the students in primary schools are below the age of 6 years or above the age of 11 years. These are among the reasons that lead to an overestimation of enrolment rates in various states and districts in the states—the estimated rates exceeding 100 per cent in many cases. However, in the case of Haryana, the extent of overestimation seems to exceed any reasonable limit. The reasons cited above may not fully explain such a high overestimation. The basic data on enrolment used as one of the inputs, hence, need to be carefully scrutinized. In view of the above, the enrolment rate estimates have been used only for the limited purpose of ranking the districts. The rankings are not likely to be vitiated unless the extent of overestimation varies widely across the districts.

Across districts, the enrolment rate is the highest in Mahendragarh and Rewari (112.39 per cent), followed by Gurgaon (86.78 per cent), Ambala and Yamunanagar (84.33 per cent), and Karnal, Panipat, and Sonipat (84.21 per cent). Faridabad has the lowest rate of enrolment (57.39 per cent) for both boys (61.88 per cent) and girls (52.04 per cent). Enrolment among girls is lower than that among boys in all the districts. Enrolment in urban areas is higher than in rural areas in all the districts.

1.2.2 Drop-out Rate

Ideally the drop-out rates should be estimated by tracing the children enrolled at the lower levels of the primary classes till they complete their primary education. In the absence of the required information, some scholars have estimated the drop-out rate as the difference between the number of children enrolled in Class I five years ago and the number of children enrolled in Class V now. The enrolment in Class I has been taken as the universe and the percentage difference between this and the number of children reaching Class V is taken as the estimate of the drop-out rate.

The drop-out rate for the state as a whole is about 18.66 per cent. Gender disparity in drop-out rates is quite high, the drop-out rate among girls at 30.31 per cent is almost three times that among boys at 9.62 per cent. Ambala and

Yamunanagar (combined) have an unbelievably low drop-out rate of 0.14 per cent. Gurgaon, too, has a low drop-out rate of 4.97 per cent. Mahendragarh and Rewari (combined) have negative drop-out rates among both boys and girls, reflecting the low reliability of the basic data.

1.2.3 Teacher–Student Ratio

The quality of teaching influences enrolment, drop-out rate, and achievement in education. However, it is an elusive concept that is difficult to conceptualize and measure in quantitative terms. In the absence of any suitable indicator for the quality of teaching, indicators such as teacher–student ratio and availability of other infrastructure are analysed.

On average, there are 47 students per teacher in the state. The ratio is high in Kurukshetra (60.15), Gurgaon (59.82), Kaithal (58.16), and Mahendragarh (58.79). The lowest ratio is seen in Rohtak (33.76). The teacher–student ratios in the districts are not very different from the optimum suggested by the Kothari Commission, that is 40 students per teacher (see Map 1.1).

The ratios presented in Table 1.E2 pertain to all primary schools, whether managed privately or by some government agency. Separate data for these two types of schools could not be gathered. Data on availability of other physical facilities are scanty and not available for any recent year.

1.2.4 Proximity of Primary Schools

As in most of the states, the geographical proximity of primary schools is no longer a problem in Haryana. Of the 7067 villages, all have a primary school within a distance of 1 km. In the absence of a further break-up of the data it is not possible to assess the number of villages with primary school within habitation.

1.2.5 Effective Literacy Rate

Data on effective literacy rate (literate among those aged 7 years and above) obtained from the 1991 and 2001 Census are given in Table 1.E3. Any person who is able to read and write with understanding in any language has been enumerated as literate. The figures reveal that 55.85 per cent of the population aged 7 years and above in the state was literate. The literacy rate of the state has increased by 13 per cent between 1991 and 2001. According to the 2001 Census the literacy rate in the state is 68.59 per cent, which is higher than the national average of 65 per cent. The literacy rate has increased in all the districts, irrespective of sex. The highest rate of literacy is found in Ambala (76.20 per cent), closely followed by Rewari (75.75 per cent), Rohtak (74.56 per cent), and Sonipat (73.71 per cent) (see Map 1.2). The districts of Bhiwani (68.17 per cent), Gurgaon (63.64 per cent),

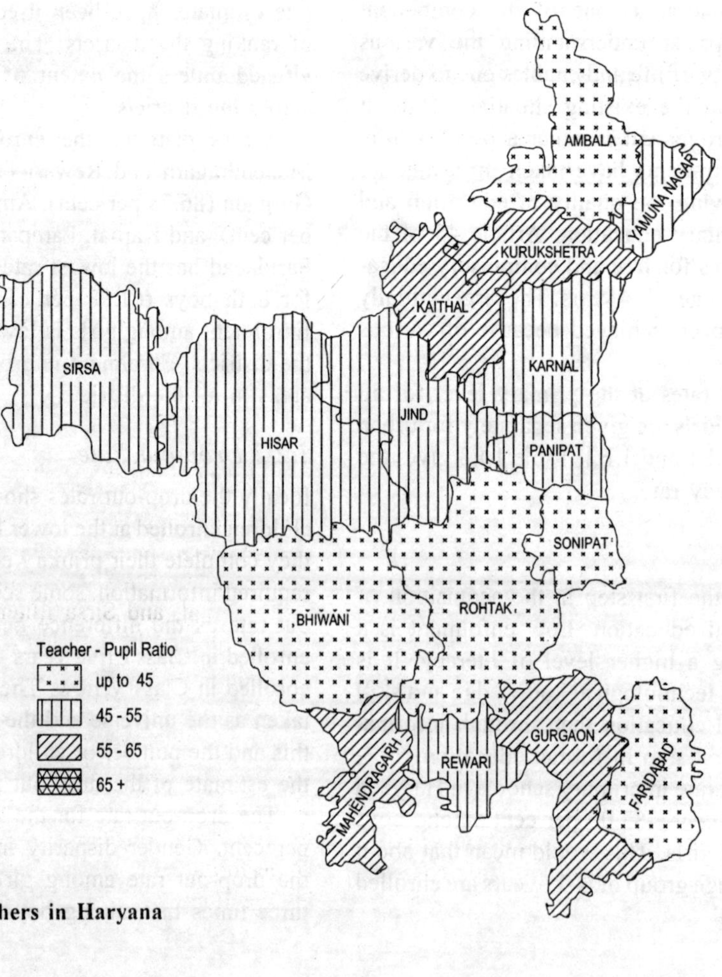

MAP 1.1: **Availability of Teachers in Haryana**

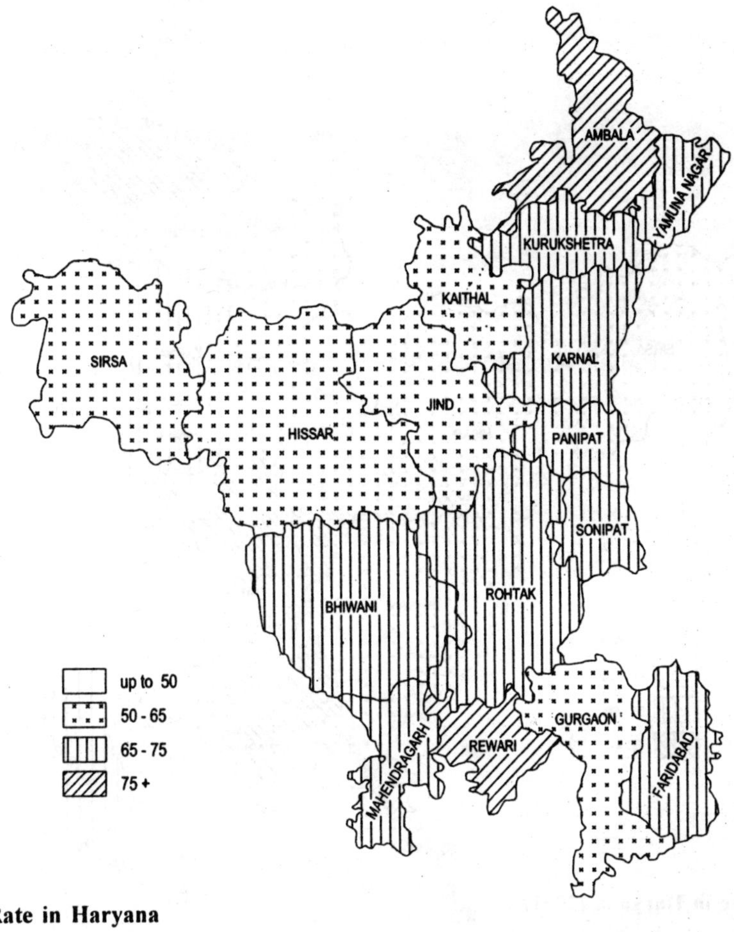

MAP 1.2: **Total Literacy Rate in Haryana**

Hissar (65.85 per cent), Jind (62.80 per cent), Kaithal (59.50 per cent), and Sirsa (61.20 per cent) have lower levels of literacy than the state average (68.59 per cent). The literacy rates are higher among males than among females in all the districts. Male literacy rate varies from a low level of 69.81 per cent in Kaithal to a high level of 89.04 per cent in Rewari. Female literacy rate is the lowest in Kaithal (47.60 per cent) and highest in Ambala (68.48 per cent). Bhiwani (53.50 per cent), Gurgaon (48.29 per cent), Hissar (50.09 per cent), Jind (48.97 per cent), Mahendragarh (54.61 per cent), and Sirsa (50.31 per cent) have low female literacy rates (see Map 1.3).

In 1991, in four out of 16 districts, the rural female literacy rate was lower than 25 per cent. These were Faridabad (22.79 per cent), Hissar (24.38 per cent), Jind (24.35 per cent), and Kaithal (23.68 per cent). The highest rural female literacy rate was found in Ambala (45.52 per cent). The female literacy rate, in urban Haryana at 64.06 per cent, was higher than that in rural areas. Across districts it varied between a low of 54.6 per cent in Kaithal and 75.52 per cent in Ambala. The difference in the literacy rates was quite wide between rural and urban areas. In 1991 in rural areas, the literacy rate was 49.85 per cent as compared to 73.66 per cent in the urban areas of the state. The gap was also wide when seen separately for males and females.

About 19.75 per cent of the population in Haryana is SC, constituting about 2.35 per cent of the total SC population of the country. As depicted in Table 1.1, the literacy level among this group is much lower than that for the total population in the state, in rural and urban areas as well as for males and females. In rural Haryana, the literacy level among SCs is marginally higher than that among SCs in the country as a whole. However, SCs in urban Haryana are lagging behind those in the country as a whole.

Haryana ranks sixteenth in male and twenty-third in female literacy among 31 states and union territories (excluding Jammu and Kashmir where the Census could not be undertaken in 1991). Keeping its economic prosperity in view, the performance of the state in literacy and primary education is not satisfactory in all the districts. In the districts of Hissar, Jind, Kaithal, and Sirsa illiterates are still in the majority. Female literacy in the rural areas of these districts is quite low. Among rural females, illiterates outnumber literates in all the districts. Literacy among rural females and SCs needs urgent and special attention. Region and population group-specific socio-cultural factors are, perhaps, responsible for keeping many girls away from school. These factors should be identified through localized surveys and taken into account while formulating and implementing action plans for micro intervention.

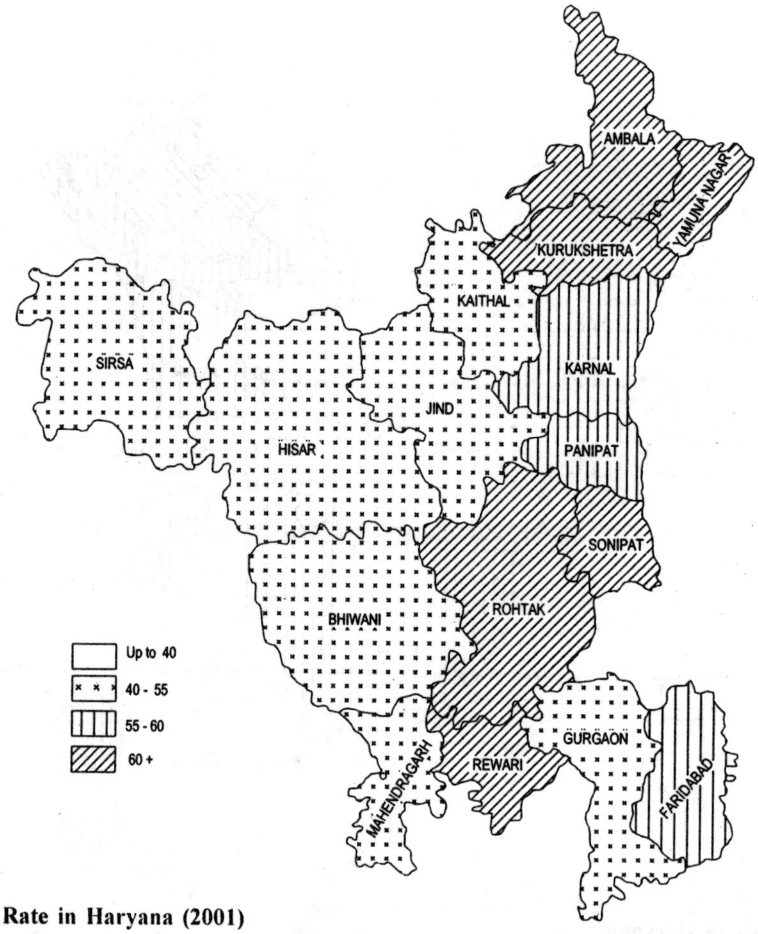

MAP 1.3: **Female Literacy Rate in Haryana (2001)**

TABLE 1.1
Literacy among Scheduled Castes in Haryana and India

Population group	All areas			Rural			Urban		
	Total	Male	Female	Total	Male	Female	Total	Male	Female
Haryana									
All population	55.85	69.10	40.47	49.85	64.78	32.51	73.66	81.96	64.06
SC Population	39.22	52.06	24.15	37.67	50.62	22.48	46.42	58.69	31.89
India									
SC population	37.41	49.91	23.76	33.25	45.95	19.46	55.11	66.60	47.29
All population	52.21	64.13	39.29	44.69	57.87	30.62	73.08	81.09	64.05

Source: Census of India, Series 1, Paper 2, 1992, Final Population Totals, New Delhi 1993.

1.3 Health Care Facilities and Health Status

The health status of the population is an important aspect of well-being. Good health, apart from being a source of vitality, is necessary for effective participation in economic and social activities leading to higher levels of human development. The individual health status and the aggregate health status of a community have multiple dimensions. The health status of a community is reflected in social indicators such as birth rate, death rate, infant and child mortality rate and life expectancy. The available health care facilities have a bearing on the achieved health status. An assessment of the adequacy of these facilities in terms of the number of hospitals, dispensaries, doctors, and other medical staff would be relevant in this context.

Population stabilization is a pre-requisite for reaping the full benefit of development in other spheres of life. A fast growing population makes it difficult to achieve the goals of providing education and health care facilities to all citizens. Realizing the adverse effect of a high growth rate of population on human development, an official family planning programme was launched in 1952. The programme succeeded in substantially reducing the death rate, birth rate, as well as the growth rate of the population. Studies undertaken by the Planning Commission and other scholars, however, indicate that reduction in fertility beyond a certain level is not possible without a reduction in infant and maternal mortality and improvement of the general health conditions of the child and mother. Accordingly, a long-term perspective, integrating all the related aspects of fertility, child and maternal mortality, nutrition and general health care facilities, has been formulated. The emphasis has, thus, shifted from family planning to family welfare. Apart from health care services for improving the general health status of the population, antenatal and post-natal care and nutrition of the child and mother have been accorded priority in the integrated family welfare programmes. The country has set itself a demographic goal of a net reproduction rate (NRR) of 1 to be achieved in the near future. The birth rate, death rate, and IMR are to reach the levels of 21, 9, and 60, respectively. It will be of interest to examine the prospect of achieving these goals in light of the current achievements.

The composition of the population in terms of age, sex, place of residence, and economic activities has a bearing on the prospects of development and is, therefore, of interest in the context of human development. It is also relevant for chalking out plans to provide facilities for education, health care, drinking water, sanitation, housing, old age security, and the like.

Sections 1.3 and 1.4 present data on the available health care facilities, current health status, and some related demographic parameters for the districts of Haryana and look into the variations in these across districts and population groups. An attempt is also made to locate the factors leading to these variations with the hope that these findings will be useful for making plans to reduce the current level of disparity.

1.3.1 Health Care Facilities

The Eighth Plan envisaged the provision of health care facilities to all by the end of the plan period. Accordingly a three-tier integrated health care system has been evolved in the states. Community health centres (CHCs), primary health centres (PHCs), and sub-centres have been built in rural areas to provide health care facilities at the doorstep. The physical targets fixed for rural areas are: (i) one sub-centre for 5000 persons in the plains and 3000 persons in the hilly and tribal areas; and (ii) one PHC for 30,000 persons in the plains and 20,000 persons in hilly and tribal areas. In urban areas, the health care system consists of hospitals, dispensaries, and health posts.

1.3.2 Poor Database

The available data on existing health care facilities are not exhaustive. Data on facilities provided by government agencies are readily available and could be gleaned from published and unpublished documents. However, a large proportion of health care facilities is provided by privately-managed hospitals, dispensaries, and private medical practitioners. Information on these is neither available from secondary sources nor has such information been collected in any survey. The information that was available—even though incomplete—has been used here to build a partial picture. Since the public and private sectors are more likely to be complementary to each other in providing health care facilities, the partial picture drawn here may not closely resemble the prevailing situation. This should be kept in view while taking decisions based on these inferences.

1.3.3 Number of Hospitals, Dispensaries, and Health Posts

Table 1.H1 gives the districtwise availability of hospitals, dispensaries, and health posts in 1991 in urban areas in the state. There are 71 hospitals, (government as well as non-government) in urban Haryana. Of these, Ambala and Hissar have 10 and 12 hospitals each, while Kurukshetra, Kaithal, Sonipat, and Mahendragarh have one hospital each.

Seen in relation to the size of the urban population, there is one hospital for 1.78 lakh persons in Sonipat, while in Bhiwani one hospital caters to only 22,000 persons. Sonipat is, however, better served by other health care facilities. The availability of hospitals should preferably be seen in relation to other health care facilities and also the prevailing morbidity conditions in the population.

There are 191 dispensaries in the state. A few districts such as Ambala, Rohtak, Faridabad, and Hissar have 19 or more dispensaries each while Kaithal, Rewari and Mahendragarh have four or fewer dispensaries each. There are only 16 health posts in the whole state, the largest number, five, in Rohtak while as many as seven districts do not have a health post.

1.3.4 Sub-centres, Public Health Centres, and Community Health Centres

Haryana has a rural economy and more than 75 per cent of the population lives in rural areas. Rural health care facilities, therefore, assume importance. The health care facilities provided by the government are not uniform across the districts. In rural areas, sub-centres are the lowest units of the health care establishment of the government, at the middle level are PHCs, and at the top level are CHCs. Table 1.H2 presents the districtwise data regarding the number of sub-centres, PHCs, and CHCs per lakh rural population. At the state level, there are 2293 sub-centres, with one lakh population being served by 18.48 sub-centres. The variation across districts is not very wide, Bhiwani has 20.78 sub-centres per lakh population while Kurukshetra has 15.17 sub-centres per lakh population (see Map 1.4).

The accepted norm is one PHC for every 30,000 rural population. In Haryana, 2.80 PHCs serve one lakh rural population on an average, which is close to the accepted norm. Among the districts, Bhiwani (3.29 per lakh population) is nearest to the norm. Other districts close to the norm are Rohtak (3.09 per lakh population), Jind (3.01 per lakh

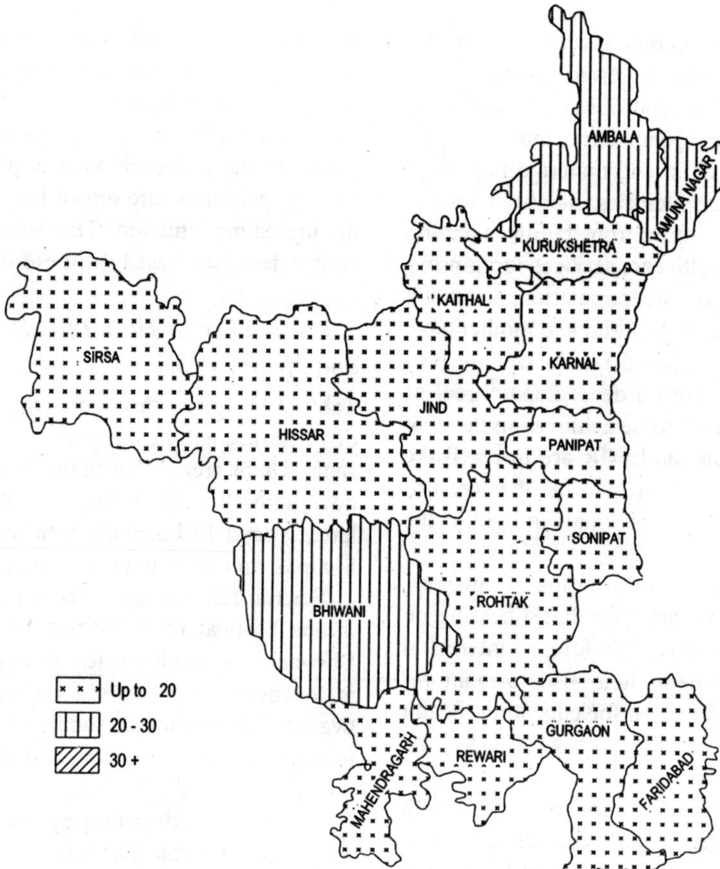

MAP 1.4: **Availability of Sub-centres in Haryana**

population), and Hissar (3.09 per lakh population). Gurgaon, with 2.19 PHCs per lakh population, is the most deficient in this respect.

1.3.5 Family Welfare Centres

In urban areas, family welfare centres (FWCs) provide maternity and child health care services. There are 56 FWCs in urban Haryana. On an average, there are 1.38 such centres per lakh urban population. The highest concentration of FWCs is seen in Mahendragarh (5.91 per lakh population), followed by Kurukshetra (3.89 per lakh population) and Ambala (2.77 per lakh population), while the lowest is in Faridabad (0.70 per lakh population).

NUMBER OF DOCTORS AND PARAMEDICAL PERSONNEL

There are 1395 doctors in position in various government dispensaries and hospitals in Haryana. The largest number of such doctors is in Faridabad (200), followed by Hissar (167), Rohtak (120), and Gurgaon (116). The lowest number (38) is in Kaithal. Seen in relation to the size of the district population, Faridabad has 13.54 doctors in position per lakh population followed by Sonipat (10.60), Kurukshetra (10.28), Karnal (10.27), and Gurgaon (10.12). Rewari (6.26) and Rohtak (6.63) are the most deficient districts in this respect (see Map 1.5).

1.4 Related Demographic Parameters

1.4.1 Population Density

Table 1.H3 presents data on population density, sex ratio, and the percentage of the SC and urban population. The density of population in Haryana is 372 persons per sq. km. It is much higher in urban areas (3561) than in rural areas (288). Across districts, Faridabad has the highest density of population (646) while the lowest (211) is seen in Sirsa. Ambala (486), Yamunanagar (465), Karnal (456), Panipat (475), Sonipat (560), and Faridabad (646) have high population densities. The districts adjoining Delhi and those near the national highway number 1 (Sher Shah Suri Marg) have higher population densities than other districts.

In urban areas, Panipat is the most densely populated with 8288 persons per sq. km. while Faridabad is the most thinly populated district with 1954 persons per sq. km. The other low density districts are Sirsa (2756) and Kurukshetra (2893).

1.4.2 Sex Ratio

A declining sex ratio (measured as the number of females per thousand males) is one of the features of India's demographic profile. The sex ratio in India has declined to 929 females per thousand males in 1991 from 936 females per thousand males in 1981. Haryana has a sex ratio of 865, much lower than the national average. Across districts the sex ratio is high in

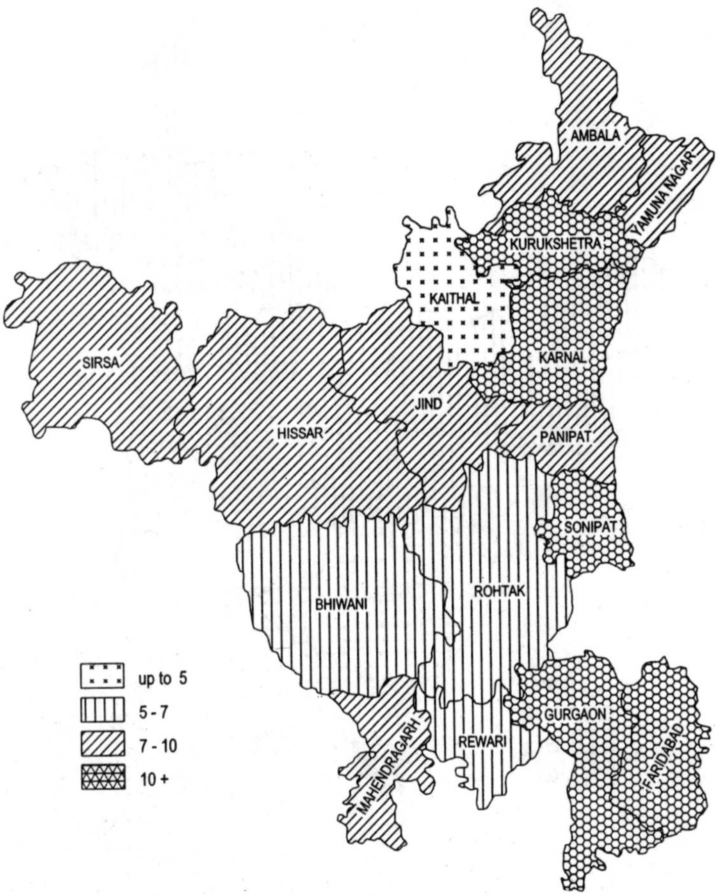

MAP 1.5: **Number of Doctors in Position per lakh Population in Haryana**

Rewari (927), Mahendragarh (910), Sirsa (885), and Ambala (885). In fact Haryana is a low sex ratio state—only Arunachal Pradesh has a sex ratio (of 860) lower than that of Haryana. The neighbouring states of Punjab (882) and Uttar Pradesh (879) also have low sex ratios. Across districts, the sex ratio is high in Ambala (885), Yamunanagar (883), Rewari (927), Mahendragarh (910), and Sirsa (885). It is low in Sonipat (841), Faridabad (828), and Jind (838).

1.4.3 Scheduled Caste Population

The SCs constitute 19.75 per cent of the state population and 2.35 per cent of the total SC population in the country. In urban areas, only 14.20 per cent of the population is SC, as compared to 21.56 per cent in rural areas. The SC population is widely distributed across the districts. In Sirsa, SCs comprise as high as 26.65 per cent of the district population while in Gurgaon their proportion is lower at 13.59 per cent. The proportion of SC population is higher in rural areas as compared to that in urban areas in all the districts; the gap is wider in districts such as Ambala, Yamunanagar, Karnal, and Panipat which are more urbanized. This is, perhaps, a reflection of the fact that the SC population, with a lower level of education and skill, finds it difficult to adjust to the urban way of life. There is no ST population in Haryana.

1.4.4 Level of Urbanization

The state of Haryana is agriculturally well-developed and the major part of the state's income is derived from agricultural activities. However, the level of urbanization is not low (see Map 1.7). The urban population constitutes 24.63 per cent of the total population of the state, which is only marginally lower than the country's average of 25.71 per cent. Haryana occupies ninth position amongst all states in the level of urbanization (see Box 1.1). Faridabad has the highest level of urbanization (48.57 per cent), followed by Ambala (35.54 per cent), Yamunanagar (33.69 per cent), Karnal (27.46 per cent), and Panipat (27.16 per cent). In the least urbanized district, Kaithal, about 14.70 per cent of the population lives in urban areas.

1.4.5 Pattern of Work Participation

About 30 per cent of the population in Haryana participates in full time economic activities as main workers—the percentages for males and females are 48.26 and 6.01 per cent, respectively. Participation as marginal workers is much lower, at 0.25 per cent for males and 4.75 per cent for females. This is perhaps, an indication of a lower incidence of unemployment and poverty in the state; this is also corroborated by data from other sources. There is no wide variation in participation rate across districts. The highest rate of participation as main workers is observed in Hissar (30.92 per cent), while the lowest is in Rewari (24.05 per cent). The percentage of male main workers varies between 50.75 per cent in Ambala and

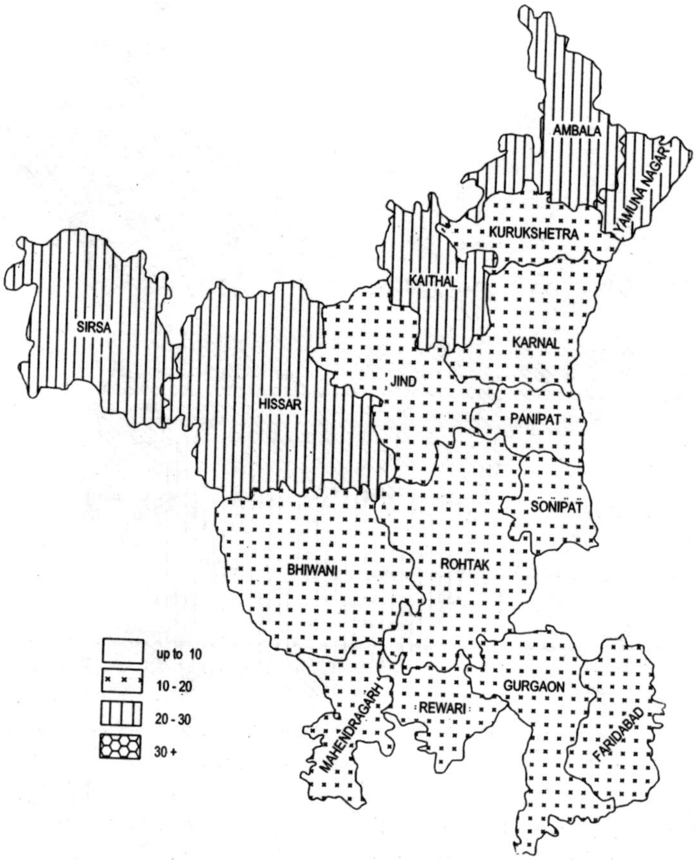

MAP 1.6: **Percentage of SC Population to Total Population in Haryana**

42.18 per cent in Rewari, while for females it is between 8.57 per cent in Bhiwani and 2.20 per cent in Yamunanagar. About 38.77 per cent of the total main workers are cultivators while another 19 per cent of them participate as agricultural labourers. Across districts, the percentage of cultivators ranges between 54.79 per cent in Bhiwani and 21.44 per cent in Ambala. The most urbanized district of Faridabad has 26.32 per cent of main workers as cultivators. Female cultivators constitute 46.64 per cent of female main workers, which is higher than the corresponding figure for males (37.92 per cent). Proportionate participation as agricultural labourers is also higher among females at 25.04 per cent, than among males at 18.35 per cent. Cultivators and agricultural labourers together account for 57.77 per cent of the total main workers in the state. The proportion of workers engaged in household industry is much lower at 1.53 per cent of the total main workers. Among males, this proportion ranges between 2.7 per cent in Panipat and 0.93 per cent in Faridabad, and among females between 6.7 per cent in Yamunanagar and 0.61 per cent in Rohtak.

Data obtained from census records indicate that less than three per cent of the females in Haryana are main workers. However, in the agrarian economy of the state the majority of the women in the working age are seen working shoulder to shoulder with the men in the fields. A study of the census enumeration procedure may resolve this paradox. According to the definition adopted in the census, a person is a cultivator if he or she ploughs the field. Since women in Haryana do not plough the field they are not enumerated as cultivators. On the other hand, a person is enumerated as an agricultural labourer if he or she works on fields owned by others and receives wages. This means that all those women who work in their own fields and carry out operations such as weeding, hoeing, thinning, reaping, threshing, and winnowing are not enumerated as either cultivators or agricultural labourers. This leads to a low estimate of the female work participation rate. Data for rural and urban areas are presented separately in Tables 1.H4 and 1.H5.

1.4.6 Size of Household and Dependency Ratio

A household in Haryana has on an average six to seven persons. The average size varies between the narrow range of 5.8 persons in Ambala and Faridabad and 6.9 persons in Mahendragarh. Households are marginally larger in rural areas (6.6) than in urban areas (5.5). These data are presented in Table 1.H6.

The age–sex composition of the population has a bearing on its future growth pattern. The current status indicates that the proportion is high need of those who care to bring them up (those below 15 years) and as well as of those aged 60 and

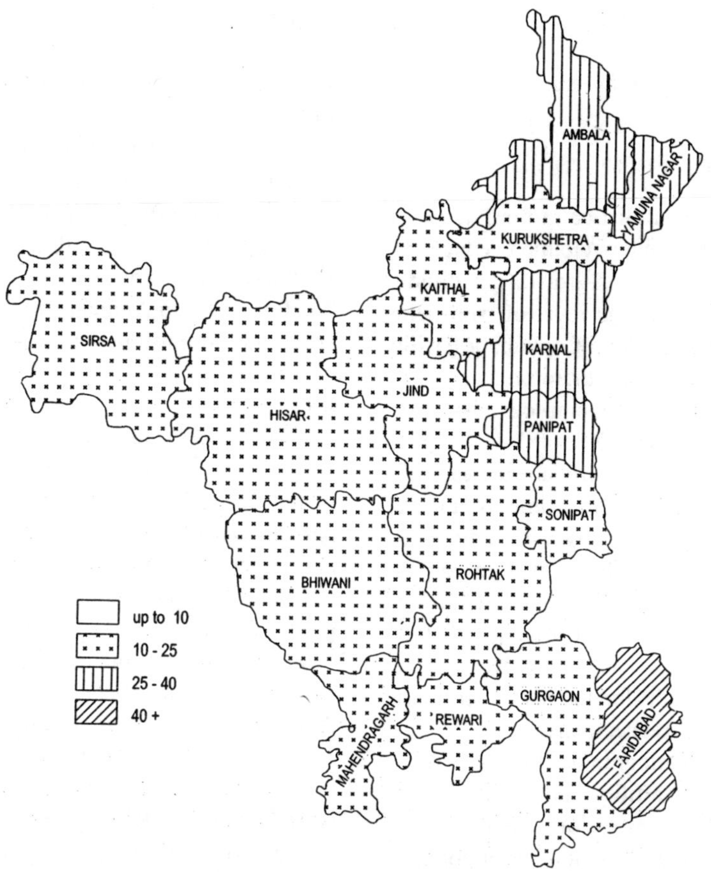

MAP 1.7: **Percentage of Urban Population to Total Population in Haryana**

above who cannot work and need economic support. The parameters total dependency ratio (TDR) and old age dependency ratio (OADR) reflect these aspects of the population. They have been computed from the 1981 Census data. The two ratios are defined as follows:

$$\text{Total Dependency Ratio} = \frac{\text{Population below age 15 years + Population above age 60 years}}{\text{Population in age group 15–59 years}} \times 1000$$

$$\text{Old Age Dependency Ratio} = \frac{\text{Population above age 60 years}}{\text{Population in age group 15–59}} \times 1000$$

At the state level, the TDR is 92.73 per cent, 93.43 per cent among males and 91.93 per cent among females. The TDR is marginally higher for males than for females. It is as high as 104.21 per cent in Bhiwani and much lower, 81.84 per cent, in Ambala. In the case of male dependency, Bhiwani has 105 male dependents per hundred males in the working age group. The lowest male dependency ratio is in Ambala (80.92 per cent). This district is highly urbanized and attracts male population in the working age group as in-migrants. Faridabad also has a low male dependency ratio at 85.27 per cent, perhaps, for similar reasons. Female dependency is the highest in Bhiwani (102.99 per cent) and the lowest in Ambala (82.92 per cent).

In all the districts, the TDR is higher in rural areas than in urban areas. This is also true when seen separately for the male and female population. The highest TDR in rural areas is 108.55 per cent in Bhiwani. Among urban areas, too, Bhiwani has the highest total dependency at 84.11 per cent.

Whereas the TDR accounts for both young and old dependents, the OADR represents the proportion of old (aged 60 years and above) persons dependent on the working age population. In Haryana, there are about 12 old age dependents per hundred persons in the working age, while in the case of males and females these figures are 13 and 11, respectively. Among the districts, the highest OADR is seen in Mahendragarh (13.76 per cent), closely followed by Bhiwani (13.12 per cent) and the lowest is in Faridabad (10.36 per cent). This ratio is higher among males than among females in all the districts. This is also true for rural areas.

There is a large difference between the OADR in rural and urban areas. The highest OADR in rural areas is 14.21 per cent in Rohtak and Mahendragarh, while in the urban areas it is the highest in Mahendragarh (11.14 per cent). The migration of persons in the working age from rural to urban areas and their return to their rural homes after retirement tends to lower this ratio in urban areas. The OADRs has also been increasing in both rural and urban areas.

1.5 Growth of Population

A fast growing population makes it difficult to provide even the basic necessities like food, shelter, clothing, education, and health care to all. The benefits of growth get divided among too many people and hence the level of well-being cannot be raised to any significant extent. Containing fertility and the growth of the population are, therefore, necessary preconditions for raising the level of human development.

The country aspires to attain an NRR of 1 in the near future. The birth rate, death rate and IMR are to reach the levels of 21, 9, and 60, respectively, by that time. A study of the trends and the current rate of growth of population and the parameters influencing it will throw light on the feasibility of achieving these targets. The decadal rates of growth of population in Haryana in 1971–81 and 1981–91 were 28.75 per cent and 27.40 per cent, which were higher than the rates for India as a whole for the same periods at 25 per cent and 23.51 per cent, respectively.

A number of social and demographic factors have a bearing on the realized rate of fertility and the growth of population. These include the number of females in the reproductive age group, 15–44 years, the number of potential mothers and the proportion married among them and thus, exposed to the risk of child bearing, and their age at marriage. The prevailing mortality rate among children is known to influence the reproductive behaviour of couples and, in turn influence the realized fertility and the growth of population. Moreover, child mortality rates, being sensitive to available health care facilities, are also important indicators of the well-being of the population. Factors such as the proportion of girls away from school also influence the realized fertility rate. A girl who drops out of school early (or is not enrolled in school) is likely to be married off early, thus contributing to an early onset of fertility. The realized fertility rate will also depend, to a large extent, on the level of knowledge among the couples about the need for and the means of ensuring a small family through appropriate choice of age at marriage and efficient use of available contraceptive methods. It is easier to spread this awareness among educated couples. A study of these factors and their influence is relevant for human development.

1.5.1 Proportion of Married Females and Mean Age at Marriage

Table 1.H7 presents data on the number of females in the age group 15–44 years, the percentage of married females in different age groups, and their mean age at marriage for all the districts of Haryana by place of residence at the time of the 1981 Census.

In this state, about 82.84 per cent of the females in the age group 15–44 years are married. Their mean age at marriage is around 16.7 years. The mean age at marriage is lower in rural areas (16.5 years) than in urban areas (17.8 years). The proportion of married females in the age group 15–19 years is 47.62 per cent in the state, ranging between 20.63 in Ambala and 69.08 per cent in Jind. The peak child bearing age is 20–4 years, and in this age group nearly 89.22 per cent of the females are married, the figure ranging between 76.70 per cent in Ambala and 96.12 per cent in Jind. In rural areas, the proportion of married females in this prime child-bearing age group is higher than that in urban areas in all the districts.

About 7 per cent of the girls in the age group 10–14 years are married, indicating a wide prevalence of child marriage in the state. This proportion is the highest in Jind (15.75 per cent), followed by Hissar (12.14 per cent), and Bhiwani (11.03 per cent). As compared to other districts, these districts also have a higher proportion of married females in the age group 15–19 years.

Across districts, the mean age at marriage ranges between 15.7 years in Jind and 17.8 years in the urbanized district of Ambala. In rural areas, it ranges from 15.5 years in Jind to 17.4 years in Ambala. In urban areas, it is higher than that in rural areas in all the districts. The lowest age at marriage is 16.7 years in Bhiwani and the highest is 18.5 years in Ambala (marginally above the statutory minimum of 18 years). In all other districts it is marginally below the statutory minimum. Quite a large number of marriages take place before the age of 18 years, in both rural and urban areas.

1.5.2 Life Expectancy, Death Rate, and Child Mortality

Expectation of life at birth in Haryana is 59.5 years for females, which is shorter than that for males at 61.5 years. In terms of expectation of life for males, Haryana ranks third among the major states after Kerala (65.9) and Punjab (63.0). The performance in terms of expectation of life for females is, however, not so impressive—the state ranks eighth among the major states. This is, perhaps, a consequence of a somewhat lower status accorded to women in the society.

The state experiences a death rate of around 8.2 per thousand persons, which is marginally lower than the national average of 9.8. A large proportion of these deaths, in Haryana as well as in other states, occurs in childhood. A scrutiny of the mortality conditions of children would be revealing. Infant mortality rates estimated from SRS data indicate that about 68 deaths occur in childhood out of a thousand live births in Haryana. The corresponding figure for the nation is much higher at 80 deaths. In terms of IMR, Haryana ranks fifth among the major states for which such estimates are available. The neighbouring states of Uttar Pradesh (93), Rajasthan (77), and Himachal Pradesh (75) have much higher levels of IMR, while Punjab has a much lower IMR at 53 and ranks second after Kerala.

Estimates of IMR from SRS data, though more reliable, are available for the nation and the major states. The small sample size, however, does not permit estimation at a lower level of disaggregation.

Four standard estimates of child mortality, viz., q(1), q(2), q(3), and q(5), obtained from the data collected in the 1981 and 1991 Censuses have been used to assess the relative positions of districts. The estimate q(i) represents the expected number of deaths before reaching age i, out of one thousand live births. Table 1.H8 presents the estimates of child mortality, q(i), by sex for all districts. Figures for 1981 are ungraduated estimates while those for 1991 are graduated estimates.

In the state as a whole in 1981, the level of mortality q(1) was 94 per thousand live births. It was higher among girls (119) than among boys (89). In rural areas q(1) was 101, 97, and 126 among persons, males, and females respectively. These are much higher than the corresponding rates 62, 59, and 65 in urban areas. Mortality before age 1 year was the highest in Gurgaon (109) and lowest in Ambala (75). The level of mortality, q(5), was 138 for the state as a whole, ranging between 180 in Gurgaon and 112 in Sirsa. The corresponding average for the country was much higher at 152. It was higher in rural (150) than in urban areas (89). Female children are exposed to a higher risk of mortality as measured by q(5) in all the districts. The achievement of Haryana in child mortality is better than that of many other states and the country as a whole. Female children, however, need more affection and care from the family and society. The 1991 Census data on IMR show a declining trend for all q(1), q(2), q(3), and q(5) for both males and females. The same trend has been observed for all the districts of Haryana. It is interesting to look at the mortality conditions of children for some population groups. Since q(2) is believed to be a more reliable estimate it has been used for the purpose of comparison.

Among the religious communities in Haryana, Muslims experience the highest incidence of child mortality, q(2), at 168 per thousand live births, followed by Hindus (124). Children of Sikh parents are exposed to the least risk of mortality at 87 per thousand live births. The figure is lower than that for Sikhs outside Haryana (92).

The capabilities and handicaps of mothers largely determine the health and mortality conditions to which children are exposed. Tables 1.2 and 1.3 compare child mortality rates by education and occupation of mother. As expected, child mortality is seen to decrease with a higher level of education of the mother. Mortality is high among those children whose mothers work as agricultural labourers and other manual workers in rural Haryana. In the prevailing work environment, these mothers are unable to take adequate care of their children. Hence, their children, deprived of maternal care, are exposed to a higher risk of morbidity and death.

The spread of education among mothers and future mothers, an improvement in the working environment of female workers, along with an improvement in general health care facilities, will go a long way in reducing child mortality in Haryana.

TABLE 1.2
Estimated Child Mortality in Haryana by Level of Education of Mother

Education of mother	Child mortality q(2)		
	Total	Male	Female
Illiterate	132	128	137
Literate but below middle	106	109	103
Middle but below matriculate	74	74	75
Matriculate but below graduate	58(48)	58(49)	58(46)
Graduate & above	36	29	42
All levels	124	121 (107)	127

Note: Figures in parentheses are graduated estimates.

Source: Census of India, 1981, Fertility and Child Mortality Estimates of Haryana, Occasional Paper No. 10 of 1987.

TABLE 1.3
Estimated Child Mortality in Rural Haryana by Occupation of Mother

Occupation	Child mortality q(2)		
	Total	Male	Female
Main workers	140	141	140
Cultivators	133	138(112)	128(135)
Agricultural labourers	160	156	164
Manual workers	165	142	190
Non-manual workers	35(57)	55(65)	0(48)
Non-workers	129(98)	135(94)	121

Note: Figures in parentheses are graduated estimates.

Source: Census of India, 1981, Fertility and Child Mortality Estimates of Haryana, Occasional Paper No. 10 of 1987.

1.5.3 Fertility Indices

There are variations in the realized rates of fertility across districts and population groups, which are a consequence of the variation in factors determining fertility. The various indices that are used to represent the fertility levels of a population group are as follows:

General Fertility Rate (GFR): The number of children born alive during the previous year per thousand women in the child bearing age (of 15–49 years in the 1981 Census).

General Marital Fertility Rate (GMFR): The number of children born alive during the previous year per thousand married women in the child bearing age (of 15–49 years in the 1981 Census).

Total Fertility Rate (TFR): Total number of children that would have been born alive per woman, if the prevailing fertility conditions continued for the entire reproductive period.

Total Marital Fertility Rate (TMFR): Total number of children that would have been born alive per married woman, if the prevailing fertility conditions continued for the entire reproductive period.

Of these indices, TFR is regarded as a more standardized measure. Estimates of these indices derived from the data collected in the 1981 Census are presented by religious groups in Table 1.H9.

In 1981, the unadjusted GFR was 143 in the state, 153 in rural areas and 110 in urban areas. The unadjusted TFR was 4.5 in the state, with a wide rural–urban differential, 4.9 in rural and 3.3 in urban areas. In terms of TFR, fertility among Muslims is the highest (5.2), both in rural (5.6) and urban (4.8) areas. Christians in rural areas have a TFR level of 5.3, which is higher than that for Hindus. In urban areas, Hindus have a higher TFR (3.3) than Christians (2.2) (see Table 1.H9).

Bhiwani (5.4), Mahendragarh (4.9), Jind (4.8), Gurgaon (4.7), and Rohtak (4.7) had higher levels of unadjusted TFR than other districts. On the other hand, Ambala (3.5), Sonipat (4.3), and Faridabad (4.1) had lower levels of TFR. In terms of other indices also, these districts have the lowest levels of fertility. In general, rural areas have a higher level of fertility, measured by any of the indices. However, the adjusted TFR, TMFR, GFR, and GMFR in 1991 have shown a declining trend compared to 1981 levels for all the districts of Haryana (Table 1.H10).

1.6 Material Well-being

Health and education are important aspects of the quality of life. The achievements of the state in this sphere have been discussed in earlier sections. There are, however, many other aspects, no less important, which could not be included due to difficulties in conceptualization and measurement and also due to deficiencies in the data. An adequate level of income and wealth, though not sufficient, is necessary for maintaining a decent standard of living. Most of the deprivation can be traced to the inadequacy of income and wealth. Income earned and assets held by households would, thus, be a proxy for many aspects of life not covered in this profile. An adequate level of income and wealth would indicate the feasibility of leading a decent life and, therefore, a higher level of human development. A lower level of these would, of course, lead to non-fulfilment of many of the household aspirations and, therefore, correspond to a lower level of human development. An analysis of the level of income earned and assets held, as also distribution of these among the members of the community, would reveal an important aspect of human development.

1.6.1 Income and Consumption

Haryana is a small state in terms of area (44,000 sq. km) and population (164.6 lakh). Prosperity in rural areas, due to the successful green revolution and a good industrial base, has raised the per capita SDP to Rs 7502 (in 1990–1 at current prices), much higher than that of the country at Rs 4964. In terms of per capita income, Haryana ranks fifth after Delhi (Rs 10,177), Goa (Rs 8797), Punjab (Rs 8373) and Pondicherry (Rs 7746).

This average picture, however, does not reveal the disparity in income among the population. Data on income at the level of the household would be needed to assess the level of inequality and the incidence and intensity of poverty in the state. Unfortunately, such data are not available for any recent year. The National Council of Applied Economic Research (NCAER) collected data on household income in some of its occasional surveys. The latest one pertained to the year 1994.

The National Sample Survey Organization (NSSO) collects data, in its various rounds, on consumer expenditure. These are compiled and published in a grouped form, persons per thousand and average expenditure in various monthly per capita consumer expenditure (MPCE) classes. In the absence of similar data on income, data from the NSS pertaining to the year 1987–8 have been utilized to assess the extent of inequality and poverty in the state. One opinion is that since consumer expenditure is influenced by income in the past as well as income prospects in the foreseeable future, it is a better representation of welfare. The MPCE in 1987–8 in Haryana was Rs 214.81 in rural areas and Rs 255.31 in urban areas. These are higher than the corresponding figures of Rs 155.75 and Rs 249.93 for the country as a whole, making Haryana rank high among states and union territories.

Measured in terms of the Gini coefficient, the distribution of consumer expenditure in Haryana is more egalitarian, compared to that in the country as a whole, both in urban and rural areas. The estimated Gini coefficients for Haryana are 0.297 for urban and 0.281 for rural areas. The corresponding estimates for the country as a whole are 0.352 and 0.291, respectively. A higher per capita expenditure and its egalitarian distribution results in a lower incidence of poverty. As estimated by the Planning Commission, the incidence of poverty in the country in 1987–8 was about 38.86 per cent, while Haryana had a much lower proportion of the poor, only 16.64 per cent. In terms of incidence of poverty, Haryana ranks fourth among all states and union territories after Delhi (12.41 per cent), Punjab (13.20 per cent), and Himachal Pradesh (15.45 per cent).

The MPCE in 1993–4 in Haryana was Rs 385.01 in rural areas and Rs 473.92 in urban areas. These are much higher than the corresponding figures for all India at Rs 281.40 and Rs 458.04 (see Table 1.4).

In spite of the higher per capita expenditure and its egalitarian distribution in both rural and urban areas in 1993–4, the incidence of poverty is high. The percentage of population below the poverty line has increased to 25.05 per cent in 1993–4 from 16.64 per cent in 1987–8, and Haryana now ranks eighth, instead of fourth previously, among the states and union territories.

TABLE 1.4
Consumer Expenditure Gini Coefficient, and Incidence of Poverty, 1993–4

	Consumer exp. per month (Rs)		Gini coefficient		Population below the
	Rural	Urban	Rural	Urban	poverty line
Haryana	385.01	473.92	0.3007	0.2762	25.05
HP	350.63	746.93	0.2762	0.4345	28.20
Punjab	443.00	510.73	0.2645	0.2763	11.77
India	281.40	458.04	0.2816	0.3399	35.97

Sources: Report of Expert Group, An estimation of proportion and number of poor, Planning Commission 1993; Levels and Patterns of Consumer Expenditure, 5th Quinquinnial Survey, NSO 50th Round, July 1993–June 1994, Department of Statistics, GOI 1996.

The percentage of population below the specified poverty line is a measure of the incidence of poverty. Sen (1976) has devised a measure of the intensity of poverty, which shows how poor are the poor, known as the Sen Index.

1.6.2 Distribution of Landholdings

Land is a major productive asset for agriculture, which is the most importance source of livelihood in rural Haryana, as in most of the states. A study of the level and distribution of landholdings in rural areas will, therefore, be relevant in assessing the material well-being of the population. A disparity in the distribution of landholdings would closely reflect the incidence of poverty and affluence in rural areas. Data collected by the NSSO in its 32nd round, when analysed, clearly indicates a strong association between small landholdings and low income. Rural poverty is, by and large, related to the households with less than one acre of land. Keeping these findings in view, the size and distribution of landholdings in rural Haryana are presented and analysed below.

Data available from the agricultural censuses pertaining to the years 1985–6 and 1990–1 have been used here to observe the variation across districts and changes over time in the distribution of landholdings in rural Haryana. The data and estimates are presented in Tables 1.P2.1 and 1.P2.2. These data and estimates reveal the following:

1. The total number of holdings has increased to 15.3 lakhs in 1990–1 from 13.5 lakhs in 1985–6.

2. The average size of holding has declined to 2.43 ha from 2.76 ha as a result of a decrease in the total area operated from 37.14 lakh ha to 37.11 lakh ha during the same period.

3. The number of marginal, small, and semi-medium holdings has increased to 6.22 lakhs, 3.04 lakhs, and 3.36 lakhs in 1990–1 from 5.02 lakhs, 2.65 lakhs, and 2.81 lakhs, respectively, in 1985–6. There is a decrease in the number of medium and large holdings from 2.39 lakhs and 0.60 lakhs in 1985–6 to 2.23 lakhs and 0.46 lakhs in 1990–1, respectively.

4. The area operated by marginal, small, and semi-medium holdings has increased to 2.95 lakh ha, 4.63 lakh ha, and 9.44 lakh ha in 1990–1 from 2.29 lakh ha, 3.83 lakh ha, and 7.90 lakh ha in 1985–6, respectively.

5. The number of holdings operated by SC farmers has increased from 0.40 lakhs to 0.46 lakhs as also the total area operated by them (from 0.75 lakh ha to 0.76 lakh ha), during the period 1985–6 to 1990–1.

6. The average size of holdings operated by SCs has, however, decreased to 1.63 ha in 1990–1 from 1.87 ha in 1985–6.

7. The area operated by medium and large holdings has decreased to 13 lakh ha and 7.09 lakh ha in 1990–1 from 14.09 lakh ha and 9.02 lakh ha in 1985–6, respectively.

8. The largest number of holdings in 1990–1 is in Hissar (2.25 lakhs), while the smallest number is in Panipat (0.54 lakhs)

9. The largest number of holdings operated by SCs in 1990–1 is in Hissar (0.11 lakhs) while the smallest number is in Rewari (only 88).

10. The average size of holding (1990–1) is the largest in Sirsa (3.55 ha) while the smallest is in Faridabad (1.63 ha).

11. The average size of holdings operated by SCs in 1990–1 is the largest in Bhiwani (2.37 ha) and the smallest in Ambala (0.86 ha).

12. The average size of holdings operated by marginal and small farmers has increased to 0.47 ha and 1.52 ha in 1990–1 from 0.46 ha and 1.45 ha, respectively in 1985–6.

13. The average size of holdings operated by large farmers has increased to 15.43 ha from 15 ha during the period 1985–6 to 1990–1, while that operated by medium farmers has decreased from 5.90 ha to 5.86 ha.

1.7 Concluding Remarks

Prior to 1966, Haryana was a backward and underdeveloped region in the composite state of Punjab. However, after becoming a separate state, it has made rapid progress in terms of economic growth, in agriculture as well as industry. Its proximity to the national capital, Delhi, has acted as a catalyst by providing access to vast markets for its products. People and goods moving from Punjab, Himachal Pradesh, Jammu and Kashmir, and the national capital region of Delhi to other parts of the country have to pass through Haryana.

The successful green revolution has ushered in economic prosperity in rural Haryana. Rapid progress in industry has raised the income of the urban population. The distribution of income is moderately egalitarian. All these developments have kept the incidence and intensity of poverty low in the state. Thus, Haryana acquires a high score in terms of material well-being. Haryana is the first state to provide piped drinking water and electricity to all its villages.

The population in Haryana is growing at a rate higher than the national average. The factors behind this include a high proportion of marriages at lower ages and the low age of females at marriage. Child marriage is a common phenomenon in the state that contributes to an early onset of fertility.

A higher coefficient of variation (CV) of 23 per cent for rural female literacy, compared with a CV of only 12 per cent for overall literacy, suggests a fairly high degree of gender discrimination. There is an urgent need to eliminate this bias so as to improve the status of women in Haryana. The teacher–student ratio is one of the indicators which reflects the quality of education and the average in Haryana is 49, which is higher than the norm of 1 : 40. However, the CV is 16 per cent, which implies that the distribution of teachers among the districts is not very skewed (see Table 1.5).

TABLE 1.5
Average, Standard Deviation and Coefficient of Variation of Human Development Indicators

	Total literacy rate	Female literacy rate rural	Teacher–student ratio	Sub-centre per lakh pop.	Agri-labourer to total main workers	Child mortality before age of 5
AVG.	56.02	33.25	49.30	18.25	19.26	104.38
SD	6.94	7.66	7.98	1.83	6.02	62.00
CV	12.39	23.02	16.17	10.03	31.25	59.97

The early marriage of girls keeps them away from school either because of non-enrolment or discontinuance. Consequently, female literacy is low in Haryana. It is much lower in rural areas. In four out of 16 districts, rural female literacy is less than 25 per cent. Even in Ambala with the highest rural female literacy, illiterates outnumber the literates among rural females. The reasons for this seem to be more socio-cultural than economic. These factors need to be identified and studied in detail through localized surveys. Strategies for micro-intervention in these areas should take due note of these.

The performance of the state in the general health status of the population is near average as measured by indicators such as the CBR, CDR, IMR, and life expectancy. The health care facilities provided by the government are not uniform across the districts. At the state level, there are 2293 sub-centres in all, and 18.48 sub-centres serve one lakh population. The variation across districts is not very wide—Bhiwani has 20.78 sub-centres per lakh population while the corresponding figure for Kurukshetra is 15.17. The CV is only 10 per cent. The level of mortality, q(5), is 138 for the state, ranging from 180 in Gurgaon to 112 in Sirsa. It seems that inter-district variation is relatively high as far as child mortality is concerned.

About 30 per cent of the population comprise the main workers. About 38.77 per cent of the total main workers are cultivators, while another 19 per cent are agricultural labourers. However, the inter-district variation among the agricultural labourers is very high. The CV is 31 per cent.

Haryana ranks high among the states in terms of all the composite indices computed by various scholars. This is largely because of its very high score in material well-being. If Haryana succeeds in translating its economic prosperity into achievements in education and health status, it will rank higher than Punjab and Kerala. Appropriate strategies should be planned and implemented to achieve this goal. The strategy should take all the socio-cultural factors into consideration. No plan can be formulated and implemented without a reliable database. The available database on education and health status in Haryana is poor and needs to be improved.

TABLE 1.E1

Districtwise Primary School Enrolment Rate in Urban Areas (boys, girls, and total), 1990–1

State/district	Total no. of eligible children for enrolment (6–11) 1986–7			Enrolment rate		
	Boys	Girls	Total	Boys	Girls	Total
Haryana	**259,074**	**225,061**	**484,135**	**220.38**	**177.89**	**200.63**
Ambala and Yamunanagar*	37,377	33,758	71,135	142.18	122.18	132.69
Bhiwani	13,158	10,930	24,088	233.01	200.21	218.13
Faridabad	44,743	38,476	83,210	63.37	47.42	56.00
Gurgaon	15,717	13,524	29,241	218.38	192.07	206.21
Hissar	17,325	23,672	40,997	453.90	220.71	319.26
Rohtak	23,823	21,364	45,187	243.34	221.17	232.86
Sirsa	12,133	11,104	22,247	279.40	191.79	248.10
Mahendragarh and Rewari*	11,366	10,946	22,312	503.50	378.85	442.30
Jind, Kaithal, and Kurukshetra*	29,832	25,680	55,512	317.94	241.39	282.53
Karnal, Panipat, and Sonipat*	42,773	34,716	78,489	238.19	198.08	217.41

Note: * Data for these districts are not available separately.

Source: Directorate of Public Instruction, Government of Haryana.

TABLE 1.E2

Districtwise Primary School Enrolment Rate and Teacher–Student Ratio in Rural Areas (boys, girls, and total), 1990–1

State/district	Total no. of eligible children for enrolment (6–11) 1986–7			Enrolment rate			Teacher–student ratio**
	Boys	Girls	Total	Boys	Girls	Total	
Haryana	**931,073**	**789,995**	**1,721,068**	**44.82**	**46.19**	**45.45**	**47.29**
Ambala and Yamunanagar*	88,238	76,694	164,932	64.43	62.70	63.63	45.74
Bhiwani	66,356	59,614	125,970	43.95	45.63	44.75	38.16
Faridabad	65,687	54,316	120,003	61.58	55.83	58.97	40.53
Gurgaon	81,935	68,371	150,306	67.47	58.93	63.58	59.81
Hissar	109,678	93,228	202,906	24.10	22.61	23.42	51.75
Rohtak	100,659	83,809	184,468	26.62	30.43	28.35	33.76
Sirsa	50,821	43,018	93,839	33.77	41.66	37.38	52.67
Mahendragarh and Rewari*	80,448	68,545	148,993	58.53	68.19	62.98	55.42
Jind, Kaithal, and Kurukshetra*	149,027	125,264	274,291	39.28	45.20	41.98	53.28
Karnal, Panipat, and Sonipat *	138,893	116,706	255,599	42.87	43.81	43.30	47.22

Note: * Data for these districts are not available separately.
** For all areas.

Source: Directorate of Public Instruction, Government of Haryana.

TABLE 1.E3
Districtwise Effective Literacy Rate by Place of Residence and Sex

State/district	1991									2001		
	All areas			Rural			Urban			All areas		
	Male	Female	Total	Male	Female	Total	Male	Female	Total	Male	Female	Total
Haryana	**69.10**	**40.47**	**55.85**	**64.78**	**32.51**	**49.85**	**81.96**	**64.06**	**73.66**	**79.25**	**56.31**	**68.59**
Ambala	75.08	56.62	66.41	68.79	45.52	58.03	88.62	75.52	81.28	83.01	68.48	76.20
Bhiwani	70.93	35.10	54.18	69.20	30.89	51.27	78.98	54.97	67.81	81.19	53.50	68.17
Faridabad	74.15	42.12	59.77	65.53	22.79	46.12	82.67	62.12	73.56	82.49	56.80	70.79
Gurgaon	67.87	34.94	52.61	63.07	26.12	46.00	85.67	66.56	76.69	77.11	48.29	63.64
Hissar	61.41	32.12	47.87	56.48	24.38	41.65	79.45	60.25	70.55	77.62	50.09	65.85
Jind	61.07	30.12	47.00	57.26	24.35	42.35	79.30	56.91	68.98	74.69	48.97	62.80
Kaithal	54.71	28.37	42.59	51.44	23.68	38.71	73.80	54.60	64.79	69.81	47.60	59.50
Karnal	67.02	43.54	56.15	61.64	34.11	48.98	81.01	67.02	74.42	76.74	58.42	68.20
Kurukshetra	69.23	46.94	58.78	64.65	40.11	53.12	83.17	68.21	76.22	79.23	60.76	70.04
Mahendragarh	77.17	36.75	57.87	75.94	33.79	55.79	85.64	57.32	72.21	85.31	54.61	70.43
Panipat	67.04	41.17	55.17	62.82	32.29	48.87	78.13	63.92	71.54	79.16	58.48	69.75
Rewari	82.16	46.18	64.77	81.22	43.05	62.61	86.96	64.06	76.45	89.04	61.25	75.75
Rohtak	76.19	45.74	62.24	73.97	40.21	58.59	84.39	65.12	75.36	84.29	63.19	74.56
Sirsa	57.21	34.02	46.32	52.19	27.43	40.55	75.54	58.35	67.51	70.93	50.31	61.20
Sonipat	77.20	48.27	64.06	75.22	42.90	60.66	83.58	64.60	74.75	83.95	61.65	73.71
Yamunanagar	69.76	50.07	60.53	63.62	40.41	52.73	81.48	68.64	75.48	79.28	64.08	72.20

Source: Census of India, 1991 and 2001.

TABLE 1.H1
Districtwise Number of Hospitals, Dispensaries, and Health Posts in Urban Areas for Allopathy System, 1991

State/district	Number of hospitals*	Number of dispensaries*	Number of health posts
Haryana	**71**	**191**	**16**
Ambala	10	21	–
Yamunanagar	6	14	1
Kurukshetra	1	7	–
Kaithal	1	2	–
Karnal	2	11	1
Panipat	3	7	1
Sonipat	1	8	1
Rohtak	7	22	5
Faridabad	5	34	2
Gurgaon	5	11	1
Rewari	2	4	–
Mahendragarh	1	4	–
Bhiwani	9	10	2
Jind	4	8	–
Hissar	12	19	2
Sirsa	2	9	–

Note: * Includes both government and non-government.

Source: Director-General of Health Services, Government of Haryana.

Table 1.H2

Districtwise Number of Sub-centres, PHCs, CHCs, and Doctors per lakh Rural Population for Allopathy System, 1990–1

State/district	Rural population	Number of sub-centres	Sub-centres per lakh population	Number of PHCs	PHCs per lakh population	CHCs per lakh population	Doctors per lakh population
Haryana	**12,408,904**	**2293**	**18.48**	**348**	**2.80**	**0.12**	**8.47**
Ambala	719,884	146	20.28	21	2.92	0.28	8.15
Yamunanagar	544,953	112	20.55	15	2.75	0.18	8.15
Kurukshetra	487,809	84	15.17	12	2.46	–	10.28
Kaithal	700,048	115	16.43	20	2.86	0.14	4.63
Karnal	642,514	115	17.90	15	2.33	0.16	10.27
Panipat	607,156	100	16.47	16	2.64	–	7.20
Sonipat	576,841	110	19.07	15	2.60	–	10.60
Rohtak	1,423,133	284	19.96	44	3.09	0.07	6.63
Faridabad	759,727	117	15.40	19	2.50	0.13	13.54
Gurgaon	913,386	155	16.97	20	2.19	–	10.12
Rewari	528,101	102	19.31	15	2.84	0.19	6.26
Mahendragarh	597,225	115	19.26	17	2.85	–	8.21
Bhiwani	943,150	196	20.78	31	3.29	0.32	5.70
Jind	797,560	129	16.17	24	3.01	–	7.58
Hissar	1,455,081	274	18.83	45	3.09	0.21	9.05
Sirsa	712,336	139	19.51	19	2.67	0.14	7.30

Source: Director-General of Health Services, Government of Haryana.

TABLE 1.H3

Districtwise Population Density, Sex Ratio, and Percentage of Urban and Scheduled Caste Population

State/district	Total					Rural			Urban		
	CMIE index 1995	Popn density	Sex ratio	Per cent of urban popn	Per cent of SC	Popn density	Sex ratio	Per cent of SC	Popn density	Sex ratio	Per cent of SC
Haryana	**133**	**372**	**865**	**24.63**	**19.75**	**288**	**864**	**21.56**	**3561**	**868**	**14.20**
Ambala	129	486	885	35.54	22.99	326	865	28.62	4655	922	14.20
Yamunanagar	132	465	883	33.69	24.96	321	885	31.53	4126	880	12.79
Kurukshetra	139	402	879	24.01	19.77	316	883	22.79	2893	867	12.03
Kaithal	135	343	852	14.70	21.44	297	848	22.78	4190	878	10.22
Karnal	141	456	865	27.46	20.02	337	856	22.55	6503	887	13.68
Panipat	132	475	854	27.16	17.89	352	848	20.51	8288	871	13.35
Sonipat	140	560	841	23.58	17.84	440	831	18.80	4564	873	10.85
Rohtak	115	407	851	21.31	18.40	326	843	19.34	5329	881	14.72
Faridabad	133	646	828	48.57	16.06	396	842	18.94	1954	813	14.97
Gurgaon	113	417	871	20.30	13.59	341	867	13.38	3136	886	13.01
Rewari	122	403	927	15.27	19.30	348	940	19.80	3144	859	14.41
Mahendragarh	102	352	910	12.41	15.46	312	911	15.77	3486	901	16.55
Bhiwani	102	247	880	17.25	18.97	207	881	19.05	3821	875	13.29
Jind	122	357	838	17.19	19.56	299	834	20.96	5598	859	18.58
Hissar	141	281	861	21.12	23.21	224	861	24.77	4758	864	12.82
Sirsa	140	211	885	21.16	26.65	164	887	28.32	2756	876	17.38

Sources: Census of India, 1991; CMIE Index 2000, District Profile, Centre for Monitoring Indian Economy.

TABLE 1.H4

Districtwise Population, Population of Workers (Main and Marginal) as Percentage of Total Population, and Population of Workers in Household Industry (as Percentage of Main Workers) for Urban Areas

State/district	Urban population			Main workers (as percentage of urban population)			Marginal workers (as percentage of urban population)			Workers in HH industry (as percentage of main workers in urban areas)		
	Total	Male	Female	Total	Male	Female	Total	Male	Female	Total	Male	Female
Haryana	**4,054,744**	**2,170,140**	**1,884,604**	**28.08**	**48.43**	**4.65**	**0.24**	**0.07**	**0.43**	**2.31**	**2.30**	**2.44**
Ambala	396,994	206,582	190,412	28.06	48.22	6.20	0.14	0.03	0.27	2.44	2.56	1.50
Yamunanagar	276,927	147,329	129,598	27.55	48.63	3.58	0.03	0.03	0.02	2.65	2.54	4.35
Kurukshetra	154,134	82,549	71,585	27.24	46.93	4.54	0.05	0.03	0.08	2.04	2.07	1.79
Kaithal	120,637	64,229	56,408	27.52	48.83	3.25	0.43	0.08	0.82	1.89	1.83	2.89
Karnal	243,283	128,925	114,358	28.34	48.96	5.08	0.31	0.19	0.45	2.69	2.72	2.36
Panipat	226,345	120,991	105,354	29.73	51.34	4.91	0.24	0.10	0.40	5.84	5.98	4.25
Sonipat	178,025	95,042	85,983	27.25	46.45	5.26	0.17	0.08	0.26	3.29	3.46	1.53
Rohtak	385,473	204,965	180,508	27.09	46.42	5.15	0.15	0.09	0.22	1.29	1.32	0.97
Faridabad	717,513	395,667	321,846	29.83	50.41	4.53	0.14	0.05	0.26	0.91	0.90	0.96
Gurgaon	232,704	123,357	109,347	27.80	52.44	6.04	0.25	0.09	0.43	2.24	2.17	2.89
Rewari	95,200	51,198	44,002	27.25	50.66	3.25	0.74	0.18	1.40	3.89	3.50	10.60
Mahendragarh	84,644	44,523	40,121	25.35	48.20	2.91	0.98	0.18	1.86	1.64	1.47	4.54
Bhiwani	196,568	104,856	91,712	26.09	48.91	3.63	0.43	0.09	0.82	3.59	3.57	3.90
Jind	165,544	89,068	76,476	26.46	49.17	3.61	0.42	0.06	0.83	2.34	2.27	3.40
Hissar	389,553	208,962	180,591	28.46	53.05	4.68	0.36	0.03	0.74	2.18	2.11	3.02
Sirsa	191,200	101,897	89,303	28.53	53.53	3.50	0.08	0.08	0.08	2.43	2.35	3.81

Source: Census of India,1991.

TABLE 1.H5

Districtwise Population, Population of Workers (Main and Marginal) as Percentage of Total Population, and Population of Cultivators, Agricultural Labourers, and Workers in Household Industry (as Percentage of Total Main Workers) for Rural Areas

State/district	Rural population			Main workers (as percentage to rural population)			Marginal workers (as percentage of rural population)			Cultivators (as percentage of main workers in rural areas)			Agricultural labourers (as percentage of main workers in rural areas)			Workers in HH industry (as percentage of main workers in rural areas)		
	Total	Male	Female	Total	Male	Female	Total	Male	Female	Total	Male	Female	Total	Male	Female	Total	Male	Female
Haryana	**12,408,904**	**6,657,334**	**5,751,570**	**28.85**	**48.20**	**6.46**	**3.02**	**0.31**	**6.16**	**48.72**	**48.71**	**48.81**	**23.38**	**22.66**	**29.58**	**1.28**	**1.31**	**1.00**
Ambala	719,884	385,956	333,928	28.96	52.10	2.21	0.38	0.07	0.75	32.10	33.07	5.80	23.92	24.14	18.10	2.04	1.96	4.31
Yamunanagar	544,953	289,086	255,867	27.58	50.68	1.49	0.44	0.12	0.80	37.19	38.00	5.86	33.92	34.03	29.64	2.41	2.23	9.55
Kurukshetra	487,809	259,063	228,746	28.23	51.23	2.18	0.95	0.12	1.89	41.17	42.43	7.54	33.60	32.60	59.94	0.84	0.81	1.62
Kaithal	700,048	378,790	321,258	28.91	50.44	3.52	2.75	0.25	5.69	53.61	54.11	45.10	27.28	26.50	40.34	1.43	1.45	1.25
Karnal	642,514	346,131	296,383	28.74	49.91	4.01	0.70	0.09	1.40	38.11	39.18	22.52	36.77	35.26	58.75	1.77	1.65	3.43
Panipat	507,156	328,513	278,643	28.53	48.71	4.74	1.83	0.17	3.78	44.41	45.37	32.77	27.96	26.42	46.69	1.47	1.43	1.83
Sonipat	576,841	315,091	261,750	29.82	48.09	7.83	1.83	0.21	3.79	39.48	38.71	45.11	21.02	19.20	34.50	0.94	0.99	0.57
Rohtak	1,423,133	772,110	651,023	29.91	46.49	10.25	2.64	0.39	5.32	51.51	49.28	63.51	18.17	17.15	23.66	0.90	0.96	0.56
Faridabad	759,727	412,556	347,171	27.65	45.36	6.60	3.03	0.42	6.14	50.31	49.14	59.91	20.92	19.55	32.15	0.89	0.95	0.41
Gurgaon	913,386	489,263	424,123	27.74	46.01	6.67	5.34	0.34	11.11	49.22	48.07	58.38	15.98	14.38	28.67	1.19	1.21	1.05
Rewari	528,101	272,262	255,839	23.47	41.11	4.70	4.28	0.61	8.18	50.10	49.25	58.03	14.45	13.23	25.88	1.80	1.78	1.95
Mahendragarh	597,225	312,481	284,744	25.30	44.02	4.78	6.37	0.61	12.69	54.62	53.38	67.12	11.31	10.48	19.73	1.54	1.57	1.26
Bhiwani	943,150	501,522	441,628	28.22	44.63	9.60	5.48	0.63	10.99	51.98	60.61	6.46	13.88	13.48	15.98	1.16	1.31	0.41
Jind	797,560	434,946	362,514	29.78	49.14	6.56	3.79	0.31	7.97	57.16	56.46	63.46	22.69	22.09	28.16	1.55	1.64	0.76
Hissar	1,455,081	782,054	673,027	31.57	50.49	9.59	2.43	0.20	5.03	55.86	54.57	63.79	26.25	25.76	29.22	0.98	1.06	0.47
Sirsa	712,336	377,510	334,826	31.44	53.01	7.12	4.58	0.35	9.34	51.80	52.42	46.61	32.99	31.84	42.58	0.88	0.88	0.84

Source: Census of India, 1991.

TABLE 1.H6

Districtwise Average Size of Households and Dependency Ratio by Sex and Place of Residence, 1981 and 1991

State/district	All areas							Rural							Urban						
	Size of household 1991	Total dependency ratio			Old age dependency ratio			Size of household 1991	Total dependency ratio			Old age dependency ratio			Size of household 1991	Total dependency ratio			Old age dependency ratio		
		Total	Male	Female	Total	Male	Female		Total	Male	Female	Total	Male	Female		Total	Male	Female	Total	Male	Female
Haryana	**6.3**	**92.73**	**93.43**	**91.93**	**12.22**	**13.30**	**11.00**	**6.6**	**98.55**	**100.70**	**96.15**	**13.01**	**14.50**	**11.34**	**5.5**	**74.44**	**71.53**	**78.00**	**9.75**	**9.66**	**9.86**
Ambala	5.8	81.84	80.92	82.92	11.96	12.98	10.77	6.4	90.01	90.09	89.93	12.98	14.65	11.04	5.0	67.31	64.84	70.25	10.16	10.39	9.33
Yamunanagar	6.2	–	–	–	–	–	–	6.6	–	–	–	–	–	–	5.5	–	–	–	–	–	–
Kurukshetra	6.5	92.00	93.88	89.87	12.01	13.42	10.41	6.8	96.44	99.45	92.43	12.48	14.17	10.58	5.8	73.45	69.87	77.81	9.92	10.18	9.61
Kaithal	6.3	–	–	–	–	–	–	6.4	–	–	–	–	–	–	6.0	–	–	–	–	–	–
Karnal	6.2	91.09	91.25	90.90	12.37	13.56	10.99	6.5	97.83	99.03	96.43	13.15	14.76	11.28	5.6	74.29	72.05	76.96	10.42	10.58	10.23
Panipat	6.0	–	–	–	–	–	–	6.2	–	–	–	–	–	–	5.7	–	–	–	–	–	–
Sonipat	6.3	90.77	93.56	87.65	12.79	14.24	11.17	6.5	100.17	98.56	102.18	14.10	15.14	11.28	5.7	74.92	72.81	76.59	10.62	10.53	10.73
Rohtak	6.6	93.86	94.90	92.58	13.38	14.32	12.32	6.6	99.85	101.49	98.02	14.21	15.40	12.89	6.0	72.91	72.65	73.20	10.48	10.67	10.27
Faridabad	5.8	88.01	85.27	91.51	10.36	10.69	9.95	7.2	102.69	105.73	99.22	13.03	14.59	11.24	4.8	70.13	62.85	80.72	7.11	6.41	8.13
Gurgaon	6.7	95.73	95.76	95.69	12.04	12.75	11.22	7.0	100.44	101.31	99.47	12.48	13.54	11.29	5.8	78.80	77.60	81.73	10.44	10.01	10.95
Rewari	6.3	–	–	–	–	–	–	6.4	–	–	–	–	–	–	6.2	–	–	–	–	–	–
Mahendragarh	6.9	99.34	104.41	94.17	13.76	15.12	12.38	7.0	102.55	108.67	96.39	14.21	15.80	12.60	6.5	80.34	80.53	80.13	11.14	11.30	10.96
Bhiwani	6.6	104.21	105.32	102.99	13.12	14.40	11.71	6.7	108.55	110.99	105.93	13.64	15.28	11.89	6.0	84.11	80.65	88.36	10.68	10.58	10.80
Jind	6.5	96.42	99.59	92.82	11.62	13.40	9.59	6.5	98.83	103.01	94.14	11.97	13.99	9.69	6.0	82.56	80.51	85.01	9.60	10.08	9.03
Hissar	6.3	94.15	94.23	94.07	11.68	12.65	10.56	6.5	98.54	99.68	97.24	12.24	13.49	10.82	5.8	77.71	74.56	81.59	9.57	9.62	9.50
Sirsa	6.3	91.74	90.18	93.55	11.53	12.10	10.86	6.4	95.31	93.81	97.02	12.23	12.96	11.40	5.9	77.94	75.61	80.81	8.86	8.87	8.85

Source: Census of India, 1981, 1991.

TABLE 1.H7

Number of Females in the Age Group 15–44, Percentage of Married Females in Different Age Groups and Mean Age at Marriage

State/district	All areas	Urban						Rural					
	Mean age at marriage	Number of females in age group	Percentage of married females in the age group				Mean age at marriage	Number of females in age group	Percentage of married females in the age group				Mean age at marriage
	(years)	15–44	10–14	15–19	20–4	15–44	(years)	15–44	10–14	15–19	20–4	15–44	(years)
Haryana	**16.7**	**606,222**	**2.19**	**25.27**	**74.86**	**74.33**	**17.8**	**1,942,090**	**8.05**	**54.07**	**94.11**	**85.49**	**16.5**
Ambala	17.8	104,638	0.89	13.12	62.23	67.79	18.5	189,360	1.56	24.37	85.37	75.80	17.4
Kurukshetra	17.2	40,179	1.71	21.26	72.85	72.39	17.8	185,499	5.38	39.41	88.27	79.76	17.0
Karnal	17.0	74,804	1.84	22.36	71.20	72.87	17.9	183,404	6.43	51.45	93.34	84.71	16.6
Sonipat	16.7	32,533	1.49	25.42	72.43	84.21	17.8	135,068	4.89	55.24	96.66	86.97	16.5
Rohtak	16.6	59,264	2.05	23.32	67.90	70.72	17.6	201,950	5.80	55.92	96.54	86.74	16.3
Faridabad	17.0	84,318	1.76	33.95	84.19	81.41	17.9	108,993	6.71	65.99	98.03	89.90	16.4
Gurgaon	16.6	35,751	2.29	25.33	77.60	74.36	17.7	129,695	6.18	59.60	97.46	87.64	16.4
Mahendragarh	16.2	26,350	4.05	35.55	82.78	78.49	17.0	164,221	7.67	59.60	97.71	88.11	16.1
Bhiwani	16.1	29,572	3.58	40.34	85.51	79.89	16.7	145,418	12.22	68.55	98.12	89.86	16.0
Jind	15.7	27,068	5.07	31.38	85.06	77.83	17.1	155,127	17.40	75.66	98.09	91.81	15.5
Hissar	16.5	61,191	2.86	28.88	79.94	75.66	17.5	232,086	14.13	62.64	94.50	87.31	16.2
Sirsa	17.4	30,556	1.79	25.70	81.13	75.74	17.9	111,266	5.07	40.17	87.81	79.73	17.3

Source: Census of India, 1981, Fertility and Child Mortality Estimates of Haryana, Occasional Paper No. 10 of 1987.

TABLE 1.H8
Child Mortality Estimates by Districts for All Areas, 1991

State/district	q(1)			q(2)			q(3)			q(5)		
	M	F	P	M	F	P	M	F	P	M	F	P
Haryana	**57**	**54**	**52**	**59**	**66**	**62**	**67**	**68**	**64**	**71**	**80**	**73**
	(132)	(119)	(126)	(121)	(127)	(124)	(118)	(133)	(125)	(125)	(153)	(138)
Ambala	49	61	55	54	71	56	59	78	67	64	83	71
Yamunanagar	60	62	61	68	64	66	71	72	71	77	78	76
Kurukshetra	35	36	35	69	72	7	81	81	81	94	92	93
Kaithal	89	74	81	95	83	86	100	89	94	107	105	106
Karnal	42	45	44	58	52	55	59	57	58	65	69	67
Panipat	71	55	64	62	75	73	67	79	75	79	88	81
Sonipat	74	71	72	79	78	79.	83	87	85	99	91	94
Rohtak	55	40	48	57	62	59	58	64	62	71	82	76
Faridabad	49	66	56	52	69	58	53	71	62	60	73	66
Gurgaon	85	83	84	99	97	98	104	101	102	106	108	107
Rewari	64	59	61	62	65	64	72	69	71	74	81	78
Mahendragarh	44	50	47	60	69	65	86	86	86	88	100	94
Bhiwani	52	50	51	109	108	107	111	112	110	114	118	115
Jind	46	48	47	77	81	79	81	95	83	87	112	99
Hisar	54	53	54	56	57	57	66	69	68	70	79	74
Sirsa	64	65	65	66	73	67	75	77	76	80	81	80

Note: Figures are graduated estimates; figures in brackets for the year 1981 are ungraduated estimates.
Source: District Level Estimates of Fertility and Child Mortality for 1991 and their Relations with Other Variables, Occasional Paper No. 1 of 1997; Registrar General, Government of India.

TABLE 1.H9
State-level Religionwise Fertility Indices by Place of Residence

Religion	All areas				Rural				Urban			
	GFR	GMFR	TFR	TMFR	GFR	GMFR	TFR	TMFR	GFR	GMFR	TFR	TMFR
All Religions	**143**	**171**	**4.5**	**5.1**	**153**	**178**	**4.9**	**5.4**	**110**	**146**	**3.3**	**4.2**
Hindus	145	171	4.6	5.1	156	178	5.0	5.4	111	142	3.3	4.2
Muslims	164	184	5.2	5.6	165	184	5.6	5.3	158	182	4.8	5.5
Christians	101	162	2.9	5.1	144	203	5.3	7.2	85	143	2.2	4.0
Sikhs	110	159	3.6	4.9	116	166	3.8	5.1	88	132	2.8	4.2
Jains	97	137	2.9	4.1	106	144	3.9	3.9	94	135	2.7	4.3

Source: Census of India, 1981, Fertility and Child Mortality Estimates of Haryana, Occasional Paper No. 10 of 1987.

TABLE 1.H10
Districtwise Adjusted Fertility Indices

State/district	1981				1991			
	GFR	GMFR	TFR	TMFR	GFR	GMFR	TFR	TMFR
Haryana	**170**	**204**	**5.4**	**6.1**	**145**	**172**	**4.3**	**5.3**
Ambala	156	209	5.0	6.3	118	158	3.5	5.4
Kurukshetra	171	215	5.5	6.4	129	170	3.8	5.5
Karnal	173	211	5.6	6.3	149	186	4.4	5.8
Sonipat	165	194	5.3	5.9	140	169	4.2	5.2
Rohtak	169	201	5.4	6.1	145	173	4.4	5.3
Faridabad	169	195	5.2	5.7	160	188	4.8	5.8
Gurgaon	171	200	5.3	6.0	186	217	5.7	6.6
Mahendragarh	162	186	5.1	5.6	148	171	4.4	5.1
Bhiwani	186	211	5.9	6.4	145	167	4.2	5.0
Jind	178	198	5.7	6.0	151	174	4.5	5.1
Hissar	174	203	5.4	5.9	152	179	4.4	5.3
Sirsa	172	215	5.4	6.2	138	171	3.9	5.2

Note: Separate estimates for rural and urban areas are not available.

Sources: Census of India, 1981, Fertility and Child Mortality Estimates of Haryana, Occasional Paper No. 10 of 1987; District Level Estimates of Fertility and Child Mortality for 1991 and their Relations with Other Variables, Occasional Paper No. 1 of 1997.

TABLE 1.P1.1
Per Thousand Distribution of Persons across MPCE Classes and Average Monthly Consumer Expenditure per Person in Haryana

Rural areas			Urban areas		
MPCE class	Persons	Average expenditure	MPCE class	Persons	Average expenditure
00–65	10	51.32	00–90	31	79.36
65–80	11	74.04	90–110	43	101.18
80–95	45	89.22	110–35	71	124.54
95–110	58	102.36	135–60	106	147.34
110–25	62	116.29	160–85	142	172.33
125–40	85	132.41	185–215	143	199.9
140–60	104	149.71	215–55	128	238.98
160–80	120	170.54	255–310	118	283.47
180–215	161	198.09	310–85	93	348.03
215–80	174	242.61	385–520	60	440.05
280–385	96	330.14	520–700	46	606.93
385 and above	74	584.22	700 and above	19	1066.13
All classes	**1000**	**214.66**	**All classes**	**1000**	**251.76**

Source: Sarvekshana, 48th Issue, Vol. xv, No. 1, 1991.

TABLE 1.P2.1
Distribution of Number of Operational Holdings and Area Operated for All Social Groups, 1985–6 and 1990–1, and Distribution of Average Size per Holding for All Groups and SCs, 1990–1

Size-class (ha)	Number		Percentage variation in number	Area		Percentage variation in area	Av. size per holding (ha) 1990–1	
	1985–6	1990–1		1985–6	1990–1		All groups	SCs
Below 0.02	**590**	**620**	**5.1**	**7**	**10**	**42.9**	**0.02**	**0.01**
0.02–0.5	298,293	374,297	25.5	77,618	103,462	33.3	0.28	0.28
0.5–1.0	203,301	247,109	21.5	151,669	191,625	26.3	0.78	0.89
Marginal	502,184	622,026	23.9	229,294	295,097	28.7	0.47	0.50
1.0–2.0	264,722	303,718	14.7	382,778	462,634	20.9	1.52	1.80
Small	264,722	303,718	14.7	382,778	462,634	20.9	1.52	1.80
2.0–3.0	166,675	207,749	24.6	399,875	508,835	27.2	2.45	2.62
3.0–4.0	114,635	128,523	12.1	390,445	434,832	11.4	3.38	3.63
Semi-medium	281,310	336,272	19.5	790,320	943,667	19.4	2.81	2.94
4.0–5.0	81,915	84,114	2.7	356,818	374,443	4.9	4.45	4.63
5.0–7.5	106,506	91,991	–13.6	628,157	541,020	–13.9	5.88	6.39
7.5–10.0	50,621	45,693	–9.7	424,414	384,948	–9.3	8.42	8.18
Medium	239,042	221,798	–7.2	1,409,389	1,300,411	–7.7	5.86	5.88
10.0–20.0	51,373	38,038	–26.0	639,080	476,677	–25.4	12.53	14.13
> 20.0 ha	8760	7927	–9.5	262,997	232,729	–11.5	29.36	53.12
Large	60,133	45,965	–23.6	902,077	709,406	–21.4	15.43	21.42
All sizes	**1,347,391**	**1,529,779**	**13.5**	**3,713,858**	**3,711,215**	**-0.1**	**2.43**	**1.63**

Source: Agricultural Census, 1990–1, Agricultural Census Division, Ministry of Agriculture.

TABLE 1.P2.2
Districtwise Distribution of Number of Operational Holdings and Area Operated for All Social Groups and SCs in Haryana, 1985–6 and 1990–1

State/district	All social groups				Scheduled castes			
	Number		Area		Number		Area	
	1985–6	1990–1	1985–6	1990–1	1985–6	1990–1	1985–6	1990–1
Ambala	**119,809**	**83,433**	**250,105**	**156,542**	**8873**	**5589**	**11,392**	**4781**
Yamunanagar	*	56,844	*	123,519	*	4608	*	4420
Kurukshetra	122,032	61,658	321,031	143,957	1686	1170	3054	2236
Kaithal	NA	74,429	NA	200,187	*	1536	*	2319
Karnal	134,831	88,125	318,133	215,970	2170	2260	4081	3024
Panipat	*	53,972	*	100,319	*	155	*	207
Sonipat	84,956	97,143	181,402	181,501	211	313	356	471
Rohtak	126,101	141,787	329,755	318,920	632	708	767	748
Hissar	159,024	225,070	591,683	650,524	8436	11,417	16,179	24,343
Sirsa	90,239	111,391	392,597	395,022	4827	6701	10,559	12,221
Bhiwani	124,794	123,713	409,280	346,003	7786	6415	21,333	15,234
Jind	84,941	89,861	288,071	245,038	1870	2274	2302	2136
Gurgaon	105,361	110,697	203,222	206,833	842	972	914	904
Faridabad	92,260	89,292	168,505	145,807	2573	1822	2726	1736
Mahendragarh	103,043	67,108	260,074	155,185h	519	342	910	594
Rewari	*	55,256	*	125,088	*	88	*	173
Haryana	1,347,391	1,529,779	3,713,858	3,711,215	39,925	46,370	74,573	75,547

Note: * District formed after 1985–6.

Source: Agricultural Census, 1990–1, Agricultural Census Division, Ministry of Agriculture.

2 Survey Report for Haryana

The units of observation and analysis of this study are rural households. The total number of rural households selected in the sample is 1808 (of which 86 were non-response), spread over 90 villages and 11 districts in the state.

TABLE 2.1
Allocation of Sample Households in Various Strata

Stratum number	Stratum: HH category/ religion/caste	Stratum: Occupation	Selected sample households
1	Households containing at least one pregnant woman		301
2	Households containing at least one child aged less than 12 months but no pregnant women		305
3	Scheduled castes	Marginal farmer	51
4	Scheduled castes	Small farmer	46
5	Scheduled castes	Large farmer	40
6	Scheduled castes	Agricultural labourer	151
7	Scheduled castes	Other	154
8	Others	Marginal farmer	151
9	Others	Small farmer	144
10	Others	Large farmer	94
11	Others	Agricultural labourer	108
12	Others	Other	263
	Total		1808

2.1 Major Findings of Survey Data

The survey has collected data on a number of indicators in the areas of (a) income and material well-being, (b) education, and (c) health care facilities for rural Haryana. However, this chapter considers only a few selected variables for analysis. These are (i) household and per capita income, (ii) poverty line groups, (iii) asset ownership; (iv) literacy rate; (v) net enrolment rate; (vi) expenditure on morbidity; (vii) immunization; and (viii) CBR and CDR. The analysis focusses on the evaluation of intra-group differentials of these indicators. An attempt has also been made to highlight the gender disparities in the access to education and health care facilities.

2.1.1 Household and Per Capita Income

Table A2.1 presents the per capita household income according to income class and percentage of households belonging to different groups. About 18 per cent of the households belong to the high income groups of Rs 62,001—86,000 and Rs 86,000 and above and about 34 per cent of the households belong to the lowest income group of up to Rs 20,000. The intra-income group differentials are very high in rural areas. The mean per capita income of the highest income group of Rs 86,000 and above is Rs 15,658—which is about seven times higher than the mean per capita income of the lowest income group.

About 7 per cent of the households are large farmers, as compared to 23 per cent who are landless and 18 per cent who are landless wage earners. Very high intra-group income differentials are observed in the landholding groups. The mean per capita income ranges from Rs 4989 for landless wage earners to Rs 15,272 for large farmers.

Among occupation groups, the highest income of Rs 8094 is observed in the agricultural group, followed by the salaried earners, professional, and self-employed group. The lowest income of Rs 2721 is observed in the wage earners group. Among social groups, the highest per capita income of Rs 10,528 is observed for other minorities, and the lowest is seen to be Rs 3936 for the SCs.

The per capita income of the household size group up to four is Rs 7963; this is much higher than that for the household size of 5–7, viz., Rs 6413 and the household size of 8 and above, viz., Rs 5757.

Very high intra-group income differential is observed among the poverty line groups. The per capita income is as low as Rs 1389 for those living in the lower segment below poverty line group, in marked contrast to a per capita income of Rs 13,191 for those in the upper segment above the poverty line group. The per capita income of the both literate group is much higher at Rs 7574 than the income of the none literate group which is only Rs 4829. The income differential is relatively less between the female and male literate groups. Very marginal intra-group differential is observed among village development groups, with the per capita income ranging from Rs 6271 for the high village development group to Rs 6580 for the low village development group. The intra-group income differentials are very high in household income,

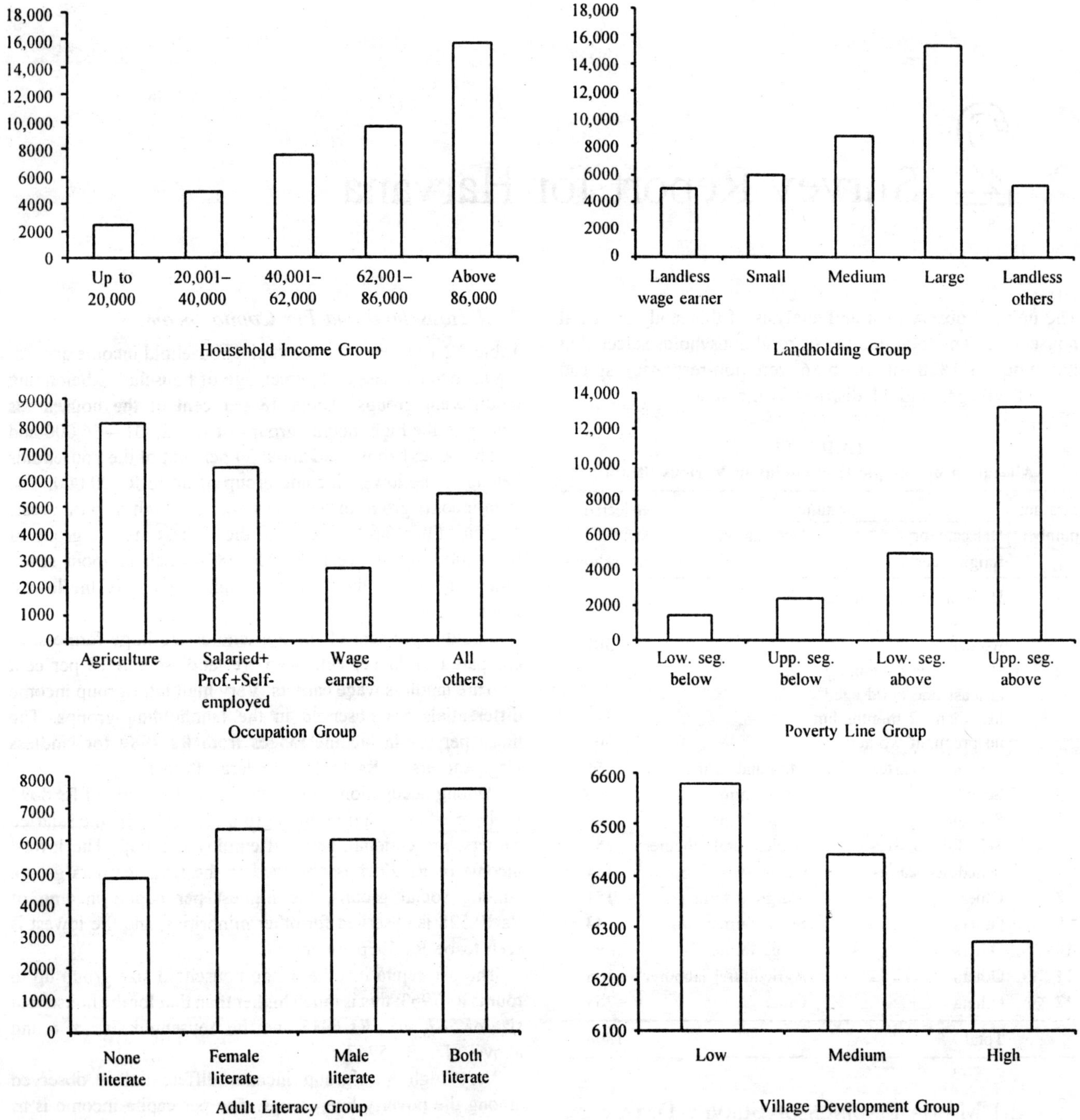

FIGURE 2.1: **Per Capita Income by Population Group (in Rs per annum)**

landholding, social, and poverty classifications (source-wise incomes are presented in Tables A.2.2 and A.2.3).

2.1.2 Asset Ownership

OWNERSHIP OF LAND AND ANIMALS

The most valuable assets for rural people are land and animals. These two assets contribute to the household income in many ways. Households in the highest income group own about 15.6 acres of land whereas those in the lowest income group own only 2.6 acres of land (see Table A2.4). Very high intra-group differentials are observed in the ownership of land among the household income groups of rural Haryana. However, a fair distribution is observed in the ownership of draught and milch animals among household income groups, except in the highest income group. On an average, 3 draught animals and 5 milch animals are reared by the highest income group.

Marginal farmers own a little less than 2 acres of land, compared to about 19 acres of land owned by large farmers. A contrasting picture is observed in the ownership of animals. It seems that landless others own more draught animals than

large farmers. Landless others have 8 draught animals whereas large farmers have only 3. Again landless others own only 2 milch animals compared with 5 milch animals owned by large farmers. However, landless wage earners own only about 2 animals.

About 3 and 7 acres of land are owned by each household in the salaried earners, professionals and self-employed group and the agricultural group, respectively. There is a marginal difference in the average landholding size between Hindus (6 acres) and Muslims (5 acres). About 8 acres of land is owned by the highest household size group, whereas only 4 acres of land is owned by the smallest household size group of up to 4 members.

The upper segment above the poverty line group owns about 9 acres of land on an average, compared to about 2 acres of land owned by the upper segment below the poverty line group. Both these groups, on an average, own three draught animals. However, the ownership of milch animals ranges from 2 for the lower segment below the poverty line group to 3 for the upper segment above the poverty line group.

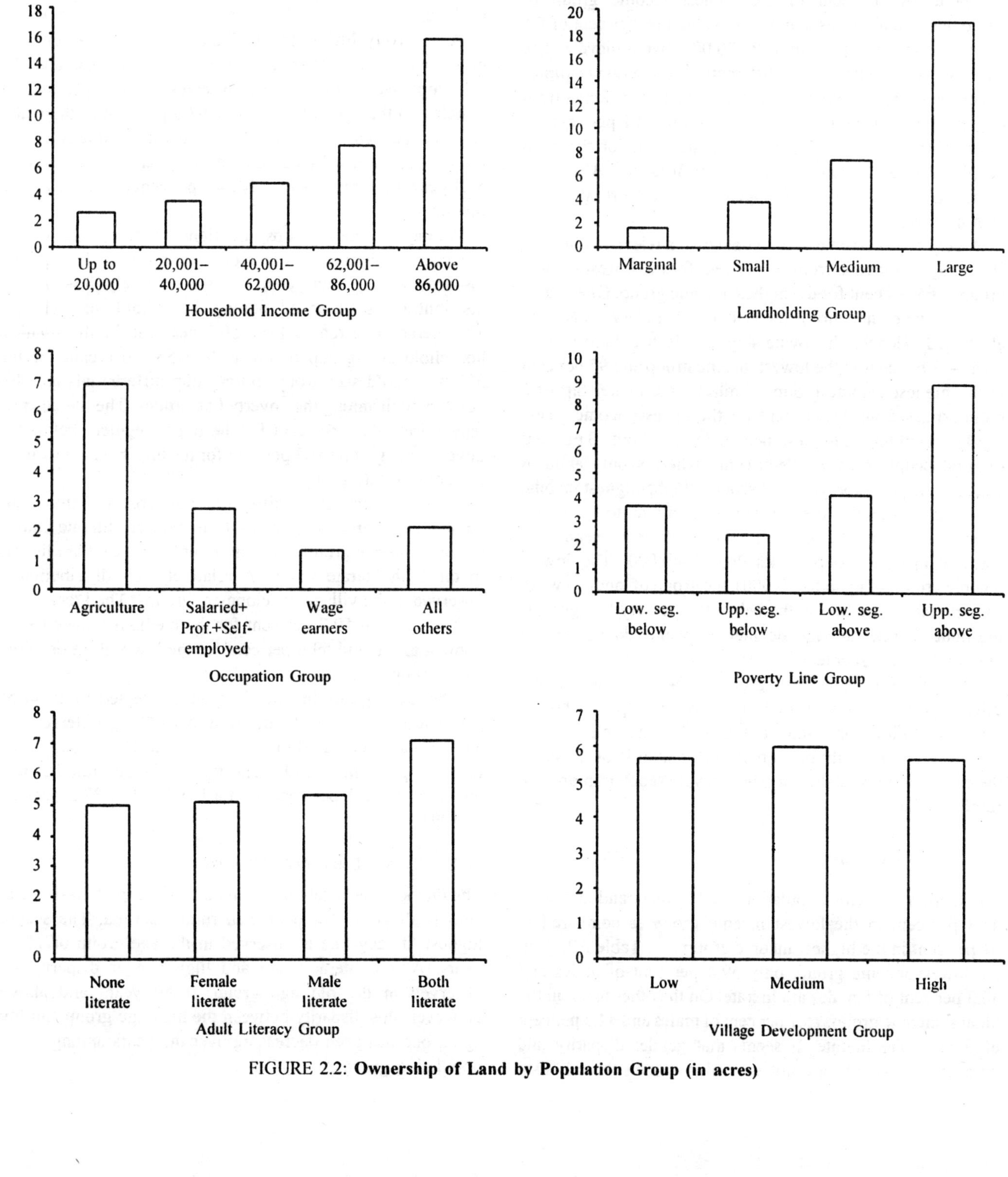

FIGURE 2.2: **Ownership of Land by Population Group (in acres)**

A more fair distribution of land as well as animals is observed among village development groups. Households in each village development group own about 6 acres of land and 2 draught and 2 milch animals.

OWNERSHIP OF HOUSEHOLD AND DURABLE ASSETS

Almost all groups of people in rural areas own a house. However, only 45 per cent of these have a separate kitchen. There are no intra- and inter-group differentials in the ownership of a house.

About 78 per cent of the highest income group of Rs 86,000 and above as compared to about 69 per cent of the lowest income group of up to Rs 20,000 own a bicycle. The intra- as well as inter-group differentials in the ownership of a bicycle are negligible in rural areas. The figures range from 61.5 per cent for the none literate group to 88.1 per cent for other minorities. The bicycle is a basic need for the rural people in order to commute over short distances. Also, as it is affordable by many in these areas most of the rural people own a bicycle.

A very high percentage of people own a television in rural Haryana, the range is from 23 per cent for the lowest income group to 65 per cent for the highest income group. One reason for the large ownership of television is that Haryana is fully electrified. Hence, the ownership of electric fans is also high—58 per cent in the lowest income group and 95 per cent in the highest income group. Similarly, the ownership of a radio ranges from 47 per cent for the lowest income group to 84 per cent for the highest income group. About 73 per cent of rural people own an electric fan whereas only about 6 per cent own a motorcycle or a scooter. In the highest income group, 23 per cent of the households own a motorcycle or a scooter as compared to about 4 per cent of the households in the low income group of Rs 20,001–40,000. The lowest income group (of up to Rs 20,000), the group of landless wage earners, the population in the below the poverty line groups, the none literate and female literate groups do not own a motorcycle or a scooter.

It is observed that intra-group as well as inter-group differentials are not very high in the ownership of a house, a bicycle, a television, a radio or transistor, and an electric fan. However, a very high intra-group differential is observed in the case of the ownership of a motorcycle/scooter among the rural population.

2.1.3 Literacy Rate

The literacy rate (for population aged 7 years and above) is 45.3 per cent in the lowest income group as compared to 61 per cent in the highest income group (see Table A2.7). In the lowest income group, only 59.4 per cent of males and 30.3 per cent of females are literate. On the other hand, in the highest income group, 75.7 per cent of males and 44.5 per cent of females are literate. It seems that gender disparity and intra-group disparity are not very high among these household income groups. Among landholding groups, the lowest literacy rate of 39.3 per cent is observed among landless wage earners. Gender disparity is also relatively high among landless wage earners. However, the intra-group variation in the access to education is not remarkably high, particularly among males. It ranges from 52.4 per cent for the landless wage earners to 68.2 per cent for the large farmers. One interesting but contradictory finding is that the literacy rate is the highest among the landless others. This is probably because a majority, if not all, of the landless others belong to the business class and, therefore, do not depend on land.

A relatively higher literacy rate is observed among the group comprising salaried earners, professionals, and the self-employed—81.4 per cent for males and 49.3 per cent for females. In the agricultural group, 68.9 per cent of the males and 37.5 per cent of the females are literate. A relatively low literacy rate is observed among the wage earners group, with 53.1 per cent of males and only 24.9 per cent of females being literate.

Among religious groups, the highest literacy rate of 72.1 per cent is observed among other minorities. The gender disparity among this group is also relatively less. A fair distribution is observed among household size groups. The literacy rate ranges from 50.2 per cent for the smallest household size group of up to 4 to 56.5 per cent for the 5–7 household size group. Intra-group differentials are also not very high among the poverty line groups. The literacy rate ranges from 45.1 per cent for the upper segment below the poverty line group to 63 per cent for the upper segment above the poverty line group.

Very high intra-group differentials are observed among the adult literacy groups. Only 18.4 per cent are literate among the none literate group whereas about 75 per cent are literate in the both literate group. A relatively fair distribution is observed in the village development groups. The literacy rate ranges between 50.7 per cent for the medium village development group and 59.6 per cent for the low village development group.

The literacy rate in rural Haryana increased to about 55 per cent in 1994 from 50 per cent in 1991. The literacy rate among males increased to 69.4 per cent in 1994 from a level of 64.78 per cent in 1991. The female literacy rate has also increased to 38.1 per cent from a low level of 32.5 per cent in 1991.

LITERACY RATE BY AGE GROUPS

The literacy rate is the highest in the age group of 10–14 years among all groups of people in rural Haryana. The second highest literacy rate is observed in the age group of 15–19 years. A low literacy rate and high gender disparity are observed in the old age group of 50 years and above. However, this disparity between the high age group and low age group has been decreasing over the years among all the population groups.

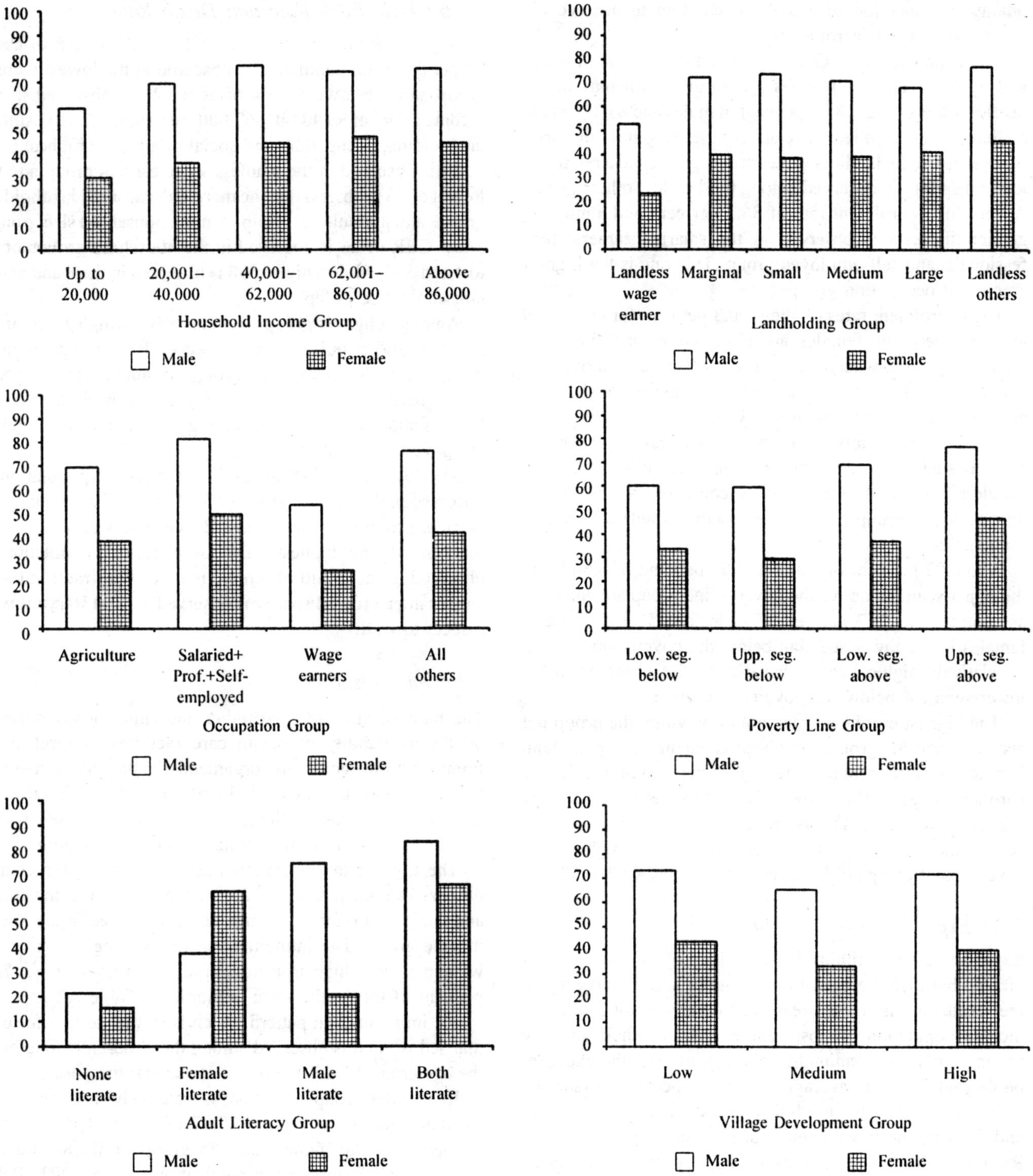

FIGURE 2.3: **Male–Female Literacy Rate by Population Group (in percentage)**

2.1.4 Enrolment Rate

The enrolment rate in the age group of 6–14 years ranges from 69.2 per cent for the lowest income group to 89.8 per cent for the high income group of Rs 62,001–86,000. In the lowest income group, 75.7 per cent of males and 63.1 per cent of females are enrolled (Table A2.8). About 89 per cent of males and 90.5 per cent of females in the high income group of Rs 62,001–86,000 are enrolled. The gender disparity index is more than one, which implies that girls are getting better opportunities, probably because of the effective New Education Policy. This policy laid emphasis on universal enrolment, universal retention, and a substantial improvement in the quality of education to enable all children to achieve the minimum level of learning (MLL).

In the landless wage earners group, 68.8 per cent of males and 49.9 per cent of females are enrolled, whereas in the landless others group, 87.8 per cent of males and 83.2 per cent of females are enrolled. A relatively higher gender disparity is observed in the landless wage earners group and a relatively lower disparity is observed among the landless others group. A very high enrolment rate of 86.2 per cent and almost no gender disparity is observed in the salaried earners, professionals, and self-employed group. This rate is the highest among all occupation groups.

High enrolment rates of about 90.3 per cent for males and 86.8 per cent for females are observed among the other minorities group, whereas low enrolment rates of about 73.6 per cent for males and 62.7 per cent for females are observed among SCs. The gender disparity is also relatively higher among SCs. Marginally higher enrolment rates of 88.9 per cent for males and 79.3 per cent for females are observed in the smallest household size group as compared to the largest household size group (80.2 per cent for males and 69.3 per cent for females).

About 92 per cent of males and 85 per cent of females in the upper segment above the poverty line group are enrolled, as compared to 71.3 per cent of males and 57.7 per cent of females in the lower segment below the poverty line group. A relatively higher gender disparity is also observed in the lower segment below the poverty line group.

The highest enrolment rate, not only within the group but also between all groups, is observed in the group of both literate—94.4 per cent of males and 93 per cent of females are enrolled. No gender disparity exists in this group. A relatively higher enrolment rate is observed in the low village development group (83.6 per cent) than in the high village development group (79.2 per cent) (see Tables A2.9 to A2.14).

2.1.5 Expenditure on Morbidity

Expenditure on morbidity is determined by not only current income but also the nature of morbidity and the urgency of the treatment. In rural areas, particularly among the low income population groups, people even sell their valuable assets such as land, animals, gold, etc. to meet the expenses on morbidity. On an average, Rs 120 is spent per person per year on short duration morbidity, like diarrhoea, cold–cough and fever by the low income groups of up to Rs 20,000 and Rs 20,001–40,000, whereas only Rs 83 is spent by the highest income group of Rs 86,000 and above. However, the greater per person expenditure on long duration morbidity, such as epilepsy, hypertension, diabetes, heart disease, mental disease, tuberculosis (TB), leprosy, and cancer, is incurred by the higher income group. It seems that intra-group variation is not very high as far as expenditure on both long and short duration morbidity is concerned (for details on short and major morbidity rates and age-wise morbidity rates see Tables A2.15 to A2.17).

2.1.6 Crude Birth Rate and Death Rate

Among household income groups, the highest CBR of about 34 per thousand population is observed in the lowest income group and the lowest CBR of about 25 is observed in the income group of Rs 40,001–62,000 (see Table A2.19). Among landholding, occupation, and social groups, the highest CBR of 37 is observed in the landless wage earners group and the lowest of 26 is observed in the marginal and small landholding groups and agricultural group. Among household size groups, a low CBR of 26 is observed in the household groups of up to 4 and 5–7, while a high of 38 is observed in the 8 and above household size group.

Among religious groups, Hindus have a high CBR of 31 per thousand population. The lowest CBR among religious groups, as well as among all groups, of about 10 is observed in the group of other minorities. On the other hand, the highest CBR of about 43 is observed among the upper segment below the poverty line group.

The lowest CDR of about 2 per thousand population is observed in the income group of Rs 40,001–62,000, marginal farmers group and low village development group. On the other hand, the highest CDR of about 23 population is observed in the group of female literate. Very high intra- as well as inter-group disparity is observed in rural Haryana with respect to CDR.

2.1.7 Immunization

The immunization of the mother and child mostly depends on the availability of health care facilities in rural areas. Immunization camps are organized by the government in the rural areas, but these are highly irregular. Even if these are organized, most of the time parents (due to their wrong beliefs) do not bring their children for immunization.

The highest immunization rate of about 90 per cent is observed among married women in the highest income group, and the lowest of about 68 per cent is observed in the lowest income group. The immunization rate among ever married women is very high in rural Haryana. On an average, 73.6 per cent of the mothers are immunized (Table A2.22).

An immunization pattern which is similar to that for ever married women is observed among the children belonging to the age group 12–23 months. It seems that the intra-group as well as inter-group variation is relatively less as far as immunization is concerned; 87.27 per cent of the children belonging to the highest income group of Rs 86,000 and above get all 8 doses of immunization such as DPT, Polio, BCG, measles, etc. (see Table A2.23), as compared to 68.67 per cent of the children belonging to the lowest income group.

2.2 Concluding Remarks

1. The per capita household income which shows the overall economic development of the households is Rs 6368 which is much higher than the national average of Rs 4485.

2. The intra-group income differentials are very high in rural areas. The mean per capita income of the highest income group of Rs 86,000 and above is Rs 15,658, which is about seven times higher than the mean per capita income of the lowest income group.

3. Very high intra-group differentials are observed in the ownership of land among different income groups. The households in the highest income group own about 15.6 acres of land whereas the lowest income group households own only 2.6 acres of land.

4. All rural groups of population own a house, but only 45 per cent of these have a separate kitchen.

5. About 65 per cent of households in highest income groups own a television as against only 23 per cent in the lowest income group.

6. The literacy rate in rural Haryana increased to about 55 per cent in 1994 from 50 per cent in 1991. The literacy rate among females increased by 5.6 percentage points during the period of 1991 to 1994 which is higher than the percentage increase for males.

7. The highest enrolment rate, not only within the group but also between all groups, is observed in the group of both literate—94.4 per cent of males and 93 per cent of females are enrolled. No gender disparity exists in this group.

8. On an average, Rs 120 is spent per person per year on short duration morbidity, like diarrhoea, cold–cough and fever by low income group whereas only Rs 83 is spent by the highest income group.

9. The immunization rate is high for the highest income group and low for the lowest income group.

The above findings suggest that Haryana is an economically developed state. However, high gender disparity in education lowers its otherwise high status among the states.

TABLE A2.1
Levels of Income and Distribution of Households by Population Group in Rural Haryana

Population group	No. of sample households	% estmtd households	Household size	Income (Rs per year)	
				Per household	Per capita
Household income					
Up to 20,000	602	33.5	5.4	12,816	2378
20,001–40,000	577	32.8	6.1	29,146	4815
40,001–62,000	259	16.2	6.5	49,235	7579
62,001–86,000	147	9.4	7.6	72,789	9622
Above 86,000	137	8.1	8.9	139,117	15,658
Landholding					
Landless wage earner	326	18.4	5.8	29,060	4989
Small	320	19.5	6.6	39,273	5988
Medium	184	12.4	7.0	61,515	8779
Large	118	7.3	8.5	129,087	15,272
Landless others	432	22.9	5.7	29,937	5243
All land owners	948	57.6	6.7	52,216	7838
All land non-owners	774	42.4	5.7	23,311	4056
Occupation					
Agriculture	719	44.0	6.7	54,041	8094
Salaried+prof.+s.empl.	392	21.9	6.3	40,380	6435
Wage earners	372	21.1	5.8	15,795	2721
All groups others	239	13.0	5.7	30,734	5419
Caste					
SCs	541	27.1	6.0	23,458	3936
Religion					
Hindus	1591	92.4		40,028	6422
Other minorities	33	2.2	6.0	63,659	10,528
Household size					
Up to 4	401	24.0	3.5	27,536	7963
5–7	867	52.0	5.9	37,712	6413
8 and above	454	24.0	9.9	57,253	5757
Poverty line					
Lower segment below	183	10.1	7.0	9,686	1389
Upper segment below	239	13.0	6.4	15,118	2373
Lower segment above	864	48.7	6.3	31,115	4909
Upper segment above	436	28.2	5.9	77,434	13,191
Adult literacy					
None literate	356	19.5	5.4	25,906	4829
Female literate	43	2.6	5.4	34,033	6315
Male literate	791	46.2	6.2	36,927	5989
Both literate	532	31.7	7.1	53,499	7574
Village development					
Low	181	10.5	6.3	41,155	6580
Medium	622	37.5	6.4	40,960	6442
High	919	52.0	6.2	38,990	6271
All groups	**1722**	**100.0**	**6.3**	**39,956**	**6368**

TABLE A2.2

Sourcewise Percentage Distribution of Household Income by Population Group in Rural Haryana

Population group	Percentage distribution w.r.t. total household income											
	Agr.+alld act.	Artisan/ ind. work	Petty trd. sm. bus.	Org. trd. bus.	Salaried empl.	Qualified prof.	Rent/int. dividend	Agr. wage	Non-agr. wage	Other sources	All sources	Total
Household income												
Up to 20,000	30.5	5.3	4.6	0.2	10.8	0.0	1.2	18.3	25.5	3.6	100.0	12,816
20,001–40,000	41.2	3.8	7.8	0.2	27.7	0.3	1.3	4.0	9.0	4.6	100.0	29,146
40,001–62,000	56.9	2.9	3.5	1.2	26.3	0.3	1.7	0.4	2.3	4.6	100.0	49.235
62,001–86,000	62.8	1.8	3.4	0.6	21.2	2.2	2.6	0.0	0.9	4.4	100.0	72.789
Above 86,000	82.3	0.8	1.6	0.7	11.7	0.0	1.2	0.0	0.0	1.7	100.0	139,117
Landholding												
Landless wage earner	3.9	1.7	0.6	0.0	2.1	0.0	0.3	33.1	56.2	2.1	100.0	15,517
Marginal	43.2	2.4	4.7	1.1	33.3	0.1	1.3	1.9	4.5	7.4	100.0	29,060
Small	71.3	1.4	2.5	0.7	17.1	0.9	1.5	0.2	0.9	3.4	100.0	39,273
Medium	84.7	0.8	0.9	0.8	8.9	0.4	0.6	0.0	0.4	2.4	100.0	61,515
Large	91.5	0.1	1.6	0.1	4.6	0.0	1.0	0.0	0.0	1.2	100.0	129,087
Landless others	5.5	9.9	14.0	1.0	54.1	1.3	4.2	1.2	2.3	6.4	100.0	29,937
All land owners	76.1	1.0	2.2	0.6	14.0	0.4	1.1	0.4	1.1	3.2	100.0	52,216
All land non-owners	5.0	7.4	9.9	0.7	38.2	0.9	3.0	11.0	18.8	5.1	100.0	23,311
Occupation												
Agriculture	89.3	0.6	1.4	0.2	4.9	0.1	0.6	0.2	0.7	2.0	100.0	54,041
Salaried+prof.+s.empl.	15.3	0.9	1.5	0.2	74.9	1.9	1.4	0.4	1.0	2.4	100.0	40.380
Wage earners	6.2	1.5	0.6	0.0	1.9	0.0	0.3	31.8	55.7	1.9	100.0	15,795
All others	14.2	19.1	29.3	4.6	3.2	0.0	8.5	1.1	2.2	17.9	100.0	30,734
Caste												
SCs	26.8	4.8	4.9	0.2	27.1	0.8	0.9	13.4	18.3	2.8	100.0	23,458
Religion												
Hindus	57.6	2.6	4.3	0.6	20.5	0.5	1.6	3.2	5.3	3.7	100.0	40,027
Other minorities	74.9	1.5	0.0	0.0	19.9	0.0	1.4	0.3	2.0	0.0	100.0	63,659
Household size												
Up to 4	50.1	3.3	5.3	0.5	20.2	1.0	2.1	4.5	7.4	5.6	100.0	27,536
5–7	58.8	2.3	3.7	0.1	20.5	0.7	1.4	3.4	5.7	3.5	100.0	37.712
8 and above	62.0	2.7	4.1	1.5	19.0	0.0	1.6	1.8	4.3	2.9	100.0	57,253
Poverty line												
Lower segment below	34.6	1.8	2.7	0.0	4.3	0.0	1.7	24.5	27.8	2.6	100.0	9686
Upper segment below	30.8	5.2	6.8	0.4	8.9	0.0	1.0	17.6	26.0	3.3	100.0	15,118
Lower segment above	45.3	4.3	5.4	1.1	25.8	0.3	1.5	3.9	8.1	4.2	100.0	31,115
Upper segment above	71.2	1.2	3.0	0.4	17.7	0.7	1.6	0.1	0.9	3.3	100.0	77,437
Adult literacy												
None literate	64.4	3.2	2.0	0.2	6.0	0.0	0.4	7.7	12.8	3.3	100.0	25,906
Female literate	65.0	1.2	4.1	0.0	0.0	0.0	5.6	6.1	7.8	10.2	100.0	34,033
Male literate	60.3	2.6	4.4	0.5	17.6	0.3	1.0	3.4	6.5	3.4	100.0	36,927
Both literate	54.5	2.4	4.4	0.9	27.6	0.9	2.3	1.1	2.2	3.7	100.0	53,499
Village development												
Low	56.2	2.7	5.0	0.7	21.4	1.5	0.8	3.3	4.6	3.6	100.0	41,155
Medium	62.5	2.4	3.4	0.4	18.0	0.6	1.5	2.9	5.2	3.2	100.0	40,960
High	56.0	2.7	4.5	0.8	21.1	0.2	1.8	3.1	5.9	4.0	100.0	38,990
All groups	**58.5**	**2.6**	**4.1**	**0.6**	**20.0**	**0.5**	**1.6**	**3.0**	**5.5**	**3.6**	**100.0**	**39,956**
Actual value	**34,046**	**16,408**	**18,663**	**29,467**	**28,354**	**33,422**	**16,722**	**7012**	**11,614**	**11,196**		**39,956**

TABLE A2.3

Average (per reporting household) Wage Income and its Share in Total Income by Population Group in Rural Haryana

Population group	Agricultural wage		Non-agr. wage		All wages		Wage as per cent of total income			Per cent of households getting 50% income from wages
	Average wage	Per cent of rep. hhs	Average wage	Per cent of rep. hhs	Average wage	Per cent of rep. hhs	Agr. wage	Non-agr. wage	All wage	
Household income										
Up to 20,000	5582	38.3	8526	34.8	9245	55.2	16.7	23.2	39.8	48.6
20,001–40,000	8801	12.1	13,282	17.9	14,830	23.2	3.6	8.2	11.8	13.6
40,001–62,000	7841	2.2	16,324	6.3	18,129	6.6	0.4	2.1	2.4	1.8
62,001–86,000	0	0.0	15,151	4.0	15,151	4.0	0.0	0.8	0.8	0.0
Above 86,000	0	0.0	18,000	0.2	18,000	0.2	0.0	0.0	0.0	0.0
Landholding										
Landless wage earner	6945	67.2	11,415	69.5	12,602	100.0	30.1	51.1	81.2	99.7
Marginal	4884	10.2	9080	13.2	9020	18.8	1.7	4.1	5.8	7.4
Small	4903	1.4	7848	4.0	7883	4.9	0.2	0.8	1.0	1.2
Medium	0	0.0	12,239	1.8	12,239	1.8	0.0	0.4	0.4	0.0
Landless others	4115	8.2	7364	8.6	6454	15.0	1.1	2.1	3.2	0.0
All land owners	4886	3.7	9008	6.0	8945	8.0	0.3	1.0	1.4	2.8
All land non-owners	6589	35.3	10,901	36.6	11,678	54.1	10.0	17.1	27.1	45.8
Occupation										
Agriculture	3705	3.3	7758	4.4	6956	6.7	0.2	0.6	0.9	0.0
Salaried+prof.+s.empl.	4730	3.4	7039	5.4	6469	8.3	0.4	0.9	1.3	0.0
Wage earners	6939	65.9	11,355	70.5	12,575	100.0	28.9	50.7	79.6	99.7
All others	3792	8.3	8222	7.4	6943	13.3	1.0	2.0	3.0	0.0
Caste										
SCs	6661	42.8	9572	40.8	10,969	61.6	12.2	16.6	28.8	49.4
Religion										
Hindus	6431	17.8	10,492	18.5	11,213	27.5	2.9	4.8	7.7	21.1
Other minorities	2634	6.2	9513	12.3	8631	15.5	0.3	1.8	2.1	3.1
Household size										
Up to 4	5557	20.1	9321	19.8	9497	31.2	4.0	6.7	10.8	23.6
5–7	6240	18.4	10,141	19.3	10,985	28.3	3.0	5.2	8.2	22.0
8 and above	8281	11.4	12,984	17.3	14,251	22.4	1.7	3.9	5.6	16.2
Poverty line										
Lower segment below	4579	47.1	7200	34.0	7402	62.2	22.3	25.3	47.5	57.9
Upper segment below	6058	39.9	9200	38.8	10,455	57.3	16.0	23.6	39.6	49.3
Lower segment above	8003	13.8	11,665	19.7	13,029	26.1	3.5	7.4	10.9	17.5
Upper segment above	4780	1.8	19,190	3.2	16,845	4.1	0.1	0.8	0.9	0.9
Adult literacy										
None literate	6100	29.7	9684	31.0	10,183	47.3	7.0	11.6	18.6	38.7
Female literate	6596	28.8	11,998	20.2	11,699	37.0	5.6	7.1	12.7	23.9
Male literate	5965	18.9	10,770	20.4	11,381	29.2	3.1	6.0	9.0	22.2
Both literate	9059	5.9	11,430	9.3	13,001	12.2	1.0	2.0	3.0	8.3
Village development										
Low	6350	19.7	10,354	16.8	9492	31.5	3.0	4.2	7.3	24.1
Medium	5932	17.9	9472	20.3	11,118	26.9	2.6	4.7	7.3	20.5
High	6736	16.1	11,462	18.4	11,694	27.3	2.8	5.4	8.2	20.8
All groups	**6375**	**17.1**	**10,558**	**18.9**	**11,219**	**27.6**	**2.7**	**5.0**	**7.7**	**21.0**

TABLE A2.4

Land and Livestock Owned by Households by Population Group in Rural Haryana

Population group	Landholdings			Draught animals			Milch animals		
	Per cent of rep. hhs	Average rep. hh	Average all groups	Per cent of rep. hhs	Average rep. hh	Average all groups	Per cent of rep. hhs	Average rep. hh	Average all groups
Household income									
Up to 20,000	32.3	2.6	0.8	10.1	2.4	0.2	67.3	1.7	1.2
20,001–40,000	53.7	3.4	1.8	15.4	2.1	0.3	74.7	2.1	1.6
40,001–62,000	80.2	4.8	3.9	23.6	2.8	0.7	87.5	2.0	1.8
62,001–86,000	89.3	7.6	6.8	26.0	2.3	0.6	91.2	2.3	2.1
Above 86,000	96.3	15.6	15.0	50.3	2.6	1.3	96.5	5.4	5.2
Landholding									
Landless wage earner	–	–	–	7.9	2.7	0.2	63.3	1.7	1.1
Marginal	100.0	1.6	1.6	11.8	2.2	0.3	90.4	1.9	1.7
Small	100.0	3.9	3.9	30.0	1.7	0.5	92.5	2.3	2.1
Medium	100.0	7.4	7.4	38.5	2.0	0.8	97.5	2.8	2.7
Large	100.0	19.0	19.0	49.8	2.8	1.4	100.0	4.8	4.8
Landless others	–	–	–	3.6	8.2	0.3	49.0	1.8	0.9
All land owners	100.0	5.8	5.8	28.6	2.1	0.6	93.3	2.6	2.5
All land non-owners	–	–	–	5.6	4.6	0.3	55.5	1.7	1.0
Occupation groups									
Agriculture	98.9	6.9	6.9	33.7	2.1	0.7	94.1	2.9	2.7
Salaried+prof.+s.empl.	40.6	2.7	1.1	6.0	6.1	0.4	67.7	1.9	1.3
Wage earners	7.5	1.3	0.1	8.4	2.6	0.2	64.8	1.7	1.1
All groups others	27.6	2.1	0.6	6.4	1.1	0.1	69.3	1.5	0.9
Caste									
SCs	22.1	3.6	0.8	9.5	2.7	0.3	62.3	1.8	1.1
Religion									
Hindus	56.5	5.8	3.3	18.6	2.5	0.5	77.5	2.3	1.8
Other minorities	78.9	7.7	6.0	32.3	1.6	0.5	90.6	3.3	3.0
Household size									
Up to 4	47.7	3.8	1.8	12.6	3.0	0.4	62.9	2.1	1.3
5–7	56.6	5.5	3.1	16.7	2.7	0.4	78.9	2.2	1.8
8 and above	69.7	7.8	5.4	29.7	1.7	0.4	89.6	2.7	2.5
Poverty line									
Lower segment below	33.3	3.6	1.2	9.9	3.1	0.3	77.6	1.7	1.3
Upper segment below	32.3	2.4	0.8	11.0	2.0	0.2	71.5	2.1	1.5
Lower segment above	54.1	4.1	2.2	17.5	2.0	0.4	74.0	1.9	1.4
Upper segment above	84.0	8.7	7.3	27.8	2.8	0.8	86.7	3.3	2.8
Adult literacy									
None literate	45.2	5.0	2.3	18.5	2.6	0.5	71.5	2.4	1.7
Female literate	57.4	5.1	3.0	18.3	4.1	0.7	73.7	2.0	1.4
Male literate	59.8	5.3	3.1	18.3	1.9	0.4	78.7	2.3	1.8
Both literate	61.9	7.1	4.4	19.7	2.8	0.6	79.8	2.5	2.0
Village development									
Low	53.9	5.7	3.1	18.1	1.9	0.3	82.2	2.2	1.8
Medium	61.5	6.0	3.7	19.2	2.6	0.5	80.8	2.2	1.8
High	55.5	5.7	3.2	18.7	2.4	0.4	74.4	2.5	1.8
All groups	**57.6**	**5.8**	**3.4**	**18.8**	**2.4**	**0.5**	**77.6**	**2.3**	**1.8**

TABLE A2.5
Amenities Available in Households by Population Group in Rural Haryana

Population group	Percentage of households owning					
	Kutcha house	Separate kitchen	Electric connection	Protected water	Piped water	Toilet
Household income						
Up to 20,000	22.3	22.9	69.5	81.3	38.9	3.5
20,001–40,000	13.4	46.9	83.6	83.0	46.1	7.5
40,001–62,000	9.0	58.8	89.3	87.9	49.0	10.3
62,001–86,000	4.6	64.5	93.1	82.2	41.2	14.2
Above 86,000	0.5	81.6	98.3	93.0	53.4	17.5
Landholding						
Landless wage earner	29.7	15.8	61.4	78.9	41.0	2.7
Marginal	9.6	44.5	79.8	82.4	41.7	5.8
Small	11.2	53.3	84.6	83.9	47.4	7.3
Medium	9.0	56.0	92.2	84.0	38.0	8.3
Large	3.4	71.9	91.0	86.3	45.3	12.7
Landless others	11.7	49.7	90.0	88.8	49.6	13.4
All land owners	9.2	53.5	85.5	83.7	43.3	7.7
All land non-owners	20.0	34.2	76.9	84.2	45.7	8.5
Occupation						
Agriculture	9.4	51.1	84.4	84.3	42.4	7.5
Salaried+prof.+s.empl.	8.7	58.4	93.3	86.8	48.7	13.5
Wage earners	29.8	16.5	61.5	77.9	40.6	3.2
All groups others	11.2	49.9	87.1	87.9	49.4	8.5
Caste						
SCs	25.1	27.9	71.5	81.8	39.4	3.7
Religion						
Hindus	13.2	46.2	83.1	84.3	44.3	8.0
Other minorities	3.2	78.1	96.1	86.2	39.8	24.7
Household size						
Up to 4	18.6	42.9	75.8	84.8	44.1	8.1
5–7	13.5	43.5	81.7	84.3	43.3	7.9
8 and above	9.6	51.6	88.2	82.4	46.7	8.3
Poverty line						
Lower segment below	24.8	17.1	67.1	79.8	35.5	2.9
Upper segment below	25.1	26.6	70.6	80.1	41.2	3.8
Lower segment above	12.7	43.2	81.7	84.4	46.7	6.3
Upper segment above	6.6	67.4	92.6	86.5	44.7	14.9
Adult literacy						
None literate	27.4	23.5	61.9	82.2	38.5	1.1
Female literate	6.8	47.4	77.2	80.5	30.2	17.8
Male literate	14.1	42.1	81.0	82.9	46.6	5.2
Both literate	5.6	63.2	95.8	86.9	45.6	15.7
Village development						
Low	18.0	48.5	78.7	73.3	23.8	6.8
Medium	13.5	46.2	80.5	85.8	49.1	8.3
High	13.1	44.1	83.5	84.8	45.0	8.1
All groups	**13.8**	**45.3**	**81.9**	**84.0**	**44.3**	**8.0**

TABLE A2.6

Consumption of Foodgrains and Utilization of PDS by Population Group in Rural Haryana

Population group	Annual household income (Rs)	Annual per capita income (Rs)	Per capita consumption of foodgrains (kg/month)	Percentage of households using PDS	Quantity of cereals (kg) bought from PDS (per hh/month)	Per cent requirement of cereals met from PDS
Household income						
Up to 20,000	12,816	2378	12.3	8.8	17.8	34.0
20,001–40,000	29,146	4815	12.3	8.2	27.0	41.3
40,001–62,000	49,235	7579	13.2	11.4	11.6	21.4
62,001–86,000	72,789	9622	13.6	5.7	18.1	34.8
Above 86,000	139,117	15,658	14.3	12.0	6.9	15.2
Landholding						
Landless wage earner	15,517	2679	12.4	9.8	23.4	33.7
Marginal	29,060	4989	12.4	9.6	16.4	37.0
Small	39,273	5988	13.1	8.7	9.3	28.4
Medium	61,515	8779	13.8	7.3	3.7	7.8
Large	129,087	15,272	14.9	10.6	6.0	9.7
Landless others	29,937	5243	11.6	8.5	33.7	45.3
All land owners	52,216	7838	13.4	8.9	10.3	23.4
All land non-owners	23,311	4056	12.0	9.1	28.6	39.8
Occupation						
Agriculture	54,041	8094	13.6	8.2	8.9	18.5
Salaried+prof.+s.empl.	40,380	6435	11.5	8.3	21.3	40.5
Wage earners	15,795	2721	12.4	9.1	23.5	33.7
All others	30,734	5419	12.9	12.7	28.5	47.7
Caste						
SCs	23,458	3936	12.5	10.7	18.3	30.2
Religion						
Hindus	40,027	6422	12.9	9.2	18.1	32.1
Other minorities	63,659	10,528	14.6	3.9	2.0	100.0
Household size						
Up to 4	27,536	7963	13.7	8.6	14.9	38.6
5–7	37,712	6413	13.0	9.0	20.6	35.9
8 and above	57,253	5757	12.3	9.4	15.8	23.2
Poverty line						
Lower segment below	9686	1389	11.6	10.2	25.3	49.5
Upper segment below	15,118	2373	12.4	10.7	20.7	31.8
Lower segment above	31,115	4909	12.4	8.2	17.9	31.7
Upper segment above	77,434	13,191	14.3	9.1	14.1	27.4
Adult literacy						
None literate	25,906	4,829	12.6	8.2	20.7	44.2
Female literate	34,033	6315	13.5	13.7	11.6	26.6
Male literate	36,927	5989	13.1	8.8	17.5	28.6
Both literate	53,499	7574	12.6	9.4	18.3	33.5
Village development						
Low	41,155	6580	13.0	12.6	19.3	21.8
Medium	40,960	6442	12.9	8.1	21.9	39.1
High	38,990	6271	12.7	8.9	15.3	33.0
All groups	**39,956**	**6368**	**12.8**	**9.0**	**18.1**	**32.4**

TABLE A2.7
Literacy Rate (per cent) and Gender Disparity by Population Group in Rural Haryana

Population group (aged 7 & above)	Literacy rates			
	Person	Male	Female	F/M
Household income				
Up to 20,000	45.3	59.4	30.3	0.51
20,001–40,000	54.7	69.9	36.2	0.52
40,001–62,000	62.4	76.7	44.7	0.58
62,001–86,000	61.7	74.5	47.1	0.63
Above 86,000	61.0	75.7	44.5	0.59
Landholding				
Landless wage earner	39.3	52.4	23.9	0.46
Marginal	57.4	72.4	39.7	0.55
Small	57.5	73.4	38.4	0.52
Medium	56.4	71.2	39.3	0.55
Large	55.5	68.2	41.2	0.60
Landless others	62.3	77.3	46.1	0.60
All land owners	56.9	71.8	39.4	0.55
All land non-owners	51.6	65.5	36.0	0.55
Occupation				
Agriculture	54.4	68.9	37.5	0.54
Salaried+prof.+s.empl.	66.6	81.4	49.3	0.61
Wage earners	40.1	53.1	24.9	0.47
All others	59.1	76.0	41.2	0.54
Caste				
SCs	45.5	60.0	29.0	0.48
Religion				
Hindus	55.9	70.3	39.3	0.56
Other minorities	72.1	84.5	59.7	0.71
Household size				
Up to 4	50.2	66.6	27.5	0.41
5–7	56.5	70.2	40.7	0.58
8 and above	54.5	69.6	38.1	0.55
Poverty line				
Lower segment below	46.9	60.6	33.5	0.55
Upper segment below	45.1	59.7	29.3	0.49
Lower segment above	54.6	69.4	37.1	0.53
Upper segment above	63.0	76.9	46.3	0.60
Adult literacy				
None literate	18.4	21.3	15.5	0.73
Female literate	52.1	38.0	62.7	1.65
Male literate	51.3	74.6	21.0	0.28
Both literate	74.8	83.4	65.5	0.79
Village development				
Low	59.6	72.9	43.4	0.59
Medium	50.7	65.3	33.8	0.52
High	57.0	71.7	40.2	0.56
All groups	**54.9**	**69.4**	**38.1**	**0.55**

TABLE A2.8

Ever Enrolment, Discontinuation, and Non-attendance Rates for Children (aged 6–14 years) by Population Group in Rural Haryana

(per cent)

Population group	Ever enrolment rate				Discontinuation rate				Non-attendance rate			
	Total	Male	Female	F/M	Total	Male	Female	F/M	Total	Male	Female	F/M
Household income												
Up to 20,000	**69.2**	**75.7**	**63.1**	**0.83**	**6.1**	**6.0**	**6.2**	**1.04**	**2.8**	**3.8**	**1.6**	**0.43**
20,001–40,000	78.5	86.1	70.3	0.82	3.0	2.2	4.0	1.81	2.7	1.7	3.9	2.28
40,001–62,000	86.2	88.3	83.7	0.95	3.5	3.5	3.5	1.02	0.8	1.4	0.0	0.00
62,001–86,000	89.8	89.0	90.5	1.02	2.7	0.9	4.5	5.07	1.9	2.9	0.9	0.30
Above 86,000	82.7	90.0	75.6	0.84	5.2	6.9	3.3	0.48	2.9	2.3	3.5	1.55
Landholding												
Landless wage earner	58.8	68.8	49.9	0.73	4.6	4.7	4.5	0.95	3.4	5.1	1.4	0.27
Marginal	81.5	84.1	78.6	0.93	5.1	4.6	5.8	1.27	1.2	2.2	0.0	0.00
Small	83.4	89.4	76.6	0.86	3.0	3.5	2.3	0.66	1.5	1.4	1.7	1.21
Medium	82.0	89.1	75.3	0.85	2.9	1.4	4.7	3.49	1.3	0.0	2.8	–
Large	81.2	85.4	76.3	0.89	6.6	8.0	4.8	0.60	3.9	4.7	3.0	0.63
Landless others	85.5	87.8	83.2	0.95	4.1	2.7	5.6	2.08	3.2	2.4	4.1	1.71
All land owners	82.2	87.1	76.9	0.88	4.1	4.0	4.3	1.07	1.7	1.8	1.6	0.89
All land non-owners	72.0	78.5	65.9	0.84	4.3	3.5	5.1	1.45	3.3	3.5	3.0	0.86
Occupation												
Agriculture	81.5	86.9	75.5	0.87	4.0	4.0	4.0	1.02	1.8	1.9	1.6	0.85
Salaried+prof.+s.empl.	86.2	86.5	85.8	0.99	3.3	3.0	3.7	1.23	2.0	0.9	3.3	3.53
Wage earners	59.6	69.6	51.1	0.73	5.3	4.8	5.9	1.21	3.2	4.8	1.3	0.26
All others	85.8	91.0	80.7	0.89	5.1	3.5	6.9	1.97	3.8	4.2	3.3	0.78
Caste												
SCs	67.9	73.6	62.7	0.85	6.0	5.1	7.0	1.36	3.3	2.6	4.0	1.55
Religion												
Hindus	80.7	85.6	75.7	0.88	3.5	2.6	4.5	1.75	2.3	2.3	2.3	0.97
Other minorities	88.1	90.3	86.8	0.96	4.0	0.0	6.3	0.00	0.0	0.0	0.0	-
Household size												
Up to 4	85.9	88.9	79.3	0.89	5.7	7.0	2.6	0.37	2.8	1.3	6.4	4.76
5–7	79.4	84.8	73.7	0.87	3.4	2.3	4.7	2.05	2.4	2.8	2.0	0.70
8 and above	74.2	80.2	69.3	0.86	5.1	5.5	4.8	0.87	1.9	2.1	1.7	0.82
Poverty line												
Lower segment below	63.2	71.3	57.7	0.81	5.8	5.3	6.2	1.17	1.6	2.6	0.7	0.26
Upper segment below	68.2	76.0	60.8	0.80	6.1	7.7	4.3	0.56	3.4	5.6	0.9	0.15
Lower segment above	80.9	85.1	76.1	0.89	4.0	2.8	5.5	1.96	2.1	1.6	2.9	1.81
Upper segment above	88.5	91.7	84.8	0.92	2.9	3.4	2.3	0.65	2.4	2.5	2.3	0.92
Adult literacy												
None literate	58.1	67.0	49.0	0.73	5.0	6.6	2.9	0.44	3.7	4.0	3.3	0.82
Female literate	76.7	85.2	66.7	0.78	4.0	0.0	9.9	0.00	0.0	0.0	0.0	–
Male literate	78.3	85.0	71.8	0.84	4.8	4.7	4.9	1.05	2.3	2.9	1.6	0.54
Both literate	93.7	94.4	93.0	0.99	2.9	1.4	4.5	3.14	1.9	1.2	2.6	2.19
Village development												
Low	83.6	86.5	80.3	0.93	3.7	1.9	6.0	3.15	1.2	2.0	0.0	0.00
Medium	75.1	81.5	68.3	0.84	5.0	7.0	2.4	0.35	2.7	2.5	2.9	1.15
High	79.2	85.0	73.6	0.86	3.7	1.9	5.7	2.97	2.3	2.5	2.1	0.85
All groups	**78.1**	**83.8**	**72.3**	**0.86**	**4.2**	**3.8**	**4.6**	**1.20**	**2.3**	**2.4**	**2.2**	**0.88**

TABLE A2.9

Factors for Non-enrolment (per cent) of Children (aged 6–14 years) and Gender Disparity by Population Group in Rural Haryana

Population group	Supply factors	Demand factors	Interest factors	Customs factors
Household income				
Up to 20,000				
Person	14.6	48.4	46.5	10.9
Gender disparity	0.73	1.12	1.06	4.75
20,001–40,000				
Person	11.7	39.1	57.8	13.9
Gender disparity	1.85	1.39	1.18	4.45
40,001–62,000				
Person	14.2	24.9	47.6	21.3
Gender disparity	0.44	1.09	1.91	–
62,001–86,000				
Person	12.5	23.4	27.9	2.2
Gender disparity	0.11	0.38	0.15	–
Above 86,000				
Person	3.0	10.3	57.7	31.5
Gender disparity	–	5.53	1.53	1.90
Landholding				
Landless wage earner				
Person	14.5	56.6	53.0	13.8
Gender disparity	0.73	1.18	1.28	4.91
Marginal				
Person	10.3	34.9	52.0	13.1
Gender disparity	1.77	1.18	0.79	2.80
Small				
Person	15.8	29.2	57.6	10.9
Gender disparity	0.38	1.30	1.08	–
Medium				
Person	11.6	14.6	36.0	22.7
Gender disparity	1.25	1.54	0.96	–
Large				
Person	16.1	19.9	57.1	28.7
Gender disparity	0.75	0.55	1.72	3.20
Landless others				
Person	5.8	36.4	38.3	3.8
Gender disparity	2.07	1.29	1.80	6.50
All land owners				
Person	13.2	26.3	51.0	16.9
Gender disparity	0.79	1.08	1.01	5.30
All land non-owners				
Person	12.3	51.4	49.2	11.2
Gender disparity	0.86	1.22	1.39	5.28
Occupation				
Agriculture				
Person	13.8	26.4	53.1	16.3
Gender disparity	0.77	0.95	1.06	9.11
Salaried+prof.+s.empl.				
Person	4.3	26.2	41.9	8.7
Gender disparity	2.71	1.55	1.37	1.54
Wage earners				
Person	14.8	56.1	52.7	14.6
Gender disparity	0.69	1.20	1.30	5.38
All others				
Person	9.5	38.8	33.0	6.4
Gender disparity	0.91	0.88	0.79	3.57
Caste				
SCs				
Person	13.6	49.5	49.6	9.6
Gender disparity	0.71	1.01	1.09	3.96
Religion				
Hindus				
Person	13.3	38.4	47.4	10.1
Gender disparity	0.78	1.26	1.29	8.62
Other minorities				
Person	–	–	57.8	0.0
Gender disparity	–	–	–	–
Household size				
Up to 4				
Person	14.5	48.1	55.1	3.9
Gender disparity	1.30	0.76	0.45	–
5–7				
Person	11.1	39.3	44.8	14.1
Gender disparity	0.82	1.12	1.54	5.41
8 and above				
Person	14.4	37.9	56.2	15.2
Gender disparity	0.76	1.42	1.04	4.47
Poverty line				
Lower segment below				
Person	10.0	46.7	53.0	12.9
Gender disparity	2.07	1.24	0.99	2.37
Upper segment below				
Person	21.5	48.5	39.6	11.6
Gender disparity	0.35	0.95	1.25	–
Lower segment above				
Person	10.8	35.5	51.2	11.6
Gender disparity	1.61	1.30	1.03	6.00
Upper segment above				
Person	9.2	19.8	59.0	28.4
Gender disparity	0.40	0.85	2.59	4.99
Adult literacy				
None literate				
Person	17.4	44.3	50.1	14.2
Gender disparity	0.91	0.93	1.06	7.37
Female literate				
Person	–	63.3	63.3	0.0
Gender disparity	–	2.01	2.01	–
Male literate				
Person	8.8	38.6	53.8	16.9
Gender disparity	0.63	1.39	1.16	3.91
Both literate				
Person	16.4	6.7	22.4	0.6
Gender disparity	1.69	0.93	1.86	–
Village development				
Low				
Person	13.5	45.8	38.5	4.4
Gender disparity	1.10	4.56	6.43	2.13
Medium				
Person	13.1	39.7	49.1	16.2
Gender disparity	0.69	1.01	0.99	6.14
High				
Person	12.2	37.6	53.0	13.6
Gender disparity	0.93	1.08	1.15	4.79
All groups				
Person	12.7	39.2	50.1	14.0
Gender disparity	0.82	1.17	1.18	5.29

(Contd.)

TABLE A2.10

Factors for Discontinuation (per cent) of Children (aged 6–14 years) and Gender Disparity by Population Group in Rural Haryana

Population group	Supply factors	Demand factors	Interest factors	Customs factors
Household income				
Up to 20,000				
Person	27.1	60.8	60.8	58.4
Gender disparity	1.01	1.03	1.03	0.78
20,001–40,000				
Person	46.7	65.6	65.6	33.9
Gender disparity	0.69	0.85	0.85	0.23
40,001–62,000				
Person	12.3	46.6	46.6	82.2
Gender disparity	–	2.91	2.91	1.00
62,001–86,000				
Person	–	40.1	40.1	76.4
Gender disparity	–	–	–	0.72
Above 86,000				
Person	35.7	58.7	58.7	63.1
Gender disparity	1.11	0.48	0.48	0.69
Landholding				
Landless wage earner				
Person	22.6	67.1	67.1	45.9
Gender disparity	1.07	0.68	0.68	0.37
Marginal				
Person	27.3	53.2	53.2	60.4
Gender disparity	0.55	1.17	1.17	0.58
Small				
Person	15.8	63.2	63.2	59.0
Gender disparity	0.79	0.76	0.76	0.48
Medium				
Person	55.6	24.3	24.3	26.3
Gender disparity	0.41	–	–	–
Large				
Person	25.7	68.6	68.6	73.3
Gender disparity	0.49	1.39	1.39	1.02
Landless others				
Person	33.4	60.8	60.8	68.8
Gender disparity	0.59	19.05	19.05	0.88
All land owners				
Person	28.4	54.7	54.7	57.8
Gender disparity	0.70	0.75	0.75	0.65
All land non-owners				
Person	28.6	63.6	63.6	58.7
Gender disparity	0.80	1.66	1.66	0.75
Occupation				
Agriculture				
Person	24.8	49.5	49.5	62.6
Gender disparity	0.82	0.46	0.46	0.62
Salaried+prof.+s.empl.				
Person	31.9	56.4	56.4	47.4
Gender disparity	2.52	5.14	5.14	0.20
Wage earners				
Person	29.1	70.9	70.9	44.4
Gender disparity	1.23	0.92	0.92	0.56
All others				
Person	35.7	69.2	69.2	77.0
Gender disparity	–	1.98	1.98	2.83
Caste				
SCs				
Person	27.1	59.7	59.7	53.5
Gender disparity	1.85	1.53	1.53	0.58
Religion				
Hindus				
Person	22.9	56.3	56.3	59.4
Gender disparity	0.78	1.45	1.45	0.65
Other minorities				
Person	100.0	–	–	–
Gender disparity	–	–	–	–
Household size				
Up to 4				
Person	51.4	57.3	57.3	46.6
Gender disparity	2.26	1.96	1.96	–
5–7				
Person	25.8	49.8	49.8	64.1
Gender disparity	1.22	1.03	1.03	0.57
8 and above				
Person	24.2	67.6	67.6	55.2
Gender disparity	0.37	1.04	1.04	0.79
Poverty line				
Lower segment below				
Person	18.1	60.4	60.4	47.2
Gender disparity	0.19	1.53	1.53	0.91
Upper segment below				
Person	29.5	82.9	82.9	68.7
Gender disparity	2.89	0.73	0.73	1.15
Lower segment above				
Person	30.0	51.9	51.9	50.8
Gender disparity	0.66	1.47	1.47	0.52
Upper segment above				
Person	33.4	46.0	46.0	75.7
Gender disparity	0.55	0.67	0.67	0.90
Adult literacy				
None Literate				
Person	20.0	62.5	62.5	68.5
Gender disparity	–	0.69	0.69	0.26
Female literate				
Person	100.0	–	–	–
Gender disparity	–	–	–	–
Male literate				
Person	30.0	51.5	51.5	56.2
Gender disparity	0.69	0.87	0.87	0.86
Both literate				
Person	23.6	77.5	77.5	60.9
Gender disparity	0.53	2.25	2.25	0.74
Village development				
Low				
Person	30.7	57.6	57.6	34.7
Gender disparity	–	1.03	1.03	0.09
Medium				
Person	33.0	67.2	67.2	58.2
Gender disparity	1.04	1.36	1.36	0.58
High				
Person	23.7	49.4	49.4	63.5
Gender disparity	0.42	1.26	1.26	0.81
All groups				
Person	28.5	58.1	58.1	58.1
Gender disparity	0.74	1.04	1.04	0.69

(Contd.)

TABLE A2.11

Proportion of Population Completing Middle and Matriculation Levels and Gender Disparity by Population Group in Rural Haryana

Population group	Middle level (aged 15+)				Matriculation level (aged 17+)			
	Total	Male	Female	F/M	Total	Male	Female	F/M
Household income								
Up to 20,000	9.6	14.7	3.8	0.26	8.2	13.4	2.5	0.19
20,001–40,000	12.4	17.0	6.6	0.39	15.2	23.8	4.8	0.20
40,001–62,000	12.5	16.5	7.4	0.45	19.3	28.8	7.3	0.25
62,001–86,000	14.1	16.8	10.9	0.65	17.4	27.6	5.9	0.21
Above 86,000	12.2	14.5	9.6	0.66	18.9	27.4	8.8	0.32
Landholding								
Landless wage earner	7.0	10.6	2.5	0.23	5.8	9.4	1.3	0.13
Marginal	12.3	17.5	6.1	0.35	16.9	26.8	4.6	0.17
Small	12.2	17.3	6.0	0.35	16.3	25.1	5.7	0.23
Medium	12.3	16.4	7.3	0.45	14.8	24.6	3.1	0.13
Large	13.7	15.2	12.0	0.79	15.8	23.3	7.0	0.30
Landless others	13.9	18.3	8.9	0.48	18.5	27.5	8.6	0.31
All land owners	12.5	16.8	7.3	0.44	16.0	25.2	5.0	0.20
All land non-owners	10.8	14.7	6.1	0.42	12.8	19.3	5.5	0.28
Occupation								
Agriculture	12.2	16.7	6.7	0.40	14.4	22.9	4.3	0.19
Salaried+prof.+s.empl.	13.6	16.6	10.0	0.60	22.6	33.2	9.5	0.29
Wage earners	7.5	10.7	3.3	0.31	6.3	10.2	1.4	0.14
All others	14.0	20.6	6.9	0.33	14.8	23.1	6.2	0.27
Caste								
SCs	9.2	13.5	3.8	0.28	10.2	15.5	3.7	0.24
Religion								
Hindus	11.9	16.1	6.9	0.43	15.4	23.8	5.5	0.23
Other minorities	19.6	21.5	17.4	0.81	13.3	19.7	5.1	0.26
Household size								
Up to 4	10.1	15.2	3.7	0.24	14.0	22.4	4.0	0.18
5–7	12.3	15.8	8.2	0.52	14.2	21.7	5.3	0.25
8 and above	11.9	16.5	6.5	0.39	15.9	24.7	5.6	0.23
Poverty line								
Lower segment below	11.7	17.3	5.2	0.30	9.4	16.1	1.8	0.11
Upper segment below	9.2	14.0	3.6	0.26	9.3	15.0	2.8	0.19
Lower segment above	12.3	16.9	6.8	0.40	14.2	22.3	4.8	0.21
Upper segment above	12.3	14.9	9.0	0.61	19.8	29.2	8.1	0.28
Adult literacy								
None literate	0.0	0.0	0.0	0.00	0.1	0.3	0.0	0.00
Female literate	7.1	0.0	11.3	0.00	1.3	0.0	2.2	0.00
Male literate	12.2	20.6	0.0	0.00	12.2	21.3	0.0	0.00
Both literate	15.7	15.9	15.6	0.98	23.7	33.3	12.8	0.38
Village development								
Low	12.3	16.0	7.6	0.48	16.3	23.8	7.4	0.31
Medium	11.9	16.4	6.4	0.39	13.2	20.5	4.5	0.22
High	11.8	15.7	7.0	0.45	15.7	24.6	5.3	0.21
All groups	**11.9**	**16.0**	**6.9**	**0.43**	**14.8**	**22.9**	**5.2**	**0.23**

TABLE A2.12
Percentage Distribution of Students (aged 6–14 years) and Gender Disparity by Type of School by Population Group in Rural Haryana

Population group	Govt schools				Govt-aided schools				Private schools			
	Total	Male	Female	F/M	Total	Male	Female	F/M	Total	Male	Female	F/M
Household income												
Up to 20,000	92.3	89.9	94.9	1.05	0.4	0.4	0.4	0.89	7.1	9.6	4.3	0.44
20,001–40,000	86.0	84.4	88.1	1.04	2.3	3.6	0.5	0.13	11.4	12.0	10.7	0.90
40,001–62,000	78.5	78.1	79.0	1.01	4.8	3.2	6.9	2.18	16.3	18.3	13.8	0.76
62,001–86,000	84.3	79.2	89.4	1.13	0.0	0.0	0.0	–	15.7	20.8	10.6	0.51
Above 86,000	74.0	66.7	82.2	1.23	0.8	1.6	0.0	0.00	25.2	31.7	17.8	0.56
Landholding												
Landless wage earner	95.7	93.9	97.9	1.04	0.3	0.6	0.0	0.00	3.9	5.5	2.1	0.38
Marginal	82.3	82.5	82.1	0.99	3.1	2.5	3.7	1.46	14.2	14.9	13.4	0.90
Small	86.7	86.5	87.1	1.01	1.2	0.0	2.8	–	12.1	13.5	10.1	0.75
Medium	86.0	78.5	94.7	1.21	1.5	2.8	0.0	0.00	12.5	18.7	5.3	0.28
Large	80.0	77.5	83.2	1.07	0.6	1.0	0.0	0.00	18.6	20.6	16.2	0.79
Landless others	80.1	75.2	85.5	1.14	2.9	5.0	0.6	0.12	16.5	19.8	12.8	0.65
All land owners	84.3	82.4	86.7	1.05	1.8	1.5	2.1	1.40	13.7	16.0	10.9	0.68
All land non-owners	86.5	83.1	90.4	1.09	1.8	3.1	0.4	0.12	11.3	13.8	8.6	0.62
Occupation												
Agriculture	87.5	85.4	90.3	1.06	0.8	0.8	0.9	1.04	11.5	13.6	8.8	0.64
Salaried+prof.+s.empl.	76.9	71.6	82.7	1.16	4.0	4.8	3.2	0.65	18.6	23.6	13.1	0.55
Wage earners	94.6	92.6	96.9	1.05	0.3	0.6	0.0	0.00	5.1	6.8	3.1	0.45
All others	77.4	77.0	77.9	1.01	3.6	4.6	2.4	0.51	18.5	18.4	18.6	1.01
Caste												
SCs	93.3	90.4	96.4	1.07	0.6	1.2	0.0	0.00	5.8	8.1	3.4	0.42
Religion												
Hindus	85.0	82.2	88.5	1.08	2.2	2.6	1.8	0.70	15.3	18.0	11.9	0.66
Other minorities	87.2	89.3	85.9	0.96	2.7	0.0	4.4	–	10.1	10.7	9.7	0.90
Household size												
Up to 4	79.0	79.7	77.4	0.97	3.2	4.5	0.0	0.00	17.8	15.8	22.6	1.43
5–7	84.0	80.7	88.0	1.09	2.0	1.9	2.0	1.06	13.8	17.4	9.3	0.54
8 and above	88.9	87.6	90.1	1.03	1.1	1.4	0.8	0.54	9.8	10.7	9.0	0.84
Poverty line												
Lower segment below	94.6	92.0	96.8	1.05	0.0	0.0	0.0	–	5.4	8.0	3.2	0.40
Upper segment below	93.5	89.2	98.3	1.10	0.9	1.0	0.9	0.89	5.6	9.8	0.9	0.09
Lower segment above	86.4	85.5	87.6	1.02	2.0	2.7	1.2	0.45	11.1	11.7	10.3	0.88
Upper segment above	74.7	71.0	79.3	1.12	2.6	2.3	2.9	1.28	22.8	26.8	17.8	0.66
Adult literacy												
None literate	91.0	88.3	94.5	1.07	0.7	0.5	0.9	1.93	8.4	11.2	4.5	0.40
Female literate	77.9	79.3	75.5	0.95	0.0	0.0	0.0	–	19.8	20.7	18.4	0.89
Male literate	89.4	88.5	90.5	1.02	0.8	1.3	0.3	0.27	9.5	10.2	8.7	0.85
Both literate	76.7	71.6	82.7	1.16	3.8	4.3	3.3	0.78	19.2	23.9	13.8	0.58
Village development												
Low	89.4	91.7	86.5	0.94	1.7	1.9	1.5	0.78	8.3	6.5	10.8	1.68
Medium	85.6	82.1	89.8	1.09	3.3	3.6	3.0	0.84	10.7	14.1	6.6	0.47
High	83.8	80.8	87.3	1.08	0.7	1.0	0.3	0.31	15.4	18.2	12.2	0.67
All groups	**85.1**	**82.6**	**88.1**	**1.07**	**1.8**	**2.1**	**1.4**	**0.69**	**12.8**	**15.2**	**10.0**	**0.66**

TABLE A2.13

Percentage Distribution of Household Annual Expenditure on Schooling (6–14 years) in Government Schools and Gender Disparity by Population Group in Rural Haryana

(Annual expenditure in rupees)

Population group	Govt schools						
	Fees	Books	Coaching	Transpt	BL	Total	#St/Rhhd
Household income							
Up to 20,000							
Person	14.3	82.8	1.3	1.7	0.0	945	1.8
Gender disparity	0.92	0.99	0.83	6.25	0.00	0.81	0.94
20,001–40,000							
Person	15.3	78.4	4.1	2.2	0.0	1053	1.8
Gender disparity	1.04	1.00	1.39	0.38	0.00	0.73	0.78
40,001–62,000							
Person	14.8	77.8	5.2	2.3	0.0	1101	1.8
Gender disparity	0.84	1.13	0.43	0.21	0.00	0.79	0.79
62,001–86,000							
Person	16.1	81.1	1.0	1.7	0.0	1547	2.2
Gender disparity	1.13	1.00	0.31	0.60	0.00	0.95	1.14
Above 86,000							
Person	11.1	86.4	1.7	0.8	0.0	1318	1.9
Gender disparity	0.92	0.98	3.03	9.22	0.00	1.36	1.10
Landholding							
Landless wage earner							
Person	13.6	82.6	1.5	2.3	0.0	841	1.8
Gender disparity	1.07	0.90	3.09	0.00	0.00	0.68	0.85
Marginal							
Person	15.5	78.4	2.8	3.2	0.0	1112	1.8
Gender disparity	0.78	1.09	0.51	0.63	0.00	0.67	0.85
Small							
Person	14.7	82.6	1.9	0.8	0.0	1149	1.9
Gender disparity	0.85	1.07	0.08	0.83	0.00	0.81	0.76
Medium							
Person	13.9	79.0	3.5	3.6	0.0	1214	1.8
Gender disparity	1.20	1.10	0.41	0.00	0.00	0.99	1.04
Large							
Person	12.1	85.5	1.5	0.9	0.0	1302	2.0
Gender disparity	0.89	0.97	11.71	0.00	0.00	1.23	0.85
Landless others							
Person	16.0	78.7	4.8	0.5	0.0	1078	1.8
Gender disparity	1.10	0.94	1.68	12.52	0.00	0.92	1.04
All land owners							
Person	14.4	80.9	2.5	2.2	0.0	1171	1.9
Gender disparity	0.89	1.07	0.43	0.36	0.00	0.85	0.85
All land non-owners							
Person	15.1	80.2	3.5	1.2	0.0	972	1.8
Gender disparity	1.10	0.92	1.97	58.33	0.00	0.82	0.95
Occupation							
Agriculture							
Person	14.1	81.5	2.5	1.9	0.0	1122	1.9
Gender disparity	0.91	1.07	0.38	0.24	0.00	0.92	0.84
Salaried+prof.+s.empl.							
Person	17.2	77.1	3.8	1.8	0.0	1186	1.8
Gender disparity	1.02	0.94	2.91	1.33	0.00	0.73	1.04
Wage earners							
Person	13.2	82.7	1.3	2.8	0.0	877	1.8
Gender disparity	1.06	0.91	2.98	8.53	0.00	0.71	0.89
All others							
Person	13.8	81.3	4.8	0.2	0.0	1166	1.9
Gender disparity	1.00	1.05	0.42	0.00	0.00	0.92	0.89
Caste							
SCs							
Person	14.8	79.9	1.1	4.2	0.0	1009	1.8
Gender disparity	0.87	1.00	3.32	1.21	0.00	0.94	0.98

(Contd.)

TABLE A2.13 (contd.)

Population group	Govt schools						
	Fees	Books	Coaching	Transpt	BL	Total	#St/Rhhd
Religion							
Hindus							
Person	14.7	80.7	2.9	1.7	0.0	1090	1.8
Gender disparity	0.96	1.02	0.85	0.79	0.00	0.84	0.91
Other minorities							
Person	15.2	79.0	0.6	5.2	0.0	1762	2.0
Gender disparity	0.97	1.06	0.00	0.56	0.00	1.37	1.53
Household size							
Up to 4							
Person	13.3	78.0	4.4	4.3	0.0	851	1.4
Gender disparity	0.76	1.14	0.00	0.74	0.00	0.33	0.41
5–7							
Person	14.7	81.4	3.3	0.6	0.0	1091	1.8
Gender disparity	0.89	1.02	1.39	0.31	0.00	0.88	0.88
8 and above							
Person	14.9	80.1	1.6	3.4	0.0	1193	2.1
Gender disparity	1.12	0.99	0.36	1.19	0.00	0.97	1.09
Poverty line							
Lower segment below							
Person	14.9	84.6	0.3	0.2	0.0	759	1.9
Gender disparity	0.97	1.00	5.26	0.00	0.00	1.20	1.24
Upper segment below							
Person	13.5	80.3	2.1	4.1	0.0	1171	1.8
Gender disparity	0.91	0.95	1.36	3.36	0.00	0.84	0.97
Lower segment above							
Person	16.1	80.1	2.4	1.5	0.0	1093	1.9
Gender disparity	1.07	1.00	1.02	0.30	0.00	0.71	0.79
Upper segment above							
Person	12.5	80.7	5.0	1.8	0.0	1227	1.8
Gender disparity	0.82	1.08	0.60	0.47	0.00	1.02	0.89
Adult literacy							
None literate							
Person	14.1	84.6	1.1	0.2	0.0	1066	1.7
Gender disparity	0.90	1.03	0.21	0.00	0.00	0.69	0.80
Female literate							
Person	9.4	83.8	3.1	3.7	0.0	1542	1.8
Gender disparity	1.32	1.00	0.82	0.46	0.00	0.31	0.58
Male literate							
Person	14.7	80.5	2.8	2.0	0.0	1006	1.9
Gender disparity	0.97	1.04	0.44	0.68	0.00	0.86	0.88
Both literate							
Person	15.5	78.5	3.8	2.3	0.0	1217	1.9
Gender disparity	0.92	0.99	1.71	0.92	0.00	1.00	0.99
Village development							
Low							
Person	13.4	83.8	0.5	2.3	0.0	1276	1.9
Gender disparity	0.96	1.00	0.00	1.92	0.00	0.53	0.71
Medium							
Person	16.1	80.3	2.7	0.9	0.0	1022	1.8
Gender disparity	0.81	1.06	0.99	0.22	0.00	1.00	0.90
High							
Person	13.9	80.0	3.7	2.4	0.0	1103	1.9
Gender disparity	1.08	1.00	0.77	0.91	0.00	0.84	0.93
All groups							
Person	14.6	80.7	2.8	1.8	0.0	1094	1.8
Gender disparity	0.96	1.02	0.86	0.81	0.00	0.84	0.89

Notes: BL: Boarding and lodging; #St/Rhhd: Number of students per rural household.

TABLE A2.14

Percentage Distribution of Household Annual Expenditure on Schooling (6–14 years) in Private Schools and Gender Disparity by Population Group in Rural Haryana

(Annual expenditure in rupees)

Population group	Private schools						
	Fees	Books	Coaching	Transpt	BL	Total	#St/Rhhd
Household income							
Up to 20,000							
Person	38.5	54.2	1.0	6.3	0.0	1794	1.5
Gender disparity	0.81	1.04	0.00	2.86	0.00	0.52	0.39
20,001–40,000							
Person	38.2	55.0	3.2	3.6	0.0	1854	1.5
Gender disparity	0.97	0.96	1.21	2.34	0.00	0.70	0.67
40,001–62,000							
Person	34.4	52.1	9.1	4.2	0.2	2561	1.6
Gender disparity	1.20	0.99	0.78	0.42	0.00	0.54	0.59
62,001–86,000							
Person	34.7	49.7	8.8	6.9	0.0	2628	1.5
Gender disparity	0.88	1.20	0.75	0.66	0.00	0.47	0.52
Above 86,000							
Person	43.9	47.6	4.8	3.7	0.0	2620	1.7
Gender disparity	0.92	0.75	5.74	8.48	0.00	0.53	0.50
Landholding							
Landless wage earner							
Person	36.1	63.0	0.8	0.0	0.0	1486	1.6
Gender disparity	0.96	1.04	0.00	0.00	0.00	0.20	0.31
Marginal							
Person	38.7	52.4	3.7	5.2	0.0	2160	1.6
Gender disparity	0.91	0.91	9.29	1.87	0.00	1.08	0.77
Small							
Person	32.6	55.5	7.2	4.7	0.0	2441	1.6
Gender disparity	0.94	1.03	0.23	6.93	0.00	0.67	0.56
Medium							
Person	39.8	54.2	1.1	4.9	0.0	2211	1.3
Gender disparity	1.30	0.83	6.27	0.00	0.00	0.14	0.24
Large							
Person	45.6	45.9	8.2	0.3	0.0	2015	1.6
Gender disparity	0.76	0.94	5.74	0.00	0.00	0.52	0.62
Landless others							
Person	37.4	48.2	7.8	6.3	0.2	2379	1.7
Gender disparity	1.10	1.06	0.50	0.82	0.00	0.61	0.59
All land owners							
Person	38.1	52.8	4.9	4.2	0.0	2229	1.5
Gender disparity	0.92	0.95	1.64	2.03	0.00	0.56	0.55
All land non-owners							
Person	37.3	49.7	7.1	5.7	0.2	2250	1.7
Gender disparity	1.09	1.03	0.54	0.89	0.00	0.56	0.54
Occupation							
Agriculture							
Person	39.4	52.6	3.9	4.1	0.0	2055	1.4
Gender disparity	0.89	0.94	1.65	3.37	0.00	0.47	0.51
Salaried+prof.+s.empl.							
Person	36.6	51.7	6.3	5.3	0.1	2916	1.8
Gender disparity	1.01	0.95	1.08	1.41	0.00	0.69	0.50
Wage earners							
Person	41.9	57.4	0.7	0.0	0.0	1239	1.5
Gender disparity	1.11	0.94	0.00	0.00	0.00	0.28	0.38
All others							
Person	35.2	48.3	10.3	6.3	0.0	1993	1.6
Gender disparity	1.17	1.20	0.53	0.11	0.00	0.65	0.89
Caste							
SCs							
Person	39.1	56.9	2.2	1.2	0.7	1353	1.3
Gender disparity	0.81	1.11	2.00	2.14	0.00	0.39	0.39

(Contd.)

TABLE A2.14 (contd.)

Population group	Private schools						
	Fees	Books	Coaching	Transpt	BL	Total	#St/Rhhd
Religion							
Hindus							
Person	38.4	51.3	5.9	4.3	0.1	2179	1.5
Gender disparity	1.01	0.96	1.18	1.12	0.00	0.52	0.53
Muslims							
Person	38.6	60.2	1.2	0.0	0.0	2327	2.7
Gender disparity	1.01	1.03	0.00	0.00	0.00	0.63	0.81
Other minorities							
Person	26.2	59.4	0.8	13.6	0.0	4321	1.4
Gender disparity	0.56	0.93	0.00	0.00	0.00	2.21	1.44
Household size							
Up to 4							
Person	32.9	54.1	8.4	4.6	0.0	2202	1.3
Gender disparity	1.33	1.15	0.00	0.00	0.00	0.36	0.60
5–7							
Person	38.5	53.7	3.0	4.9	0.0	2224	1.6
Gender disparity	0.85	0.98	1.12	3.67	0.00	0.51	0.43
8 and above							
Person	39.3	46.2	10.0	4.3	0.2	2283	1.6
Gender disparity	1.06	0.94	1.61	0.37	0.00	0.89	0.89
Poverty line							
Lower segment below							
Person	41.7	51.4	0.6	6.3	0.0	1639	1.5
Gender disparity	0.95	1.24	0.00	0.00	0.00	0.38	0.48
Upper segment below							
Person	41.7	56.6	0.0	1.7	0.0	1586	1.3
Gender disparity	1.70	0.58	0.00	0.00	0.00	0.13	0.08
Lower segment above							
Person	35.6	53.6	5.4	5.3	0.1	2243	1.6
Gender disparity	0.93	1.00	1.08	1.65	0.00	0.84	0.68
Upper segment above							
Person	39.0	50.0	6.7	4.3	0.0	2391	1.6
Gender disparity	1.02	0.94	1.07	1.49	0.00	0.45	0.53
Adult literacy							
None literate							
Person	36.4	58.0	0.0	5.7	0.0	1791	1.5
Gender disparity	0.79	0.85	0.00	0.00	0.00	0.48	0.30
Female literate							
Person	41.5	58.5	0.0	0.0	0.0	2013	1.3
Gender disparity	1.26	0.83	0.00	0.00	0.00	0.42	0.54
Male literate							
Person	37.2	57.1	1.8	3.9	0.0	1731	1.5
Gender disparity	0.94	0.98	3.16	1.50	0.00	0.73	0.73
Both literate							
Person	38.1	47.7	8.8	5.3	0.1	2762	1.7
Gender disparity	1.00	0.99	1.05	1.03	0.00	0.51	0.49
Village development							
Low							
Person	30.7	48.3	17.0	4.1	0.0	3112	2.0
Gender disparity	0.99	0.79	2.17	0.84	0.00	1.05	1.27
Medium							
Person	40.8	52.7	3.0	3.5	0.0	1983	1.6
Gender disparity	0.81	1.05	9.30	0.70	0.00	0.49	0.39
High							
Person	37.6	51.9	5.2	5.2	0.1	2269	1.5
Gender disparity	1.06	0.98	0.30	1.92	0.00	0.55	0.57
All groups							
Person	37.8	51.8	5.6	4.7	0.1	2235	1.6
Gender disparity	0.97	0.97	1.10	1.50	0.00	0.56	0.55

Notes: BL: Boarding and lodging; #St/Rhhd: Number of students per rural household.

TABLE A2.15
Short-duration and Major Morbidity Prevalence Rates and Gender Disparity by Population Group in Rural Haryana

Population group	Short-duration morbidity ('000 popn)				Major morbidity per lakh popn
	Diarr.	Cold and Cough	Fever	Total	
Household income					
Up to 20,000					
Person	37	50	98	176	7448
Gender disparity	1.00	0.98	1.35	1.24	1.06
20,001–40,000					
Person	31	54	89	165	6815
Gender disparity	0.95	0.99	1.35	1.18	1.42
40,001–62,000					
Person	19	47	74	135	6504
Gender disparity	0.99	0.93	1.57	1.23	1.23
62,001–86,000					
Person	20	37	81	132	5180
Gender disparity	0.55	1.07	1.34	1.09	1.24
Above 86,000					
Person	26	37	53	111	6266
Gender disparity	0.85	1.08	1.35	1.21	1.05
Landholding					
Landless wage earner					
Person	32	44	91	161	5627
Gender disparity	0.80	0.77	1.55	1.20	0.88
Marginal					
Person	25	52	86	155	7408
Gender disparity	1.07	1.06	1.58	1.39	1.31
Small					
Person	33	53	93	167	5998
Gender disparity	0.84	1.41	1.55	1.40	1.43
Medium					
Person	23	36	73	128	5956
Gender disparity	1.46	0.99	0.85	0.99	1.20
Large					
Person	29	39	63	125	6819
Gender disparity	0.65	1.11	1.56	1.13	1.26
Landless others					
Person	30	53	85	162	8157
Gender disparity	1.01	0.75	1.25	1.03	1.20
All land owners					
Person	28	47	82	148	6514
Gender disparity	0.95	1.17	1.38	1.27	1.31
All land non-owners					
Person	31	49	88	162	6985
Gender disparity	0.91	0.76	1.38	1.11	1.08
Occupation					
Agriculture					
Person	28	46	83	148	6744
Gender disparity	0.93	1.19	1.19	1.17	1.31
Salaried+prof.+s.empl.					
Person	25	56	82	159	6404
Gender disparity	1.52	0.90	1.62	1.31	1.08
Wage earners					
Person	31	43	92	161	5964
Gender disparity	0.77	0.80	1.70	1.27	0.96
All others					
Person	35	47	78	151	8277
Gender disparity	0.64	0.81	1.26	1.01	1.47
Caste					
SCs					
Person	31	46	84	156	7281
Gender disparity	0.87	0.93	1.70	1.28	1.11
Religion					
Hindus					
Person	27	47	83	150	6813
Gender disparity	0.88	0.96	1.40	1.19	1.19
Other minorities					
Person	15	57	180	251	3231
Gender disparity	1.55	3.35	1.06	1.36	4.15
Household size					
Up to 4					
Person	33	56	116	200	11,621
Gender disparity	1.16	1.49	1.43	1.42	1.83
5–7					
Person	24	50	93	158	6054
Gender disparity	1.33	1.05	1.38	1.31	1.22
8 and above					
Person	34	42	61	131	5811
Gender disparity	0.61	0.76	1.43	1.00	0.96
Poverty line					
Lower segment below					
Person	34	49	96	172	6830
Gender disparity	0.80	0.94	1.31	1.16	0.77
Upper segment below					
Person	39	50	79	163	6090
Gender disparity	0.98	0.72	1.47	1.14	1.01
Lower segment above					
Person	30	49	86	155	6787
Gender disparity	1.05	0.96	1.32	1.19	1.23
Upper segment above					
Person	21	44	77	136	6778
Gender disparity	0.67	1.27	1.50	1.25	1.57
Adult literacy					
None literate					
Person	34	61	96	179	6928
Gender disparity	0.75	1.39	1.20	1.20	1.22
Female literate					
Person	29	62	88	160	5227
Gender disparity	0.00	0.76	0.63	0.59	0.41
Male literate					
Person	31	43	87	155	7010
Gender disparity	1.36	0.94	1.46	1.32	1.44
Both literate					
Person	24	47	74	139	6283
Gender disparity	0.68	0.84	1.48	1.10	1.01
Village development					
Low					
Person	33	30	98	155	6456
Gender disparity	0.85	0.90	1.22	1.12	1.78

(Contd.)

(Contd.)

TABLE A2.15 (contd.)

Population group	Short-duration morbidity ('000 popn) Diarr.	Cold and Cough	Fever	Total	Major morbidity per lakh popn
Medium					
Person	28	45	94	160	7258
Gender disparity	1.04	1.03	1.36	1.24	1.27
High					
Person	29	53	74	148	6334
Gender disparity	0.88	0.97	1.45	1.19	1.07
Age (years)					
0–4					
Person	179	147	134	422	1359
Gender disparity	0.85	0.75	1.10	0.91	0.33
5–14					
Person	11	58	100	164	1715
Gender disparity	1.12	0.91	0.97	0.97	0.75

(Contd.)

TABLE A2.15 (contd.)

Population group	Short-duration morbidity ('000 popn) Diarr.	Cold and Cough	Fever	Total	Major morbidity per lakh popn
15–34					
Person	3	16	45	64	3052
Gender disparity	2.23	0.97	1.66	1.52	1.98
35–59					
Person	4	25	93	119	11,179
Gender disparity	3.79	2.05	2.16	2.30	1.33
60 & above					
Person	8	38	93	137	36,590
Gender disparity	0.60	2.28	1.67	1.70	1.07
All groups					
Person	29	48	84	153	6697
Gender disparity	0.93	0.99	1.38	1.20	1.21

TABLE A2.16

Short-duration Morbidity Prevalence Rates and Gender Disparity by Population Group in Rural Haryana

Population group	Short-duration morbidity ('000 popn) Age groups (completed years) 0–4	5–14	15–34	35–59	60+	All
Household income						
Up to 20,000						
Person	455	174	83	134	146	176
Gender disparity	0.93	1.06	1.28	2.72	1.86	1.24
20,001–40,000						
Person	465	173	64	118	177	165
Gender disparity	0.91	1.00	2.36	1.48	1.41	1.18
40,001–62,000						
Person	436	169	60	100	45	135
Gender disparity	0.87	1.08	1.24	2.59	30.27	1.23
62,001–86,000						
Person	372	142	39	134	157	132
Gender disparity	1.02	0.53	1.05	2.89	0.73	1.09
Above 86,000						
Person	269	110	55	91	122	111
Gender disparity	0.77	0.78	1.21	5.28	3.45	1.21
Landholding						
Landless wage earner						
Person	453	152	82	106	141	161
Gender disparity	0.75	1.17	1.49	1.98	3.67	1.20
Marginal						
Person	402	187	52	149	113	155
Gender disparity	0.92	1.24	1.84	2.95	0.83	1.39
Small						
Person	475	176	78	120	161	167
Gender disparity	0.97	1.07	2.82	2.15	2.28	1.40
Medium						
Person	362	140	47	97	137	128
Gender disparity	1.11	0.58	0.57	2.19	2.14	0.99
Large						
Person	301	127	64	104	108	125
Gender disparity	0.81	0.67	1.23	4.32	2.13	1.13
Landless others						
Person	460	175	58	118	144	162
Gender disparity	0.91	0.85	1.26	1.80	0.91	1.03

(Contd.)

Population group	Short-duration morbidity ('000 popn) Age groups (completed years) 0–4	5–14	15–34	35–59	60+	All
All land owners						
Person	397	165	61	122	133	148
Gender disparity	0.96	0.96	1.65	2.60	1.78	1.27
All land non-owners						
Person	457	163	69	112	142	162
Gender disparity	0.83	0.98	1.35	1.87	1.58	1.11
Occupation						
Agriculture						
Person	385	158	68	115	138	148
Gender disparity	0.97	0.80	1.55	2.48	1.62	1.17
Salaried+prof.+s.empl.						
Person	487	201	48	110	106	159
Gender disparity	0.92	0.97	2.52	2.59	1.65	1.31
Wage earners						
Person	439	153	83	118	147	161
Gender disparity	0.74	1.28	1.48	2.59	3.28	1.27
All others						
Person	420	144	48	150	163	151
Gender disparity	0.89	1.31	0.62	1.37	1.09	1.01
Caste						
SCs						
Person	446	154	60	118	150	156
Gender disparity	0.76	1.42	1.65	2.44	2.01	1.28
Religion						
Hindus						
Person	418	161	64	117	138	150
Gender disparity	0.90	0.95	1.56	2.11	1.76	1.19
Other minorities						
Person	414	332	122	247	279	251
Gender disparity	1.08	0.95	0.72	12.31	– 1.36	
Household size						
Up to 4						
Person	566	222	73	194	266	200
Gender disparity	1.16	1.51	1.23	1.77	1.26	1.42

(Contd.)

TABLE A2.16 (contd.)

Population group	Short-duration morbidity ('000 popn) Age groups (completed years)					
	0–4	5–14	15–34	35–59	60+	All
5–7						
Person	425	184	72	114	115	158
Gender disparity	0.98	1.04	1.68	2.63	1.98	1.31
8 and above						
Person	383	118	52	91	104	131
Gender disparity	0.75	0.80	1.46	2.33	1.81	1.00
Poverty line						
Lower segment below						
Person	442	163	79	118	120	172
Gender disparity	0.77	1.29	1.25	2.03	2.61	1.16
Upper segment below						
Person	444	169	67	107	126	163
Gender disparity	0.97	0.81	1.56	2.17	1.07	1.14
Lower segment above						
Person	439	155	67	120	140	155
Gender disparity	0.89	1.03	1.59	2.23	1.53	1.19
Upper segment above						
Person	354	180	54	121	140	136
Gender disparity	0.98	0.81	1.46	2.58	2.19	1.25
Adult literacy						
None literate						
Person	399	160	84	119	224	179
Gender disparity	0.85	1.42	2.38	1.54	1.41	1.20
Female literate						
Person	636	96	73	131	216	160
Gender disparity	0.82	0.39	0.91	1.79	1.05	0.59
Male literate						
Person	418	171	65	126	125	155
Gender disparity	0.91	0.91	1.39	2.91	1.79	1.32
Both literate						
Person	429	162	57	108	110	139
Gender disparity	0.96	0.83	1.49	2.08	1.78	1.10
Village development						
Low						
Person	402	161	76	110	156	155
Gender disparity	0.86	1.41	0.68	3.37	0.52	1.12
Medium						
Person	400	168	69	141	147	160
Gender disparity	0.86	1.11	1.59	1.93	1.67	1.24
High						
Person	443	161	59	105	126	148
Gender disparity	0.95	0.79	1.78	2.55	2.30	1.19
All groups						
Person	422	164	64	119	137	153
Gender disparity	0.91	0.97	1.52	2.30	1.70	1.20

(Contd.)

TABLE A2.17

Major Morbidity Prevalence Rates and Gender Disparity by Population Group in Rural Haryana

Population group	Major morbidity (per lakh popn) Age groups (completed years)					
	0–4	5–14	15–34	35–59	60+	All
Household income						
Up to 20,000						
Person	1799	1488	4412	11,533	43,746	7448
Gender disparity	0.37	3.16	1.27	1.25	0.86	1.06
20,001–40,000						
Person	1100	1903	3223	12,835	32,729	6815
Gender disparity	0.31	0.63	4.56	1.21	1.25	1.42
40,001–62,000						
Person	2368	1255	3258	10,997	31,969	6504
Gender disparity	0.08	0.77	1.43	1.50	1.21	1.23
62,001–86,000						
Person	623	1421	372	7268	36,959	5180
Gender disparity	0.08	–	–	2.21	1.11	1.24
Above 86,000						
Person	492	2969	2219	9745	36,532	6266
Gender disparity	–	0.14	2.23	1.49	1.02	1.05
Landholding						
Landless wage earner						
Person	208	648	3960	7804	39,315	5627
Gender disparity	–	1.37	1.13	0.65	1.05	0.88
Marginal						
Person	1861	1391	3053	14,537	34,938	7408
Gender disparity	0.74	0.62	2.62	1.43	1.15	1.31
Small						
Person	612	892	2172	9997	37,881	5998
Gender disparity	0.24	3.55	2.72	1.29	1.17	1.43
Medium						
Person	1538	1860	2159	10,756	29,714	5956
Gender disparity	0.62	0.99	1.52	1.52	0.96	1.20
Large						
Person	594	4207	2511	7318	40,135	6819
Gender disparity	–	0.53	2.17	2.74	1.12	1.26
Landless others						
Person	2911	2731	4095	13,776	37,651	8157
Gender disparity	0.21	0.51	2.49	1.44	0.96	1.20
All land owners						
Person	1140	1730	2450	11,243	35,546	6514
Gender disparity	0.48	0.87	2.27	1.48	1.12	1.31
All land non-owners						
Person	1680	1695	4034	11,072	38,351	6985
Gender disparity	0.20	0.59	1.72	1.12	0.99	1.08
Occupation						
Agriculture						
Person	1302	1688	2644	11,434	37,771	6744
Gender disparity	0.39	1.00	2.61	1.34	1.12	1.31
Salaried+prof.+s.empl.						
Person	1537	2230	2521	12,830	29,538	6404
Gender disparity	0.25	0.33	1.25	1.39	1.01	1.08
Wage earners						
Person	722	989	3834	8983	39,556	5964
Gender disparity	1.70	1.33	1.27	0.94	0.98	0.96

(Contd.)

TABLE A2.17 (contd.)

Population group	Major morbidity (per lakh pop) Age groups (completed years) 0–4	5–14	15–34	35–59	60+	All
All others						
Person	2327	2331	4459	10,431	39,175	8277
Gender disparity	–	0.73	3.66	1.98	1.13	1.47
Caste						
SCs						
Person	2374	1580	3097	14,192	37,954	7281
Gender disparity	0.22	0.78	2.48	1.30	0.95	1.11
Religion						
Hindus						
Person	1436	1701	3095	11,332	36,566	6813
Gender disparity	0.24	0.64	2.01	1.35	1.04	1.19
Other minorities						
Person	0	3723	0	4823	31,699	3231
Gender disparity	0.25	1.31	1.17	0.98	1.49	4.15
Household size						
Up to 4						
Person	772	1707	5934	18,981	45,965	11,621
Gender disparity	0.33	3.21	2.56	1.31	1.29	1.83
5–7						
Person	954	1656	2593	9757	38,310	6054
Gender disparity	–	0.42	2.29	1.62	1.09	1.22
8 and above						
Person	1890	1809	2452	9876	30,870	5811
Gender disparity	0.58	1.11	1.42	0.97	0.91	0.96
Poverty line						
Lower segment below						
Person	1706	1727	4104	8705	48,382	6830
Gender disparity	–	2.79	1.98	1.27	0.54	0.77
Upper segment below						
Person	962	1635	4092	11,437	33,620	6090
Gender disparity	6.27	2.77	0.77	0.82	1.18	1.01

(Contd.)

TABLE A2.17 (contd.)

Population group	Major morbidity (per lakh pop) Age groups (completed years) 0–4	5–14	15–34	35–59	60+	All
Lower segment above						
Person	1556	1534	3060	12,406	33,314	6787
Gender disparity	0.19	0.49	2.42	1.23	1.08	1.23
Upper segment above						
Person	981	2140	2275	9873	39,701	6778
Gender disparity	0.59	0.35	2.56	1.98	1.38	1.57
Adult literacy						
None literate						
Person	2063	1627	6368	8887	39,557	6928
Gender disparity	0.28	0.62	2.23	1.12	1.16	1.22
Female literate						
Person	1101	1530	658	9163	46,167	5227
Gender disparity	0.28	–	–	1.35	0.17	0.41
Male literate						
Person	1210	1591	2935	12,694	35,835	7010
Gender disparity	0.09	0.99	2.07	1.70	1.15	1.44
Both Literate						
Person	1116	2020	2290	10,337	35,890	6283
Gender disparity	0.87	0.64	1.77	0.95	1.00	1.01
Village development						
Low						
Person	1124	697	3167	11,181	44,992	6456
Gender disparity	–	0.93	5.20	1.32	1.74	1.78
Medium						
Person	870	1586	3502	13,763	36,030	7258
Gender disparity	0.48	0.19	2.68	1.78	1.03	1.27
High						
Person	1795	2035	2705	9360	35,617	6334
Gender disparity	0.35	1.34	1.25	1.00	1.00	1.07
All groups						
Person	1359	1715	3052	11,179	36,590	6697
Gender disparity	0.33	0.75	1.98	1.33	1.07	1.21

TABLE A2.18

Per Person Household Expenditure for Treatment of Illness and Gender Disparity by Population Group in Rural Haryana

Population group	Cost of short illness: Fees and medicines	Cost of short illness: Proportion of total cost	Cost of long illness: Fees and medicines	Cost of long illness: Proportion of total cost	Per sick person	Per reporting
Household income						
Up to 20,000						
Person	120	0.75	60	0.65	814	838
Gender disparity	1.05	1.12	0.91	1.27	0.86	0.88
20,001–40,000						
Person	120	0.74	65	0.64	958	978
Gender disparity	1.17	1.05	1.57	0.84	1.11	1.11
40,001–62,000						
Person	71	0.80	47	0.70	732	762
Gender disparity	1.12	1.01	0.76	1.16	0.62	0.65
62,001–86,000						
Person	94	0.72	49	0.75	952	990
Gender disparity	0.97	0.93	1.20	1.11	0.97	0.90

(Contd.)

Population group	Cost of short illness: Fees and medicines	Cost of short illness: Proportion of total cost	Cost of long illness: Fees and medicines	Cost of long illness: Proportion of total cost	Per sick person	Per reporting
Above 86,000						
Person	83	0.82	52	0.70	833	833
Gender disparity	1.54	1.06	1.45	0.97	1.38	1.38
Landholding						
Landless wage earner						
Person	119	0.70	50	0.62	903	923
Gender disparity	1.03	1.14	0.56	1.28	0.64	0.67
Marginal						
Person	96	0.78	61	0.72	825	842
Gender disparity	1.40	0.95	1.04	1.11	0.79	0.82
Small						
Person	107	0.75	46	0.59	777	790
Gender disparity	1.17	1.09	2.25	1.02	1.58	1.52

(Contd.)

Table A2.18 (contd.)

Population group	Cost of short illness		Cost of long illness			
	Fees and medi-cines	Pro-portion of total cost	Fees and medi-cines	Pro-portion of total cost	Per sick person	Per rep-orting
Medium						
Person	89	0.79	41	0.74	699	725
Gender disparity	1.10	0.97	1.23	1.00	1.03	1.06
Large						
Person	99	0.80	69	0.72	1011	1042
Gender disparity	1.40	0.96	0.99	0.94	0.79	0.74
Landless others						
Person	110	0.76	76	0.67	943	974
Gender disparity	0.96	1.11	1.33	0.97	1.10	1.12
All land owners						
Person	99	0.77	53	0.68	816	836
Gender disparity	1.25	1.01	1.32	1.00	1.01	1.00
All land non-owners						
Person	114	0.73	64	0.65	928	955
Gender disparity	1.00	1.12	0.99	1.08	0.92	0.95
Occupation						
Agriculture						
Person	99	0.78	54	0.67	806	823
Gender disparity	1.16	1.00	1.28	0.93	0.98	0.97
Salaried+prof.+s.empl.						
Person	106	0.72	64	0.66	1011	1034
Gender disparity	1.28	1.13	1.11	1.00	1.03	1.06
Wage earners						
Person	120	0.71	50	0.63	847	874
Gender disparity	1.12	1.14	0.63	1.28	0.65	0.66
All others						
Person	97	0.82	69	0.71	844	876
Gender disparity	0.83	1.00	2.00	1.12	1.35	1.38
Caste						
SCs						
Person	103	0.74	55	0.66	760	782
Gender disparity	1.18	1.15	0.82	1.14	0.73	0.74
Religion						
Hindus						
Person	101	0.75	0.59	0.66	879	903
Gender disparity	1.07	1.06	1.17	1.03	0.98	0.99
Other minorities						
Person	320	0.83	16	0.59	509	509
Gender disparity	2.33	0.93	2.88	1.11	0.69	0.69
Household size						
Up to 4						
Person	153	0.75	81	0.78	702	746
Gender disparity	1.25	1.05	1.94	0.99	1.06	1.09
5–7						
Person	108	0.74	58	0.63	969	988
Gender disparity	1.34	1.07	1.06	0.96	0.87	0.87
8 and above						
Person	84	0.77	48	0.67	828	836
Gender disparity	0.85	1.05	1.05	1.14	1.10	1.09
Poverty line						
Lower segment below						
Person	112	0.70	47	0.59	693	705
Gender disparity	0.86	1.10	0.65	1.38	0.85	0.82

(Contd.)

Table A2.18 (contd.)

Population group	Cost of short illness		Cost of long illness			
	Fees and medi-cines	Pro-portion of total cost	Fees and medi-cines	Pro-portion of total cost	Per sick person	Per rep-orting
Upper segment below						
Person	103	0.75	55	0.61	913	936
Gender disparity	1.08	1.16	1.00	1.30	0.99	1.02
Lower segment above						
Person	110	0.77	59	0.67	881	893
Gender disparity	1.08	1.06	1.32	0.93	1.07	1.07
Upper segment above						
Person	93	0.75	59	0.73	874	920
Gender disparity	1.48	0.98	1.24	0.99	0.79	0.81
Adult literacy						
None literate						
Person	123	0.69	63	0.69	910	951
Gender disparity	1.15	1.14	0.62	1.12	0.51	0.51
Female literate						
Person	121	0.66	66	0.77	1268	1643
Gender disparity	0.80	0.87	1.55	1.52	3.77	4.37
Male literate						
Person	105	0.76	55	0.68	786	799
Gender disparity	1.14	1.04	1.50	1.20	1.05	1.07
Both literate						
Person	95	0.79	57	0.64	922	939
Gender disparity	1.15	1.06	1.14	0.82	1.13	1.12
Village development						
Low						
Person	109	0.81	87	0.61	1,353	1,392
Gender disparity	0.90	1.02	2.57	1.20	1.45	1.41
Medium						
Person	111	0.79	56	0.68	775	792
Gender disparity	1.14	1.09	1.02	1.15	0.81	0.83
High						
Person	99	0.71	52	0.68	832	856
Gender disparity	1.19	1.05	1.01	0.93	0.94	0.93
Age (years)						
0–4						
Person	242	0.76	10	0.74	771	771
Gender disparity	0.83	1.06	0.18	0.88	0.53	0.53
5–14						
Person	98	0.76	14	0.53	841	863
Gender disparity	0.90	1.08	0.34	1.41	0.46	0.44
15–34						
Person	52	0.74	37	0.64	1233	1253
Gender disparity	1.08	1.00	1.75	0.85	0.89	0.89
35–59						
Person	102	0.76	109	0.66	981	1006
Gender disparity	2.27	1.03	1.28	1.11	0.96	1.00
60 & Above						
Person	128	0.73	237	0.73	650	670
Gender disparity	1.53	1.20	1.09	1.01	1.02	1.03
All groups						
Person	105	0.75	57	0.67	861	884
Gender disparity	1.14	1.06	1.17	1.03	0.96	0.97

TABLE A2.19
Fertility Rate by Population Group in Rural Haryana

Population group	Crude birth rate per '000	TFR (15–49)	Average children ever born to ever married women			Crude death rate
			Boys	Girls	Total	
Household income						
Up to 20,000	34	5.2092	1.6	1.6	3.2	6
20,001–40,000	30	4.4151	1.7	1.5	3.1	7
40,001–62,000	25	3.1359	1.5	1.2	2.8	2
62,001–86,000	30	3.5967	1.4	1.3	2.7	8
Above 86,000	30	3.1143	1.3	1.2	2.5	3
Landholding						
Landless wage earner	37	5.7291	1.6	1.5	3.1	8
Marginal	26	3.9669	1.6	1.4	3.1	2
Small	26	3.7861	1.6	1.4	3.0	7
Medium	28	3.5333	1.5	1.3	2.8	3
Large	29	3.2004	1.4	1.2	2.6	3
Landless others	35	4.5633	1.5	1.4	3.0	7
All land owners	27	3.6276	1.6	1.4	2.9	4
All land non-owners	36	5.0738	1.6	1.5	3.0	8
Occupation						
Agriculture	26	3.5545	1.6	1.4	3.0	4
Salaried+prof.+s.empl.	32	4.2535	1.6	1.4	3.0	4
Wage earners	36	5.5551	1.6	1.5	3.1	9
All others	35	4.4176	1.4	1.3	2.6	6
Caste						
SCs	36	5.2521	1.6	1.5	3.2	9
Religion						
Hindus	31	4.1057	1.5	1.4	2.9	6
Other minorities	10	1.5643	1.5	1.7	3.2	5
Household size						
Up to 4	26	3.0543	1.2	0.9	2.1	14
5–7	26	4.0127	1.7	1.5	3.3	4
8 and above	38	4.9438	1.5	1.4	2.9	4
Poverty line						
Lower segment below	31	5.7731	1.8	2.1	3.9	6
Upper segment below	43	6.4452	1.7	1.6	3.2	4
Lower segment above	31	4.1399	1.6	1.4	3.0	5
Upper segment above	23	2.7817	1.4	1.1	2.6	6
Adult literacy						
None literate	38	5.8057	1.7	1.7	3.4	8
Female literate	15	2.4050	1.4	1.6	3.1	23
Male literate	30	5.1544	1.7	1.4	3.2	4
Both literate	29	2.9310	1.3	1.2	2.6	4
Village development						
Low	29	3.7604	1.7	1.4	3.1	2
Middle	28	3.7808	1.6	1.5	3.0	8
High	33	4.5724	1.6	1.4	2.9	4
All groups	**30**	**4.1908**	**1.6**	**1.4**	**3.0**	**5**

TABLE A2.20
Contraceptive Prevalence Rate for Ever Married Women by Population Group in Rural Haryana

Population group	Termination method % EMW	Vasectomy users % to all	Spacing method % EMW	Loop/CopT user % to all	% EMW using methods
Household income					
Up to 20,000	32.0	4.7	6.3	0.0	38.3
20,001–40,000	37.5	6.0	7.0	22.0	44.6
40,001–62,000	43.1	1.7	4.7	28.5	47.8
62,001–86,000	33.3	4.3	8.9	37.1	42.3
Above 86,000	37.1	2.4	9.3	30.1	46.3
Landholding					
Landless wage earner	32.3	3.6	5.2	5.3	37.5
Marginal	40.7	5.7	5.9	26.2	46.6
Small	44.3	3.8	4.9	17.2	49.2
Medium	33.5	2.3	7.1	41.9	40.6
Large	34.3	0.0	7.6	15.6	41.9
Landless others	31.2	7.2	11.0	18.5	42.2
All land owners	39.2	3.5	6.1	25.7	45.3
All land non-owners	31.7	5.5	8.3	14.7	40.0
Occupation					
Agriculture	39.4	2.3	5.7	27.1	45.2
Salaried+prof.+s.empl.	35.4	9.5	10.7	23.0	46.1
Wage earners	33.0	4.9	4.9	5.2	37.9
All others	31.1	1.3	8.2	12.6	39.2
Caste					
SCs	33.7	4.4	4.9	4.6	38.7
Religion					
Hindus	38.1	4.1	6.4	18.4	44.5
Other minorities	36.2	0.0	27.8	51.8	63.9
Household size					
Up to 4	31.1	7.6	7.7	21.8	38.8
5–7	41.6	3.8	6.9	12.7	48.5
8 and above	31.8	3.3	6.7	30.8	38.5
Poverty line					
Lower segment below	32.8	6.8	4.4	0.0	37.3
Upper segment below	31.7	4.2	6.4	5.6	38.1
Lower segment above	35.8	4.7	6.7	19.5	42.5
Upper segment above	40.6	2.6	8.5	31.5	49.1
Adult literacy					
None literate	35.7	0.7	3.8	10.0	39.5
Female literate	32.8	9.1	10.7	27.7	43.6
Male literate	41.2	5.1	4.1	14.8	45.3
Both literate	31.3	4.3	11.3	24.2	42.6
Village development					
Low	44.6	4.2	9.3	32.7	53.9
Middle	35.7	2.4	6.0	13.6	41.7
High	35.1	5.5	7.2	21.9	42.3
All groups	**36.3**	**4.2**	**6.9**	**20.7**	**43.3**

TABLE A2.21
Reasons for Non-adoption of Birth Control Measures by Population Group in Rural Haryana

(*per cent*)

Population group	Non-adoption	Reasons for not using birth control measures					
		Demand factors	Want son	Health factors	Supply factors	Household factors	Lack of knowledge
Household income							
Up to 20,000	60.4	34.2	16.2	7.0	2.0	18.8	29.6
20,001–40,000	55.6	42.1	16.1	6.9	2.3	16.5	24.9
40,001–62,000	50.5	55.7	14.3	1.0	2.4	8.7	26.3
62,001–86,000	65.4	45.6	18.9	6.6	1.9	12.7	24.5
Above 86,000	47.1	66.7	21.0	1.8	0.3	3.4	13.6
Landholding							
Landless wage earner	62.5	40.7	15.6	8.6	2.6	17.7	22.7
Marginal	53.4	40.5	13.9	7.0	1.0	17.0	31.0
Small	50.8	42.8	16.3	5.9	3.0	16.2	27.4
Medium	59.4	43.0	19.9	5.3	2.2	12.7	26.2
Large	58.1	61.3	16.6	1.0	1.0	12.7	16.8
Landless others	57.8	41.1	17.7	4.2	1.9	11.0	27.9
Land owners	54.7	45.6	16.6	5.2	1.9	14.9	26.2
Land less	60.0	40.9	16.7	6.3	2.2	14.2	25.4
Occupation							
Cultivators	54.8	42.7	16.1	5.3	2.0	16.5	26.7
Salaried+prof.+s.empl.	53.9	42.3	20.6	5.3	1.7	10.6	27.7
Wage earners	62.1	41.5	14.6	8.6	2.9	17.9	22.7
All others	60.8	52.8	15.2	2.4	1.4	9.5	25.0
Caste							
SCs	61.3	41.3	19.6	7.5	2.0	10.7	26.3
Religion							
Hindus	55.5	45.0	17.0	6.0	2.2	10.5	26.4
Other minorities	36.1	63.7	19.4	0.0	0.0	6.8	29.4
Household size							
Up to 4	61.2	52.4	15.7	3.6	0.0	7.9	23.4
5–7	51.5	33.2	17.5	8.1	3.9	18.2	30.4
8 and above	61.5	51.4	16.1	3.9	0.9	13.7	21.9
Poverty line							
Lower segment below	63.4	32.8	17.9	8.5	0.2	27.0	23.0
Upper segment below	57.7	33.2	12.6	5.0	3.1	21.2	31.3
Lower segment above	57.8	45.0	16.1	5.9	2.2	13.0	26.3
Upper segment above	50.7	54.6	19.9	3.7	2.0	6.4	22.5
Adult literacy							
None literate	60.5	31.0	18.5	7.1	1.8	23.1	27.7
Female literate	56.4	51.3	9.8	0.0	3.0	14.3	36.5
Male literate	54.7	38.5	17.1	7.0	2.7	18.4	25.9
Both literate	57.4	54.4	15.6	3.9	1.4	6.8	24.2
Village development							
Low	46.1	52.5	17.7	6.7	1.5	5.8	16.8
Medium	58.3	41.8	16.7	7.6	2.4	18.5	24.6
High	57.7	43.7	16.4	4.0	1.8	13.2	28.2
All groups	**56.7**	**43.7**	**16.6**	**5.6**	**2.0**	**14.6**	**25.8**

TABLE A2.22
Distribution of Ever Married Women Having Delivery in Previous Year by Population Group in Rural Haryana

Population group	EMW having delivery previous year	Post-natal care received	Attended by trained person	Place of delivery			Immunization %
				Hospital	CHC/PHC	Home	
Household income							
Up to 20,000	18.2	12.9	57.8	5.5	4.6	90	68.2
20,001–40,000	17.8	25.7	60.1	10.7	5.7	83.7	72.3
40,001–62,000	13.8	19.1	61.4	4.1	8	87.8	73.4
62,001–86,000	15.6	15	68.7	9.1	1.5	89.4	77.1
Above 86,000	17.4	41.1	73.9	20.4	5.8	73.9	89.6
Landholding							
Landless wage earner	21.2	16.2	50.4	3.7	3.7	92.6	58.1
Marginal	14.1	22.1	55.1	5	6.4	88.6	84.3
Small	14.7	19.9	71.8	7	4.2	88.8	75.3
Medium	15.6	22.7	60.2	13.9	2.8	83.3	66.5
Large	15.2	26.2	62.9	10.8	3.9	85.3	78.8
Landless others	19.7	20.7	68.9	13	8.2	78.8	82.1
Land owners	14.8	22.3	63	8.8	4.4	86.8	76.2
Landless	20.4	18.5	60.1	8.6	6	85.4	70.6
Occupation							
Cultivators	14.6	20.5	64	8.7	3.6	87.7	72.5
Salaried+prof.+s.empl.	17.9	23.3	72.2	12.3	7	80.7	90.3
Wage earners	20.3	15.9	50.4	3.6	3.5	92.9	57.4
All others	19	23.8	55.9	11.1	9.5	79.4	76.1
Caste							
SCs	20.8	18.9	57.2	5.1	5.9	88.9	71.0
Religion							
Hindus	17	20.1	62.7	8.8	5.6	85.6	74.7
Other minorities	5.1	88.8	100	77.5	0	22.5	100.0
Household size							
Up to 4	12.2	22	68.7	18.8	0.7	80.5	72.7
5–7	15	20.3	58.9	7.6	7.2	85.3	70.2
8 and above	21.5	20.4	62.5	7.2	4.4	88.4	76.9
Poverty line							
Lower segment below	23.3	15.2	51.1	1.8	2.8	95.3	69.2
Upper segment below	21.2	15.1	62.3	5.6	6.1	88.2	65.4
Lower segment above	16.5	21.4	62.1	9.6	6.5	83.9	76.3
Upper segment above	12.3	28.7	69.5	15.7	2.6	81.7	77.1
Adult literacy							
None literate	21.4	7.5	60.5	3.5	2.1	94.3	50.3
Female literate	7.7	40.8	66.7	33.3	0	66.7	48.3
Male literate	17.8	15.7	56.7	4.9	3.8	91.3	73.9
Both literate	14.8	34.5	68.9	16.1	9	75	88.5
Village development							
Low	16.2	19.6	56.4	6.5	2.9	90.6	77.7
Middle	15.5	16.1	69.9	7.8	3.6	88.6	67.2
High	18.1	23.4	57.5	9.6	6.5	83.9	76.8
All groups	**17**	**20.5**	**61.7**	**8.7**	**5.2**	**86.2**	**73.6**

TABLE A2.23

Percentage of Children (aged 12–23 months) Immunized and Gender Disparity by Population Group in Rural Haryana

Population group	Percentage of children (12–23 months)				
	DPT 3 doses	Polio 3 doses	BCG 1 dose	Measles 1 dose	All 8 doses
Household income					
Up to 20,000					
Person	75.11	73.37	84.32	73.87	68.67
Gender disparity	0.78	0.82	0.85	0.78	0.79
20,001–40,000					
Person	81.01	81.01	85.22	74.73	73.70
Gender disparity	0.96	0.96	0.94	0.90	0.92
40,001–62,000					
Person	70.75	70.75	70.75	70.75	70.75
Gender disparity	0.79	0.79	0.79	0.79	0.79
62,001–86,000					
Person	80.45	80.45	89.12	81.50	72.82
Gender disparity	0.86	0.86	1.11	1.30	1.01
Above 86,000					
Person	90.77	87.91	93.00	92.35	87.27
Gender disparity	0.85	0.80	0.89	0.88	0.79
Landholding					
Landless wage earner					
Person	69.19	69.19	81.10	65.09	60.40
Gender disparity	0.99	0.99	0.83	0.90	0.91
Marginal					
Person	73.51	71.22	76.92	72.85	70.56
Gender disparity	0.75	0.80	0.83	0.77	0.81
Small					
Person	73.19	73.19	77.48	73.19	69.75
Gender disparity	0.85	0.85	1.08	0.94	0.92
Medium					
Person	78.27	78.27	82.08	81.59	77.78
Gender disparity	0.73	0.73	0.83	0.82	0.71
Large					
Person	86.01	82.30	88.89	86.01	79.42
Gender disparity	0.92	0.85	0.97	1.06	0.93
Landless others					
Person	91.93	91.45	95.56	81.95	81.95
Gender disparity	0.95	0.96	0.90	0.89	0.89
All land owners					
Person	77.07	75.91	80.77	77.93	74.08
Gender disparity	0.82	0.81	0.93	0.89	0.84
All land non-owners					
Person	82.97	82.68	89.86	75.31	73.46
Gender disparity	0.95	0.96	0.87	0.89	0.88
Occupation					
Agriculture					
Person	77.07	75.65	80.64	78.74	74.05
Gender disparity	0.81	0.80	0.93	0.89	0.82
Salaried+prof.+s.empl.					
Person	87.81	87.35	87.39	83.77	83.77
Gender disparity	0.97	0.98	0.89	0.91	0.91
Wage earners					
Person	70.06	70.06	81.63	66.08	61.52
Gender disparity	0.97	0.97	0.82	0.88	0.88
All others					
Person	83.42	83.42	95.94	69.15	69.15
Gender disparity	0.74	0.74	0.91	0.79	0.79
Caste					
SCs					
Person	80.37	80.37	89.30	80.92	77.81
Gender disparity	0.86	0.86	0.89	0.90	0.88
Religion					
Hindus					
Person	81.01	79.99	86.63	78.63	74.90
Gender disparity	0.86	0.86	0.92	0.89	0.84
Other minorities					
Person	76.16	76.16	76.16	76.16	76.16
Gender disparity	1.53	1.53	1.53	1.53	1.53
Household size					
Up to 4					
Person	72.81	72.04	75.45	65.38	62.74
Gender disparity	0.78	0.80	0.85	0.76	0.69
5–7					
Person	79.66	77.97	85.22	78.73	73.86
Gender disparity	0.84	0.83	0.90	0.83	0.81
8 and above					
Person	80.33	80.33	84.92	78.76	77.26
Gender disparity	0.92	0.92	0.94	1.01	0.96
Poverty line					
Lower segment below					
Person	69.56	69.56	81.03	69.10	66.15
Gender disparity	0.70	0.70	0.81	0.69	0.62
Upper segment below					
Person	78.91	75.93	87.87	77.44	68.48
Gender disparity	0.90	1.00	0.93	0.91	1.06
Lower segment above					
Person	80.77	80.59	83.54	75.52	74.91
Gender disparity	0.93	0.93	0.93	0.92	0.93
Upper segment above					
Person	79.12	77.26	83.85	83.85	77.26
Gender disparity	0.78	0.73	0.89	0.89	0.73
Adult literacy					
None literate					
Person	59.85	59.85	73.76	68.63	58.14
Gender disparity	0.84	0.84	0.94	0.99	0.79
Female literate					
Person	86.35	86.35	100.00	69.05	69.05
Gender disparity	1.25	1.25	1.00	1.81	1.81
Male literate					
Person	78.70	77.38	81.70	74.00	72.09
Gender disparity	0.81	0.79	0.84	0.76	0.75
Both literate					
Person	89.04	88.14	90.37	85.21	84.31
Gender disparity	0.97	0.98	1.01	0.99	1.01
Village development					
Low					
Person	70.83	70.83	77.11	66.85	63.71
Gender disparity	1.04	1.04	1.04	1.18	1.08
Medium					
Person	70.80	68.67	78.10	72.54	64.71
Gender disparity	0.93	0.92	1.02	1.02	0.96
High					
Person	86.37	86.19	89.13	82.17	82.17
Gender disparity	0.82	0.83	0.84	0.79	0.79
All groups					
Person	79.07	78.20	83.85	77.04	73.87
Gender disparity	0.86	0.86	0.91	0.89	0.85

(Contd.)

3 Village Study in Haryana
Rattangarh and Bhoda Hoshnak

3.1 Selection of Districts

From the twelve selected sample districts of the United Nations Development Programme (UNDP) household survey, two districts were selected for a qualitative study of villages. While selecting the districts, economic variations and socio-cultural differences between the various villages were taken into account. The CMIE index of development for the districts was used to determine the economic variations, assuming the all-India index of development to be 100.

Two districts, one with a high index of 293 and the other with a low index of 196, were selected in order to compare a well-developed district with an undeveloped district. While selecting the districts, care was taken to exclude areas adjacent to the larger urban towns and adjoining districts in order to study the impact of socio-cultural and economic indicators. Thus, the two districts of Kurukshetra in the north and Hissar in the south-west were identified.

Kurukshetra is the smallest district in the state occupying an area of 2.75 per cent of the state. It is located in the northern part of Haryana, and is surrounded by Karnal in the south, Kaithal in the south-west, Yamunanagar in the north-east, and Ambala in the extreme north—connecting the district with the state capital, Chandigarh. After the reorganization of the district, Kurukshetra is left with only two *tehsils*, Pahwa and Thanesar.

The other district of this study, Hissar, is on the south-west of the state, surrounded by Jind in the east, Sirsa in the west, Punjab in the north, and Rajasthan in the south. Hissar has the largest area compared to any other district in Haryana.

The two districts present the following variations. While the rural literacy rate in Hissar is 41.6 per cent, Kurukshetra has a rural literacy rate of 53.1 per cent, which is above the state average of 49.8 per cent. Similarly, the female literacy rate in Kurukshetra is 40.1 per cent, while Hissar is far behind with a literacy rate of only 24.4 per cent, which is lower than the state average of 32.5 per cent. Considering the fact that all the villages have schools within a distance of 1 km, the lower literacy level in Hissar can be attributed to socio-cultural factors. This trend is discernible in primary school enrolment ratios. While the percentage of main workers in Hissar is only marginally higher than that in Kurukshetra, the female work participation rate is nearly three times in Hissar than that in Kurukshetra. This indicates the economic need for female employment in Hissar district. However, there is no variation in the work participation rate of male workers, though it is marginally higher than the state average.

TABLE 3.1
Profile of Selected Districts

Indicators	Haryana	Selected districts	
		Kurukshetra	Hissar
CMIE index of development (All India = 100)	136	293	196
Sex ratio	874	883	861
Area (in per cent)	100	2.75	10.27
Population (1991 census) (in million)	16.318	0.635	1.835
Rural indicators			
Population (in million)	12.272	0.481	1.447
Population growth rate between 1981 and 1991 (in per cent)	21.57	16.76	20.49
Main workers (percentage of total population)			
Total	28.66	27.99	30.92
Male	48.26	50.19	50.18
Female	6.01	2.75	8.55
Literacy (aged 7 yrs and above) (in per cent)			
Total	49.8	53.1	41.6
Male	64.8	64.6	56.5
Female	32.5	40.1	24.4
Primary school enrolment rate (in per cent)			
Total	45.5	42.0	23.4
Boys	44.8	39.3	24.1
Girls	46.2	45.2	22.6
Percentage of villages with a school within 1 km	100 (7067)	100 (398)	100 (510)

3.1.1 Selection of Villages

Nine villages were identified in each district for the household survey, from which one village each was selected for this study. Keeping in view the constraints, villages were selected so as to avoid big villages and villages in the urban vicinity, and to cover as many religious/caste variations as possible to observe the socio-economic and cultural effects. Villages with an average of 250 households were identified from the given list. Thus, Rattangarh village in Shahabad block of Thanesar tehsil of Kurukshetra district and Bhoda Hoshnak village in Agroha block of Hissar district were surveyed and the analysis is presented in this chapter.

3.2 Profile of Village Rattangarh in Kurukshetra

3.2.1 *Location*

Rattangarh village is located in Shahabad block of Kurukshetra district in Haryana. It lies mid-way between the district headquarters and the district of Ambala towards the north. By virtue of its location on the GT Karnal highway, and being closer to the block headquarters (Shahabad, at a distance of 2 km), there is urbanization in a certain sense in this village.

TABLE 3.2
Distribution of Households by Caste, Rattangarh

Caste	No. of households	Percentage of households
Scheduled caste (SC)	139	52.1
Upper caste (UC)	103	38.6
Other backward caste (OBC)	18	6.7
Minority community (MC)	7	2.6
	267	100.0

Notes: Scheduled caste: This also includes a few converted Sikhs and Balmikis along with the harijans; Upper caste includes jats, brahmins, and khatris; OBC includes the service sector castes like khatis, kumhars, gadriyas, barbers, etc.

Rattangarh village has 267 households, of which 52.1 per cent (139 households) are SCs. About 39 per cent (103 households) are categorized as the upper castes and include 45 jats, 15 khatris, 13 brahmins, and 13 jat Sikhs. There are 18 households belonging to OBCs and 7 are Muslim households. The housing pattern is contiguous, but residents of the village live in separate enclaves. Most of the houses of the upper castes are located next to the roadside. The old SC colony is located in the newly established colony at the rear of the village; it has been established through the 'Indira Awas Yojana' in 1977. There is an additional enclave of about 40 to 50 households, occupied by the ethnic Sikhs, in close proximity to this village. However, as this enclave comes under a different village panchayat, this community was not included in the qualitative study.

There seems to be a fair amount of inter-caste dependence in the economic and social activities in the village. For example, the upper castes are the land owners in this village whereas SCs and backward castes are the wage labourers. There is a long tradition of dependence of the SCs on the landed high caste families in the village. There is also a kind of bonded contract between the SC workers and the landowners. For example, the study team found that about Rs 5000 was being paid in advance to the SC households in exchange for one adult's one full year's work on both the household and the farm. These unwritten contracts are so binding that even for a single day's absence—either due to sickness or other engagements—the landlord debits Rs 50. In another contract, Rs 30,000 was advanced in exchange for six years of adult male work with the landlord. The other family members are, however, not a party to such contracts. The bonded labour is served with food for the whole day. Such incidents appear not very uncommon in this village. This was apparent from the response of the SC families to a question relating to the status and nature of employment. The answer was 'zamindar ka kaam' which means a bonded-like work contract.

The seven Muslim households comprise migrants who visit this village on a regular basis for a long duration of time and are involved in honey collection from the forests. These families do not appear to have integrated into the social scene of this village. A number of migrant households from central Uttar Pradesh belonging to the backward classes have settled in the rented houses owned by the SCs in the new SC colony. While all these migrant families work as labourers in the nearby sugar, alcohol, and acid manufacturing factories, only a few SCs work in these industries. Most of the SCs work as wage labourers and a few are engaged in service occupations.

Nearly all the cultivable land is irrigated mainly by tubewells. The soil is fertile and the yield is good. The major *kharif* crops grown are paddy, cotton, sugarcane, and sunflower, and the major *rabi* crops are wheat and mustard. All the big landlords sell not only their own crops but also help in marketing the produce of the smaller cultivators. The daily wage rate in this village is Rs 50 for males and Rs 30 for females. There is no incidence of child labour in this village. While men undertake heavier field jobs such as ploughing, operating tractors, carrying loads, etc., the women are engaged in laborious work related to agriculture such as sowing, weeding, cotton picking, transplanting, potato cleaning, etc.

3.2.2 *Education*

The village primary school was established in 1955. At present there are about 200 children studying in classes up to the fifth standard. All the five teachers in the school, four of whom are females, come from outside the village to teach daily. Although it is a *pucca* building, there are no door or window fixtures in the school building. The school is located in a low-lying area that gets flooded during the rainy season because of which the school is often closed during the monsoon. Even though the village got an electricity connection in the early 1950s, the school has not been provided with a connection till now. There is a toilet with an overhead tank for the use of the staff. The hand pump inside the school complex provides drinking water.

According to the principal of the school, who is a woman, almost all the children from the SCs and backward castes in the village are enrolled in the school. However, an almost equal number of children from the upper castes attend the private primary school at Shahabad. All the currently enrolled children are residents of this village. Over 50 per cent of the students studying in the village primary school are from the SCs and the other half is equally divided between the backward and the upper castes.

TABLE 3.3

Castewise Enrolment of Children in Government Primary School, Rattangarh

Class	Total			Backward caste			Scheduled caste			Others		
	M	F	T	M	F	T	M	F	T	M	F	T
I	30	14	44	5	4	9	21	8	29	4	2	6
II	24	19	43	2	5	7	18	8	26	4	6	10
III	23	22	45	6	4	10	10	13	23	7	5	12
IV	18	23	41	5	7	12	11	12	23	2	4	6
V	14	15	29	4	3	7	5	7	12	5	5	10
Total	**109**	**93**	**202**	**22**	**23**	**45**	**65**	**48**	**113**	**22**	**22**	**44**

Each student is charged a fee of 75 paise per month towards the welfare of children and Rs 5 is charged as an annual donation from every child. An admission fee of Rs 25 is charged from children who wish to get re-admitted. There are special schemes for SC children, especially girls, who are provided four metres of cloth for uniform per year and Rs 10 per month as stipend. Both SC boys and girls get an annual amount of Rs 10 for stationery expenses but no incentive is given for books. The fees in the private school in the town vary between Rs 35 and Rs 50 per month, and Rs 90 per month has to be paid for transport charges.

None of the Muslim children seems to be studying in these schools. One very interesting feature with regard to higher education is that about 20 to 25 SC boys are studying in college whereas very few boys and girls belonging to the upper castes do so. The upper caste children seem to discontinue education after high school. The pattern of higher education among the SCs is perhaps the result of high expectations raised through the job reservation policy of the government for the SCs.

3.2.3 Health Infrastructure

Since the village is only 2 km from the block headquarters, villagers can access both the public and private health care facilities, whether for preventive, promotive or curative care. Till recently, an auxiliary nurse mid-wife (ANM) would regularly visit the village to provide antenatal care and immunization on the first wednesday of each month. Since 1993, however, a sub-centre has been constructed opposite the village across the GT Karnal road and an ANM, who has to cover 35 other surrounding villages as well, has been posted there since May 1994. The sub-centre provides, besides the clinic space, a two-room accommodation for the ANM. The approach to the sub-centre is blocked due to stagnant water (between the road and the sub-centre) in an area of about 15 to 20 ft. This could be seen all along the road across the village up to Shahabad. It appears that water draining from Shahabad town gets accumulated all along the roadside throughout the year, breeding germs and mosquitoes. On all the other three sides, fields surround the sub-centre and a small pathway is evidently used for defecation. It is clear as to why people do not visit this sub-centre to receive health care.

The ANM does not stay in this sub-centre. She travels 5 km daily to reach the sub-centre. Her contention is that the sub-centre should be a part of the village and not outside as it makes it unsafe to reside. As far as the villagers are concerned, the existence of this sub-centre is pointless. The ANM provides her routine services in the primary school premises. For mild ailments, there are two registered medical practitioners (RMPs) residing in the village who are available to the people in the morning and evening; they have their own clinics located in the neighbouring village. Very often, to avoid delays in seeking treatment, the villagers visit private practitioners in the nearby town as their experiences with the public health facilities have been very disappointing. According to the ANM, there is an immense need for a lady helper, especially for delivery cases. However, there seems to be no such provision at present.

Deliveries are normally conducted by a trained birth attendant residing in the village. There are a trained dai and a nurse in the village. The old woman who has been practising as dai for the last two decades had undergone a six-week training organized by the state government about 10–15 years ago. As she is more experienced, people have more confidence and trust in her as compared to the nurse who has come to the village only recently. Moreover, since the nurse is employed in a private nursing home, she is not available when the people need her.

In addition, a male multipurpose worker (MPW), a resident of the village, has been working for the last thirty years and maintaining a record of the incidence of malaria in the village;

he assists the ANM during her routine vaccination visits. On the whole, public health care facilities are not available to the residents of this village.

POTABLE WATER

The Corporation has been supplying drinking water to the villagers since 1988. At one end of the village, a well (which is about 650 ft deep) has been bored for the purpose. Pipes are connected at different points in the village so that there is an easy access to drinking water for all the households. About 20 such water connections have been provided at convenient points and water is supplied for about four hours a day. About 20–5 households, at their own personal expense, have extended the individual connections inside the households, though the authorities do not officially permit such a practice.

Up to the time that piped water was made available, the villagers generally used well water. Some of the well-to-do households have installed hand pumps inside their premises. Since piped water became available, people have ceased using other sources.

SANITATION

The surroundings of the village, especially the roadside, are never dry. It appears that the drainage water from the nearby town flows in this direction and gets accumulated in the ditches on either side of the road, which then becomes a breeding place for mosquitoes. There is no pipe fitted with stop corks to regulate the supply. There is also no arrangement for garbage disposal and garbage is heaped at convenient places. The zamindar gets it lifted at times by harijans by paying for it and uses it as manure in his fields. According to the 'sarpanch' of the village, garbage is one of the major factors reponsible for creating unhygienic conditions in the village.

The upper caste households, who generally live in concrete houses, have separate toilets in their backyards, outside the main house, and these toilets are equipped with flushing facilities and overhead tanks to store water. Faecal matter is disposed of through 'sok da gadda' system, which essentially means digging a hole a few feet below the ground surface with bricks laid all around the wall; through the pores in the wall the defecated matter is absorbed and dries up. No government subsidy has been received in any form by the upper castes for this purpose, but some of the SC households have apparently been provided a subsidy in the form of materials for construction. However, a majority of the SCs continue to use the open field behind their houses for defecation. Women folk and children in these households use a corner of the open space around the house to urinate. It is common among children to defecate in areas where garbage is thrown.

Some of the infrastructure facilities provided to the villagers include:

1. An anganwadi centre has been operation since 1987 for pre-school children between the ages of 3 and 6 years. As it has no building of its own, it is functioning in one of the rooms of the school. About 75 children of the village from the SCs, khatris of the upper castes, and backward castes attend this centre. The proportion of female children is higher in the anganwadi. If they can afford it, the villagers send their children to nurseries and the kindergarten in the town.

2. Nutrition supplements given in the anganwadi include baked soybean (sweet and salted), jaggery coated wheat and roasted wheat, and milk powder with sugar. In addition, a weekly stock of ready sweet mix pack meant for children between 6 months and one and a half years of age is given to the mothers of these children.

3. The ANM visits the centre once a month for antenatal care and immunization.

4. A post office is located in a room in the post master's house since 1961. It provides additional facilities like registration, parcel booking, money order despatch, etc., and once a day the mail is cleared.

5. A mini-cooperative bank located in Chhapra, about 6 km from the village, serves the villagers by providing both crop and non-crop loans to members. About 20–5 farmers benefit from this scheme. A steel almirah manufacturing unit run by a resident in the village also benefits from the mini bank non-crop loan scheme at a reasonable interest rate.

3.2.4 Focus Group Discussion

In all, five focus group discussions (FGDs) were conducted, three of which were for women in the reproductive age group, while one each was for males and elderly women in the village. Out of the three female FGDs, one was exclusively conducted for the SC women. In the other two FGDs, the participants were mostly from the high caste jats, brahmins, and Sikhs. A large proportion of upper caste participants belonged to joint families. Of the two upper caste FGDs held for women, one group was relatively very young, about 18–28 years old. The other group was relatively older, with ages ranging between 24 and 45 years. For the SC women's FGD, the age range was 28–40 years.

As an overview, there were very clear differences in the viewpoints, attitudes, aptitudes, cultural practices, and desires between the SCs and the relatively high caste Hindus. An attempt is made here to present these differences in a comparative perspective.

As far as the lifestyle and standard of living are concerned, the upper castes were relatively better-off. Many are landed and in service jobs. Although most of the particpting women, even among the upper castes, were illiterate, their points of view were considerably different from those of the SC women who were also illiterate. It appears that the be-havioural and attitudinal differences emerge from the prosperity of the higher castes, which is a result of their cultivation and landholding patterns. Practically all the SC families of the FGD participants reported as working for *dehadi* which literally means working on daily wages. The dehadi, however, also includes a kind of bonded labour contract system, which has been explained earlier. The relatively rich have substantial food stocks and do not depend on the market for their day-to-day foodgrain purchases whereas the SC families have to depend on daily wages for their daily needs. They were in such a bad position that they were not even able to purchase their supplies of sugar from the Public Distribution System (PDS). The PDS wheat supplied for distribution was being diverted to the flour-mill owned by the PDS manager next door and the flour was being sold at Rs 5.50 per kg.

EDUCATION

The value of education is appreciated by both the communities. Education is a major input of human resource development among the high castes. They like to educate even the girls up to a certain standard. The upper castes prefer to send their children only to the private school in the nearby town. They are willing to pay for and are capable of meeting the higher cost of education. In these communities, education is seen as an alternative to land—they expect jobs outside the farms but also know about the difficulty in obtaining these jobs.

The SCs of this village also recognize the value of schooling. However, they are not able to afford the high cost of sending their children to the private school. They are entirely dependent on the government school in the village. Although the participants were not satisfied with the physical facilities (their children have to even carry a small jute rag to school to sit on) and sanitary conditions in the school, they are forced to send their children there because they value education. Some women, even among the SCs, stated that they arrange for private tuition for their children. Among the high castes, not only do the women provide private tuition, they also provide a better environment for their children in their homes for studies.

Among the SCs and backward castes there has been a reported withdrawal of girls from studies. This is due to two reasons: (i) high demand for labour during certain periods when girls also work in the fields; and (ii) they are entrusted with the care of younger children so that the mother can work. Although there were no reports of people trying to re-admit their children in school, the participants reported that re-admission is not only discouraged but they have to pay a re-admission fee as well, which is about Rs 25. Some SC women also complained that there was a nominal monthly fee, which was collected on a regular basis. The SC women appreciated the supply of four metres of cloth for uniform for girls but complained that the cost of books was high and should be subsidized. The upper caste participants in the two FGDs, however, made no such demands. The upper castes are less likely to withdraw girl children from school, at least up to a certain level, whereas the withdrawal of girl children is more common among the lower castes.

Both the upper and lower castes use the government high school, which is located in a nearby town. It was also found that it is the SC boys who continue to go for higher studies to colleges. It appears that there is a need for a flexible or dynamic school system, essentially to provide for the easy re-admission of those SC children who drop out for various social and economic reasons.

An FGD was conducted for a mixed group of male members who belonged mostly to the upper castes and were landed and relatively older. Four of the seven members were literate. The discussion with them on education was fairly clear-cut. The men had more definite views about girls studying only up to the fifth standard. They were unwilling to send girls to the neighbouring town for middle and high school level education. Much of the remaining discussion centred around the education of boys. They recognized the importance of education in the modern day world. They also recognized that education would increase work efficiency in many types of work, including agriculture. For example, they would be in a better position to identify better seeds, sow them in the right proportion, and operate modern machinery. The main complaint was about the very bad quality of primary education in the village. From their point of view, sending even boys outside for higher level studies was risky. They complained that very often teachers misused the services of children by asking them to fetch fruits, beverages, and other items. At the higher level, while the boys are in town, their parents are incapable of keeping a watch on them. It is often feared that their sons may bunk classes and fool around in the town, often spending the money meant for their studies.

A few, however, conveyed that children tend cattle after returning from school. Sometimes when demand is at a peak, children are withdrawn from school to work on the family farms. Often when both the parents work as wage labourers, the children are withdrawn from school because their parents cannot supervise them. Men placed more emphasis on the need for a home environment conducive to studies and supervision of studies at home. They were relatively more concerned than women about their children going out of control. There was also a complaint that even the zamindar's children, though they were educated up to the BA level, could not get a job, even with 75 per cent marks.

Analysis of school drop-outs. Nine children, mostly girls between 9 and 14 years of age, who had discontinued schooling before completing their primary (Class V) education any time during the previous three years were contacted in the village, so as to understand the conditions which led them to do so. In the case of the respondents who were unable to express themselves, the problems were discussed with any responsible adult member of the household. As the upper castes value educating both boys and girls up to a certain minimum level, even at a higher cost, there seemed little possibility of their children dropping out at the primary level.

The keenness of parents to send their cnildren to school is reflected in the situation where younger brothers and sisters of drop-outs in most of these households were attending school. However, the drop-out children seem to have reconciled to their condition as drop-outs—a majority of them expressed their desire to get trained in 'sewing' which would help them to support themselves. In one case, a 14 year old girl was asked to discontinue by the teacher saying that 'she was grown up to study in Class V'. Such social pressures also discourage them from continuing their schooling and deter them psychologically from getting re-admitted. However, these drop-outs denied any kind of caste discrimination in school.

That the upper castes value education as part of the development of the child, and thus are particular about educating both girls and boys is reflected from the fact that not even a single child was found among these castes who had discontinued before completing primary level education in the recent past. Hence, all the nine children canvassed belonged to SC households whose parent/parents were engaged in wage work.

diseases. For example, some of them reported drinking water, stagnant water, environmental sanitation, and unhygienic conditions as some of the causes of sicknesses. Teething was also given as an important cause of diarrhoea among children. They were aware of the need for rehydration in children suffering from diarrhoea. Some of them also knew about oral rehydration solution (ORS) and many reported the practice of giving ginger water to children as a home remedy. A number of gynaecological complaints were discreetly mentioned with the major complaints being back and joint pains, which they related to the family planning methods adopted. The upper caste women were particular about the need for more nutritious food during pregnancy and reported going for regular post-natal checks and pre-natal immunization and taking iron and folic acid tablets.

The high caste women were also very particular about using hot water, soap, and a clean blade to perform safe

TABLE 3.4
Identification of Respondents, Rattangarh

Sl. no.	Sex	Age years	Caste	Class studied up to	Parents' occupation		Parents' education level	
					Father	Mother	Father	Mother
1.	G	14	SC	4	AWL	AWL	P	NIL
2.	G	10	SC	2	WL	HHW	P	NIL
3.	G	14	SC	4	WL	WL	P	NIL
4.	G	9	SC	1	AWL	AWL	NIL	NIL
5.	G	12	SC	4	WL	WL	P	NIL
6.	G	14	SC	4	NAWL	AWL	P	NIL
7.	G	9	SC	2	AWL	AWL	NIL	NIL
8.	G	10	SC	4	AWL	AWL	NIL	NIL
9.	G	12	SC	3	AWL	AWL	P	NIL

Note: G: girl; AWL: agriculture wage labour; NAWL: non-agriculture wage labour; WL: wage labour; NIL: no formal education; P: primary education.

Even among the SCs, there is a tendency to withdraw girls as there are hardly any drop-outs among the boys in the primary school.

However, the education of parents did not seem to have any effect on children as their poverty stood foremost, and eight of the nine children aged between 9 and 14 years had discontinued studies at different stages, varying from Class I to Class IV, due to economic pressure at home. With the passage of time, there is a tendency among children to lose interest in studies, and the urge among parents to re-admit them also diminishes when they think of paying the re-admission fee of Rs 25 per child. Some of the reasons for discontinuing school include the mother's illness and taking care of siblings, etc.

HEALTH

The upper caste participants were relatively well informed about the origin, cause, transmission, and manifestation of

deliveries. These women often travel to Ambala which is about 20 km away to receive many types of health care. These families seem to make elaborate arrangements for child delivery and they are also aware of a number of different types of home remedies and traditional medication. However, the trend has now shifted towards modern medical treatment even

TABLE 3.5
Reasons for Dropping Out of School before Completing Primary Education, Rattangarh

Reason for discontinuing	Response (no.)	Response (per cent)
Economic difficulty at home	8	89
Not interested in studies	3	33
To take care of siblings	2	22
Mother's illness	1	11
Poor health	1	11

when the families are located far away. They also reported fairly regular bathing and changing of clothes. The maintenance of hygiene is satisfactory among these castes.

As compared to the upper castes, the SC and ST women's group presented a bleak picture of health, inadequate access to food and nutrition, and lack of resources for the maintenance of personal hygiene and sanitation. They reported that most of the time they eat '*rotis* with tea and *chatni*' which lack proteins and other vitamin supplements. They even reported having been forced to eat vegetables such as potatoes that were rotten and which would cause sickness. Another major problem was the inability to have a bath daily because of their work schedule that started very early in the day and ended late in the night. As reported earlier, practically all of them work. One major complaint from the SC women was a very high exposure to mosquito bites. Many women complained about body and joint pains, mostly originating from tedious work. They reported difficulties in the management of pregnancies because they would be working until almost the day of delivery and would start working again within 9 to 10 days after the delivery. Therefore, antenatal, natal, and post-natal care are almost non-existent. There was also no pre-natal immunization or taking of iron and folic acid tablets; nor was there any report of going in for special treatment in the nearby hospital.

The men reported that although the houses were kept clean, the roads and immediate environment were not. They were willing to pay only if some institution such as the municipality undertook this work. An unhygienic environment was reported as the cause of the widely prevalent fever. They reported that the doctors, who were making a good amount of money, did not make any diagnosis. One of the main factors reported as a source of disease was the use of fertilizers and pesticides in cultivation. One stated, '*Bimari kudrat ki den nehin hai. Anaj mein bimari hai.*' They were of the opinion that some of the pesticides were of sub-standard quality, which could cause a greater danger to their health.

The main complaint was that even the pregnant women were not attended to properly by the health department. The ANM did not visit the village, although there is a sub-centre there. Immunizations are not conducted in the village and the men reported that they took their children to the nearby town for immunization. This was confirmed by reports from the female FGDs. It was alleged that the government doctors often give only prescriptions; very often they also give irrelevant and useless medicines. For example, one participant stated that when she went to get medicine for fever, a blood test was not conducted and only four or five white tablets were given. Such seemingly undependable medication appears to drive these people to seek expensive private health care. The men reported that home remedies were very popular in the past but many of the raw materials for the home remedies had lost their medicinal values due to the extensive use of fertilizers and pesticides. Cases of measles are never taken to a modern practitioner. Instead, they are taken to the main mandir in the nearby village.

Results of free listing of diseases. Twenty adult, married women between the ages of 21 and 70 years were selected at random to seek information about their knowledge and understanding of the common illnesses, along with their symptoms and causes. Of those interviewed, ten women were below 30 years, another eight were between 31 and 45 years of age, and the remaining two were about 45 years of age. A proforma was canvassed for the purpose.

The respondents were women belonging to different castes: nine belonged to the upper castes and seven represented the SCs. The rest were from the other castes. A majority of the women interviewed were illiterate, with the exception of three upper caste women of whom one (aged 22 years) had completed middle school education and the other two were somewhat literate.

It was decided to initially record the spontaneous replies and then do some probing with respect to diseases of children, women, the elderly, etc. Very often, the responses clearly indicated their reluctance to talk about illness as if it was a stigma. They said, 'we are not suffering from any illness', 'what do we know of illness'. Thus, mild probing like 'you might have heard of some child in the neighbourhood falling sick' was unavoidable. Still there was some resistance from the respondents. Some said 'we do not know about others'. Thus, it was only after a lot of effort that their knowledge and understanding about illnesses could be listed.

In general, the responses of the participants did not vary much, both in terms of type and quality. The only exception to this were the educated upper caste women who listed names of chronic illnesses such as enlarged liver pleurisy, and typhoid with their broad symptoms and causes, which perhaps was a reflection of their education.

The widespread knowledge about an illness is perhaps suggestive of its prevalence in the environment. Among the short-duration illnesses, a majority of the respondents listed fever (80 per cent), followed by malaria (70 per cent), and cold and cough (65 per cent). It was observed that women in the younger age group (less than 30 years of age) more commonly listed illnesses like vomiting and loose motion (55 per cent), and pneumonia (50 per cent). Stomach-ache was listed mainly by the SCs (35 per cent). Possibly this reflects their intake which often lacks minerals, proteins, and vitamins. A few also listed headache (30 per cent) and measles (25 per cent). It is interesting to observe that while the upper caste women were able to name uncommon illnesses, they failed to list even the broad symptoms associated with these. The lower caste women engaged in wage work were able to link the broad symptoms associated with an illness more confidently. Thus, possibly, the working women seem to have a better opportunity to widen their knowledge than the upper caste women who restrict themselves to their homes.

TABLE 3.6
Prevalence Rate of Illness, Rattangarh

(*n* = 20)

Local name	Approximate English equivalent	No. of response	Per cent
Bukhar	Fever	16	80
Jukam and khansi	Cold and cough	13	65
Orsa	Pneumonia	9+1	50
Ulti and dasth	Vomiting and diarrhoea	11	55
Malaria	Malaria	14	70
Khasra	Measles	5	25
Sar dard	Headache	6	30
Peeth ka dard	Back ache (upper)	2	10
Kamar ka dard	Back ache (lower)	2	10
Pait dard	Stomach ache	7	35
Badan dard	Body ache	1	5
Rasoli	Abcess	1	5
Kamjori	Anaemic	1	5
Tapedic	Tuberculosis	4	20
Sans ki bimari	Breathing problem	8	40
Blood pressure	Blood Pressure (low)	4	20
Moti jara	Typhoid	1	5
Choti maatha	Chicken Pox	3	15
Kali khansi	Whooping Cough	3	15
Gal gotu	Diphtheria	1	5
Polio	Polio	6	30
Par chawan	Malnourishment	1	5
Gale dard	Throat pain	1	5
Ankhon se sambandith	Eye-related problem	5	25
Kan se sambandith	Ear-related problem	2	5
Daant se sambandith	Toothache	10	25
Jodon ka dard	Joint Pain	4	20
Piliya	Jaundice	2	10
Pleurisy	Pleurisy	1	5
Jigar ki bimari	Enlarged liver	1	5
Cancer	Cancer	1	5
Dil ki bimari	Heart problem	3	15

Often the perceived causes of some of the commonly listed illnesses such as fever, cold and cough, pneumonia, vomiting, diarrhoea, joint pain, and asthmatic problem, were associated with climatic changes, while the symptoms in a few cases were self-explanatory (see Table 3.7). Malaria was the disease that was most clearly identified with its symptoms and causes.

Despite the efforts to probe women's illnesses by suggestion, symptoms, etc., the women were generally unwilling to co-operate except in one case where a pregnant woman confessed to having severe backache, accepting it to be natural. The other illnesses listed were jaundice, heart problem, chickenpox, measles, tuberculosis (TB) and some diseases that could be prevented by vaccines.

The symptoms reported for most of the illnesses did suggest something plausible. For example, for chest congestion the symptom given was fast breathing (pasli chalna), pain in the chest, etc.; for low blood pressure the symptoms given were giddy feeling, swelling all over, headache, etc.; while the causes for common illnesses like cold and cough, fever, vomiting and diarrhoea were very often associated with the climate; and malaria was identified as being caused by mosquitoes, stagnant water, etc.

TABLE 3.7
Symptoms and Perceived Causes of Common Illnesses, Rattangarh

Name of illness	Symptoms	Perceived causes
Fever	(a) Body hot (5)	(a) Exposure to cold/hot weather (4) (b) Severe cold (2) (c) Change of climate (1)
Cold and cough (self explanatory)	(a) Running nose (2) (b) Blocked nose (2)	(a) Extreme climate: if very hot/cold and monsoon (1)
Pneumonia	(a) Heavy breathing (6) (b) Chest congestion (2) (c) Fever (2) (d) Pain in chest (1)	(a) Winter (4) (b) Bathing in winter with cold water (2)
Vomiting/diarrhoea (self explanatory)	(a) Lumpy stools, green in colour (1)	(a) Due to heat (2) (b) Among infants when teething (1) (c) Poor hygiene (2) (d) Change of season (2) (e) Improper food habits (2) (f) Weakness (resulting in poor health digestion) (1)
Malaria	(a) Fever with shivering (10) (b) Body hot (2) (c) Alternate day fever (1)	(a) Poor hygiene (1) (b) Mosquito bite (7)
Measles	(a) Continuous fever (4) (b) Rashes (4)	(a) Change of season (1) (b) Freckles (1)
Headache (self explanatory)		(a) Exposure to cold air in winter and heat in summer (2)
Stomach ache		Not known
Tuberculosis	(a) Persistent cough (3) (b) Fever (3) (c) Blood in sputum (1) (d) Nose and eyes blocked (1)	(a) Chewing tobacco and smoking tobacco/hookka (3) (b) Exposure to cold (1)
Breathing problem (asthmatic)	(a) Gasping for breath (5)	(a) Exposure to cold (b) Neglected Cough (1)
Blood pressure (low)	(a) Headache (1) (b) Swelling in the body (1) (c) Giddy feeling (1) (d) Sinking feeling (1)	(a) Weakness (2) (b) Worries (1) (c) Malnutrition (1) (d) Old age (1)
Polio	(a) Limbs are not	(a) Exposure during fever (1) properly formed (5)
Joint pain		(a) Old age (3) (b) Winter (1)

Note: Figures in parentheses are the number of those reporting.

SOCIAL SECURITY

Most of the upper caste women seemed to have an independent saving behaviour. Many also reported having bank accounts in the nearby town. They specifically denied having participated in the Mahila Samridhi Yojana operated by the post office. They also believed that children were not to be depended upon in their old age.

The SC group, on the other hand, mentioned taking frequent loans from the local landlords. The small amounts were often interest free but any amount beyond Rs 100 would incur an interest of 5 per cent per month. Thus, as even the day-to-day life was difficult, it was difficult to save for one's old age. 'Who wishes to think about the future?' was a sentiment expressed by one participant. They thought that public pensions might be forthcoming. The SC participants were happy that plots for constructing houses were given to them. However, plot-holders go through some harrowing experiences from which the local sarpanch seems to bail them out. The group felt that education may lead to their children taking care of them later in life. They believed 'We work for dehadi as long as we can and later children are there to do the dehadi and take care of us'. This group particularly mentioned the lack of resources and property as a major cause for the splitting of joint families. The incidence of alcohol consumption among the SCs appears to be relatively low, although not non-existent. Alcohol consumption in these villages appears to be a status symbol and is thus, relatively more prevalent among the upper castes. The SC women also hoped that there may be new factory jobs created for them which would ensure 'bandhi' which means a regular source of income. Traditionally, they depend on the landlord for regular employment which is, however, more in the nature of bondage rather than help.

While the SC and backward caste women expressed the desire that their daughters should get sewing machines, the upper caste women desired that their children, especially daughters, get sewing jobs. This suggests that many of the upper caste families may also be having machines and their daughters might have undergone some sort of training. According to the information provided by the post office authorities, over 100 sewing machines have been received by them and these have been distributed mostly among women belonging to SC and backward castes which seems to have a high potential to help poor families, especially women, by providing them with some sort of social security. Since most of the male participants were landed, they reported natural calamities as the main source of damage to their levels of living and their efforts in generating income. The best social security according to these men was their ability to survive the shocks of natural calamities and have access to loans to ward off the evil times. They were of the opinion that the old people would be taken care of in a better way only if they kept substantial cash and property with them. However, some also suggested that if they took care of their parents then their sons would also take care of them. They said that there was not much of monetary interaction between them and their wives. They undertake and earn substantially from dairy activities. This group of men, it may be noted, are landed, whose wives are most likely to own milch animals. However, the importance of children and old age security are not totally dispensed with. They reported having high expectations from their sons right from the day they were born.

A group of elderly women aged 60 to 75 years was called to discuss the issues of social security and old age problems. There were 10 women of whom eight were widows, two were SCs, three were from the backwards castes, and the rest belonged to the upper castes. They felt that in this FGD they could express their views about any issues that they wished to discuss. Each one of them provided very rich information regarding their lifestyles in old age. Most reported that they undertake many different types of work, such as cleaning, wood collection, feeding and taking care of the grandchildren, milking of animals, and watch and ward work. The old SC women also reported that they undertake some special type of seasonal wage earning work and earn Rs 20 per day through potato sorting.

The elderly women seemed to value physical fitness the most. They were of the opinion that as long as they were in a position to move around they could take care of themselves. But they suspected problems once they were immobile. Their lifelong savings and earnings seemed to have been spent mostly on arranging marriages. They were not able to save any cash or gold. They did, however, mention that 'land is the best security' followed by their own children.

The most frequently reported sicknesses were joint pain, bodyache, headache, pain in the limbs and arms, and respiratory problems. Some reported to be suffering from high blood pressure and blindness. At least two women reported that their sons were taking great care of them and that they were spending substantial amounts to provide them the required treatment. One SC woman was admitted to a hospital when she was sick and Rs 6000 was spent to get her treated. Another lady had a cataract operation at a cost of Rs 1100 in a private hospital. One old woman who was identified as the sarpanch's mother placed a high value on her son-in-law's help and had unclear feelings about family support by others. These old women often quoted psychological and family tensions as reasons for their sickness. At one time many of these women were enrolled for old age pension, but at the time of this study, only three women were receiving a pension of Rs 100 per month from the government. Most of them felt that Rs 200 would be a fair amount for them as old age pension. Finally, they said, 'if our men were alive things would have been different'.

UNDP SAMPLE HOUSEHOLDS REVISITED

In this village only five households were selected for the quantitative survey—there was no response from one as the family had migrated to the town. The information recorded for the rest of the households was complete in itself and the team's revisit only confirmed that probing was done fairly exhaustively while canvassing. This would not have been possible if the villagers and the respondents had not been helpful and co-operative.

3.3 Profile of Village Bhoda Hoshnak in Hissar

3.3.1 Location

The village 'Bhoda Hoshnak' is located in Agroha block of Fatehabad tehsil in Hissar district of Haryana. It is situated at a distance of about 190 km from Delhi, on national highway no. 10 on the Delhi–Sirsa stretch.

Geographically, the village is located in the north-west part of the state, surrounded by Punjab in the north and Rajasthan in the south-west. The districts of Jind, Sirsa, and Bhiwani surround the village in the east, west, and south, respectively. Like many other villages of Haryana, this village is also connected to the main road by a metalled road 200 m long and about 2 m wide.

3.3.2 History and Origin

The origin of the village dates back to some two and a half centuries when a few Muslims and khatis, belonging to the other backward castes, arrived here to settle down for farming

TABLE 3.8
Locational details, Bhoda Hoshnak

Important details	Place	Distance from the village (km)	Particulars
Block headquarters	Agroha	4	Nearest town, telephone exchange
Tehsil headquarters	Fatehabad	29	
District headquarters	Hissar	25	Railway station

activities and named the village 'Hushnak' after the great-grandfather of one of the Muslims. With the growth of farming in the village, the service sector expanded the village further. The kumhars (the clay pot makers), the harijans who provided personal services to the landed class, and some more khatis who by profession were engaged in carpentry work established themselves with the upper caste or landed households and gradually settled down in the village. The turmoil during the partition period forced the Muslims to dispose of their landed property before leaving the country. A major share of such land was bought by the landlords of the upper caste jats and Sikhs of the neighbouring area. It is believed that some Muslims who were desperate to leave the country disposed of their land at whatever price it fetched. In the bargain, some kumhars also managed to acquire some land, which elevated their social status in the village. It appears that a few harijans who could not resist the temptation also bought small pieces of land of sizes one and two acres by selling off whatever little possessions they had so that dependence on landlords for their survival would be reduced. Thus, the landed class comprises mainly jats, brahmins, kumhars, and khatis who, by virtue of being original settlers, own large farms in and around the village. However, the few SCs with their marginal farms were unable to sustain themselves and continued to work as wage labourers on others' farms. With the departure of the Muslims, the Hindus were keen to replace the Muslim name and changed it to 'Hoshnak' from 'Hushnak', which has no specific significance. In November 1966, when Haryana state was formed by splitting the erstwhile Punjab, the Sikhs (a few in number) of the village migrated to the newly-formed Punjab state, thus allowing the upper caste to enrich themselves by acquiring the landed property of these Sikhs and further widen the gap between those with large landed property and the rest.

There are three entrances to the village from the main road. The middle entrance connects the inhabitants of the village with a motorable road. The early settlers, that is the kumhars and khatis, live in close proximity to this road. On either side of this road, one can see a narrow pathway, of which one leads to the SC cluster and the other provides entry to the school and anganwadi centre. The housing pattern is contiguous and people of different castes live in clusters. In the background is a canal flowing from the Bhakra dam since 1972, stretching through the entire length of the village. The fields are located on either side of the canal. A few inhabitants of the village reside on the other side of the main road, where their fields are situated.

3.3.3 Demographic and Ethnic Composition

The village has a total population of 1280 persons distributed among 212 households. People of different castes reside in this village. The castewise distribution of the households is given in Table 3.9.

TABLE 3.9
Distribution of Households by Caste, Bhoda Hoshnak

Religion/caste	No. of households	Per cent
Hindus		
Upper caste	64	30.2
(i) Jats	49	
(ii) Brahmins	9	
Rajputs	6	
Scheduled castes	35	16.5
(i) Harijans	35	
Other backward castes	108	50.9
(i) Kumhar	88	
(ii) Khatis	12	
(iii) Others	8	
Minority community (muslims)	5	2.4
Total Households	212	100.0

Kumhars belonging to the other backward castes are in the majority, followed by the upper caste jats, and harijans belonging to the SC. In addition to these, a few khatis (12) of the backward caste, brahmins, and banwaris of the upper castes, and a handful of Muslim families inhabit the village. However, the landed khatis and the kumhars are the dominant castes along with the upper caste landlords.

3.3.4 Land Utilization

The geographical area of the village is spread over 395 ha as per the official records of the 'patwari', of which over four-fifths of the area is under crop cultivation (see Table 3.10).

Ninety per cent of the cultivated area is irrigated as per the official records. However, in reality the fields farther away from the canal are often not actually irrigated as most of the canal water is absorbed by the soil before it reaches these fields and tubewell water, being saline, is not fit for irrigation in many cases.

There are two crop seasons in a year. In the kharif season, mainly bajra, cotton and gram are grown, while in the rabi

TABLE 3.10
Land Utilization, Bhoda Hoshnak

Pattern in use	Area (ha.)	Per cent
Geographical area of which	395	100
(a) Net area sown	331	83.79
(b) Area irrigated	293	74.17
Land not for cultivation	26	6.68
Pond/canal	37	9.36
Others	1	0.25

season mainly wheat and mustard are grown. Between the kharif and rabi seasons, that is April–June, some vegetables are also grown. In the kharif season, at the time of this study, the farmers had decided to grow cotton on a larger area as it was more profitable because of a 200 per cent increase in the market prices in the previous season.

3.3.5 Occupation and Economic Well-being

Nearly 95 households (45 per cent) in the village own land. This includes the upper caste jats, brahmins, and banwaris and the kumhars and khatis of the other backward castes. A few harijans of the SCs have small fragmented holdings that hardly help them to sustain themselves. Some of them do not even cultivate their land, as they are not able to afford the inputs such as seeds, irrigation, fertilizers, etc. Hence, for their sustenance, they undertake wage work on other farms in the village where men are paid Rs 50 per day and women are paid Rs 30 per day. In addition, the employer provides the wage labourers with lunch and tea. Those men who are looking for wage work generally prefer to go to the town for non-farm work, such as helper's jobs in shops or for semi-skilled jobs like construction work, carpenter's jobs, etc., which fetch them an amount of Rs 80–100 per day. It is interesting to know that the kumhars who are traditional pot makers and the khatis who are carpenters by profession are not following their traditional occupations. They are either landlords cultivating their own land or have their small enterprises in the village like 'kirana' shop, electrician's shop, vegetable hawking or carrying loads in their rickshaws, etc.

The relatively older women in the economically poor households support themselves by doing lighter work like cutting fodder for the landed households in the neighbourhood, and in return they get paid Rs 10–15 in cash or kind. The women of the upper caste/landed households restrict themselves to household activity and do not go out for work. However, the household activities include cattle care and visiting their own farm, in addition to their regular domestic duties of cooking, childcare, cleaning, etc. There is no practice of sending children for wage labour in the village. However, a few children visit others' farms to cut grass, which enables them to feed the cattle at home free of cost. At the outset, there seems to be a lot of interdependence between the different communities in the village.

3.3.6 Education Infrastructure

Due to good political affiliation, the village is equipped with a high school run by the state government since 1989. It was originally a primary school, which was started in the year 1955, and upgraded to the middle level in 1981.

TABLE 3.11
Children Enrolled in Government Primary School, Bhoda Hoshnak

	Class					Total
	I	II	III	IV	V	
Total students						
Total	60	41	40	42	27	210
Boys	37	24	23	25	15	124
Girls	23	17	17	17	12	86
Scheduled castes						
Total	10	6	7	3	1	27
Boys	5	4	5	2	1	17
Girls	5	2	2	1	0	10
Backward castes						
Total	26	19	15	16	8	84
Boys	16	10	10	10	4	50
Girls	10	9	5	6	4	34
Others						
Total	24	16	18	23	18	99
Boys	16	10	8	13	10	57
Girls	8	6	10	10	8	42

Over two-thirds of the children in the village attend the village primary school. Of these, a large proportion (59 per cent) are boys. A relatively larger proportion of children belong to the upper castes, including jats, brahmins, and rajputs. The primary school has nine rooms, of which three rooms are not in use as the walls and the floor are not plastered. In all, five teachers were sanctioned for the primary school. One position was lying vacant for the previous few months prior to the time of this study. There were three female teachers and one male teacher in the primary section, which is managed by the principal of the middle school. The principal of the primary school stated that they were unable to provide even a 'dari' to the students as the funds due to the primary section are often not released by the management.

Despite easy access to the village primary school, the children between 6 and 14 years of age whose parents were illiterate did not attend school as there was a lack of motivation. On the other hand, a few children (aged 6–8 years) whose mothers were literate were being sent out to a private primary school in the nearby town.

Nearly 50 per cent of the children in the village continue education beyond the primary level and a majority of these seem to be boys belonging to the upper castes. However, based on the cross-sectional data on enrolment, only some broad trends can be interpreted.

TABLE 3.12
Enrolment in the Government High School Bhoda Hoshnak, 1994–5

	Class					Total	Per cent
	VI	VII	VIII	IX	X		
Total enrolment							
Total	28	26	32	36	24	146	100.0
Boys	17	21	24	34	20	116	72.5
Girls	11	5	8	2	4	30	27.5
No. enrolled from the village							
Total	21	20	25	25	16	107	100.0
Boys	12	15	18	23	12	80	74.8
Girls	9	5	7	2	4	27	25.4
Student from other villages							
Total	7	6	7	11	8	39	100.0
Boys	5	6	6	11	8	36	92.3
Girls	2	–	1	–	–	3	7.7

The middle school has ten rooms and two staff rooms, separate for males and females; in addition, there is an office room and a principal's room. The school is provided with electricity, and drinking water is provided by filling earthen pots in the summer. However, in the winter (November–March), there seems to be no facility for storing water except for one/two pitchers in the office room for the use of the staff. The children of this village go back home during break-time and return to the school for the afternoon session. Though there is a separate toilet facility for boys and girls, it is badly maintained, as there is a shortage of water.

3.3.7 Health Infrastructure

The only public health care facilities available to the villagers are antenatal care and immunization provided by the ANM, who visits the village once a month for a few hours.

There are three RMPs (private) who have their shops in the village, and who offer consultancy services along with medicines and injections when needed, at a cost varying between Rs 8 and Rs 20 per visit. Two of these RMPs stay outside the village and keep their clinics open during the day. One RMP residing in the village provides home visits during emergency calls. On an average, about 8–10 patients visit them everyday for common and minor ailments such as cold, cough, malaria, typhoid, etc. A few essential drugs like analgesics, paracetamols, and anti-histamines are stocked in their clinics. The practitioner residing in the village keeps a few Ayurvedic medicines and Hamdard products, for treatment of women's diseases like white discharge, problems related to irregular menses, etc., and claims that they are quite effective.

For attending to deliveries in the village, an elderly woman, nearing sixty years of age, performs the dai's job. Even though she has never been trained, people in the village seem to place a lot of confidence in her for not only conducting deliveries but also treating the ailing infants by carrying them on her lap, as according to the villagers she seems to possess some superpower. Of late, the educated youth (men) of the village are choosing to visit qualified doctor's clinics in the town, especially for maternal care for their spouses, which includes antenatal, natal, and post-natal care.

3.3.8 Water, Sanitation, and General Surroundings

Since 1972, the Municipal Corporation has been supplying drinking water through community pipes located at eight points all around the village. Each pipe is connected with a 'T' pipe so that two taps are fitted to each connection. Twice a day water is supplied for about a couple of hours. Before the piped water became available, rainwater was stored in a pond constructed on the other side of the road. This was used exclusively for drinking and a well adjacent to the pond was used for washing, bathing, etc. The pond at the entrance of the village is used only to meet the requirements of the livestock.

In the absence of any community cleaning or garbage disposal system, the general surroundings appear to be quite unhygienic. To add to this, the heaps of dung cakes which have been stacked like pyramids by every household, constantly spread their smell all around the village. Further, the garbage of the households is collected in any vacant area around the house where very often the children defecate. This gets accumulated unless some landlord gets it lifted once or twice a year to be used as manure in the field. However, a few landed households seem to have constructed a toilet in a corner of their house. The general practice among male adults is to use the field to defecate and females and children use the corner of the houses to urinate. Personal hygiene is practised only to the extent possible because of the constraints of buying soap, storing water, etc., and hence many of the villagers are not very particular about it.

3.3.9 Electricity

Since 1972 the village has electricity, and every household in the village has a connection for which it pays a fixed amount of Rs 10 per month. The supply is regular and steady. Nearly 80 per cent of the households have consumer durables, like TV, fan, immersion rod to heat water in winter, etc. A few of them have mixers, heaters, irons, washing machines, etc. but these are sparingly used.

3.3.10 Type of House

There are very few *kutcha* houses in this village. In the semi-pucca houses, the walls are made of clay and the roof of stone slabs. The floor is given a smooth finish with mud mixed with dung. There are a few pucca multi-storied structures in this village, which belong mostly to the upper castes or landed community. A few of these structures which have come up recently belong to the kumhars of the village who have sold part of their agricultural land and with the money earned have managed to construct *pucca* concrete houses. Some of the men in this community are construction workers. The boundary walls of these pucca houses, up to 10 ft in height, are made with clay mud and bricks, and huge wooden doors are fitted at the entrance. The main house has pucca walls of concrete and the roof is made of stone slabs supported by steel. The lime wash, which is whitish-green in colour, gives a facelift to these houses. In these pucca houses even the floor is cemented.

The poorer households have only one room, which is a multi-purpose room, and the buffaloes are tied just outside the room. Separating the two areas is just a small mud wall, about 2–3 ft in height. The pucca houses which belong to the economically better-off households have at least 2–3 rooms meant for living, a kitchen, a verandah, a store room and some open space where they generally spread cots. On the other end of the boundary wall, there are animal sheds, which are made with mud and brick. The animals are tied in the open during the day, and at night they are shifted to the shed to protect them from the cold. Some of the other infrastructure facilities in the village include the following.

1. An anganwadi centre is being run since 1987 in the mini co-operative bank complex in the village and is being attended by about 30–5 children in the pre-school age group (3–6 years). An anganwadi worker who is trained for the purpose visits the centre six days a week. Nutritional supplements are provided to these children and also to expectant mothers and infants. The supplements include puffed soyabean (sweet and salted), *panjiri* made from roasted wheat ground with sugar, etc. The stocks of these food items are replenished quarterly. As a result, sometimes they get stale and are not fit for consumption. The villagers, especially the SC women, complained that their children do not get their due share, and when the mothers go to collect their infants' share they are insulted. As these women do not benefit, they seem to dislike it, and the others do not seem to be interested in it. On the other hand, the anganwadi worker claims that she often falls short of the requirements, partly because of the improper storing facility and partly because some products get stale soon.

2. Financial assistance is provided for growing crops, small business ventures like opening a shop, trading in agricultural implements, etc. by the mini co-operative bank located in the village. Any responsible citizen of the village is eligible to become a member by paying a membership charge of Rs 11. A member can draw loans up to Rs 10,000 against merely a note. Recoveries are made twice a year and according to the collecting authority, normally there are no defaulters and some amount of delay on genuine grounds is condoned. At present, 405 persons are enrolled as members in this village and the outstanding disbursements are around Rs 3,800,000. Of the members enrolled, nearly 48 are from 20 SC households and the rest of the 357 members are from the other castes.

3. Since 1952, a post office has been functioning on a small scale in one of the rooms of the residence of the post master. It provides facilities for registration, sending parcels, UPC mailing, daily delivery and clearance, and saving schemes. Seventeen persons have recurring deposits, ten persons have savings accounts and one person has a time deposit. Special schemes for women like 'Mahila Samridhi Yojana'—under which women can save up to Rs 300 per annum and earn an interest of 25 per cent per annum—are also provided. Three women have accounts under this scheme.

4. The various government schemes that are being implemented or have been implemented at least for some time in the village include the Jawahar Rojgar Yojana (JRY), Antodaya, Literacy Mission, Adult Education Programme, and Pensions scheme. According to one of the senior village bureaucrats very few people in the village have benefited from these schemes. While the Literacy Mission has picked up well and eligible citizens are receiving pensions, the Adult Education Programme which was implemented between 1985 and 1990 has not been effective because of the lack of motivation among the male members. At present the two schemes that seem to be working are the JRY and the Literacy Mission. Under the former, some employment opportunities are provided in the town and a few menfolk from kumhar families are participating. The effect of the Literacy Mission is apparent from the increased enrolment in the schools in the last few years.

3.3.11 Focus Group Discussions

Four FGDs were organized in the village, two for women in the reproductive age group, who had at least one child in the school-going age group and/or a child below five years of age. A third one was organized among men whose spouses were below 35 years of age, and the fourth was held among elderly women who were above sixty years of age. In the first three FGDs, human development issues relating to health and education were discussed, while issues relating to social security were focussed on in all the FGDs, with a greater thrust in the FGD held for elderly women.

Of the two FGDs among women, one was organized among the women belonging to the SC category who worked as wage labourers in agriculture with little or no landholdings. In all, there were six participants, aged 22–30 years, who were illiterate. The other FGD was held among women of the upper castes and backward castes combined who were generally landed but mostly illiterate, except for one woman who was educated up to the middle standard. These were relatively older than those who participated in the previous FGD and their ages were in the range of 22–35 years of age. These women restricted their activity to the work at home, which included feeding, milking, cleaning the animals and own farm work during leisure time. There were a total of seven participants in the FGD. Their higher economic status is due to the secondary occupations of their spouses, for example, service, non-agricultural wage labour jobs in town, etc.

Six out of the eight participants in the men's FGD were literate and represented the different caste groups of the village, namely, the upper castes, backward castes and SCs. They were between the age of 22 and 35 years and were landed. Four of the eight participants in the men's FGD were employed in the service sector.

In the FGD organized for the elderly women, eight women participated. They were aged between 62 and 90 years. Two women represented the upper castes and the rest were from the backward castes. All of them lived with their families and none of them were literate. A few of them suffered from poor vision and breathing problems.

As an overview it may be said that the participants in all the groups, irrespective of their literacy status, had a fairly good knowledge about the world outside their purview. This was clearly reflected in their responses as well as in their attitudes, behaviour, and interest in the various issues related to health, education, and social security, raised during the discussions.

EDUCATION

Education as a part of child rearing, seems to be a long accepted fact by the women of the landed caste who are sending both sons and daughters to the government high school in the village. They expressed the view that the absence of a senior secondary school in the village is an impediment to the further education of girls as they are not sent outside the village. The only woman belonging to the upper caste, who was around 28 years of age and educated up to the middle standard, seemed to value the quality of education and thus preferred to send all her three children to a private primary school in a nearby town though it cost Rs 95 per child per month—of which Rs 35 was paid as tuition fee and Rs 60 as transport cost as compared to 50 paise in the government primary school which is taken as 'parent–teachers fund'. The women claimed that children are taught etiquette in the public school and this is often missing in government schools. Interestingly, the private schools grant Rs 50 per month as scholarship in order to attract good students. One child from the village is benefiting from this scheme.

As against this, the women participants in the FGD organized for the SCs valued the need for education up to a minimum level, that is, to make their children literate, as they did not want their children to be like them who can only 'angootha tek', that is give a 'thumb impression'. Very often they fail to achieve even this goal because of their inability to buy school uniforms for their children, without which the children are not allowed to sit in the class and thus drop out. However, the boys and girls fulfilling the above condition seem to be receiving a monthly stipend of Rs 10 and Rs 15, respectively from the authorities. It is believed that a re-admission amount of Rs 25 has to be paid if a child wants to go back to school, which the parents are often unable to raise and hence the children have to discontinue studies.

In the FGD organized for men most of whom had children in the school-going age, the landed class viewed education as a part of the child's development and thus valued both boys' and girls' education equally.

The men belonging to the upper castes clearly indicated that educating boys would benefit them in four ways. One, boys are the heirs to the family; educating them would improve the environment in the household and thereby elevate the family's social status. Two, they would be able to manage their farms more efficiently with better understanding. Third, they would be more confident about handling finances independently and could open their own shops in the future. Last, it would add to the confidence of the parents as unlike them the educated son would be in a position to communicate with officials more easily and effectively.

Analysis of school drop-outs: Ten children who had dropped out from school during the previous three years before completing their primary education were selected randomly to understand the factors responsible for discontinuing education through a formatted questionnaire. To seek this information discussions were held with each respondent separately to avoid a bias as far as possible. In the cases where the child was not in a position to respond, efforts were made to discuss this with any adult member of the household.

The children were aged between 9 and 14 years and had dropped out between classes III and V. Nine out of the ten children interviewed were girls of which one girl was from the SC community, and among the rest there was an equal number belonging to the upper castes and backward castes. The only boy interviewed was from the backward castes. This also suggests that a larger number of girls dropped out compared to boys.

Interestingly, it was observed that the education and occupation of the parents did seem to influence their children's education. In the cases where both the parents were illiterate and were engaged in own farming activities there was insufficient motivation for children to study, as neither of the parents was in a position to participate in any form as far as the school activities were concerned, and hence the children gradually to lost interest in studies and discontinued at their own will and convenience (Table 3.14). This is evident from the fact that in these households the siblings, irrespective of sex, are currently studying. On the other hand, the two girls who had educated parents and whose fathers were involved in office jobs dropped out from school while in class V, as they felt that the teacher was harassing them by beating and abusing them. This was perhaps the normal atmosphere that prevailed in the school and because of a better environment at home these children could not adjust to the school atmosphere.

That the SC girl discontinued studies due to economic reasons is confirmed by the fact that the girl still desired to continue education whenever possible. Some of the other reasons for dropping out include: girls wanting to settle down

TABLE 3.13
Details of Drop outs, Bhoda Hoshnak

(*no. of drop outs = 10*)

Sl. no.	Sex (yrs)	Age	Caste	Education		Occupation		Siblings currently studying (nos)*		Class in which dropped out
				Father	Mother	Father	Mother	Boys	Girls	
1.	F	14	BC	Nil	Nil	Cul	HHW	–	–	Fifth
2.	F	10	UC	AP	Nil	Cul	HHW	–	1	Fourth
3.	M	14	BC	Nil	Nil	Cul	HHW	1	NS	Fifth
4.	F	12	BC	Nil	Nil	Cul	HHW	NS	NS	Fifth
5.	F	12	SC	Nil	Nil	Cul	HHW	NS	NS	Sixth
6.	F	13	BC	Nil	Nil	Cul	HHW	3	–	Fifth
7.	F	10	UC	Nil	Nil	Cul	HHW	2	–	Fourth
8.	F	9	UC	M	P	Service	HHW	1	–	Fourth
9.	F	9	UC	HS	BP	Service	HHW	2	–	Third
10.	F	12	BC	M	Nil	Service	HHW	–	–	Fifth

Notes: Nil: illiterate; NS: not studying; UC: upper caste; BC: backward caste; P: primary (–); —Not in the school going age; AP: above primary; M: middle; Cul: cultivator; HS: higher secondary; HHW: household wife. * Indicates number attending school.

TABLE 3.14
Primary Reason for Dropping Out of School by Education of Parents

Parents literacy status	No. of responses	Occupation of father	Reason codes					
			1	2	3	4	5	6
Neither of the parents literate	6	All cultivators	3	1	1	1		
Father literate and mother illiterate	2	Cultivator; salaried job		1			1	
Both parents literate	2	Both in salaried job					1	1

Reason Codes:

1: no interest in studies; 2: health problem (self or others); 3: economic reason; 4: household work including own farm work and cattle care; 5: scared of teacher (beating/abuse); 6: waited to shift to urban area.

in life, failure in exams, household work, need to shift to urban area for education, etc.

While the two upper caste girls whose parents were literate had set their ambition on becoming teachers, a majority of the girls (five out of nine) were interested in learning sewing and tailoring to keep themselves occupied. The boy aspired to get into the family occupation of furniture-making.

Both the men and women in the wage labour class belonging to the SC preferred to educate even the boys only up to the primary level. They felt educating them beyond that would cost a lot and they did not want to take any risk in investing in education as the return on investment, in terms of assured employment, is unsure. A relatively older woman in the FGD clearly stated, 'we already see a lot of unemployment among boys in 20–5 age group'. Thus, a few men suggested that after their high school education, boys could pursue some technical or vocational courses to help them to find employment if the facilities are provided.

A few of the well-to-do landed class men expressed their concern about the poor quality of teaching in schools which may be responsible for their boys losing interest in studies and getting into bad company. Educating girls as much as boys, at least up to high school level was considered important by the landed castes for two reasons. One, it would help them to have better perspectives on life. Two, their status in the marriage market would go up as educated grooms prefer educated brides. Nevertheless, there is always a tendency to withdraw girls first, in case of any emergency and as far as possible, the parents resist withdrawing boys at least before the primary level. The mothers belonging to the landed castes suggested that some knitting and stitching training may be useful for the girls waiting to be married after their high school which they often complete by 16–17 years of age. They are married only after 19 years of age.

HEALTH

It is interesting to observe that the women in the FGDs, though illiterate, were not ignorant with regard to the health of their family members. They could well associate poor sanitation, stagnant water, mosquito breeding, extreme climate, and bad drinking water with the illnesses surrounding them.

The SC women who were engaged in wage work pointed out that poor nutrition was also one of the important causes for their ill health. Unlike the landed/upper caste women, they normally consume 'bajre ki roti' with chhaj (butter milk) or tea which perhaps lack most of the mineral and vitamin supplements needed for the kind of work they perform.

Irrespective of caste, the women said that the most common children's diseases were cold, cough, pneumonia, fever, and diarrhoea. The children in the upper caste/landed households seem to be looked after better by their mothers as these mothers generally do not work outside their homes and perhaps have some leisure time compared to the SC women. For example, some women from the upper caste treat their children with home remedies during their illness. For diarrhoea they give a clove baked in fire and powdered with sugar/milk. Sometimes they prepare a sugar and salt water solution which they call ORS. For any mild fever or ache they first give treatment at home by giving 'Kromocin' meaning Crocin, Anacin, etc., and if the symptoms do not get cured, only then they go to a doctor in the nearby town for treatment—they go to the private clinic of a doctor in the nearby town for treatment of minor ailments, and for serious ailments, treatment is sought in the private nursing home at the district headquarters rather than in the district hospital run by the government. As one of the women commented, 'Government hospitals do not take care of the patients properly'. That even the wage workers prefer to seek treatment in private clinics at a very high cost is evident from the response of one of the woman participants in the SC focus group discussion who had recently got her seven-year old son treated for a serious stomach infection. She seems to have spent over Rs 1500 on the treatment, which was raised by borrowing from the upper caste landed folks at an interest of 3 per cent per month. Both women and men responded that malaria and typhoid common illnesses suffered by the young and the old.

The male participants, even though they appeared to be more rational than their female counterparts, did seem to have a strong belief in religious healers and often turn to 'jadh fus' and 'tabiz' when their children are sick, along with seeking treatment in a doctor's clinic. When asked about female-related illnesses, the relatively older men did not seem to hesitate to express their concern about the common health problems of middle-aged women in the village and clearly indicated that 'vayu', gastric problem; 'bavasir', piles; and 'ulas', dislocation of uterus were the common and grave problems. However, according to these men, cancer was more prevalent among men who consumed alcohol and tobacco (smoking)—around 3–4 persons had died in the last few years in the village. 'Dama', which refers to breathing problem, was common among the elderly women.

The upper caste/landed caste men, often being the heads of the households and decision-takers, categorically revealed that for any maternal care the women of these households were taken to the private nursing homes at the district headquarters which is about 25 km from the village, and that they went for regular check ups and for pre-natal, natal, and post-natal care. These women also seemed to be supplementing their diet during pregnancy by taking milk, *dalia* etc.

On the other hand, a majority of the women of the village consulted the local 'untrained dai' for their pregnancy-related problems and delivery which in normal cases was conducted at home. These women did not seem to take any special care during their pregnancies. However, in case of any complications, they were confident that the dai would advise them of the right time to go to hospital.

One of the upper caste men expressed the view that he always felt a risk whenever he went for any treatment in the private nursing homes as the treatment is given before any diagnostic tests are done and patients are kept in the dark about the disease for which they are being treated. This is a reflection on the service rendered by these doctors who charge exorbitant amounts of money and are not answerable to anyone.

Results of the free listing of illnesses. The free listing pro forma was canvassed at random among 20 women to gauge their knowledge about illnesses and their symptoms and perceived causes. These respondents were ever married women between the age of 20 and 75, most of whom were illiterate. Only two of them were literate; one was the youngest woman from the kumhar community who had completed primary education and the other one was a jat woman aged 27 years who had studied up to the middle standard and was in charge of the Adult Education Programme functioning between 1985 and 1990.

A few of the most common illnesses listed were malaria (70 per cent), cold and cough (55 per cent), breathing problems (55 per cent), and joint pains (50 per cent). The respondents represented the different castes. The other backward caste women constituted 65 per cent of the respondents and they listed 27 types of illnesses. The frequency of responses to these illnesses is presented in Table 3.16.

A majority of the respondents were unable to perceive the causes of the illnesses they had listed. A few who responded traced the cause to climate and air, which included cold weather, monsoon or change in seasons and 'hava ki kharabi' (polluted air) was a common reply. Interestingly, problems related to eyes were associated with the use of fertilizer in agriculture resulting in poor quality food crops. Three respondents listed polio and the perceived cause was related to 'injection during fever'. 'Drinking and smoking' were stated to cause TB, and the men in the FGD had the view that they resulted in cancer.

Many of the respondents listed the names of the illnesses, but only a few could elaborate on the symptoms related to these illnesses, except in the case of malaria (85 per cent) and breathing problems (82 per cent) where a majority stated more or less the same symptoms. This perhaps suggests that most

TABLE 3.15
Frequency of Illnesses Listed

Illness		With probe		Without probe		Combined	
Local name	English equivalent	Nos	per cent	Nos	per cent	Nos	per cent
Malaria	Malaria	6	30	8	40	14	70
Jhukam and Khansi	Cold and Cough	5	25	6	30	11	55
Dama	Breathing problem	7	35	4	20	11	55
Jodon ka dard	Joint pain	5	25	5	25	10	50
Orsa	Pneumonia	6	30	1	5	7	35
Bukhar	Fever	–	–	6	30	6	30
Dasth	Diarrhoea	1	5	5	25	6	30
Ori/Khasra	Measles	3	15	3	15	6	30
Sar dard	Headache	2	10	3	15	5	25
Charma rog	Skin problem	2	10	2	10	4	20

Note: Other illnesses listed include typhoid, menstruation problem, delivery complications, jaundice, gastric, cancer, piles, TB, polio, stomach problems, etc.

of the information about of the illness percolated from their friends and neighbours. This is confirmed from the FGDs where most of the illnesses listed in Table 3.16 were covered by the participants.

The frequency of listing of illnesses gives an idea about their prevalence in the village. This broadly confirms the findings of the FGDs, where cold, cough, pneumonia, and fever were listed as common illnesses suffered by children.

SOCIAL SECURITY

Elderly women below the age of 70 years generally seemed to be active and contributed to the household activity, subject to their limitations. While some of them managed the household by preparing food, milking the cows, working in the farm, etc., a few others undertook only light work such as churning butter from milk or any other work given to them by their daughters-in-law, and enjoyed leisure at other times.

TABLE 3.16
Frequency of Responses to Symptoms and Perceived Causes of Illnesses, Bhoda Hoshnak

Name of illness	Symptoms	Perceived causes
Malaria	(a) Shivering followed by fever (85 per cent)	(a) Mosquito (20 per cent)
Cold and cough	(Self explanatory)	(a) Climatic change (30 per cent)
Breathing	(a) Breathlessness (82 per cent) (b) Cough (40 per cent)	(a) During climate change (40 per cent) (b) Old age (10 per cent)
Joint pain	(a) Unable to walk (40 per cent) (b) Pain all over (40 per cent)	(a) Cold weather (20 per cent) (b) Change in climate (20 per cent)
Pneumonia	(a) Heavy breathing (37 per cent) (b) Wheezing sound from nose (28 per cent)	(a) Exposure to winter (33 per cent)
Fever	(a) Pain in limbs	(a) Exposure to cold weather (10 per cent) (b) Getting wet (10 per cent)
Diarrhoea	(a) Watery stools (50 per cent)	
Measles	(a) Fever and rashes all over body (80 per cent)	(a) Summer heat (25 per cent)
Headaches	(Self explanatory)	(a) Pollution in the air
Skin problems	(a) Boils (50 per cent) (b) Watery excretion (25 per cent) (c) Redness (25 per cent)	(a) Monsoon (25 per cent)
Eye problems	(a) Losing vision (b) Redness in eyes	Foodgrains/crops quality deterioration because of fertilizer
Polio	Disability of limbs (100 per cent)	Injection during Fever (100 per cent)
TB	(a) Persistent cough	Drinking and smoking

Note: Figures in parentheses give the percentage of respondents.

According to these women, the greatest asset one could have is cash as it is likely to earn them more respect. However, they expressed the view that none of them had cash for varied reasons. One woman said, 'all the cash has been spent on marriages of sons/daughter, where is the cash? All of it we have spent'. A woman whose husband was in service, received a pension but the balance, after meeting the expenses, was kept in the bank and was not in her hand. All the women eligible for pension receive pension regularly and the post master distributes it at their door-step.

Culturally, the oldest couple/oldest person (if active) in the household is consulted on any major decision in the household and thus the social status of the elderly among the landed community is fairly high as compared to those belonging to the landless class.

One woman belonging to the backward caste (kumhar) confessed that she had some land because of which her son was looking after her well.

Because of their status in their households these women are looked after properly by their daughters-in-law when they are sick. Some level of domination is felt by some of these older women whose daughters-in-law are educated. One of them stated, 'I was sent to school but because of father's early death I discontinued' thus regretting that she was not literate. Another woman commented, 'if I was educated I would be talking like you and working like you in office'.

The younger women in the landed households upper castes, were unable to visualize any kind of problems in their old age, since their needs were being taken care of by their spouses. But the SC women, who did not even have assets and were struggling by doing wage work, responded that their children were their sole hope in old age, 'as we take care of our fathers-in-law and mothers-in-law today, in the long run our children will take care of us'. This is their only hope for the future.

The men confidently said that 'rural women consider family as their wealth' and men as heads of the households planned in terms of re-investing in business, spending on daughters' marriages, buying jewellery, and investing in land which comes in handy in their old age. Above all they still 'depend on children to be looked after in old age', but the idea of their sons not getting educated or becoming alcoholic disturbs the men immensely. Alcohol-related violence seems to be common in the households and in the village.

UNDP SAMPLE HOUSEHOLDS REVISITED

In all, twenty households selected in the village for the present Rural Rapid Appraisal (RRA) study were those originally selected for the detailed quantitative survey, under the UNDP project, 'Qualitative Study of Human Development—Village Bhoda Hoshnak, District Hissar, Haryana'. Necessary probing was done wherever required and it was found that the information recorded earlier was mostly correct except for some marginal change in the age in one household.

3.4 Conclusion and Policy Implications

3.4.1 Conclusion

This section makes a comparative analysis of Rattangarh village of Kurukshetra and Bhoda Hoshnak village of Hissar.

Rattangarh village is urbanized as the district of Kurukshetra is well developed. The village is closer to the capital and is located near the GT Karnal highway, which connects the national capital with the state capital. Besides, this is the transit road linking the Himachal Pradesh capital, Shimla, which is a tourist centre. Rattangarh village is closer to the block headquarters, which is just 2 km from the village. Kurukshetra is the smallest district in terms of area, hence it is an administratively compact unit. There is only one well-managed primary school in the village, which is mainly utilized by the SCs, who are in a majority. The economically well-off send their children to the nearest private primary schools or government high schools and colleges in the block headquarters. As regards health infrastructure, though there is a sub-centre in the village, which is functioning well, the villagers seem to prefer the private practioners (at affordable cost) at the block headquarters because of good service as well as easy access due to public transport facilities. The PHC is also accessible at the block headquarters. The villagers are economically better placed because of employment opportunities in the sugar factories, breweries, and office complexes at the block headquarters. The land in the village is fertile and there are large agricultural holdings belonging to the upper caste jats, on whose farms, the uneducated SCs work as wage labourers. In the village itself, there are steel furniture factories run by the jat Sikhs, which provide additional employment opportunities to the villagers.

In contrast, Bhoda Hoshnak village in Hissar is not so well located although it is on the Delhi–Sirsa national highway no. 10, which is not as hectic as the GT Karnal highway. The block headquarters is only 4 km from the village; however, there is little development and less industrial activity since it has been established very recently. Relatively, the land here is not so fertile and the landholdings are small. This village was re-established after the Partition and experienced disturbances during the reorganization of the composite state of Punjab in 1966. Unlike the village in Kurukshetra, the roads here are not well developed and the public transport facility is also not comparable. The houses are mostly semi-pucca with hardly any sanitation facilities, whereas in the Kurukshetra village a majority of the landlords have houses resembling urban bungalows with modern sanitation facilities and the SC families have been provided with housing units under the Indira Awas Yojana. There is a primary school as well as a high school in this small Hissar village, both run by the state government. As a result of this, there are many educated youths who have no employment opportunities as the district is not industrially well developed. On the health front, in the Bhoda Hoshnak village, there is hardly any government health infrastructure available. The ANM visits the village anganwadi centre at regular intervals and provides preventive and promotive health care. There are three private RMPs in the village, two of whom do not reside in the village but have their clinics here. For any major ailments, the villagers have to go to the PHC at the block headquarters, which is 4 km from the village and which does not seem to be functioning well, according to the villagers. In case of emergencies, the villagers have to approach the private practioners at the block headquarters or the facilities at the district headquarters, which is 25 km away. Due to poor public transport facilities, the villagers do not find access to these convenient.

There are some common features in both the villages. Both the villages are electrified and have piped water supply. Road facilities exist in both villages. The literacy level in both villages is comparable for the economically well-off groups. In both villages, there is very little media interaction at the community level. There are no welfare activities carried out by non-government agencies and the general hygiene and sanitary conditions are poor.

3.4.2 Policy Recommendations

1. In the Hissar village, road, public transportation, and communications facilities need to be improved.

2. There is a need to promote health and hygiene education through awareness camps in both the villages, more so in Bhoda village, for better environment and sanitary conditions. At the same time, the government's subsidized sanitation promotion activities should be introduced at the household and institutional levels.

3. The government health infrastructure and its supervision need to be strengthened and monitored.

4. By shifting some industries from the neighbourhood districts, employment opportunities should be increased for the educated youths particularly in the Hissar village.

5. Drainage facilities should be introduced under various government schemes, such as IRDP, JRY, which will not only improve the living conditions of the villagers but also provide employment opportunities.

6. A household survey should be conducted in Rattangarh village to ascertain the reasons for the success of Indira Awas Housing Scheme and the scheme should be implemented it in Bhoda Hoshnak.

7. Appropriate rural folk media, based on local culture and customs and local language, should be introduced to create public awareness on all developmental activities.

HIMACHAL PRADESH

Himachal Pradesh occupies 1.81 per cent of the total land area of India but comprises only 0.61 per cent of its population. The state also has an average household size that is less than the national average and a sex-ratio that is favourable to females Though more than half of the households belong to the low-income groups and only 2.9 per cent fall in the high-income bracket, it has been noted that 97.2 per cent of households have their own house. However, only 11.8 per cent and 3.3 per cent of the population respectively possess a bicycle and motorcycle or scooter—this is because of the rugged terrain and the absence of motorable roads.

The average size of operational holdings has declined from 1.54 hectares to 1.20 hectares even though their number has been steadily increasing. As regards literacy, the state ranks third in the country with a literacy rate of 77 per cent though the male–female and rural–urban differences in literacy are relatively high. The total primary school enrolment rate is 92.3 per cent. And even though the enrolment of girls is higher than that of boys, their drop-out rate is also larger in all districts except Shimla.

Himachal Pradesh has achieved many of its goals for the health sector which include the establishment of 39.2 sub-centres and 3.8 primary health centres (PHCs) per lakh population. The state has a comparatively high life expectancy of 62.8 years. Though 67.1 per cent of ever-married women in the state are immunized, the immunization of children aged 12–23 months is only 57.2 per cent and is characterized by a high gender disparity. Though Himachal Pradesh has made progress in health care and education as compared to other Indian states, it still requires much government intervention for overall development.

4 Secondary Data Report for Himachal Pradesh

4.1 General Profile of the State

Himachal Pradesh is situated in the northern part of the country. It is surrounded by Jammu and Kashmir in the north and north-west, Punjab in the south and south-west, Haryana in the south, and Tibet in the east. It has an area of 55,673 sq. km, sharing 1.81 per cent of the land area and 0.61 per cent of the population of the country. In 1991, the population density of the state was 93 persons per sq. km and the total population was 51.7 lakh. Himachal Pradesh is predominantly a rural state; about 91 per cent of the population lives in rural areas. In 1981, only 58 towns were reported in the state. Out of a total of 969,018 households, 861,445 households are located in rural areas while only 107,573 households are in urban areas. Among religious communities in the state, the Hindus dominate. At the time of the 1981 Census, Hindus accounted for 95.8 per cent of the population followed by Muslims (1.6 per cent), Buddhists (1.2 per cent), and Sikhs (1.2 per cent). Christians and Jains constituted 0.1 per cent and 0.02 per cent, respectively, of the population. The Scheduled Castes (SCs) comprise 25.34 per cent of the states' population and the Scheduled Tribes (STs) another 4.22 per cent.

The economy of Himachal Pradesh is basically agrarian. The industrial base is weak. The latest Census enumeration indicates that 66 per cent of the main workers are engaged in agriculture (63 per cent as cultivators and 3 per cent as agricultural labourers), earning about 40 per cent of the state domestic product (SDP). The agricultural activities in the state are largely dependent on the monsoon. Foodgrains are the major agricultural product; the output is around 11 to 14 lakh tonnes per year. In the drought year of 1987–8 output dipped to 8.72 lakh tonnes. In the year 1991–2, the per capita foodgrain production in the state was higher (260.88 kg) than the all-India average of 199.22 kg. Apart from foodgrains, cultivation of fruits and vegetables is also undertaken on a large scale, giving the farmers good returns.

The workforce participation rate (main and marginal workers as percentage of total population) in the state is 42.82 per cent, which is higher than the national average of 37.46 per cent. The workforce participation rate among males (50.64 per cent) is marginally lower than the national average of 51.55 per cent. The female workforce participation rate at 34.82 per cent is, however, higher than the national average of 22.26 per cent. Out of the 31 states and union territories, Himachal Pradesh ranks seventh in the female workforce participation rate. The six states and union territories with female workforce participation rate higher than that of Himachal Pradesh are Dadra and Nagar Haveli (48.79 per cent), Mizoram (43.52 per cent), Manipur (38.96 per cent), Nagaland (37.96 per cent), Arunachal Pradesh (37.49 per cent), and Meghalaya (34.93 per cent).

The performance of the state in achieving literacy is quite impressive. The effective literacy rates (literates as per cent of population aged 7 years and above) in the state—which are 86 per cent among males and 67 per cent among females—are higher than the national averages of 75.85 per cent among males and 54.16 per cent among females. The females of this state are at par with the general population of the country in terms of literacy.

The health status of the population, for males and females, in Himachal Pradesh is better than that in the country as a whole. The life expectancy at birth (for the period 1981–5) was 60.4 years for all persons as compared to the national average of 58.6 years (for 1991). The male life expectancy (58.5 years) is almost at par with the national average (58.9 years) while the female life expectancy in the state at 62.9 years is higher than the national average at 59.1 years. The females per thousand males ratio in the state is 976. Only two states, Kerala (1036) and Pondicherry (979), have a larger proportion of females. Himachal Pradesh is the only state where the number of females is growing at a faster rate than males since 1941. This is perhaps, a reflection of access to better health care facilities for females.

According to the Sample Registration Survey (SRS) estimates for the year 1991, the crude birth rate (CBR), crude death rate (CDR), and infant mortality rate (IMR) for the state are 28.4, 8.9, and 75, respectively, as compared to the national averages of 29.3, 9.8, and 80. The annual exponential growth rate of the population between 1981 and 1991 for the state was 1.89 per cent as compared to the national average of 2.14 per cent. The rate of growth of population in Himachal Pradesh is the fifth lowest observed among 31 states and union territories. The states and union territories with a rate of growth of population lower than that of Himachal Pradesh are

Orissa (1.83 per cent), Goa (1.49 per cent), Tamil Nadu (1.43 per cent), and Kerala (1.34 per cent). The level of urbanization is quite low in the state. Only 8.69 per cent of the total state population lives in urban areas, as compared to the national average of 25.73 per cent. In terms of the level of urbanization, Himachal Pradesh ranks second from the bottom among 31 states and union territories. Only Dadra and Nagar Haveli has an urbanization level of 8.47 per cent which is lower than that of Himachal Pradesh. The average household size in the state is 5.34 persons as compared to the national average of 5.52 persons.

The state's per capita income (per capita net SDP) for the year 1990–1 is Rs 4790 (1990–1 prices) as compared to the national average of Rs 4964 (per capita net national product, at 1990–1 prices) for the same year. The Centre for Monitoring the Indian Economy (CMIE) relative index of development for the state is 75. Hence, the development index is 25 less than the all-India index. The states of Punjab (199) and Bihar (43) have the highest and the lowest indices of development, respectively. Out of a total of 12 districts in the state, only three districts have a CMIE index higher than the state average (see Map 4.1). These are Solan (132), Shimla (128), and Una (77). The district of Chamba (46) has the lowest index of development followed by Kinnaur (49), Mandi (56), Sirmaur (65), Kangra (66), Hamirpur (68), Bilaspur (69), Kullu (70), and Lahul and Spiti (74). The incidence of poverty in the state is, however, quite low—it was 9.12 per cent in 1987–8 against the national average of 29.23 per cent in the same year. Punjab is the only state with incidence of poverty lower than that of Himachal Pradesh. The recent information on poverty line groups shows that the state has 28.2 per cent of its total population below the poverty line. Table 4.1 compares some important indicators for the state and the country.

4.2 Education

In this section, an attempt has been made to assess the current level of knowledge of the people in the state of Himachal Pradesh. Knowledge may be acquired through formal education as well as through informal contacts. Limitations of conceptualization, measurement, and data availability compel us to consider only formally acquired knowledge and to confine the analysis to indicators such as enrolment and drop-out ratios at the primary level and the effective literacy rate achieved.

4.2.1 Enrolment Rate

Tables 4.E1 and 4.E2 present districtwise primary school gross enrolment rates in each district for rural and urban areas. Gross enrolment ratio is defined as the number of students enrolled as a percentage of the eligible children. The discussion here is confined to primary school enrolment due to

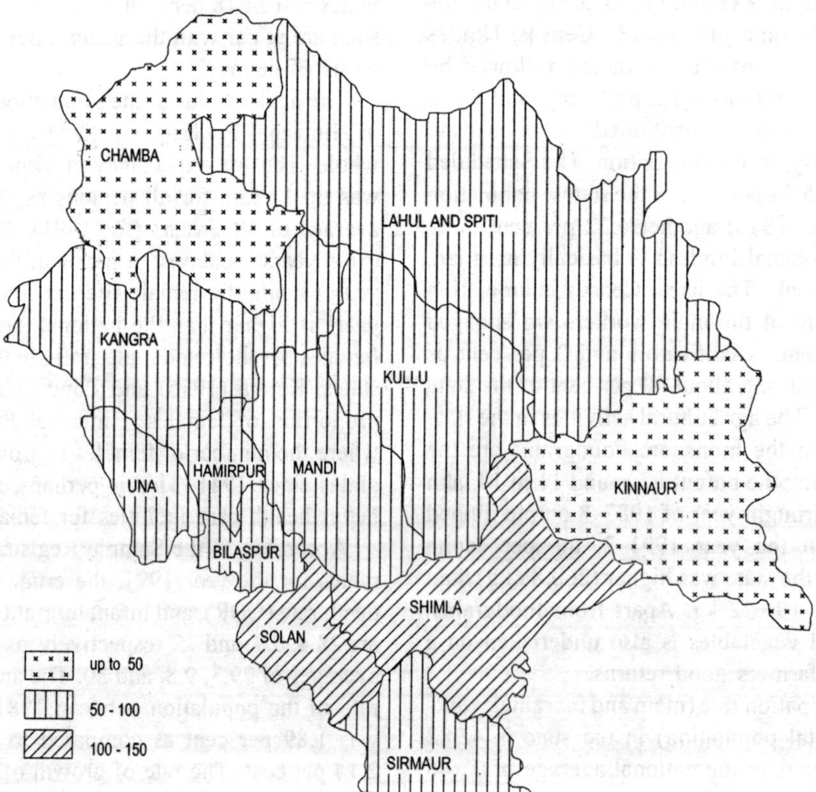

MAP 4.1: Levels of Economic Development in Himachal Pradesh

TABLE 4.1

Socio-economic Indicators for Himachal Pradesh and India

Indicators	Himachal Pradesh	All India
Area (Sq. km)	55,673	3,065,027
No. of districts	12	452
No. of blocks	69	5774
No. of villages (inhabited)	16,997	580,702
Total no. of UA* and town	55	3699
Total no. of towns	58	4615
Number of households	969,018	152,009,467
Population (persons)	5,170,877	838,583,988
Population (males)	2,617,467 (50.62)	435,216,358 (51.90)
Population (females)	2,553,410 (49.38)	403,367,630 (48.10)
SC population	1,310,296 (25.34)	138,223,277 (16.48)
ST population	218,349 (4.22)	67,758,380 (8.08)
Literacy rate (total)	77.13	65.38
Literacy rate (males)	86.02	75.85
Literacy rate (females)	68.08	54.16
Work force participation rate (total)	2,214,379 (42.82)	314,147,422 (37.46)
Work force participation rate (males)	1,325,394 (50.64)	224,372,007 (51.55)
Work force participation rate (females)	888,985 (34.82)	89,775,415 (22.26)
Main workers (total)	1,779,100 (34.41)	285,948,545 (34.10)
Main workers (males)	1,284,679 (49.08)	221,666,784 (50.93)
Main workers (females)	494,421 (19.36)	64,281,761 (15.94)
Cultivators (total)	1,125,311 (63.25)	110,702,346 (38.71)
Cultivators (males)	695,618 (54.15)	88,480,942 (39.92)
Cultivators (females)	429,693 (86.91)	22,221,404 (34.57)
Marginal workers (total)	435,279 (8.42)	28,198,877 (3.36)
Marginal workers (males)	40,715 (1.56)	2,705,223 (0.62)
Marginal workers (females)	394,564 (15.45)	25,493,654 (6.32)
Non-workers (total)	2,956,498 (57.18)	524,436,566 (62.54)
Non-workers (males)	1,292,073 (49.36)	210,844,351 (48.45)
Non-workers (females)	1,664,425 (65.18)	313,592,215 (77.74)
Decadal variation of population (%)		
1971–81	23.71	24.66
1981–91	20.79	22.72
1991–2001	18.00	21.35
Annual exponential growth rate (1981–91) (%)	1.89	2.14
Crude birth rate	28.4	29.3
Crude death rate	8.9	9.8
Infant mortality rate	75	80
Sex ratio	976	929
Urban population	449,196 (8.69)	217,611,012 (25.95)
Household size	5.34	5.52
Population density	93	274
Life expectancy at birth (total)	60.4	58.6
Life expectancy at birth (males)	58.5	58.1
Life expectancy at birth (females)	62.9	59.1
Foodgrain production ('000 tonnes) (1991–2)	1349	167,065
Per capita income (1990–1) (Rs)	4790	4964
Incidence of poverty (1987–8) (%)	9.12	29.90

Notes: *UA: Urban Agglomeration All figures are for the year 1991 unless mentioned otherwise; Life Expectancy figures for Himachal Pradesh are for the year 1981–5 and all-India figures are for the year 1986–91; All-India figures are excluding that for the state of Jammu and Kashmir except for CBR, CDR, IMR, life expectancy, foodgrain production, per capita income and incidence of poverty; Figures in parentheses are percentages to total population, except for cultivators, which are expressed as percentage of main workers.

Sources: Census of India, 1991, Series-1, Paper-2, 1992, Final Population Totals, New Delhi, 1993; District Level Estimates of Fertility and Child Mortality for 1991 and their Relations with Other Variables, Occasional Paper No. 1 of 1997, Office of the Registrar General, India; Economic Survey 1991–2, Government of India, Ministry of Finance; Report of Expert Group, An Estimation of Proportion and Number of Poor, Planning Commission, 1993.

non-availability of data. The eligible population for primary school enrolment is taken to be those in the age group 6 to 11 years. This has been estimated on the basis of the observed growth rate of population in the age group 0–6 years between 1981 and 1991. The distribution of population by age groups is not yet available from the 1991 Census.

$$(\text{POPLN 6–11 YR})_{1991} \quad \frac{(\text{POPLN 0–6 YR})_{1991}}{(\text{POPLN 0–6 YR})_{1981}} \times (\text{POPLN 6–11 YR})_{1981}$$

These estimates have been obtained separately for boys and girls for rural and urban areas of each district. The estimates for districts and the state can be derived by simple aggregation. The number of students enrolled when divided by the eligible population in the respective category gives the corresponding gross enrolment ratio.

The primary school gross enrolment ratios for Himachal Pradesh in all areas are 92.3 per cent, 94.6 per cent and 89.8 per cent respectively for total, boys and girls. The rural–urban

BOX 4.1
Profile of Himachal Pradesh

Item	Unit	Year	Himachal Pradesh		Highest		Lowest		India
			Rank	Actual	State	Actual	State	Actual	Actual
CMIE index	No.	1995	9	113.88	Punjab	171.92	Bihar	91.31	100
HDI indicators (Pal and Pant)		1993	–	–	Punjab	0.793	Bihar	0.503	1
(Shiva Kumar)		1991	9	0.425					
(Tilak)		1991	9	0.462					
PCY (at 1980–1 prices)	Rs	1992–3	7	2137	Punjab	3730	Bihar	1142	2226
Urban population	%	1991	16	8.7	Maharashtra	38.7	HP	8.70	2739
Literacy	per '000	1991	3	771	Kerala	898	Bihar	385	522
Life expectany	Years	1986–90	3	62.8	Kerala	69.5	MP	53.0	57.7
HHs in Electrified dwelling	%	1988–9	1	83.9	HP	83.9	Bihar	4.5	26.9
Annual PC consumption of electricity	KWh	1991	11	217	Punjab	703	Assam	96	299
Road length	per '000/sq. km	1991	14	459	Kerala	3567	MP	321	621
No. of beds in hospitals	'0000	1993	7	71.6	Kerala	255.0	MP	26.3	68.3
No. of dispensaries	'0000	1990	5	4.1	Gujarat	15.2	MP	0.4	3.4
Regd. med. practitioners	'0000	1992	–	–	Karnataka	77.7	UP	24.7	28.9
Agriculture									
Cereals (per capita)	kg	1993–4	4	227.8	Punjab	1016.3	Kerala	32.0	193.7
Pulses (per capita)	kg	1993–4	15	2.0	MP	48.8	Kerala	0.6	157.0
Total oil seeds (per capita)	kg	1993–4	15	0.9	MP	66.5	Kerala	0.4	24.6
Milk availability (per capita per day)	g	1991	4	280	Punjab	672	Assam	0.5	218
Manufacturing									
Share in net value added from manufacturing	%	1993	–	–	Maharashtra	22.8	Punjab	4.1	100.0
Regd. working factories	%	1993	16	0.63	Bihar	20.8	HP	0.6	100.0
Share in employment of regd. working factories	%	1993	16	0.63	Maharashtra	14.7	HP	0.6	100.0

Sources: CMIE Index 2000, District Profile, Centre for Monitoring Indian Economy; *Statistical Abstract*, 1992, Central Statistical Organization, Government of India.

disparity in enrolment is only marginal. The gross enrolment ratios in urban areas are 85.1 per cent, 87.3 per cent, and 82.7 per cent respectively for total, boys, and girls. The corresponding figures for rural areas are 92.8 per cent, 95.2 per cent, and 90.3 per cent. The total enrolment for all areas ranges between 75.2 per cent in Chamba to 108.8 per cent in Lahul and Spiti. For all other districts it varies from 80 per cent to 98 per cent. In urban areas, the gross enrolment ratio varies from a minimum of 44.5 per cent (Hamirpur) to a maximum of 124.3 per cent (Kullu). In rural areas, it varies from a minimum of 75.5 per cent in Chamba to a maximum of 108.8 per cent in Lahul and Spiti. One reason for the higher estimates of gross enrolment ratio in rural areas is perhaps, the enrolment of children aged more than 11 years in larger numbers in primary schools—increasing the extent of over-estimation in rural areas as compared to that in urban areas.

GENDER DIFFERENTIAL

The enrolment ratios among girls are generally lower than those among boys. Only in three districts, Kangra, Hamirpur and Kinnaur, is the gross enrolment ratio among girls higher than that among boys for all areas. The enrolment ratios among boys and girls differ by 29.9 per cent in Chamba to 0.6 per cent in Una. In urban areas, the gross enrolment ratio among girls is higher than that among boys in five districts, namely Chamba, Hamirpur, Una, Kullu, and Shimla. In other districts, the difference ranges from 27 per cent in Kangra to 1.5 per cent in Sirmaur. In rural areas, the enrolment ratio among girls is higher than that among boys in four districts, Kangra, Hamirpur, Bilaspur, and Kinnaur. The difference between the gross enrolment ratio among boys and girls varies between 32.4 per cent in Chamba and 1.1 per cent in Una.

Thus, in terms of enrolment, girls are not behind boys everywhere in the state.

URBAN–RURAL DIFFERENTIAL

The total gross enrolment ratios in urban areas are higher than those in rural areas in Kullu (40.5 per cent), Kangra (14.8 per cent), Bilaspur (9.3 per cent), and Sirmaur (3.6 per cent); the figures in parentheses indicate the urban–rural differences in enrolment. For six districts, gross enrolment ratios in urban areas are lower than those in rural areas and the difference ranges from 57.1 per cent (Hamirpur) to 5.9 per cent (Chamba).

One possible reason for obtaining a primary school gross enrolment ratio of more than 100 per cent could be the underestimation of eligible population for primary school enrolment from the observed ratio of growth in the 0–6 year population between 1981 and 1991. Children in the age group 6–11 years are taken to be eligible for primary school enrolment. However, children of age more than 11 years are often enrolled in primary schools, especially in rural areas.

4.2.2 Drop-out Rate

Enrolment in school, though necessary, is not sufficient for the spread of literacy and education; to achieve this, continuation in school is necessary for at least some period. There are several reasons for children dropping out of school. Unattractive way of teaching in the school, disinterest of students and parents, and poverty have often been cited as reasons for dropping out.

Due to the non-availability of the rural–urban breakup of enrolment figures for the early years, it is not possible to estimate drop-out ratios for rural and urban areas separately. The primary school drop-out ratio for Himachal Pradesh was 32.5 per cent in 1989–90. The drop-out ratio among girls (35.4 per cent) was higher than that among boys (30.0 per cent). Out of the 12 districts in the state, the drop-out ratio among girls was lower than that among boys only in Shimla district; for the rest of the 11 districts the drop-out ratio was higher among girls.

4.2.3 Teacher–Student Ratio

Table 4.E2 gives the districtwise teacher–student ratio at the primary level in Himachal Pradesh. The teacher–student ratio gives the average number of students per teacher in the district. On an average, there are 35 students per teacher at the primary level in the state. The teacher–student ratio varies from 11.44 in Lahul and Spiti to 38.16 in Mandi. These are, however, outliers, and 9 of the 12 districts have teacher–student ratios in the range of 33.73 to 36.91.

4.2.4 Literacy Rate

The overall effective literacy rate (defined as the number of literates as a percentage of population aged seven years and above) in Himachal Pradesh has increased from 51.17 per cent in 1981 to 63.86 per cent in 1991, and the figures are 75.36 per cent for males and 52.13 per cent for females in 1991 as compared to 64.27 per cent for males and 37.72 per cent for females in 1981. The effective literacy rate in Himachal Pradesh is higher than the all-India average. Table 4.E3 gives the districtwise effective literacy rates for males and females for the years 1991 and 2001 (see Map 4.2).

Effective literacy rate for the state of Himachal Pradesh increased by 12.69, 11.09, and 14.41 percentage points for total, male, and female population, respectively, between 1981 and 1991. The rate of change is higher between 1991 and 2001. The literacy rate has increased by 13.27, 10.66, and 14.97 percentage points, respectively for total, male, and female population between 1991 and 2001. The corresponding increases for the country (excluding Jammu and Kashmir and Assam) are 8.41, 7.41, 9.47 percentage points for total, male, and female population, respectively.

Himachal Pradesh ranks eleventh, twelfth, and eleventh, respectively for total, male, and female effective literacy rates among 31 states and union territories in India.

The highest literacy rates were recorded in district Hamirpur (in 1991)—74.88 per cent among total population, 85.11 per cent among males, and 65.90 per cent among females (see Map 4.3); and the lowest in district Chamba—44.70 per cent, 59.96 per cent, and 28.57 per cent for total population, males, and females, respectively. Out of the 12 districts in the state, seven districts, Chamba, Mandi, Kullu, Lahul and Spiti, Solan, Sirmaur and Kinnaur, have literacy rates lower than the state average. However, except for Chamba and Sirmaur, the remaining 10 districts have achieved literacy rates higher than the national average. Six districts have male literacy rate lower than the state average. These are Chamba, Kullu, Lahul and Spiti, Solan, Sirmaur, and Kinnaur. Again, only in Chamba and Sirmaur are the male literacy rates lower than the national average. In the case of female literacy rate, eight districts, Chamba, Mandi, Kullu, Lahul and Spiti, Shimla, Solan, Sirmaur and Kinnaur, have literacy rates lower than the state average. Four districts, namely Chamba, Kullu, Lahul and Spiti, and Sirmaur, have female literacy rates lower than the national average female literacy rate.

URBAN–RURAL DIFFERENTIAL

The effective literacy rates for rural areas are 61.86 per cent, 73.89 per cent, and 49.79 per cent, respectively for total population, males, and females; while for the urban population the corresponding rates are 84.17 per cent, 88.97 per cent, and 78.32 per cent. The urban–rural differential in the state is quite wide (22.31 per cent). The maximum urban–rural differential in the state is observed in Chamba (41.74 per cent), while the minimum differential is seen in Una (7.55 per cent).

The lowest literacy rate in rural areas is seen in Chamba (41.39 per cent) and the highest in Hamirpur (74.09 per cent). For the other districts it ranges from 48.27 per cent to 70.26 per cent. Only Kangra, Hamirpur, Una, and Bilaspur have rural literacy rates higher than the state average. Among males the lowest literacy is seen again in Chamba (57.44 per cent)

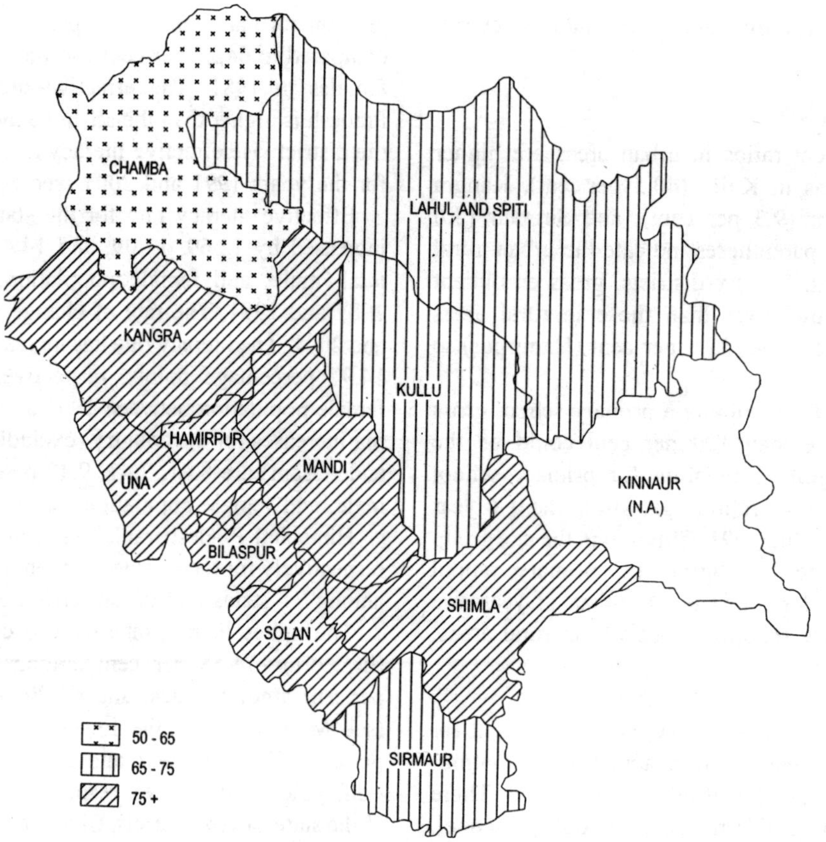

MAP 4.2: **Total Literacy Rate in Himachal Pradesh (2001)**
Note: Data for Kinnaur is not available.

and the highest is in Hamirpur (84.59 per cent). For the rest of the districts it ranges from 60.55 per cent to 80.70 per cent. Kangra, Hamirpur, Una, Bilaspur, and Mandi have rural male literacy rates higher than the state average. Among females, the minimum literacy rate is in Chamba (24.48 per cent) and the maximum is in Hamirpur (65.05 per cent). For the remaining districts it ranges from 34.32 per cent to 60.67 per cent. Kangra, Hamirpur, Una, and Bilaspur have rural female literacy rates higher than the state average.

In urban areas, the minimum total literacy rate is observed in Una (77.81 per cent) and the maximum is in Shimla (86.96 per cent). For the rest of the districts it varies from 80.04 per cent to 86.57 per cent. Six districts, (Hamirpur, Bilaspur, Mandi, Kullu, Shimla, and Solan) have total literacy rates higher than the state average. The male literacy rate in urban areas is the minimum in Kangra (84.85 per cent) and the maximum in Hamirpur (91.81 per cent). For the rest of the districts, it ranges between 85.67 per cent and 91.56 per cent. Hamirpur, Bilaspur, Mandi, Kullu, and Shimla have urban male literacy rates higher than the state average. The urban female literacy rate is the minimum in Una (69.39 per cent) and the maximum in Shimla (81.98 per cent). For the rest of the districts it varies from 73.62 per cent to 80.50 per cent. Hamirpur, Mandi, Kullu, Shimla, and Solan have urban female literacy rates higher than the state average.

GENDER DIFFERENTIAL

Though the overall literacy rate for all areas in the state is 63.86 per cent, there is a wide gap in literacy rates among males and females. The male–female differential in the state is of the order of 23.23 per cent, 24.10 per cent, and 10.65 per cent for all areas, rural areas, and urban areas, respectively. The male–female differential for all areas varies from 18.73 per cent in Kangra to 33.73 per cent in Lahul and Spiti. Among rural areas, the male–female differential varies from 19.18 per cent in Kangra to 33.73 per cent in Lahul and Spiti. Among urban areas, it varies from 8.23 per cent in Solan to 16.40 per cent in Una. Table 4.2 gives the male–female differential in effective literacy rates for all areas, rural areas, and urban areas. The disparity is quite high in rural areas as compared to urban areas.

FACTORS AFFECTING LITERACY RATE

The enrolment and drop-out ratios are likely to influence the achieved rate of literacy. These in turn are influenced by factors such as physical access to school, number of students per teacher, and other population group specific socio-cultural factors. In an attempt to explain the inter-district variation in the literacy rate, a number of regression equations involving these variables have been estimated and their statistical properties examined. Two of these equations are presented below.

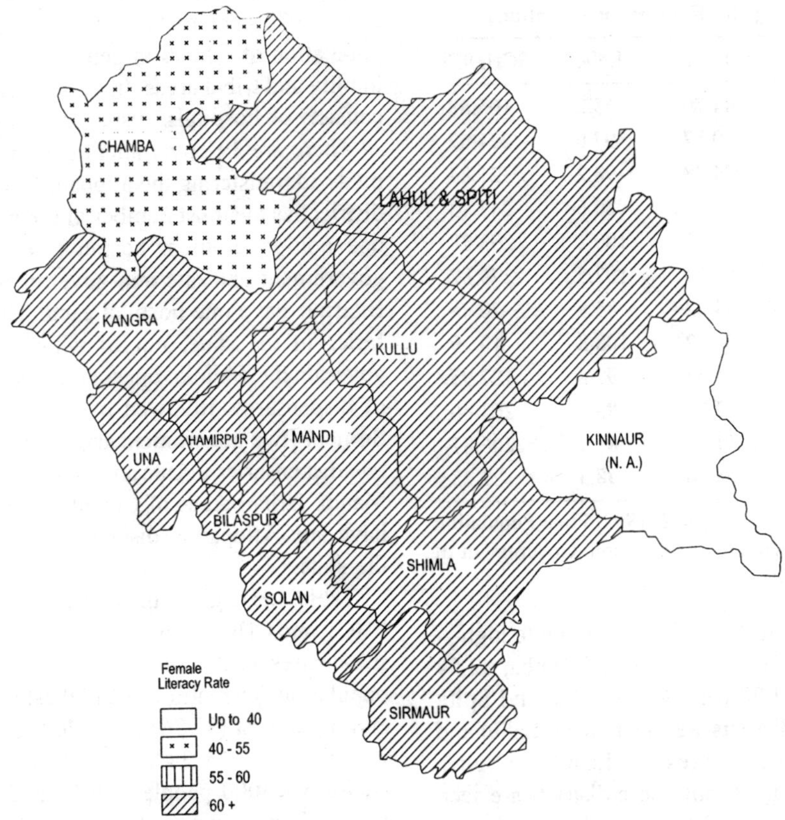

MAP 4.3: **Female Literacy Rate in Himachal Pradesh (2001)**
Note: Data for Kinnaur is not available.

$$ELR = 51.700 + 0.054 * SCHDEN \quad (4.1)$$
$$\qquad\qquad\qquad\quad (2.77)$$
$$R^2 = 0.43$$

$$ELR = 17.095 + 0.371 * ENR + 0.055 * SCHDEN \quad (4.2)$$
$$\qquad\qquad\qquad (2.15) \qquad\qquad (3.31)$$
$$R^2 = 0.63$$

where:
ELR = Effective literacy rate (all areas),
ENR = Primary school gross enrolment ratio (all areas),
SCHDEN = Primary school per thousand sq. km

The geographical proximity of primary schools (SCHDEN) and enrolment ratio (ENR) together explain more than 60 per cent of the variation in the literacy rate (ELR). Correlation and regression are, however, only indicative. Plausible causal chains need to be constructed to ascertain the influence of one variable on another. The existence of schools within reach and the enrolment of children in these schools are known prerequisites for the spread of literacy.

Other estimated regression equations, not presented here, indicated that factors such as number of primary schools per lakh population and student–teacher ratio have only a marginal influence on the achieved level of literacy in this state.

The overall performance of the state in achieving literacy is quite good. However, the districts with high concentrations of SCs and STs are noticeably behind the other districts in terms of the literacy rate. The districts with low literacy rates are Chamba (44.70 per cent), Sirmaur (51.62 per cent), Kullu (54.82 per cent), Lahul and Spiti (56.82 per cent), and Kinnaur (58.36 per cent). The percentage of SCs and STs

TABLE 4.2
Male–Female Differential in Effective Literacy Rate in Himachal Pradesh, 1991

(per cent)

State/district	All areas	Rural	Urban
Himachal Pradesh	23.23	24.10	10.65
Chamba	31.39	32.96	11.30
Kangra	18.73	19.18	9.20
Hamirpur	19.21	19.54	11.31
Una	20.14	20.44	16.40
Bilaspur	21.42	21.71	13.29
Mandi	27.53	28.52	11.13
Kullu	31.11	32.20	11.59
Lahul and Spiti*	33.73	33.73	–
Shimla	24.21	26.71	8.48
Solan	23.98	25.83	8.23
Sirmaur	24.75	26.23	12.05
Kinnaur*	30.00	30.00	–

Note: * Totally rural districts.
Source: Estimated by the author.

TABLE 4.3
Data Used in Estimating the Regression Equations

Districts	ELR	ENR	SCHDEN
Chamba	44.70	75.2	105.88
Kangra	70.57	97.0	224.02
Hamirpur	74.88	98.2	321.84
Una	70.91	80.6	247.13
Bilaspur	67.17	100.1	293.78
Mandi	62.74	102.5	275.82
Kullu	54.82	85.9	70.38
Lahul and Spiti	56.82	108.8	10.29
Shimla	64.61	97.4	187.95
Solan	63.30	85.8	263.86
Sirmaur	51.62	81.2	206.81
Kinnaur	58.36	98.3	22.23

Sources: Census of India, Series-1, Paper-2, 1992, Final Population Totals, New Delhi, 1993; Directorate of Education, Government of Himachal Pradesh, Shimla, 1992.

among the total population of these districts are quite high—31.79 per cent in Sirmaur, 50.12 per cent in Chamba, 82.54 per cent in Kinnaur, and 84.08 per cent in Lahul and Spiti. Enrolment ratios for these districts are low (except Lahul and Spiti), and drop-out ratios are high (except Lahul and Spiti). In terms of physical access to school, these districts are seen to lag behind the others. Gender disparity in literacy is also pronounced in these districts—Sirmaur (24.75 per cent), Kinnaur (30 per cent), Kullu (31.11 per cent), Chamba (31.39 per cent), and Lahul and Spiti (33.73 per cent). Special effort is needed to raise the literacy level in these districts, especially among females, SCs, and STs. Improvements in physical access to school and other related infrastructure are necessary in these districts. Population group specific socio-cultural factors may have a role to play in determining enrolment and drop-out and need to be studied and taken account of while formulating policies for micro-intervention.

4.3 Health Care Facilities and Health Status

Health and population control are among the priority objectives of the Eighth Plan, which envisages that adequate health care facilities should be available to the entire population by the end of the plan period. Within the Health for All strategy, the health status of the underprivileged is proposed to be improved through a community-based system with about 30,000 persons as the basic unit for primary health care.

Primary health care will be the main instrument for achieving the target of Health for All by 2000. Accordingly, a three-tier system of health care comprising community health centres (CHCs), PHCs, and sub-centres has been built up in rural areas. These institutions are supposed to provide integrated primary health care and family welfare services to the people at their doorsteps. The government has fixed a target to set up one sub-centre for every 5000 persons in general, and for every 3000 persons in hilly and tribal areas; one PHC for a population of 30,000 in general, and one for 20,000 persons in hilly and tribal areas. In urban areas, the health care system consists of hospitals, dispensaries, and health posts.

There are 39 government and three non-government hospitals administering the allopathic system in the state. Shimla district has the most number of government hospitals (10) and one non-government hospital, followed by Kangra (eight government and one non-government). Hamirpur, Una, and Bilaspur have one hospital each. There are in all 23 dispensaries in the state, out of which 22 are managed by the government. Shimla, once again, has the largest number (12) of dispensaries followed by Solan (three government), and Sirmaur (two government and one non-government); there are two dispensaries in Una and one each in Kangra, Bilaspur, and Mandi. Urban areas of Chamba, Hamirpur and Kullu do not have any Allopathic dispensary. There is no health post in the state.

Table 4.H1, gives the districtwise number of sub-centres, PHCs, and CHCs in the rural areas in the state. There are 1851 sub-centres in the state or 39.20 sub-centres per lakh rural population. The ratio is the highest (92.67) in Lahul and Spiti and the lowest (33.76) in Kullu. For the rest of the districts, it varies between 34.09 and 49.11. The target of one sub-centre per 3000 people in hilly and tribal areas has already been achieved in the state.

There are 183 PHCs in the state or 3.88 PHCs per lakh population. The ratio is the highest (12.78) in Lahul and Spiti and the lowest (2.31) in Hamirpur. The target of one PHC per 20,000 population in hilly and tribal areas has been achieved in only three districts, namely Lahul and Spiti, Shimla, and Kinnaur, out of the 12 districts in the state. District Chamba is close to achieving the target of one PHC per 20,000 population.

The state has 26 CHCs or 0.55 CHCs per lakh population. The ratio is the highest (6.39) in Lahul and Spiti and the lowest (0.29) in Una and Sirmaur. For the rest of the districts, it varies from 0.36 to 4.21. Bilaspur and Solan do not have any CHC.

Table 4.H2 gives the districtwise number of doctors and paramedical staff posts sanctioned and in position. There are in all 1179 doctors' posts sanctioned in the state out of which 1126 doctors are in position, that is, there is a shortfall of 53 (4.5 per cent). District Solan has the largest shortfall of doctors (16.82 per cent) followed by district Shimla (7 per cent). Doctors' posts sanctioned per lakh population is 22.8 for the state as a whole. The ratio is the highest in Lahul and Spiti (105.45) and the lowest in Kangra (17.21). For the remaining districts, it varies from 18.51 to 56.12.

There are in all 6593 paramedical staff posts sanctioned in the state and 5769 paramedical staff in position, a shortfall of 824 (12.50 per cent). Solan has the largest shortfall of 126 paramedical staff and Una has the lowest shortfall of 14. In percentage terms, Solan has the maximum shortfall of 20.72 per cent and Mandi has the minimum shortfall (3.34 per cent) of paramedical staff posts sanctioned. Paramedical staff posts sanctioned per lakh population is the largest in Lahul and Spiti (345.11) and the smallest in Una (99.14). It has been seen that doctors and paramedical staff posts sanctioned per lakh population is the highest for Lahul and Spiti. The district, however, is very thinly populated.

Table 4.H2 shows districtwise family welfare centres (FWCs) in the state. There are in all 46 FWCs in the state. District Shimla has the largest number (12) and the districts of Una, Kullu, Lahul and Spiti, and Kinnaur have the smallest number (one each). Hamirpur does not have any FWC. In terms of FWC per lakh population, the ratio is the highest for the district of Lahul and Spiti (3.20) and the lowest for the district of Una (0.26).

Table 4.H2 gives the districtwise number of doctors and paramedical staff. Data presented are for the state as a whole and include both the allopathic and indigenous systems of medicine. The details in respect of the different systems could not be obtained. Availability of medical staff (doctors and paramedical) is the highest in Kangra, which also has the largest number of PHCs, and CHCs, doctors, and paramedical staff. Shimla has the largest number of hospitals, dispensaries, FWCs, and medical staff. Lahul and Spiti does not have any hospital or dispensary. There are in all 1348 staff nurses in the state.

4.4 Related Demographic Parameters

Table 4.H3 shows the districtwise population density, sex ratio, and percentage of urban, SC, and ST population in the state by place of residence.

4.4.1 Population Density

According to the 1991 Census enumeration, the population density for all areas in Himachal Pradesh is 93 persons per sq. km as compared to the all-India figure of 267 persons per sq. km. Hamirpur is the most densely populated district with 330 persons per sq. km while Lahul and Spiti has only two persons per sq. km. Kinnaur (11), Kullu (55), and Chamba (60) are the other three districts with population density less than the state average. In rural areas of the state, there are only 85 persons per sq. km, with a maximum of 314 in Hamirpur and a minimum of two in Lahul and Spiti. Kinnaur (11), Kullu (51), and Chamba (56) are the other districts with population density less than the state average for rural areas. The population density for urban areas in the state is 1665 persons per sq. km. The maximum density is observed in Shimla (2492) and the minimum density in the district of Una (823). Bilaspur (960), Solan (1437), Chamba (1441), Kullu (1508), and Hamirpur (1626) have population density less than the state average for urban areas.

4.4.2 Sex Ratio

One of the basic demographic characteristics of a population is its sex composition. The sex composition is affected by many factors such as the differentials in the mortality condition of males and females, sex selective migration, and sex ratio at birth. The sex ratio is measured as the number of females per 1000 males in the population.

The sex ratio in India is adverse to females and has been declining over the decades. The marginal improvement noticed during 1971–81 has not been maintained during 1981–91. For the country as a whole, the sex ratio declined from 934 in 1981 to 929 in 1991. The reasons for the adverse sex ratio in the country include preference for the male child and consequent neglect of female babies—manifest in different health and nutritive conditions between males and females—leading to differential mortality conditions and lower expectation of life at birth for females.

Kerala is the only state with a sex ratio (1040) favourable to females. Himachal Pradesh with a current sex ratio of 976, and an increasing trend since 1941 is approaching a sex ratio favourable to females.

Some districts like Hamirpur (1105), Kangra (1024), Una (1017), Mandi (1013), and Bilaspur (1002) already have a sex ratio favourable to females. The sex ratio in rural areas of the state is 990. Five districts have a sex ratio more than 1000, namely, Kangra (1029), Hamirpur (1123), Una (1024), Bilaspur (1013), and Mandi (1025). The sex ratio is lower in urban areas (831). The higher sex ratio in rural areas is partly due to male migration from rural to urban areas in search of employment.

4.4.3 Scheduled Caste Population

The SC population is 25.34 per cent of the total population in the state (Table 4.H3). A large majority (93.67 per cent) lives in rural areas. The highest concentration of SCs is in Solan (31.27 per cent of the total district population) while Lahul and Spiti has only 7.11 per cent of SCs. In rural areas, the SC population on an average is 25.99 per cent, varying between 32.84 per cent in Solan and 7.11 per cent in Lahul and Spiti. In urban areas, it is 18.47 per cent, varying between 21.08 per cent in Sirmaur and 14.52 per cent in Kullu.

4.4.4 Scheduled Tribe Population

According to the 1991 Census, 4.22 per cent of the state's population belongs to STs. Most of them (97.52 per cent) are in rural areas. They are concentrated in Lahul and Spiti (76.97 per cent of the total district population). Other districts with a sizeable ST population are Kinnaur and Chamba with 55.58 per cent and 28.35 per cent, respectively (see Map 4.4). In rural areas, STs constitute 4.51 per cent of the population and they are largely concentrated in Lahul and Spiti (76.97 per cent), Kinnaur (55.58 per cent), and Chamba (30.37 per cent). In urban areas, they constitute a low proportion of 1.20 per cent of the total urban population of the state.

4.4.5 Urbanization

Table 4.H3 depicts the pattern of urbanization in the districts. Himachal Pradesh, being a hilly state, has a very low level

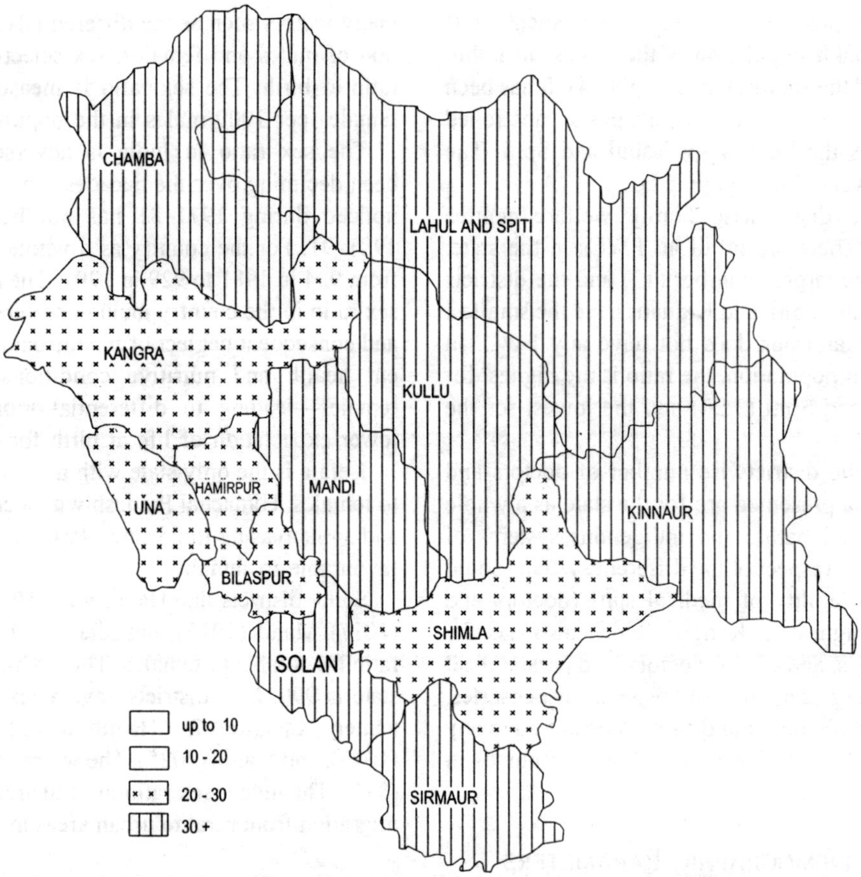

MAP 4.4: **Percentage of SCs and STs to Total Population in Himachal Pradesh**

of urbanization. Out of the total population of 52 lakh, 91.31 per cent lives in rural areas. The rest (that is, 8.69 per cent) lives in urban areas of the state.

In most of the districts, the percentage of urban population is very low, except in Solan and Shimla. The lowest (5.05 per cent) urban population is in Hamirpur. Shimla, being the capital of the state, has the highest (20.43 per cent) urban population, followed by Solan district.

4.4.6 Work Participation

According to the 1991 Census, there are 1,779,100 main and 435,320 marginal workers in the state. This means that there are 34.41 per cent main and 8.42 per cent marginal workers and the remaining 57.17 per cent are non-workers in the state. Among males, 49.08 per cent are main workers and 1.56 per cent are marginal workers. Among females, the corresponding figures are 19.36 per cent and 15.45 per cent. Male and female non-workers in the state are 49.36 per cent and 65.19 per cent respectively. Of the total main workers, 63.25 per cent are cultivators, 3.30 per cent are agricultural labourers, 1.43 per cent are engaged in household industries, and the remaining 32.02 per cent are engaged in other activities. Of the male main workers, 54:15 per cent are cultivators, 3.81 per cent agricultural labourers, 1.70 per cent are engaged in household industry and the remaining 40.34 per cent are engaged in other activities. Of the female main workers, 86.91 per cent are cultivators, 1.98 per cent are agricultural labourers, 0.72 per cent are engaged in household industry and the remaining 10.39 per cent are engaged in other activities.

The maximum percentage of main workers is seen in Lahul and Spiti (54.18 per cent), and the minimum in Una (27.46 per cent). Among the male main workers, the maximum percentage is in the district of Lahul and Spiti (63.60 per cent) and the lowest is in the district of Hamirpur (41.91 per cent). Among the female main workers, the maximum percentage is seen in Lahul and Spiti (42.64 per cent) and the minimum in Una (7.36 per cent).

The maximum percentage of marginal workers is in Chamba (16.03 per cent) and the minimum is in Kinnaur (5.10 per cent). For the remaining districts, the percentage varies from 5.50 per cent to 13.57 per cent. Among the male marginal workers, the maximum percentage is in the district of Lahul and Spiti (5.30 per cent), and the minimum is in district Una (0.77 per cent). For the remaining districts, it varies from 0.85 per cent to 2.64 per cent. Among the female marginal workers, the maximum percentage is in Chamba (30.14 per cent), and the minimum is in Kinnaur (9.64 per cent). For the remaining districts, it varies between 10.54 per cent and 24.78 per cent.

In Himachal Pradesh, 63.25 per cent of the total main workers are cultivators. The maximum percentage of cultivators is observed in Kullu (78.14 per cent), and the minimum in Lahul and Spiti (51.69 per cent). In the remaining districts the percentage varies from 52.51 per cent to 73.73 per cent. There are 54.15 per cent male cultivators in Himachal Pradesh. The maximum percentage of cultivators is in Kullu (70.89 per cent), and the minimum in Lahul and Spiti (38.42 per cent). For the remaining districts, the percentage varies between 40.72 per cent and 64.20 per cent. There are 86.91 per cent female cultivators in the state. The maximum percentage is in Mandi (92.36 per cent), and the minimum is in Una (74.41 per cent). For the other remaining districts, it varies from 75.91 per cent to 92.15 per cent.

The proportion of agricultural labourers is very small in the state, constituting only 3.30 per cent of total main workers. Male and female agricultural labourers are 3.81 per cent and 1.98 per cent of the total male and female main workers, respectively. The percentage of workers engaged in household industry is even lower than that of the agricultural labourers (1.43 per cent). Of the male and female workers, 1.70 per cent and 0.72 per cent, respectively, are engaged in household industries.

Table 4.H4 presents districtwise, sexwise, main and marginal workers as a percentage of total population and workers in household industry as a percentage of main workers for urban areas. In urban areas, out of a population of 449,196 persons, 33.39 per cent are main workers, 1.60 per cent are marginal workers, and the remaining 65.01 per cent are non-workers. The maximum number of main workers is in Shimla (39.43 per cent) and the minimum is in district Kangra (27.52 per cent). For the remaining districts, it varies from 29.14 per cent to 37.60 per cent. Out of a male population of 245,274 in urban areas, 51.92 per cent are main workers, 0.44 per cent marginal workers, and the remaining 47.64 per cent are non-workers. The maximum number of male main workers is in Shimla (58.08 per cent) and the minimum in district Kangra (44.73 per cent). For the remaining districts, it varies from 45.02 per cent to 56.50 per cent. Out of a total female population of 203,922 in urban areas, 11.10 per cent are main workers, 2.98 per cent marginal workers, and the remaining 85.92 per cent are non-workers. Female main workers are the maximum in Shimla (13.74 per cent), and the minimum are in Una (6.68 per cent), while for the remaining districts it varies from 8.09 per cent to 13.49 per cent.

Among the marginal workers in urban areas, the maximum are in Bilaspur (2.91 per cent) and the minimum are in Kullu (0.15 per cent). For the remaining districts it varies from 0.39 per cent to 2.47 per cent. Among the male marginal workers, the maximum is in district Kangra (0.55 per cent), and the minimum is in district Kullu (0.08 per cent). For the remaining districts, it varies from 0.19 per cent to 0.52 per cent. Among the female marginal workers, the maximum are in Bilaspur (5.79 per cent) and the minimum in Kullu (0.25 per cent). For the remaining districts, it varies from 0.51 per cent to 5.15 per cent. The percentage of workers engaged in household industry as a proportion of the total population is very small (1.25 per cent). The maximum proportion engaged in household industry is in Kullu (4.92 per cent) and the minimum is in Shimla (0.40 per cent). For the remaining districts, the figure varies from 0.79 per cent to 2.69 per cent. Among the male workers engaged in household industries, the maximum proportion is in district Kullu (4.46 per cent) and the minimum in district Shimla (0.37 per cent). For the rest of the districts it varies between 0.69 per cent and 2.9 per cent of the total population. Among female workers engaged in household industries, the maximum proportion is in Kullu (7.38 per cent) and the minimum in Shimla (0.54 per cent). For the remaining districts, it varies from 0.68 per cent to 1.68 per cent of the total population. Similar data for rural areas are available in Table 4.H5. Of the total rural population of 4,721,681 males, 34.50 per cent are main workers, 9.07 per cent are marginal workers, and the remaining 56.43 per cent are non-workers in the state. The maximum percentage of main workers in the state is in Lahul and Spiti (54.18 per cent) and the minimum in Una (27.30 per cent). For the remaining districts, it varies from 27.55 per cent to 47.32 per cent. Out of a rural male population of 2,372,193 persons, 48.79 per cent are main workers. Among the male main workers, the maximum percentage is in district Lahul and Spiti (63.60 per cent), and the minimum in district Hamirpur (41.68 per cent). For the remaining districts it varies from 44.75 per cent to 58.85 per cent. Out of the rural female population of 23,49,488 females, there are 20.08 per cent main workers in the state. Among the female main workers, the maximum percentage is observed in Lahul and Spiti (42.64 per cent) and the minimum in Una (7.42 per cent). For the remaining districts, it varies from 10.83 per cent to 34.51 per cent.

There are, in all, 9.07 per cent marginal workers in the state. The highest percentage is in the district of Chamba (17.22 per cent) and the minimum in district Kinnaur (5.10 per cent). For the remaining districts, it varies from 5.89 per cent to 14.21 per cent. There are 1.67 per cent male marginal workers in the state. The highest percentage is in Lahul and Spiti (5.30 per cent) and the minimum in Una (0.83 per cent). For the remaining districts, it varies from 0.91 per cent to 2.82 per cent. There are 16.53 per cent female marginal workers in the state. The maximum percentage is in the district of Chamba (32.33 per cent) and the minimum is in the district of Kinnaur (9.64 per cent). For the remaining districts, it varies from 11.24 per cent to 25.82 per cent.

Cultivators (68.58 per cent) constitute the majority among the main workers in the state. Agricultural labourers and workers in the household industries are 3.48 per cent and 1.45 per cent of the total main workers respectively.

4.4.7 Household Size and Dependency Ratio

Table 4.H6 gives the districtwise, sexwise, household size and dependency ratio by place of residence. Household size is defined as the average number of persons per household. According to the 1991 Census, the household size for the state is 5.34, which is smaller than the national average. The size of households is the largest in Sirmaur (5.78 persons) and the smallest in Kinnaur (4.34 persons). In rural areas of the state, the average household size is 5.48 persons. The largest average household size is in Sirmaur (5.95) and the smallest is in Kinnaur (4.34 persons). In urban areas, the average household size is 4.18 persons, with the largest in Una (4.96 persons) and the smallest in Shimla (3.72 persons).

The dependency ratio is defined as the economically inactive population as a percentage of the economically active population. The population between the ages of 15 and 59 years is considered as economically active and the rest as economically inactive.

According to the 1981 Census, the dependency ratio for the state as a whole is 47.08 per cent. It is the highest in Hamirpur (51.36 per cent) and the lowest in Lahul and Spiti (36.73 per cent). The dependency ratio among males in the state as a whole is 48.04 per cent—the highest percentage is in Hamirpur (56.42 per cent) and the lowest is in Lahul and Spiti (32.88 per cent). For the remaining districts, it varies from 38.83 per cent to 52.86 per cent. The female dependency ratio of the state as a whole is 46.10 per cent. The maximum female dependency ratio is in the district of Mandi (47.24 per cent) and the minimum is in the district of Lahul and Spiti (41.75 per cent). For the remaining districts, it varies from 44.20 per cent to 47.02 per cent.

In rural areas, the dependency ratio for the state as a whole is 47.87 per cent. The highest is in Hamirpur (51.84 per cent) and the lowest is in Lahul and Spiti (36.73 per cent). For the remaining districts, it varies from 41.87 per cent to 50.21 per cent. The dependency ratio among males in rural areas is 49.19 per cent. The highest is in Hamirpur (57.39 per cent) and the lowest is in Lahul and Spiti (32.88 per cent). For the remaining districts, it varies from 38.83 per cent to 53.59 per cent. The dependency ratio among females is 46.53 per cent. The highest is in Mandi (47.70 per cent) and the lowest is in Lahul and Spiti (41.75 per cent). For the remaining districts, it varies from 45.32 per cent to 47.25 per cent.

In urban areas, the dependency ratio is 37.55 per cent. The highest is in Una (44.19 per cent) and the lowest is in Shimla (31.09 per cent). For the remaining districts, it varies from 35.23 per cent to 42.14 per cent. The dependency ratio among males in urban areas is 35.49 per cent. The highest is in Una (44.62 per cent) and the lowest is in Shimla (27.79 per cent). For the remaining districts, it varies from 31.87 per cent to 41.23 per cent. The dependency ratio among females is 40.13 per cent. The highest is in Una (43.71 per cent) and the lowest is in Shimla (36.04 per cent). For the remaining districts, it varies from 39.51 per cent to 43.60 per cent.

Old age dependency ratio is defined as the population aged 59 years and above as a percentage of the population between 15 and 59 years. The old age dependency ratio is 7.50 per cent for the state and varies between 9.86 per cent in Una and 6.00 per cent in Kullu. Among males, it is 8.31 per cent. The highest is seen in Una (11 per cent) and the lowest in Lahul and Spiti (5.65 per cent). Among females, the old age dependency ratio averages at 6.68 per cent, ranging between 9.40 per cent in Kinnaur and 5.59 per cent in Kullu.

In rural areas, the average is 7.70 per cent. The old age dependency ratio is 8.59 per cent for males and 6.80 per cent for females. The highest values for all persons, males and females are in the districts of Una (10 per cent), Una (11.25 per cent), and Kinnaur (9.40 per cent), respectively, while the lowest values are in Kullu (6.13 per cent), Lahul and Spiti (5.65 per cent), and Kullu (5.68 per cent).

In urban areas, the average is 5.06 per cent, 5.16 per cent among males and 4.93 per cent among females. The highest values for all persons, males and females are recorded in Una—8.15 per cent for all three categories. The lowest values for all persons, males and females—3.51 per cent, 3.70 per cent, and 3.23 per cent, respectively—are recorded in Shimla.

Among all areas in the state, six districts have the dependency ratio for females higher than that for males and two districts have old age dependency ratio for females higher than that for males. In rural areas, in six districts the dependency ratio for all, and in two districts the old age dependency ratio, were higher for female than for males. Among urban areas, nine districts out of ten (Kinnaur and Lahul and Spiti are totally rural districts) have a total dependency ratio and three districts have old age dependency ratio for females more than that for males. District Una has the same old age dependency ratio for both males and females. This shows that discrimination against the girl child is less in Himachal Pradesh compared to some other parts of the country and this leads to lower child mortality among girls than that among boys and hence to a higher dependency ratio for females. The situation with respect to the old age dependency ratio is different. The old age dependency ratio for females is less than that for males, which indicates that the mortality among females at higher ages is more than that of males and this leads to a lower old age dependency ratio for females.

4.4.8 Fertility

Table 4.H7 gives the districtwise number of females in the age group 15–44 years and the percentage of married females in different age groups. These data pertain to the year 1981. Data for 1991 are not yet available. The percentage of married females in the age group 10–14 years is quite low in the state (1.49 per cent, 0.38 per cent and 1.56 per cent respectively for all areas, urban areas and rural areas). Only Sirmaur district has a sizeable percentage (7.70 per cent) of married females in the 10–14 years age group, followed by Chamba (2.48 per cent) and Solan (2.42 per cent). In the 15–19 years age group, the percentages of married females are 31.54, 14.93, and 32.82 respectively for all areas, urban areas, and rural areas. In Sirmaur district, the percentage of married females in the age group 15–19 years is quite high (53.66 per cent) followed by Bilaspur (45.22 per cent), Mandi (44.25

per cent), and Solan (43.12 per cent). In 20–4 years age group, the percentages of married females are 86.14, 63.89, and 88.34, respectively, for all areas, urban areas, and rural areas. In Bilaspur district, the percentage of married females in the age group 20–4 years is quite high (94.13 per cent). In the 15–44 years age group, married females are 77.48 per cent, 68.89 per cent, and 78.22 per cent of the female population in that age group for all areas, urban areas, and rural areas, respectively. The percentage of married females in the state, in the age group of 15–44 years, is the highest in Sirmaur (85.75 per cent) and the lowest in Lahul and Spiti (62.60 per cent).

4.4.9 Infant and Child Mortality

Table 4.H8 shows estimates of infant and child mortality. According to the 1981 Census enumeration, the IMR is 92. The estimates of child mortality for children aged two, three, and five are 123, 124, and 139 per thousand respectively. The decline in child mortality between ages two and three is quite sizeable. The level of urbanization, education, and health facilities across the districts are among the factors that influence child mortality. The IMR varies from 69 (Hamirpur) to 138 (Kinnaur). The child mortality for children aged two varies from 86 (Hamirpur) to 191 (Kinnaur). For children aged three, the rate varies from 89 (Hamirpur) to 194 (Kinnaur). The mortality rate of children aged five varies from 96 (Hamirpur) to 220 (Kinnaur) (see Map 4.5). It varies between 100 and 150 in Kangra, Mandi, Una, Bilaspur, and Solan. In Chamba, Lahul and Spiti, Kullu, Shimla, and Sirmaur the rate is as high as 150 to 200. Hamirpur ranks highest in terms of the literacy rate, for both males and females. Kinnaur is one of the low literacy districts in the state. This, perhaps, indicates that with the spread of literacy, child mortality is likely to go down. Infant and child mortality among girls are generally lower than those among boys, except for Lahul and Spiti for aged two and Una and Bilaspur for aged five.

It is interesting to note that in urban areas the lowest child mortality rates are not seen in Hamirpur but in Mandi and the highest rates are in Una. In urban areas, female child mortality rates are also generally lower than that of males, except for Bilaspur and Shimla (for infants); Hamirpur, Bilaspur, and Mandi (for aged two), Bilaspur (for aged three), and Bilaspur, Kangra, and Kullu (for aged five). In Bilaspur, female child mortality in urban areas is consistently higher than male child mortality.

In rural areas, the lowest child mortality rates are in Hamirpur and the highest in Kinnaur. In rural areas, child mortality rates for females are generally lower than those for males, except in Una and Lahul and Spiti (for infants) and (aged two) and Una and Bilaspur (aged five). The child

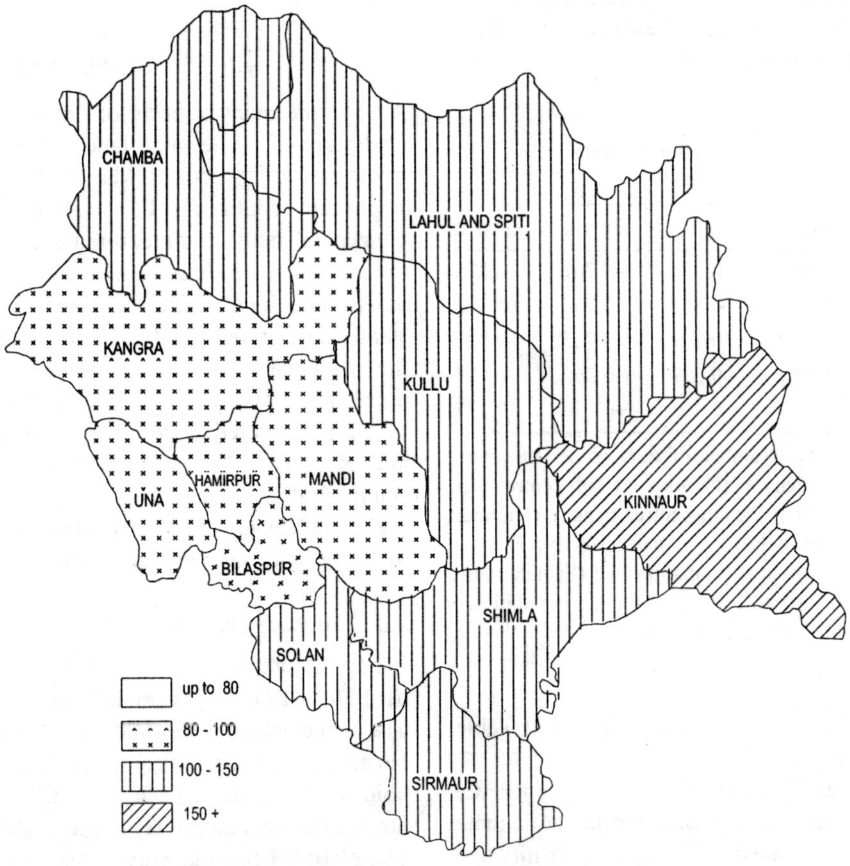

MAP 4.5: **Child Mortality Rate in Himachal Pradesh**

mortality rates have been reducing over time, as seen from 1991 Census data.

Table 4.H9 gives the districtwise adjusted fertility indices. Data for rural and urban areas are not available separately. According to the 1981 Census results, gross fertility rate (GFR), gross marital fertility rate (GMFR), total fertility rate (TFR), and total marital fertility rate (TMFR) estimates for Himachal Pradesh are 130, 166, 4.0, and 5.0 respectively (for definitions of fertility rates see Section 1.5.3). The GFR and TFR are the highest in Chamba and the lowest in Lahul and Spiti. The GMFR and TMFR are the highest in Kinnaur and the lowest in Bilaspur. However, in 1991 these rates had declined in all the districts.

FACTORS AFFECTING FERTILITY AND CHILD MORTALITY

Despite good performance in education and health, there is wide inter-district variation in fertility and child mortality rates in the state. Some districts like Hamirpur have a better record while Kinnaur requires micro-intervention to improve its record. A search for interrelation among various indicators and policy variables will be useful in the formulation and implementation of action plans. Availability of health care facilities such as doctors, PHCs, and sub-centres, their geographical proximity, literacy (especially female literacy), and female work participation rate are among the factors likely to have an impact on child mortality and marital fertility. Simple correlation coefficients between these variables and q(1), q(2), q(5), TMFR, and GMFR have been computed and studied here using data for the districts in the state.

TABLE 4.4
Correlation Coefficients between Some Selected Indicators

	q(1)	q(2)	q(5)	TMFR	GMFR
DOC	–0.682	–0.593	–0.778	–0.701	–0.825
SUB	–0.743	–0.669	–0.857	–0.732	–0.822
PHC	–0.584	–0.513	–0.701	–0.725	–0.821
FELR	–0.765	–0.581	–0.692	–0.362	–0.505
WPART	0.285	0.214	0.465	–0.039	0.177

Notes: DOC: Doctors density (Number of doctors per thousand sq. km); SUB: Sub-centres density (Number of sub-centres per thousand sq. km); PHC: Primary health centres density (Number of PHCs per thousand sq. km); FELR: Female effective literacy rate; WPART: Female work force participation rate (Female main and marginal workers as a percentage of total female population); q(i): Probability of death of a child before attaining age i (i = 1, 2, 5).

The estimated correlation coefficients displayed in Table 4.4 indicate the following:

1. Improved health care facilities (DOC, SUB, and PHC) tend to reduce child mortality and marital fertility. Adequate health care facilities are prerequisites for reduced fertility and child mortality.

2. Higher level of literacy among females, and lower child mortality and marital fertility. This corroborates the positive association between child mortality and level of education of mother observed in the data collected in the 1981 Census (Table 4.5). Children are largely taken care of by mothers. Educated mothers can understand medical advice better and utilize available health care facilities better. Children of educated mothers are, therefore, exposed to a lower risk of mortality.

3. Higher work participation rates among females seem to increase child mortality and marital fertility, though the magnitude of the correlations estimated here are low. A large majority of the female workers are employed in low paid jobs in unorganized sectors. In the prevailing working conditions these mothers fail to take adequate care of their children. Such children are consequently exposed to a higher risk of mortality. That the occupation of the mother does influence child mortality is corroborated by data collected in the 1981 Census pertaining to a number of states (Table 4.6). The situation in Himachal Pradesh is not likely to be different. High child mortality, in turn, is one of the factors that contribute to higher marital fertility.

The spread of education among working mothers, better access to health care facilities, and improvement in working conditions of females may reduce child mortality and marital fertility and thus lead to a higher level of human development in the state.

4.5 Material Well-being

Among the many aspects of quality of life, education and health are of prime importance. These have been discussed in the preceding sections. Many other aspects, though no less important, could not be covered due to difficulties in conceptualization and measurement as well as deficiencies in the available database. An adequate level of income and assets, though not sufficient, is necessary for leading a decent standard of living. Most of the deprivations can be traced to the inadequacy of income and assets. Income earned and assets held by people would, thus, be a proxy for other aspects of life not covered in this profile. Adequate levels of income and assets would indicate the feasibility of having a decent standard of living and a higher level of human development while inadequacy of these would necessarily correspond to a lower level of human development.

4.5.1 Income and Expenditure

Per capita income in Himachal Pradesh is Rs 4790 (per capita net SDP at 1990–1 prices). It is lower than that in the country as a whole, which is Rs 4964 (per capita net national product). No agency collects and compiles data on income at the household level regularly. Data on distribution of income among households are, therefore, not available for any recent year. The National Sample Survey Organization (NSSO) collects data on consumer expenditure in its various rounds on a

TABLE 4.5

Estimated Child Mortality by Education of Mother, 1981

Education of mother	Estimated child mortality											
	All areas				Rural areas				Urban areas			
	q(1)	q(2)	q(3)	q(5)	q(1)	q(2)	q(3)	q(5)	q(1)	q(2)	q(3)	q(5)
Illiterate	146 (103)	138	141 (153)	153	147 (103)	139	142	154	104	112	110 (119)	125
Literate but below middle	137× (72)	105 (88)	98	101	140× (73)	106 (89)	99	101	78 (68)	87	81 (90)	92
Middle but below matriculate	83@	86	76	76	87+ (59)	89 (70)	78	79	46	67 (59)	64	67
Matriculate but below graduate	61	65	62	60	64	69	69	68	46	53 (46)	50	50
Graduate and above**												

Notes: × Graduation is not possible for All areas and Rural areas (Male); @ Graduation is not possible for All areas (Person, Male); + Graduation is not possible for Rural areas (Male); ** Because of the small numbers involved, the estimates for the graduate and above category could not be worked out; Figures in parentheses are graduated estimates.

Source: Census of India, 1981, Child Mortality Estimates of India, Occasional Paper No. 5 of 1988.

TABLE 4.6

Statewise Child Mortality Estimate q(2) by Occupation of Female Main Workers

State	Occupation					
	Rural				Urban	
	Cultivators	Agricultural labourers	Manual workers	Non-manual workers	Manual workers	Non-manual workers
Andhra Pradesh	119	133	127	110	106	53
Bihar	123	161	146	89	123	46
Gujarat	102	149	140	90	109	58
Haryana	133	160	165	64	115	34
Karnataka	107	137	111	97	120	69
Kerala	74	88	84	42	78	33
Madhya Pradesh	165	208	211	137	151	119
Maharashtra	126	169	157	90	126	50
Orissa	163	179	328	133	155	97
Punjab	87	128	120	43	91	56
Rajasthan	162	298	183	101	130	67
Tamil Nadu	112	143	151	85	143	63
Uttar Pradesh	147	197	166	105	120	60
West Bengal	93	113	130	68	114	53
India	136	157	147	88	128	55

Note: Child mortality estimates by occupation have been worked out only for the major states (with 10+ million population); * In urban areas, cultivators and agricultural labourers have been included under manual workers.

Source: Census of India, 1981, Child Mortality Estimates of India, Occasional Paper No. 5 of 1988.

regular basis. These are available separately for population groups resident in rural and urban areas in states and union territories in a groupwise form. Persons per thousand and mean expenditure are published for various per capita expenditure classes. In the absence of data on household income for any recent year, the NSSO data on consumer expenditure pertaining to the year 1987–8 have been used to assess the level of material well-being in this state as a whole. Inadequate sample size does not permit further disaggregation of NSSO data on consumer expenditure.

TABLE 4.7

Consumer Expenditure, Gini Coefficient (1993–4) and Population below Poverty Line

	Consumer expenditure per month		Gini coefficient		Population below poverty line
	Rural	Urban	Rural	Urban	1993–4
Himachal Pradesh	350.63	746.93	0.2762	0.4345	28.20
Punjab	443.00	510.73	0.2645	0.2763	11.77
Rajasthan	322.39	424.73	0.2599	0.2904	27.41
Bihar	218.30	353.03	0.2239	0.3070	54.96
India	281.40	458.04	0.2816	0.3399	35.97

Source: The Report of the Expert Group on Estimation of Proportion and Number of the Poor, Planning Commission, 1993, Level and Pattern of Consumer Expenditure; 5th Quinquennial Survey NSSO Fiftieth Round (July 1993–June 1994), Department of Statistics, Government of India, 1996.

The monthly per capita consumer expenditure (MPCE) in rural Himachal Pradesh was Rs 209.61 in 1987–8. It increased to Rs 350.63 in 1993–4. In urban areas, the expenditure in 1987–8 was Rs 345.70. It increased to Rs 746.93 in 1993–4. These figures are higher than the average for the country as a whole at both points of time. The all-India consumer expenditure in 1987–8 was Rs 155.75 and Rs 249.93 for rural and urban areas, respectively. It increased to Rs 281.40 in rural areas and Rs 458.04 in urban areas in 1993–4.

To observe the inequality in consumer expenditure, the Gini coefficient, which is the most popular measure of inequality, has been estimated. In 1987–8, the ratio was 0.27 for rural and 0.30 for urban areas. In 1993–4, the ratio was the same as it was in 1987–8 for rural areas, while in urban areas it increased to 0.43. Over this period the inequality has remained the same in rural areas while it has increased in urban areas.

4.5.2 Distribution of Landholdings

The current income status reflects one aspect of material welfare. Data on consumer durables and productive assets held by households would reflect income prospects and thus indicate another aspect of material welfare. Data on these are not available for any recent year. However, agriculture being the main source of livelihood of the majority of the population, an analysis of the pattern of landholdings may prove interesting. Land is the major productive asset for those engaged in agriculture. The disparity in the distribution of income expenditure in rural areas would closely correspond to the disparity in the distribution of landholdings. The NSSO, in presenting the data collected in its 32nd round on employment and unemployment, provided a cross classification of 'Rural Households with Principal Industry–Agriculture' by per capita expenditure as well as per capita land possessed. This tabulation clearly indicated that low income and small landholdings are strongly associated. Rural poverty is, by and large, concentrated among the households with less than one acre of land. It is against this backdrop that an attempt has been made to analyse the number of categories of farmers, the areas operated and trends, using the data available from the Agricultural Censuses of 1985–6 and 1990–1.

During the period 1985–6 to 1990–1, the number of operational holdings increased from 638,000 to 844,000 and the area operated increased from 980,000 hectares to 1,015,000 hectares. However, the average size of operational holdings declined from 1.54 hectares to 1.20 hectares for all social classes of farmers. Among SC farmers, the number of operational holdings increased from 180,000 to 189,000 and area operated from 134,000 hectares to 138,000 hectares. There was a marginal decline in the average size of holdings (from 0.74 hectares to 0.73 hectares during 1985–6 to 1990–1). Among ST farmers, the number of operational holdings increased from 32,000 to 34,000, the area operated from 38,000 hectares to 40,000 hectares, accompanied by a marginal decline in the average size of holdings (from 1.19 hectares to 1.16 hectares) during the same period. Table 4.8 gives the number of operational holdings, area operated, and the average size of the holdings for various social classes of farmers.

The proportion of marginal farmers increased from 61.6 per cent in 1985–6 to 63.7 per cent in 1990–1, whereas for the remaining categories there was a declining trend during the same period. The category of semi-medium farmers operates the largest area, that is, 25.7 per cent of the total operated area (11.4 per cent farmers). Marginal farmers operate 21.5 per cent of the total operated area. Table 4.9 gives the distribution of the farmers of all social classes by their number of operational holdings, area operated and average size of the holdings for the year 1985–6 and 1990–1.

During 1985–6 to 1990–1, the average size declined for all the farmer categories, except for that of large farmers where it increased from 15.83 hectares in 1985–6 to 18.11 hectares in 1990–1.

Most of the landholdings in the state belong to individuals. During 1990–1, for all social classes of farmers, 99.1 per cent of the holdings were owned by individuals accounting for 97.9 per cent of the total operated area; 0.7 per cent holdings

TABLE 4.8

Number of Operational Holdings, Area Operated, and Average Size by Social Class

	No. of holdings ('000)	Area operated ('000 hectares)	Average size (hectares)
All farmers			
1980–1	638	980	1.54
1985–6	753	980	1.30
1990–1	844	1015	1.20
Scheduled castes			
1985–6	180	134	0.74
1990–1	189	138	0.73
Scheduled tribes			
1985–6	32	38	1.19
1990–1	34	40	1.16

Sources: All-India Report on Agricultural Census, 1985–6, Department of Agriculture and Co-operation, Ministry of Agriculture, Government of India, New Delhi, 1992; Provisional Results of Agricultural Census 1990–1, Directorate of Economics and Statistics, Shimla.

TABLE 4.9

Number of Operational Holdings, Area Operated, and Average Size for All Farmers, 1985–6 and 1990–1

Farmer class	No. of holdings ('000)		Area operated ('000 hectares)		Average size (hectares)	
	1985–6	1990–1	1985–6	1990–1	1985–6	1990–1
Marginal (< 1 ha.)	463	538	201	218	0.43	0.41
Small (1–2 ha.)	155	168	223	228	1.44	1.36
Semi-medium (2–5 ha.)	92	96	255	261	2.77	2.72
Medium (5–10 ha.)	36	37	208	207	5.78	5.66
Large (> 10 ha.)	6	6	95	100	15.83	18.11
Total	753	844	980	1015	1.30	1.20

Sources: All-India Report on Agricultural Census, 1985–6, Department of Agriculture and Co-operation, Ministry of Agriculture, Government of India, New Delhi, 1992; Provisional Results of Agricultural Census 1990–1, Directorate of Economics and Statistics, Shimla.

accounting for 1.4 per cent of area were jointly held and 0.2 per cent belonged to institutions which account for 0.8 per cent of the total operated area in the state. The average size of holdings is the largest for institutional holdings and the smallest for individual holdings. Distribution of holdings by size would thus, largely correspond to distribution of farmers by size of their holdings. Table 4.10 gives distribution of holdings and area operated by type of holdings for all social classes of farmers, SCs, and STs.

TABLE 4.10

Percentage Distribution of Holdings and Area Operated by Type of Holding for All Social Classes

(per cent)

Type of holdings	All social classes		Scheduled castes		Scheduled tribes	
	Number	Area	Number	Area	Number	Area
Individual	99.1	97.9	99.3	98.4	99.5	99.2
Joint	0.7	1.4	0.7	1.6	Neg.	0.1
Institutional	0.2	0.8	Neg.	Neg.	0.5	0.7
Total	100.0	100.0	100.0	100.0	100.0	100.0

Note: Neg.: Negligible.

Source: Provisional Results of 1990–1 Agricultural Census, Directorate of Economics and Statistics, Shimla.

Table 4.P2 gives the distribution of operational holdings for all social classes of farmers, SCs, and STs corresponding to marginal farmers in each district. Average size of landholdings for marginal farmers of all social classes in the state is 0.41 hectares. Among SC and ST marginal farmers in the state, the average size of holding is 0.40 hectares and 0.45 hectares, respectively.

The average size of landholdings for small farmers of all social classes in the state is 1.36 hectares; the largest is in Solan (1.54 hectares) and the smallest is in Mandi (1.07 hectares). Among SC small farmers in the state, the average size of holding is 1.38 hectares; the largest is in Solan (1.45 hectares) and the smallest is in Lahul and Spiti (1.32 hectares). Among ST small farmers in the state, the average size is 1.43 hectares; the largest is in Shimla (1.90 hectares) and the smallest is in Solan (1.13 hectares).

The average size of landholdings for semi-medium farmers of all social classes in the state is 2.72 hectares. The largest average size is in Solan (2.85 hectares) and the smallest is in Shimla (2.52 hectares). Among SC semi-medium farmers in the state, the average size of holding is 2.63 hectares, ranging between 2.79 hectares in Solan and 2.63 hectares in Chamba and Hamirpur. Among ST semi-medium farmers in the state, the average size is 2.71 hectares, ranging between 3.21 hectares in Shimla and 2.71 hectares in Chamba.

Table 4.P2.1 gives data for medium farmers. The average size of landholdings for medium farmers of all social classes in the state is 5.66 hectares. For SC and ST medium farmers in the state the average size of holding is 5.54 hectares and 5.39 hectares.

Table 4.P2.2 gives data pertaining to large farmers. The average size of landholdings for large farmers of all social classes in the state is 18.11 hectares. For among SC and ST large farmers in the state, the average size of holding is 13.73 hectares and 16.94 hectares.

4.6 Government Programmes and Policies

A higher level of human development as a goal has been accorded high priority in the Eighth Five Year plan. Already many government programmes and policies are being implemented in the state with assistance from the Central Government and international donor agencies. The main thrust of all these programmes and policies is to raise the level of living of the people, especially those who have been left behind in the earlier stages of development, so as to bring them at par with the mainstream of the society. The important programmes and policies currently being implemented in the state are discussed in this section. The current status of various population sub-groups in the state in terms of identified areas of social concerns is assessed in subsequent sections.

4.6.1 Public Distribution System

In order to make the public distribution system (PDS) more effective and targeted to the vulnerable sections of the population, besides foodgrains other essential commodities such as, sugar, cloth, edible oils, pulses, salt, tea leaves, exercise books, school stationery and kerosene oil are being distributed through fair price shops. Nearly 80 per cent of these shops are being run by co-operative societies which ensure their fair functioning.

4.6.2 Education

The Eighth Plan has given priority to the universalization of elementary education and complete eradication of illiteracy in the age group 15–35 years through the National Literacy Mission (NLM). Adequate provision of freeships and scholarships to the poor and meritorious students, with a bias in favour of those from SCs, STs and other backward communities, has been made. This is expected to raise the level of education among these sections of society. As on 31 March 1992, there were 7547 government primary schools functioning in the state. The Directorate of Primary Education is engaged in continuing efforts to raise the quality of teaching. The provision of at least one primary school within a radius of 1 to 1.5 km is expected to make primary education physically accessible to every child. The facility of Integrated Education of Handicapped Children is being provided at Shimla, Nahan, Dharamsala, and Chamba.

4.6.3 Health and Family Welfare

After the Alma-Ata declaration in 1978, Health For All has become a major social concern of the government. In Himachal Pradesh, the Department of Health and Family Welfare provides services such as public health, control of communicable diseases, health education, family welfare and maternal and child care through a network of 39 civil hospitals, 18 CHCs, 17 rural hospitals (upgraded PHCs), 191 PHCs, 196 civil dispensaries, 1851 sub-centres, and 46 maternal and child health centres.

Facilities for treatment by homeopathy and other Indian systems of medicine are available in two regional hospitals, one tribal hospital, nine district hospitals, one natural care unit, and 522 ayurvedic dispensaries.

4.6.4 Nutrition Programme

The special nutrition programme being implemented by the Social and Women's Welfare Department aims at providing supplementary nutritive diet to children below six years and expectant and nursing mothers belonging to the poor sections of the society. This programme is expected to benefit 133,000 children and 30,000 expectant and nursing mothers.

4.6.5 Social Welfare

Many other social welfare programmes are being implemented with different weaker sections of the society as target groups. These include: old age and widow pension; child welfare; and women's welfare.

1. Old age and widow pension: Under this scheme, a pension of Rs 60 per month is provided to those persons aged above 60 years with annual income less than Rs 2000 and no one to support them. This pension is also provided to those with children, if their monthly income does not exceed Rs 1000. There is, however, no age limit for widows for receiving this pension.

2. Child welfare: Orphans, semi-orphans and destitute children receive boarding, lodging, and education facilities up to matriculation (Class 10) free of cost.

3. Women's welfare: There are many programmes in the state which aim to bring women into the mainstream of development and to make them economically independent. These programmes include the following.

State Homes

Destitute women and girls are offered free boarding and lodging and training in crafts, tailoring, embroidery etc. at state homes. A financial assistance (currently Rs 3000 per woman) is also provided for rehabilitation at the end of training.

Working Women's Hostel

Working women's hostels, constructed with 75 per cent grant-in-aid from the Central Government and 25 per cent grant-in-aid from the state government, provide residential accommodation at subsidized rates to women working away from their homes.

Marriage Grant to Destitute Girls

A marriage grant of up to Rs 2500 per beneficiary is being given to the girl or her parents/guardians if their annual income does not exceed Rs 7500.

Assistance for Self Employment to Women

In order to encourage entrepreneurship among women, financial assistance of Rs 1000 to Rs 2000 is given to women with adequate knowledge in any trade or with training/diploma in that particular trade if her annual income does not exceed Rs 7500. This is expected to encourage entrepreneurship among women. This is perhaps, one of the factors contributing to the higher work participation rate among women in this state.

4.6.6 Welfare of the Handicapped

Facilities such as artificial limbs, scholarships, and vocational training are offered to handicapped persons. A marriage grant of Rs 5000 is given to those who marry handicapped persons. Old age pension in the shape of disability relief (currently Rs 60 per month) is provided to all physically handicapped persons, irrespective of age. All lepers in the state receive a rehabilitation allowance of Rs 60 per month.

4.6.7 Welfare of Backward Classes

Current welfare programmes for SCs, STs, and other backward classes include:

1. Scholarships for technical education. Each trainee from backward classes receives a scholarship of Rs 100 per month.
2. Award for inter-caste marriage. The system of awards for inter-caste marriages aims to discourage untouchability and associated social evils and to eradicate these in the long run.
3. Housing subsidy. In order to improve the living conditions of backward classes, construction and repair of their houses are subsidized.
4. Drinking water supply scheme. Village-based schemes are being undertaken in the villages with a concentration of SC which are not covered by the Public Health Department for providing safe drinking water.

4.7 Concluding Remarks

Himachal Pradesh is a predominantly agrarian economy. Since it does not have a considerable industrial base, its economic progress is not impressive. The per capita income of the state, Rs 2137, is lower than the national average of Rs 2226. The percentage of the state's population living below the poverty line is 28.4 per cent, placing the state at eighth position out of 17 major states. There exists a great amount of variation among the districts with respect to literacy, health care, child mortality etc. To get an idea of the difference among the districts, the value of the coefficient of variation (CV) has been calculated and presented in Table 4.11.

The percentage of literates in the state (63.86 per cent) is well above the national average (52.21 per cent). In terms of literacy, the female population of Himachal Pradesh is at par with the general population of the country. Urban–rural and female–male disparity in literacy are relatively low in the state. The district level variation with respect to literacy is the lowest (44.7 per cent) in Chamba and the highest (74.88 per cent) in Hamirpur. The CV is 13.66, which is relatively low.

The female literacy rate for rural areas is 49.79 per cent. Like the total literacy rate, female literacy rate is also the lowest in Chamba (24.48 per cent) and the highest in Hamirpur (65.05 per cent). The variation in female literacy (25.45) is much more than that for total literacy. There exists a large level of gender disparity in the literacy rate. A gap of 23.23 per cent in the total literacy rate exists between males and females, which is even higher for rural literacy. There are, on an average, 32 students per teacher at the primary level in the state. The ratio varies from 11 in Lahul and Spiti to 38 in Mandi. The CV is 23.3, showing relatively less variation among districts.

The state has achieved better health care facilities in terms of sub-centres and PHCs per lakh population. The average number of sub-centres and PHCs per lakh population is 39.2 and 3.88, respectively. In the SC and ST dominated districts of Lahul and Spiti, Kinnaur, and Chamba, sub-centres and PHCs per lakh population are more in number than in other districts. The ratio of doctors per lakh population is 23 and the CV is 76. This shows very high variation among the districts due to better allotment of doctors in sparsely populated settlements in the above mentioned districts.

The percentage of agricultural labourers to total main workers is only 3.3 per cent. The districtwise percentage of agricultural labourers is also very low. It is the highest in Una (7.96 per cent) and the lowest in Chamba (1.07 per cent). Child mortality for the state is 90, and is the highest in Kullu (114) and the lowest in Mandi (73). The CV among the districts is as high as 46.6. The level of urbanization, education and health facilities across the districts are among the factors that influence child mortality.

TABLE 4.11

Average, Standard Deviation, and Coefficient of Variation of Human Development Indicators

	Total literacy	Student–Teacher ratio	Female literacy rural	Sub-centres per lakh pop.	Doctors per lakh pop.	Child mortality	Agriculture labourers	CMIE index
Avg.	61.71	32.36	46.18	44.43	31.98	76.50	3.41	75.00
SD	8.43	7.54	11.75	15.45	24.37	35.65	2.09	26.19
CV	13.66	23.30	25.45	34.78	76.20	46.61	61.30	34.92

The CMIE index of development for the state is 75. There exists a vast differential (CV is 34.9) in terms of development among the districts. Solan has the highest development index of 132 and the lowest index of 46 is observed for Mandi.

The state has achieved most of its goals in terms of literacy and health care facilities. Since it is a hilly state and opportunities for industrialization and urbanization are limited, there is a need to develop the agricultural sector, particularly plantation crops and sericulture. There is also a need to develop small-scale household and cottage industries by using the local raw material. This will help to improve the economic condition of the people. To reduce the differences among the population, there is a need for a greater level of participation of the people in various developmental projects.

TABLE 4.E1

Districtwise Primary School Gross Enrolment Rate in Urban Areas (boys, girls, and total)

State/district	Total no. of eligible children for enrolment (universe 6–11)*			Enrolment rate (per cent)		
	Boys	Girls	Total	Boys	Girls	Total
Himachal Pradesh	**26,595**	**23,604**	**50,199**	**87.3**	**82.7**	**85.1**
Chamba	1886	1737	3623	66.2	73.3	69.6
Kangra	3809	3417	7226	123.9	96.9	111.1
Hamirpur	1475	1387	2862	43.2	45.9	44.5
Una	2321	1979	4300	45.6	47.9	46.7
Bilaspur	970	847	1817	121.3	94.6	108.9
Mandi	2888	2649	5537	94.5	87.4	91.1
Kullu	1158	1107	2265	119.8	129.0	124.3
Lahul and Spiti	–	–	–	–	–	–
Shimla	6952	5958	12,910	87.4	89.9	88.6
Solan	2622	2323	4945	77.8	69.0	73.7
Sirmaur	2514	2200	4714	85.2	83.7	84.5
Kinnaur	–	–	–	–	–	–

Note: * Estimated from 1981 population of 6–11 years age group by applying the growth rate observed in 0–6 years age group between 1981 and 1991.

Source: Directorate of Education, Government of Himachal Pradesh, Shimla.

TABLE 4.E2

Districtwise Primary School Gross Enrolment Rate in Rural Areas (boys, girls, and total)

State/district	Total no. of eligible children for enrolment (universe 6–11) *			Enrolment rate (per cent)			Teacher–student ratio
	Boys	Girls	Total	Boys	Girls	Total	All Areas
Himachal Pradesh	**339,185**	**322,331**	**661,516**	**95.2**	**90.3**	**92.8**	**34.98**
Chamba	28,177	27,862	56,039	91.6	59.2	75.5	28.62
Kangra	78,667	71,699	150,366	93.2	99.8	96.3	36.91
Hamirpur	23,756	22,583	46,339	98.4	104.9	101.6	36.42
Una	25,778	24,144	49,922	84.1	83.0	83.5	36.37
Bilaspur	19,421	18,127	37,548	99.5	99.7	99.6	36.84
Mandi	50,098	48,529	98,627	106.8	99.5	103.2	38.16
Kullu	21,372	20,404	41,776	87.4	80.1	83.8	35.62
Lahul and Spiti	1690	1568	3258	110.8	106.6	108.8	11.44
Shimla	34,049	33,119	67,168	101.2	97.0	99.1	33.73
Solan	25,033	24,242	49,275	89.9	84.0	87.0	36.39
Sirmaur	26,548	25,753	52,301	90.3	71.3	80.9	34.83
Kinnaur	4595	4301	8896	98.0	98.5	98.3	22.94

Note: * Estimated from 1981 population of 6–11 years age group by applying the growth rate observed in 0–6 years age group between 1981 and 1991.

Source: Directorate of Education, Government of Himachal Pradesh, Shimla.

TABLE 4.E3

Districtwise Effective Literacy Rate by Place of Residence and Sex, 1991 and 2001

(per cent)

State/district	All areas (1991)			Rural (1991)			Urban (1991)			All areas (2001)		
	Male	Female	Total	Male	Female	Total	Male	Female	Total	Male	Female	Total
Himachal Pradesh	**75.36**	**52.13**	**63.86**	**73.89**	**49.79**	**61.86**	**88.97**	**78.32**	**84.17**	**86.02**	**67.10**	**77.13**
Chamba	59.96	28.57	44.70	57.44	24.48	41.39	88.50	77.20	83.13	77.22	50.00	63.73
Kangra	80.12	61.39	70.57	79.85	60.67	70.04	84.85	75.65	80.39	88.19	74.00	80.68
Hamirpur	85.11	65.90	74.88	84.59	65.05	74.09	91.81	80.50	86.57	90.86	76.41	83.16
Una	81.15	61.01	70.91	80.70	60.26	70.26	85.79	69.39	77.81	88.49	74.85	81.09
Bilaspur	77.97	56.55	67.17	77.10	55.39	66.08	90.68	77.39	84.65	87.13	70.53	78.80
Mandi	76.65	49.12	62.74	75.31	46.79	60.80	91.56	80.43	86.42	86.67	65.36	75.86
Kullu	69.64	38.53	54.82	67.82	35.62	52.37	90.63	79.04	85.62	84.55	61.24	73.36
Lahul and Spiti	71.78	38.05	56.82	71.78	38.05	56.82	–	–	–	82.76	61.00	73.17
Shimla	75.96	51.75	64.61	71.54	44.83	58.61	90.46	81.98	86.96	87.72	70.68	79.68
Solan	74.67	50.69	63.30	72.53	46.70	60.18	88.52	80.29	84.86	85.35	67.48	77.16
Sirmaur	63.20	38.45	51.62	60.55	34.32	48.27	85.67	73.62	80.04	79.73	60.93	70.85
Kinnaur	72.04	42.04	58.36	72.04	42.04	58.36	–	–	–	–	–	–

Source: Directorate of Census Operations, Government of Himachal Pradesh, Shimla.

TABLE 4.H1

Districtwise Number of Sub-centres, PHCs, and CHCs per lakh Rural Population for Allopathy System, 1991

State/district	Sub-centres			PHCs		CHCs	
	Total rural population	Number of sub-centres	Sub-centres per lakh population	Number of PHCs	PHCs per lakh population	Number of CHC	CHC per lakh population
Himachal Pradesh	**4,721,681**	**1851**	**39.20**	**183**	**3.88**	**26**	**0.55**
Chamba	363,397	155	42.65	18	4.95	4	1.10
Kangra	1,114,723	386	34.63	30	2.69	5	0.45
Hamirpur	346,442	136	39.26	8	2.31	2	0.58
Una	345,997	119	34.39	9	2.60	1	0.29
Bilaspur	278,652	95	34.09	11	3.95	–	–
Mandi	720,603	281	39.00	28	3.89	5	0.69
Kullu	281,421	95	33.76	10	3.55	1	0.36
Lahul and Spiti	31,294	29	92.67	4	12.78	2	6.39
Shimla	491,272	219	44.58	30	6.11	2	0.41
Solan	334,989	164	48.96	14	4.18	–	–
Sirmaur	341,621	137	40.10	15	4.39	1	0.29
Kinnaur	71,270	35	49.11	6	8.42	3	4.21

Source: Directory of Medical, Public Health and Hospitals in Himachal Pradesh, Directorate of Health Services, Government of Himachal Pradesh, Shimla.

TABLE 4.H2

Districtwise Number of Doctors and Paramedical Staff Posts Sanctioned and in Position, 1991

State/district	Total population	Doctors posts sanctioned	Doctors in position	Doctors per lakh population	Para-medical staff posts sanctioned	Para-medical staff in position	Para-medical staff per lakh population	Family welfare centres per lakh population
Himachal Pradesh	**5,170,877**	**1179**	**1126**	**22.80**	**6593**	**5769**	**127.50**	**0.89**
Chamba	393,286	89	89	22.63	537	439	136.54	1.27
Kangra	1,174,072	202	197	17.21	1266	1107	107.83	0.34
Hamirpur	369,128	69	68	18.69	439	404	118.93	0.00
Una	378,269	70	67	18.51	375	361	99.14	0.26
Bilaspur	295,387	63	63	21.33	322	306	109.01	1.69
Mandi	776,372	160	155	20.61	868	839	111.80	1.03
Kullu	302,432	65	62	21.49	365	334	120.69	0.33
Lahul and Spiti	31,294	33	32	105.45	108	91	345.11	3.20
Shimla	617,404	200	186	32.39	1060	864	171.69	1.94
Solan	382,268	107	89	27.99	608	482	159.05	1.31
Sirmaur	379,695	81	79	21.33	494	411	130.10	0.79
Kinnaur	71,270	40	39	56.12	151	131	211.87	1.40

Note: * Calculated on the basis of posts sanctioned.

Source: Directory of Medical, Public Health and Hospitals in Himachal Pradesh, Directorate of Health Services, Government of Himachal Pradesh, Shimla.

TABLE 4.H3

Districtwise Population Density, Sex Ratio, and Percentage of Urban and SC, and ST Population

State/district	All areas						Rural				Urban			
	CMIE index 1995	Popn density	Sex ratio	Per cent of urban popn	Per cent of SC	Per cent of ST	Popn density	Sex ratio	Per cent of SC	Per cent of ST	Popn density	Sex ratio	Per cent of SC	Per cent of ST
Himachal Pradesh	**113.88**	**93**	**976**	**8.69**	**25.34**	**4.22**	**85**	**990**	**25.99**	**4.51**	**1665**	**831**	**18.47**	**1.2**
Chamba	98.59	60	949	7.60	19.17	28.35	56	953	19.88	30.37	1441	902	18.11	3.79
Kangra	119.54	205	1024	5.05	21.17	0.14	195	1029	21.51	0.14	1729	934	14.65	0.15
Hamirpur	115.11	330	1105	6.15	23.68	0.06	314	1123	24.09	0.05	1626	870	17.38	0.3
Una	116.05	246	1017	8.53	22.47	0.01	231	1024	22.69	0.01	823	939	20.04	0.04
Bilaspur	116.36	253	1002	5.67	25.82	2.7	242	1013	26.15	2.8	960	836	20.36	1.1
Mandi	111.14	197	1013	7.18	28.98	1.21	184	1025	29.69	1.25	1930	869	19.84	0.76
Kullu	96.32	55	920	7.00	28.93	3.61	51	931	30.0	3.22	1508	784	14.52	8.8
Lahul and Spiti	167.96	2	817	–	7.11	76.97	2	817	7.11	76.97	–	–	–	–
Shimla	115.10	120	894	20.43	27.13	0.71	97	943	29.33	0.61	2492	726	18.54	0.11
Solan	131.94	197	909	12.37	31.27	0.64	176	922	32.84	0.69	1437	821	20.14	0.32
Sirmaur	118.63	134	897	10.03	30.18	1.61	122	899	31.20	1.76	2135	874	21.08	0.27
Kinnaur	140.26	11	856	–	26.87	55.58	11	856	26.87	55.58	–	–	–	–

Sources: Directorate of Census Operations, Government of Himachal Pradesh, Shimla, 1991; CMIE Index 2000, District Profile, Centre for Monitoring Indian Economy.

TABLE 4.H4

Districtwise Population, Workers (Main and Marginal) as Percentage to Total Population, Workers in Household Industry for Urban Areas as Percentage to Total Main Workers, 1991

State/district	Total population			Main workers			Marginal workers			Workers in HH industry		
	Total	Male	Female	Total	Male	Female	Total	Male	Female	Total	Male	Female
Himachal Pradesh	**449,196**	**245,274**	**203,922**	**33.39**	**51.92**	**11.10**	**1.60**	**0.44**	**2.98**	**1.25**	**1.24**	**1.33**
Chamba	29,889	15,717	14,172	30.95	48.43	11.57	1.59	0.48	2.82	1.35	1.42	1.04
Kangra	59,349	30,690	28,659	27.52	44.73	9.09	0.61	0.55	0.67	1.18	1.09	1.65
Hamirpur	22,686	12,132	10,554	29.30	45.02	11.22	1.58	0.47	2.85	1.22	1.34	0.68
Una	32,272	16,646	15,626	29.14	50.23	6.68	0.63	0.19	1.10	1.77	1.85	1.05
Bilaspur	16,735	9113	7622	33.81	50.97	13.29	2.91	0.50	5.79	2.69	2.91	1.68
Mandi	55,769	29,832	25,937	31.74	49.35	11.49	2.38	0.41	4.63	0.79	0.69	1.28
Kullu	21,011	11,776	9235	37.60	56.50	13.49	0.15	0.08	0.25	4.92	4.46	7.38
Lahul and Spiti	–	–	–	–	–	–	–	–	–	–	–	–
Shimla	126,132	73,086	53,046	39.43	58.08	13.74	2.47	0.52	5.15	0.40	0.37	0.54
Solan	47,279	25,964	21,315	34.14	53.68	10.34	1.40	0.50	2.48	1.22	1.28	0.86
Sirmaur	38,074	20,318	17,756	29.42	48.06	8.09	0.39	0.28	0.51	2.15	2.28	1.25
Kinnaur	–	–	–	–	–	–	–	–	–	–	–	–

Source: Directorate of Census Operations, Government of Himachal Pradesh, Shimla, 1991.

TABLE 4.H5

Districtwise Population, Workers (Main and Marginal) as Percentage to Total Population, Cultivators, Agricultural Labourers, Workers in Household Industry for Rural Areas as Percentage to Total Main Workers (Total, Male, and Female), 1991

State/district	Total population			Main workers			Marginal workers			Cultivators			Agricultural labourers			Workers in HH industry		
	Total	Male	Female	Total	Male	Female	Total	Male	Female	Total	Male	Female	Total	Male	Female	Total	Male	Female
Himachal Pradesh	**4,721,681**	**2,372,193**	**2,349,488**	**34.50**	**48.79**	**20.08**	**9.07**	**1.67**	**16.53**	**68.58**	**59.59**	**90.64**	**3.48**	**4.07**	**2.03**	**1.45**	**1.75**	**0.70**
Chamba	363,397	186,042	177,355	32.68	51.59	12.84	17.22	2.82	32.33	71.79	68.01	87.70	1.14	1.12	1.26	1.23	1.33	0.79
Kangra	1,114,723	549,331	565,392	27.55	44.75	10.83	7.16	1.37	12.77	55.04	48.44	81.53	6.14	6.78	3.55	2.39	2.51	1.91
Hamirpur	346,442	163,197	183,245	29.91	41.68	19.42	12.68	2.37	21.87	64.85	49.41	94.35	1.89	2.49	0.74	1.87	2.54	0.58
Una	345,997	170,936	175,061	27.30	47.66	7.42	6.50	0.83	12.04	57.03	53.50	79.12	8.12	8.74	4.23	2.28	2.34	1.86
Bilaspur	278,652	138,442	140,210	30.87	45.73	16.19	14.21	2.46	25.82	71.24	62.88	94.54	1.38	1.69	0.53	1.42	1.73	0.56
Mandi	720,603	355,914	364,689	37.91	47.17	28.87	8.71	1.89	15.37	78.13	67.75	94.67	1.49	1.71	1.13	1.22	1.65	0.53
Kullu	281,421	145,753	135,668	42.80	52.93	31.91	5.89	0.91	11.24	82.81	76.47	94.10	2.28	2.71	1.53	0.83	0.99	0.55
Lahul and Spiti	31,294	17,224	14,070	54.18	63.60	42.64	10.76	5.30	17.43	51.69	38.42	75.91	5.15	3.60	7.98	0.77	0.72	0.85
Shimla	491,272	252,811	238,461	44.02	52.99	34.51	6.33	1.21	11.76	73.19	61.58	92.09	4.01	4.99	2.41	0.50	0.73	0.11
Solan	334,989	174,274	160,715	35.10	52.43	16.31	11.30	1.70	21.70	62.21	55.13	86.90	2.20	2.37	1.59	1.32	1.52	0.65
Sirmaur	341,621	179,875	161,746	41.30	54.95	26.12	7.16	1.51	13.44	77.22	70.09	93.91	3.50	4.16	1.96	1.01	1.33	0.24
Kinnaur	71,270	38,394	32,876	47.32	58.85	33.85	5.10	1.22	9.64	54.49	40.72	82.45	5.13	4.96	5.46	2.80	3.57	1.24

Source: Directorate of Census Operations, Government of Himachal Pradesh, Shimla, 1991.

TABLE 4.H6

Average Size of Households (1991) and Dependency Ratio by Sex and Place of Residence, 1981

State/district	All areas							Rural							Urban						
	Size of house-hold	Total dependency ratio			Old age dependency ratio			Size of house-hold	Total dependency ratio			Old age dependency ratio			Size of house-hold	Total dependency ratio			Old age dependency ratio		
	1991	Total	Male	Female	Total	Male	Female	1991	Total	Male	Female	Total	Male	Female	1991	Total	Male	Female	Total	Male	Female
Himachal Pradesh	**5.34**	**47.08**	**48.04**	**46.10**	**7.50**	**8.31**	**6.68**	**5.48**	**47.87**	**49.19**	**46.53**	**7.70**	**8.59**	**6.80**	**4.18**	**37.55**	**35.49**	**40.13**	**5.06**	**5.16**	**4.93**
Chamba	5.33	45.79	45.46	46.14	6.70	7.46	5.89	5.42	46.28	45.97	46.61	6.80	7.59	5.96	4.42	39.08	38.69	39.51	5.30	5.64	4.91
Kangra	5.38	47.97	50.27	45.71	7.66	8.85	6.48	5.42	48.32	50.76	45.92	7.74	8.97	6.54	4.62	41.26	41.23	41.30	5.97	6.62	5.26
Hamirpur	5.34	51.36	56.42	46.95	9.28	10.65	8.10	5.40	51.84	57.39	47.09	9.44	10.91	8.18	4.57	42.14	40.94	43.60	6.35	6.35	6.36
Una	5.35	49.75	52.86	46.72	9.86	11.00	8.75	5.39	50.21	53.59	46.96	10.00	11.25	8.80	4.96	44.19	44.62	43.71	8.15	8.15	8.15
Bilaspur	5.62	48.91	50.81	47.02	8.45	9.36	7.54	5.72	49.39	51.55	47.25	8.58	9.58	7.60	4.38	39.27	37.23	41.80	5.78	5.41	6.25
Mandi	5.41	48.37	49.51	47.24	7.12	7.82	6.41	5.52	49.19	50.71	47.70	7.28	8.08	6.49	4.24	38.01	35.88	40.67	5.06	4.89	5.27
Kullu	5.27	44.72	44.32	45.15	6.00	6.38	5.59	5.42	45.44	45.40	45.49	6.13	6.55	5.68	3.81	35.23	31.87	39.95	4.35	4.41	4.27
Lahul and Spiti	4.82	36.73	32.88	41.75	6.49	5.65	7.59	4.82	36.73	32.88	41.75	6.49	5.65	7.59	–	–	–	–	–	–	–
Shimla	5.00	42.68	41.34	44.20	6.38	6.84	5.86	5.48	44.83	44.25	45.47	6.92	7.51	6.27	3.72	31.09	27.79	36.04	3.51	3.70	3.23
Solan	5.37	46.84	47.25	46.39	7.23	7.96	6.45	5.64	48.05	48.97	47.07	7.58	8.41	6.72	3.99	36.79	34.24	40.07	4.30	4.57	3.96
Sirmaur	5.78	45.69	44.96	46.52	6.94	7.90	5.83	5.95	46.15	45.46	46.93	7.09	8.15	5.89	4.62	40.87	39.77	42.16	5.32	5.41	5.21
Kinnaur	4.34	41.87	38.83	45.32	7.77	6.33	9.40	4.34	41.87	38.83	45.32	7.77	6.33	9.40	–	–	–	–	–	–	–

Source: Directorate of Census Operations, Government of Himachal Pradesh, Shimla, 1981 and 1991.

TABLE 4.H7

Number of Females in the Age-group 15–44 and Percentage of Married Females in Different Age Groups

State/district	Urban					Rural				
	Number of females in age group	Percentage of married females in the age group				Number of females in age group	Percentage of married females in the age group			
	15–44	10–14	15–19	20–4	15–44	15–44	10–14	15–19	20–4	15–44
Himachal Pradesh	**72,985**	**0.38**	**14.93**	**63.89**	**68.89**	**846,801**	**1.56**	**32.82**	**88.34**	**78.22**
Chamba	5175	0.68	14.96	59.00	65.47	61,119	2.60	42.16	90.82	80.82
Kangra	11,471	0.11	12.06	62.58	66.94	207,627	0.37	19.67	84.22	72.98
Hamirpur	3333	0.33	14.38	74.60	71.92	69,155	0.52	27.01	92.91	77.15
Una	5338	0.48	11.88	68.47	68.96	62,235	0.31	15.68	78.21	70.85
Bilaspur	2536	0.68	23.76	66.98	71.88	50,898	1.80	46.22	95.5	83.77
Mandi	10,561	0.37	16.47	63.43	69.96	127,954	1.46	46.40	93.98	83.46
Kullu	3630	0.50	16.86	66.38	68.82	46,755	0.64	31.66	87.78	78.39
Lahul and Spiti	–	–	–	–	–	6585	0.94	15.36	60.26	62.6
Shimla	17,525	0.32	13.75	59.69	67.98	89,676	1.32	32.57	85.51	77.93
Solan	7338	0.59	18.84	69.84	72.25	56,329	2.58	45.87	91.89	82.39
Sirmaur	6077	0.40	15.14	65.54	69.31	56,347	8.40	57.99	94.34	87.52
Kinnaur	–	–	–	–	–	12,125	1.26	23.63	69.94	67.63

Source: Directorate of Census Operations, Government of Himachal Pradesh, Shimla, 1991.

TABLE 4.H8
Child Mortality Estimates by Districts for All Areas, 1991

State/district	q(1)			q(2)			q(3)			q(5)		
	M	F	P	M	F	P	M	F	P	M	F	P
Himachal Pradesh	**84** (101)	**81** (89)	**82** (92)	**90** (133)	**82** (113)	**86** (123)	**95** (138)	**89** (119)	**92** (124)	**98** (142)	**92** (136)	**95** (139)
Chamba	109	93	104	110	98	106	112	107	111	113	114	113
Kangra	79	74	77	89	84	87	97	92	95	100	99	100
Hamirpur	65	65	65	70	69	70	76	74	75	82	79	81
Una	70	74	72	79	76	77	84	83	84	92	97	96
Bilaspur	70	71	71	74	72	73	77	74	75	80	84	82
Mandi	69	69	69	84	74	79	86	78	82	92	87	90
Kullu	101	102	102	108	109	109	114	112	114	115	116	116
Lahul and Spiti	61	56	59	100	78	94	107	91	100	124	118	122
Shimla	112	77	104	118	102	110	123	107	116	133	119	126
Solan	87	81	84	97	85	94	102	92	97	105	99	101
Sirmaur	94	93	94	111	104	107	116	102	109	124	111	118
Kinnaur	124	122	123	134	192	134	153	192	144	159	212	152

Note: Figures in parentheses are for the year 1981.

Sources: District Level Estimates of Fertility and Child Mortality for 1991 and their Relations with Other Variables: Occasional Paper No. 1 of 1997, Office of the Registrar General, India; Directorate of Census Operations, Government of Himachal Pradesh, Shimla, 1991.

TABLE 4.H9
Districtwise Adjusted Fertility Indices

State/district	1981				1991			
	GFR	GMFR	TFR	TMFR	GFR	GMFR	TFR	TMFR
Himachal Pradesh	**152**	**194**	**4.7**	**5.8**	**118**	**158**	**3.6**	**5.3**
Chamba	161	202	4.9	6.0	148	193	4.5	6.0
Kangra	146	198	4.8	5.9	109	153	3.4	5.3
Hamirpur	136	176	4.3	5.2	97	129	3.0	4.3
Una	142	197	4.9	6.3	110	157	3.5	5.3
Bilaspur	151	181	4.5	5.4	112	142	3.3	4.6
Mandi	157	189	4.6	5.5	119	154	3.5	4.9
Kullu	157	201	4.9	6.2	137	178	4.0	5.8
Lahul and Spiti	130	204	4.2	6.0	122	195	3.8	6.2
Shimla	152	197	4.7	6.1	119	162	3.5	5.7
Solan	156	191	4.6	5.6	122	160	3.5	4.9
Sirmaur	160	187	4.9	5.6	150	190	4.5	6.0
Kinnaur	153	223	4.9	6.7	136	192	4 0	6.2

Source: Directorate of Census Operations, Government of Himachal Pradesh, Shimla, 1991.

TABLE 4.P1

Distribution of Persons across MPCE Classes for Rural and Urban Areas and Gini Ratio of Consumption Expenditure, 1987–8

Rural areas			Urban areas		
MPCE class	Persons	Average expenditure in MCPE class	MPCE class	Persons	Average expenditure in MCPE class
00–65	5	38.15	00–90	0	–
65–80	13	73.77	90–110	0	–
80–95	36	88.20	110–135	40	124.50
95–110	50	102.24	135–160	63	145.47
110–25	75	118.02	160–185	55	169.28
125–40	95	132.26	185–215	134	199.74
140–60	133	150.04	215–255	141	234.85
160–80	108	169.74	255–310	94	287.27
180–215	165	195.92	310–385	198	340.12
215–80	152	241.76	385–520	125	443.05
280–5	99	319.99	520–700	94	604.16
385 and above	69	574.71	700 and above	56	998.61
All classes	1000	209.61	All classes	1000	345.70

Note: Gini Ratio for Rural areas = 0.271
Gini Ratio for Urban areas = 0.296
FGT Index of Poverty for Rural Areas = 0.0123
FGT Index of Poverty for Urban Areas = 0.0014
Source: NSS Consumer Expenditure Survey.

TABLE 4.P2

Districtwise Distribution of Landholdings by Agricultural Operational Land Owned, Marginal Farmers, 1990–1

State/district	Total		SC		ST	
	Number of holdings	Total land owned*	Number of holdings	Total land owned*	Number of holdings	Total land owned*
Himachal Pradesh	**538,039**	**218,041.00**	**148,746**	**58,847.00**	**20,911**	**9451.00**
Chamba	43,728	19,849.00	5827	2601.00	12,636	5822.00
Kangra	162,772	56,431.00	33,161	10,780.00	36	11.00
Hamirpur	42,005	18,179.00	11,260	4136.00	0	0.00
Una	41,263	15,711.00	8726	3220.00	0	0.00
Bilaspur	26,462	13,308.00	8710	4133.00	652	343.00
Mandi	86,711	35,926.00	29,104	11,530.00	914	436.00
Kullu	42,021	16,139.00	12,906	4901.00	1678	486.00
Lahul and Spiti	1767	918.00	250	132.00	1517	786.00
Shimla	47,168	20,513.00	19,114	7991.00	224	85.00
Solan	19,405	9760.00	8345	4297.00	83	46.00
Sirmaur	19,426	9004.00	9024	4162.00	179	97.00
Kinnaur	5311	2303.00	2319	964.00	2992	1339.00

Note: * Land owned is in hectares.

Source: Provisional Results of Agricultural Census, 1990–1, Directorate of Economics and Statistics, Government of Himachal Pradesh, Shimla.

TABLE 4.P2.1

Districtwise Distribution of Landholdings by Agricultural Operational Land Owned, Medium Farmers, 1990–1

State/district	Total		SC		ST	
	Number of holdings	Total land owned*	Number of holdings	Total land owned*	Number of holdings	Total land owned*
Himachal Pradesh	**36,539**	**206,925.76**	**2261**	**12,527.40**	**1081**	**5,831.21**
Chamba	751	3844.98	20	96.69	159	789.46
Kangra	7151	41,537.00	219	1219.00	0	0.00
Hamirpur	2541	14,203.31	35	199.52	0	0.00
Una	3862	23,156.12	123	715.09	0	0.00
Bilaspur	1243	6514.04	35	177.05	48	245.89
Mandi	2815	14,776.72	117	581.36	64	363.22
Kullu	757	4083.00	22	121.00	6	31.00
Lahul and Spiti	219	1125.41	1	4.32	218	1121 09
Shimla	5985	31,340.94	385	2165.92	15	85.89
Solan	5145	30,025.82	720	3935.96	11	50.86
Sirmaur	5589	33,664.81	577	3273.76	86	527.92
Kinnaur	481	2653.61	7	37.73	474	2615.88

Note: * Land owned is in hectares.

Source: Provisional Results of Agricultural Census, 1990–1, Directorate of Economics and Statistics, Government of Himachal Pradesh, Shimla.

TABLE 4.P2.2

Districtwise Distribution of Landholdings by Agricultural Operational Land Owned, Large Farmers, 1990–1

State/district	Total		SC		ST	
	Number of holdings	Total land owned*	Number of holdings	Total land owned*	Number of holdings	Total land owned*
Himachal Pradesh	**5528**	**100,092.44**	**175**	**2401.99**	**79**	**1338.40**
Chamba	34	900.43	0	0.00	1	26.17
Kangra	1127	30,739.00	12	189.00	0	0.00
Hamirpur	212	4208.76	0	0.00	0	0.00
Una	1221	21,109.81	17	198.05	0	0.00
Bilaspur	50	719.54	0	0.00	0	0.00
Mandi	78	981.07	0	0.00	1	19.11
Kullu	28	352.00	0	0.00	1	11.00
Lahul and Spiti	10	171.66	0	0.00	10	171.66
Shimla	653	7944.01	19	213.49	2	40.10
Solan	565	8915.84	50	718.53	1	10.45
Sirmaur	1506	23,270.43	77	1082.92	19	280.02
Kinnaur	44	779.89	0	0.00	44	779.89

Note: * Land owned is in hectares.

Source: Provisional Results of Agricultural Census, 1990–1, Directorate of Economics and Statistics, Government of Himachal Pradesh, Shimla.

5 Survey Report for Himachal Pradesh

The units of observation and analysis of this study are rural households. The total number of rural households selected in the sample is 1210 (of which 35 were non-response), spread over 65 villages and eight districts in the state.

TABLE 5.1
Allocation of Sample Households in Various Strata

Stratum number	Stratum: HH category/ religion/caste	Stratum: Occupation	Selected sample households
1	Households containing at least one pregnant woman		113
2	Households containing at least one child aged less than 12 months but no pregnant women		116
3	Scheduled castes	Marginal farmer	88
4	Scheduled castes	Small farmer	25
5	Scheduled castes	Large farmer	0
6	Scheduled castes	Agricultural labourer	87
7	Scheduled castes	Other	81
8	Others	Marginal farmer	251
9	Others	Small farmer	85
10	Others	Large farmer	44
11	Others	Agricultural labourer	104
12	Others	Other	216
	Total		1210

5.1 Major Findings

The survey has collected a number of indicators in the areas of income and material well-being, education, and health care facilities for rural Himachal Pradesh. However, here we consider a few selected variables for analysis. These are (i) household and per capita income; (ii) poverty line groups; (iii) asset ownership; (iv) literacy rate; (v) net enrolment rate; (vi) expenditure on morbidity; (vii) immunization; and (viii) CBR; and (viii) CDR.

The analysis focuses on an evaluation of the intra-group differentials for these indicators. An attempt has also been made to highlight the gender disparity in accessing education and health care facilities.

5.1.1 Household and Per Capita Income

The household income for rural Himachal Pradesh is Rs 23,973 and the per capita income is Rs 4168. Among the household income groups, the per capita income in the up to Rs 20,000 income group is Rs 2165. It increases to Rs 4717 in the Rs 20,001–40,000 income group, which is more than double of the former group. The per capita income of the household income groups Rs 40,001 to Rs 62,000 and Rs 62,001 to Rs 86,000 is Rs 6276 and Rs 9593, respectively. In the landholding groups, the per capita income of the households increases with an increase in landholding. The landless wage earners have the lowest per capita income (Rs 2104) preceded by marginal (Rs 3910), small (Rs 4781), and medium (Rs 6177) landholders. The per capita income of all landowners (Rs 4175) and all land non-owners (Rs 4067) shows that the difference between the two categories is very small. This may be due to the fact that the land non-owners are the salaried class or professionals employed in the villages. They may be outsiders so they do not possess any land at the place of employment.

The per capita income of the people varies according to the occupation of the head of the household. The highest per capita income (Rs 5637) was reported for the salaried, professional, and self-employed group followed by other occupations (Rs 1968), and cultivators (Rs 3537). Wage earners have the lowest per capita income of Rs 2752. The per capita income of SC households is only Rs 3554, while for the higher castes it is Rs 4422. In the household size group, this need not to explain that as the household size increases the household income increases but the per capita income decreases.

The per capita income by the poverty line group shows a very clear picture about rural Himachal Pradesh. People belonging to the lower segment below the poverty line group have a household income of Rs 7774 and a per capita income of Rs 1163, with a very large household size (6.7). The per capita income of the upper segment below the poverty line group is Rs 2286, while the per capita income of the lower segment above the poverty line group is Rs 4190. For the upper segment above the poverty line group, the per capita income is Rs 9429 which is around eight times more than that for the lower segment below the poverty line group. This indicates clearly that there exists a vast disparity between the rich and the poor people in the state.

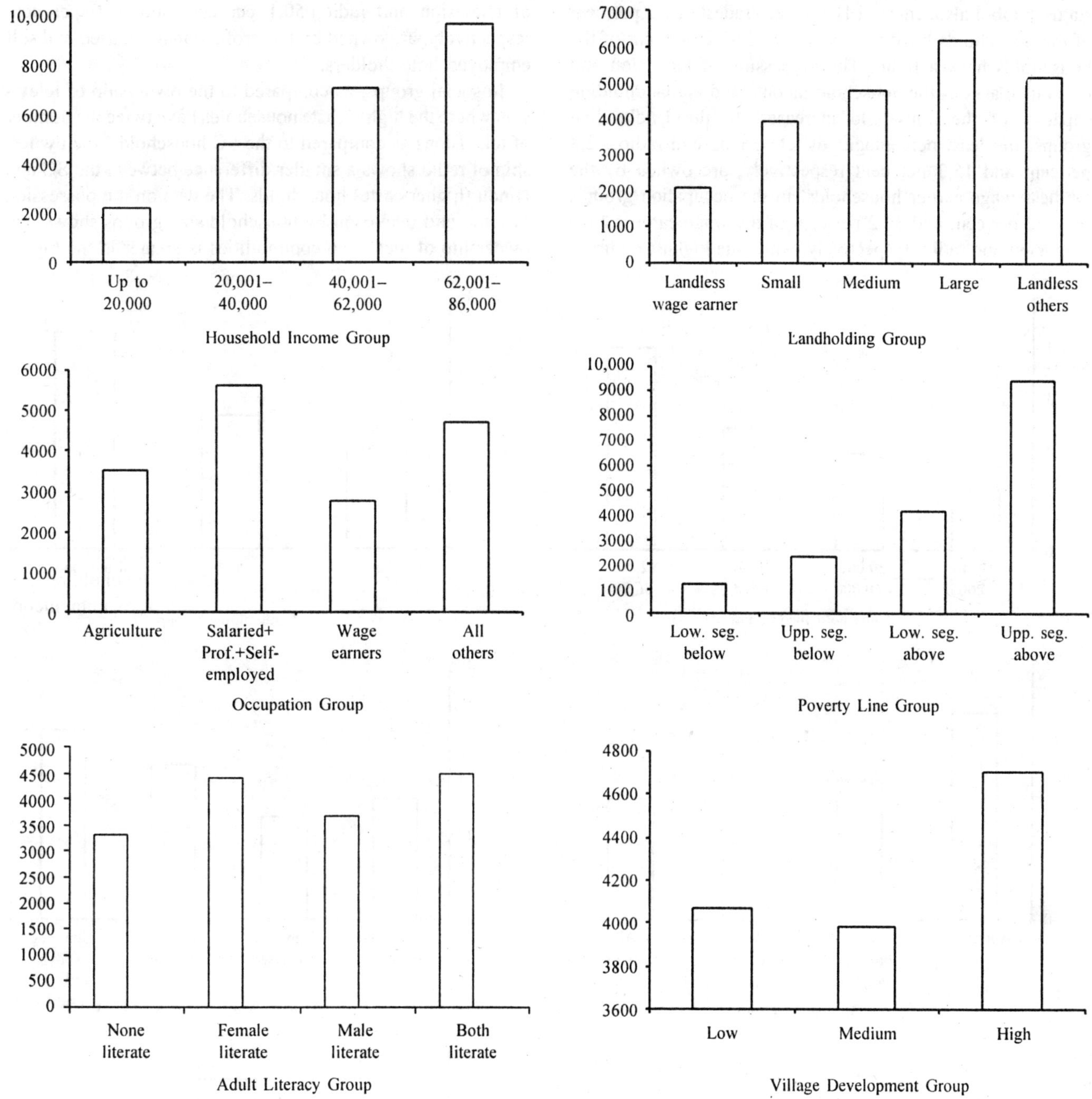

FIGURE 5.1: **Per Capita Income by Population Group (in Rupees per annum)**

The per capita income by adult literacy group shows that households with both male and female literate and households with the female literate have more per capita income than the households in which only the male is literate. The per capita income of the village development groups does not show a clear picture as the village development level goes up, although the household income increases with an increase in the level of the village development.

5.1.2 Asset Ownership

This section discusses the asset ownership of people of different groups in rural Himachal Pradesh, including ownership of house. The ownership of house shows that 97.2 per cent households have their own houses. Among all the population groups, only 81.1 per cent of the landless wage earners have their own house. These landless wage earners may be the people who have migrated in from other areas, working in various development projects having no houses of their own. It further shows that only 90.3 per cent of all land non-owners have houses.

The possession of television and radio in rural India, apart from being a medium of information and entertainment, is a status symbol also. In rural Himachal Pradesh, 27.9 per cent of the households have a television and 47.2 per cent of the households have a radio. The possession of television and radio increases as the household income and the landholding capacity of the household increases. In the landholding groups, the least percentages of televisions and radios, 2.8 per cent and 15.3 per cent respectively, are owned by the landless wage earner households. In the occupation groups, only 72 per cent and 33.2 per cent of the wage earners have television and radio, respectively, while the highest numbers of television and radio, 50.1 per cent and 61.9 per cent respectively, are owned by the professional, salaried and self employed householders.

In social groups, as compared to the ownership of television where the higher caste households have twice the number of televisions as compared to the SC households, the ownership of radio shows a smaller difference between the SC and Hindu (higher caste) households. The data on the possession of radio and television by household size groups shows that ownership of these two commodities is greater in the bigger

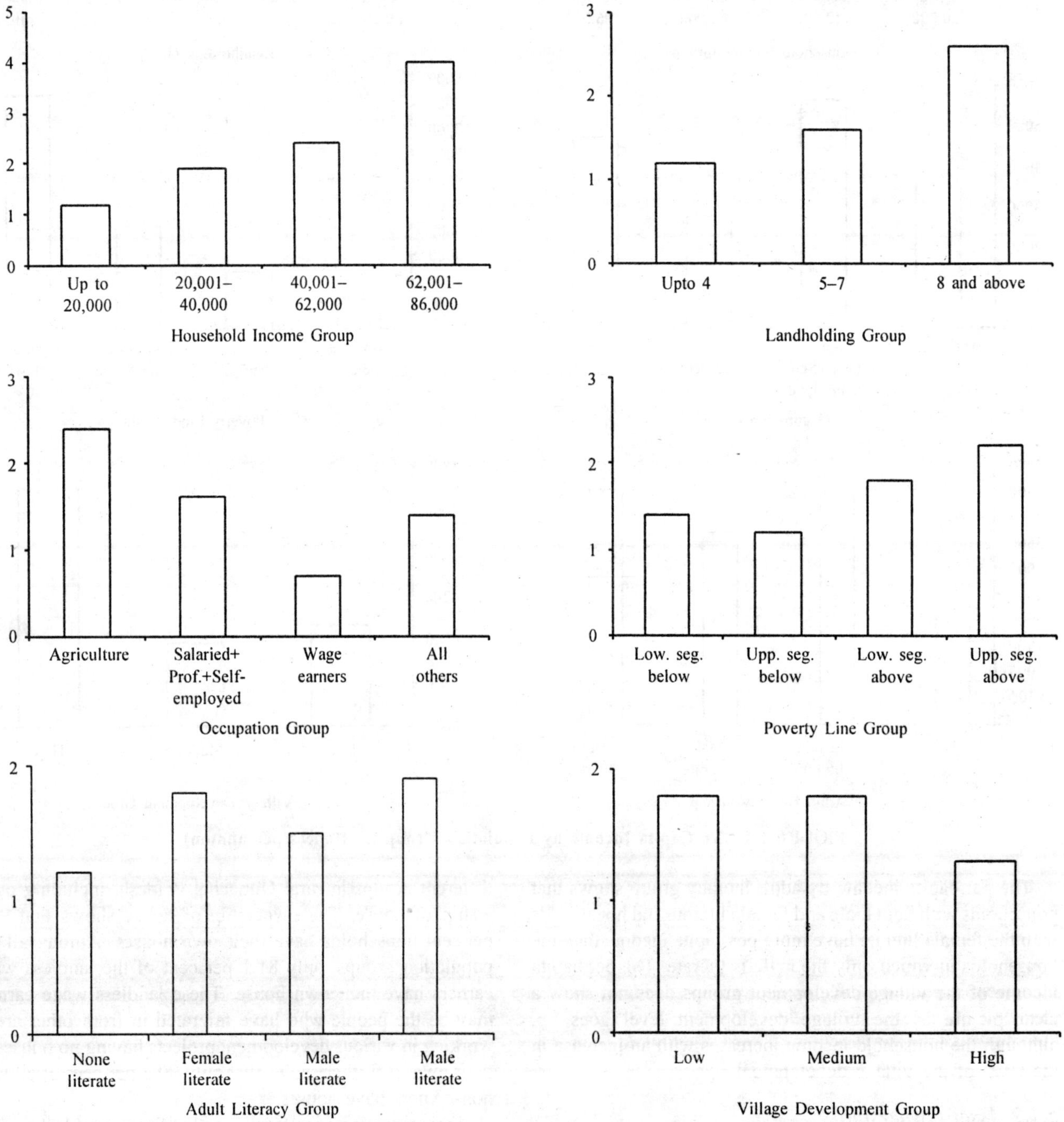

FIGURE 5.2: **Ownership of Land by Population Group (in acres)**

households, and the ownership of television increases more in the small households than the ownership of radio. 42.5 per cent of the households in the low developed villages have a radio; this percentage increases to 46.9 per cent in the medium developed villages and 54.5 per cent in the highly developed villages. In case of ownership of television, 17.9 per cent of households in the low developed villages have television. This percentage increases to 30.8 in the medium developed villages and 36.7 in the highly developed villages. This indicates that the ownership of television has become higher in the developed villages than the ownership of radio, presumably because of the high price of television as compared to that of the radio.

The ownership of electric fans is also a status symbol and depends on the economic position of the households. It is also determined by many other factors, from which the electrification of the household and the climatic condition of the region are more important. Himachal Pradesh being a hilly state, the annual temperature experienced is below 15° C in the districts lying between the north to north-eastern and southern districts of the state such as Chamba, Kangra, Mandi, Shimla and Solan, and also the districts of Lahul and Spiti, Kinnaur and Sirmaur. In this temperature, the use of electric fans is, thus, limited. In spite of the fact that the state is highly electrified (88 per cent of all households have electricity) (see Table A5.5), only 37.1 per cent of the total households have electric fans. Even then, this is a high proportion.

A bicycle is an essential asset for the rural people, although this depends on the income and occupation of the people and, at times, on the relief of the area. In rural Himachal Pradesh, only 11.8 per cent of the households have a bicycle, which is a very small figure.

Like the possession of a bicycle, the possession of a motorcycle/scooter also depends on the topography and the terrain of the region, as also the economic condition, occupation and landholding status of the household. In Himachal Pradesh, which has mostly a rugged terrain, only 3.3 per cent households own a motorcycle or scooter, in spite of the fact that it is a moderately developed state. The table shows that households having a higher income own a greater percentage of motorcycles or scooters than the lower income groups. The salaried, professionals and the self-employed households own a higher percentage of motorcycles or scooters than the cultivators and wage earners. Among the village development groups, the ownership of the vehicles increases with the development of the villages.

5.1.3 Literacy Rate

The total literacy rate of rural Himachal Pradesh is 68.2 per cent. The male literacy rate is 79.4, while for females the literacy rate is only 57.0 per cent. In the household income groups, the least literacy rate for both males and females is reported in the income group of up to Rs 20,000 (see Table A5.7). As the household income increases the literacy rate increases and the gender disparity becomes lower. In the occupation groups, there exist vast differences. The wage earners have the lowest literacy rate of 60.1 per cent, followed by cultivators with a 61.8 per cent literacy rate, and the salaried have the highest literacy rate of 79.7 per cent. There is a vast difference in the literacy rate found between the SCs (63.47 per cent) and the Hindus (70.5 per cent). The gender disparity in these two segments of the population is also very high. The differences in literacy among segments in the poverty line groups and adult literacy groups are prominent. The total literacy rate of 62.1 per cent in the lower segment below the poverty line group increases to 64.5 per cent in the upper segment below the poverty line group. The two segments above the poverty line have literacy rates of 69.7 per cent and 75.1 per cent respectively, which are both above the state average.

The literacy rate in the adult literacy group shows that 64.5 per cent of the total population in the female literate households are literate, as compared to 55.7 per cent of male literate households and only 21.2 per cent of none literate households. The gender disparity in male literate households is highest (0.28), which indicates that the high literacy rate of female literate households is an advantage in making other members of the family literate.

5.1.4 Ever Enrolment Rate (EER)

Ever enrolment rate of children in the age group of 6–14 years in elementary education for the state is reported to be 92.7 per cent. For boys, the ever enrolment rate is 95.5 per cent, while for girls the EER is 90.0 per cent, that is, 5.5 per cent less than that for the boys. The household income plays an important role in the determination of enrolment. However, the data on EER shows a decline of enrolment with an increase in income. The lowest EER in the income groups, seen in the high income group of Rs 62,001 to Rs 86,000 income group, may be due to the small sample size. But the gender disparity in the high income group is less and the EER for girls is higher than that for boys. Landholding, which is another indicator of well-being, is positively related with EER. The most important aspect in this group is that the landless wage earners have a high EER as compared to the landholders.

The EER by occupational groups shows that the other occupations group has the highest (97.4 per cent) enrolment, followed by the salaried, professionals and self-employed group (97.0 per cent). Cultivators have a distinct third position (89.1 per cent), followed by wage earners (88.5 per cent). Although the overall EER in Himachal Pradesh is very high, the SCs have a very low rate (88.6 per cent) as compared to the Hindus (higher castes). The EER by household size groups reveals that the enrolment in the bigger households is lower than in the smaller household size groups, but the discontinuation and non-attendance rate in the smaller households is higher than that in the bigger households.

The data on the EER by adult literacy groups shows that the EER is highest where both the male and female head of

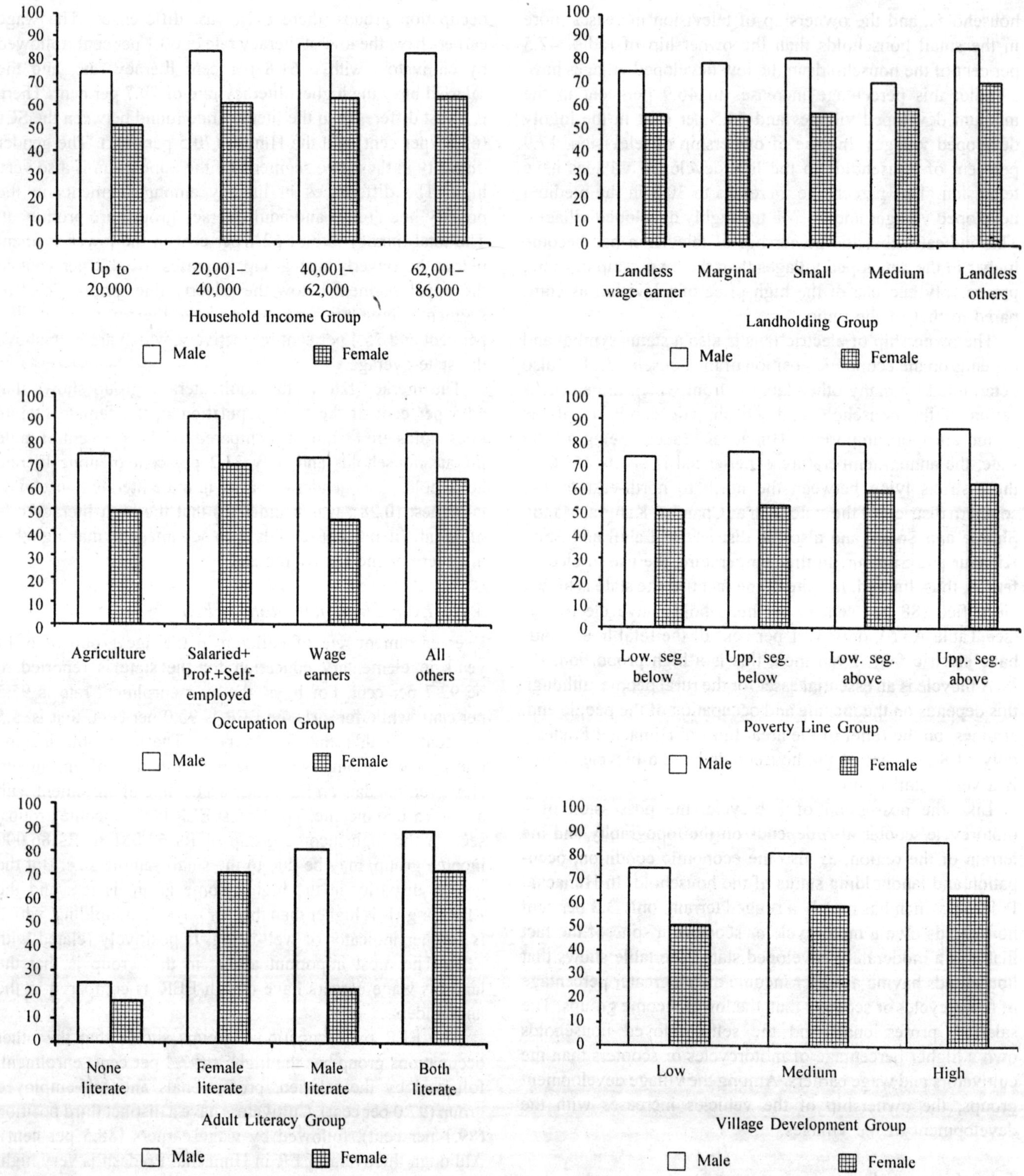

FIGURE 5.3: Male–Female Literacy Rate by Population Group (in percentage)

the households are literate (97.9 per cent), followed by the female literate households (97.4 per cent). Male literate households have a distinct third position with a low (86.3 per cent) enrolment, followed by households in the none literate group (80.0 per cent).

5.1.5 Expenditure on Morbidity

Table A5.18 gives information about per person expenditure on both short-term and long-term morbidity in terms of fees and medicines. The information on expenditure on per sick and per reporting house is also given in the same table. The

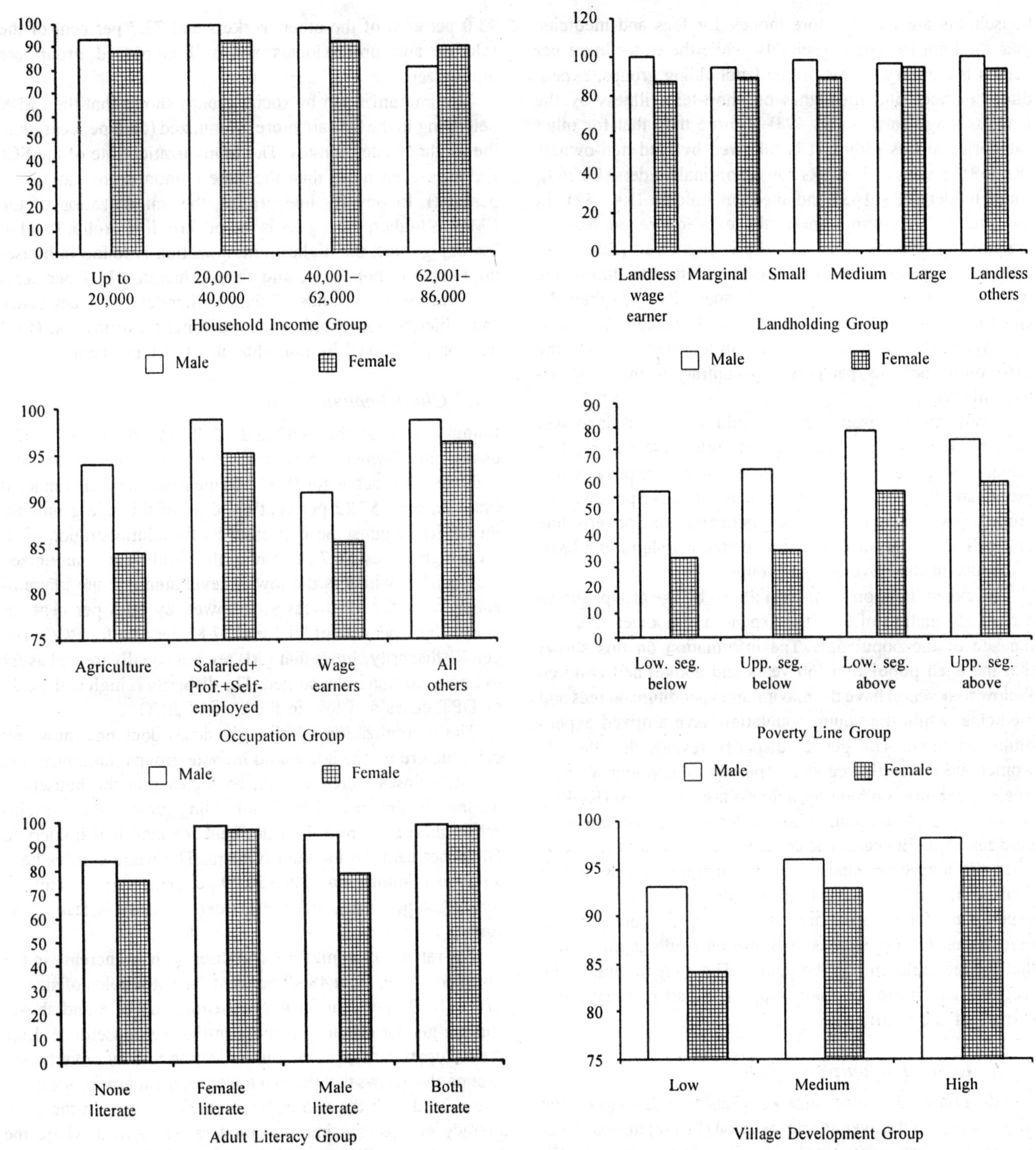

FIGURE 5.4: **Male–Female Ever Enrolment Rate by Population Group (percentage)**

expenditure on short-term morbidity for the state is Rs 256, and the per-head expenditure on girls is more than that for the boys. For long-term illness, the expenditure is Rs 209 and the gender disparity is less. The expenditure per sick per household is Rs 1295.

The expenditure in terms of fees and medicine for both short-term and long-term illness varies for the various population groups. It is determined by the household income, occupation of the head of the household and the landholding size. The pattern of expenditure shows that the low income households are paying more money for fees and medicine than the high income households, while the expenditure per person is contrary to this. In the landholding groups, expenditure on fees and medicines on short-term illness by the landless wage earners (Rs 498) is more than that for other categories in this group. It is followed by land non-owners (Rs 368), landless others (Rs 296), marginal holders (Rs 269), small holders (Rs 163) and medium holders (Rs 147). In the case of long-term illness, the expenditure on fees by landholding groups does not show any clear picture. In occupation groups also, in the case of short-term illness, the wage earners are spending more money (Rs 348) than the cultivators (Rs 218) and salaried, professionals and self-employed (Rs 237). In the case of long-term illness the expenditure per sick per person is contrary to that in short-term illness.

In poverty line groups the expenditure per sick increases from Rs 1017 in the lower segment below the poverty line group to Rs 1026 in the upper segment below the poverty line group, and Rs 1192 in the lower segment above poverty line group to Rs 1456 in the upper segment above the poverty line group. There is no discrimination of the people on the basis of gender in the poverty line groups.

The expenditure on short-term illness by age groups shows a clear cut picture of how the expenditure is determined by the age of the population. The information on this shows that the aged population (60 years and above) and children (below four years) have the maximum expenditure on fees and medicine, while the young population have a mixed expenditure on them. The gender disparity reveals that the old women are discriminated as compared to the young women. The expenditures on long-term illness are the highest (Rs 407) for the aged population, followed by that for people aged between 35 to 59 years. The children have mixed expenditure since the long-term illnesses are comparatively few among them. The information of gender disparity on long-term expenditure for the girls are less. The expenditure per sick reveals that the per sick expenditure on adults is more than that for the children and the young. This may be due to the fact that adults are the main supporters and primary bread earners of the family.

5.1.6 Mother Immunization Rate

The data on mother immunization (Table A5.22) shows that 67.1 per cent of the ever married women (EMW) in rural areas of the state are immunized. The immunization of EMW increases steadily with an increase in the household income. Similarly, in the case of the landholding groups, it rises from 64.5 per cent in the marginal landholding households to 86.2 per cent in the medium sized landholdings. In occupation groups, the wage earners have the lowest immunization rate of 49.9 per cent, while 66.9 per cent of the cultivators, 73.0 per cent of the other workers and 73.7 per cent of the salaried and professionals and self employed group are immunized.

The immunization by social groups shows that the EMW belonging to the SCs are more immunized (68.6 per cent) than the (higher caste) Hindus. The immunization rate of the SCs EMW is even more than the state immunization rate (67.1 per cent). In poverty line groups, the immunization of the EMW is higher, the higher is the poverty line group. In adult literacy groups, the highest immunization is found in households having both male and female literate (74.7 per cent) followed by households of female literates (67.4 per cent). Male literate households have a distinct third position (51.7 per cent) followed by none-literates (47.1 per cent).

5.1.7 Child Immunization

Immunization of children aged 12–23 months consists of 8 doses, out of which 3 doses each are for diphtheria and polio and one dose each is for BCG and measles. In rural Himachal Pradesh, only 57.22 per cent children of this age group are immunized against these diseases by the administration of all these eight doses. 66.7 per cent of the children are immunized for measles, which is the lowest level amongst the immunization rates for all diseases, followed by 69.8 per cent for polio, 70.87 per cent of DPT and 77.81 per cent for BCG. The gender disparity shows that girls are not equally treated as far as immunization is concerned. The disparity is high in the case of DPT doses and low in the case of BCG.

The immunization by all eight doses does not show any clear picture by the household income groups. Immunization by BCG doses increases with an increase in the household income. In the case of the landholding groups, the immunization increases from 53.5 per cent for marginal holders to 64.66 per cent for medium holders. The wage earners have a higher immunization rate (50.29 per cent) than the cultivators (48.4 per cent), and the gender disparity is less in the former case.

The rate of immunization increases with an increase in the household size, from 48.47 per cent for households of size up to 4 to 61.70 per cent for the household size of 8 and above. But the gender disparity is more in the big households. Like the occupation groups, the immunization rate by poverty line groups also shows that the two lower segment groups are more immunized than the two upper segment groups. In the adult literacy groups, the immunization rate is lowest where the households are illiterates (22.2 per cent), followed by the male literate households (39.26 per cent) and female literate households (56.22 per cent). The immunization rate is the highest (64.33 per cent) where both the male and female head of the households are literates. The illiterates have a lower immunization rate and the gender disparity is the lowest among them as compared to the literate groups.

TABLE A5.1
Levels of Income and Distribution of Households by Population Group in Rural Himachal Pradesh

Population group	No. of sample households	% estmtd households	Household size	Income (Rs per year) Per household	Per capita
Household income					
Up to 20,000	663	53.6	5.1	11,121	2165
20,001–40,000	373	30.9	6.0	28,291	4717
40,001–62,000	132	11.2	7.1	49,399	6976
62,001–86,000	38	2.9	7.5	71,935	9593
Landholding					
Landless wage earner	33	2.8	4.7	9994	2104
Marginal	932	76.3	5.6	21,812	3910
Small	130	10.1	7.3	35,002	4781
Medium	49	3.9	8.1	49,918	6175
Landless others	72	6.1	3.9	20,101	5138
All land owners	1120	91.1	5.9	24,657	4175
All land non-owners	105	8.9	4.2	16,967	4067
Occupation					
Agriculture	446	35.4	5.9	20,875	3537
Salaried+prof.+s.empl.	284	23.8	6.2	34,841	5637
Wage earners	240	19.3	5.3	14,650	2752
All groups others	255	21.4	5.4	25,428	4698
Caste					
SCs	336	27.5	5.5	19,560	3554
Religion					
Hindus	1182	96.5	–	23,933	4176
Household size					
Up to 4	377	31.5	3.2	18,454	5822
5–7	599	49.5	5.8	23,626	4079
8 and above	249	18.9	9.9	34,069	3425
Poverty line					
Lower segment below	237	18.5	6.7	7774	1163
Upper segment below	249	20.1	5.9	13,464	2286
Lower segment above	460	37.9	5.8	24,376	4190
Upper segment above	279	23.4	4.8	45,160	9429
Adult literacy					
None literate	162	13.2	3.9	12,972	3318
Female literate	81	6.7	5.2	22,940	4385
Male literate	322	26.0	5.4	19,639	3663
Both literate	660	54.1	6.5	28,881	4474
Village development					
Low	401	32.4	5.7	23,162	4073
Medium	557	45.4	5.9	23,551	3986
High	267	22.2	5.5	26,026	4710
All groups	**1225**	**100.0**	**5.8**	**23,973**	**4168**

TABLE A5.2

Sourcewise Distribution of Household Income by Population Group in Rural Himachal Pradesh

Population group	Percentage distribution w.r.t. total household income											
	Agr.+alld act.	Artisan/ ind. work	Petty trd. sm. bus.	Or. trd. bus.	Salaried empl.	Qualified prof.	Rent/int./ dividend	Agr. wage	Non-agr. wage	Other sources	All sources	Actual value
Household income												
Up to 20,000	42.0	5.1	3.1	0.1	10.3	0.3	1.3	1.4	27.4	9.0	100.0	11,121
20,001–40,000	35.9	7.5	3.1	1.1	31.6	0.5	1.5	0.1	9.3	9.5	100.0	28,291
40,001–62,000	31.1	5.6	1.8	0.5	42.9	0.0	1.2	0.0	7.7	9.2	100.0	49,399
62,001–86,000	42.3	0.0	2.7	4.0	41.2	2.3	0.2	0.0	1.3	6.0	100.0	71,935
Landholding												
Landless wage earner	2.0	0.2	0.0	0.0	3.0	0.0	0.0	2.6	92.1	0.0	100.0	9994
Marginal	33.6	6.1	2.9	1.0	30.5	0.5	1.4	0.5	14.2	9.2	100.0	21,812
Small	54.6	2.0	2.2	0.4	26.9	0.0	1.3	0.1	5.7	6.9	100.0	35,002
Medium	57.3	1.8	1.4	6.2	19.5	0.0	0.3	0.0	3.5	10.1	100.0	49,918
Landless others	7.0	20.8	12.0	0.0	40.2	1.6	2.2	0.3	0.6	15.3	100.0	20,101
All land owners	39.6	5.0	2.6	1.4	28.7	0.4	1.3	0.4	11.8	8.9	100.0	24,657
All land non-owners	6.1	17.1	9.8	0.0	33.4	1.3	1.8	0.7	17.3	12.5	100.0	16,967
Occupation												
Agriculture	78.0	1.5	1.3	0.5	6.7	0.1	0.5	0.3	7.8	3.3	100.0	20,875
Salaried+prof.+s.empl.	19.0	0.6	0.8	0.2	74.8	1.2	1.0	0.0	1.9	0.6	100.0	34,841
Wage earners	21.1	1.2	0.3	0.0	3.7	0.0	0.1	2.1	69.9	1.6	100.0	14,650
All others	19.2	21.8	10.4	4.7	2.9	0.0	3.6	0.1	3.5	33.8	100.0	25,428
Caste												
SCs	29.8	8.3	2.4	0.1	27.5	0.2	0.5	1.2	24.7	5.4	100.0	19,560
Religion												
Hindus	37.7	4.9	3.1	1.2	29.5	0.5	1.4	0.4	12.1	9.3	100.0	23,932
Household size												
Up to 4	35.9	3.4	3.1	0.3	26.3	1.4	2.1	0.5	12.7	14.3	100.0	18,454
5–7	35.7	7.6	3.9	2.1	28.9	0.2	1.3	0.5	12.4	7.5	100.0	23,626
8 and above	42.1	4.5	1.4	0.7	31.8	0.1	0.8	0.2	11.1	7.3	100.0	34,069
Poverty line												
Lower segment below	54.5	6.3	2.0	0.3	6.5	0.0	0.8	1.4	23.5	4.7	100.0	7774
Upper segment below	41.3	5.8	3.7	0.1	11.2	0.0	1.3	1.5	27.4	7.7	100.0	13,464
Lower segment above	37.0	7.1	2.8	0.5	28.0	0.5	1.3	0.3	14.1	8.5	100.0	24,376
Upper segment above	34.6	4.5	3.3	2.4	37.6	0.6	1.5	0.0	4.9	10.6	100.0	45,160
Adult literacy												
None literate	49.5	4.7	1.4	0.0	7.9	0.1	0.8	1.2	23.2	11.1	100.0	12,972
Female literate	34.0	3.7	1.0	0.0	11.3	0.0	1.9	0.0	7.1	40.9	100.0	22,940
Male literate	43.2	4.5	3.0	0.6	20.3	0.2	0.8	0.7	21.3	5.6	100.0	19,639
Both literate	34.6	6.5	3.5	1.8	36.0	0.6	1.5	0.2	8.4	6.9	100.0	28,881
Village development												
Low	42.5	3.5	3.5	1.9	22.8	0.3	1.3	0.2	11.7	12.3	100.0	23,162
Medium	36.5	5.2	1.6	0.9	30.6	0.0	1.4	0.6	13.8	9.4	100.0	23,551
High	32.8	9.6	5.2	1.2	34.2	1.5	1.4	0.1	9.5	4.5	100.0	26,026
All groups	**37.5**	**5.7**	**3.1**	**1.3**	**29.0**	**0.5**	**1.3**	**0.4**	**12.1**	**9.1**	**100.0**	–
Actual value	**9747**	**13,886**	**14,492**	**28,978**	**21,942**	**17,901**	**8271**	**2828**	**8468**	**13,285**	–	**23,973**

TABLE A5.3

Average (per reporting household) Wage Income and its Share in Total Income by Population Group in Rural Himachal Pradesh

Population group	Agricultural wage		Non-agr. wage		All wages		Wage as per cent of total income			Per cent of households getting 50% income from wages
	Average wage	Per cent of rep. hhs	Average wage	Per cent of rep. hhs	Average wage	Per cent of rep. hhs	Agr. wage	Non-agr. wage	All wage	
Household income										
Up to 20,000	2689	5.3	6253	44.3	6038	48.2	1.3	24.9	26.2	29.3
20,001–40,000	2127	1.0	9156	26.2	9083	26.6	0.1	8.5	8.5	6.4
40,001–62,000	0	0.0	17,644	19.6	17,644	19.6	0.0	7.0	7.0	6.0
62,001–86,000	450	3.2	12,112	6.9	8462	10.1	0.0	1.2	1.2	0.0
Landholding										
Landless wage earner	1575	15.0	8937	93.7	8608	100.0	2.4	83.8	86.1	100.0
Marginal	2788	3.3	7706	36.7	7450	39.2	0.4	13.0	13.4	19.9
Small	2143	1.2	7147	25.5	7023	26.3	0.1	5.2	5.3	3.8
Medium	450	2.3	6321	24.8	5815	27.2	0.0	3.1	3.2	0.0
Landless others	4000	1.3	4009	2.8	4006	4.1	0.3	0.6	0.8	0.0
All land owners	2680	3.0	7617	34.6	7364	36.9	0.3	10.7	11.0	17.1
All land non-owners	1958	5.5	8626	31.0	8223	33.8	0.6	15.8	16.4	31.0
Occupation										
Agriculture	1416	4.0	4953	30.0	4533	34.1	0.3	7.1	7.4	0.0
Salaried+prof.+s.empl.	2356	0.6	6836	8.7	6555	9.3	0.0	1.7	1.8	0.0
Wage earners	3860	7.4	9607	96.9	9590	100.0	1.9	63.5	65.5	94.9
All others	1949	1.1	6037	13.3	5873	14.0	0.1	3.2	3.2	0.0
Caste										
SCs	3120	6.6	9200	47.8	8658	53.1	1.1	22.5	23.5	33.1
Religion										
Hindus	2744	3.1	7654	34.3	7381	36.8	0.4	11.0	11.3	18.3
Household size										
Up to 4	2354	3.3	7372	28.9	7042	31.3	0.4	11.5	12.0	21.4
5–7	2904	3.4	7435	35.9	7166	38.6	0.4	11.3	11.7	19.1
8 and above	1893	2.7	8727	39.2	8612	40.3	0.1	10.0	10.2	11.3
Poverty line										
Lower segment below	1475	6.6	3890	42.7	3757	46.8	1.3	21.4	22.6	25.8
Upper segment below	3088	6.0	6611	50.7	6338	55.8	1.4	24.9	26.3	30.4
Lower segment above	4152	1.7	9406	33.2	9276	34.5	0.3	12.8	13.1	16.3
Upper segment above	1064	0.8	13,224	15.2	12,943	15.6	0.0	4.5	4.5	5.4
Adult literacy										
Literate	2526	5.7	7092	38.5	6701	42.9	1.1	21.1	22.2	26.3
Female literate	0	0.0	7685	19.2	7685	19.2	0.0	6.4	6.4	13.7
Male literate	2562	5.0	7394	51.3	7156	54.8	0.7	19.3	20.0	28.0
Both literate	2609	2.2	8192	26.9	7942	28.5	0.2	7.6	7.8	12.3
Village development										
Low	2998	1.3	6764	36.3	6683	37.4	0.2	10.6	10.8	17.9
Medium	2478	5.6	8336	35.5	7802	39.7	0.6	12.6	13.2	19.6
High	2779	1.2	7810	28.8	7816	29.2	0.1	8.6	8.8	16.5
All groups	**2571**	**3.2**	**7699**	**34.3**	**7434**	**36.6**	**0.3**	**11.0**	**11.4**	**18.4**

TABLE A5.4

Land and Livestock Owned by Households by Population Group in Rural Himachal Pradesh

Population group	Landholdings			Draught animals			Milch animals		
	Per cent of rep. hhs	Average rep. hh	Average all groups	Per cent of rep. hhs	Average rep. hh	Average all groups	Per cent of rep. hhs	Average rep. hh	Average all groups
Household income									
Up to 20,000	88.4	1.2	1.1	53.5	2.3	1.2	82.1	2.5	2.1
20,001–40,000	92.9	1.9	1.7	57.5	2.1	1.2	88.7	2.3	2.0
40,001–62,000	96.6	2.4	2.3	51.4	2.7	1.4	90.4	3.0	2.7
62,001–86,000	100.0	4.0	4.0	80.2	2.1	1.7	100.0	3.0	3.0
Landholding									
Landless wage earner	–	–	–	17.0	1.6	0.3	53.6	6.9	3.7
Marginal	100.0	1.0	1.0	56.1	2.2	1.2	88.7	2.2	2.0
Small	100.0	3.6	3.6	81.0	2.5	2.1	99.2	3.4	3.4
Medium	100.0	6.8	6.8	85.4	2.9	2.5	95.2	4.1	3.9
Landless others	–	–	–	3.3	2.0	0.1	33.6	1.7	0.6
All land owners	100.0	1.7	1.7	60.3	2.3	1.4	90.2	2.5	2.2
All land non-owners	–	–	–	7.5	1.7	0.1	39.8	3.9	1.5
Occupation									
Agriculture	98.0	2.4	2.3	70.6	2.3	1.6	92.3	2.6	2.4
Salaried+prof.+s.empl.	92.5	1.6	1.5	47.3	2.1	1.0	86.8	2.3	2.0
Wage earners	85.7	0.7	0.6	53.5	2.4	1.3	82.4	2.4	2.0
All groups others	83.0	1.4	1.2	41.7	2.3	0.9	76.7	2.7	2.1
Caste									
SCs	88.6	1.2	1.1	51.9	2.3	1.2	78.5	2.5	2.0
Religion									
Hindus	91.7	1.7	1.6	57.0	2.3	1.3	85.8	2.5	2.1
Household size									
Up to 4	85.4	1.2	1.0	38.0	2.1	0.8	73.6	2.0	1.5
5–7	92.0	1.6	1.5	57.6	2.2	1.3	89.3	2.4	2.2
8 and above	98.3	2.6	2.6	79.7	2.5	2.0	96.6	3.3	3.2
Poverty line									
Lower segment below	92.4	1.4	1.3	64.4	2.4	1.5	86.8	2.9	2.5
Upper segment below	88.5	1.2	1.1	60.3	2.3	1.4	85.4	2.5	2.2
Lower segment above	91.6	1.8	1.6	54.8	2.2	1.2	87.2	2.2	1.9
Upper segment above	91.6	2.2	2.0	45.7	2.3	1.1	82.9	2.7	2.3
Adult literacy									
None literate	84.3	1.2	1.0	48.8	2.1	1.0	75.2	2.4	1.8
Female literate	90.6	1.8	1.6	53.2	2.0	1.1	87.4	2.1	1.8
Male literate	92.2	1.5	1.4	63.9	2.3	1.5	85.6	2.7	2.3
Both literate	92.3	1.9	1.7	53.5	2.3	1.2	88.2	2.5	2.2
Village development									
Low	94.6	1.8	1.7	68.4	2.4	1.6	89.4	2.6	2.3
Medium	92.7	1.8	1.7	54.8	2.3	1.3	87.5	2.5	2.2
High	82.8	1.3	1.1	38.5	1.9	0.7	76.7	2.4	1.9
All groups	**91.1**	**1.7**	**1.5**	**55.6**	**2.3**	**1.3**	**85.7**	**2.5**	**2.2**

TABLE A5.5

Amenities Available in Households by Population Group in Rural Himachal Pradesh

Population group	Percentage of households having					
	Kutcha house	Separate kitchen	Electric connection	Protected water	Piped water	Toilet
Household income						
Up to 20,000	65.4	71.6	82.8	72.3	68.6	11.9
20,001–40,000	54.2	91.6	93.1	78.5	76.2	17.4
40,001–62,000	37.8	90.0	96.9	69.9	66.6	28.0
62,001–86,000	44.8	94.0	90.9	66.1	63.5	17.7
Landholding						
Landless wage earner	79.2	34.2	75.1	71.2	65.4	2.8
Marginal	60.6	80.6	87.4	73.6	70.4	14.7
Small	47.5	94.6	92.2	74.5	71.9	20.3
Medium	37.1	92.7	86.8	76.5	74.1	16.9
Landless others	46.6	70.4	92.7	76.0	70.0	32.3
All land owners	57.7	82.8	88.1	73.8	70.8	15.5
All land non-owners	55.7	60.3	87.2	74.5	68.5	23.1
Occupation						
Agriculture	63.3	79.1	80.8	70.0	66.7	17.0
Salaried+prof.+s.empl.	42.6	90.5	97.9	77.6	75.1	20.0
Wage earners	72.1	67.9	81.1	67.4	63.2	7.0
All groups others	51.6	84.9	95.0	82.1	78.6	19.1
Caste						
SCs	69.6	73.5	86.1	75.2	72.8	13.6
Religion						
Hindus	58.3	81.3	88.1	73.9	71.5	15.8
Household size						
Up to 4	60.7	77.3	86.8	73.7	70.5	14.6
5–7	58.8	82.4	89.2	75.9	72.8	15.5
8 and above	49.0	83.2	86.7	68.8	64.7	20.9
Poverty line						
Lower segment below	63.4	70.5	77.6	75.4	70.5	15.5
Upper segment below	65.7	72.6	84.5	67.6	64.4	7.8
Lower segment above	57.6	84.7	90.9	75.9	73.0	15.6
Upper segment above	45.8	90.2	94.4	74.7	71.9	25.0
Adult literacy						
None literate	77.8	56.0	62.4	63.0	60.6	8.3
Female literate	53.6	87.0	97.6	81.3	80.6	11.2
Male literate	66.8	75.5	81.4	66.9	62.8	10.1
Both literate	48.6	88.9	96.2	79.0	75.5	21.7
Village development						
Low	65.3	78.5	82.7	72.4	71.6	9.0
Medium	53.3	80.3	89.1	69.7	65.0	15.5
High	54.9	85.8	93.4	84.5	80.5	28.3
All groups	**57.5**	**80.9**	**88.0**	**73.9**	**70.6**	**16.2**

TABLE A5.6

Consumption of Foodgrains and Utilization of PDS by Population Group in Rural Himachal Pradesh

Population group	Annual household income (Rs)	Annual per capita income (Rs)	Per capita consumption of foodgrains (kg/month)	Percentage of households using PDS	Quantity of cereals (kg) bought from PDS (per hh/month)	Per cent requirement of cereals met from PDS
Household income						
Up to 20,000	11,121	2165	17.6	73.8	40.3	40.6
20,001–40,000	28,291	4717	17.4	78.9	44.1	42.4
40,001–62,000	49,399	6976	17.0	77.4	56.1	44.1
62,001–86,000	71,935	9593	16.5	65.7	47.3	32.7
Landholding						
Landless wage earner	9994	2104	15.2	69.8	54.0	63.8
Marginal	21,812	3910	17.2	78.1	42.0	41.7
Small	35,002	4781	18.7	68.4	56.4	38.1
Medium	49,918	6175	17.0	68.5	53.1	31.8
Landless others	20,101	5138	17.9	66.4	41.1	57.3
All land owners	24,657	4175	17.4	76.4	43.7	40.3
All land non-owners	16,967	4067	17.0	67.4	45.2	59.6
Occupation						
Agriculture	20,875	3537	17.5	73.6	41.4	37.0
Salaried+prof.+s.empl.	34,841	5637	17.3	79.0	50.9	46.7
Wage earners	14,650	2752	16.9	73.5	43.2	43.7
All others	25,428	4698	17.8	77.0	40.0	40.5
Caste						
SCs	19,560	3554	17.6	77.6	43.0	42.2
Religion						
Hindus	23,932	4176	17.4	75.7	45.6	41.5
Household size						
Up to 4	18,454	5822	19.3	73.9	27.1	39.8
5–7	23,626	4079	17.8	77.7	45.9	43.8
8 and above	34,069	3425	15.7	72.9	66.3	38.4
Poverty line						
Lower segment below	7774	1163	17.0	74.9	45.0	38.1
Upper segment below	13,464	2286	17.3	74.4	47.2	41.1
Lower segment above	24,376	4190	17.4	76.7	45.2	43.5
Upper segment above	45,160	9429	17.8	75.4	37.7	41.1
Adult literacy						
None literate	12,972	3318	16.8	72.0	31.5	42.1
Female literate	22,940	4385	17.5	80.3	37.4	37.9
Male literate	19,639	3663	18.0	77.2	38.2	38.1
Both literate	28,881	4474	17.2	75.2	50.3	43.1
Village development						
Low	23,162	4073	16.9	76.2	38.0	35.9
Medium	23,551	3986	17.1	74.5	46.4	41.3
High	26,026	4710	18.6	77.1	47.1	50.8
All groups	**23,973**	**4168**	**17.4**	**75.6**	**43.8**	**41.4**

TABLE A5.7
Literacy Rate (per cent) and Gender Disparity by Population Group in Rural Himachal Pradesh

Population group	Literacy rate (aged 7 and above)			
	Total	Male	Female	F/M
Household income				
Up to 20,000	62.8	74.2	51.4	0.69
20,001–40,000	71.9	83.2	60.8	0.73
40,001–62,000	74.7	86.6	62.9	0.73
62,001–86,000	73.0	82.6	63.6	0.77
Landholding				
Landless wage earner	67.2	75.5	56.5	0.75
Marginal	67.6	79.2	55.7	0.70
Small	69.3	81.6	57.7	0.71
Medium	65.2	71.1	59.6	0.84
Landless others	78.0	85.7	70.7	0.82
All land owners	67.8	79.2	56.4	0.71
All land non-owners	74.3	81.9	66.4	0.81
Occupation				
Agriculture	61.8	74.0	49.5	0.67
Salaried+prof.+s.empl.	79.7	90.0	69.5	0.77
Wage earners	60.1	72.4	45.3	0.63
All others	72.2	82.6	63.3	0.77
Caste				
SCs	63.4	75.1	50.4	0.67
Religion				
Hindus	68.3	79.5	57.1	0.72
Household size				
Up to 4	63.4	76.0	50.3	0.66
5–7	70.8	82.3	58.6	0.71
8 and above	66.9	76.4	58.4	0.76
Poverty line				
Lower segment below	62.1	74.0	50.5	0.68
Upper segment below	64.5	75.8	53.0	0.70
Lower segment above	69.7	80.2	59.8	0.75
Upper segment above	75.1	86.8	62.6	0.72
Adult literacy				
None literate	21.2	24.7	17.3	0.70
Female literate	64.5	46.6	71.4	1.53
Male literate	55.7	80.7	22.7	0.28
Both literate	80.1	88.8	71.9	0.81
Village development				
Low	62.3	73.8	50.8	0.69
Medium	69.4	80.5	58.5	0.73
High	74.5	85.0	63.2	0.74
All groups	**68.2**	**79.4**	**57.0**	**0.72**

TABLE A5.8
Ever Enrolment, Discontinuation, and Non-attendance Rates for Children (aged 6–14 years) by Population Group in Rural Himachal Pradesh

(*per cent*)

Population group	Ever enrolment rate				Discontinuation rate				Non-attendance rate			
	Total	Male	Female	F/M	Total	Male	Female	F/M	Total	Male	Female	F/M
Household income												
Up to 20,000	90.6	93.4	87.7	0.94	2.9	2.8	3.1	1.10	4.2	4.0	4.4	1.11
20,001–40,000	96.0	99.1	92.6	0.93	1.7	1.2	2.2	1.74	3.1	3.7	2.4	0.66
40,001–62,000	94.7	97.7	92.0	0.94	0.0	0.0	0.0	0.00	2.4	2.3	2.5	1.08
62,001–86,000	86.2	80.9	89.6	1.11	0.0	0.0	0.0	0.00	3.4	0.0	5.3	-
Landholding												
Landless wage earner	94.8	100.0	87.9	0.88	3.0	5.0	0.0	0.00	6.0	10.1	0.0	0.00
Marginal	92.1	94.5	89.5	0.95	2.1	1.6	2.8	1.81	3.7	3.2	4.3	1.35
Small	93.3	98.1	88.9	0.91	2.2	4.3	0.0	0.00	2.3	2.9	1.7	0.59
Medium	95.2	96.1	94.6	0.98	0.0	0.0	0.0	0.00	0.0	0.0	0.0	-
Landless others	96.9	100.0	94.1	0.94	1.7	0.0	3.4	0.00	6.3	9.9	2.7	0.28
All land owners	92.5	95.1	89.8	0.94	2.0	1.8	2.2	1.20	3.3	3.0	3.6	1.20
All land non-owners	96.2	100.0	92.2	0.92	2.2	2.0	2.4	1.19	6.2	10.0	1.9	0.19
Occupation												
Agriculture	89.1	93.9	84.3	0.90	3.3	3.4	3.2	0.92	3.9	2.6	5.3	2.00
Salaried+prof.+s.empl.	97.0	98.8	95.2	0.96	0.0	0.0	0.0	0.00	3.0	3.6	2.4	0.67
Wage earners	88.5	90.9	85.6	0.94	3.3	2.6	4.2	1.64	4.3	5.7	2.4	0.43
All others	97.4	98.6	96.3	0.98	1.4	0.7	2.1	2.89	2.9	3.2	2.6	0.81
Caste												
SCs	88.6	91.9	84.8	0.92	3.8	2.3	5.7	2.53	3.6	3.5	3.6	1.01
Religion												
Hindus	93.1	79.9	74.8	0.94	2.0	1.8	2.3	1.28	3.5	3.4	3.6	1.06
Household size												
Up to 4	95.4	97.4	92.7	0.95	4.3	1.8	8.1	4.52	8.3	8.8	7.6	0.87
5–7	93.0	95.1	90.8	0.95	1.7	2.1	1.2	0.59	3.0	2.8	3.3	1.16
8 and above	91.2	95.2	88.1	0.93	1.6	1.5	1.7	1.18	2.3	2.0	2.5	1.23
Poverty line												
Lower segment below	89.5	92.4	86.7	0.94	5.4	6.1	4.5	0.74	4.4	4.0	4.8	1.19
Upper segment below	90.9	94.4	87.4	0.93	1.1	0.7	1.5	2.16	3.2	4.2	2.1	0.50
Lower segment above	95.0	97.6	92.5	0.95	0.9	0.7	1.1	1.69	3.0	1.7	4.3	2.49
Upper segment above	95.2	96.9	93.2	0.96	1.1	0.0	2.4	0.00	3.9	6.1	1.0	0.17
Adult literacy												
None literate	80.0	83.7	75.9	0.91	4.0	2.9	5.4	1.89	9.1	6.2	12.6	2.02
Female literate	97.4	98.1	96.9	0.99	2.2	3.4	1.3	0.39	5.1	7.8	3.0	0.39
Male literate	86.3	94.0	78.0	0.83	3.8	3.2	4.7	1.46	5.4	5.8	4.8	0.83
Both literate	97.9	98.5	97.4	0.99	0.8	0.7	0.9	1.23	1.5	1.3	1.7	1.29
Village development												
Low	88.4	93.1	84.2	0.90	2.7	2.7	2.6	0.97	4.6	4.4	4.7	1.08
Medium	94.4	95.9	92.8	0.97	2.4	2.2	2.5	1.12	2.7	2.1	3.3	1.52
High	96.7	98.1	94.9	0.97	0.4	0.0	0.8	0.00	3.5	5.0	1.6	0.32
All groups	**92.7**	**95.5**	**90.0**	**0.94**	**2.0**	**1.8**	**2.2**	**1.20**	**3.5**	**3.5**	**3.5**	**0.98**

TABLE A5.9

Factors for Non-enrolment (per cent) of Children (aged 6–14 years) and Gender Disparity by Population Group in Rural Himachal Pradesh

Population group	Supply factors	Demand factors	Interest factors	Customs factors
Household income				
Up to 20,000				
Person	13.8	66.4	24.9	4.2
Gender disparity	1.78	1.01	0.96	–
20,001–40,000				
Person	–	58.8	18.7	2.8
Gender disparity	–	1.21	–	–
40,001–62,000				
Person	–	51.9	5.1	–
Gender disparity	–	1.23	–	–
62,001-86,000				
Person	–	–	42.2	–
Gender disparity	–	–	–	–
Landholding				
Landless wage earner				
Person	–	46.9	–	–
Gender disparity	–	–	–	–
Marginal				
Person	10.4	67.3	23.9	3.6
Gender disparity	1.53	1.13	0.79	–
Small				
Person	–	39.7	16.4	4.1
Gender disparity	–	–	–	–
Landless others				
Person	45.7	–	54.3	0.0
Gender disparity	–	–	–	–
All land owners				
Person	8.8	61.4	22.0	3.5
Gender disparity	1.34	1.11	0.80	–
All Land non-owners				
Person	23.9	22.4	28.3	0.0
Gender disparity	–	–	–	–
Occupation				
Agriculture				
Person	3.4	56.6	21.7	4.3
Gender disparity	1.20	1.11	0.79	–
Salaried+prof.+s.empl.				
Person	–	48.0	10.8	0.0
Gender disparity	–	1.06	–	–
Wage earners				
Person	24.5	81.0	30.2	3.6
Gender disparity	2.08	1.16	0.81	–
All others				
Person	12.3	25.1	14.6	0.0
Gender disparity	–	–	–	–
Caste				
SCs				
Person	11.3	66.9	24.6	0.0
Gender disparity	1.44	1.15	1.11	–
Religion				
Hindus				
Person	10.3	61.7	21.3	3.7
Gender disparity	1.42	0.96	0.95	0.00
Household size				
Up to 4				
Person	19.9	53.9	21.6	22.5
Gender disparity	–	1.94	–	–
5–7				
Person	13.3	64.5	27.2	1.9
Gender disparity	2.29	1.02	0.71	–
8 and above				
Person	2.2	55.2	16.3	1.2
Gender disparity	–	1.11	–	–
Poverty line				
Lower segment below				
Person	15.7	66.7	18.8	9.4
Gender disparity	0.84	1.04	1.07	–
Upper segment below				
Person	10.6	63.4	35.9	0.0
Gender disparity	–	0.74	1.06	–
Lower segment above				
Person	2.9	59.0	13.8	0.0
Gender disparity	–	2.32	0.97	–
Upper segment above				
Person	–	27.2	17.7	0.0
Gender disparity	–	1.14	–	–
Adult literacy groups				
None literate				
Person	17.8	72.9	22.6	6.4
Gender disparity	1.04	0.74	0.22	–
Male literate				
Person	7.8	66.4	21.0	0.9
Gender disparity	–	1.47	1.56	–
Both literate				
Person	–	23.5	31.0	6.4
Gender disparity	–	1.54	2.22	–
Village development				
Low				
Person	9.5	66.8	16.4	1.7
Gender disparity	0.54	0.84	1.15	–
Medium				
Person	8.9	51.6	25.8	7.0
Gender disparity	–	2.02	0.87	–
High				
Person	9.8	48.3	44.6	0.0
Gender disparity	–	0.56	0.48	–
All groups				
Person	9.4	59.8	22.3	3.3
Gender disparity	1.45	1.07	0.82	–

(Contd.)

TABLE A5.10

Factors for Discontinuation (per cent) of Children (aged 6–14 years) and Gender Disparity by Population Group in Rural Himachal Pradesh

Population group	Supply factors	Demand factors	Interest factors	Customs factors
Household income				
Up to 20,000				
Person	14.5	74.5	74.5	49.8
Gender disparity	1.91	1.14	1.14	0.69
20,001–40,000				
Person	–	75.8	75.8	69.5
Gender disparity	–	2.56	2.56	0.49
Landholding				
Landless wage warner				
Person	–	–	–	100.0
Gender disparity	–	–	–	–
Marginal				
Person	13.7	81.2	81.2	48.0
Gender disparity	1.18	1.10	1.10	0.95
Small				
Person	–	52.1	52.1	100.0
Gender disparity	–	–	–	–
Landless others				
Person	–	100.0	100.0	–
Gender disparity	–	–	–	–
All land owners				
Person	11.7	77.0	77.0	55.5
Gender disparity	1.70	1.22	1.22	0.72
All land non-owners				
Person	–	51.5	51.5	48.5
Gender disparity	–	–	–	–
Occupation				
Agriculture				
Person	12.6	76.9	76.9	55.2
Gender disparity	1.22	1.23	1.23	0.68
Wage earners				
Person	13.0	84.4	84.4	44.0
Gender disparity	–	1.55	1.55	0.37
All others				
Person	–	51.4	51.4	72.3
Gender disparity	–	–	–	0.64
Caste				
SCs				
Person	8.1	75.8	75.8	50.5
Gender disparity	–	1.61	1.61	0.53
Religion				
Hindus				
Person	11.1	77.5	77.5	53.3
Gender disparity	1.59	1.26	1.26	0.66
Household size				
Up to 4				
Person	24.7	100.0	100.0	49.6
Gender disparity	0.33	1.00	1.00	0.99
5–7				
Person	–	58.9	58.9	56.8
Gender disparity	–	1.46	1.46	0.35
8 and above				
Person	12.8	73.0	73.0	57.8
Gender disparity	–	1.09	1.09	0.76
Poverty line				
Lower segment below				
Person	17.0	70.2	70.2	58.3
Gender disparity	2.70	1.02	1.02	0.97
Upper segment below				
Person	–	100.0	100.0	66.7
Gender disparity	–	1.00	1.00	0.50
Lower segment above				
Person	–	62.1	62.1	37.9
Gender disparity	–	–	–	–
Upper segment above				
Person	–	100.0	100.0	46.1
Gender disparity	–	–	–	–
Adult literacy				
None literate				
Person	39.0	80.3	80.3	58.7
Gender disparity	0.64	2.00	2.00	1.29
Female literate				
Person	32.9	100.0	100.0	67.1
Gender disparity	–	1.00	1.00	–
Male literate				
Person	–	69.0	69.0	47.6
Gender disparity	–	1.05	1.05	0.90
Both literate				
Person	–	71.4	71.4	62.1
Gender disparity	–	2.71	2.71	0.31
Village development				
Low				
Person	8.3	85.1	85.1	50.0
Gender disparity	–	1.42	1.42	1.08
Medium				
Person	13.6	71.8	71.8	55.7
Gender disparity	0.86	1.52	1.52	0.32
High				
Person	–	–	–	100.0
Gender disparity	–	–	–	–
All groups				
Person	10.7	74.9	74.9	54.9
Gender disparity	1.71	1.36	1.36	0.63

(Contd.)

TABLE A5.11

Proportion of Population Completing Middle and Matriculation Levels and Gender Disparity by Population Group in Rural Himachal Pradesh

Population group	Middle level (aged 15+)				Matriculation level (aged 17+)			
	Total	Male	Female	F/M	Total	Male	Female	F/M
Household income								
Up to 20,000	14.0	17.6	10.4	0.59	11.0	14.8	7.2	0.49
20,001–40,000	15.9	20.0	12.1	0.60	16.7	22.5	11.1	0.49
40,001–62,000	13.4	14.6	12.3	0.85	21.9	30.5	13.3	0.44
62,001–86,000	14.8	13.4	16.3	1.21	23.4	33.7	13.2	0.39
Landholding								
Landless wage earner	11.5	15.4	6.7	0.43	8.6	8.0	9.3	1.16
Marginal	14.7	18.4	11.1	0.60	14.7	20.3	9.1	0.45
Small	14.0	17.1	10.9	0.63	16.3	23.4	9.5	0.41
Medium	13.0	12.3	13.7	1.12	18.0	23.5	12.6	0.54
Landless others	16.6	14.6	18.3	1.25	21.1	24.4	18.0	0.74
All land owners	14.5	17.8	11.2	0.63	15.2	20.9	9.6	0.46
All land non-owners	14.8	14.9	14.8	0.99	16.7	18.2	15.3	0.84
Occupation								
Agriculture	12.5	15.1	9.9	0.66	12.9	18.3	7.7	0.42
Salaried+prof.+s.empl.	18.1	21.1	15.3	0.72	22.8	30.5	15.2	0.50
Wage earners	13.1	17.1	8.3	0.48	7.5	10.1	4.5	0.44
All others	14.6	18.3	11.6	0.64	17.0	23.7	11.5	0.49
Caste								
SCs	14.3	19.0	9.2	0.48	12.1	15.4	8.6	0.56
Religion								
Hindus	14.5	17.8	11.4	0.64	15.4	20.9	10.0	0.46
Household size								
Up to 4	14.2	18.6	9.9	0.53	14.2	20.9	7.8	0.37
5–7	15.7	19.1	12.3	0.64	15.3	20.5	10.1	0.49
8 and above	12.6	14.3	11.1	0.78	15.9	20.9	11.2	0.53
Poverty line								
Lower segment below	11.9	15.6	8.4	0.54	10.7	13.9	7.6	0.55
Upper segment below	15.3	18.7	11.8	0.63	10.0	14.3	5.8	0.41
Lower segment above	14.9	17.9	12.0	0.67	16.3	22.8	10.2	0.45
Upper segment above	15.3	17.8	12.8	0.72	22.0	28.8	15.2	0.53
Adult literacy								
Female literate	12.0	0.0	15.3	0.00	7.6	0.0	10.0	0.00
Male literate	10.2	17.3	0.0	0.00	8.5	14.9	0.0	0.00
Both literate	18.1	20.6	15.8	0.77	20.5	26.9	14.4	0.53
Village development								
Low	12.2	16.5	7.8	0.47	12.5	19.2	5.6	0.29
Medium	15.1	18.2	12.1	0.67	15.6	21.0	10.6	0.51
High	16.4	17.9	14.9	0.83	18.4	22.3	14.4	0.65
All groups	**14.5**	**17.6**	**11.4**	**0.65**	**15.3**	**20.7**	**9.9**	**0.48**

TABLE A5.12

Percentage Distribution of Students (aged 6–14 years) and Gender Disparity by Type of School and Population Group in Rural Himachal Pradesh

Population group	Govt schools				Govt-aided schools				Private schools			
	Total	Male	Female	F/M	Total	Male	Female	F/M	Total	Male	Female	F/M
Household income												
Up to 20,000	97.0	96.3	97.7	1.01	0.0	0.0	0.0	–	2.9	3.4	2.3	0.68
20,001–40,000	92.7	92.9	92.3	0.99	0.3	0.0	0.6	–	6.6	6.6	6.6	1.00
40,001–62,000	93.5	90.3	96.7	1.07	1.2	1.3	1.1	0.80	5.3	8.3	2.2	0.26
62,001–86,000	72.5	52.7	83.6	1.59	1.8	0.0	2.8	–	25.7	47.3	13.5	0.29
Landholding												
Landless wage earner	100.0	100.0	100.0	1.00	0.0	0.0	0.0	–	0.0	0.0	0.0	–
Marginal	95.8	94.9	96.8	1.02	0.1	0.2	0.0	0.00	3.9	4.5	3.2	0.72
Small	96.0	95.5	96.5	1.01	1.2	1.2	1.1	0.91	2.8	3.2	2.4	0.74
Medium	93.7	96.2	92.0	0.96	0.8	0.0	1.4	–	3.9	3.8	4.0	1.06
Landless others	77.0	75.0	79.0	1.05	1.8	0.0	3.5	–	21.2	25.0	17.5	0.70
All land owners	95.4	94.5	96.4	1.02	0.3	0.3	0.2	0.71	4.1	4.8	3.2	0.67
All land non-owners	85.0	84.7	85.3	1.01	1.2	0.0	2.4	–	13.8	15.3	12.2	0.80
Occupation												
Agriculture	96.2	96.6	95.7	0.99	0.4	0.4	0.4	1.06	3.0	2.6	3.4	1.31
Salaried+prof.+s.empl.	92.3	89.9	94.7	1.05	0.8	0.7	1.0	1.49	6.9	9.4	4.3	0.46
Wage earners	97.1	96.7	97.7	1.01	0.0	0.0	0.0	–	2.9	3.3	2.3	0.68
All others	93.1	91.2	94.8	1.04	0.0	0.0	0.0	–	6.5	8.0	5.2	0.64
Caste												
SCs	97.7	97.7	97.7	1.00	0.3	0.0	0.7	–	1.7	1.7	1.6	0.90
Religion												
Hindus	94.5	93.6	95.4	1.02	0.4	0.3	0.4	1.29	4.9	5.7	4.1	0.71
Other minorities	94.1	90.1	100.0	1.11	0.0	0.0	0.0	–	5.9	9.9	0.0	0.00
Household size												
Up to 4	94.7	92.3	98.5	1.07	0.0	0.0	0.0	–	4.7	6.7	1.5	0.23
5–7	93.8	93.5	94.1	1.01	0.5	0.6	0.5	0.86	5.5	5.7	5.4	0.96
8 and above	95.9	95.0	96.7	1.02	0.2	0.0	0.4	–	3.7	5.0	2.5	0.50
Poverty line												
Lower segment below	97.7	97.3	98.1	1.01	0.0	0.0	0.0	–	2.3	2.7	1.9	0.72
Upper segment below	99.7	100.0	99.3	0.99	0.0	0.0	0.0	–	0.3	0.0	0.7	–
Lower segment above	92.4	91.2	93.7	1.03	0.4	0.0	0.8	–	6.8	8.4	5.1	0.61
Upper segment above	88.1	86.2	90.5	1.05	1.3	1.9	0.6	0.29	10.1	11.0	8.9	0.81
Adult literacy												
None literate	100.0	100.0	100.0	1.00	0.0	0.0	0.0	–	0.0	0.0	0.0	–
Female literate	97.4	98.1	96.8	0.99	0.0	0.0	0.0	–	1.8	0.0	3.2	–
Male literate	96.9	97.7	95.7	0.98	1.0	0.6	1.5	2.40	2.1	1.6	2.8	1.70
Both literate	92.2	89.9	94.5	1.05	0.2	0.3	0.1	0.50	7.3	9.5	5.1	0.53
Village development												
Low	94.9	94.2	95.6	1.01	0.1	0.0	0.2	–	4.5	5.3	3.7	0.70
Medium	95.8	95.0	96.6	1.02	0.4	0.4	0.4	1.06	3.6	4.3	3.0	0.70
High	91.7	90.8	92.8	1.02	0.7	0.6	0.7	1.22	7.7	8.6	6.4	0.74
All groups	**94.6**	**93.7**	**95.5**	**1.02**	**0.4**	**0.3**	**0.4**	**1.29**	**4.8**	**5.6**	**3.9**	**0.70**

TABLE A5.13

Percentage Distribution of Household Annual Expenditure on Schooling (6–14 years) in Government Schools and Gender Disparity by Population Group in Rural Himachal Pradesh

(Annual expenditure in rupees)

Population group	Govt schools						
	Fees	Books	Coaching	Transpt	BL	Total	#St/Rhhd
Household income							
Up to 20,000							
Person	10.1	88.2	0.6	0.0	1.0	1381	1.9
Gender disparity	1.00	0.98	0.35	0.00	0.00	0.84	0.92
20,001–40,000							
Person	8.3	90.4	1.0	0.3	0.0	1597	1.8
Gender disparity	0.95	1.00	1.02	0.00	3.68	0.81	0.86
40,001–62,000							
Person	8.3	84.0	0.2	5.4	2.1	2088	2.2
Gender disparity	1.02	1.12	0.00	0.35	0.00	1.09	1.08
62,001–86,000							
Person	20.8	79.2	0.0	0.0	0.0	1289	1.6
Gender disparity	3.22	0.82	0.00	0.00	0.00	4.80	2.80
Landholding							
Landless wage earner							
Person	7.6	90.1	2.3	0.0	0.0	1025	2.0
Gender disparity	1.36	1.01	0.00	0.00	0.00	0.50	0.69
Marginal							
Person	9.0	88.9	0.5	0.8	0.8	1484	1.8
Gender disparity	1.05	1.00	0.34	0.37	4.07	0.84	0.90
Small							
Person	12.5	85.9	0.6	1.0	0.0	2039	2.2
Gender disparity	0.83	1.01	0.52	0.00	0.00	1.15	1.04
Medium							
Person	6.9	83.9	0.0	4.3	4.8	1979	2.9
Gender disparity	1.31	1.20	0.00	0.17	0.00	1.17	1.37
Landless others							
Person	7.1	87.6	4.6	0.7	0.0	1411	1.8
Gender disparity	0.93	0.93	3.69	0.00	0.00	0.94	1.07
All land owners							
Person	9.5	88.2	0.5	1.0	0.9	1570	1.9
Gender disparity	1.02	1.00	0.57	0.57	1.63	0.91	0.95
All land non-owners							
Person	7.2	88.4	3.9	0.5	0.0	1265	1.9
Gender disparity	1.04	0.95	2.25	0.00	0.00	0.78	0.90
Occupation							
Agriculture							
Person	9.4	89.7	0.3	0.6	0.0	1553	2.0
Gender disparity	0.87	1.00	1.24	0.00	0.00	0.81	0.87
Salaried+prof.+s.empl.							
Person	9.5	86.5	1.6	2.0	0.5	1747	1.8
Gender disparity	1.30	1.00	0.99	0.35	0.00	0.84	1.00
Wage earners							
Person	9.9	89.7	0.3	0.0	0.0	1094	1.8
Gender disparity	1.22	0.98	0.00	0.00	0.00	0.79	0.77
All others							
Person	8.7	87.3	0.4	0.6	3.0	1654	2.0
Gender disparity	0.84	1.01	0.60	0.00	2.10	1.23	1.14
Caste							
SCs							
Person	9.2	89.1	0.4	1.3	0.0	1402	1.7
Gender disparity	1.16	0.99	0.15	1.13	0.00	0.79	0.75

(Contd.)

TABLE A5.13 (contd.)

Population group	Govt schools						
	Fees	Books	Coaching	Transpt	BL	Total	#St/Rhhd
Religion							
Hindus							
Person	9.4	88.4	0.8	0.8	0.7	1550	1.9
Gender disparity	1.02	0.99	0.84	0.73	2.84	0.91	0.95
Household size							
Up to 4							
Person	9.2	86.6	0.7	0.3	3.1	1283	1.4
Gender disparity	0.95	0.93	0.00	2.26	0.00	0.66	0.67
5–7							
Person	8.6	89.2	0.7	1.2	0.3	1438	1.8
Gender disparity	1.05	1.01	1.44	0.44	0.00	0.83	0.90
8 and above							
Person	10.4	87.3	0.9	0.9	0.6	1961	2.4
Gender disparity	0.97	1.02	0.72	0.90	0.04	1.17	1.17
Poverty line							
Lower segment below							
Person	11.8	88.1	0.0	0.0	0.0	1398	2.0
Gender disparity	0.89	1.02	0.00	0.00	0.00	0.82	0.97
Upper segment below							
Person	8.6	90.5	0.8	0.0	0.1	1468	2.0
Gender disparity	1.20	0.99	0.21	0.00	3.28	0.91	0.91
Lower segment above							
Person	8.7	88.0	1.1	0.6	1.6	1666	1.9
Gender disparity	1.04	0.98	1.10	0.77	2.65	0.97	0.99
Upper segment above							
Person	8.9	85.6	0.7	4.0	0.8	1585	1.6
Gender disparity	1.01	1.04	1.21	0.60	0.00	0.82	0.82
Adult literacy							
None literate							
Person	8.3	91.2	0.5	0.0	0.0	1196	1.8
Gender disparity	1.01	1.01	0.00	0.00	0.00	0.65	0.80
Female literate							
Person	8.2	91.8	0.0	0.0	0.0	1576	2.1
Gender disparity	1.01	1.00	0.00	0.00	0.00	1.19	1.28
Male literate							
Person	8.7	89.3	0.0	0.0	2.0	1356	1.8
Gender disparity	1.01	0.95	0.00	0.00	0.00	0.81	0.74
Both literate							
Person	9.9	86.8	1.2	1.6	0.6	1707	1.9
Gender disparity	1.02	1.02	0.90	0.59	0.03	0.94	1.03
Village development							
Low							
Person	8.5	89.5	0.9	0.6	0.6	1588	2.0
Gender disparity	1.16	1.02	0.05	0.20	0.00	0.92	1.04
Medium							
Person	10.2	87.4	0.2	0.8	1.4	1522	1.9
Gender disparity	0.90	0.99	0.00	0.75	3.62	0.95	0.96
High							
Person	8.8	87.7	1.6	1.9	0.1	1543	1.8
Gender disparity	1.12	0.98	1.93	0.88	3.84	0.78	0.78
All groups							
Person	9.3	88.2	0.7	0.9	0.8	1548	1.9
Gender disparity	1.02	1.00	0.85	0.62	1.65	0.90	0.94

Notes: BL: Boarding and lodging; #St/Rhhd: Number of students per rural household.

TABLE A5.14

Percentage Distribution of Household Annual Expenditure on Schooling (6–14 years) in Private Schools and Gender Disparity by Population Group in Rural Himachal Pradesh

(Annual expenditure in rupees)

Population group	Private schools						
	Fees	Books	Coaching	Transpt	BL	Total	#St/Rhhd
Household income							
Up to 20,000							
Person	38.8	55.2	0.0	6.0	0.0	2251	1.5
Gender disparity	0.84	0.89	0.00	0.00	0.00	0.84	0.62
20,001–40,000							
Person	34.9	63.2	0.9	1.0	0.0	1930	1.3
Gender disparity	0.78	1.16	0.00	2.56	0.00	0.81	0.86
40,001–62,000							
Person	22.5	70.9	3.4	3.3	0.0	4086	1.3
Gender disparity	0.98	1.04	0.00	1.56	0.00	0.29	0.27
62,001–86,000							
Person	23.9	36.7	0.0	7.9	31.5	6295	1.7
Gender disparity	1.67	1.78	0.00	0.00	0.00	0.08	0.51
Landholding							
Marginal							
Person	30.5	63.7	1.9	3.8	0.0	2447	1.3
Gender disparity	0.95	0.97	0.00	5.33	0.00	0.56	0.63
Small							
Person	37.5	60.3	0.0	2.2	0.0	1296	1.1
Gender disparity	1.32	0.83	0.00	1.40	0.00	0.72	0.76
Medium							
Person	35.0	65.0	0.0	0.0	0.0	872	1.0
Gender disparity	0.57	1.37	0.00	0.00	0.00	1.44	1.52
Landless others							
Person	36.9	61.9	0.0	1.2	0.0	2794	1.7
Gender disparity	0.75	1.16	0.00	3.53	0.00	0.85	0.71
All land owners							
Person	29.1	56.5	1.3	4.8	8.3	2759	1.3
Gender disparity	1.09	1.15	0.00	1.80	0.00	0.40	0.62
All land non-owners							
Person	36.9	61.9	0.0	1.2	0.0	2794	1.7
Gender disparity	0.75	1.16	0.00	3.53	0.00	0.85	0.71
Occupation							
Agriculture							
Person	30.9	61.0	0.0	8.1	0.0	1776	1.2
Gender disparity	1.41	0.67	0.00	0.00	0.00	1.24	1.15
Salaried+prof.+s.empl.							
Person	27.6	53.1	2.0	4.9	12.4	3767	1.4
Gender disparity	0.96	1.46	0.00	0.61	0.00	0.29	0.44
Wage earners							
Person	41.5	58.5	0.0	0.0	0.0	1284	1.5
Gender disparity	0.52	1.43	0.00	0.00	0.00	0.33	0.52
All others							
Person	34.9	64.7	0.0	0.5	0.0	2724	1.7
Gender disparity	0.91	1.05	0.00	1.66	0.00	0.60	0.71
Caste							
SCs							
Person	32.9	67.1	0.0	0.0	0.0	1570	1.0
Gender disparity	0.47	1.33	0.00	0.00	0.00	0.40	0.68
Religion							
Hindus							
Person	30.5	57.2	1.1	4.3	6.9	2760	1.4
Gender disparity	1.02	1.17	0.00	1.60	0.00	0.49	0.66

(Contd.)

TABLE A5.14 (contd.)

Population group	Private schools						
	Fees	Books	Coaching	Transpt	BL	Total	#St/Rhhd
Household size							
Up to 4							
Person	43.5	56.5	0.0	0.0	0.0	1721	1.1
Gender disparity	0.28	1.60	0.00	0.00	0.00	0.05	0.14
5–7							
Person	29.7	65.6	0.5	4.1	0.0	2584	1.4
Gender disparity	1.02	0.93	0.00	3.99	0.00	0.82	0.85
8 and above							
Person	27.8	44.5	2.4	5.4	19.9	3956	1.5
Gender disparity	1.39	1.57	0.00	0.12	0.00	0.23	0.58
Poverty line							
Lower segment below							
Person	37.2	47.9	0.0	14.8	0.0	2299	1.4
Gender disparity	0.99	0.64	0.00	0.00	0.00	1.82	0.70
Upper segment below							
Person	27.3	72.7	0.0	0.0	0.0	1100	1.0
Gender disparity	0.00	0.00	0.00	0.00	0.00	0.00	0.00
Lower segment above							
Person	33.8	48.9	0.6	3.7	13.1	2821	1.5
Gender disparity	0.92	1.60	0.00	0.24	0.00	0.39	0.59
Upper segment above							
Person	24.6	71.0	2.1	2.3	0.0	2934	1.3
Gender disparity	1.11	0.99	0.00	1.31	0.00	0.39	0.64
Adult literacy							
Female literate							
Person	29.6	70.4	0.0	0.0	0.0	1588	1.0
Gender disparity	0.00	0.00	0.00	0.00	0.00	0.00	0.00
Male literate							
Person	32.6	67.4	0.0	0.0	0.0	1125	1.2
Gender disparity	0.74	1.16	0.00	0.00	0.00	1.11	1.28
Both literate							
Person	30.4	56.5	1.2	4.5	7.4	3111	1.5
Gender disparity	1.05	1.13	0.00	1.95	0.00	0.40	0.52
Village Development							
Low							
Person	35.7	62.9	1.4	0.0	0.0	2056	1.6
Gender disparity	0.96	1.06	0.00	0.00	0.00	0.54	0.72
Medium							
Person	26.3	51.8	0.0	6.0	16.0	3527	1.4
Gender disparity	0.89	1.64	0.00	0.40	0.00	0.33	0.66
High							
Person	32.4	61.1	2.1	4.4	0.0	2623	1.3
Gender disparity	1.08	0.86	0.00	23.44	0.00	0.62	0.57
All groups							
Person	30.5	57.5	1.1	4.1	6.7	2766	1.4
Gender disparity	1.02	1.16	0.00	1.67	0.00	0.47	0.64

Notes: BL: Boarding and lodging; #St/Rhhd: Number of students per rural household.

TABLE A5.15
Short Duration and Major Morbidity Prevalence Rates and Gender Disparity by Population Group in Rural Himachal Pradesh

Population group	Short duration morbidity ('000 popn)				Major morbidity per lakh popn
	Diarr.	Cold and Cough	Fever	Total	
Household income					
Up to 20,000					
Person	51	290	20	348	10,867
Gender disparity	1.00	1.31	1.19	1.25	1.26
20,001–40,000					
Person	42	241	16	287	11,910
Gender disparity	0.93	1.29	1.34	1.24	1.21
40,001–62,000					
Person	45	246	13	290	10,382
Gender disparity	1.05	1.32	1.46	1.30	1.18
62,001–86,000					
Person	25	164	44	219	10,868
Gender disparity	0.42	0.90	0.80	0.76	1.53
Landholding					
Landless wage earner					
Person	44	352	31	408	16,838
Gender disparity	0.47	1.10	0.79	1.08	1.18
Marginal					
Person	49	267	20	322	10,870
Gender disparity	1.06	1.31	1.28	1.26	1.27
Small					
Person	31	214	15	255	10,663
Gender disparity	0.82	1.32	0.51	1.19	1.10
Medium					
Person	32	185	17	217	7798
Gender disparity	0.58	1.44	4.73	1.44	1.89
Landless others					
Person	60	349	6	398	17,030
Gender disparity	0.99	1.52	–	1.46	1.21
All land owners					
Person	45	255	19	307	10,614
Gender disparity	0.98	1.30	1.18	1.24	1.27
All land non-owners					
Person	54	350	15	401	16,962
Gender disparity	0.83	1.35	1.30	1.31	1.20
Occupation					
Agriculture					
Person	40	249	15	293	9,506
Gender disparity	0.71	1.34	1.16	1.22	1.14
Salaried+prof.+s.empl.					
Person	36	214	20	259	11,406
Gender disparity	1.12	1.35	1.54	1.29	1.34
Wage earners					
Person	58	294	23	358	10,297
Gender disparity	1.10	1.21	0.87	1.22	1.22
All others					
Person	59	315	19	376	13,918
Gender disparity	1.11	1.30	1.27	1.28	1.31
Caste					
SCs					
Person	48	269	17	321	10,497
Gender disparity	0.78	1.46	1.26	1.35	1.26

(Contd.)

Population group	Short duration morbidity ('000 popn)				Major morbidity per lakh popn
	Diarr.	Cold and Cough	Fever	Total	
Religion					
Hindus					
Person	44	260	18	309	10,985
Gender disparity	0.96	1.32	1.14	1.26	1.28
Household size					
Up to 4					
Person	55	318	28	381	16,189
Gender disparity	1.32	1.51	1.02	1.47	1.39
5–7					
Person	45	282	18	335	11,355
Gender disparity	1.02	1.27	1.26	1.22	1.24
8 and above					
Person	43	199	15	243	7779
Gender disparity	0.72	1.28	1.29	1.18	1.25
Poverty line					
Lower segment below					
Person	57	274	18	331	9678
Gender disparity	0.93	1.11	1.50	1.10	1.05
Upper segment below					
Person	48	260	18	315	9251
Gender disparity	1.02	1.39	1.10	1.29	1.31
Lower segment above					
Person	42	260	18	309	11,349
Gender disparity	0.94	1.35	1.30	1.30	1.29
Upper segment above					
Person	41	250	22	297	13,742
Gender disparity	0.99	1.38	0.89	1.28	1.38
Adult literacy					
None literate					
Person	50	309	12	355	11,905
Gender disparity	1.48	1.44	1.62	1.48	1.35
Female literate					
Person	.39	310	27	359	11,250
Gender disparity	1.76	1.00	0.45	1.02	0.96
Male literate					
Person	58	276	18	337	9806
Gender disparity	0.82	1.36	0.99	1.26	1.44
Both literate					
Person	41	243	19	292	11,357
Gender disparity	0.97	1.29	1.36	1.24	1.20
Village development					
Low					
Person	48	280	16	332	12,222
Gender disparity	0.90	1.35	1.29	1.26	1.27
Medium					
Person	45	234	21	287	9604
Gender disparity	0.93	1.26	1.00	1.19	1.41
High					
Person	45	294	17	339	12,332
Gender disparity	1.16	1.34	1.68	1.34	1.05

(Contd.)

TABLE A5.15 (contd.)

Population group	Short duration morbidity ('000 popn) Diarr.	Cold and Cough	Fever	Total	Major morbidity per lakh popn
Age groups (years)					
0–4					
Person	138	332	15	451	2285
Gender disparity	0.80	0.90	1.28	0.87	0.27
5–14					
Person	34	267	21	314	4618
Gender disparity	1.00	0.94	1.47	0.98	0.88
15–34					
Person	28	220	14	256	7555
Gender disparity	0.82	1.50	0.62	1.34	1.18

(Contd.)

TABLE A5.15 (contd.)

Population group	Short duration morbidity ('000 popn) Diarr.	Cold and Cough	Fever	Total	Major morbidity per lakh popn
35–59					
Person	35	286	23	330	17,141
Gender disparity	1.76	1.84	2.05	1.82	1.62
60 and above					
Person	66	258	21	320	34,365
Gender disparity	1.13	1.47	0.77	1.38	1.24
All groups					
Person	46	261	19	313	11,024
Gender disparity	0.96	1.31	1.18	1.25	1.26

TABLE A5.16

Short Duration Morbidity Prevalence Rates and Gender Disparity by Population Group in Rural Himachal Pradesh

Population group	Short duration morbidity ('000 popn) Age groups (completed years) 0–4	5–14	15–34	35–59	60+	All
Household income						
Up to 20,000						
Person	497	336	293	377	344	348
Gender disparity	0.86	0.93	1.45	1.66	1.55	1.25
20,001–40,000						
Person	411	294	229	299	316	287
Gender disparity	0.81	1.08	1.27	1.90	1.41	1.24
40,001–62,000						
Person	443	314	229	297	273	290
Gender disparity	0.96	1.03	1.21	2.45	1.14	1.30
62,001–86,000						
Person	343	177	196	195	275	219
Gender disparity	0.66	0.45	0.74	2.22	0.38	0.76
Landholding						
Landless wage earner						
Person	458	495	326	416	300	408
Gender disparity	0.70	0.90	1.36	1.35	1.77	1.08
Marginal						
Person	459	319	268	342	331	322
Gender disparity	0.92	0.99	1.30	1.89	1.33	1.26
Small						
Person	400	280	185	260	270	255
Gender disparity	0.60	1.15	1.29	1.55	1.77	1.19
Medium						
Person	305	189	142	260	303	217
Gender disparity	1.08	1.93	2.18	1.51	1.32	1.44
Landless others						
Person	585	372	408	358	354	398
Gender disparity	1.11	0.86	2.23	2.00	1.27	1.46
All land owners						
Person	445	305	249	327	318	307
Gender disparity	0.86	1.00	1.30	1.84	1.38	1.24
All land non-owners						
Person	535	418	378	379	343	401
Gender disparity	0.97	0.86	1.90	1.69	1.36	1.31
Occupation						
Agriculture						
Person	426	310	235	297	297	293
Gender disparity	0.72	1.06	1.23	1.71	1.72	1.22
Salaried+prof.+s.empl.						
Person	434	255	194	284	238	259
Gender disparity	0.82	0.89	1.70	2.52	0.68	1.29
Wage earners						
Person	491	351	298	389	378	358
Gender disparity	1.06	0.89	1.38	1.35	1.53	1.22
All others						
Person	481	358	336	401	405	376
Gender disparity	1.00	1.04	1.25	1.92	1.37	1.28
Caste						
SCs						
Person	397	317	281	352	304	321
Gender disparity	0.93	1.05	1.38	1.89	1.81	1.35
Religion						
Hindus						
Person	442	314	254	325	314	309
Gender disparity	0.87	0.98	1.37	1.81	1.44	1.26
Household size						
Up to 4						
Person	622	354	331	388	437	381
Gender disparity	0.94	0.97	1.47	2.46	1.28	1.47
5–7						
Person	513	350	278	342	306	335
Gender disparity	0.92	1.05	1.34	1.56	1.28	1.22

(Contd.)

TABLE A5.16 (contd.)

Population group	Short duration morbidity ('000 popn) Age groups (completed years)					
	0–4	5–14	15–34	35–59	60+	All
8 and above						
Person	356	242	181	259	256	243
Gender disparity	0.80	0.95	1.40	1.89	1.64	1.18
Poverty line						
Lower segment below						
Person	454	324	259	396	310	331
Gender disparity	0.85	0.89	1.30	1.28	1.63	1.10
Upper segment below						
Person	461	297	280	308	342	315
Gender disparity	0.88	0.97	1.48	1.89	1.42	1.29
Lower segment above						
Person	402	330	258	323	300	309
Gender disparity	0.78	1.09	1.40	2.07	1.40	1.30
Upper segment above						
Person	585	284	228	308	345	297
Gender disparity	1.13	0.90	1.15	2.11	1.20	1.28
Adult literacy						
None literate						
Person	440	367	323	337	342	355
Gender disparity	1.42	1.05	1.46	2.06	2.18	1.48

(Contd.)

TABLE A5.16 (contd.)

Population group	Short duration morbidity ('000 popn) Age groups (completed years)					
	0–4	5–14	15–34	35–59	60+	All
Female literate						
Person	428	315	363	366	433	359
Gender disparity	0.79	0.77	0.76	1.33	2.18	1.02
Male literate						
Person	484	345	271	354	333	337
Gender disparity	0.78	0.87	1.70	1.67	1.09	1.26
Both literate						
Person	442	286	238	316	295	292
Gender disparity	0.84	1.10	1.22	1.92	1.23	1.24
Village development						
Low						
Person	521	335	268	345	306	332
Gender disparity	0.86	1.04	1.24	2.06	1.54	1.26
Medium						
Person	372	280	236	313	327	287
Gender disparity	0.85	0.93	1.23	1.68	1.46	1.19
High						
Person	536	349	283	346	324	339
Gender disparity	0.91	0.99	1.79	1.79	1.02	1.34
All groups						
Person	451	314	256	330	320	313
Gender disparity	0.87	0.98	1.34	1.82	1.38	1.25

TABLE A5.17

Major Morbidity Prevalence Rates and Gender Disparity by Population Group in Rural Himachal Pradesh

Population group	Major morbidity (per lakh popn) Age groups (completed years)					
	0–4	5–14	15–34	35–59	60+	All
Household income						
Up to 20,000						
Person	2442	4724	7819	16,918	32,981	10,867
Gender disparity	0.23	0.92	1.37	1.33	1.48	1.26
20,001–40,000						
Person	1848	5626	8093	17,296	39,218	11,910
Gender disparity	0.15	1.23	0.94	1.92	0.98	1.21
40,001–62,000						
Person	3108	3202	7705	15,858	31,162	10,382
Gender disparity	0.68	0.18	1.23	1.42	1.29	1.18
62,001–86,000						
Person	2955	1308	3474	23,398	36,933	10,868
Gender disparity	–	–	0.67	2.58	1.34	1.53
Landholding						
Landless wage earner						
Person	5677	11,822	19,348	20,567	35,660	16,838
Gender disparity	–	0.80	1.62	1.48	1.35	1.18
Marginal						
Person	2002	3906	7378	17,520	35,379	10,870
Gender disparity	0.50	0.86	1.06	1.60	1.25	1.27
Small						
Person	3287	4618	7483	14,500	33,303	10,663
Gender disparity	–	0.72	1.68	1.35	1.03	1.10

(Contd.)

Population group	Major morbidity (per lakh popn) Age groups (completed years)					
	0–4	5–14	15–34	35–59	60+	All
Medium						
Person	3860	1563	2997	15,770	20,889	7798
Gender disparity	–	0.72	2.39	9.86	1.26	1.89
Landless others						
Person	0	15,015	11,987	19,473	45,599	17,030
Gender disparity	–	0.90	1.68	1.15	1.34	1.21
All land owners						
Person	2289	3892	7,108	16,949	33,761	10,614
Gender disparity	0.29	0.89	1.13	1.67	1.22	1.27
All land non-owners						
Person	2227	13,819	14,635	19,868	43,622	16,962
Gender disparity	–	0.88	1.59	1.26	1.38	1.20
Occupation						
Agriculture						
Person	3302	3232	5179	14,721	30,117	9,506
Gender disparity	0.33	0.76	1.03	1.31	1.39	1.14
Salaried+prof.+s.empl.						
Person	1588	5359	9722	16,138	36,657	11,406
Gender disparity	0.76	0.65	1.14	2.35	1.06	1.34
Wage earners						
Person	2053	3546	9484	15,983	33,077	10,297
Gender disparity	–	0.78	1.73	1.45	0.87	1.22

(Contd.)

TABLE A5.17 (contd.)

Population group	Major morbidity (per lakh popn) Age groups (completed years)					
	0–4	5–14	15–34	35–59	60+	All
All others						
Person	1622	7029	6997	24,106	41,151	13,918
Gender disparity	–	1.26	0.96	1.52	1.29	1.31
Caste						
SCs						
Person	2274	4788	7584	17,439	30,875	10,497
Gender disparity	–	1.29	0.98	2.09	0.98	1.26
Religion						
Hindus						
Person	1436	1701	3095	11,332	36,566	6,813
Gender disparity	0.33	0.15	1.13	0.76	0.68	0.70
Household size						
Up to 4						
Person	5825	5516	8261	23,688	40,900	16,189
Gender disparity	–	1.15	1.07	1.31	1.63	1.39
5–7						
Person	2275	5376	8236	16,412	37,435	11,355
Gender disparity	0.69	0.81	1.26	1.60	1.04	1.24
8 and above						
Person	1573	3101	6099	13,003	25,510	7,779
Gender disparity	0.11	1.08	1.19	2.20	1.23	1.25
Poverty line						
Lower segment below						
Person	3054	6018	7036	15,731	29,212	9,678
Gender disparity	0.11	0.71	1.44	1.28	1.32	1.05
Upper segment below						
Person	951	4952	6314	14,597	30,515	9,251
Gender disparity	1.71	1.09	1.32	1.43	1.39	1.31
Lower segment above						
Person	2161	3285	8790	16,082	37,495	11,349
Gender disparity	0.10	1.12	1.22	1.83	1.06	1.29

(Contd.)

TABLE A5.17 (contd.)

Population group	Major morbidity (per lakh popn) Age groups (completed years)					
	0–4	5–14	15–34	35–59	60+	All
Upper segment above						
Person	3376	5023	7035	22,106	35,835	13,742
Gender disparity	0.89	0.67	0.80	1.71	1.39	1.38
Adult literacy						
None literate						
Person	0	2801	7398	16,318	37,274	11,905
Gender disparity	0.89	1.51	2.74	1.52	1.30	1.35
Female literate						
Person	2780	4524	8027	18,183	38,159	11,250
Gender disparity	–	1.17	2.74	0.66	1.38	0.96
Male literate						
Person	1518	4694	7707	16,107	25,138	9806
Gender disparity	–	1.08	1.41	1.81	1.15	1.44
Both literate						
Person	2886	4985	7484	17,614	36,633	11,357
Gender disparity	0.37	0.72	1.06	1.69	1.23	1.20
Village development						
Low						
Person	2173	5909	8840	18,965	35,572	12,222
Gender disparity	0.13	1.01	1.08	1.81	1.32	1.27
Medium						
Person	2402	3629	5736	15,650	31,415	9604
Gender disparity	0.51	0.94	1.68	1.58	1.36	1.41
High						
Person	2170	4545	9630	17,796	39,198	12,332
Gender disparity	–	0.52	0.94	1.43	0.96	1.05
All groups						
Person	2285	4618	7555	17,141	34,365	11,024
Gender disparity	0.27	0.88	1.18	1.62	1.24	1.26

TABLE A5.18

Per Person Household Expenditure for Treatment of Illness and Gender Disparity by Population Group in Rural Himachal Pradesh

Population group	Cost of short illness		Cost of long illness			
	Fees and medicines	Proportion of total cost	Fees and medicines	Proportion of total cost	Per sick person	Per reporting
Household income						
Up to 20,000						
Person	286	0.94	119	0.78	1096	1212
Gender disparity	1.04	0.99	1.17	1.08	0.92	0.89
20,001–40,000						
Person	248	0.86	146	0.79	1226	1297
Gender disparity	1.19	0.92	1.27	1.04	1.05	1.07
40,001–62,000						
Person	205	0.74	112	0.80	1082	1120
Gender disparity	0.90	1.14	1.02	1.07	0.87	0.84
62,001–86,000						
Person	236	0.99	267	0.76	2465	2564
Gender disparity	0.38	0.99	2.52	1.01	1.65	1.76

(Contd.)

Population group	Cost of short illness		Cost of long illness			
	Fees and medicines	Proportion of total cost	Fees and medicines	Proportion of total cost	Per sick person	Per reporting
Landholding						
Landless wage earner						
Person	498	0.93	137	0.82	814	875
Gender disparity	0.50	1.10	0.80	1.07	0.67	0.58
Marginal						
Person	269	0.91	130	0.79	1195	1279
Gender disparity	1.15	1.00	1.23	1.06	0.97	0.98
Small						
Person	163	0.78	112	0.73	1059	1167
Gender disparity	0.66	1.18	1.67	0.97	1.51	1.36
Medium						
Person	147	0.97	115	0.71	1483	1568
Gender disparity	0.82	0.99	1.73	1.15	0.91	0.99

(Contd.)

Table A5.18 (contd.)

Population group	Cost of short illness		Cost of long illness			
	Fees and medi-cines	Pro-portion of total cost	Fees and medi-cines	Pro-portion of total cost	Per sick person	Per rep-orting
Landless others						
Person	296	0.74	246	0.83	1449	1628
Gender disparity	1.46	0.51	1.13	1.13	0.94	0.86
All land owners						
Person	249	0.90	126	0.78	1191	1278
Gender disparity	1.04	1.02	1.28	1.05	1.01	1.01
All land non-owners						
Person	368	0.82	208	0.83	1226	1357
Gender disparity	0.86	0.69	1.08	1.11	0.90	0.81
Occupation						
Agriculture						
Person	218	0.92	119	0.72	1259	1431
Gender disparity	1.00	1.03	1.22	1.06	1.06	1.05
Salaried+prof.+s.empl.						
Person	237	0.77	124	0.82	1092	1160
Gender disparity	1.27	0.90	1.41	1.02	1.05	1.02
Wage earners						
Person	348	0.93	114	0.81	1109	1154
Gender disparity	0.77	1.05	0.80	1.03	0.65	0.67
All others						
Person	267	0.97	177	0.82	1278	1336
Gender disparity	1.24	0.98	1.49	1.08	1.13	1.11
Caste						
SCs						
Person	265	0.81	130	0.80	1244	1286
Gender disparity	0.94	0.98	1.29	1.11	1.02	1.00
Religion						
Hindus						
Person	250	0.88	130	0.77	1183	1271
Gender disparity	1.02	0.98	1.32	1.07	1.03	1.02
Household size						
Up to 4						
Person	328	0.91	209	0.80	1295	1404
Gender disparity	1.62	1.00	1.11	0.97	0.80	0.84
5–7						
Person	276	0.89	136	0.78	1199	1299
Gender disparity	0.95	1.04	1.49	1.11	1.20	1.17
8 and above						
Person	188	0.86	83	0.77	1074	1129
Gender disparity	0.85	0.84	1.08	1.03	0.86	0.82
Poverty line						
Lower segment below						
Person	298	0.95	98	0.77	1017	1157
Gender disparity	0.89	0.92	1.14	1.18	1.08	1.02
Upper segment below						
Person	236	0.88	94	0.73	1026	1157
Gender disparity	1.22	1.18	1.04	1.01	0.80	0.79

(Contd.)

Table A5.18 (contd.)

Population group	Cost of short illness		Cost of long illness			
	Fees and medi-cines	Pro-portion of total cost	Fees and medi-cines	Pro-portion of total cost	Per sick person	Per rep-orting
Lower segment above						
Person	232	0.88	135	0.79	1192	1248
Gender disparity	1.06	0.86	1.35	1.02	1.05	1.04
Upper segment above						
Person	280	0.84	200	0.81	1456	1523
Gender disparity	1.00	1.12	1.38	1.04	1.00	1.00
Adult literacy groups						
None literate						
Person	281	0.95	139	0.85	1173	1310
Gender disparity	1.32	1.04	1.86	1.05	1.38	1.36
Female literate						
Person	266	1.11	123	0.76	1099	1151
Gender disparity	0.77	0.56	0.34	0.99	0.35	0.34
Male literate						
Person	243	0.94	111	0.71	1140	1246
Gender disparity	0.88	1.06	1.57	1.03	1.09	1.15
Both literate						
Person	257	0.84	139	0.80	1226	1308
Gender disparity	1.07	0.99	1.23	1.06	1.02	0.99
Village development						
Low						
Person	261	0.94	145	0.76	1188	1289
Gender disparity	1.10	1.00	1.38	1.03	1.09	1.09
Medium						
Person	244	0.90	118	0.79	1231	1338
Gender disparity	0.95	1.02	1.38	1.10	0.98	0.94
High						
Person	275	0.81	140	0.81	1141	1193
Gender disparity	1.10	0.90	0.94	1.03	0.89	0.89
Age groups (years)						
0–4						
Person	359	0.89	17	0.63	787	927
Gender disparity	0.71	0.95	0.09	1.18	0.34	0.34
5–14						
Person	168	0.95	26	0.74	566	648
Gender disparity	0.86	1.00	1.06	1.18	1.20	1.11
15–34						
Person	192	0.84	87	0.78	1161	1219
Gender disparity	1.13	0.89	1.10	1.02	0.93	0.87
35–59						
Person	332	0.89	243	0.76	1418	1508
Gender disparity	1.34	1.17	1.48	1.02	0.91	0.93
60 and above						
Person	410	0.92	407	0.83	1184	1285
Gender disparity	0.94	0.87	1.23	1.11	1.00	1.03
All groups						
Person	256	0.89	131	0.78	1194	1285
Gender disparity	1.03	0.98	1.26	1.05	1.00	0.99

TABLE A5.19
Fertility Rate by Population Group in Rural Himachal Pradesh

Population group	Crude birth rate per '000	Crude death rate	TFR (15–49)	Average children ever born to ever married women		
				Boys	Girls	Total
Household income						
Up to 20,000	20	6	2.4507	1.5	1.4	3.0
20,001–40,000	26	5	3.2560	1.5	1.3	2.8
40,001–62,000	22	9	2.4261	1.4	1.3	2.7
62,001–86,000	28	9	2.5818	1.4	0.9	2.3
Landholding						
Landless wage earner	12	0	1.1900	1.8	1.3	3.0
Marginal	22	8	2.7444	1.5	1.4	2.9
Small	25	5	3.0905	1.4	1.2	2.6
Medium	22	1	2.1062	1.4	1.2	2.7
Landless others	30	5	3.6244	1.3	1.3	2.7
All land owners	22	7	2.7389	1.5	1.4	2.9
All land non-owners	24	3	2.8007	1.5	1.3	2.8
Occupation						
Agriculture	25	9	3.1838	1.5	1.4	2.8
Salaried+prof.+s.empl.	24	9	2.8907	1.5	1.3	2.8
Wage earners	20	2	2.3609	1.5	1.3	2.8
All others	17	3	2.1045	1.5	1.4	2.9
Caste						
SCs	21	6	2.6313	1.5	1.3	2.9
Religion						
Hindus	22	6	2.6813	1.5	1.4	2.8
Household size						
Up to 4	14	14	1.4373	1.3	1.0	2.3
5–7	18	5	2.4011	1.6	1.4	3.1
8 and above	33	5	3.9249	1.4	1.5	2.8
Poverty line						
Lower segment below	23	8	2.9283	1.6	1.6	3.2
Upper segment below	25	4	3.2361	1.5	1.5	3.0
Lower segment above	23	6	2.7363	1.4	1.3	2.8
Upper segment above	17	9	2.0369	1.5	1.1	2.6
Adult literacy						
None literate	19	12	2.8385	1.4	1.4	2.8
Female literate	15	2	1.6229	1.3	1.7	3.1
Male literate	20	8	3.5677	1.8	1.4	3.2
Both literate	24	5	2.7211	1.4	1.3	2.7
Village development						
Low	21	5	2.7369	1.5	1.4	2.9
Middle	26	9	3.0389	1.4	1.3	2.8
High	17	4	2.1239	1.6	1.3	2.9
All groups	**22**	**6**	**2.7313**	**1.5**	**1.4**	**2.8**

TABLE A5.20
Contraceptive Prevalence Rate for Ever Married Women by Population Group in Rural Himachal Pradesh

Population group	Termination method % EMW	Vasectomy users % to all	Spacing method % EMW	Loop/CopT user % to all	% EMW using methods
Household income					
Up to 20,000	52.2	27.5	4.1	30.8	56.3
20,001–40,000	51.0	25.2	6.7	40.1	57.7
40,001–62,000	43.7	29.2	6.8	10.4	50.5
62,001–86,000	43.6	38.3	2.2	0.0	45.8
Landholding					
Landless wage earner	69.2	16.4	0.0	0.0	69.2
Marginal	51.5	27.8	4.7	29.9	56.2
Small	46.1	30.1	6.6	14.1	52.7
Medium	38.7	35.7	2.5	0.0	41.2
Landless others	52.4	17.0	15.4	41.1	67.7
All land owners	49.9	28.1	5.1	28.2	55.0
All land non-owners	58.4	16.7	9.9	41.1	68.3
Occupation					
Agriculture	48.6	22.8	3.3	42.3	51.9
Salaried+prof.+s.empl.	53.4	27.1	7.7	31.6	61.1
Wage earners	51.2	28.1	2.9	27.0	54.1
All others	49.3	33.5	8.1	20.4	57.4
Caste					
SCs	54.0	23.9	4.1	39.8	58.2
Religion					
Hindus	50.4	28.2	5.3	29.5	55.7
Household size					
Up to 4	50.6	38.3	3.6	0.0	54.2
5–7	55.5	26.1	5.9	41.9	61.4
8 and above	42.4	21.1	5.6	21.4	48.0
Poverty line					
Lower segment below	50.8	30.4	2.6	23.3	53.3
Upper segment below	54.3	22.6	4.6	32.0	58.9
Lower segment above	47.7	25.3	7.2	35.1	54.9
Upper segment above	51.6	32.9	5.5	16.9	57.1
Adult literacy					
None literate	45.8	34.0	2.3	0.0	48.1
Female literate	57.2	19.3	3.5	33.5	60.8
Male literate	56.5	29.3	1.6	34.1	58.1
Both literate	48.1	26.6	7.4	30.3	55.5
Village development					
Low	49.4	25.0	4.5	40.2	53.9
Middle	47.8	30.9	5.5	18.7	53.3
High	58.9	23.3	6.5	40.1	65.4
All groups	**50.5**	**27.3**	**5.4**	**29.7**	**55.9**

TABLE A5.21
Reasons for Non-adoption of Birth Control Measures by Population Group in Rural Himachal Pradesh

(*per cent*)

Population group	Non-adoption	Reasons for not using birth control measures: Demand factors	Want son	Health factors	Supply factors	Household factors	Lack of knowledge
Household income							
Up to 20,000	43.4	37.4	12.0	10.0	6.4	8.5	17.3
20,001–40,000	43.1	41.7	11.3	8.4	5.1	9.7	19.4
40,001–62,000	51.9	40.4	7.9	10.7	4.7	9.4	20.5
62,001–86,000	48.3	68.7	3.6	9.3	0.0	6.8	8.0
Landholding							
Landless wage earner	30.8	32.7	0.0	10.8	11.8	0.0	23.1
Marginal	43.8	39.7	10.9	10.2	6.1	8.0	19.2
Small	47.3	45.3	9.5	7.6	5.0	13.3	13.5
Medium	58.8	33.8	22.1	5.2	2.6	13.7	12.8
Landless others	32.3	43.6	9.3	13.1	0.0	7.3	25.2
Land owners	45.0	39.9	11.4	9.4	5.6	9.3	17.8
Landless	31.7	39.9	6.1	12.3	4.1	4.8	24.5
Occupation							
Cultivators	48.1	37.1	15.2	8.3	4.7	8.3	19.5
Salaried+prof.+s.empl.	38.9	37.2	11.6	9.4	8.3	17.3	19.0
Wage earners	45.9	44.5	6.5	12.5	4.9	4.8	15.7
All others	42.6	43.2	8.2	8.7	4.7	5.7	17.0
Caste							
SCs	41.8	44.8	10.4	10.8	4.6	7.1	16.0
Religion							
Hindus	44.3	39.9	11.3	9.0	5.7	9.1	18.0
Household size							
Up to 4	45.8	48.0	9.9	8.3	2.6	6.2	18.1
5–7	38.6	41.5	8.9	11.3	6.0	7.6	15.3
8 and above	52.0	33.3	14.6	8.1	6.7	12.6	21.4
Poverty line							
Lower segment below	45.6	29.4	12.7	7.7	9.9	11.2	23.8
Upper segment below	40.9	42.4	10.7	13.3	5.9	7.1	16.8
Lower segment above	45.5	40.2	11.8	8.1	3.3	9.1	15.8
Upper segment above	43.2	52.2	7.7	11.0	4.4	8.6	17.1
Adult literacy							
None literate	51.9	37.4	11.0	7.6	10.9	11.5	17.5
Female literate	39.2	48.7	9.5	8.0	6.0	9.3	16.1
Male literate	41.9	30.5	14.6	12.5	7.5	5.3	19.9
Both literate	44.5	42.6	10.2	8.9	4.0	10.1	17.8
Village development							
Low	46.1	40.1	13.7	8.5	9.9	10.8	12.8
Medium	46.7	40.3	8.5	9.0	3.8	9.9	21.5
High	34.6	38.1	14.2	13.4	1.5	2.9	18.9
All groups	**44.1**	**39.9**	**11.2**	**9.5**	**5.6**	**9.1**	**18.1**

TABLE A5.22

Distribution of Ever Married Women Having Delivery the Previous Year by Population Group in Rural Himachal Pradesh

Population group	EMW having delivery previous year	Post-natal care received	% immunization	Attended by trained person	Place of delivery		
					Hospital	CHC/PHC	Home
Household income							
Up to 20,000	12.4	18.9	60.6	25.2	12.4	0.6	87
20,001–40,000	15	24	70.3	38	9.5	1.7	88.9
40,001–62,000	14	26.2	71.7	35.6	16.5	5	78.5
62,001–86,000	15.2	22.8	81.2	11.4	11.4	0	88.6
Landholding							
Landless wage earner	7	0	64.5	0	0	0	100
Marginal	13.4	23.2	72.5	29.2	10.8	2	87.2
Small	14.1	18.9	86.2	33.5	16.7	0	83.3
Medium	13.8	11	79.2	39.2	11	0	89
Landless others	17.8	31.9	67.2	47.8	26.4	0	73.6
Land owners	13.5	22	65.1	31.1	11.9	1.6	86.5
Landless	14	26.2		39.3	21.7	0	78.3
Occupation							
Cultivators	16.5	16.7	66.9	27.9	7.9	0	92.1
Salaried+prof.+s.empl.	14	34.8	73.7	45.6	19.9	2.3	77.8
Wage earners	10.8	13.5	49.9	17.5	4.6	1.9	93.5
All others	10.6	23.8	73	31.6	19.6	3.4	77
Caste							
SCs	12.1	22.9	68.6	35.2	7	3.7	89.2
Religion							
Hindus	13.2	23.6	66.3	31.7	12.7	1.6	85.7
Household size							
Up to 4	8.9	32.3	59.3	40.9	11.3	0	88.7
5–7	11.1	26.1	62.9	34.6	15.9	0.8	83.4
8 and above	20.4	16	72.9	26.4	10	2.5	87.4
Poverty line							
Lower segment below	15.2	16.7	64.5	24.3	7.1	0	92.9
Upper segment below	13.7	16.5	68.3	30.3	16.6	2.6	80.8
Lower segment above	13.1	25.2	68.8	30.6	8.3	2.3	89.3
Upper segment above	11.7	33.7	64.9	50.8	28.4	0	71.6
Adult literacy							
None literate	12.5	19.9	47.1	20.7	0	4	96
Female literate	7.6	22.1	67.4	48.2	14.4	0	85.6
Male literate	13.6	20.7	51.7	21	2.5	2.6	94.9
Both literate	14.3	23.1	74.7	35.6	17.4	0.9	81.7
Village development							
Low	12.2	15.5	58.6	23.6	7.1	0	92.9
Middle	15.1	28.1	71.3	36.4	12.4	1.1	86.4
High	11.6	15.7	68.6	30.7	22.6	5.2	72.2
All groups	**13.5**	**22.3**	**67.1**	**31.6**	**12.5**	**1.5**	**86**

TABLE A5.23

Percentage of Children (aged 12–23 months) Immunized and Gender Disparity by Population Group in Rural Himachal Pradesh

Population group	Percentage of children (12–23 months)				
	DPT 3 doses	Polio 3 doses	BCG 1 dose	Measles 1 dose	All 8 doses
Household income					
Up to 20,000					
Person	72.33	73.89	76.46	65.20	57.17
Gender disparity	0.86	0.89	0.94	0.90	0.87
20,001–40,000					
Person	67.34	67.44	77.04	64.03	53.50
Gender disparity	0.83	1.00	0.97	1.02	0.84
40,001–62,000					
Person	78.67	78.67	88.49	78.08	74.79
Gender disparity	0.66	0.66	0.92	0.81	0.72
62,001–86,000					
Person	76.50	42.87	76.50	76.50	42.87
Gender disparity	0.00	0.00	0.00	0.00	0.00
Landholding					
Landless wage earner					
Person	66.77	66.77	66.77	66.77	66.77
Gender disparity	0.00	0.00	0.00	0.00	0.00
Marginal					
Person	67.22	67.95	73.71	63.57	53.50
Gender disparity	0.73	0.79	0.86	0.83	0.71
Small					
Person	74.32	71.10	87.73	70.30	66.04
Gender disparity	0.93	1.34	1.08	1.03	1.16
Medium					
Person	81.03	64.66	88.56	88.56	64.66
Gender disparity	0.79	1.12	1.01	1.01	1.12
Landless others					
Person	88.12	88.12	88.12	70.86	70.86
Gender disparity	1.26	1.26	1.26	1.19	1.19
All land owners					
Person	69.88	68.77	77.29	66.43	56.32
Gender disparity	0.75	0.87	0.89	0.86	0.79
All land non-owners					
Person	85.34	85.34	85.34	70.33	70.33
Gender disparity	1.30	1.30	1.30	1.19	1.19
Occupation					
Agriculture					
Person	57.08	55.65	66.59	55.26	48.40
Gender disparity	0.56	0.67	0.84	0.70	0.67
Salaried+prof.+s.empl.					
Person	81.53	75.28	83.09	76.69	64.02
Gender disparity	0.96	1.09	0.90	0.91	0.92
Wage earners					
Person	71.28	74.85	81.65	66.67	50.29
Gender disparity	1.04	1.14	1.15	1.26	0.89
All others					
Person	78.91	81.38	85.80	72.07	68.29
Gender disparity	0.76	0.81	0.86	0.89	0.86
Caste					
SCs					
Person	69.67	71.84	77.79	63.34	49.18
Gender disparity	0.80	0.86	0.83	0.89	0.81
Religion					
Hindus					
Person	69.98	68.88	77.26	65.57	55.65
Gender disparity	0.76	0.87	0.89	0.86	0.79
Household Size					
Up to 4					
Person	76.04	76.04	82.10	54.53	48.47
Gender disparity	1.04	1.04	1.19	1.90	1.60
5–7					
Person	69.33	69.32	76.69	66.70	54.78
Gender disparity	0.65	0.71	0.77	0.80	0.59
8 and above					
Person	71.34	68.97	78.01	69.36	61.70
Gender disparity	0.86	1.07	1.01	0.87	0.98
Poverty line					
Lower segment below					
Person	79.15	79.15	79.15	67.77	67.77
Gender disparity	0.93	0.93	0.93	0.80	0.80
Upper segment below					
Person	59.83	62.43	67.38	59.72	50.71
Gender disparity	0.99	1.07	1.24	1.01	1.05
Lower segment above					
Person	71.12	71.12	81.15	71.52	60.50
Gender disparity	0.72	0.83	0.83	0.85	0.69
Upper segment above					
Person	81.04	67.46	85.25	62.10	44.30
Gender disparity	0.64	0.82	0.80	0.93	1.02
Adult literacy					
None literate					
Person	34.31	34.31	45.82	33.73	22.22
Gender disparity	1.41	1.41	2.14	0.93	1.02
Female literate					
Person	56.22	71.89	87.57	56.22	56.22
Gender disparity	0.50	0.68	0.86	0.50	0.50
Male literate					
Person	65.07	65.07	68.28	45.37	39.26
Gender disparity	0.58	0.58	0.66	0.66	0.43
Both literate					
Person	75.81	73.45	81.93	75.04	64.33
Gender disparity	0.86	0.99	0.95	0.93	0.90
Village development					
Low					
Person	55.19	55.64	69.19	54.06	44.28
Gender disparity	0.73	0.98	0.93	1.02	1.11
Medium					
Person	78.58	77.24	81.68	77.88	67.91
Gender disparity	0.77	0.85	0.89	0.91	0.76
High					
Person	75.65	73.28	81.14	60.61	52.58
Gender disparity	0.91	0.97	0.95	0.78	0.78
All groups					
Person	70.87	69.83	77.81	66.68	57.22
Gender disparity	0.78	0.89	0.91	0.88	0.81

(Contd.)

6 Village Level Study in Himachal Pradesh: Batran and Bhullang

6.1 Introduction

A qualitative study of two villages, Batran in Hamirpur district and Bhullang in Kullu district—was undertaken in 1993–4 as part of the project, 'Developing Indicators of Human Resource Development'. As per the objective of the study, one advanced district, namely, Hamirpur and one backward district, namely, Kullu were selected for research.

Hamirpur is one of the most advanced districts, educationally as well as socially. It has been declared as the first fully-literate district in the state. Its sex ratio of 1162 females per thousand males is the highest and this is because a high proportion of males are employed in the armed services; the major source of income is transfer income. Both the districts have fully electrified villages. Kullu, however, ranks among the backward districts of the state.

6.2 Batran Village

6.2.1 Location of the Village

Batran village is located on the slopes of the lower hills of Himachal Pradesh, situated in *tehsil* and block Nadaun of border district Hamirpur, adjoining Hoshiarpur district of Punjab.

The village is spread over a vast area and has three major hamlets. The nearest town is Kangu, at a distance of 6 km. For major necessities the villagers go to Kangu, and for marketing purposes they go to Nadaun which is at a distance of 10 km. The district headquarter, Hamirpur is about 38 km away and the state capital Shimla is at a distance of about 200 km.

The district is characterized by a short summer from April to June, displaying a maximum temperature of 40°C. July and August are the rainy months, while winters are long, starting from November and extending to mid-March. The maximum day temperature in the extreme winter is around 15°C.

6.2.2 Historical Background

The period of settlement at the present site is estimated to be around 150 years. The first people to settle here were rajputs from Rajasthan. There were in all about eleven rajput villages. They first tried to settle in the Kangra district, near Nadaun and then went on to Kamlah. From Kamlah, a few of them moved to this present site while others established themselves at other sites. In fact, the present name of the village is popularly believed to be derived from the name of the head of the group which moved to this site, although various other legends are also attached to the ways in which the village name originated. The other castes came to settle later, according to the services needed by the inhabitants of the time. Today, the language spoken by the villagers is Punjabi, but according to the prescribed school curriculum of Himachal Pradesh, the written language is Hindi.

6.2.3 General Characteristics

All the villagers are Hindu. This is apparent in the presence of three Shiva temples in the village of which the oldest is the Sada Shiva temple, surmised to be more than a hundred years old. Once in a year a *bhandara* (a community feast) is held. The few food items are donated by the villagers, irrespective of caste or creed. Usually, people from all castes go to the Shiva temples on days of religious importance as well as on occasions like marriage, birth, etc. There is a pujari in only one of these temples where a 'sarai' shelter is also under construction.

The construction of houses in the village, however, has marked similarities. Almost all houses have two rooms in the middle, one side store, a kitchen, and a bathroom. In front of the rooms there is a verandah, facing an open courtyard. The constructed building thus has a U-shape but if the verandah is included, it acquires a square shape.

Most of the houses in the village have *pucca* walls, but some houses, especially those belonging to low castes, have *kutcha* walls which have been properly plastered with mud from both sides. The walls in the rooms are whitewashed and are lined with calendars of deities and photographs of family members or of currently famous cine stars.

All the houses are constructed on raised platforms and have kutcha floors. A few of the houses, belonging to both SCs and rajputs, have pucca floors. The kutcha floors in all the houses are beautifully plastered with a mixture of mud and gobar and are coloured with paint.

No household has a smokeless chullah. The fuel used is firewood. The chullah is covered with a mixture of soil and cowdung at least once a week. The practice of placing the chullah in the open courtyard is absent here. The smoke in the kitchen is let out from a space left between the wall and the thatched roof, making the whole kitchen blackish. The kitchen is generally large and also serves as a dining room for the family where mats are spread out to sit and eat on. Drinking water is stored in covered earthen pots. The villagers do not usually sleep on the floor but on cots or double beds.

Almost all the houses, have a separate cattle shed, usually at a distance from the living place. The fodder is also kept in the cattle shed though the fuel wood is kept inside the kitchen.

6.2.4 Population

There are approximately 175 households in the village, consisting of 93 rajputs, 58 SCs, 9 other SCs, that is kabir panthi, 10 barber, 10 sunar, and 1 brahmin.

DOMINANT CASTE

The rajputs may have maintained their dominance in the village due to the following factors: (i) since their ancestors established the village, most of the cultivable land is owned by them; (ii) for generations, their ancestors have been serving in the army, and even today almost all the rajput households have usually one male member in the army; (iii) the number of rajput households is numerically dominant over the other caste households.

6.2.5 Occupation

AGRICULTURE AND ALLIED ACTIVITIES

The total geographical area of the village is 950 acres, out of which 235 acres is currently fallow, while the rest of the land, though unirrigated, has double cropping.

On private lands, there are a few plantations of *galgal* (a citrus fruit used for pickle), lemon, and mango. The crops grown are high yielding variety (HYV) wheat and desi *makka*. Crops such as rice, sugarcane, ginger and mustard are also sown in a small area.

ANIMAL HUSBANDRY

Almost all the households own cattle, of which, buffaloes and cows are domesticated for milk, goats for meat, and sheep for wool. All these cattle are of *desi* or local variety. Among the milk-yielding animals, the buffalo is the most common while cows are also kept by a few households. A milk co-operative was recently set up to facilitate milk collection. However, this centre manages to collect only 40 litres of milk every day and since there is not much surplus milk in the village, it does not seem to be an economically viable initiative.

Bullocks are also kept by households with medium and large holdings. Their reproduction is carried out through artificial insemination. Also, one bull is usually left free to roam about for breeding purposes. About 38 cows have been artificially inseminated since April 1997. In addition, sheep and goats are also inseminated.

A veterinary hospital has been functioning in a rented building in the village since 1974. The doctor goes door to door for cattle vaccinations. The vaccinations are given for haemorrhage septicemia (HS), rinderpest (RP), foot and mouth disease (FMD), and validated and qualified herd (VQ) and are given at the outbreak of epidemics. The target for RP is 1200 and that for FMD is 200 per year. Except for FMD, for which charges are Rs 2 on an average, six to seven cases are attended to in the hospital every day. In the summers and rainy season, the number of cases goes up to 25. In general, the people are not familiar with the symptoms of these diseases and only when the case becomes chronic or when the cattle stop eating, does it become a matter of concern to them. Otherwise, treatment is tried at home for 2–3 days, then cattle are brought to the hospital. Here, medicines are administered for 3–5 days in the hospital and in chronic cases a longer treatment has to be followed.

Although the supply of medicines is sufficient, some of the injections are not available in the hospital and have to be prescribed. Vaccinations and inseminations are sufficient. However, there is scarcity of fodder in this area.

TABLE 6.1
Average Price of Cattle, Batran

(Rupees)

Buffalo	5000 to 7000
Cow (jersey)	8000 to 12,000
Cow (desi)	1000 to 1500
Goat	700 to 800
Sheep	300 to 400

SERVICES

There are about 150 service class people working mostly in the army, the majority of whom are rajputs; the others work in private factories in Ludhiana (hosiery business), Delhi, Bombay, etc. and other miscellaneous jobs. The village has produced one medical graduate, two BEd teachers, 10–15 graduates, and about 100 matriculates. There are only four employees from the village working as teachers and in the post office.

Many lower caste labourers from this village are working with the contractors outside the village for extracting resin of the *cheel* tree. For this work they do not mind going to far off places, even as far as Dehradun, Jammu, etc. Women and children do not go for paid labour work inside or outside the village, but women have to work more on their own fields and take care of cattle as their men folk are usually out of the village for jobs. Men folk other than rajputs do agriculture and non-agriculture wage labour in the village. Sometimes they may go out if there is a scarcity of jobs within the village. There are about 25 shops, which are run by the people of the village itself.

The government wage rate for an unskilled worker is Rs 24 but the villagers earn about Rs 40–5 from both the government as well as private contractors. Males and females are paid equally. The villagers estimated that about 25 among the educated youth are unemployed, if the cut off point is taken as matriculation.

CHILD LABOUR

All the village children study up to the matriculation level at least. So there is no incidence of paid or unpaid child labour in this village. But children in some of the households, in their spare time, do help their parents by working in the fields or grazing the cattle. The age at which they start helping in this and other household work, is usually above 10 years.

6.2.6 *Infrastructural Facilities*

The villagers feel that more progress should be made in the provision of infrastructural facilities as after the merger of this village with Himachal Pradesh, upper Himachal takes the major share of funds.

TABLE 6.2
Time Calendar, Batran

Amenities/services	Year of establishment
Sada shiv temple	(period unknown)
Gugga (snake god) temple	Since long
Primary school	1948
Co-operative society	1948
PDSC ration shop	1948
Bus	1952
Post office	1955
Electricity	1967
Fully electrified	1987
Shiv temple	1967
Sub centre	1968
Radio	1971
Veterinary hospital	1974
Middle school	1978
Television	1980
High school	1985
Two wheeler scooter	1988
Drinking water (piped)	1989
Gobar gas plants	1990
Refrigerator	1991
Rain shelter	1991
Hand pump	1992
Desi wine shop	1992
Metalled road (started in 1948)	1993
LPG cooking gas	1993
Telephone (school and post office)	1994
Milk co-operative (collection centre)	1994

SHOPS

There are 27 shops in the village: grocery (5), tea stall with sweets (4), tailor shops (4), cosmetic shops (3), confectionery (2), books and stationery (2), barber (2), shoe repair (1), wine shop (1), vegetable shop (1), cycle repair shop (1), and goldsmith (1). About 21 shops have started functioning only in the last five years. The oldest among the shops is one started in 1970. Most of these shops are in rented buildings. Four shops were being run by women in this village.

MULTIPURPOSE CO-OPERATIVE SOCIETY

One multipurpose co-operative society has been functioning in this village since 1948. The name of this society is Krishi Sehkri Simiti, Batran. The items sold through this society are both controlled and uncontrolled rate items. The controlled rate items are rice, wheat, *atta*, cloth, kerosene oil, tea, sugar, fertilizer, note books, etc. The uncontrolled items are pulses, salt, detergents, *agarbatties*, etc. Not only Batran but some other villages are also covered by this society. The total number of ration cards is 406, out of which, 35 come under the Antodya scheme. All the items are sold on cash down basis but fertilizer is given on loan only to poor farmers. This society is open for six days a week, seven hours per day (10 AM to 5 PM). This society has its own building, and has enough space for sale and storage. The society has kept one salesman and one secretary on payment basis. They do not face any kind of problems on account of supply.

DRINKING WATER

There are four sources of drinking water in the village: (i) *baurrie*, (ii) well, (iii) hand pump, and (iv) piped water. Baurries are the oldest source of water for the village people. The word baurrie means spring. There are 3–4 baurries in the whole village, at a distance from each other. There are three baurries on one side of the village and one on another side, if we take the main leading road running through the village as a dividing line. The portion of the village which has only one baurrie has lesser houses, while the larger part of the village is on the other side of the road where three baurries are located.

These three baurries are located in Baukher, Tilla gram, and Parla gram hamlets. The first baurrie in Baukher area, is a small, round, and not very deep kutcha pit. There is no cover over it and the water is not clean. One can see big insects, and other dirt flowing in it. The surrounding walls of the baurrie are covered thickly with creepers and green algae. Adjoining it, a small nala flows. The baurrie is in a deep furrow between two hills, one of which is an inhabited area. In this area, there are a few SC households along with rajput households and one house of a lohar. In the absence of any other source of water near this area, all the households use this water for drinking purposes.

The second source of water is wells. There are two wells, of which only one is used throughout the year. The water level is at about 10 ft. This well is pucca with a roof over it. This well is located in a populated area where there are mostly nai households and a few rajput households. This water is clean and no algae was seen inside the well, since the villagers put bleaching powder in it to clean the water. Households of all castes from this area use this water. The other well is not in use at all and the households in these areas bring water from the hand pumps.

Three hand pumps were installed by the government in 1992 at a water level of 135 ft. All these hand pumps are on the roadside and at a good distance from each other. They are used by all castes. The SC households are far away from the roadside where the hand pumps are located, and thus, they face difficulty in taking water from these. Discussions with the villagers led to the conclusion that this water is the safest.

Piped water came into the village in 1989. People do not use this water for drinking, though they may take it for drinking purposes of cattle or for other household use. The reason for this, according to the villagers, is that as this water comes from the nala where the villagers go for defecation, this water is not clean for drinking. The lifted water passes through three tanks where it is treated to make it germ free.

DRAINAGE

The village is located on the slopes of the lower hills of Himachal Pradesh. Waterlogging in general is not a problem. The texture of the soil being sandy, the drainage water does not flow into the streets and gets absorbed in the soil instead. In the rainy season, the drain water tends to collect at one place in some fields. If a proper drainage system is developed, these fields can be utilized for second cropping. The rain water usually flows through the foot paths or streets. These being kutcha, a lot of soil erosion takes place every year.

SANITATION

There is no separate place for garbage disposal. The garbage of the household consists of cowdung, in houses where cattle are kept and other kitchen refuse. Cowdung is thrown into the fields for manure purposes along with other refuse. Where they do not have any fields or cattle, the garbage is thrown in the jungle. The roadside was never seen littered with garbage and the village usually looked clean.

A sanitation campaign has been in progress in this village for the past few years. About 100 households have flush toilets. However, only 25 per cent of these are utilized. The reasons for the non-use of the others were: (i) some of them collapsed within a few months of installation; (ii) many beneficiaries could not afford a wall or cover it for privacy; (iii) other non-users were not habituated to this kind of facility and preferred the open fields.

Instead of giving the total subsidy money of Rs 1200 to the general castes and Rs 1500 to the SCs, for toilet construction, the block office got the latrines installed through a private contractor. The block authorities in their enthusiasm did not wait for applications to come in, rather they authorized the contractor to install the latrines for those willing to provide space for it. Moreover, the demand for this facility was not created by any kind of motivation for hygiene or education regarding its benefits. The villagers welcomed it as a free benefit. However, now, they expect the government to construct concrete flooring and walls to enclose it, before they use it. People who do not use this facility, defecate in the forest area.

There is no big sewer near the village though 4–5 nalas flow and originate in the village. One of these nalas is perennial and drinking water facility is provided by uplifting water from this nala. The potential of the other nalas is small but if they are properly intercepted they can be developed as minor irrigation projects.

TRANSPORT

A metalled road from Nadaun to Salouni passes through this village. In addition, there are about eight buses plying each way through, which stop at the village bus stop, which also acts as a rain shelter and was constructed by the government in 1991.

6.2.7 Education

PRIMARY SCHOOL

A primary school was established in the village in 1948. This helped in solving the problem of non-enrolment and drop-out. The enrolment rate is 100 per cent in this village and there have been no drop-outs in the last few years up to the middle level. There were 191 students in the primary school in November 1994, out of which one third were from the SCs. This ratio is almost similar to the ratio of the number of households of each caste. There were seven teachers (five males and two females). The Classes IV and V have two sections, so that each section of a class has an independent teacher. There is one parent teacher association (PTA) for this school, which meets after every three months and pays Rs 90 per month to partially meet the expenses of one female *ad hoc* teacher and the electricity bill. There are no toilets, but drinking water is vailable. There are four rooms in all, with a verandah in front. Other infrastructure in the school is good. There is no government scheme of free books, uniform, or mid-day meal. Very rarely does any student go to a public school outside the village.

HIGH SCHOOL

In the building adjoining the primary school, there is a ten year old high school. It has nine rooms. There are eight teachers in this school. There are no toilets and everyone has to go out to the jungle. There is only one female teacher although the need was expressed for at least two.

The teachers felt that their numbers are inadequate to handle the large size of classes. In Class IX there were 92 students in one section. The library in the school is almost non-functional except for the newspapers for the teachers. There is a shortage of furniture and the students sit on the ground in the open space. In the classrooms there are neither desks nor mats. There is no discrimination on gender or caste basis and no difference in intelligence could be seen among the students on a caste basis. Boys and girls remain in different groups; though there is co-education, there is no interaction between them. A first aid box is available in the school. Mostly the boys play some sports or games.

6.2.8 Health Facilities

PRIVATE PRACTITIONER

There is only one private practitioner in this village. Earlier his brother, having a Bachelor of Ayurvedic Medicine (BAMS) degree, was also practising at the same shop. This practitioner has no qualification or experience of working with a proper doctor and has learnt about some medicines from his brother. The private practitioner gets two to four patients every day suffering from cold–cough, temperature, and stomach problems. Males of 12 to 60 years age group come to him. Patients usually take medicines after waiting for 2 to 4 days of the illness though educated people come earlier. He also makes home visits. Patients usually go to Kangu or Nadaun for medication.

SUB-CENTRE

A sub-centre has been functioning in this village since the last 38 years, catering to the needs of nine villages. The sub-centre is located on the main road of Batran. The total population covered by this centre in 1994 was 3865. The centre has two employees, one multiple health worker (MHW) and one auxiliary nurse mid-wife (ANM). The centre is open from 3.00 PM to 5.00 PM every day, excluding holidays, and on every Thursday it remains open throughout the day. On the other days, the workers visit the households in the morning shift. This centre is attached to the Kangu dispensary, which is located at a distance of 6 km, where proper indoor and outdoor facilities are available. The PHC for this area is at Thoreta, 9 km away. However, the patients do not go to the PHC. From the Kangu dispensary they go to Hamirpur or are further referred to PGI Chandigarh and sometimes they go to Shimla.

During the field visits the health workers give antenatal and post-natal care, guidance about dehydration solution, motivation for immunization as well as family planning. Antenatal care includes tetanus toxoid (TT) immunization, BP checking, and distribution of iron tablets. The ANM informed the team that more than half of the patients do not consume the full quantity of tablets prescribed and given. Some of them complain of constipation due to this medicine. They also agreed that immunization of mother and child is around 100 per cent and they ensure that the gap between two doses of polio/DPT is not more than two months. In schools they immunize girls of Classes VI and X every year. From the birth register, they keep a proper record of eligible children and the immunization given in the counterfoil of the child card. Vitamin A solution is also given every six months to the eligible children. Iodine in salt is checked in at least four samples every month in the area of this sub-centre at the outlet points. Since the villagers usually keep the salt in open containers, iodine may evaporate, but no case of goitre has been detected.

There is no provision for delivery cases in the centre and the ANM is not available after duty hours. So the deliveries are generally done by the local dais, of whom only one is trained. These workers claim that the dais are trained and a disposable kit is supplied to them though, rarely. At the time of delivery generally old and dirty clothes are used in spite of the best efforts of the ANM. Everybody promises to use washed clothes, but this promise is not usually kept. The practice of throwing away the first milk has been totally stopped and the child is put to feed after about an hour or two only.

Family planning methods such as Nirodh and oral pills are usually distributed when the workers go on field visits. Sometimes people come to the centre also to collect these. The MHW is more respected and trusted as he distributes some medicines also. The supply of medicines is sufficient. The reported cases of diseases recalled by the workers were diarrhoea, stomach problems, temperature, cold–cough, headache, cuts and wounds, body pain and white discharge, excessive bleeding, menopause, periods disturbances, stomach ache in girls at puberty, pneumonia, and worms.

Many cases of skin problems were observed for which most people take private medicine or go to the dispensary at Kangu, hence these cases are not reported at the centre. Sometimes the medicines are prescribed and for any reaction caused by these, Avil tablets are taken. The number of patients per day is around 10, with the maximum number being 25.

TABLE 6.3
Family Planning Methods, Batran

Total population	3865
Eligible couples	1095
Spacing methods total	163
(a) Pills	16
(b) IUD	79
(c) Nirodh	68
Termination	254
Female sterilization	217
Male sterilization	37

About 58 per cent of the couples practise family planning. Among the rest, grown up children or husbands working at far away places were the reasons expressed by most for not practising family planning.

The sub-centre building consists of two rooms, a store, bathroom, toilet and an open courtyard. When some women were contacted at the household level, it was revealed that people visit this centre for minor ailments, for first aid only. They go directly to the dispensary at Kangu for other illnesses. They did not confirm the household visits of the health workers. Many of them do not know about the delivery kits being supplied by the centre. Some women still put their children to breast feed after 2 to 3 days, and many do not know about dehydration solutions or iodized salt, which is contrary to the claim of the health workers.

6.2.9 *Social Issues—Customs and Practices*

FOOD HABITS

Rice, wheat, maize, and pulses are the main foodgrain items. Non-vegetarian food is consumed by all castes. All males consume non-vegetarian food occasionally, while about half of the females are pure vegetarian. Vegetables are cooked less frequently, as this area does not produce much of vegetables. Due to its shortage, milk is consumed mainly in the form of tea.

ALCOHOLISM

Almost all males consume alcohol occasionally, and a large number of them, mainly army personnel or policemen, are regular drinkers. In the evenings, a few persons are seen roaming around in a drunken state.

DRESS

The dressing pattern of this border village is quite similar to that of Punjab. Men, both old and young, wear kurta pyjamas, mostly made of terrycot cloth. In winters they wear a woolen coat over it. A number of men wear trousers with a shirt when going out. Many young men wear pants at home too. Both women and girls, wear salwar kameez. Women generally dress in bright colours and synthetic and fashionable cloth. Young married women are familiar with beauty parlours and tend to wear make-up even at home. Women in general wear silver ornaments with very little gold which usually consists of either a marriage ring, or a nosepin or earrings. Girls get their noses pierced at a very young age. All married women up to their middle age, wear *payals* on their feet. Girls before marriage do not cover their heads with a dupatta but after marriage they observe purdah.

MARRIAGE AND DEATH CUSTOMS

Marriages do not take place within the village and among relations. The custom of not marrying into the four gotras, that is, father's, mother's, father's mother and mother's mother is followed in all castes. The marriage ceremonies are performed according to Hindu rites. The marriageable age for boys is 22–3 years; sometimes it is as late as 28–9 years. For girls, the marriage age is 18–19 years. Marriage expenses are similar for both males and females, being Rs 40,000 and Rs 100,000 for SC and general castes, respectively. As part of the dowry, scooter, refrigerator, and mixie, are given by many. There is no case of inter-caste marriage or inter-religious marriage.

The practice of polyandry or polygamy is not at all practiced in this village. A few males have gone in for second marriage after the death of their first wife. There are no illicit relations reported, but the villagers remarked that there may be a few such cases.

The villagers celebrate a son's birth by distributing sweets and/or giving clothes to close relations. There are no puberty functions. The purdah system is still prevalent here, irrespective of the caste. Most of the men are serving outside the village as mentioned earlier, therefore, many households are headed by women. The main control of the households still rests with the non-residential husbands. The women have to take the day-to-day decisions and manage agriculture and house, cook, clean, purchase cattle, and take care of other household needs. The men folk keep a good relationship with the women. Decisions such as buying clothes, or visiting the parents are taken only after obtaining the husband's consent. Movement within the village or to the nearby town for any work is not restricted. Women attend to the school teachers, the patwari, gram sewak, and other officials if needed.

There was no case of suicide reported in this village and the village has never witnessed major violence leading to deaths. Though this village has the traditional joint family system, recently, a change has been observed because of economic compulsions. Even if one of the brother's earnings is not equivalent to that of the others, he will be forced to leave the joint family. Where the head of the household is the main person who controls the finances, the joint family is still surviving.

PANCHAYAT SECRETARY

The Panchayat secretary has two Panchayats under him. He visits the village on the 9th and 23rd of every month. His work involved conducting the Integrated Rural Development Programme (IRDP) and other backward caste (OBC) survey and preparing the voters list along with his normal duties. Seven cases under IRDP have been cleared in recent years. The income and expenses of the panchayat with source of income and pattern of expenditure are presented in Table 6.4. A chuHah tax is collected from all the households, and in 1993–4 this collection was Rs 1085. The other source of income is from the panchayat land.

6.2.10 *Summary of Focus Group Discussions*

Four FGDs were organized, two for women in the reproductive age group, one for elderly women above 55 year of age and one, for married men belonging to different castes.

Two FGDs for women in the reproductive age group were conducted. The first had eight participants, two were from the (nai) barber caste and the rest were SCs. The age group was between 21–9 years. All had studied up to the primary school level, two up to the middle level and only one up to the matriculation level. In the group, except for three women whose spouses were engaged in service, tailoring, and the third unemployed—the others along with their spouses were agricultural workers. Of the eight participants only two lived in joint families, others have nuclear families.

The second FGD was for upper caste women in the age group of 24–30 years, having minimum primary school education and living in rajput joint families. All of them were

TABLE 6.4
Funds and Expenditure, Batran

Year	Income	Funds raised	Expenditure	Purpose
1986–7	10,000	BDO	8697	Marriage/house
1988–9	15,000	BDO	15,003	Construction of streets
1992–3	40,000	BDO	46,039	Construction of streets
1992–3	4410	Panchayat	4410	Small bridge
1993–4	4000	Panchayat	3982	Bus stop
1993–4	4433	Panchayat	4433	Small bridge
1993–4	1000	Panchayat	1010	On panchayat ghar
1993–4	10,000	BDO	10,164	Small bridge
1993–4	15,000	BDO	15,046	Small bridge
1993–4	2000	Panchayat	2000	Cleaning panchayat ghar
1993–4	2000	Panchayat	2000	Repairing of High School walls
1993–4	10,000	BDO	10,000	Community centre in one hamlet.
1994–5	10,000	BDO	10,004	Construction of baurrie (source of drinking water)
1994–5	10,000	BDO	10,003	Small bridge
1994–5	20,000	BDO	20,002	Small bridge

Note: BDO: Block development office.

agricultural workers, while most of their spouses were engaged in service.

The FGD for elderly women had 11 participants—six rajputs, three SCs, and two who were landless. Of these three were living with their husbands and the rest in joint families. All of them were engaged in small household jobs (minor jobs like baby sitting, sweeping, cooking, etc.). Five were suffering from diseases like BP, pain in the feet, headache, neck pain, poor eyesight, and sinking heart. About one-third confided that their sons treated them well and took care of them, the others seemed desperate and talked emotionally on the same subject. Regarding their expectations from the government, all of them were vocal about their demands for regular pensions, although no one wanted staying arrangements or rations. The main reason for this expectation was the impression that the RRA team had called them to this meeting to consider some old age pensions.

The FGD for married men in the age group of 25–35 years, was reasonably good although participation of some of the members was not adequate. This may be due to the fact that this group was not homogeneous. Out of the seven participants, five were rajputs and two SCs. The occupational structure also varied—three were cultivators, one had a private business, one owned a tea stall, one supervised the water supply works and the last was illiterate, had no land and was thus engaged in wage labour.

6.2.11 Findings of Focus Group Discussions

EDUCATION

All participants in the FGDs were keen to educate their children. The commonly perceived advantages from education were: an improvement in general awareness, ease while travelling, creates more confidence, improves the prospects of service, business, and marriage.

The SC women reported that an educated person can engage in some self-employed work which will, in turn, improve the quality of life. For them, it was also a means of getting service sector employment for the boys and a good match for the girls.

The upper class women perceived that an educated person can do better cultivation, hence it enhances the status of the family and improves the social behaviour of the children.

Male group participants expected that the educated ones would look after their parents well, raise the family income, help the younger children in education and would get better technical jobs.

Even the old women recognized the importance of education as helpful in travelling and enhancing general awareness.

The male participants came out with some disadvantages; they felt that educated boys may get influenced by negative peer pressure, especially in the company of children from well-to-do families. This may influence them to develop negative attitudes towards rural life.

The general belief is that parents' education does not affect the child's studies, rather the children of uneducated parents are themselves motivated to study more.

Financial constraints or poverty is the major reason for drop-outs from school in all the groups. Parents find it difficult to provide uniforms, books, stationery, etc. Two of the groups correlated weakness in studies with the high drop-out rates—which are higher for the girls after matriculation than for the boys. This is also due to the fact that the school for higher studies is not in the village and there are problems associated with girls travelling outside the village. However, both men and women agreed that if a higher education facility were to be available in the village, girls would also continue their studies.

Along with studying, girls start helping a little in the household from the age of 7–8 years, while boys start doing minor shopping errands, cattle care and providing secondary help in cultivation and labour work from the age of 12–13 years. They are paid half the wage of an adult. However, children are not withdrawn from school to earn money, before completing their matriculation. The children who are involved in wage labour, do so during the holidays.

About 4–5 students from well-to-do families go to private English-medium schools at Kangu. The participants said that government education facilities are better than private, because of financial affordability. In all the groups, participants demanded the establishment of an anganwadi which would be helpful in pre-school education. Another common demand was the construction of toilets in the school.

HEALTH

Almost all households of the lower castes have modern septic latrines constructed by the block development office (BDO) on full subsidy. The upper caste had to pay Rs 300 and the remaining cost was subsidized. As a result, many upper caste households still do not have such toilets. The utilization of these toilets was extremely restricted due to the following reasons: (i) there is no privacy as these can not be covered; (ii) a full bucket of water is needed each time for which one has to go a long distance; (iii) the older generation is not habituated to using modern toilets; (iv) a good number of these got damaged within a few months due to faulty design. About three-fourth of the population goes to the forest or nala catchment for defecation.

The SCs drink water drawn mainly from the baurrie and in the summer some even drink tap water which is considered to be dirty. The upper castes, some OBCs, and SCs drink hand pump water, considered to be the best in the village. Some OBCs and SCs also drink water from open wells.

Due to the difficulty in collecting water, personal hygiene (bathing, washing clothes, etc.) is not maintained. This is seen mainly in the labour class. Women generally keep better hygiene, as they stay at home. After defecation or before cooking/eating, etc. they wash hands with ash or mud. Only a few employee households use soap.

The villagers do not have the habit of drinking boiled water. However, only when doctors recommended it during any illness, is boiled water consumed. After delivery, women usually drink boiled water for a month. Diarrhoea, fever, and stomach problems are considered to be water-borne diseases. A rich diet, good quality drinking water, and cleanliness of house and eatables reduces the risk of sickness. Women participants said that personal hygiene also affects health. They recognized the effect of seasonal variation in the pattern of diseases. In winters, diseases such as cold, cough, and fever dominate, in the rainy season malaria, and in summers fever and typhoid. They said that excessive or heavy work did not affect health.

The participants did not know much about contagious diseases. Some of them reported eye flu and TB to be contagious, which was spread by sharing utensils, clothes, etc. Dietary restrictions are usually observed only when recommended by the doctors during illness otherwise, they consume a normal diet.

Women were aware that a weak child is likely to get more diseases. The causes of disease conceptualization were contradictory. They believe in many different kinds of explanations of sickness. Effect of bacteria, *devta's* anger, mental tensions, evil eye (*nazar*) and misdeeds of previous births were given as the possible explanations for different kinds of diseases. Disabilities are seen as the result of misdeeds of a last birth and a child's crying as the effect of an evil eye. However, only a few believe in evil spirits or other supernatural explanations.

It was believed that infant deaths are because of God's wishes, non-treatment of ailment, deficiency of diet, mothers' weakness and mothers' carelessness. Non-immunization and diarrhoea are the major causes for infant mortality according to upper caste women.

Premature delivery, miscarriage, and still births were reported to occur due to women's weakness or a weak uterus. The SC women remarked that women were more prone to sickness than men as they worked more and consumed a poor diet. They said that food is served first to children, then to male members and the leftover is for female members. Men gave an additional reason for women's sickness as weakness due to pregnancies.

Male participants were not aware of women-specific diseases as women usually do not tell their husbands about such diseases. With further probing they named sexually transmitted diseases (STD) and AIDS as the sexual diseases.

Scheduled caste women interpreted the causes of congenital abnormalities as God's wish or mishandling of delivery by a local dai. The men's group considered cancer, paralysis, AIDS and TB as incurable if not detected at an early stage. Another typical observation by this group was that women whose husbands stay with them regularly, conceive more and have to get abortion occasionally. This adversely affects their health. Such abortions are generally performed by the local dai.

Poor health and frequent germ attacks were correlated to misdeeds in a previous birth. All believed in the effects of the evil eye (nazar) on children and effects of tension, but did not believe in evil spirits. The diseases common in children were fever, eye infections, stomach problems, dizziness, cold, cough, headache, leg pain, diarrhoea, vomiting, and skin problems.

The old age illnesses were headache, stomach problems, joint pain, poor eyesight, back pain, swelling of feet/body, fever, tension, tooth problems, low BP, sinking heart, cold, cough, leucorrhoea and skin problems. Women suffer more from back pain (specially sterilized women), excessive bleeding, leucorrhoea, prolapsed uterus swelling, gastric problems, cancer, etc. Other common diseases reported by males were pneumonia, malaria, dysentery, piles, eye flu, TB, diabetes, etc.

There is no practice such as polygamy or polyandry and hence there is no risk of STD. Seeking treatment after falling ill mainly depends upon the amount of cash in hand.

Home remedies are tried when the villagers cannot afford proper medical treatment. Headache, fever, cold, cough, are many a times treated through home remedies. Adults do not usually rest, during and after illness.

Pregnant women work normally till delivery, but avoid lifting heavy loads specially during the last month. After delivery, minor household work is attended to after 15 days and routine work starts after a month.

The deliveries are mostly attended by the local dais who are not trained. Dais never make use of the kits supplied by the sub-centre. The cord is cut by sterilized scissors or by a blade taken from the household. The mother-in-law and other elderly women do not usually allow a hospitalized delivery. Further, the ANM does not attend to any delivery.

All expecting women procure and consume vitamins, iron tablets and TT immunizations from the public health facility. The ANM visits the households to motivate family planning acceptance, but for all antenatal and post-natal care the beneficiaries go to the sub-centre. The public health facility is the main source of preventive and curative services. For all types of illnesses, patients (including infants) go to the public dispensary at Kangu. Medicines are usually prescribed but for minor ailments some medicines are given by the dispensary or the sub-centre. The participants wanted longer working hours of the sub-centre.

The incentive money for sterilization is welcomed and it is spent on providing a good diet for women. Proper care is taken during sterilization, but there is no post-operative care. Colostrum is not given to the child, and the child is usually put to breast feed after 2–3 days of spoon feeding milk other than that of the mother.

Participants were divided almost equally on the role of educated women to prevent and cure illness. Men said that an educated woman would avoid breast feeding and will spend the maximum time on herself. On the other hand, some SC and all upper caste women recognized the positive role of women's education. The educated female will keep the children and house clean and seek immediate and proper medical help in case of illness.

SOCIAL SECURITY

Participants were worried about old age but no one was saving any money for it. The reason being that they live hand to mouth. Savings and gold are considered as the best old age security. Generally, nobody in the village helps if someone loses an earning member. The male child was considered the main financial security and the female child for help in nursing. Women keep only Rs 10 to 20 for emergencies.

In the old age focus group, two-thirds of the participants confided that their sons did not take care of them. Still, all of them feel that sons are the best security. Also, owning land did not change their status if the quality of land was poor. During their illness, daughters-in-law generally look after them. All members of the older age group expected the government to give them pension. Although the old women do not get social respect within the family or community, grand children are generally affectionate. Intra-family conflicts are common and frequent in all households. The reasons reported were, not getting food on time, drinking habit of men, acute poverty, joint family problems, children's education and needs, women's disobedience, household necessities, kitchen needs, illness, etc.

Inter-family conflicts sometimes occur due to property, drinking, etc. They are solved in the Panchayat. The villagers could not recall any police case for such conflicts.

6.2.12 Free Listing of Illnesses

A morbidity schedule on free listing of illnesses was canvassed in this village among twenty married women of 25 to 65 years of age. The women were from the following age groups: 25 to 35 years (6), 36 to 45 years (9), 46 to 55 years (4) and sixty five-year old (1). Out of the 14 rajput women, seven were illiterate, four had studied up to primary level and only three reached above primary level. The lone 50 year-old woman carpenter was illiterate, and of the five SC women, one was illiterate, two had studied up to primary level, and others up to middle and above. These women from different hamlets of the village were interviewed individually. They were asked the illness pattern in the village for the past 2–4. First they were asked to recall the illness (without probes), once they exhausted the list then some probes like seasonality, gender, age (children, old age, women-specific disease with emphasis on reproductive morbidity) were used to facilitate the respondent. Though the village is quite spread out, the inter-family/intra-family interaction is very good. This may be due to better literacy and employment levels. Most of the women reported acute illnesses only but a few reported chronic ones also. Stomach problems (diarrhoea, dysentery, gastric, worms, etc.) and cold–cough were reported by almost all (95 per cent).

The other major diseases were fever (85 per cent), body/back pain (55 per cent), joint pain (50 per cent), malaria (40 per cent), skin problems (35 per cent), and eye infection (30 per cent). The women-specific diseases reported were leucorrhoea (20 per cent) and irregular menses (5 per cent). The remaining diseases reported were mainly chronic.

About half of the respondents could state the perceived causes of illness, while others could not identify the cause. They identified stomach problems due to diet; malaria due to mosquitoes; skin problems due to heat; joint/body pain because of old age or weakness; cold–cough due to winter cold;

jaundice because of the summer heat; back ache as an after-effect of sterilization or delivery; high BP due to worry, low BP because of weakness; and leucorrhoea due to weakness.

TABLE 6.5
Prevalence Rate of Illness, Batran

(*N* = 20)

Local name	Standard name	No.	Percentage
Diarrhoea, dysentery, gastric, worms, etc.	Stomach problems	19	95
Sardi, jukam, sore throat	Cold, cough	19	95
Bukhar	Fever	17	85
Sharir dard/kamar dard	Body pain/joint pain	11	55
Joron ka dard	Joint pain	10	50
Malaria	Malaria	8	40
Charam rog, kharas	Skin problem	7	35
Ankh dard/cataract	Eye infection/cataract	6	30
Safed pani	Leuccorrhoea	4	20
Sir dard	Headache	4	20
Dama/sans ki bimari	Asthma/bronchitis	3	15
Pneumonia	Pneumonia	3	15
Khasra/mata	Measles/chicken pox	2	10
BP ghatna/badhna	BP low/high	2	10
Jor dard	Arthrhitis	1	5
Typhoid	Typhoid	1	5
Peelia	Jaundice	1	5
Mahwari disturb	Irregular menses	1	5
Dil ka dard	Heart attack	1	5
Cancer	Cancer	1	5
Lakwa	Paralysis	1	5
Hernia	Hernia	1	5
Kaledu	Mumps	1	5

6.3 Bhullang Village

6.3.1 Location

The tehsil and district in which village Bhullang is located as well as the nearest town (18 km away), are known by the name Kullu. Kullu town is also the district headquarters and is about 9 km from the Mandi–Kullu national highway No. 21. The nearest bus stop on this highway is at Mohal, from where a kutcha foot path leads to the village, situated on the top of a hill. The distance from one corner of the village to the other is about 5 km. There is another road from Kullu to Dora Nala. A part of the village is nearer to this road and is easily approachable, though there is a hilly river between the road and the village, so that in the rainy season the village is not approachable from this side. It is about 90 km from the nearest railway station of Joginder Nagar, which is almost out of reach for this population. The state capital Shimla is about 200 km away.

The village is at a height of approximately 1400 meters or more. The upper part of the village experiences snowfall in the winter months of January to March. In April, the weather becomes warmer and the snow melts. The months of May–June are the hottest with the mercury rising above 30°C. The rainy season starts by June end and extends up to early August. The remaining months are pleasantly cool and by December light woollen clothes are required.

6.3.2 Land Area

DISTRIBUTION

The total geographical area of the village is 154 hectares, which does not include the unmeasured third class forest area. The cultivable area is 128 hectares, out of which only one hectare is irrigated, four hectares is permanently fallow, 22 hectares is nala, paths, residential area, etc. The community land is about three hectares. There is no separate land for grazing. All the households have some land. The village consists of 16 small villages or hamlets.

LAND USE

The village has orchards of apple, *kinnu* (a hybrid citrus fruit), plum, almonds, and gal gal, etc. The third class forest in the village has trees such as *kail*, *deodar*, pinus (*cheel*), and rubenia, etc. The hill is not widely covered by these trees, but trees such as kail can be mainly seen in pockets, described as jungle by the inhabitants. Even these trees remain green at the top only, because the lower branches have been cut off by the villagers for fuel purposes. Quite a large part of the village hill is barren.

The steep slope of the hill and the absence of thick forest causes excessive soil erosion. The field beds have stones boundaries but on the top of the boundaries grass is grown which helps in preventing soil erosion. The soil conservation department has planted quite a few rubenia trees as well as grasses such as feactica, steacria to stop further soil erosion. The rubenia plant is quite useful as the leaves are used as fodder for sheep and goats while the skin of the soft branches is used to make ropes and the remaining hard wood is used as fuel.

SOIL EROSION

The soil in this village is generally sandy loam and erosion (sheet and galli) takes place. The Department of Soil Conservation Works and the Forest Department take care of soil conservation in arable and non-arable land, respectively. The community type arable land is given drainage laying treatment like galli control, check dams, check walls, guide walls, etc. In addition to these engineering works, vegetative structures like contour-vegetated edges and edges/shrubs including grasses are laid out on community as well as individual private land.

Rubenia plants which are soil binding and useful for fodder and fuel purposes are planted along the drainage line and the boundary lines of the individual farms. The community works are undertaken purely by the public departments, whereas work on the farmers' land is executed by the farmers themselves on a 50 per cent subsidy and 50 per cent loan basis. The loan is to be paid after five years in ten-yearly, interest-free instalments. The rates per hectare to the individual farmer is Rs 4000 and the upper limit of the total amount is Rs 6000.

6.3.3 General Characteristics of the Village

The hill adjacent to the village is overshadowed on two sides by a mountain fully covered with snow. On the third side of the hill, flows a nala (Dora nala) while river Beas flows from the fourth side after a small stretch of plain area—Mohal. The surroundings are generally dry, but for two to three months between December and March, the upper part is covered with snow. When the snow melts the paths get muddy and water flows from some paths.

TEMPLE

A temple of Naina Devi is situated where the Goddess came riding on a pig and killed the Rakshas who were troubling the villagers. This portion of the village is called Sur. Since then, every year villagers take the idols of the Goddess and other Gods from one storage place to this place for worship. The celebration and worship goes on for a week. Not only the villagers but even a few outsiders visit this temple during this week.

HOUSES

The houses are constructed within the farms. There is no proper inhabited village. Every family lives at a place fairly distant from the others. At some places, two to four houses are adjoining each other because the same family stay separately in these houses. Generally, the houses are made of wood. The ground floor walls are sometimes made of stone but the roof, floor and walls of the first floor are made of wood. On the top there is a sloping roof of slates, useful during snowfall. The ground floor is usually used for cattle while the upper part is used for all the households activities. In poorer houses, there is only one room which is used for all purposes including keeping cattle. People sleep on the floor. They spread a *chatai* (mat) and old clothes on the floor to sleep on. Recently, some people have started using beds also, as the beds have been given as part of the dowry in some cases.

The villagers think that their ancestors came to this place from Prasher in Mandi district, where the legendary rishi Prasher lived. There is no legend attached either to the origin of the village or to the name of the village. The Naina Devi temple is an ancient temple. Since the building is wooden, it can be assumed that the structure is of recent origin.

6.3.4 Population

The village consists of 16 small villages or hamlets. The number of SC households is 183 and upper castes is 104. These castes are well distributed among different segments. There are 238 upper caste males and 262 females; 445 SC males and 432 females; 4 ST males and 4 females. The religion of all the households is Hinduism. The castes are SC, ghumar, badhai, thani, lohar, sonar, brahmin, bhat, and rajput, etc.

Though the upper castes and SCs were equally distributed earlier and had equal share in property, that is, land in the village; over generations, the SC population has become greater in number than the upper castes due to the higher birth rate. Thus the land held by SC is more fragmented, whereas all the upper caste families own larger pieces of land. So in terms of economic status, the upper castes are better-off, but in terms of political influence or power the SCs have an upper edge.

MIGRATION

Migration both in and out is negligible in this village. About two or three families have migrated in from Lahul and Spiti district and the same number have migrated out due to the employment opportunities. The families migrating in have purchased part of the land of some other families. The forest area and other community land have been encroached upon by the adjoining cultivators. This encroachment went on up to 1980.

6.3.5 Occupation

Cultivation is the main occupation of the villagers. All castes have cultivable pieces of land, even though the holdings are very small. Males, females, and children of all castes participate equally in cultivation. The crops grown are maize, wheat, *kodra* (a coarse cereal that remains unaffected by disease for years together), paddy, *mah* (black gram), *rajmah*, potato, vegetables, *sarson*, etc. The main crops are maize and wheat which cover about 70 per cent of the gross cropped area.

Non-agricultural wage labour is the next occupation undertaken by men, and by women of the SCs more than those from the upper castes. Animal husbandry is also an important part of the economic life of almost each household in this village, the cattle being raised for household use only. Children usually graze the cattle. Some SC males are engaged in basket making and a few men are carpenters by profession.

Of the six persons in service, three are in the Police (two hawaldars and one constable); one multipurpose health worker working in this village itself, one female (daughter-in-law) teaching on a temporary basis in the village primary school and one peon in the Forest Department.

Family child labour is fairly prevalent among all castes. The girl child, apart from household chores, also grazes the cattle. The male child helps in the fields, grazes the cattle, and also collects the fuel wood.

The village experienced drought conditions continuously from 1984 onwards. Even during this period, nobody migrated out. The effect of this drought was felt more by cattle and quite a number died due to hunger and thirst. The villagers themselves managed to survive by some means or the other.

As there is no migration at all from the village, there is no seasonal effect on the wage rates in the village. The usual wage rate in both agricultural and non-agricultural labour is Rs 25 for the males and females, while children are paid half of this. Even the forest guard employs local children and pays them half of the adult's rate but in the records he shows that a full rate is paid. Their age is always noted in the records to be above 18 years.

Altogether, there are about 10 people who have studied beyond Class X, six of them are employed as mentioned earlier. The remaining are unemployed and live in the village. So far, no one from the village has become an officer or an influential person.

ANIMAL HUSBANDRY

Animal husbandry is almost a part and parcel of each household. The domestic animals in the village are cow, bullock, horse, mule, sheep, goat, etc. while pet dogs are kept to guard sheep and goats. The cows, bullocks, and sheep are kept by almost all the households for domestic use only. There are no milk co-operatives or wood collection centres, etc. The milk and wood is consumed within the individual households. Sometimes, milk is sold by some to neighbours with the hope of obtaining the same concession when their own cattle dry up.

6.3.6 Infrastructural Facilities

TABLE 6.6
Amenities and Services, Bhullang

Amenities	Place	Distance (km)
Approach road	Mohal	9
Bus stop	Mohal	9
Railway station	Surinder nagar	90
Post office	Mohal	9
Community television	No	NA
Community radio	No	NA
Library/reading room	No	NA
Electric street lights	No	NA
Bank	Mohal	9
Co-operative credit society	Mohal	9
Regulated market/mandi	Mohal	9
Pharmacy/drug outlet	Mohal	9
Sources of drinking water	(a) Piper water	NA
for all costs	(b) Baurrie	NA

TABLE 6.7
Time Calendar, Bhullang

Infrastructure	Year
Naina devi temple	Since 500 years
Radio	1960
Primary school	1960
Primary school building	1970
Electricity	1977
Drinking water	1978
Sub-centre	1989
Flour mill	1989
TV	1990
Telephone to Panchayat	1992
PDS (ration depot)	1992
Mahila mandal	1992
Private toilets	1992
Building for sub-centre	1993
Yuvak mandal	1995

SHOPS

There is one flour mill in the village and four grocery shops. There is also a ration depot. Only urgent necessities are purchased in the village, otherwise the villagers go to nearby places such as Mohal, Bhuntar, Kullu for shopping.

WATER SUPPLY

There are a few water storage tanks and channels (*kools*) in the village, which are constructed by the Department of Water Conservation. Under Jawahar Rozgar Yojana (JRY), the village panchayat has also constructed tanks. This water not being sufficient for the use of the inhabitants, the tank is not used for irrigation. Piped water is supplied to parts of the village from some of these storage tanks and others are directly accessed to fetch water for household needs as well as for cattle use. There is no problem of water logging and salinity or alkalinity in this village.

DRINKING WATER

Tap water is available in all the hamlets but it is in short supply. All castes use tap water for drinking. There are natural streams also, where cattle drink water and clothes are washed. The taps are at common places and sometimes water is wasted as people forget to turn off the taps.

PUBLIC DISTRIBUTION SYSTEM AND CO-OPERATIVE CREDIT SOCIETY

The PDS has its depot in Mohal. This scheme started functioning in this village only in October 1992. At present the number of ration cards issued are: SC (173) and other castes (106). Items sold include sugar, wheat, rice, palmoline, cloth, and kerosene oil, on control rate; while pulses, oils, soap, washing powder, copies, cement, and cloth on free sale.

There is no co-operative credit society in the village. Some of the villagers are members of the Mohal Co-operative Credit Society. There is no money-lender in the village. Small amounts can be borrowed from the neighbours without interest.

GOVERNMENT/NON-GOVERNMENTAL ORGANIZATION SCHEMES

Widows and old and blind people get a government pension. Many people got loans under the IRDP. Indira Awaas Yojana Scheme is also available in this village. In the rainy season, some houses collapsed in the recent past and the people got between Rs 5000 and Rs 6000 as government aid, irrespective of the cost of rebuilding.

6.3.7 *Educational Facilities*

The sole government primary school in this village has three rooms. Of the four teachers, one male and one female teacher are employed on *ad hoc* basis, the other two male teachers are regular. A part-time worker (*jal wahak*) is also employed for distributing drinking water, cleaning, etc.

TABLE 6.8
Classwise Break up of students in Bhullang Primary School

Class	All			Scheduled Castes		
	Total	M	F	Total	M	F
1st	34	24	10	25	15	10
2nd	40	23	17	29	12*	17
3rd	28	13	15	16	7	9
4th	13	8	5	2	0	2
5th	14	10	4	6	5	1
Total	**129**	**79**	**50**	**77**	**41**	**36**

Note: * One is ST.

As there are only three rooms, Class V alone gets an independent room, Classes I and II as well as Classes III and IV share the other rooms. In winters, the students of all classes sit in the open at one place, though there is an open space on the other side also. The practice of preparing eligible student's list was stopped some five or six years ago, and hence the teachers do not have any record of the enrolment rate.

The fee and building fund of Re 1, 10 paise as Red Cross fund, Rs 2 which is compulsory under the Sanchyaka scheme are collected monthly. Under the Sanchayaka scheme, the money deposited by children during their primary education is paid to them along with interest for higher studies. A parent-teacher (PT) fund of Rs 4 is taken annually.

There is no toilet facility in the school, so the students and teachers use the foot paths or nearby jungle. When the part-time worker is not available, the students clean the black board and rooms. It was observed that teachers also send the children for petty personal work, sometimes outside the village.

Scheduled castes get scholarships but there is no free distribution of uniform, books, stationery, mid-day meals, etc. The regular teachers were satisfied with the salary and job conditions, but the *ad hoc* teachers expected a higher salary. *Durries* for the students have been provided recently.

The SC and other caste students sit together and they do not abuse each other by caste in the school. When they fight, they abuse each other by their father's name. Students do not bathe or wash clothes regularly. According to the students, one or the other teacher remains on leave.

A PTA, with the village pradhan as its chairman, holds a meeting once a year. Only a few parents attend such meetings.

TABLE 6.9
Sanchayaka Scheme and Other Funds, Bhullang

Name of scheme	Earlier balance	Saving 1.1.94 to 24.12.94	Total
Building fund	5505.15	1330.00	5627.15
Red cross	1398.82	132.70	1411.02
Sanchayaka	11715.70	3093.00	11954.70

The school building is very small and the children sit on the floor. Many children drop out even before completing primary school. Only a few from this village study beyond the primary level. Education after matriculation has not started in this village.

The National Literacy Programme started in the village was successful in identifying the target population and even distributed books to some. However, in later stages it was a total failure in this village. There are about 8–10 boys who have studied up to matriculation in this Panchayat and three of them could secure jobs, while the others are employed in their own family occupation.

6.3.8 *Social Issues—Customs and Practices*

FOOD HABITS

Generally people take meals twice a day. The food items consumed are rice, wheat, maize, pulses, meat, and vegetables.

Everybody gets a sufficient amount of food throughout the year.

ALCOHOLISM

Drinking is common here. Mostly men prepare it at home. There are occasional inter/intra family conflicts after having drinks. Even the old women drink. Smoking is common amongst men, but many married women also smoke.

COOKING CHULLAH

There are no gobar gas plants in the village, but there are two or three improved chullahs. As this is a forest area, wood is mainly used as fuel.

DRESS

Males wear kurta pyjama and females wear salwar kameej and *pattu* over it. Women do not observe purdah, girls wear frocks up to 3–4 years of age.

MARRIAGE CUSTOMS

The marriageable age of boys is 15–16 years and for girls it is 17–18 years. So usually the wife is elder to the husband by a year or two. The parents arrange some marriages. Otherwise the boy and girl elope for a few days and when they come back the community performs the marriage ceremony. Most of the marriages take place within the village. If any relative lives outside the village, then some girls are married there. About 100 people make a marriage party, mostly from the same caste only. Dowry consists of a bedding, a pattu, few utensils, and some gold ornaments. Sometimes people spend up to Rs 10,000 on marriages. If a woman is childless, the man may marry a second time. Parents generally live with the younger child. Property is usually divided after the death of the parents.

CEREMONIES

As the girls are generally married within the village, parental property is divided between the siblings. The married girls touch the feet of the relatives in respect. Sweets are distributed at the birth of a son, but not at the birth of a daughter. They perform a *mundan* ceremony for boys. The dead are burned, but a child less than a year is buried after death. The status of women is comparatively better as they get a share of the parental property. If the husband or in-laws do not treat her well, she gets married again.

POLYANDRY OR POLYGAMY

Polyandry or polygamy is practiced openly. A few men had second marriages and in cases where their first wife was alive they usually deserted the first one. As marriages can take place within the village, when a couple wants to marry, they run away for few days and when they come back the villagers accept them as married. Even if a married woman wants to live with somebody else, she pays the cost of the earlier marriage to her first husband.

FAMILY STRUCTURE

The joint family system prevails here. All sons usually remain together till the father is alive but immediately after his death, the joint family splits into nuclear families, headed by each son. In case the children are young at the time of the father's demise, they stay together up to their marriage and who so ever gets married sets up a separate household.

INTER-CASTE/INTER-RELIGION MARRIAGES

As there is a single religion in this village, there is no case of inter-religion marriages, however, inter-caste marriages are common. Society accepts these marriages up to the extent that they are not actively opposed. However if an upper caste male or female marries a low caste person, the upper caste parents will break off their relations with their child. Recently, in the case of a rajput girl marrying an SC boy, her parents cut off all relations with her.

FAIRS AND FESTIVALS

All the traditional Hindu festivals are celebrated in the village separately by scheduled castes and the upper castes. A week-long fair is organized at the temple every year in which people from other villages participate along with the local residents. The upper castes worship inside the temple, but the SCs are not allowed to go near the deity.

PANCHAYAT SECRETARY

The Panchayat earns its income from donations, house tax, land revenue, government help, and JRY. The money collected is spent on school buildings, constructing pucca passages, keeping a chowkidar, and other expenditures.

TABLE 6.10
Income of Bhullang Panchayat

(Rupees)

Year	Jawahar rozgar yojana	Panchayat house tax	Government aid
1991–2	11,700	209	–
1992–3	12,313	2092	3000
1993–4	28,719	1387	30,000
1994–5	14,770	197	10,000

6.3.9 Health

PRIVATE PRACTIONER

No medical practitioner of any system of medicine was available. For private medical help Mohal is sometimes visited. Generally people prefer the public hospital at Kullu or the sub-centre in the village.

SUB-CENTRE

The sub-centre situated in the heart of Bhullang, covers 47 small villages. These villages are very small in terms of population. The total population of all these villages was 2840 as on 4 May 1992. The MHW who belongs to one of these villages is very popular with the masses. All the villagers accord him the status of a doctor. He keeps many medicines and injections. Generally, he provides curative services, apart from preventive/promotive ones. He refers the patients to Kullu hospital if he cannot diagnose the illness. The hospital authorities prescribe medicines, which are given to the patient through the MHW. Sometimes, he prescribes the medicines and buys these from the open market against payment. As there is no private doctor in the village, he fills in an important gap. As he is not well trained in curative health, serious problems sometimes occur because of his wrong diagnosis or wrong medication.

The ANM is not as popular—her visits are fewer as she comes from Kullu. The villagers need occasional visits of doctors to this sub-centre.

There was one case of leprosy in this village. He used to live separately and is no more now. When this disease was detected, his family built him a small house and provided him the necessities of life. Many old people have weak vision. Two years ago one woman died of cancer. There are 4–5 cases of polio. There is no anganwadi or mid-day meal scheme in the village.

6.3.10 Summary of Focus Group Discussions

Four focus group discussions were held to ascertain the status with respect to education, health, and social security. The details of the participants in these focus groups are as follows:

CURRENTLY MARRIED YOUNG MALES

The focus group was held for 100 minutes with seven SC and three upper caste male participants in the age group 22–35 years. All were literate except for three SCs. A count of their children varied from 2 to 5 and all of them have at least one son. Three of them did not have daughters and half of them live in joint families. All of them are occupied in cultivation and two of them in wage labour. One of the participants had TB five years ago and another complained of joint pain, all others were healthy. Except for one, all have cultivable land either in their or their spouse's name. The rating of this focus group was very satisfactory.

SCHEDULED CASTE MARRIED WOMEN WITH CHILDREN LESS THAN 5 YEARS OLD

The focus group was held for 90 minutes with nine SC participants, in the age group of 20 to 30. The education level was middle (1), primary (1), below primary (1), and illiterate (6). All of them were living in nuclear families and helped in cultivation along with household work. The number of children varied from 1 to 3. The participants had two sons and one daughter (3); only two daughters (2); one son (1); and one son, one daughter (2). The rating of the focus group was satisfactory.

WOMEN WITH SCHOOL-GOING CHILDREN

The focus group was held with eight SC and one rajput participant for 90 minutes. The age group of the participants was 29 to 40 years. Only one of them was educated up to Class IV. The number of children in their family varied from 3 to 6. All of them have at least one son. All except one have daughters also. Six of them were from nuclear families. All of them help in cultivation along with household work. Four of them reported weak eye sight. No one owned land in their own or their spouse's name. The rating of this group was satisfactory.

ELDERLY WOMEN

The focus group was held with nine participants for 95 minutes. All the participants were illiterate SCs aged between 59 to 70 years. Six of them were married and three were widows. The number of living children varied from one to eight. Two of them had only daughters and the rest had both sons and daughters. The widow who had only one daughter is living with her daughter and the other widow having only daughters lives with the daughters. All others live with their sons. All of them still help in the fields and do some household work. Four of them were ill due to asthma, TB, goitre, and cough. Three of them have land in their names or in their husbands' names. The rating of the focus group was satisfactory.

6.3.11 Findings of Focus Group Discussions

EDUCATION

The village is widely spread out with an inadequate education facility and it is educationally backward. The population covered by the primary school, is not much; because of difficult terrain, the school is not easily accessible. After the primary level, further education facility is a long distance away. Most of the participants viewed education positively in the sense that it makes one civilized, develops the brain, increases the chances of getting jobs and improves marriage prospects. The men and young women think that it improves the quality of life, with lesser chances of being cheated, enables one to shop smartly and maintain better cleanliness, personal hygiene, etc. The male participants believed that education makes a person more confident to talk to others in business dealings, cultivation, and cattle care. The educated person can understand when the cattle are sick or which medicine is suitable and can seek medical help from the correct person. Some of the female participants stated that an educated person could be helpful in educating the next generation, could shop with confidence, could look for gainful wage labour and maintain accounts. The elderly women thought that the educated get more respect. There is no disadvantage of education, but a few males feared that if the educated do not get employment, they would hesitate to become involved in wage labour. The expectations from boys and girls after education are, respectively, better financial support and a better life after marriage. In the primary school, the number of rajput girls is far less than the rajput boys. When asked, the male participants reported that in a natural way births of girls are lesser than those of boys in rajput families. There is no practice of infanticide or foeticide or any other visible cause.

Most of the participants were of the view that the main reason for drop-outs or non-enrolment is the problem in arranging the fee, books, uniform, etc. due to acute poverty. The other major reasons are a lack of interest, or weakness in, or failure in studies and also spending time in household work and cattle grazing. Male participants attributed the drop-out rate to the parents' illiteracy. Lack of proper facilities, long distance, and need for training girls in household work before marriage were the reasons expressed by some of the women participants. Girls are withdrawn at a higher rate as compared to boys. Male participants further stated that when the educated youth could not get employment, they even lost interest in the family occupation of cultivation or wage labour. Such a situation created disinterest in the parents to enroll and educate their children. They also expressed the view that if any earning member dies then also children are withdrawn and the consent of the children is generally not taken. Even if the child wants to study, the final decision lies with the parents.

In case of need at home, the elder child is asked to take leave, irrespective of gender. Parents do not provide them many teaching aids, though they are motivated to do the home work given by the teachers. Children are involved in some activity between the age of 7 to 12. Girls do more household work and start early. Education in the school is, however, satisfactory and the students enjoy the teacher's company. Most of the parents did not expect that their children would get any job after education but they did send them to school so that child could learn to talk, behave, respect elders, work properly, keep the house tidy and for the development of brain. After dropping out, girls are engaged in stitching, cattle grazing, sweeping, fetching water, etc. Some of the participants reported that there was no problem in admissions up to the high school level. In the primary school, there are problems of less number of rooms, inadequate mats and lack of water supply, inadequate number of teachers, lack of fencing around the school building and lack of proper passages to school. There is no toilet facility in the school. The general perception voiced is that nobody cares and they get nothing from the government, even though most of the students get free books, etc. They demanded that text books and uniforms should be provided free by the government for the poor. Government schools are considered as good. The male participants demanded mid-day meals for students and balwadis in different hamlets.

The reasons for fewer students being present during the visit of this team were explained as extreme winter and non-availability of necessities like firewood in the school and a lack of woollen clothes possessed by the school-going children.

HEALTH

Only a few households have constructed modern toilets, which are also not usable during extreme winters. Most of the people defecate in their own fields. Others go to the forest or use the passages. Though there is a government water supply, it is not sufficient, especially in summers. Many drink water from the baurrie, a natural source of water. In winters, people drink lukewarm water and boiled water only if recommended by the doctor. The shortage of water and extreme winters change standards of personal hygiene. Due to shortage of water or money for soap, the women bathe after two to six days and sometimes wash their hair after a month. Clothes are changed only on an occasion or for a visit outside the village or after 15 days to one month. Most of the villagers know that better sanitation, hygiene and a proper diet ensure good health. They also know that polluted water can cause illness. They cannot control most of these. The effect of seasonal variation on the disease pattern was recognized by most. In winters, cold, cough and fever are more common, while in the summers, headache, stomach ache, loose motion, vomiting, and skin problems are more prevalent. Most of them were aware of communicable diseases. Some of the communicable diseases reported were skin problems, TB, cough, loose motion, vomiting, leprosy, and eye infection. Such diseases spread by sleeping in the same room as the infected person or sharing drinking and eating utensils. Actually, no such precaution is followed as the living space is less. Only in cases of leprosy care is taken to seclude the affected.

They believe that diseases occur due to natural causes (bacterial), evil spirit, devta's anger, evil eye (nazar), lack of proper diet and weakness. Nobody believed in the misdeeds of previous birth. The women with school-going children reported that menopause and excess menses also lead to diseases. Tension and excess work can cause illness. In the free listing the diseases reported were TB (because of poor cleanliness and weakness), diarrhoea (due to summer season and contaminated water), headache, stomach ache (because of eating hot and cold items simultaneously), cold (winter), leucorrhoea, worms, excess menses, cough, asthma (because of smoking), joint pain, skin problems, scabies, loose motion/vomitting, fever, headache, indigestion, ear pain, stomach pain after delivery, blood in cough, etc. Women are more prone to sickness and women's diseases are white discharge, cold–cough, stomach ulcer, stomach problems after delivery, dizziness, cancer, back ache and headache, TB, excess menses, ulcer in the uterus, and irregular menses. Most of the women inform their husbands about women-specific diseases. Dietary restrictions are observed at the recommendation of doctors. Married women reported precautions during illness as not eating potato, cabbage, rajmah and ghee, while rice water and non-veg soup is consumed. They generally do not take rest during or after illness. In families where there are other members to help, some do take rest. Cancer, heart palpitation, mental cases, etc. were considered as incurable diseases. Some participants remarked that cancer, leprosy, TB etc., if treated at the initial stage are curable. Similarly, mental diseases if present from birth are not curable but if the cause is evil spirit, then they are curable. The old age participants occasionally have illnesses as headache, stomach ache, joint pain, weak eyesight, hearing problem, breathlessness, cold, cough, goitre, incapacity to climb the hill or to do physical work, fever, chest pain, arm pain, etc.

Premature births and miscarriages occur due to negligence of the mother's illness, lifting heavy weight during pregnancy, and improper diet. The causes for infant deaths are assumed to be lack of adequate diet taken by the pregnant mother, effect of evil spirits or pregnant mothers not getting immunized. They could not think of any cause of maternal death except the improper birth of the child. Women generally do not increase their diet during pregnancy because they cannot digest it or afford it.

Women work till the day of delivery, and afterwards if there is no helping hand, they start the necessary household work 2–3 days later. Otherwise they resume work after 10 to 12 days. The women start cultivation or wage labour after one to three months of delivery. Mostly the deliveries take place in the village with the help of a dai (midwife), who may or may not be trained. Most deliveries occur in the living room but sometimes the cattle shed is specially chosen to maintain the cleanliness of the living room. Few use washed bed sheets, most use old and unwashed bed sheets. A new blade is used to cut the cord. A sitting posture (on stones) is always used to facilitate the delivery. In case of a difficult delivery, the woman has to be taken to the public hospital at Kullu. Due to the difficult way some women even die on the way. Some men have married for the second time, for the first wife could not have a male child. After falling ill they start medication with a lapse of 5–6 days. They first try home remedies and seek devta's permission. If the disease is not due to the devta's anger, only then do they seek medical treatment. If a child is ill, professional medical treatment is sought early unlike the response to the illness of adults. Most patients (approximately one third do not do so) first ask the devta, if the disease is due to him before they go to the sub-centre. Further, if referred they generally visit the public hospital at Kullu or PHC, Bhunter. The role of devta is recognized by almost all, some approach him first, others approach him if not cured by the doctors. Money is also a consideration in seeking treatment; if they have money, treatment is started early, otherwise they wait for long period. In case of emergencies the villagers approach the MHW who is posted in the village, for medication.

The participants complained that the public hospital staff does not respect the poor and preferential treatment is accorded to the better off. However, the sub-centre staff is nice to them.

SOCIAL SECURITY

When an earning member of a family dies, the other family members have only each other to depend on. Others in the village are not in a position to help. For a few days, relatives extend some help. To tackle emergencies like snowfall season, the villagers keep a stock of firewood, cereals, etc. It is very rare to find anybody with a savings account. Women keep small amounts of Rs 10 to Rs 50 separately for emergencies, usually without the knowledge of their husbands. Within the village a small amount can be raised as loan with an interest as high as 10 per cent per month. Both boys and girls can help their parents financially in old age. Widows are accorded less social status in the family and society. Women are not independent enough to do even small shopping for themselves, as they have to ask for money and permission from their husbands. All prefer a government loan and want the IRDP loan to be waived off. Money is considered as the best old age security, but they are unable to save. The next security is dependence on children. Even in old age people have to work, as possession of land, gold or money does not significantly change a person's status with respect to his children looking after his needs. Old people do worry about the future, but are confused about the type of worry. Most of them are loved by their children and grand-children. During sickness the old women are looked after very well.

Intra-family conflicts do occur in most of the families, the causes being affairs related to children, drinking habits (women also drink), financial constraints, children's education, home work, women speaking in the presence of their husband, etc. The women always have to submit first in case of such conflicts. They consider their husband as *parmeshwar* (God). These conflicts are solved naturally or the elders help to make a compromise by shouting at both. Sometimes inter-family conflicts occur due to land disputes and this requires police intervention.

6.3.12 Morbidity Schedule—Free Listing of Illness

A morbidity schedule on free listing of illness was canvassed in this village among 20 married women of ages 25 to 70 years. The age groups were 25 to 35 years (11), 36 to 45 years (7), 56 years (1) and 70 year (1). There were 14 illiterate and one fourth class pass SC women, 3 illiterate carpenter women and 2 illiterate rajput women. The women were interviewed from different hamlets, widely spread over the village. The women were individually asked to recall the illness prevalent in the recent past, that is, the last two to four years in this village without probes. When they exhausted the names, some probes like seasonality, gender, age (children, old age, women-specific diseases with focus on reproductive morbidity) were used to facilitate the respondent. As the village is widely spread on the hill and has 17 hamlets, the inter-family/intra-family interaction of the people is limited, so that less number of diseases were reported and only those experienced within the limited circle were reported. Only a few women reported chronic diseases, most of them recalled only acute illnesses like fever without symptom (65 per cent); diarrhoea

(65 per cent); cold–cough, skin problem, joint pain (55 per cent each). Leucorrhoea was reported by 60 per cent of the women. Other major illnesses were asthma, chest infection, backache/body pain, excess menses, headache, and stomach ache/worms.

Causes of chest infection and cold–cough were reported as being due to very low temperature in winters; asthma due to old age or weakness; leucorrhoea due to weakness, eating sour food or eating food that was believed to be hot in ayurvedic terms of reference; excess bleeding due to cold, cancer in women due to white discharge followed by pink discharge; back pain after sterilization, TB due to early marriage. The lack of personal hygiene in activities such as bathing, cleaning clothes, etc. due to the lack of water and the extreme winters.

TABLE 6.11
Prevalence Rate of Illness, Bhullang

(*N = 20*)

Local name	Standard name	No.	Percentage
Bukhar	Fever without symptoms	13	65
Pechish, tatian	Dysentery, Diarrhoea	13	65
Safed pani	Leucorrhoea	12	60
Najla, jukam	Cold, cough	11	55
Khaj, phora phinsi	Skin problem	11	55
Jor dard	Joint pain	11	55
Dama	Asthma	6	30
Chhati jam	Chest infection/pain	6	30
Kamar/sharir dard	Backache/body pain	6	30
More/less bleeding	Excess/improper menses	6	30
Sir dard	Headache	5	25
Pet dard/keerre	Stomach ache/worms	5	25
TB	TB	3	15
Ulti	Vomiting	3	15
Cancer	Cancer	3	15
Lakwa	Polio/paralysis	2	10
Kharas/bavasir	Skin Problem/piles	2	10
Post delivery weakness	Anaemic	2	10
Pet me pani bharna	Stomach problem	2	10
Poor eye sight	Eye weak	1	5
Chakar ana	Dizziness	1	5
Bache na hona	Sterility	1	5
Dant dard	Toothache	1	5

6.3.13 Drop-outs at Primary Level

This village is educationally very backward. The RRA team could locate and interview ten drop-out students. The number might be greater, but they were either not available during the stay or some of them could not be identified due to the difficult topography of the village. The sample students dropped out between 1990 to 1995, but seven of them dropped in 1994 and 1995. Half of them were males. As this was a Hindu village, all the drop-outs were Hindus. The castes they belonged to were rajput (3), harijan (6) and diwan (OBC) (1). The occupation of their parents was cultivation. Except for one of the fathers listed as literate, the fathers and mothers of all drop-outs were illiterate. The drop-out students could estimate the annual household income as Rs 1500 (5), Rs 2000 (1), Rs 4000 (1) and do not know (3). To reach the school, they used to travel on foot, one km (2), two km (4), three km (1), four km (2) and seven km (1). The school timings were reported as 9.00 AM to 3.00 PM or 10.00 AM to 4.00 PM. They studied up to Class I (3), II (5), III (1) and IV (1). The length of stay in the school was two years (4), three years (4), four years (1) and five years (1).

The reasons for drop-out were reported as financial constraints (7), failure in examination (1), eye problem (1) and need for sheep grazing (1). After dropping-out, the males were engaged in labour work in the forest (3) and handloom weaving (2); the females were engaged in cattle grazing (2), cultivation (2), and labour work with the irrigation department (1). None of them described the teachers as bad and all named a favourite teacher. Except three all said that the teachers encouraged them if they had any queries. Only one girl reported that the books were boring and tough. Three girls used to quarrel in the classrooms. The high caste students and economically forward used to treat four students badly by calling them poor or by calling their father's name.

None of the drop-outs said that going to school was a waste and all desired that their younger siblings should study. When asked about their plans of adopting any occupation once they grew up, the occupations they reported were cultivation (4), handloom weaving (4), and unsure (2). Only four replied that they feel handicapped without education. Most of them expressed that if they had got more education, they could have been better at handloom weaving. All of them expressed the view that they would like to go to school.

PUNJAB

Punjab is one of the prosperous states in India with the third highest per capita income. The incidence of poverty in the state is also much lower as compared to other states in the country. There are no marked rural–urban variations—6.35 per cent people are below the poverty line in rural Punjab as against 5.75 per cent in its urban areas (1999–2000). Thirty per cent of the state's population resides in urban areas. A survey reveals that 55 per cent of the state's male population is working but female work participation rate is as low as 3 per cent. It may also be noted that 30 per cent of the main workers are cultivators. Agriculture accounts for 44 per cent of the state economy, while manufacturing and tertiary sectors contribute about 28 per cent each to the gross state domestic product.

The state, though rich in economic terms, does not reveal the same picture in the other parameters of human development, 58.5 per cent of the state's population is literate with wide inter-district, rural–urban, and male–female disparity. Nevertheless, it is better placed than many other states in India. Not only has there been a rise in the literacy rate with increasing income and increasing level of village development, the gender disparity is also getting reduced. The enrolment rates also reveal a correspondence with increasing household incomes.

There has been a growth in infrastructural facilities in the health sector. Medical institutions—hospitals, CHCs, PHCs, and sub-centres—have been increased as also the number of para-medical staff. Even though Punjab is one of the more developed states of India, it still requires development for removing disparities in, for example, its male–female, rural–urban ratios in health and literacy.

7 Secondary Data Report for Punjab

7.1 A Profile of the State

When India became independent, Punjab like Bengal, was partitioned between India and Pakistan. The eastern part was included in India while the western part went to Pakistan. Eight princely states of east Punjab were grouped into one single state PEPSU—Patiala and the East Punjab States Union—with Patiala as the capital. PEPSU state was merged with Punjab in 1956. Present day Punjab came into being when the states were reorganized in 1966.

7.1.1 Locational Characteristics

The state is surrounded by Jammu and Kashmir in the north, Himachal Pradesh in the north-east, Haryana, Chandigarh, and Uttar Pradesh in the east and south-east, Rajasthan in the south-west, and Pakistan in the west and north-west. From the physiographic point of view, Punjab may be divided into three regions: (i) the hilly tracts, (ii) the foothill plains, and (iii) the flat plains. The flat plains, comprising the major part of the state of Punjab, are formed out of the alluvium deposits of five rivers—Ravi, Beas, Sutlej, Chenab, and Jhelum. These deposits are alternate beds of clay and sand, making the land fertile. On the basis of convenience, the Punjab plain is divided into two regions: (i) North Punjab Plain, consisting of the districts of Gurdaspur, Amritsar, Ferozpur, Faridkot, and Bathinda; and (ii) Bisht Doab and East Punjab Plain, comprising the districts of Hoshiarpur, Kapurthala, Jalandhar, Ludhiana, Sangrur, and Rupnagar. As far as drainage is concerned, Punjab is mainly drained off by the Ravi, Beas, Sutlej, and Ghaggar rivers. The Ravi, Beas, and Sutlej are perennial rivers and their sources are located in the glacial region of the Himalayas, whereas the Ghaggar river flows along the eastern and southern boundary of the state and is seasonal. There are *choes* in the Bisht Doab, a tract between Beas and Sutlej.

The climate of Punjab is of the semi-arid type. It is transitional between the arid climate of Rajasthan and the humid climate of Himachal Pradesh. Unfortunately, the anti-cyclone with its high pressure does not allow the moisture-laden monsoon winds to rise higher so as to condense and shower rainfall. High summer temperature and evaporation are other characteristics of the climate. Though the temperature conditions are more or less uniform, rainfall in the state exhibits no such uniformity. It decreases from north and north-east to south-west. The sub-mountainous tract receives about 100 cm of average annual rainfall, which decreases to only 30 cm in the south-west region. There are also extreme variations in rainfall from year to year, which adversely affect agriculture. It is to combat this truancy of rainfall that Punjab is increasing its network of canals.

7.1.2 Population Characteristics

The total area of the state is 50,362 sq km. and its population is about two crore. Thus, on an average 403 persons live in one sq. km. The area and the population of the state form 1.5 per cent and 2.4 per cent, respectively, of the total area and population of India. Of the total population of 2 crore in the state, 29.55 per cent live in urban areas. Thus, Punjab has a higher level of urbanization than the country as a whole (25.71 per cent). The number of females per thousand males in Punjab has increased marginally from 879 in 1981 to 882 in 1991 but it is much lower than the national average of 929. Sex-ratios in the neighbouring states of Uttar Pradesh (879) and Haryana (865) are also low. It may be noted that about 28 per cent of the total population in the state belong to Scheduled Castes (SCs), accounting for about 4 per cent of the SC population in the country. There is no Scheduled Tribe (ST) population in the state. The majority of the population is constituted by Sikhs (60.75 per cent), followed by Hindus (36.93 per cent), Christians (1.10 per cent), and Muslims (1.00 per cent). About 78 per cent of the Sikhs in the country live in Punjab (Census of India 1981).

7.1.3 Social and Demographic Aspects

The crude birth rate (CBR) for the state was 28.6 per thousand in 1991 which is marginally lower than the national average of 29.3. The infant mortality rate (IMR) was 53 per thousand in 1991, much lower than the national average of 80. In fact, Punjab ranks second to Kerala by this indicator. (The gap between the first and the second positions is, however, quite wide—Kerala has an IMR of 17 per thousand live births.) The life expectancy at birth for males and females for the period 1981–8 is estimated at around 63.0 and 64.7 years, respectively, next only to that of Kerala, which has the longest expectation of life in the country. The crude death rate (CDR) is estimated to be around 8.0 per thousand as compared to 6.0 in Kerala and 9.8 for the country as a whole.

The decennial growth rate of population in Punjab dropped to 20.81 per cent during 1981–91 from 23.89 per cent during 1971–81. This implies that the exponential growth rate is 1.89 per cent per annum. This rate is 2.11 per cent for the country.

The level of fertility as measured by the total fertility rate (TFR) is lower than the national average. It declined to 3.2 in 1989 from 4.0 in 1981. The corresponding figures for the country are 4.5 and 3.9 for these two time points. The CBR has also shown a declining trend from 30.3 per thousand in 1981 to 28.6 per thousand in 1991. Nearly 85 per cent of the births in the state are reported to be attended by trained personnel as compared to only 42.3 per cent in the country. The level of child mortality in the state as measured by q(5) was 111 per thousand live births. This is lower than the national average of 152.

The effective literacy rate which was 48.2 per cent in 1981 rose to 58.5 per cent in 1991—higher than the national average of 52.2 per cent. Even in the rural areas of Punjab, the literacy rate is around 52.8 per cent which is marginally higher than the overall literacy rate at the national level. Female literacy in the state (50.4 per cent) is much higher than the national average (39.3 per cent). The gap between male and female literacy is quite low—15.3 percentage points against 24.8 percentage points at the national level. Box 7.1, discusses the place of Punjab in relation to other states in India. All the districts are, however, not equally advanced and developed in terms of all the parameters of social development. This study makes an attempt to assess the variation in achievements across the 12 districts in Punjab.

BOX 7.1
Profile of Punjab

Item	Unit	Year	Punjab		Highest		Lowest		India
			Rank	Actual	State	Actual	State	Actual	Actual
CMIE index	No.	1995	1	171.9	Punjab	171.9	Bihar	43	100
HDI indicators (Pal and Pant)		1993	1	0.793	Punjab	0.793	Bihar	0.503	1
(Shiva Kumar)		1991	2	0.744	Kerala	0.651	UP	0.110	1
(Tilak)		1991	2	0.586	Kerala	0.775	UP	0.292	1
PCY (at 1980–1 prices)	Rs	1992–3	1	3932	Punjab	3730	Bihar	1142	2226
Urban population	%	1991	5	29.7	Maharashtra	38.7	HP	8.70	2573
Literacy	per '000	1991	6	585	Kerala	898	Bihar	385	522
Life expectany	Years	1986–90	2	65.2	Kerala	69.5	MP	53.0	57.7
HHs in electrified dwellings	%	1988–9	2	71.6	HP	83.0	Bihar	4.5	26.9
Annual PC consumption of electricity	KWh	1991	1	70.3	Punjab	703	Assam	96	299
Road. length	per '000/sq. km	1991	4	1078	Kerala	3567	MP	321	621
No. of beds in hospitals	'0000	1993	8	69.5	Kerala	255.0	MP	26.3	68.3
No. of dispensaries	'0000	1990	3	7.3	Gujarat	15.2	MP	0.4	3.4
Regd. med. practitioners	'00000	1992	–	–	Tamil Nadu	82.9	UP	24.7	28.9
Agriculture									
Cereals (per capita)	kg	1993–4	1	1016.3	Punjab	1016.3	Kerala	32.0	193.7
Pulses (per capita)	kg	1993–4	12	3.5	MP	48.5	Kerala	0.6	15.0
Milk availability (per capita per day)	g	1991	9	11.0	MP	66.5	Kerala	0.4	24.6
Manufacturing									
Share in net value added from manufacturing	%	1993	1	71.8	Punjab	71.8	Assam	0.03	12.3
Regd. working factories	%	1993	1	672	Punjab	672	Assam	0.05	218
Share in employment of regd. working factories	%	1993	10	4.1	Maharashtra	22.8	Punjab	4.1	100
Regd working factories			8	5.4	Bihar	20.8	HP	0.6	100
Share in employment of regd. working factories			11	4.0	Maharashtra	14.7	HP	0.6	100

Sources: CMIE Index 1995, District Profile, Centre for Monitoring Indian Economy; *Statistical Abstract*, 1992, CSO, Government of India.

7.1.4 The Economy

The economy of the state is basically agrarian with three fourth of the population engaged in agriculture, cultivating 83.5 per cent of its geographical area. About half of the state domestic product (SDP) is earned from agriculture and allied activities. The agriculture sector including livestock is expected to grow by 3.20 per cent per annum in the Eighth Plan period (*Economic Survey* 1995–6).

The state is one of the most developed in agriculture in terms of total foodgrain production and productivity. The total area under crops has increased considerably since 1970–1. The main factors responsible for this are (i) uncultivated land being brought under the plough and (ii) change in the cropping pattern. The cropping intensity in the state was 185 during 1995–6. The agriculture scene in the state is still dominated by paddy–wheat rotation. The percentage of area under these two crops to gross cropped area has increased from 47.36 during 1970–1 to 70.67 during 1995–6.The production of total foodgrains in Punjab increased from 73.05 lakh tonnes (1970–1) to 201.07 lakh tonnes (1995–6) (*Economic Survey* 1996–7), which is largely attributed to the increased productivity in the state. Despite having only 1.54 per cent of the geographical area of the country, the state continues to be the largest contributor to the central pool of foodgrains for more than last one decade. The total contribution of foodgrains to the central pool has increased from 68.0 lakh tonnes in 1980–1 to 107.6 lakh tonnes during 1995–6 (73 lakh tonnes of wheat and 34.6 lakh tonnes of rice). Fertilizers, the most important input, played a very important role in enhancing agricultural production and ushering in the green revolution in the state. Since the introduction of high yielding varieties (HYVs), the consumption of chemical fertilizers has been increasing steadily. Fertilizer consumption per hectare of gross cropped area in Punjab has increased from 113 kg in 1980–1 to 163 kg per hectare in 1990–1. The state has a relatively higher per capita consumption of petroleum products as compared to other states owing to a fairly high level of mechanization of agriculture and a wide network of roads. The larger size of the operational holdings makes large-scale mechanization of agriculture profitable.

Twenty-one per cent of Punjab's net SDP comes from the industry and mining sectors. The performance in the field of industry is also not less impressive. Per capita SDP from the manufacturing factory sector at current prices was about Rs 507 crore as against Rs 336 crore for India as a whole in 1987–8. In fact, the state of Punjab ranks third among the major states of India in terms of net value added by the manufacturing factory sector, the first and second being Maharashtra and Gujarat respectively. Important industrial items produced in the state are bicycle parts, sewing machines, hand tools, machine tools, auto-parts, electronic items, sports, surgical and leather goods, hosiery, knitwear, fasteners, nuts and bolts, textiles, sugar, and vegetable oils.

The per capita net domestic product is quite high at Rs 3751 (at 1980–1 prices), lower only to that of Goa (Rs 4604) and Delhi (Rs 4838) in 1990–1. The percentage of population below the poverty line is quite low (7.20 per cent in 1993–4). In India as a whole, nearly 30 per cent of the population is below the poverty line. Punjab is thus one of the advanced states in terms of economic prosperity. The Centre for Monitoring the Indian Economy (CMIE) index of relative development is 211 for the state as against the all-India index of 100 in 1991.

7.1.5 Infrastructure

An efficient rail and road network has facilitated much of the economic development in Punjab by providing easy accessibility to most areas of the state. To make the green revolution a complete success in Punjab, one of the basic prerequisites was the development of a good transport system. Without its efficient transport system, modern agricultural inputs such as chemical fertilizers, diesel, farm implements, insecticides, and HYV seeds could not have been made available in many areas of the state. Punjab has a total railway route length of 3636.19 km. Out of this, only 259.56 km is of narrow gauge while the rest, 3376.63 km, is of broad guage. The length of railways per 100 sq. km is almost double the all-India average. The border and strategically important state of Punjab is served by 964 km of the national highways. While providing improved road transport facilities, the state transport system caters efficiently to the needs of agriculture and industrial production (from the point of production to the point of consumption) and also to passenger transport.

A look at the road map of Punjab convinces even a casual observer that the greater part of Upper Bari Doab, Bisht Jullander Doaba, and Malwa plain have high accessibility, having been made accessible through the construction of link roads. Furthermore, one finds that all villages in the state have electricity.

7.2 Government Programmes and Policies

The development of human resources is both a means and an end. Education and improved health status, while being desirable in themselves, are also important components of social and economic development. Recognizing this, special efforts have been made through the various five year plans to accelerate the pace of human development. A major theme of the Seventh Plan (1985–90) has been the integration of human development programmes with other programmes. Some progress has been made towards this. First, integration between different intra-sector activities has been promoted, for example between health care and family welfare. Second, integration between health, education, and related sectors has been pursued, for example, between child care and pre-primary education, between education, health, and nutrition in the Integrated Child Health Care and Enrolment and Retention in the School Health Programme. Third, human resource development is being integrated with other development activities such as the National Rural Employment Programme (NREP) and the Rural Landless Employment

Guarantee Programme (RLEGP) by using their funds for the construction of school and health centre buildings.

7.2.1 *Education*

Education is an effective means for transforming the society through human development. An appropriate educational system cultivates knowledge, skills, positive attitude, awareness and a sense of responsibility towards rights and duties, and imparts people an inner strength to fight oppression, humiliation, and inequality.

Under the Seventh Plan, the thrust areas in the education sector were the following.

1. Universal elementary education.
2. Eradication of illiteracy in the age group 15–35 years.
3. Vocationalization and skill-training programmes at different levels of education.
4. Upgradation of standards and modernization at all stages of education and effective links with gainful employment; a special emphasis on science, environment and value orientation.
5. Spread of education of high quality and excellence in every district in the country.
6. Removal of obsolescence and modernizing technical education, especially to meet emerging requirements.

The National Education Policy was adopted in May 1986, and its Programme of Action was adopted in August 1986. These called for comprehensive efforts to cover a wide range of concerns and comprised long-term as well as medium-term measures. Among the areas envisaged for concerted action are the following.

1. Early childhood care and education and integrated child development service (ICDS).
2. Universalization of elementary education through formal and non-formal methods so as to realize the goals by 1995.
3. Reduction of wastage through involvement of local community in the management of elementary education.
4. Vocationalization of education in order to divert 10 and 25 per cent of students at the plus two stage to the vocational stream by 1990 and 1995, respectively.
5. Selective support to research and development (R & D) infrastructure in the higher education system, including the Council of Strengthening of Infrastructural Facilities in Science and Technology (COSIST) programme and critical areas of research.
6. Cultural heritage and curriculum.
7. Media and educational technology.

Some of these objectives are time-bound and target-specific while others would take time to get fully incorporated into the national education system.

The educational facilities in the state have been expanded and upgraded during the past decades. A good network of 12,945 primary schools, 1377 middle schools, 2418 high schools, and 257 senior secondary schools has been established by collective efforts of the government and privately-managed educational institutions. The state now has a primary school in every village, a middle school within 2 km and a high/senior secondary school within 2.5 km of every village. The situation is better than the norm fixed by the Government of India, viz., one km for a primary school, 3 km for a middle school and 5 km for a high and higher secondary school.

UNIVERSALIZATION OF ELEMENTARY EDUCATION

The target indicated in the National Education Policy was the achievement of universal primary education up to the age of 11 years by 1990 and education of all children up to 14 years of age by 1995. A major effort in the Seventh Five Year Plan was to extend formal school education facilities, organize meaningful non-formal education programmes, and improve the quality, relevance, effectiveness, and usefulness of elementary education. Special attention was to be paid to the promotion of education among girls, first generation learners, and children belonging to the SCs.

The state has a network of 12,755 government primary schools, 80 aided private primary schools and 100 unaided private schools and 500 branches with 47,800 teachers to cope with the requirements of primary education. Every inhabited revenue village has been provided with a government primary school. To meet the requirement of new colonies or habitations, 25 government primary schools have been opened during the Seventh Five Year Plan.

Deficiencies in infrastructure facilities in the government primary schools are inducing parents to shift their wards to private primary schools. Physical deficiencies reported in the state in 1988 were to the extent of 27,448 class rooms and other materials, costing about Rs 10 crore, at the primary school stage, construction of 15 middle and 30 high school buildings; repair of 10 middle and 20 high school unsafe buildings, and additional accommodation for 100 middle and 300 high schools at a cost of Rs 313 crore.

OPERATION BLACKBOARD

Operation Blackboard seeks to eliminate disparities in educational facilities and improve teaching quality in publicly-funded schools. The focus has been on the underprivileged, economically weak, and educationally disadvantaged sections of the society.

Under this scheme, facilities of classrooms, furniture for students and teachers, blackboards, drinking water and lavatories etc. are being provided in the government primary schools. For construction of school buildings envisaged under Operation Blackboard, funds are being supplemented from NREP and RLEGP in addition to the normal budget provisions of the state government.

SCIENCE EDUCATION

The importance of science education has been highlighted in the Seventh Plan. It was proposed to update and modernize science teaching, improve laboratories and libraries in schools, and ensure high quality science teaching through a large-scale, in-service orientation programme for the subject teachers.

Out of 2171 government high/senior secondary schools,

1167 schools are reported to be without science laboratories. To provide 1000 science laboratories at a cost of Rs one lakh per laboratory, a sum of Rs 1000 lakh was provided for the state under the Seventh Plan.

A new scheme for scholarships to children belonging to riot-affected families has been introduced. An allocation of Rs 3 lakh was made in 1988–9 for this purpose.

NAVODAYA VIDYALAYA

In order to make available facilities for quality education to rural children and to make up for the absence of good quality schools in rural areas, a major effort in the Seventh Plan was to provide residential model schools in all the districts of the country.

In Punjab, five Navodaya Vidyalayas—one each at Longowal (Sangrur), Baring Khera (Faridkot), Bondi (Ludhiana), Pujewal (Hoshiarpur), and Goindwal (Amritsar)—have been set up for the physical and mental development of talented children in rural areas.

There are six Adarsh schools managed and financed by the Punjab School Education Board. The department has a proposal to take over the administration of these schools and to open 18 such new schools.

TEACHERS' TRAINING

With the introduction of the 10+2 system of education and changed syllabi in the state, it has become imperative to impart in-service training to the teachers especially in science and mathematics. Three in-service teacher-training centres had been functioning before the launch of the Seventh Plan. Two more centres, at Ludhiana and Gurdaspur, have been opened in 1985–6. During 1987–8, three centres (at Amritsar, Bathinda and Hoshiarpur) were opened. The annual capacity of an in-service teacher training centre is 1500. The existing strength of the teaching staff in the middle and high schools is around 50,000. It is, therefore, essential that one in-service training centre is set up in each district to cope with the requirement of teachers' training.

ERADICATION OF ADULT ILLITERACY

Eradication of illiteracy in the age group 15–35 years is a major thrust area in the Seventh Plan. It is one of the components of the Minimum Needs Programme (MNP). The objective is to achieve hundred per cent coverage of adults in the age group of 15–35 years by 1995 through non-formal education. The National Literacy Mission launched during 1988–9, incorporating all on-going programmes of adult literacy and education, is being continued. Special emphasis will be given to post-literacy follow-up and continuing education through Jana Shikhshan Nilayams (JSN). The proposed allocation for the year 1988–9 for adult education was Rs 10 lakh in the state.

HIGHER EDUCATION

At higher levels of education, the attempt was to improve standards and to make courses more relevant and flexible, linking these to current development needs. According to the National Policy on Education 1986, urgent steps are being taken to protect the higher education system from 'degradation'.

To foster linkages between universities' development sectors and the society, the University Grants Commission has emphasized redesigning of courses, introduction of computer education, biotechnology, environmental science, and other inter-disciplinary areas. In the state, against the Seventh Five Year Plan target of introducing 50 new courses, the department has introduced 37 courses during the first three years of the plan. To maintain these 37 courses along with additional staff created during these years, a sum of Rs 107 lakh was proposed for the 1988–9 plan outlay.

7.2.2 Health Care

Improvement in the health status of the population is a basic requirement for raising the standard of living and developing human resources. The role of the government in this field is critical in the following areas: (i) provision of primary health care facilities in rural areas; (ii) drug policy; (iii) programme for control of major diseases; (iv) provision of family planing, maternal and child health (MCH), immunization, and related services.

With a view to achieving health for all by AD, 2000 the rural health component of the MNP has the following objectives: (i) establishment of one sub-centre for a population of 5000 in the plains and 3000 in tribal and hill areas by 1990 (100 per cent coverage); (ii) one primary health centre (PHC) for 30,000 population in the plains and 20,000 in tribal and hill areas by 1990 (100 per cent coverage); (iii) establishment of one community health centre (CHC) for a population of one lakh or one community developed (CD) Block by 1990 (50 per cent coverage).

PRIMARY HEALTH CARE

The establishment of a network of health centres in rural areas has been the objective of primary health care. Comprehensive health care services are being organized for this purpose. Health and family welfare services are being provided in an integrated manner for their optimal utilization. Efforts are being made for inter-sectoral health action, that is, coupling of health with health related sectors such as nutrition, housing, water supply, sanitation, and education.

Community participation in health and family welfare is a well-recognized need. All-out efforts are being made to enhance community participation in health programmes by involving non-governmental organizations (NGOs) and formal and non-formal village institutions.

Sub-centres constitute the base of the health structure in the state. The services of one male and one female worker are available in these centres. The number of sub-centres has increased from 2105 in 1979–80 to 2603 in 1984–5 and 2852 in 1990–1. There was one sub-centre for every 5000 rural population at the end of the Seventh Plan. To cope with the increasing population, and also to maintain the already realized goal of providing one sub-centre for every 5000 population, there was a target of opening 250 sub-centres in the rural areas of the state during the Annual Plan 1988–9. An outlay of Rs 114 lakh was proposed for this purpose.

During the Sixth Five Year Plan period, emphasis was laid on the opening of subsidiary health centres (SHCs) (dispensary) in rural areas, and by 1984–5 one SHC existed in the state for every 8000 rural population. Earlier, one PHC was available for over one lakh rural population. Now, according to new guidelines, one PHC is to be provided for every 30,000 rural population. It was proposed to set up more PHCs by upgrading SHCs during the Seventh Five Year Plan. For this purpose, a sum of Rs 1630 lakhs was provided for the period 1985–90.

As per the guidelines of the Government of India, 10 CHCs were established during 1982–3 at upgraded PHC or sub-divisional hospitals to provide specialist services in medicine, surgery, gynaecology, and paediatrics to the rural masses. During the Seventh Five Year Plan period, it was proposed to establish 60 CHCs at upgraded PHCs and other important urban hospitals at a cost of Rs 160 lakhs. The additional requirement of staff for one CHC would be four doctors (specialists), three staff nurses, one dresser, and two Class IV employees, costing about Rs 1.20 lakh annually for staff etc. and a non-recurring expenditure of Rs 0.20 lakh, besides a building component of Rs 2.5 lakh for the CHC.

During the previous plans, 111 rural hospitals (25/30 bedded) were sanctioned. Many of these either have inadequate buildings or are lying incomplete because of a lack of resources in the community. To complete these buildings and to make them functional during the Annual Plan 1988–9, an outlay of Rs 50 lakh was sanctioned.

It is proposed to start the training and continuing education of PHC staff, including medical officers, as per the guidelines of the Government of India so as to keep their knowledge up-to-date. Some categories of para-medical staff will also be given reorientation at these health and family welfare training centres. To provide additional buildings, machinery, and equipment for this purpose, an outlay of Rs 5.25 lakh was proposed under this scheme for the year 1988–9.

DRUG POLICY

A substantial part of health care needs is supplied by the private sector. In fact, private expenditure on health care is about twice as large as total public expenditure. The effectiveness of the private system depends, among other things, on the quality of medical education and the cost and availability of drugs. Hence, drug policy is an important issue for the health care delivery system. It is proposed to strengthen drug control in the state by providing drug inspectors, intelligence-cum-legal cells, assistant drug controllers, zonal assistant drug controllers, strengthening of testing laboratories and supporting ministerial staff at headquarters. An outlay of Rs 15 lakh was proposed in the Annual Plan 1988–9.

DISEASE CONTROL

The major disease control programmes for communicable and non-communicable diseases are implemented as centrally-sponsored schemes with 50 per cent cost sharing by the states.

A modified plan of operation under the National Malaria Eradication Programme (NMEP) was implemented in the state with effect from 1 April 1977. Under this scheme, the entire rural area was brought under remedial insecticides such as DDT, BHC, and Malathion. A sum of Rs 350 lakh as state share was proposed to meet the operational cost of the spray and also for the purchase of insecticides and medicine and equipment (M and E).

Under the NMEP scheme in urban areas, all the towns with a population of more than 40,000 are to be covered. During the Sixth Plan, eight towns with a population of more than 40,000 were taken up for this purpose till 31 March 1984. Another five towns were proposed to be covered during 1984–5. A sum of Rs 50 lakh was proposed in the Annual Plan 1988–9 as state share to meet the cost of larvicides and purchase of M and E and vehicles.

The national tuberculosis (TB) control programme aims to detect active TB cases in an early stage by sputum examination at the peripheral health centres and their treatment through an organized district TB control programme. Tuberculosis is prevalent among the poor, who live in slums and congested places. A sum of Rs 37 lakh was proposed as state share for the Annual Plan 1988–9 to provide anti-TB drugs free of cost to poor patients.

The national programme for the control of blindness was launched in 1976. The creation of a District Eye Mobile Team primarily for the school-going children serves a very useful purpose. During the year 1988–9 it was proposed to continue three existing eye mobile teams, one each in Gurdaspur, Faridkot, and Ludhiana. For this purpose an outlay of Rs 17 lakh was proposed for the year 1988–9.

OTHER PROGRAMMES

1. Strengthening of state health and district laboratories

Laboratory investigations play an important role in the diagnosis of various diseases. Technical staff, machinery and equipment, and chemical reagents are essential for this purpose. A sum of Rs 2 lakh was earmarked for strengthening of laboratories in district hospitals at Jalandhar, Sangrur, Ferozpur, and Hoshiarpur during the Annual Plan 1988–9.

2. Establishment of health equipment and maintenance repair unit

The state hospitals have equipment worth more than Rs 25 crore. It has been proposed to establish equipment and repair and maintenance units in all the districts.

3. Expanded programme on immunization

The expanded programme on immunization aims at protecting mothers and children from dreadful diseases such as tetanus, diphtheria, whooping cough, polio, TB, measles, and typhoid. These diseases can be prevented by immunization with potent vaccines administered at the proper age and time. A sum of Rs 4 lakh was proposed in 1988–9 for minimum additional staff and for purchase of equipment.

4. Hospital treatment of diarrhoea diseases by oral dehydration therapy
Diarrhoea in children in the age group 0–5 years is quite common and it is one of the major causes of morbidity and mortality. This can be considerably reduced if the child is saved from dehydration. Under this scheme, it is proposed to procure oral rehydration solution (ORS) powder packets for distribution through health functionaries working in the field.

5. Grant of additional incentives and compensation out of state fund to acceptors of sterilization
In addition to motivation and incentives provided by the Government of India, additional incentive at the rate of Rs 50 per acceptor is granted to acceptors of sterilization from state resources.

6. Providing independent feeders for continuous electric supply to hospitals
An uninterrupted supply of electricity is essential for storing life-saving drugs, vaccines, etc. at the proper temperature so that they do not lose their potency. It is proposed to provide independent feeders and generator sets at district and other important hospitals.

7. Strengthening of school health services
With effect from 1 August 1981, the programme of medical check-up of school-going children by the existing medical and para-medical staff of the PHCs, CHCs, and civil hospitals is in operation all over the state.

7.2.3 Nutrition

Lack of proper nutritive diet for the children from poor families is affecting the physical and psychological development of such children. Special nutrition programmes have been introduced in as many as 43 ICDS projects in the state. With the revised cost per day of nutritive diet at 65 paise per child, 95 paise per pregnant woman, and Rs 1.15 per day for the severely malnourished child, the average cost per beneficiary works out to 69 paise. Taking into consideration the anticipated number of 286,000 beneficiaries to be covered during the year 1988–9 an outlay of Rs 393 lakh was proposed.

Under the special nutrition programme, expectant and nursing mothers and children below 6 years are covered. Ex-pectant and nursing mothers are provided a nutritional diet for 180 days in a year under the Nutrition Diet Scheme. At the rate of Rs 207 per beneficiary, a sum of Rs 3.88 lakh was proposed for 1988–9.

7.2.4 Employment Generation and Poverty Alleviation

In order to reduce the incidence of rural poverty, three broad policy options have been pursued. First, to increase the asset holdings of the poor, redistributive land reform measures have been adopted and special programmes of assistance for creation of better productive asset bases have been introduced. Second, augmentation of wage incomes has been sought through expansion of employment in agricultural and non-agricultural activities in rural areas, and special employment generation programmes have been initiated to provide supplementary employment. Third, provision for improved access of the poor to important services like education and health has been sought to be made through other programmes such as the MNP.

Further, efforts have been made to minimize the erosion of the real incomes of the poor due to price rise, by ensuring supplies of food grains and other essential commodities through the public distribution system (PDS). Most of these programmes, which have been in operation for some time, have received renewed emphasis during the Seventh Plan.

1. Integrated Rural Development Programme (IRDP)
The IRDP, which was started in 1980, aims at improvement of the economic conditions of the rural poor living below the poverty line. During the Seventh Five Year Plan, this programme covered those households whose annual income was up to Rs 4800. Under this programme, the state government and the Government of India are providing capital subsidy to the extent of 33.3 per cent on a matching basis. Loans for particular ventures are being offered by commercial banks.

2. Training of Rural Youth for Self Employment (TRYSEM)
This scheme aims at equipping rural youth with necessary skills and technology to enable them to seek self-employment. The training courses are based on the concept of 'learning by doing' and are offered in selected trades in such activities that lead to self-employment. It was proposed to impart training to 5000 persons during 1988–9. The training infrastructure of such institutions will be further strengthened, for which necessary provision was made in the plan.

3. Development of Women and Children in Rural Areas (DWCRA)
Under this scheme, assistance is to be provided either to individual women, or to those organized into homogeneous groups to take up economically viable activities. The programme also provides support services and child care facilities. The scheme was initiated in Punjab during 1984–5. An amount of Rs 6.08 lakh was utilized for this purpose during 1985–6. The outlay for 1988–9 was fixed at Rs 9 lakh for providing assistance to 170 groups of women.

4. National Rural Employment Programme
This programme is financed by the Government of India and the states on a matching basis. Started in April 1977 as a non-plan scheme, 'Food for Work Programme', it was renamed NREP in 1980. The major emphasis being on generation of additional employment, 50 per cent of the funds are to be utilized as wages and the balance for materials. The programme has three basic objectives.

1. Generation of additional gainful employment for unemployed persons, both men and women, in rural areas.
2. Creation of durable assets (for strengthening rural infrastructure) that would result in rapid growth of the rural economy and steady rises in the income levels of the rural poor.
3. Improvement of nutritional status and living standard of the rural poor.

This programme is being implemented mainly by two departments, viz., Rural Development and Panchayats and the Forest Department. For 1988–9, a sum of Rs 600 lakh was proposed to generate nearly 22 lakh man-days of work under this scheme in the state.

5. Rural Landless Employment Guarantee Programme

This programme was launched during 1983–4 with the objective of providing employment to at least one member of every landless labour household for up to 100 days in a year. Under this centrally-sponsored scheme, 18.02 lakh of man-days of employment was created during 1986–7, exceeding the target of 15 lakh man-days set initially. An outlay of Rs 7.6 crore was proposed for 1988–9 for the implementation of the programme at an accelerated pace, to generate an additional employment of 25 lakh man-days.

7.3 Education in Punbjab

Education is an integral part of the overall level of human development. The progress of a society depends not only on its natural and capital resources but also to a large extent on its stock of human capital. Current productivity depends on the quality of education and skills of the population. The content and quality of education received by the younger generation determine the pace of further development. It is, therefore, relevant in the context of human development, to assess the level and prospects of education of the people. This section describes the educational profile of the state of Punjab, disaggregated at the level of districts. Due to data limitations, this profile is confined to the literacy rate and primary education only. Data on enrolment and drop-out rates at the primary school level, teacher–student ratio, and effective literacy rate, have been compiled and analysed.

7.3.1 Enrolment Rate

The enrolment rates for the districts in the state are given for urban and rural areas in Tables 7.E1and 7.E2. The data on enrolment have been obtained from the Punjab Department of Education while the number of eligible children in the age group 6–11 years in 1990–1 has been estimated assuming that the growth rate observed during 1971–81 in the relevant age group persists.

According to these estimates, larger proportions of girls are enrolled in school in seven out of twelve districts in Punjab. This makes the average enrolment rate for girls (89.3 per cent) marginally higher than that for boys (88.9 per cent). The enrolment rate is also found to be favourable to rural children in many districts, the difference being about 10.9 percentage points for the state as a whole. Around 89 per cent of the children in the state (both boys and girls) are enrolled in school.

The enrolment rate is 96.72 per cent in Amritsar, followed by Hoshiarpur (95.02 per cent), and Bathinda (93.93 per cent). These three districts have an enrolment rate higher than the state average (89.14 per cent). Faridkot, however, has an estimated enrolment rate of 115.11 per cent.

In urban Punjab, enrolment is low in Ludhiana, Hoshiarpur, and Sangrur. In Ludhiana enrolment among girls (79.16 per cent), is higher than that among boys (73.20 per cent). Ludhiana is the most urbanized district in Punjab where child labour is quite remunerative. A probe into the sex composition of child labour may be helpful in explaining this gender disparity in enrolment. In rural Amritsar and Patiala enrolment among girls is low. It is also low among boys in rural Kapurthala.

Many of the estimated enrolment rates exceed 100 per cent, indicating that the procedure adopted leads to gross overestimates. In urban areas of Gurdaspur, enrolment rate for girls is estimated to be as high as 167.8 per cent. The reason may lie in the method of estimating the number of children in the age group 6–11 years and also in the basic data on enrolment used as input. Children in the age group 6–11 years do not constitute the proper universe for enrolment in primary schools. Many children beyond this age group are in primary schools. The basic data on enrolment is believed to be inflated for various reasons.

7.3.2 Drop-out Rate

Ideally the drop-out rates should have been estimated by tracing the children enrolled at the lower levels of primary classes till they complete their primary education. In the absence of the required information an attempt has been made here to estimate the drop-out rates as the difference between the number of children enrolled five years ago (1986–7) in Class I and the number of children enrolled now (1990–1) in Class V. The enrolment in Class I has been taken as the universe, and the percentage difference between this and the number reaching Class V is taken as the estimated drop-out rate.

The overall drop-out rate for the state, according to these estimates, is quite high at 24.56 per cent. It is 25.11 per cent for girls and 24.09 per cent for boys. Amritsar, Ferozpur, Patiala, Sangrur, Bathinda, and Faridkot have very high rates of drop out. Drop-out rates in Ludhiana, both among boys (18.10 per cent) and girls (16.80 per cent), are also high. The drop-out rates in other districts are much lower, ranging between 3 and 7 per cent.

In most districts, the drop-out rate is higher for girls than for boys. Only in Ludhiana, Gurdaspur, and Jalandhar is the rate lower for girls. The rural–urban differences in drop-out rates could not be studied due to the non-availability of data on enrolment, which is needed for estimating these rates.

Gurdaspur has a negative drop-out rate among girls, making the overall drop-out rate negative. This is perhaps, a reflection on the unreliability of these estimates, arising out of the estimation procedure adopted. One can only hope that the dimensional order of these estimates is right and the extent of underestimation does not vary widely across the districts.

7.3.3 Teacher–Student Ratio

The quality of teaching is likely to influence enrolment, drop-out, and achievement in education. This is, however, an elusive concept, difficult to conceptualize and measure in quantitative terms. In the absence of any suitable indicator for the quality of teaching, physical indicators such as teacher–student ratio and availability of infrastructure can be analysed.

On an average there are 42 students per teacher in the state. The teacher–student ratio is high in Faridkot (51), Bathinda (49), and Jalandhar (45). In the districts of Hoshiarpur, Rupnagar, Kapurthala, and Gurdaspur, a teacher on an average has to take care of fewer students (33–5). The teacher–student ratio in the districts is not far from the optimum suggested by the Kothari Commission, namely 40 students per teacher (see Map 7.1). Data on availability of other physical facilities are scanty and not available for any recent year.

7.3.4 Proximity of Primary Schools

The geographical proximity of primary schools is no longer a problem in Punjab. Of the 12,795 villages all have a primary school within a distance of 1 km. In the absence of a further break-up of these data it is not possible to assess the number of villages with a primary school within habitation.

7.3.5 Effective Literacy Rate

Data on effective literacy rate (literates among those aged 7 years and above) obtained from the Census of India, 1991 and 2001 are given in Table 7.E3. Any person who is able to read and write with understanding in any language has been enumerated as literate. The figures reveal that 58.51 per cent of the population aged 7 years and above in the state is literate. In 1991 the highest rate of literacy was found in Hoshiarpur (70.74 per cent), closely followed by Jalandhar (68.45 per cent), Rupnagar (68.14 per cent), and Ludhiana (67.35 per cent). The districts of Amritsar (58.09 per cent), Ferozpur (48.01 per cent), Sangrur (46.16 per cent), Bathinda (43.03 per cent), and Faridkot (49.42 per cent) had lower levels of literacy than the state average (58.51 per cent). The literacy rates were higher among males than among females in all the districts. Male literacy was the highest in Hoshiarpur (79.31 per cent) and varied from a low of 50.55 per cent in Bathinda to 79.31

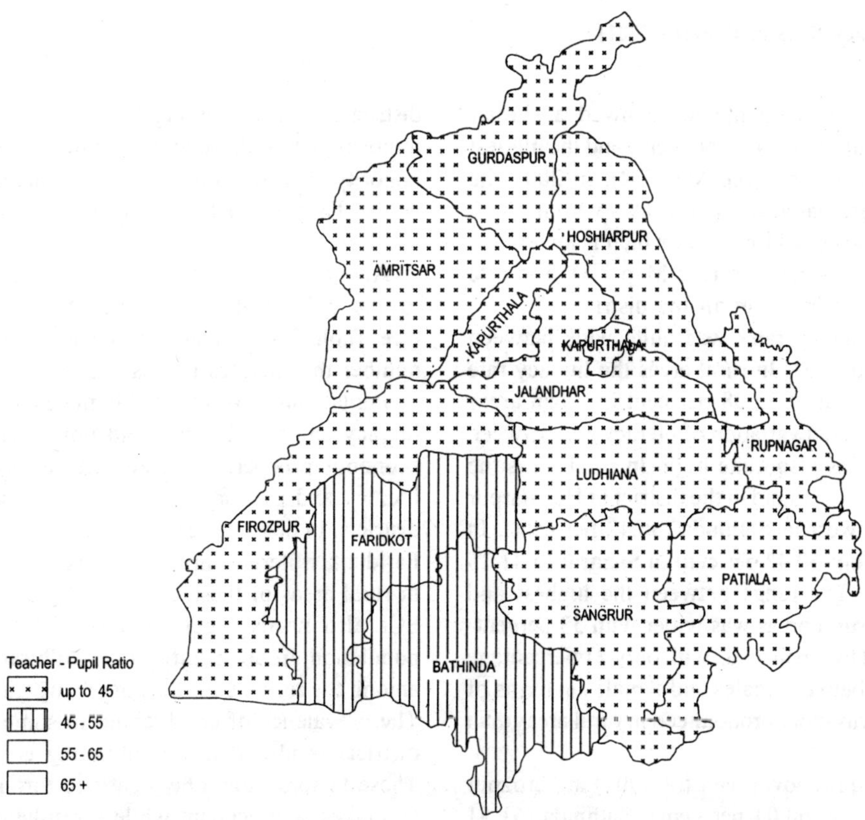

MAP 7.1: **Availability of Teachers in Punjab**

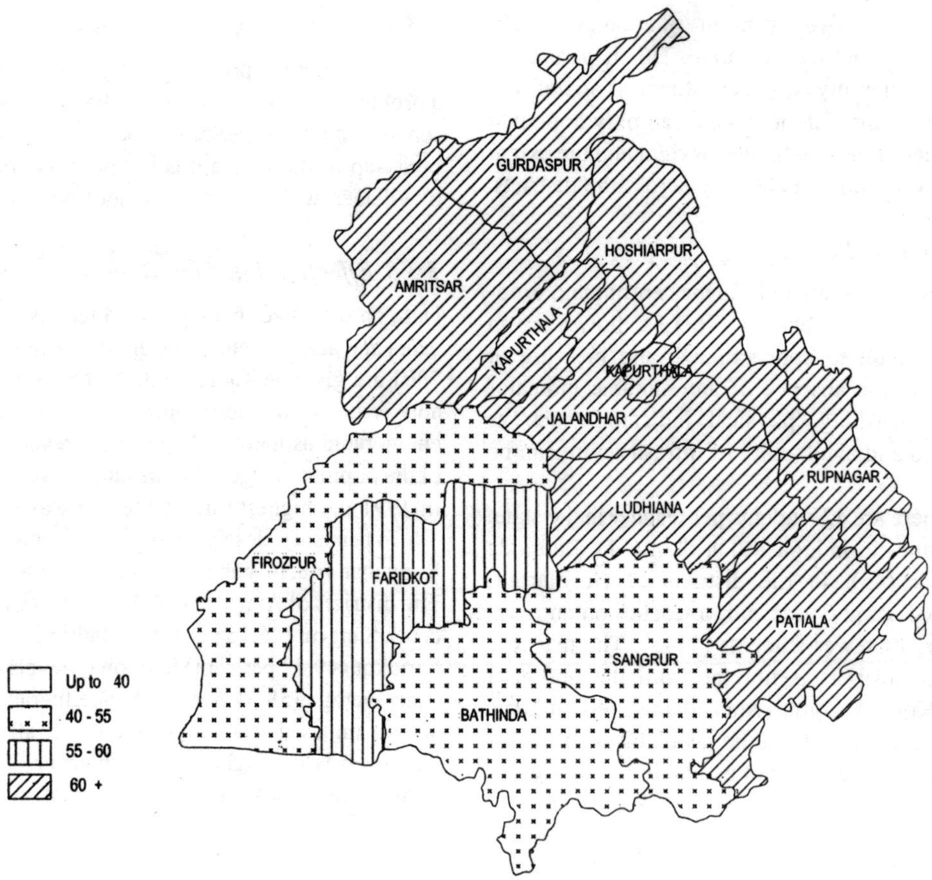

MAP 7.2: **Female Literacy Rate in Punjab (2001)**

per cent in Hoshiarpur. Female literacy showed a similar trend—the lowest in Bathinda (34.51 per cent) and the highest in Hoshiarpur (61.48 per cent) (see Map 7.2). In 2001 the literacy rate for the state has increased to 69.95 from 58.57 in 1991. The rate of change is 11 per cent which is lower than the national average of 13 per cent (see Map 7.3). The rate of change is higher for females in all the districts.

The difference in literacy rates was quite wide between rural and urban areas in 1991. In rural areas the literacy rate was 52.77 per cent as against 72.08 per cent in urban areas of the state. The inter-district variation of literacy rate between rural and urban areas was also quite high. In rural areas the highest level of literacy was found in the district of Hoshiarpur (69.22 per cent) and lowest in Bathinda (36.42 per cent). In urban areas it varied from 60.42 per cent in Sangrur to 81.15 per cent in Rupnagar. The range between the highest and lowest literacy rate in rural areas was wider with 33 percentage points as compared to urban areas with only 21 percentage points. The difference between males and females in terms of effective literacy rate was more pronounced in rural areas than in urban areas.

The literacy rate is quite low (even for 2001) in Ferozpur (61.42 per cent), Sangrur (60.04 per cent), Bathinda (61.51 per cent), and Faridkot (63.43 per cent) compared to other districts. Literates among females in these districts are in a minority, while those among males have only a very slender majority. The situation in the rural areas of these districts is worse. These districts are also characterized by low enrolment and high drop-outs.

About 28 per cent of the population in Punjab belongs to the SCs. Literacy among this group is much lower (see Table 7.1). Except among urban males, illiterates out-number the literates in this group.

Punjab ranks twenty-first in male and fourteenth in female literacy among 32 states and union territories. Keeping its economic prosperity in view, the performance of the state in literacy and primary education is not satisfactory in all the districts. In districts such as Ferozpur, Sangrur, Bathinda, and Faridkot, illiterates are still in the majority. Female literacy in rural areas of these districts is quite low. Literacy among SCs also needs urgent and special attention. Region and population group specific socio-cultural factors are, perhaps, among the reasons for keeping many girls away from school. The prevalence of child labour in some of the industrialized districts is also a factor inhibiting enrolment and literacy. These factors should be identified through localized surveys and taken into account while formulating and implementing action plans for micro-intervention.

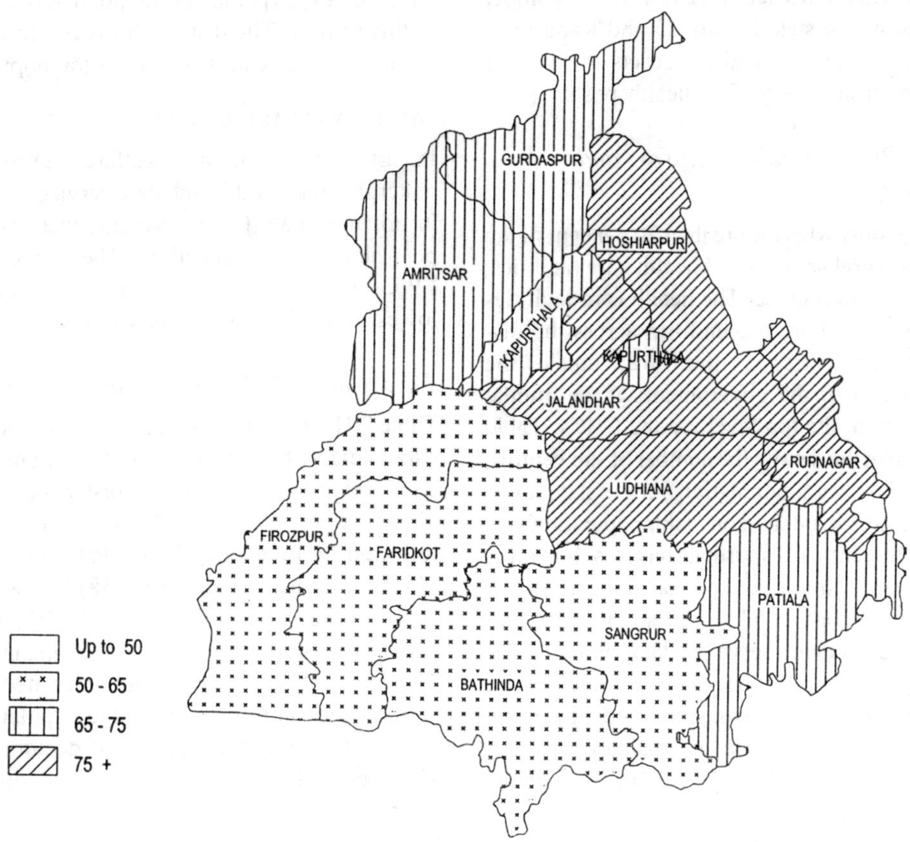

MAP 7.3: **Total Literacy Rate in Punjab (2001)**

TABLE 7.1
Literacy Among Scheduled Castes in Punjab

Population group	All areas			Rural			Urban		
	Total	Male	Female	Total	Male	Female	Total	Male	Female
All population in Punjab	58.51	65.66	50.41	52.77	60.71	43.85	72.08	77.26	66.12
SC population in Punjab	41.09	49.82	31.03	39.55	48.54	29.20	47.04	54.76	38.14
SC population in India	37.41	49.91	23.76	33.25	45.95	19.46	55.11	66.60	47.29
All population in India	52.21	64.13	39.29	44.69	57.87	30.62	73.08	81.09	64.05

Source: Census of India, 1991.

7.4 Health Care Facilities and Health Status

Health status is one of the important components of the overall level of human development. In recent years, social indicators representing health status have received due importance in the construction of composite indices of development. The achieved health status of any population group would depend on the availability of health care facilities. Taking stock of such facilities would be relevant for the formulation and implementation of policies relating to health—including identification of areas needing micro-intervention. Sections 7.4 and 7.5 review the available health care facilities and some related demographic parameters in the state before attempting an assessment of the achieved health status.

7.4.1 Number of Hospitals, Dispensaries, and Health Posts

Table 7.H1 gives the districtwise availability of government hospitals, dispensaries, and health posts in urban areas. There are 130 government hospitals in urban Punjab. Of these 20 are located in Amritsar while the smallest district, Kapurthala, has only four. Seen in relation to the size of the urban population, there is one hospital for 73,000 persons in Ludhiana, while in Ferozpur one hospital caters to only 35,000 persons. The availability of hospitals should preferably be seen in relation to other health care facilities and the prevailing morbidity conditions in the population.

There are 221 dispensaries in the state. A few districts such as Ludhiana, Jalandhar, and Patiala have more dispensaries while Ferozpur and Faridkot districts have fewer. The number of health posts in the whole state is only 23 and Kapurthala and Faridkot have no health post. In other districts, the number of health posts varies from one to four health posts.

7.4.2 Sub-centres, Public Health Centres, and Community Health Centres

Punjab has a rural economy where more than 70 per cent of the population lives in the rural areas. Rural health care facilities, therefore, assume great importance. The health care facilities provided by the government are not uniform across the districts. In rural areas, sub-centres are the lowest unit of the health care establishment of the government; at the middle level are the PHCs, and at the top level are the CHCs. Table 7.H2 and Map 7.4 present the data on the number of sub centres, PHCs, and CHCs per lakh rural population. At the state level, there are 2852 sub-centres in all, and one lakh population was served by nearly 20 sub-centres. Kapurthala has 50 sub-centres per lakh rural population while Ludhiana has only seven.

The accepted norm is one PHC for every 30,000 rural population. In Punjab, 2.93 PHCs serve one lakh rural population on an average. This figure is close to the accepted norm. Among the districts, Gurdaspur (3.36) has already achieved the norm. Other districts close to the norm are Hoshiarpur (3.16), Rupnagar (3.22), Patiala (3.23), and Faridkot (3.10). Kapurthala, with 2.08 PHCs per lakh rural population, is the most deficient in this respect. The district, however, has the largest number (50.62) of sub-centres per lakh rural population.

FAMILY WELFARE CENTRES

In urban areas, family welfare centres (FWCs) provide maternity and child health care services. There are 124 FWCs in urban Punjab. On an average, there are two such centres per lakh urban population. The highest concentration of FWCs is seen in Amritsar (3.16 per lakh population) and the lowest is in Bhatinda (1.14 centres per lakh population).

7.4.3 Number of Doctors and Paramedical Personnel

Table 7.H3 indicates the number of doctors, nurses, and other paramedical staff in the districts of Punjab. In Punjab there are 13,457 doctors who administer the allopathic system of treatment. The largest number of doctor is in Amritsar (2814) followed by Ludhiana (2290), Patiala (2273), and Jalandhar (1621). The lowest number (258) is observed in Rupnagar.

There are 7662 staff nurses in Punjab, with the districtwise variation ranging from 1921 in Ludhiana to 68 in Bathinda. The availability of doctors and other medical staff should be seen in relation to the size of the population in the districts. Table 7.H3 gives the number of doctors and other medical staff per lakh population across the districts. Among the

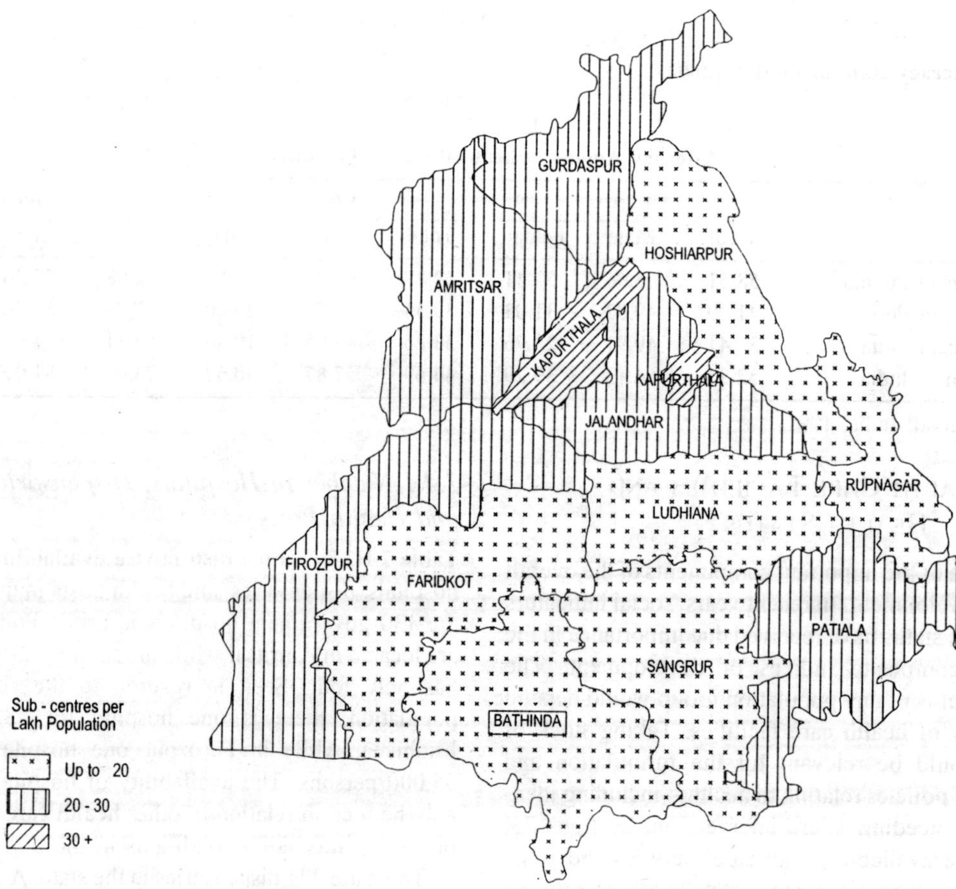

MAP 7.4: **Availability of Sub-centres in Punjab**

districts, Ludhiana seems to be better served by doctors and other medical staff, while districts such as Ferozpur and Rupnagar are deficient in this respect.

7.5 Related Demographic Parameters

7.5.1 Population Density and Sex Ratio

A knowledge of certain demographic parameters such as population density, urbanization, sex ratio, and composition of population in terms of religious and ethnic groups is useful for formulating policies to provide basic necessities like housing, water supply, sanitation, health care facilities, and education to various groups of population. A study of these parameters across districts and population groups would, therefore, be relevant in the context of human development.

Table 7.H4 presents data on population density, sex ratio, and the proportion of urban and SC population. The density of population in Punjab is 403 persons per sq. km. It is much higher in urban areas (4159) than in rural areas (292). Ludhiana has the highest density of population (641), while the density of population is lowest (274) in Ferozpur. Gurdaspur (493), Amritsar (492), Ludhiana (641), Jalandhar (596), Rupnagar (439), and Patiala (414) have population densities higher than the state average. Among the rural areas, Jalandhar has the highest density (399). Ludhiana, which is one of the million plus cities of the country, reported the highest level of urban density of population (6305), followed by Gurdaspur (5058), Jalandhar (4995), and Sangrur (4941). The density is low in urban areas of Kapurthala (2164), and Bathinda (2290). At the state level, the population density in urban areas is 4159 persons per sq. km. One of the major issues in India's demographic profile is the declining sex ratio. In India as a whole, the sex ratio is 929, which has declined from 936 in 1981. In the state of Punjab the sex ratio, 882 females per thousand males, is lower than the national average. Even in Gurdaspur (903) and Hoshiarpur (919), with high proportions of females, the sex ratio remains well below the all-India level. Sex ratios in the neighbouring states of Uttar Pradesh (879) and Haryana (865) are also low.

7.5.2 Scheduled Caste Population

The SCs constitute 28.31 per cent of the state population and 4.15 per cent of the total SC population in the country. In urban areas, only 19.69 per cent of the population is SC, as compared to 31.93 per cent in rural areas. The SC population is widely distributed across the districts. In Jalandhar, SCs constitute as high as 39.08 per cent of the district population while in Ferozpur the population is much lower at 21.80 per cent. The proportion of SC population is higher in rural areas of all the districts; the gap is wider in districts such as Amritsar, Ludhiana, Jalandhar, Rupnagar, and Patiala that are more urbanized (see Map 7.5). This is perhaps, a

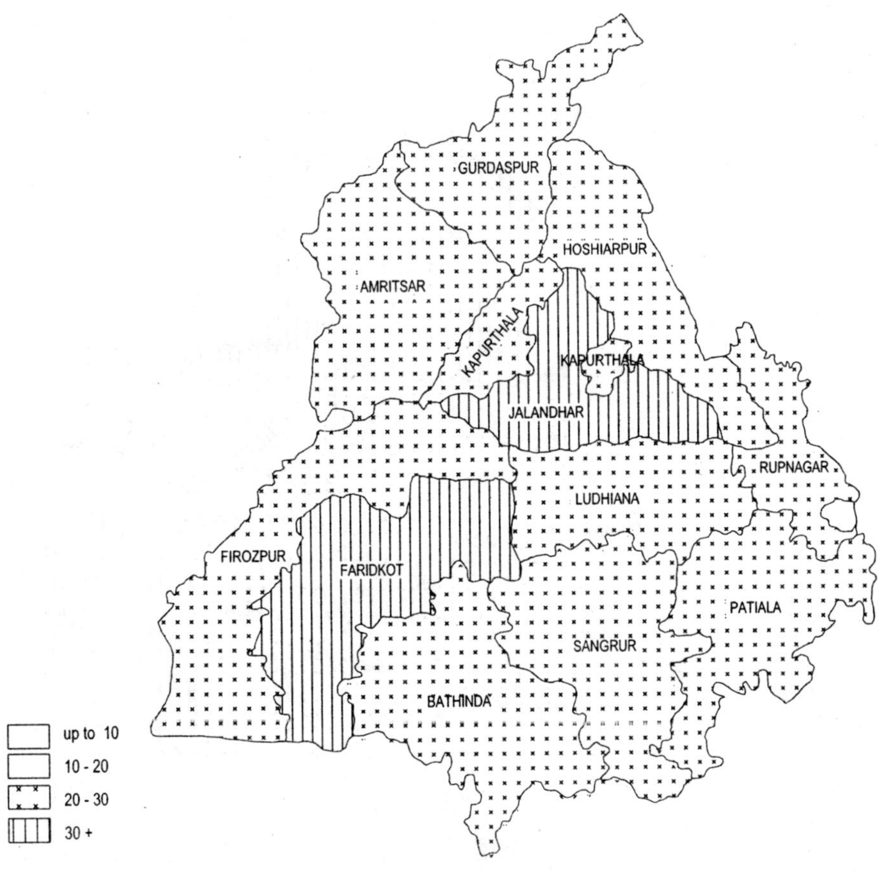

MAP 7.5: **Percentage of SC Population to Total Population in Punjab**

corroboration of the fact that the SC population with lower levels of education and skills finds it difficult to adjust to urban ways of life. There is no ST population in Punjab.

7.5.3 Level of Urbanization

Punjab is agriculturally well-developed and the major part of the state income is derived from agriculture and allied activities. However, the level of urbanization is not low. The urban population constitutes 29.55 per cent of the total population, which is higher than the average of 25.71 per cent for India. Ludhiana has the highest level of urbanization (50.28 per cent), followed by Jalandhar (35.96 per cent), Amritsar (34.09 per cent), and Patiala (29.90 per cent). In the least urbanized district, Hoshiarpur, about 15 per cent of the population lives in urban areas (see Map 7.6).

7.5.4 Pattern of Work Participation

About 30 per cent of the population in Punjab (54.12 per cent of males and 2.79 per cent of females) participates in full time economic activities. Participation as marginal workers is much lower, 0.10 per cent among males and 1.61 per cent among females. This is perhaps, an indication of a lower incidence of unemployment and poverty in the state, which is also corroborated by data from other sources. The variation in participation rate is not wide across the districts. The highest percentage of main workers is in Ludhiana (31.26 per cent), while the lowest is in Hoshiarpur (27.84 per cent). The percentage of male main workers varies in the narrow range of 56.13 per cent in Sangrur to 50.79 per cent in Hoshiarpur, while for females it varies between 1.92 per cent in Sangrur and 3.45 per cent in Kapurthala. About 31.44 per cent of the total main workers are cultivators; another 23.82 per cent participate as agricultural labourers. Female cultivators constitute only 8.72 per cent of female main workers. The proportionate participation as agricultural labourers is almost equal among males (23.80 per cent) and females (24.36 per cent). The proportion of workers engaged in the household industry is much lower at 1.33 per cent of the total main workers. Cultivators and agricultural labourers together account for 55.26 per cent of the total main workers in the state. Across districts, the percentage of cultivators ranges between 43.34 per cent in Bathinda and 20.00 per cent in the most urbanized district of Ludhiana. The variation in districtwise distribution of female main workers may be obtained from Map 7.7. Similar data for urban and rural areas are presented separately in Tables 7.H5 and 7.H6.

7.5.5 Size of Household and Dependency Ratio

The average household in Punjab has five to six persons with not much variation across districts. Households are marginally larger in rural areas (6.10) than in urban areas (5.61).

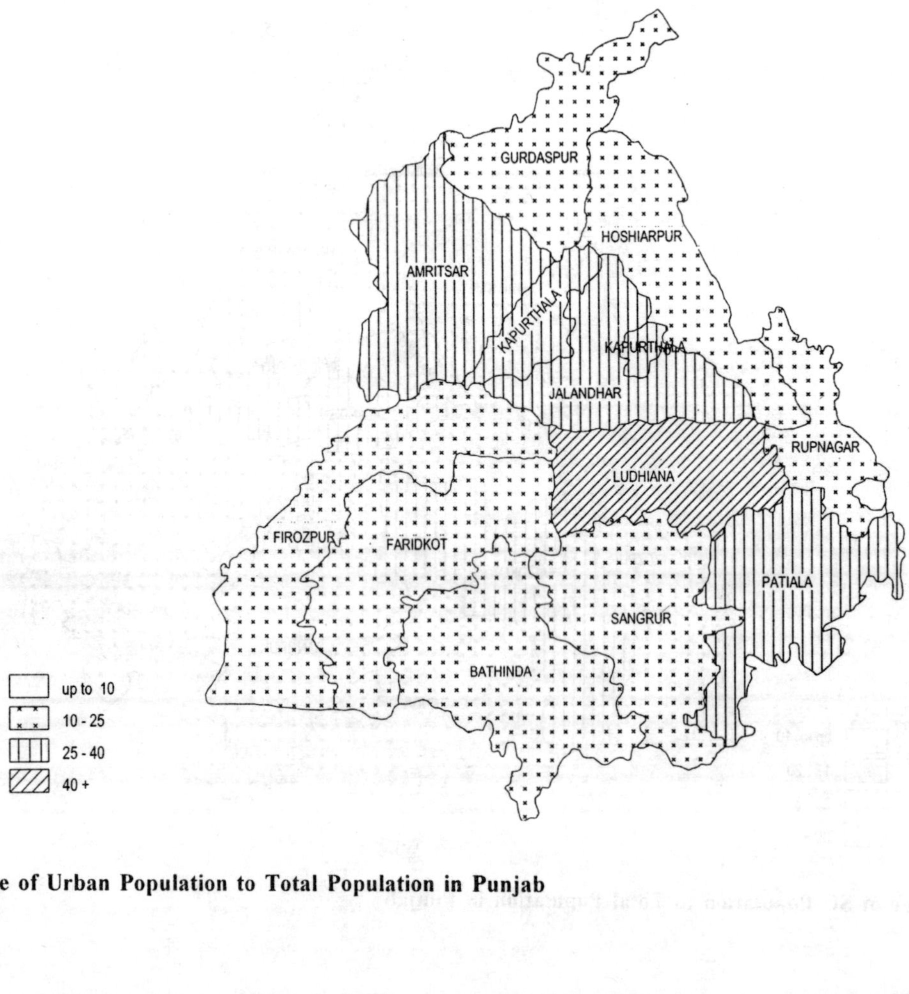

MAP 7.6: **Percentage of Urban Population to Total Population in Punjab**

The age–sex composition of the population has a bearing on its future growth pattern. The current age–sex status indicates the proportion of the population that needs care, viz., those below 15 years, and the proportion to be supported economically, viz., those aged 60 years and above, cannot work. The total dependency ratio and the old age dependency ratio reflect these aspects of the population.

Table 7.H7 presents these data and the dependency ratios. The total dependency ratio has been computed as the number of persons in the age group 0–14 years and above 60 years per hundred persons in the age group 15–59 years. These data relate to 1981. Agewise data from the 1991 Census are not yet available. Similarly, the old age dependency ratio has been computed as the number of persons aged 60 years and above per hundred persons in the age group 15–59 years. At the state level, the total dependency ratio is 80.83 per cent, which means that there are nearly 81 dependent persons per hundred persons in the working age group 15–59 years. The dependency ratio is higher for males than for females. It is as high as 87.27 per cent in Gurdaspur and only 71.85 per cent in Ludhiana. In the case of male dependency, Gurdaspur had 91 male dependents per hundred males in the working age group. The lowest male dependency is observed in Ludhiana (70.19 per cent). This district is more urbanized, attracting male population in the working age group as in-migrants. This partly explains the lower male dependency ratio in this district. Female dependency is the highest in Ferozpur (87.30 per cent) and the lowest in Ludhiana (73.51 per cent).

In all the districts, the dependency ratio is higher in the rural areas than in the urban areas. This is also true when seen separately for the male and female population. The highest dependency ratio in rural areas is 90.83 per cent in Gurdaspur. In urban areas, Hoshiarpur has the highest dependency ratio (82.24 per cent). This is much lower than the highest ratio observed in rural areas.

Whereas the total dependency ratio accounts for both young and old dependents, the old age dependency ratio represents the number of old (aged 60 years and above) persons dependent on the working age population. In Punjab, in the total population there are 14 aged dependents per hundred persons in the working age, while in the case of males and females the figures are 15 and 13 aged dependents respectively. Among the districts, the highest old age dependency ratio is in Hoshiarpur (17.33 per cent) and the lowest is in Patiala (12.10 per cent). The old age dependency ratio among males is higher than that among females in all the districts.

There is a big difference between the old age dependency ratios in rural and urban areas. The highest old age dependency of both the sexes in rural areas is 18.79 per cent in Hoshiarpur while it is the highest in the urban areas of the same district at only 12.87 per cent. The migration of persons in the working age from rural to urban areas and their return migration to rural homes after retirement tends to lower the old age dependency ratio in urban areas.

7.6 Population Growth

The country aspires to attain a net reproduction rate (NRR) of 1 in the near future. The birth rate, death rate and IMR are expected to reach the levels of 21, 9, and 60. A look into the trends and current ratio of growth of population and the parameters influencing it will throw light on the feasibility of achieving these targets. The decadal rates of growth in Punjab for 1971–81 and 1981–91 were 23.89 per cent and 20.81 per cent, respectively; these were lower than the rates for India for the same decades at 25 per cent and 23.51 per cent.

A number of social and demographic factors have a bearing on the realized rate of fertility and growth of population. These include the number of females in the reproductive age group (15–44 years), that is, the potential mothers; the proportion among them who are married and thus exposed to the risk of child bearing; and their age at marriage. The prevailing mortality rate among children is known to influence the reproductive behaviour of couples and thus has a bearing on the realized fertility and growth of population. Moreover, child mortality rates being sensitive to available health care facilities are also important indicators of well-being of the population. Factors such as the proportion of girls who are away from school also influence the realized fertility rate. A girl who has dropped out of school early (or not enrolled in school) is likely to be married off early, thus contributing to an early onset of fertility. The realized fertility rate also depends, to a large extent, on the level of knowledge among the couples about the need for and the means of ensuring a small family by appropriate choice of age at marriage and efficient use of available contraceptive methods. It is easier to induce these motivations and practices among educated couples. A look at these factors and the ways of influencing these are relevant in the context of human development.

7.6.1 Proportion of Females Married and Mean Age at Marriage

Table 7.H8 presents data on the number of females in the age group 15–44 years, the percentage of married females in different age groups and their mean age at marriage for all the districts of Punjab by place of residence at the time of the 1981 Census.

In this state, about 69.20 per cent of the females in the age group 15–44 years are married. Their mean age at marriage is around 18.9 years with not much difference between rural and urban areas. The proportion of married females in the age group 15–19 was 13.42 per cent in the state, ranging between 8.45 per cent in Hoshiarpur and 20.72 per cent in Bathinda. The peak childbearing age is 20–4 years, and in this age group about 68 per cent of the females are married. The figure ranges between 77.09 per cent in Bathinda and 62.82 per cent in Gurdaspur. In rural areas, the proportion of married females in this prime childbearing age group is marginally higher than that in urban areas in most of the districts.

About one per cent of the girls in the age group 10–14 years are married indicating some prevalence of child marriage in the state. The proportion is the highest in Bathinda (1.71 per cent), followed by Sangrur (1.47 per cent), Rupnagar (1.30 per cent), and Ferozpur (1.26 per cent). These districts have a higher proportion of married females in the age group 15–19 years as well. High drop-out rates in these districts support the contention that girls away from school are married off early. If this is indeed true then, raising enrolment and retention of girls in school would be one of the ways of influencing the age at marriage and the fertility rate.

There is not much variation in the mean age at marriage across districts, and between rural and urban areas. The highest mean age at marriage is 19.40 years in rural Hoshiarpur while the lowest, 18.30 years, is seen in urban Rupnagar and urban Patiala. All the means are very close to the statutory minimum of 18 years. Quite a large number of marriages must be taking place before the age of 18 years, both in rural and urban areas of almost all the districts.

7.6.2 Death Rate and Child Mortality

The expectation of life at birth in Punjab is 64.7 years for females, which is longer than that for males at 63.0 years. In terms of expectation of life, Punjab ranks second to Kerala among the major states. The state experiences a death rate of around 8 per thousand persons, which is marginally lower than the national average of 9.8. A large proportion of these deaths, in Punjab as well as in other states, occurs in childhood. A scrutiny of the mortality conditions of children would be revealing. Infant mortality rates estimated from sample registration system (SRS) data indicate that about 53 deaths out of one thousand live births in Punjab occur in childhood. The corresponding figure for the nation is much higher at 80. In terms of IMR, Punjab ranks second to Kerala among the major states for which such estimates are available. The gap between the first and the second is, however, quite wide. Kerala has a low IMR of 17. The neighbouring states of Punjab, viz., Uttar Pradesh (93), Rajasthan (77), Himachal Pradesh (75), and Haryana (68), have much higher levels of IMR.

Estimates of IMR from SRS data, though more reliable, are available only for the nation and the major states. The small sample size does not permit estimation at a lower level of disaggregation.

Four standard estimates of child mortality, viz., q(1), q(2), q(3), and q(5), obtained from data collected in the 1981 Census have been used to assess the relative positions of districts and other population groups. The estimate q(i) represents the expected number of deaths out of one thousand live births before reaching age i years.

In the state as a whole the level of mortality q(1) was 77 per thousand live births in 1981. It is higher among girls (79) than among boys (74). In rural areas, q(1) is 85, 83, and 90 among persons, males, and females, respectively. These are higher than the corresponding rates 53, 51, and 55 in urban areas. Mortality before age one year is highest in Kapurthala (92) and lowest in Ludhiana (66).

The level of mortality q(5), for the state as a whole is 111, ranging between 129 in Sangrur to 94 in Ludhiana. The corresponding figure for the country is much higher at 152. It is higher (124) in rural areas than in urban areas (73). Female children are exposed to a higher risk of mortality as measured by q(5). The achievement of Punjab in reducing child mortality is better than that of many other states and the country as a whole, though it is not commendable keeping its economic prosperity in view. However, it is observed from 1991 child mortality rates that q1, q2, q3, and q5 all have been declining compared to 1981 levels. In this part the q1 and q2 are graduated which cannot be compared with q3 and q5 which are ungraduated for the year 1981.

It is of interest to look into the mortality conditions of children for different population groups. Since q(2) is believed to be a more reliable estimate, it has been used for the purpose of comparison here.

Among religious communities in Punjab, Christians experience the highest incidence of child mortality q(2) at 108, followed by Sikhs (98), Muslims (96), and Hindus (88). Sikhs residing away from Punjab have a lower level of q(2), the figure for the country being 92. Out-migrants are generally at a higher level of socio-economic status in terms of education and income, which lowers the level of child mortality.

Mothers' capabilities and handicaps largely determine the health and mortality conditions to which children are exposed. Tables 7.2 and 7.3 tabulate child mortality rates by the education level and the occupation of the mother. As expected, child mortality is seen to decrease with a rise in the level of education of the mother.

Mortality is high (128) among children whose mothers work as agricultural labourers in rural Punjab, followed by children of manual workers. Mothers working as agricultural labourers and other manual workers are unable to take adequate care of their children. Their children, deprived of maternal care, are exposed to a higher risk of morbidity and death.

TABLE 7.2
Estimated Child Mortality q(2) by Level of Education of Mother in Punjab

Education of mother	Child mortality q(2)		
	Total	Male	Female
Illiterate	122(106)	125(101)	118
Literate but below middle	97	99	95(85)
Middle but below matriculate	75	79	70
Matriculate but below graduate	54	60	48
Graduate and above	29	31	26
All levels	**109(94)**	**112 (90)**	**105(98)**

Note: Figures in parentheses are graduated estimates.

Source: Census of India, 1981, Fertility and Child Mortality Estimates of Haryana, Occasional Paper No. 10 of 1987.

TABLE 7.3
Estimated Child Mortality by Occupation of Main Workers in Rural Punjab

Occupation	Child mortality q(2)		
	Total	Male	Female
Main workers	131(107)	127	135(111)
Cultivators	100(87)	118(59)	81(109)
Agricultural Labourers	157(128)	147	167(126)
Manual workers	120	109	133
Non-manual workers	43	86(53)	–
Non-workers	119(94)	123(100)	115

Note: Figures in parentheses are graduated estimates.

Source: Census of India, 1981. Fertility and Child Mortality Estimates of Punjab, Occasional Paper No. 10 of 1988.

The spread of education among mothers and future mothers and improvement of the working environment of female workers along with general health care facilities will go a long way in further reducing child mortality in Punjab.

7.6.3 Fertility Indices

There are variations in the realized rate of fertility across districts and other population groups. There are a consequence of variation in the factors that determine fertility. The various indices that are used to represent the fertility levels of a population include: general fertility rate (GFR), general marital fertility rate (GMFR), TFR, and total marital fertility rate (TMFR). For definitions of these rates see Section 1.5.3

Of these indices, TFR is regarded as a more standardized measure. Estimates of these indices (derived from the data collected in the Census of India, 1981 and 1991) are presented by religious groups in Table 7.H10 and across all the districts in Table 7.H11. In 1981, GFR was 98 in the state—104 in rural areas and 84 in urban areas. TFR was 3.2 in the state with wide rural–urban differential. Fertility among Muslims is the highest in terms of TFR (4.6), while in rural areas Christians have a TFR level of 4.8, which is higher than that for Muslims. Sikhs had the lowest level of fertility in the state as measured by many of these indices. The adjusted TFR, TMFR, GFR, and GMFR for 1991 show a declining trend for state and for all the districts as well.

Ferozpur (3.8), Sangrur (3.5), Gurdaspur (3.6), and Bathinda (3.6) have higher levels of TFR. On the other hand, Ludhiana and Jalandhar have lower levels of TFR, 2.5 and 2.7, respectively. In terms of other indices also these two districts have the lowest levels of fertility. In general, rural areas have higher levels of fertility with respect to all the indices as compared to urban areas.

7.7 Material Well-being

Among the major aspects of quality of life, health and education are very important. The achievements of the state in this sphere have been discussed in earlier sections. There are, however, many other aspects, no less important, which could not be included due to difficulties in conceptualization and measurement and deficiencies in the data. An adequate level of income and wealth, though not sufficient, is necessary for leading a decent standard of living and for a higher level of human development. Most of the deprivations can be traced to the inadequacy of income and wealth. Income earned and the assets held by households would, thus, be a proxy for many aspects of life not covered in this profile. A lower level of these would of course lead to non-fulfilment of many aspirations and thus indicate a lower level of human development. An analysis of the level of income earned and the assets held, as also distribution of these among the members of the community, reveal an important aspect of human development.

7.7.1 Income and Consumption

The per capita income in Punjab is Rs 3751 (in 1990–1 at 1980–1 prices), which is next to that in Delhi (Rs 4838) and Goa (Rs 4604). Per capita income is, however, an aggregate measure and does not reveal the distributional aspect. No agency collects data on income at the household level on a regular basis. The National Council for Applied Economic Research (NCAER) in some of its occasional surveys collected such data, the latest one pertaining to 1980–1. Data on distribution of income among households are, therefore, not available for any recent year. The National Sample Survey Organization (NSSO), in its various rounds, collects data on consumer expenditure on a more or less regular basis. These are available separately for population groups residing in urban and rural areas in states and union territories in grouped form—persons per thousand and mean expenditure in various expenditure classes. In the absence of data on household income, the data on consumer expenditure obtained from the NSSO pertaining to 1987–8 have been used to assess the level of material well-being in the state as a whole. The inadequate sample size does not permit further disaggregation of the NSSO data on consumer expenditure. One opinion is that consumer expenditure is a better indicator of material well-being since it is influenced by the past income as well as prospects of income in the foreseeable future. If so, the use of consumer expenditure is indeed more appropriate.

The monthly per capita consumer expenditure (MPCE) in 1987–8 in Punjab was Rs 244.28 for rural areas and Rs 267.44 for urban areas. These are higher than the corresponding figures of Rs 155.75 and Rs 249.93 for the country as a whole. Punjab ranks high among states and union territories in this respect. In 1993–4, the MPCE in Punjab was Rs 433.00 in rural areas and Rs 510.73 in urban areas. These are higher than the corresponding figures for earlier years.

Measured in terms of the Gini coefficient, the distribution of consumer expenditure in Punjab is more egalitarian in urban punjab and almost at par in rural areas compared to the country as a whole. Estimated Gini coefficients for Punjab are 0.275 for urban and 0.295 for rural areas. The corresponding estimates for the country as a whole are 0.352 and 0.291, respectively. Higher per capita expenditure and its egalitarian distribution resulted in a lower incidence of poverty. As estimated by the Planning Commission, the incidence of poverty in the country in 1987–8 was about 30 per cent. Punjab has a much lower proportion of the poor, only 7.20 per cent. The proportion was the lowest among states and union territories. According to the 1993–4 estimates, a much lower proportion of the population in Punjab's rural and urban areas is poor, that is, 12.11 and 6.7 per cent, respectively. However, due to the use of different methodologies, these figures are not directly comparable.

The percentage of population below the specified poverty line is a measure of the *incidence* of poverty, that is, how many are poor. Sen (*Econometrica* 1976) devised a measure of the *intensity* of poverty, that is, how poor are the poor: According to the indices of both Sen Poverty Index (P_s) and Foster, Greer, and Thorbecke (FGT), poverty is more intense in urban than in rural Punjab.

Table 7.4
Intensity of Poverty in Punjab

	P_S	FGT
Rural areas	0.0361	0.0069
Urban areas	0.0434	0.0078

Source: Computed from NSS data for 1993–4.

TABLE 7.5
Consumer Expenditure, Gini Coefficient (1993–4) and Population below Poverty Line

	Consumer expenditure		Gini coefficient		Percentage below
	Rural	Urban	Rural	Urban	poverty line
Punjab	433.0	510.73	.2645	.2763	11.77
Rajasthan	322.3	424.73	.2599	.2904	27.41
Bihar	218.3	353.03	.2239	.3070	54.96
All India	281.40	458.04	.2816	.3399	35.97

Source: Computed from NSS data for 1993–4.

Tables 7.4 and 7.5 show the data on consumer expenditure and the population below the poverty line in the major states in India, and also present a comparative picture with the all-India average. This clearly shows that Punjab is better placed as compared to its neighbouring states not only in terms of the poverty line but also in terms of rural and urban variations.

The data on operational holdings and average holdings reveal the following:

1. The total number of holdings has increased to 11.2 lakhs in 1990–1 from 10.9 lakhs in 1985–6.

2. The average size of holding has declined to 3.61 hectares from 3.77 hectares as a result of a decrease in the total area operated from 41.0 lakh hectares to 40.3 lakh hectares during the same period.

3. The number of marginal and medium holdings has increased while there has been a decrease in the number of small semi-medium and large holdings. The trend observed in Punjab is different from that observed elsewhere in the country and warrants further scrutiny and analysis.

4. The marginal holdings constitute the largest proportion (26.47 per cent), followed by semi-medium (25.86 per cent), medium (23.41 per cent), small (18.25 per cent), and large holdings (6.00 per cent).

5. The proportion of area operated is highest for medium holdings (40.22 per cent), followed by large (26.70 per cent), semi-medium (20.87 per cent), small (8.14 per cent), and marginal holdings (4.07 per cent).

6. The largest number of holdings are in Amritsar (11.10 per cent), followed by Gurdaspur (10.14 per cent), Ferozpur (10.05 per cent), Faridkot (9.59 per cent), Bathinda (9.16 per cent), and Sangrur (9.13 per cent). The smallest number is in Ropar (4.80 per cent).

7. The average size of holding is the largest in Bathinda (4.71 hectares), followed by Faridkot (4.50 hectares), Sangrur (4.38 hectares), and Ferozpur (4.19 hectares). The lowest average size is in Ropar (2.32 hectares).

8. Among holdings operated by SC farmers, the number of marginal and small holdings accounted for 67 per cent of the total holdings while land operated by them was only 30.52 per cent of the total.

9. Holdings operated by the SCs are concentrated in Hoshiarpur (15.54 per cent), followed by Jalandhar (10.17 per cent), and Bathinda (10.12 per cent). The lowest proportion of SC holdings is in Kapurthala (4.43 per cent).

10. The largest size of holding operated by the SCs is in Jalandhar (2.53 hectares) followed by Kapurthala (2.29 hectares) and Ludhiana (2.17 hectares). These are smaller than the average size of holding in the state (3.61 hectares).

7.8 Concluding Remakrs

Punjab is one of the economically prosperous states in India. This prosperity is largely a consequence of the successful green revolution. The per capita income in 1990–1 (at 1980–1 prices) was quite high at Rs 3751. The state also ranks high in terms of per capita consumer expenditure. Higher average income and expenditure and its egalitarian distribution resulted in a low incidence of poverty. The proportion of the poor in Punjab at 7.20 per cent is the lowest among all states and union territories. This gives Punjab a high score in human development in terms of material well-being.

About 58.51 per cent of the population (65.66 per cent of males and 50.41 per cent of females) were enumerated as literate in the 1991 Census. Punjab is ahead of the country as a whole in terms of overall literacy. It, however, ranks twenty-first in male and fourteenth in female literacy among the 32 states and union territories. Keeping its economic prosperity in view, its performance in literacy falls short of expectation. The performance of some of the districts such as

Ferozpur, Patiala, Sangrur, Bathinda, and Faridkot is not satisfactory. Rural female literacy in these districts is low and needs well-planned micro-intervention. The strategy should include motivation campaigns to raise the female age at marriage and improve enrolment and retention of girls in school. Efforts to raise adult literacy may be of help in motivating the parents to send their children to school and to keep them there till the completion of their primary education.

The performance of the state in terms of CBR, CDR, IMR, and expectation of life is better than that of the country. In fact, Punjab ranks next to Kerala in terms IMR and expectation of life. Kerala, however, is much ahead of Punjab and there is scope for improvement in these areas (Table 7.6).

Child mortality is low in Punjab both among males and females. However, across the districts, it is higher in Kapurthala and Sangrur than in other districts of Punjab. Female child mortality is higher than male child mortality in all the districts from age one itself. The female children in Punjab need more care and affection from the society and family.

A wide disparity persists in Punjab in child mortality between rural and urban areas. This is despite a highly developed transport infrastructure and a widespread network of health care facilities, even in rural Punjab. The reasons for the persistence of this disparity, perhaps, are more social than economic and need a careful probe.

The overall performance of Punjab in human development is quite high. Shiva Kumar (*Economic and Political Weekly* October 1991), and Tilak (IASSI Quarterly 1991) have ranked Punjab next to Kerala among the major Indian states. However, there always remains scope for further improvements in the quality and content of the lives of the people.

TABLE 7.6

Some Indicators of Health Status in Punjab, Kerala, and India, 1997

States	Crude birth rate (per '000 persons)	Crude death rate (per '000 persons)	Infant mortality rate (per '000 live births)	Life expectancy at birth (1992–6)	
				Male (years)	Female (years)
India	27.2	8.2	71	60.1	61.4
Kerala	17.9	6.2	12	70.2	75.8
Punjab	23.4	7.4	51	66.4	68.6

Source: Compendium of India's Fertility and Mortality Indicators, 1971–97, based on the Sample Registration System (SRS), Registrar General, India.

TABLE 7.E1

Districtwise Primary School Enrolment Rate in Urban Areas (boys, girls, and total), 1990–1

State/district	Total no. of eligible children for enrolment (6–11) 1986–7			Enrolment rate		
	Boys	Girls	Total	Boys	Girls	Total
Punjab	**346,432**	**298,442**	**644,874**	**77.79**	**86.48**	**81.81**
Gurdaspur	21,734	19,058	40,792	147.37	167.79	156.91
Amritsar	50,287	42,903	93,190	78.32	84.82	81.31
Ferozpur	22,431	20,334	42,765	89.5	78.91	84.46
Ludhiana	74,832	61,710	136,542	44.58	52.92	48.35
Jalandhar	41,348	35,442	76,790	82.76	92.88	87.43
Kapurthala	9,007	9,113	18,120	80.84	82.76	81.8
Hoshiarpur	12,113	10,307	22,420	62.16	71.04	66.24
Rupnagar	13,384	10,262	23,646	78.23	85.05	81.19
Patiala	30,507	30,012	60,519	43.16	91.13	66.95
Sangrur	25,529	20,999	46,528	63.35	63.77	63.54
Bathinda	19,536	15,989	35,525	127.68	123.09	125.62
Faridkot	25,724	22,313	48,037	120	107.94	114.38

Source: Directorate of Public Instruction, Government of Punjab.

TABLE 7.E2

Districtwise Primary School Enrolment Rate (boys, girls, and total) and Teacher–Student Ratio in Rural Areas, 1990–1

State/district	Total no. of eligible children for enrolment (6–11)*			Enrolment rate			Teacher–student ratio**
	Boys	Girls	Total	Boys	Girls	Total	
Punjab	**898,167**	**774,437**	**1,672,604**	**93.29**	**92.04**	**92.71**	**42**
Gurdaspur	88,988	75,970	164,958	71.63	121.16	94.44	35
Amritsar	107,999	87,794	195,793	103.32	59.87	83.84	44
Ferozpur	80,456	66,515	146,971	88.25	96.96	92.19	44
Ludhiana	72,355	61,013	133,368	102.79	106.89	104.67	42
Jalandhar	82,951	70,537	153,488	87.85	92.46	89.97	45
Kapurthala	31,320	26,453	57,773	77.95	81.98	79.8	34
Hoshiarpur	74,898	64,168	139,066	95.52	104.41	99.62	33
Rupnagar	42,041	37,602	79,643	89.63	91.76	90.64	34
Patiala	85,801	94,069	179,870	97.33	73.93	85.09	40
Sangrur	79,106	66,054	145,160	92.01	85.93	89.24	43
Bathinda	75,677	61,980	137,657	86.92	84.12	85.66	49
Faridkot	76,575	62,282	138,857	115.67	114.98	115.36	51

* for Government and non-Government schools together; ** for all areas.

Source: Directorate of Public Instruction, Government of Punjab.

TABLE 7.E3

Districtwise Effective Literacy Rate by Place of Residence and Sex and Number of Villages by Distance from School

State/district	All areas			Rural			Urban			All areas 2001	Total number of villages	Number of villages by distance from school less than 1 km
	Male	Female	Total	Male	Female	Total	Male	Female	Total			
Punjab	**65.66**	**50.41**	**58.51**	**60.71**	**43.85**	**52.77**	**77.26**	**66.12**	**72.08**	**69.95**	**12,795**	**12,795**
Gurdaspur	69.56	53.33	61.84	66.57	49.51	58.44	79.92	66.77	73.69	74.19	1626	1626
Amritsar	65.07	50.10	58.09	57.80	40.49	49.74	78.91	68.26	73.93	67.85	1242	1242
Ferozpur	56.88	38.11	48.01	51.17	30.91	41.59	74.77	60.75	68.16	61.42	1162	1162
Ludhiana	72.47	61.23	67.35	69.93	54.99	62.95	74.89	67.74	71.71	76.54	979	979
Jalandhar	74.87	61.33	68.45	71.34	55.91	63.99	81.05	71.09	76.37	77.91	1256	1256
Kapurthala	70.03	55.83	63.31	66.11	51.04	58.90	80.79	70.03	75.84	73.56	699	699
Hoshiarpur	79.31	61.48	70.74	78.33	59.43	69.22	84.61	73.07	79.16	81.40	1623	1623
Rupnagar	76.45	58.54	68.14	73.02	52.87	63.66	86.46	75.03	81.15	78.49	917	917
Patiala	65.93	50.33	58.62	59.76	42.08	51.51	80.29	69.05	74.97	69.96	1462	1462
Sangrur	53.73	37.86	46.16	48.94	33.04	41.57	67.29	52.66	60.42	60.04	718	718
Bathinda	50.55	34.51	43.03	44.02	27.81	36.42	73.11	57.67	65.87	61.51	527	527
Faridkot	56.43	41.50	49.42	50.84	35.51	43.65	73.10	59.14	66.52	63.34	584	584

Sources: Directorate of Public Instruction, Government of Punjab, 1991; Census of India, 2001.

TABLE 7.H1

Districtwise Number of Govt Hospitals, Dispensaries, Health Posts, and Family Welfare Centres per lakh Urban Population in Urban Areas for Allopathy System

State/district	Number of hospitals	Number of dispensaries	Number of health posts	Urban population	Family welfare centres*	Family welfare centres per lakh population
Punjab	**130**	**221**	**23**	**5,993,225**	**124**	**2.07**
Gurdaspur	10	12	1	386,412	5	1.29
Amritsar	20	18	4	853,831	27	3.16
Ferozpur	11	8	3	384,400	10	2.60
Ludhiana	17	37	3	1,242,781	22	1.77
Jalandhar	14	38	2	728,802	15	2.06
Kapurthala	4	12	0	166,605	2	1.20
Hoshiarpur	6	11	2	222,138	5	2.25
Rupnagar	6	15	1	232,317	6	2.58
Patiala	14	33	1	566,973	9	1.59
Sangrur	9	11	3	417,994	11	2.63
Bathinda	10	17	3	351,133	4	-1.14
Faridkot	9	9	0	439,839	8	1.82

Note: * Family Welfare Clinics + Maternity and Child Health Care Centres.

Source: State Bureau of Health Intelligence, Directorate of Health and Family Welfare, Government of Punjab, Chandigarh.

TABLE 7.H2
Districtwise Number of Sub-centres, PHCs, and CHCs per lakh Rural Population for Allopathy System, 1991

State/district	Sub-centres			PHCs		CHCs	
	Total rural population	Number of sub-centres	Sub-centres per lakh population	Number of PHCs	PHCs per lakh population	Number of CHCs	CHCs per lakh population
Punjab	**14,288,744**	**2852**	**19.96**	**419**	**2.93**	**43**	**0.30**
Gurdaspur	1,370,320	284	20.73	46	3.36	4	0.29
Amritsar	1,650,729	332	20.11	45	2.73	5	0.30
Ferozpur	1,223,417	249	20.35	35	2.86	4	0.33
Ludhiana	1,228,813	88	7.16	32	2.60	4	0.33
Jalandhar	1,297,985	261	20.11	34	2.62	2	0.15
Kapurthala	480,042	243	50.62	10	2.08	5	1.04
Hoshiarpur	1,232,890	242	19.63	39	3.16	4	0.32
Rupnagar	683,286	133	19.46	22	3.22	2	0.29
Patiala	1,329,269	270	20.31	43	3.23	4	0.30
Sangrur	1,292,126	257	19.89	38	2.94	1	0.08
Bathinda	1,208,830	238	19.69	35	2.90	4	0.33
Faridkot	1,291,037	255	19.75	40	3.10	4	0.31

Note: Data available on 1.4.1991.

Source: State Bureau of Health Intelligence, Directorate of Health and Family Welfare, Government of Punjab. Chandigarh.

TABLE 7.H3
Districtwise Number of Doctors, Nurses, and Other Paramedical Staff per lakh Population, 1991

State/district	Population	Doctors	Nurses	Mid-wives	Dais	Lady health visitors
Punjab	**20,281,969**	**66.34**	**37.77**	**62.34**	**170.14**	**6.99**
Gurdaspur	1,756,732	35.97	58.00	109.80	229.63	8.31
Amritsar	2,504,560	112.35	43.04	68.07	237.12	14.93
Ferozpur	1,607,817	28.11	45.46	49.19	211.28	3.35
Ludhiana	2,471,594	92.65	77.72	87.10	142.49	6.87
Jalandhar	2,026,787	79.97	38.37	47.61	168.44	5.22
Kapurthala	646,647	46.85	15.92	51.96	234.44	6.80
Hoshiarpur	1,455,028	47.21	28.65	104.25	222.67	16.01
Rupnagar	915,603	28.17	22.28	63.12	158.25	4.69
Patiala	1,896,242	119.86	39.86	39.97	135.47	4.53
Sangrur	1,710,120	38.06	12.68	33.85	110.63	3.15
Bathinda	1,559,963	38.65	4.35	33.78	156.28	2.82
Faridkot	1,730,876	50.43	20.68	46.85	63.49	3.69

Source: State Bureau of Health Intelligence, Directorate of Health and Family Welfare, Government of Punjab, Chandigarh.

TABLE 7.H4
Districtwise Population Density, Sex Ratio, and Percentage of Urban and Scheduled Caste Population

State/district	All areas				Rural			Urban		
	Popn density	Sex ratio	Per cent of SC	Per cent of urban popn	Popn density	Sex ratio	Per cent of SC	Popn density	Sex ratio	Per cent of SC
Punjab	**403**	**882**	**28.31**	**29.55**	**292**	**888**	**31.93**	**4159**	**868**	**19.69**
Gurdaspur	493	903	24.70	22.00	393	905	25.35	5058	895	22.36
Amritsar	492	873	28.01	34.09	337	871	32.68	4416	876	18.97
Ferozpur	274	894	21.80	23.91	212	896	22.70	4079	882	18.91
Ludhiana	641	844	24.74	50.28	386	879	35.32	6305	812	14.27
Jalandhar	596	899	39.08	35.96	399	907	44.57	4995	885	29.31
Kapurthala	396	896	29.46	25.76	309	910	31.71	2164	857	22.97
Hoshiarpur	375	919	33.32	15.27	325	925	34.77	2716	890	25.30
Rupnagar	439	870	24.57	25.37	341	870	27.20	2830	870	16.83
Patiala	414	880	23.60	29.90	299	874	28.59	4194	895	11.93
Sangrur	335	870	26.83	24.44	258	867	29.43	4941	881	18.80
Bathinda	281	880	29.27	22.51	224	876	31.31	2290	893	22.25
Faridkot	302	882	34.08	25.41	230	880	37.17	3671	887	25.02

Source: Census of India, 1991.

TABLE 7.H5

Districtwise Urban Population of Workers (Main and Marginal) as Percentage to Urban Population, Workers in Household Industry for Urban Areas as Percentage to Total Main Workers in Urban Areas

State/district	Urban population			Main workers (as percentage to urban population)			Marginal workers (as percentage to urban population)			Workers in HH industry (as percentage to main workers in urban areas)		
	Total	Male	Female	Total	Male	Female	Total	Male	Female	Total	Male	Female
Punjab	**5,993,225**	**3,208,611**	**2,784,614**	**29.96**	**52.22**	**4.31**	**0.10**	**0.04**	**0.17**	**1.72**	**1.64**	**2.88**
Gurdaspur	386,412	203,866	182,546	27.28	48.49	3.59	0.04	0.03	0.05	0.70	0.67	1.15
Amritsar	853,831	455,175	398,656	30.20	53.07	4.09	0.00	0.00	0.00	0.61	0.54	1.79
Ferozpur	384,400	203,669	180,731	28.64	50.47	4.04	0.37	0.14	0.63	1.90	1.69	4.83
Ludhiana	1,242,781	685,983	556,798	32.26	55.70	3.39	0.00	0.00	0.00	0.32	0.28	1.17
Jalandhar	728,802	386,573	342,229	29.52	51.49	4.58	0.15	0.06	0.26	4.89	4.87	5.18
Kapurthala	166,605	89,731	76,874	30.74	52.86	4.93	0.10	0.04	0.17	1.74	1.59	3.64
Hoshiarpur	222,138	117,559	104,579	28.83	49.83	5.23	0.17	0.02	0.33	2.02	2.01	2.23
Rupnagar	232,317	124,226	108,091	30.31	50.25	7.39	0.01	0.01	0.01	1.52	1.56	1.10
Patiala	566,973	299,263	267,710	29.23	50.19	5.80	0.06	0.03	0.09	2.65	2.45	4.63
Sangrur	417,994	222,199	195,795	29.23	52.03	3.35	0.19	0.03	0.36	2.12	2.06	3.28
Bathinda	351,133	187,259	163,874	29.39	51.46	4.18	0.20	0.06	0.35	1.87	1.87	1.99
Faridkot	439,839	233,108	206,731	29.42	51.57	4.44	0.20	0.07	0.34	1.96	1.86	3.27

Source: Census of India,1991.

TABLE 7.H6

Districtwise Rural Population, Workers (Main and Marginal) as Percentage to Rural Population, Cultivators, Agricultural Labourers, Workers in Household Industry for Rural Areas

State/district	Rural population			Main workers (as percentage to rural population)			Marginal workers (as percentage to rural population)			Cultivators (as percentage to main workers in rural areas)			Agricultural labourers (as percentage to main workers in rural areas)			Workers in HH industry (as percentage to main workers in rural areas)		
	Total	Male	Female	Total	Male	Female	Total	Male	Female	Total	Male	Female	Total	Male	Female	Total	Male	Female
Punjab	**14,288,744**	**7,569,423**	**6,719,321**	**30.11**	**54.92**	**2.16**	**1.10**	**0.12**	**2.21**	**42.81**	**43.79**	**14.99**	**30.75**	**30.37**	**41.46**	**1.17**	**1.09**	**6.18**
Gurdaspur	1,370,320	719,477	650,843	28.05	52.04	1.54	0.25	0.08	0.44	36.66	37.30	12.97	31.26	31.51	21.96	0.66	0.59	3.26
Amritsar	1,650,729	882,328	768,401	30.90	56.05	2.03	0.01	0.01	0.01	42.24	43.25	10.31	33.49	33.31	39.20	0.37	0.31	2.17
Ferozpur	1,223,417	645,095	578,322	30.83	55.72	3.06	2.28	0.20	4.59	50.40	51.69	24.08	33.92	32.62	60.52	0.73	0.70	1.39
Ludhiana	1,228,813	654,056	574,757	30.24	55.32	1.69	0.00	0.00	0.00	39.24	40.19	3.81	28.21	28.37	22.21	0.66	0.61	2.63
Jalandhar	1,297,985	680,520	617,465	29.22	53.57	2.38	0.90	0.12	1.75	34.09	35.20	6.52	31.59	31.11	43.39	2.08	1.97	4.59
Kapurthala	480,042	251,299	228,743	29.83	54.30	2.96	1.52	0.15	3.01	41.16	42.25	19.23	26.26	25.52	41.25	1.30	1.22	3.02
Hoshiarpur	1,232,890	640,566	592,324	27.66	50.97	2.46	1.17	0.27	2.14	35.24	36.20	13.76	26.11	25.98	29.17	2.46	2.27	6.77
Rupnagar	683,286	365,445	317,841	29.10	52.79	1.85	0.89	0.12	1.78	38.15	38.56	24.51	20.47	20.70	12.76	1.63	1.60	2.66
Patiala	1,329,269	709,313	619,956	29.90	54.60	1.64	0.62	0.16	1.14	40.86	41.71	8.59	30.95	30.69	41.10	1.50	1.38	5.93
Sangrur	1,292,126	692,162	599,964	31.45	57.45	1.46	1.69	0.13	3.49	50.69	51.36	20.29	29.73	29.53	38.49	1.19	1.14	3.68
Bathinda	1,208,830	642,590	566,240	31.67	57.45	2.40	2.74	0.20	5.62	52.95	54.28	16.93	30.76	29.90	54.29	1.19	1.11	3.41
Faridkot	1,291,037	686,572	604,465	31.80	57.17	2.98	1.83	0.11	3.79	47.37	48.63	20.09	36.66	35.78	55.69	0.92	0.86	2.31

Source: Census of India, 1991.

TABLE 7.H7

Districtwise Size of Households and Dependency Ratio by Sex and Place of Residence

State/district	All areas							Rural							Urban						
	Average size of household	Total dependency ratio			Old age dependency ratio			Average size of household	Total dependency ratio			Old age dependency ratio			Average size of household	Total dependency ratio			Old age dependency ratio		
		Total	Male	Female	Total	Male	Female		Total	Male	Female	Total	Male	Female		Total	Male	Female	Total	Male	Female
Punjab	**5.90**	**80.83**	**81.66**	**80.00**	**14.06**	**15.05**	**13.07**	**6.10**	**85.04**	**86.67**	**85.40**	**15.78**	**16.92**	**14.62**	**5.61**	**71.66**	**69.97**	**73.29**	**10.51**	**10.65**	**10.35**
Gurdaspur	6.09	87.27	90.53	84.05	14.67	16.14	13.14	6.11	90.83	94.56	87.10	15.41	17.08	13.75	6.01	75.53	77.31	73.76	12.01	13.07	11.08
Amritsar	5.96	83.53	84.54	82.40	14.05	14.51	13.08	6.12	90.48	92.91	88.05	15.70	16.95	14.45	5.69	71.24	70.73	71.75	10.98	11.47	10.49
Ferozpur	5.94	86.57	86.16	87.30	13.43	14.12	12.70	6.02	89.48	89.11	89.85	14.24	15.30	13.19	5.69	77.96	76.82	79.09	10.74	10.37	11.11
Ludhiana	5.77	71.85	70.19	73.51	13.10	13.49	12.70	6.15	77.41	78.79	76.04	16.31	17.45	15.17	5.45	64.94	59.83	70.04	9.01	8.72	9.31
Jalandhar	5.82	80.36	86.20	74.51	14.82	16.41	13.23	5.90	85.56	90.12	81.02	17.26	18.89	15.64	5.69	71.78	70.83	72.72	10.68	10.68	10.68
Kapurthala	5.81	81.81	84.27	79.35	14.04	15.09	12.99	5.90	85.54	89.76	81.32	15.06	16.56	13.56	5.56	73.86	72.96	74.75	11.86	12.05	11.68
Hoshiarpur	5.62	83.91	88.17	79.64	17.33	19.34	15.35	5.65	88.99	91.20	86.79	18.79	20.55	17.03	5.46	82.24	72.35	92.12	12.87	13.02	12.73
Rupnagar	5.68	79.58	78.98	80.17	14.77	16.17	13.38	6.06	83.19	83.47	82.92	16.66	18.45	14.87	4.80	67.37	64.48	70.27	8.52	8.81	8.23
Patiala	6.05	78.69	78.70	78.68	12.10	13.36	10.83	6.34	83.63	84.32	82.94	13.15	14.92	11.38	5.47	67.94	66.59	69.28	9.81	10.00	9.61
Sangrur	6.13	77.58	77.13	78.03	14.18	15.02	13.34	6.22	84.20	71.38	97.02	13.87	15.84	11.89	5.84	77.22	76.21	78.23	11.71	12.19	11.24
Bathinda	5.96	80.77	80.79	80.75	13.28	14.24	12.32	6.07	82.89	83.78	82.00	14.44	15.72	13.17	5.59	73.95	71.33	76.57	9.52	9.55	9.49
Faridkot	6.10	81.22	82.42	79.99	14.29	14.80	13.77	6.16	82.15	84.20	80.10	15.06	15.99	14.14	5.94	77.17	76.90	77.44	10.76	11.09	10.42

Source: Census of India, 1991.

TABLE 7.H8

Number of Females in the Age-group 15–44 years, Percentage of Married Females in Different Age Groups and Mean Age at Marriage, 1981

State/district	All Areas	Rural						Urban					
	Mean age at marriage (years)	Number of females in age group 15–44 ('000)	Percentage of married females in the age group			Mean age at marriage (years)	Number of females in age group 15–44 ('000)	Percentage of married females in the age group				Mean age at marriage
			10–14	15–19	20–4	15–44			10–14	15–19	20–4	15–44	
Punjab	**18.90**	**10,468**	**0.99**	**13.47**	**68.73**	**68.88**	**18.80**	**25,135**	**1.00**	**13.29**	**66.50**	**69.99**	**18.90**
Gurdaspur	18.70	729	0.89	9.65	60.27	66.53	18.90	2435	0.77	10.95	63.65	65.63	18.70
Amritsar	19.10	1581	0.58	10.71	64.01	68.79	19.10	2919	0.61	10.64	66.37	67.46	19.20
Ferozpur	18.90	641	1.27	18.2	67.79	70.98	18.60	2029	0.85	6.04	41.12	63.02	19.00
Ludhiana	19.20	1906	1.16	12.75	67.91	63.42	19.20	2253	1.05	9.90	60.69	62.14	19.20
Jalandhar	18.80	1359	0.93	10.66	64.99	68.24	18.90	2345	0.63	9.41	65.37	67.38	18.70
Kapurthala	19.00	353	0.84	11.60	65.85	68.44	18.90	820	0.98	10.17	61.70	65.66	19.10
Hoshiarpur	18.80	385	0.72	7.95	59.45	68.11	19.40	2230	0.59	8.52	63.84	65.71	18.80
Rupnagar	18.40	348	2.07	14.39	77.94	72.26	18.90	1129	1.11	13.88	72.58	70.84	18.30
Patiala	18.40	1065	0.43	11.94	63.81	69.33	18.80	2309	1.10	18.36	75.30	71.31	18.30
Sangrur	18.80	698	1.07	16.26	69.79	71.38	18.90	2289	1.59	17.78	73.20	71.55	18.80
Bathinda	18.60	644	1.43	20.93	76.01	74.81	18.60	2094	1.78	20.66	77.47	73.08	18.60
Faridkot	19.10	759	1.56	18.88	70.88	72.27	18.70	2283	0.75	14.24	70.69	70.68	19.20

Source: Census of India, 1981.

TABLE 7.H9

Child Mortality Estimates by Districts for All Areas, 1991

State/district	q(1)			q(2)			q(3)			q(5)		
	Male	Female	Total	Male	Female	Total	Male	Female	Total	Male	Female	Total
Punjab	**81** (74)	**53** (79)	**74** (77)	**89** (98)	**63** (90)	**81** (94)	**95** (100)	**79** (105)	**88** (102)	**97** (109)	**82** (118)	**92** (111)
Gurdaspur	75	74	75	76	84	81	82	91	86	96	101	99
Amritsar	48	50	49	56	57	57	59	58	59	65	60	61
Firozpur	58	63	61	67	69	68	72	74	74	76	79	77
Ludhiana	42	47	45	46	51	47	51	56	53	59	61	60
Jalandhar	56	51	53	59	58	59	66	65	64	70	69	69
Kapurthala	96	94	95	106	104	105	115	113	114	124	121	122
Hoshiarpur	80	85	82	87	89	88	92	93	90	101	99	100
Rupnagar	59	60	60	66	64	63	71	69	70	77	74	76
Patiala	69	59	64	74	69	72	79	71	78	81	73	80
Sangrur	54	51	53	71	76	75	74	77	76	78	80	79
Bathinda	69	74	72	72	78	75	79	84	81	84	91	87
Faridkot	54	51	53	56	60	58	60	64	62	68	65	67

Note: Figures in parentheses are for the year 1981.

Source: District Level Estimates of Fertility and Child Mortality for 1991 and their Relations with Other Variables: Occasional Paper No. 1 of 1997; Office of the Registrar General, India.

TABLE 7.H10

State-level Religionwise Fertility Indices by Place of Residence

Religion	All areas				Rural				Urban			
	GFR	GMFR	TFR	TMFR	GFR	GMFR	TFR	TMFR	GFR	GMFR	TFR	TMFR
All religions	**98**	**138**	**3.2**	**4.3**	**104**	**147**	**3.5**	**4.6**	**84**	**117**	**2.8**	**3.6**
Hindus	99	137	3.2	4.2	113	155	3.8	4.8	85	188	2.6	3.5
Muslims	136	178	4.6	5.7	131	173	4.5	5.7	143	186	4.6	5.8
Christians	129	179	4.4	5.5	138	191	4.8	5.9	97	137	2.9	4.0
Sikhs	97	138	3.2	4.4	100	143	3.4	4.5	80	113	2.5	3.5

Source: Fertility and Child Mortality Estimates of Punjab, Census of India, 1981, Occasional Paper No. 10, 1988, Office of the Registrar General, India.

TABLE 7.H11
Districtwise Adjusted Fertility Indices

State/district	All areas							
	1981				1991			
	GFR	GMFR	TFR	TMFR	GFR	GMFR	TFR	TMFR
Punjab	**151**	**212**	**4.9**	**6.6**	**124**	**167**	**3.8**	**5.8**
Gurdaspur	161	236	5.5	7.5	118	168	3.7	5.7
Amritsar	158	224	5.3	7.2	126	171	4.0	5.8
Ferozpur	161	223	5.2	6.9	139	181	4.2	5.9
Ludhiana	142	200	4.6	6.3	100	132	3.0	4.7
Jalandhar	141	204	4.7	6.4	116	164	3.6	6.0
Kapurthala	149	216	5.0	6.8	113	157	3.4	5.4
Hoshiarpur	144	212	5.0	6.6	115	165	3.7	6.2
Rupnagar	145	198	4.8	6.2	129	172	4.0	5.7
Patiala	157	217	5.1	6.6	132	174	4.0	5.9
Sangrur	153	208	5.0	6.4	130	170	4.0	5.6
Bathinda	152	202	4.8	6.1	130	167	3.9	5.6
Faridkot	152	210	4.9	6.5	126	164	3.8	5.6

Note: Rates seem to be overestimated.
Source: Fertility and Child Mortality Estimates of Punjab, Census of India, 1981, Occasional Paper No. 10, 1988, Office of the Registrar General, India; District Level Estimates of Fertility and Child Mortality for 1991 and their Inter-Relations with Other Variables: Occasional Paper No. 1 of 1997; Office of the Registrar General, India.

TABLE 7.P1
Per Thousand Distribution of Persons across MPCE Classes and Average Monthly Consumer Expendture per person in Punjab

Urban			Rural		
MPCE class (Rs)	Per '000 distribution of person	Av. consumption expenditure per person for a period of 30 days	MPCE class (Rs)	Per '000 distribution of person	Av. consumption expenditure per person for a period of 30 days
Less than 90	13	76.63	Less than 65	4	57.27
90–110	17	99.92	65–80	4	76.49
135–60	117	147.17	95–110	54	103.97
160–85	100	171.26	110–25	74	117.87
185–215	138	198.25	125–40	70	133.14
215–55	133	232.46	140–60	87	148.39
255–310	144	281.57	160–80	94	169.73
310–85	90	341.4	180–215	163	199.26
385–520	109	441.25	215–80	194	245.06
520–700	48	587.76	280–385	125	321.64
> 700	21	871.68	> 385	114	609.29
All classes	**1000**	**269.95**	**All classes**	**1000**	**244.19**

Source: Sarvekshana, 48th Issue, Vol. XV, No. 1, 1991.

TABLE 7.P2.1

Distribution of Number of Operational Holdings and Area Operated for All Social Groups, 1985–6 and 1990–1 and Average Size per Holding for All Social Groups and SCs, 1990–1

Size class (ha.)	Number		Area (in ha.)		Av. size per holding (1990–1)	
	1985–6	1990–1	1985–6	1990–1	All groups	SCs
Below 0.02	**0**	**10,148**	**0**	**130**	**0.01**	**0.02**
0.02–0.5	116,632	136,098	36,384	45,510	0.33	0.34
0.5–1.0	139,627	149,422	102,186	118,584	0.79	0.78
Marginal	**256,259**	**295,668**	**138,570**	**164,224**	**0.56**	**0.52**
1.0–2.0	207,639	203,842	310,971	328,215	1.61	1.35
Small						
2.0–3.0	183,188	175,519	456,259	445,274	2.54	2.37
3.0–4.0	107,649	113,269	383,578	396,267	3.50	3.38
Semi-medium	**290,837**	**288,788**	**839,837**	**841,541**	**2.91**	**2.63**
4.0–5.0	104,214	96,363	462,512	428,672	4.45	4.35
5.0–7.5	99,340	107,115	634,187	667,916	6.24	5.84
7.5–10.0	56,561	58,003	492,363	525,223	9.06	8.60
Medium	**260,142**	**261,481**	**1,589,062**	**1,621,811**	**6.20**	**5.40**
10.0–20.0	59,769	55,842	815,844	781,855	14.00	12.90
20 and above	13,784	11,330	409,608	295,037	26.04	27.73
Large	**73,553**	**67,172**	**1,225,452**	**1,076,892**	**16.03**	**14.75**
All sizes	**1,088,430**	**1,116,951**	**4,103,892**	**4,032,683**	**3.61**	**1.75**

Source: 'Provisional Data on Number and Areas of Operational Holdings, Agricultural Census, 1990–1, Government of Punjab, Chandigarh.

TABLE 7.P2.2

Districtwise Distribution of Number and Area of Operational Holdings in Punjab for All Social Groups, 1985–6 and 1990–1 and Average Size per Holding for All Social Groups and SCs, 1990–1

District	Number		Area (in ha)		Av. size per holding (1990–1)	
	1985–6	1990–1	1985–6	1990–1	All groups	SC
Hoshiarpur	6824	8376	9653	13,995	2.67	1.67
Jalandhar	5526	5479	13,610	13,857	3.31	2.53
Ludhiana	2849	3100	5793	6720	3.56	2.17
Ferozpur	3270	3443	5766	6486	4.19	1.88
Amritsar	4454	4744	6159	7863	3.29	1.66
Gurdaspur	4683	5082	8752	8358	2.35	1.64
Kapurthala	2200	2388	4625	5460	3.8	2.29
Bathinda	5579	5455	7609	7688	4.71	1.41
Patiala	3560	4635	5963	8567	3.78	1.85
Sangrur	4146	3891	6055	5250	4.38	1.35
Ropar	2564	2666	3033	4110	2.32	1.54
Faridkot	3823	4627	6054	6152	4.50	1.33
Punjab	49,478	53,886	83,072	94,506	3.61	1.75

Source: 'Provisional Data on Number and Area of Operational Holdings, Agricultural Census, 1990–1, Government of Punjab, Chandigarh.

8 Survey Report for Punjab

The units of observation and analysis of this study are rural households. The total number of rural households selected in the sample is 1373 (of which 70 were non-response), spread over 70 villages and eight districts in the state.

TABLE 8.1
Allocation of Sample Households in Various Strata

Stratum number	Stratum: HH category/ religion/caste	Stratum: Occupation	Selected sample households
1	Households containing at least one pregnant woman		251
2	Households containing at least one child aged less than 12 months but no pregnant women		360
3	Scheduled castes	Marginal farmer	8
4	Scheduled castes	Small farmer	14
5	Scheduled castes	Large farmer	20
6	Scheduled castes	Agricultural labourer	126
7	Scheduled castes	Other	116
8	Others	Marginal farmer	76
9	Others	Small farmer	79
10	Others	Large farmer	115
11	Others	Agricultural labourer	98
12	Others	Other	110
	Total		1373

8.1 Major Findings

8.1.1 Inter-group Differentials

The distribution of sample households in relation with their socio-economic characteristics is presented in Table A8.1. This shows that about one half of the sample households belonged to the lower income group (less than Rs 20,000 per annum). Another 15 per cent of the households belonged to the category with annual income more than Rs 62,000. Distribution *vis-à-vis* land ownership shows that all land owners accounted for 44.3 per cent households, while 55.7 per cent of the households did not have any land. The distribution according to occupational characteristics reveals that the main occupation of about 40 per cent was agriculture while one-fifth were self-employed. It must be noted that a sizeable percentage of sample households (25 per cent) were wage earners.

The distribution *vis-à-vis* religious affiliation shows that 28 per cent of the households were Hindus. It must be noted that in Punjab, the majority of the inhabitants follow Sikhism. A sizeable percentage of households (50.6 per cent) were of medium size, while about one-fifth were joint or extended families. The overall development of the state is reflected through the distribution of households by village development category which shows that only 5.6 per cent of the sample households belonged to less developed villages while 41.6 per cent were from highly developed villages.

8.1.2 Per Capita Income

In rural Punjab as a whole the per capita income was quite high at Rs 6380 as compared to Rs 4485 for rural India. It may be noted that landowners in the state have a higher total household income, and their per capita income is more than double that of non-landowners. This is largely because of increased land productivity in the state. Household and per capita income by religion do not show much disparity indicating that people from all religions are equally rich or poor. However, data show that in small sized households the per capita income is higher than that in the joint family households. It is also interesting to find that there is little variation in households and per capita income in relation to village development categories (see Tables A8.2 to A8.4 for sources of income).

8.1.3 Asset Ownership

The ownership of consumer durables in the state is presented in Table A8.5, which shows wide variation in the ownership of different assets. While 80 and 75 per cent of the households owned a bicycle and electric fan respectively, the ownership of TV and radio is more limited as only 38 per cent of the sample households own these assets. Similarly, ownership of motor cycle is observed only among 13 per cent of the rural households. It may be noted that the ownership of these items is much higher in rural Punjab as compared to other states in the country.[1] As expected, the ownership of these assets shows a close correspondence with income and land ownership. The

[1] Detailed statewise information is presented in NCAER, *India: Human Development Report* (1999).

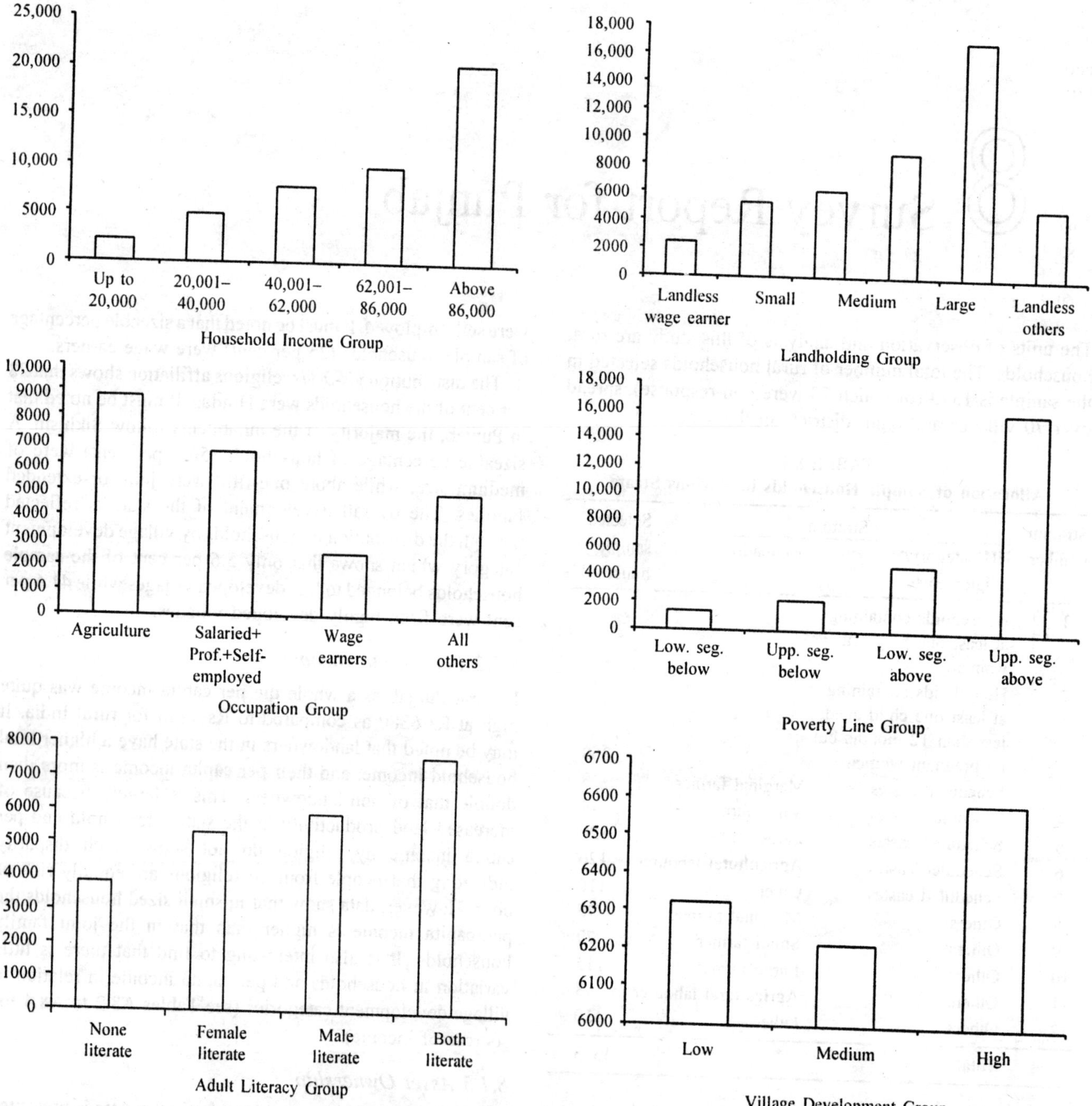

FIGURE 8.1: **Per Capita Income by Population Group (in Rupees per annum)**

ownership of assets does not vary among households practising different religions. However, it may be noted that such ownership is relatively less among SCs, who are considered to be at the bottom rung in the social hierarchy. It may also be noted that the ownership of television and radio shows a manifold increase in both literate group households as compared to the none literate group. Similarly, village development shows an association with the ownership of assets, though in terms of per capita income, there is hardly any variation between the highly developed and less developed villages (see Tables A8.6 and A8.7 for household amenities and PDS consumption).

8.1.4 Agricultural and Non-agricultural Wages

In rural Punjab as a whole, agriculture wage income accounts for three per cent of the total household income while the contribution from non-agricultural wages is five per cent. It may also be noted that 22 per cent of sample households earned more than 50 per cent of their income from wages. It is interesting to note that even in an agriculturally advanced state, the landless wage earners earn 52 per cent of their total income from non-agricultural activities signifying the importance of non-agricultural activities in the state economy.

8.1.5 Literacy Rate

According to the 1991 Census, Punjab has a literacy rate of 52.8 per cent, while the present survey puts this rate at 60.2 per cent—68.2 per cent for males and 51.2 per cent for females. Inter-group differentials reveal that the literacy rates increase with an increase in household income, for both males and females. Literacy rate *vis-à-vis* land owning categories shows that among non-landowners,the literacy rate is higher for males. Similarly, the self-employed have higher literacy rates as compared to those whose main occupation is agriculture. Yet

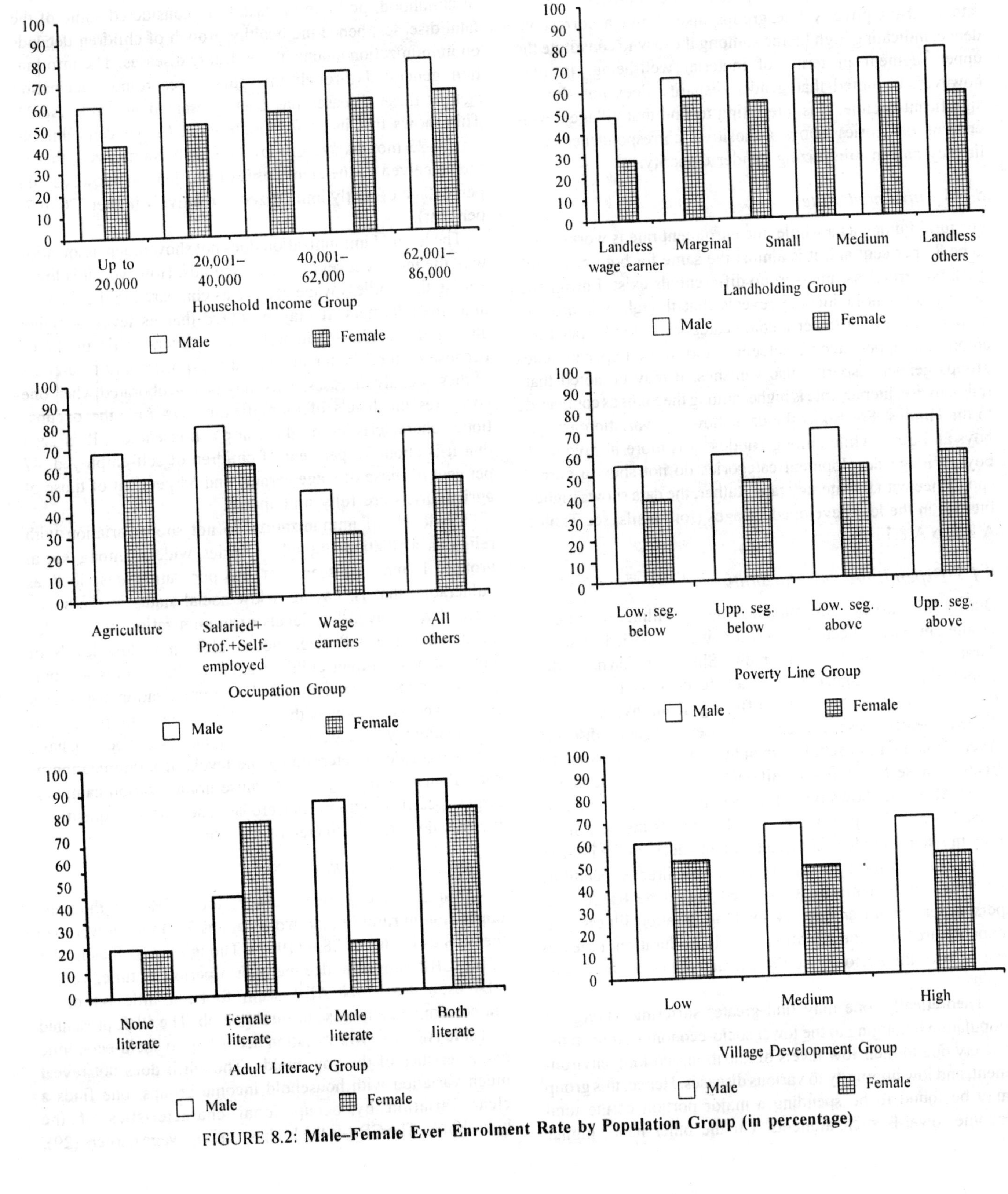

FIGURE 8.2: **Male–Female Ever Enrolment Rate by Population Group (in percentage)**

one finds that among the self-employed, gender disparity is higher. Literacy *vis-à-vis* occupational characteristics reveals that it is least among wage earners, and more so among females.

Religionwise, the literacy rates do not show much variation. However, among social groups, the literacy rate is much lower among the SCs as compared to the non-SCs. Literacy rate *vis-à-vis* poverty line groups also shows a correspondence, indicating high literacy among those who constitute the upper segment in terms of material well-being. It may, however, be noted that gender disparity does not show a significant decline. It is interesting to find that village development categories show a positive correspondence with literacy and in minimizing gender disparity.

8.1.6 Enrolment Rate

For rural Punjab as a whole, the enrolment rate is worked out to be 87 per cent and it is almost the same for both boys and girls. Nevertheless, inter-group differentials exist. Enrolment rate by household income reveals that though it is around 80 per cent among lower income categories, it is 97 per cent among the upper income category; and in the upper income groups gender disparity also vanishes. It may be noted that religionwise, literacy rate is higher among the Sikhs as compared to the Hindus. For Sikhs the data shows no variation among boys and girls, while among Hindus, it is more in favour of boys. Village development categories do not show a correspondence with the literacy rate. Rather, the data shows higher literacy in the less developed villages (for details, see Tables A.8.9 to A.8.13).

8.1.7 Expenditure on Morbidity

During this survey, information related to ailments and cost of ailment was collected. Later, this was classified as short-duration and long-duration morbidity. Short-duration morbidity comprised cold, cough, diarrhoea, and fever; and long- duration morbidity included people suffering from hypertension, diabetes, heart disease, TB, leprosy, cancer, and mental diseases. Average annual household expenditure (per sick person) for treating these two types of ailments has been presented in Table A8.17. It shows that in rural Punjab, the total cost per person is Rs 1703 per annum, which includes the cost of not only medicine and fees but also takes into account the indirect expenditure on food, travel, and stay. The direct expenditure on short-duration morbidity worked out to be Rs 203 per person per annum and Rs 44 for long-duration illness. The expenditure on short-duration and long-duration illnesses varies with the socio-economic characteristics of the households.

Theoretically, one may find greater suffering among the population belonging to the lower socio-economic strata in the society due to their low levels of nutrition, working environment, and low immunity to various diseases. Hence, this group may be found to be spending a major portion of the total income towards such ailments. On the other hand, higher income groups might be spending a large sum due to quality care towards ailments but this may not amount to a major proportion of the total income (for short and major morbidy rate see Tables A.8.14 to A.8.16).

8.1.8 Immunization

In childhood, polio and measles are considered some of the fatal diseases; hence the healthy growth of children depends on immunization against these deadly diseases. The information generated through this survey regarding vaccination against these diseases has been presented in Table A8.22. This shows that in rural Punjab about 62 per cent children (in 12–23 months age group) were fully immunized, that is, they received all the eight doses of vaccination. However, the percentage of partly immunized is relatively higher (70 to 75 per cent).

The level of immunization does not show much association with the income level of the households. However, it is lower among the landless wage earners as compared to the medium and small farmers. It may be noted that its level is higher among the landless and not wage earners. This might be because of their better literacy and exposure and awareness of these deadly diseases. This may be corroborated when one compares the levels of immunization *vis-à-vis* the occupational characteristics of the sample households. It is seen that it is about 72 per cent of children of self-employed, 47 per cent of those of wage earners and 64 per cent of those of agriculturists are fully immunized.

The levels of immunization do not show variation with religious affiliation, though it varies widely among social groups. It may be seen that the population described as vulnerable, that is, having a low social status in the social hierarchy, received low levels of immunization. It may also be noted that small sized households show low levels of immunization among children aged 12–23 months as compared to medium sized households. Immunization also shows a positive association with adult literacy and more so with female literacy. Village development, however, does not have much of a role in determining the levels of immunization in rural Punjab. This might be because immunization camps or target-specific programmes were launched more frequently in the less developed villages of the state.

8.1.9 Crude Birth Rate

According to the present survey, the CBR per thousand population in rural Punjab works out as 22, much lower than the SRS estimates of 28.6 (1992). Though the SRS estimates of the CBR showed a decline over a period of time, yet the HDI estimates of NCAER seem to be a little bit of an underestimate in the case of rural Punjab. The CBR presented in Table A8.18 shows variation according to socio-economic characteristics of the households. Though it does not reveal much variation with household income groups, one finds a clear variation by occupational characteristics of the households. The CBR is the highest among wage earners (29),

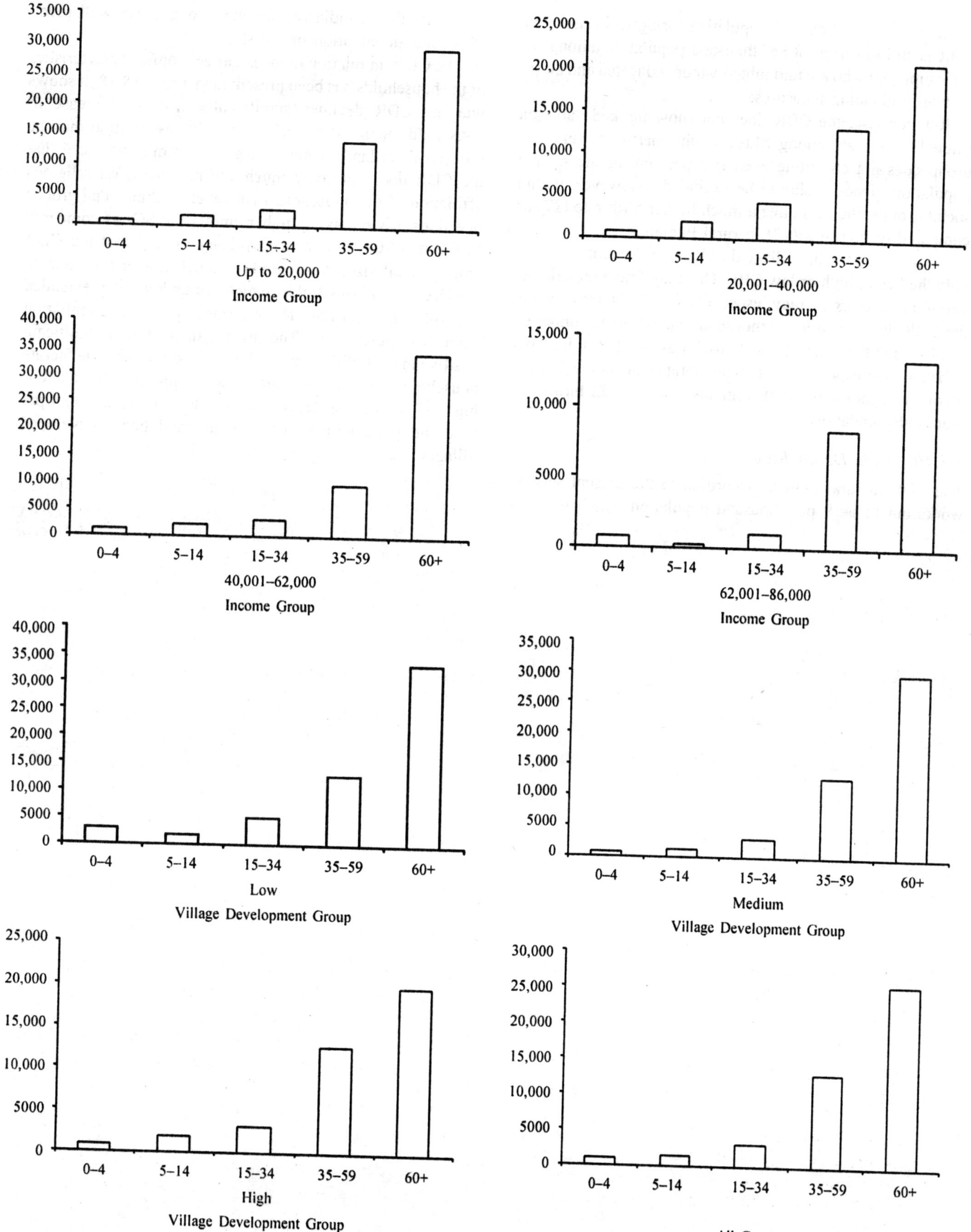

FIGURE 8.3: **Major Morbidity Prevalence Rate by Age and Population Group (per lakh population)**

while it is 23 per thousand population for agriculturists. The CBR is still lower at 18 per thousand population among the self-employed who are undoubtedly more educated and aware of family planning measures.

Religionwise, the CBR does not show marked variation (though it is high among Muslims, this particular religious group does not constitute even five per cent of the sample population, hence it should be excluded). However, within social groups, the SCs have a much higher birth rate (27) as compared to non-SCs (17) in rural Punjab.

It may be noted that village development categories do not hold the key to high or low CBR. One may find a remarkable variation *vis-à-vis* literacy, especially female literacy, where the CBR declines to 9 per thousand population as compared to 27 among the none-literate households. A CBR of 9 seems to be an underestimate for female literate category as in both literate categories, the CBR remains at around 22 births per thousand population.

8.1.10 Crude Death Rate

The CDR in rural Punjab, according to the present survey, works out to be 9 per thousand population which is much lower than the all-India average and it corresponds well, given the economic situation of the state.

The CDR, in relation to the socio-economic characteristics of the households has been presented in Table A8.18. It shows that the CDR declines significantly with an increase in household income. Similarly, a positive association may be seen *vis-à-vis* land owning categories. It may be noted that the CDR does not show much variation *vis-à-vis* religious affiliation of the households. However, within social groups one finds it is relatively higher among the SCs as compared to the non-SCs. It is also surprising to find that the CDR among small sized households is much higher than that in the large sized households, which are undoubtedly extended or joint family set-ups. The reasons for such differentiation need to be researched. The present data show a significant positive impact of literacy on the CDR; among female literate households, the CDR is much lower. Similarly, the CDR is high (17) in the less developed villages as compared to 9 per thousand population in the medium and better developed villages.

TABLE A8.1
Levels of Income and Distribution of Households by Population Group in Rural Punjab

Population group	No. of sample households	% estmtd households	Household size	Income (Rs per year)	
				Per household	Per capita
Household income					
Up to 20,000	557	41.8	5.1	11,702	2313
20,001–40,000	385	29.6	5.9	28,488	4846
40,001–62,000	170	13.7	6.5	49,603	7655
62,001–86,000	88	6.9	7.4	72,477	9779
Above 86,000	103	7.9	7.7	155,246	20,240
Landholding					
Landless wage earner	310	21.2	5.5	13,554	2472
Marginal	178	13.9	5.4	28,474	5280
Small	171	12.9	6.2	38,594	6248
Medium	131	10.6	6.8	60,291	8886
Large	98	7.0	8.2	139,177	16,993
Landless others	415	34.5	5.4	27,499	5076
All land owners	578	44.3	6.4	56,538	8840
All land non-owners	725	55.7	5.4	22,190	4077
Occupation					
Agriculture	496	37.6	6.5	57,020	8804
Salaried+prof.+s.empl.	264	21.5	5.5	36,360	6560
Wage earners	323	22.2	5.5	13,982	2533
All groups others	220	18.7	5.4	27,031	4992
Caste					
SCs	134	9.0	5.8	24,201	4196
Religion					
Hindus	362	28.0	–	35,975	6327
Other minorities	884	68.3	5.9	39,158	6584
Household size					
Up to 4	358	29.2	3.3	24,286	7469
5–7	660	52.4	5.9	35,978	6125
8 and above	285	18.4	10.0	62,419	6242
Poverty line					
Lower segment below	185	13.6	6.2	8151	1309
Upper segment below	212	14.6	6.0	13,291	2218
Lower segment above	635	47.7	6.0	28,913	4832
Upper segment above	271	24.1	5.4	85,496	15,976
Adult literacy					
None literate	305	22.3	5.0	18,991	3815
Female literate	70	5.3	5.7	30,194	5319
Male literate	325	25.4	5.2	30,331	5856
Both literate	603	47.0	6.7	50,807	7608
Village development					
Low	78	5.6	5.6	35,452	6320
Medium	686	52.8	5.8	36,082	6217
High	539	41.6	6.0	39,377	6588
All groups	**1303**	**100.0**	**5.9**	**37,418**	**6380**

TABLE A8.2

Sourcewise Percentage Distribution of Household Income by Population Group in Rural Punjab

Population group	Percentage distribution w.r.t. total household income										
	Agr.+alld act.	Artisan/ ind. work	Petty trd. sm. bus.	Or. trd. bus.	Salaried empl.	Qualified prof.	Rent/int./ dividend	Agr. wage	Non-agr. wage	Other sources	All sources
Household income											
Up to 20,000	23.0	7.7	9.6	0.2	16.2	0.1	2.2	15.2	21.8	3.9	100.0
20,001–40,000	36.6	4.4	6.4	0.4	33.3	1.2	2.0	4.1	7.5	4.1	100.0
40,001–62,000	56.8	3.5	6.4	0.3	23.0	0.7	1.9	1.1	4.0	2.4	100.0
62,001–86,000	62.2	6.6	2.0	0.8	24.3	0.0	0.3	0.4	1.5	1.9	100.0
Above 86,000	80.3	0.8	1.2	0.2	13.8	0.4	3.1	0.1	0.0	0.2	100.0
Landholding											
Landless wage earner	2.9	0.7	0.7	0.2	3.7	0.1	0.4	33.4	57.3	0.7	100.0
Marginal	47.2	8.5	3.3	1.0	26.2	0.1	4.3	0.9	4.2	4.2	100.0
Small	73.2	3.8	3.9	0.6	13.9	0.6	0.3	0.6	1.9	1.3	100.0
Medium	90.8	1.6	0.7	0.0	5.9	0.0	0.5	0.0	0.1	0.5	100.0
Large	94.3	0.0	0.4	0.2	3.8	0.5	0.4	0.1	0.0	0.2	100.0
Landless others	4.8	8.1	13.4	0.3	58.0	1.3	5.6	1.7	1.4	5.4	100.0
All land owners	81.8	2.5	1.6	0.4	9.9	0.3	1.0	0.3	1.1	1.1	100.0
All land non-owners	4.4	6.4	10.4	0.2	45.4	1.0	4.4	9.0	14.4	4.3	100.0
Occupation											
Agriculture	92.3	0.9	0.6	0.0	4.1	0.3	0.5	0.2	0.4	0.6	100.0
Salaried+prof.+s.empl.	7.7	0.5	0.9	0.0	87.3	1.5	0.3	0.9	0.7	0.1	100.0
Wage earners	5.2	0.8	0.7	0.2	3.5	0.1	0.4	32.0	56.5	0.6	100.0
All others	9.9	23.0	29.3	2.2	5.0	0.1	13.0	1.6	2.9	13.0	100.0
Caste											
SCs	18.6	5.9	4.4	0.0	33.5	0.0	0.2	9.7	23.0	4.6	100.0
Religion											
Hindus	48.2	5.5	8.0	0.5	24.9	0.0	1.4	2.6	6.9	2.1	100.0
Other minorities	60.4	3.2	3.2	0.3	20.1	0.7	2.5	3.1	4.5	2.1	100.0
Household size											
Up to 4	45.3	2.3	5.9	0.3	24.0	1.4	4.2	4.4	7.8	4.4	100.0
5–7	51.7	4.9	4.1	0.3	25.6	0.1	2.1	3.4	6.1	1.6	100.0
8 and above	70.5	2.8	4.3	0.3	13.6	0.7	0.9	2.1	3.1	1.8	100.0
Poverty line											
Lower segment below	24.9	3.5	5.3	0.0	2.1	0.2	0.1	24.2	33.8	5.9	100.0
Upper segment below	30.0	9.1	8.7	0.0	12.5	0.1	1.4	18.3	18.6	1.3	100.0
Lower segment above	43.2	4.9	6.7	0.5	27.0	0.4	2.4	3.8	8.0	3.3	100.0
Upper segment above	69.2	2.5	2.6	0.3	19.9	0.7	2.1	0.2	1.0	1.3	100.0
Adult literacy											
None literate	42.7	3.0	1.3	0.0	7.4	0.0	5.6	15.4	18.9	5.7	100.0
Female literate	63.7	2.4	1.2	0.0	21.6	0.0	0.0	2.7	3.3	5.1	100.0
Male literate	49.7	5.1	8.4	0.6	19.5	1.3	1.2	3.6	8.6	2.0	100.0
Both literate	60.3	3.6	4.1	0.3	24.8	0.4	2.0	0.9	2.2	1.4	100.0
Village development											
Low	60.0	1.7	3.5	1.5	19.1	0.1	0.0	2.9	8.4	2.8	100.0
Medium	54.6	3.9	3.9	0.5	21.5	0.4	3.3	3.6	6.1	2.2	100.0
High	57.8	3.8	5.4	0.0	22.0	0.7	1.1	2.7	4.4	2.1	100.0
All groups	**56.3**	**3.8**	**4.5**	**0.3**	**21.6**	**0.5**	**2.1**	**3.2**	**5.5**	**2.2**	**100.0**

TABLE A8.3

Average (per reporting household) Wage Income and its Share in Total Income by Population Group in Rural Punjab

Population group	Agricultural wage		Non-agr. wage		All wages		Wage as per cent of total income			Per cent of households getting 50% income from wages
	Average wage	Per cent of rep. hhs	Average wage	Per cent of rep. hhs	Average wage	Per cent of rep. hhs	Agr. wage	Non-agr. wage	All wage	
Household income										
Up to 20,000	4648	34.7	7179	32.4	8150	48.3	13.8	19.9	33.7	42.4
20,001–40,000	7242	14.6	12,919	15.1	15,859	19.0	3.7	6.8	10.6	13.0
40,001–62,000	8832	5.8	15,936	11.2	18,304	12.5	1.0	3.6	4.6	2.7
62,001–86,000	13,476	1.8	15,373	6.3	18,426	6.6	0.3	1.3	1.7	0.3
Above 86,000	8112	1.4	0	0.0	8112	1.4	0.1	0.0	0.1	0.0
Landholding										
Landless wage earner	5684	72.3	9254	76.2	11,166	100.0	30.3	52.1	82.4	99.4
Marginal	4753	4.8	10,742	10.2	10,936	12.1	0.8	3.9	4.7	6.0
Small	8279	2.7	12,454	5.3	16,213	5.4	0.6	1.7	2.3	0.7
Medium	0	0.0	12,000	0.5	12,000	0.5	0.0	0.1	0.1	0.0
Large	12,329	1.1	0	0.0	12,329	1.1	0.1	0.0	0.1	0.0
Landless others	4144	10.1	7337	4.9	6046	12.8	1.5	1.3	2.8	0.0
All land owners	6401	2.5	11,315	4.8	12,465	5.7	0.3	1.0	1.2	2.1
All land non-owners	5400	33.8	9073	32.1	10,282	46.0	8.2	13.1	21.3	37.9
Occupation										
Agriculture	6154	1.9	8712	2.5	10,237	3.2	0.2	0.4	0.6	0.0
Salaried+prof.+s.empl.	4052	7.7	8220	2.9	5909	9.3	0.9	0.7	1.5	0.0
Wage earners	5724	71.0	9375	76.6	11,251	100.0	29.1	51.4	80.5	99.0
All others	4071	9.4	9461	7.6	7614	14.5	1.4	2.7	4.1	0.0
Caste										
SCs	5115	41.8	10,199	49.7	12,550	57.4	8.8	20.9	29.8	44.2
Religion										
Hindus	4888	17.1	10,011	22.6	11,568	26.8	2.3	6.3	8.6	20.5
Other minorities	5658	19.2	9063	17.6	10,048	26.7	2.8	4.1	6.9	20.6
Household size										
Up to 4	4398	22.1	8400	20.4	8897	30.2	4.0	7.1	11.1	25.4
5–7	5687	19.4	9216	21.5	10,590	29.1	3.1	5.5	8.6	22.5
8 and above	6815	17.9	11,707	14.9	13,513	21.9	1.9	2.8	4.7	15.2
Poverty line										
Lower segment below	3878	46.3	5895	42.4	6545	65.6	22.0	30.7	52.7	59.8
Upper segment below	6106	36.3	7732	29.0	9256	48.1	16.7	16.9	33.5	41.0
Lower segment above	6307	15.7	11,662	18.1	13,957	22.2	3.4	7.3	10.7	15.8
Upper segment above	5605	3.4	13,972	5.6	14,953	6.5	0.2	0.9	1.1	1.3
Adult literacy										
None literate	5602	47.4	7894	41.4	9885	59.9	14.0	17.2	31.2	51.6
Female literate	6227	11.8	7796	11.8	8697	19.0	2.4	3.0	5.5	9.4
Male literate	4183	23.5	9747	24.4	9865	34.1	3.2	7.8	11.1	25.4
Both literate	7484	5.8	12,198	8.4	13,407	10.9	0.9	2.0	2.9	7.5
Village development										
Low	–	22.3	9367	29.1	10,891	33.5	2.6	7.7	10.3	23.8
Medium	6150	19.4	9663	20.6	11,265	28.3	3.3	5.5	8.8	22.9
High	4795	20.1	8797	18.0	9370	27.2	2.5	4.0	6.5	20.6
All groups	**5454**	**19.9**	**9314**	**20.0**	**10,477**	**28.1**	**2.9**	**5.0**	**7.9**	**22.0**

TABLE A8.4

Land and Livestock Owned by Households by Population Group in Rural Punjab

Population group	Landholdings			Draught animals			Milch animals		
	Per cent of rep. hhs	Average rep. hh	Average all groups	Per cent of rep. hhs	Average rep. hh	Average all groups	Per cent of rep. hhs	Average rep. hh	Average all groups
Household income									
Up to 20,000	22.3	2.3	0.5	13.1	1.4	0.2	64.7	1.9	1.2
20,001–40,000	42.3	4.2	1.8	23.1	2.7	0.6	76.0	2.6	2.0
40,001–62,000	70.2	7.7	5.4	45.0	1.5	0.7	83.8	3.1	2.6
62,001–86,000	85.0	11.6	9.8	40.5	1.6	0.6	92.5	3.2	2.9
Above 86,000	88.2	16.8	14.8	59.6	1.5	0.9	92.4	4.3	4.0
Landholding									
Landless wage earner	–	–	–	4.0	1.4	0.1	60.3	1.9	1.2
Marginal	100.0	1.6	1.6	41.0	1.5	0.6	89.4	2.3	2.1
Small	100.0	3.9	3.9	46.3	1.9	0.9	96.0	2.9	2.8
Medium	100.0	7.9	7.9	66.1	1.6	1.1	98.2	3.6	3.6
Large	100.0	25.3	25.3	63.6	1.4	0.9	99.3	4.7	4.6
Landless others	–	–	–	6.0	3.8	0.2	57.7	1.9	1.1
All land owners	100.0	7.5	7.5	52.1	1.6	0.8	95.0	3.2	3.0
All land non-owners	–	–	—	5.3	3.1	0.2	58.7	1.9	1.1
Occupation									
Agriculture	95.5	8.6	8.2	55.7	1.6	0.9	96.4	3.5	3.4
Salaried+prof.+s.empl.	20.1	2.6	0.5	8.7	4.4	0.4	61.8	1.8	1.1
Wage earners	4.6	1.6	0.1	4.7	1.5	0.1	62.1	1.9	1.2
All groups others	16.4	4.0	0.7	11.8	1.3	0.2	61.3	1.8	1.1
Caste									
SCs	15.9	3.1	0.5	8.1	9.4	0.8	64.7	2.2	1.4
Religion									
Hindus	40.7	8.0	3.2	24.3	2.8	0.7	71.9	2.6	1.9
Other minorities	48.1	7.4	3.5	27.8	1.4	0.4	76.8	2.7	2.1
Household size									
Up to 4	36.1	4.3	1.6	16.4	1.6	0.3	58.5	2.1	1.2
5–7	44.0	7.0	3.1	25.1	1.9	0.5	77.6	2.7	2.1
8 and above	58.4	11.7	6.8	43.9	1.6	0.7	92.8	3.1	2.9
Poverty line									
Lower segment below	19.2	2.0	0.4	17.2	1.4	0.2	66.7	2.0	1.3
Upper segment below	26.3	3.3	0.9	15.7	1.6	0.3	71.7	2.0	1.4
Lower segment above	41.4	5.6	2.3	24.0	2.0	0.5	75.4	2.6	2.0
Upper segment above	75.3	11.3	8.5	41.3	1.6	0.6	80.0	3.4	2.7
Adult literacy									
None literate	25.9	3.9	1.0	17.8	1.6	0.3	66.4	2.1	1.4
Female literate	58.5	4.9	2.9	29.0	5.0	1.5	84.5	2.6	2.2
Male literate	40.1	6.7	2.7	20.3	1.7	0.3	74.0	2.6	1.9
Both literate	53.8	9.0	4.8	32.7	1.5	0.5	78.1	2.9	2.3
Village development									
Low	55.8	5.4	3.0	33.7	1.7	0.6	86.8	2.2	1.9
Medium	46.0	6.8	3.1	25.5	2.0	0.5	77.4	2.8	2.1
High	40.6	8.9	3.6	25.7	1.4	0.4	69.9	2.6	1.8
All groups	**44.3**	**7.5**	**3.3**	**26.0**	**1.8**	**0.5**	**74.8**	**2.6**	**2.0**

TABLE A8.5

Ownership of House and Selected Consumer Durables by Population Group in Rural Punjab

Population group	Percentage of households owning					
	House	Bicycle	Television	Radio transistor	Electric fan	Motorcycle/ scooter
Household income						
Up to 20,000	96.6	71.4	23.0	27.0	61.2	2.9
20,001–40,000	97.2	85.2	42.9	37.1	80.9	11.3
40,001–62,000	98.7	83.3	53.0	46.2	88.0	21.1
62,001–86,000	99.2	93.4	49.9	49.6	89.9	28.0
Above 86,000	99.3	88.8	69.6	66.0	95.7	50.5
Landholding						
Landless wage earner	97.2	70.3	13.5	16.6	50.7	0.2
Marginal	97.4	82.0	37.5	41.1	74.7	10.3
Small	99.6	87.6	34.6	31.1	83.7	12.8
Medium	100.0	84.7	49.2	49.2	91.5	20.6
Large	100.0	90.4	62.4	57.8	90.0	47.1
Landless others	95.6	78.8	47.8	42.8	79.9	13.8
All land owners	99.1	85.6	43.4	42.8	83.8	19.3
All land non-owners	96.2	75.5	34.7	32.8	68.8	8.7
Occupation						
Agriculture	99.5	84.9	40.6	42.2	84.2	20.1
Salaried+prof.+s.empl.	94.4	83.7	56.2	46.2	81.2	17.4
Wage earners	97.3	71.0	15.0	17.8	52.0	0.5
All others	97.2	76.5	42.3	40.2	79.0	10.5
Caste						
SCs	96.5	78.8	31.8	34.8	63.9	1.7
Religion						
Hindus	96.7	78.7	36.9	41.3	71.0	11.2
Other minorities	98.0	81.1	39.9	36.9	78.1	14.7
Household size						
Up to 4	96.0	68.8	28.2	33.2	67.7	8.9
5–7	97.7	83.0	38.4	35.5	77.5	12.0
8 and above	99.3	89.3	55.5	48.9	81.9	24.6
Poverty line						
Lower segment below	97.9	71.8	16.7	21.9	52.3	2.8
Upper segment below	96.7	71.0	30.7	30.5	67.6	3.1
Lower segment above	97.5	84.6	39.5	37.4	77.8	10.7
Upper segment above	97.7	81.0	53.9	49.8	88.7	30.9
Adult literacy						
None literate	97.0	56.5	9.0	15.3	52.6	1.7
Female literate	97.9	66.0	24.9	23.8	67.9	8.3
Male literate	97.3	85.4	25.9	27.6	75.5	5.8
Both literate	97.8	89.8	61.0	54.4	87.1	23.6
Village development						
Low	98.0	62.5	24.5	41.0	55.5	2.7
Medium	97.6	81.1	35.6	36.3	74.9	11.6
High	97.3	81.0	44.2	38.0	78.8	17.1
All groups	**97.5**	**80.0**	**38.6**	**37.3**	**75.4**	**13.4**

TABLE A8.6

Amenities Available in Households by Population Group in Rural Punjab

Population group	Percentage of households having					
	Kutcha house	Separate kitchen	Electric connection	Protected water	Piped water	Toilet
Household income						
Up to 20,000	26.7	34.6	72.5	95.0	22.7	11.8
20,001–40,000	17.0	50.3	88.0	95.0	20.2	19.9
40,001–62,000	9.6	64.6	94.1	99.7	22.2	24.9
62,001–86,000	5.7	62.7	93.9	97.0	8.7	31.6
Above 86,000	3.5	76.6	97.9	99.3	23.4	42.4
Landholding						
Landless wage earner	35.4	27.5	62.6	95.3	27.9	5.3
Marginal	16.3	57.5	84.8	97.0	18.6	27.2
Small	13.3	59.5	88.1	96.4	17.3	14.1
Medium	12.9	58.6	94.3	99.0	20.5	25.0
Large	6.3	71.2	99.3	99.2	17.9	41.8
Landless others	14.0	46.3	87.7	94.7	19.8	21.7
All land owners	13.0	60.6	90.3	97.6	18.6	25.2
All land non-owners	22.2	39.1	78.1	94.9	22.9	15.5
Occupation						
Agriculture	12.2	58.6	90.3	97.9	17.6	25.3
Salaried+prof.+s.empl.	11.1	52.7	90.5	94.8	18.0	23.6
Wage earners	34.9	28.4	63.0	95.5	28.1	6.0
All others	18.1	48.4	86.3	94.8	22.7	20.6
Caste						
SCs	27.7	38.1	67.6	92.8	33.8	8.0
Religion						
Hindus	24.0	42.7	82.4	93.9	36.0	16.5
Other minorities	14.9	52.6	84.9	97.1	15.1	22.0
Household size						
Up to 4	20.4	40.5	78.8	96.7	21.3	21.4
5–7	19.0	50.2	83.9	95.3	22.3	15.9
8 and above	11.9	57.4	90.1	97.6	16.9	28.5
Poverty line						
Lower segment below	31.6	28.0	65.5	95.5	28.0	7.9
Upper segment below	28.6	40.8	76.6	94.0	20.1	10.4
Lower segment above	16.0	50.1	85.9	95.9	19.6	20.2
Upper segment above	8.2	62.6	93.3	98.2	20.3	31.5
Adult literacy						
None literate	35.6	24.1	61.7	96.9	29.7	9.5
Female literate	19.1	42.9	82.9	97.3	18.1	6.2
Male Literate	18.6	36.8	81.1	95.8	21.5	14.9
Both literate	9.4	67.5	95.3	95.8	16.9	28.8
Village development						
Low	41.1	27.2	73.8	94.4	46.1	2.2
Medium	16.1	49.9	82.9	94.9	19.0	17.2
High	17.4	50.3	85.7	97.9	20.1	25.5
All groups	**18.1**	**48.8**	**83.5**	**96.1**	**21.0**	**19.8**

TABLE A8.7

Consumption of Foodgrains and Utilization of PDS by Population Group in Rural Punjab

Population group	Annual household income (Rs)	Annual per capita income (Rs)	Per capita consumption of foodgrains (kg/month)	Percentage of households using PDS	Quantity of cereals (kg) bought from PDS (per hh/month)	Per cent requirement of cereals met from PDS
Household income						
Up to 20,000	11,702	2313	13.4	6.6	31.6	12.2
20,001–40,000	28,488	4846	14.1	5.0	19.9	4.0
40,001–62,000	49,603	7655	15.1	5.3	5.8	1.0
62,001–86,000	72,477	9779	14.8	5.4	15.8	2.4
Above 86,000	155,246	20,240	16.0	3.5	15.7	1.8
Landholding						
Landless wage earner	13,554	2472	13.6	9.1	17.3	7.0
Marginal	28,474	5280	15.8	4.1	63.9	11.5
Small	38,594	6248	15.3	1.5	13.4	0.9
Medium	60,291	8886	14.8	3.0	4.9	0.5
Large	139,177	16,993	16.2	5.2	9.6	1.5
Landless others	27,499	5076	12.8	6.4	24.0	7.4
All land owners	56,538	8840	15.5	3.3	30.4	3.8
All land non-owners	22,190	4077	13.1	7.4	20.9	7.2
Occupation						
Agriculture	57,020	8804	15.5	3.9	30.8	4.3
Salaried+prof.+s.empl.	36,360	6560	13.2	5.7	26.3	6.8
Wage earners	13,982	2533	13.7	8.7	17.3	6.5
All others	27,031	4992	13.2	5.4	20.7	5.9
Caste						
SCs	24,201	4196	13.1	10.5	16.3	5.6
Religion						
Hindus	35,975	6327	13.8	9.1	12.9	4.2
Other minorities	39,158	6584	14.5	3.8	32.8	5.8
Household size						
Up to 4	24,286	7469	15.7	5.3	26.7	8.6
5–7	35,978	6125	14.2	6.3	24.3	6.3
8 and above	62,419	6242	13.7	4.2	12.5	1.5
Poverty line						
Lower segment below	8151	1309	13.1	3.0	16.3	3.4
Upper segment below	13,291	2218	12.9	8.4	32.7	12.5
Lower segment above	28,913	4832	14.3	6.6	23.5	6.0
Upper segment above	85,496	15,976	15.9	3.4	12.3	1.7
Adult literacy						
None literate	18,991	3815	13.9	4.2	24.0	5.2
Female literate	30,194	5319	16.3	3.4	79.8	10.5
Male literate	30,331	5856	14.4	5.4	14.3	3.5
Both literate	50,807	7608	14.1	6.6	23.9	6.0
Village development						
Low	35,452	6320	15.1	4.5	120.0	91.0
Medium	36,082	6217	13.7	1.7	33.5	2.0
High	39,377	6588	14.8	10.8	16.0	8.4
All groups	**37,418**	**6380**	**14.3**	**5.6**	**23.4**	**5.5**

TABLE A8.8
Literacy Rate (per cent) and Gender Disparity by Population Group in Rural Punjab

Population group	Literacy rate (aged 7 and above)			
	Total	Male	Female	F/M
Household income				
Up to 20,000	51.3	60.1	42.5	0.71
20,001–40,000	62.0	70.2	52.3	0.75
40,001–62,000	64.1	70.5	56.3	0.80
62,001–86,000	68.7	74.6	61.4	0.82
Above 86,000	72.0	79.2	64.1	0.81
Landholding				
Landless wage earner	38.5	48.2	28.1	0.58
Marginal	61.9	65.7	57.6	0.88
Small	62.7	70.3	54.1	0.77
Medium	63.5	70.5	55.6	0.79
Large	67.3	73.1	60.6	0.83
Landless others	67.8	77.6	56.9	0.73
All land owners	63.6	69.6	56.7	0.81
All land non-owners	57.0	66.9	46.2	0.69
Occupation				
Agriculture	62.7	68.4	56.2	0.82
Salaried+prof.+s.empl.	71.6	80.1	62.1	0.78
Wage earners	39.0	48.7	28.7	0.59
All others	64.5	75.2	52.5	0.70
Caste				
SCs	46.5	57.5	34.6	0.60
Religion				
Hindus	61.7	71.7	50.8	0.71
Other minorities	60.9	68.1	52.8	0.78
Household size				
Up to 4	51.4	64.5	35.9	0.56
5–7	61.5	67.9	54.4	0.80
8 and above	62.9	71.1	54.0	0.76
Poverty line				
Lower segment below	46.1	54.7	38.4	0.70
Upper segment below	53.3	59.9	46.5	0.78
Lower segment above	62.7	70.6	53.5	0.76
Upper segment above	67.4	74.9	58.3	0.78
Adult literacy				
None literate	18.7	18.9	18.5	0.97
Female literate	55.4	39.3	68.1	1.73
Male literate	52.9	75.9	19.6	0.26
Both literate	77.1	82.5	71.4	0.87
Village development				
Low	57.0	60.7	53.1	0.87
Medium	59.3	67.9	49.4	0.73
High	61.8	69.6	53.2	0.76
All groups	**60.2**	**68.2**	**51.2**	**0.75**

TABLE A8.9
Ever Enrolment, Discontinuation, and Non-attending Rates for Children (aged 6–14 years) by Population Group in Rural Punjab

(per cent)

Population group	Ever enrolment rate				Discontinuation rate				Non-attendance rate			
	Total	Male	Female	F/M	Total	Male	Female	F/M	Total	Male	Female	F/M
Household income												
Up to 20,000	83.3	86.5	79.9	0.92	6.6	5.2	8.2	1.60	2.0	1.3	2.8	2.12
20,001–40,000	85.8	87.7	83.5	0.95	5.0	5.2	4.7	0.90	1.9	1.4	2.5	1.73
40,001–62,000	88.9	89.6	87.9	0.98	5.4	6.7	3.6	0.53	2.6	2.6	2.5	0.95
62,001–86,000	95.5	95.9	95.0	0.99	3.8	4.5	2.9	0.66	4.3	3.7	5.1	1.37
Above 86,000	97.1	97.6	96.6	0.99	2.9	0.0	5.8	0.00	0.7	0.0	1.4	–
Landholding												
Landless wage earner	74.2	81.3	66.7	0.82	6.1	4.4	8.1	1.83	1.5	2.6	0.1	0.05
Marginal	89.9	87.1	93.3	1.07	3.7	6.0	1.1	0.19	4.8	2.8	7.0	2.49
Small	90.0	85.6	94.2	1.10	7.4	8.0	6.8	0.85	2.8	2.2	3.4	1.58
Medium	93.6	95.8	90.7	0.95	6.5	4.4	9.3	2.12	1.3	1.5	1.0	0.64
Large	95.4	96.1	94.5	0.98	1.4	0.0	3.0	0.00	0.6	0.0	1.2	–
Landless others	89.2	91.6	86.2	0.94	5.7	5.0	6.7	1.32	1.8	0.9	3.0	3.25
All land owners	91.9	90.7	93.2	1.03	4.8	4.8	4.9	1.03	2.6	1.7	3.6	2.13
All land non-owners	83.1	87.6	77.9	0.89	5.9	4.8	7.2	1.49	1.7	1.5	1.9	1.27
Occupation												
Agriculture	92.3	92.2	92.5	1.00	5.0	4.5	5.5	1.22	2.9	1.8	4.1	2.20
Salaried+prof.+s.empl.	90.5	91.6	89.3	0.98	3.8	1.4	6.6	4.58	2.8	1.4	4.4	3.05
Wage earners	73.6	79.4	67.5	0.85	5.8	4.3	7.8	1.81	1.5	2.5	0.1	0.05
All others	89.0	91.6	85.7	0.94	8.0	10.3	4.9	0.48	0.0	0.0	0.0	–
Caste												
SCs	72.9	81.0	64.0	0.79	10.1	8.2	12.8	1.57	0.7	1.1	0.0	0.00
Religion												
Hindus	85.3	90.3	79.5	0.88	6.1	5.7	6.7	1.18	1.0	0.7	1.3	1.74
Other minorities	88.5	89.0	88.0	0.99	5.0	4.5	5.6	1.25	2.6	2.1	3.3	1.60
Household size												
Up to 4	92.6	91.3	95.1	1.04	6.1	4.9	8.1	1.64	1.1	0.0	3.2	–
5–7	86.4	88.3	84.3	0.96	5.6	5.7	5.4	0.96	2.5	1.8	3.3	1.79
8 and above	86.1	89.8	82.5	0.92	4.8	2.7	7.0	2.63	1.6	1.6	1.5	0.91
Poverty line												
Lower segment below	78.5	81.9	75.6	0.92	8.5	6.6	10.3	1.56	2.2	2.5	1.9	0.75
Upper segment below	84.5	89.7	78.8	0.88	6.0	4.6	7.7	1.68	2.4	1.4	3.7	2.72
Lower segment above	88.4	88.4	88.3	1.00	4.6	4.6	4.5	0.98	2.0	1.4	2.7	1.99
Upper segment above	94.0	95.3	92.3	0.97	4.2	4.2	4.3	1.03	2.0	1.7	2.4	1.43
Adult literacy												
None literate	67.7	71.2	64.1	0.90	8.3	8.6	7.8	0.91	2.2	2.4	2.0	0.85
Female literate	94.2	94.5	94.0	0.99	7.8	5.1	11.3	2.20	0.0	0.0	0.0	–
Male literate	89.8	93.8	85.3	0.91	8.5	8.4	8.6	1.03	2.0	1.3	2.8	2.10
Both literate	95.2	95.0	95.4	1.00	2.5	1.7	3.5	2.04	2.4	1.7	3.4	2.01
Village development												
Low	88.9	85.2	94.2	1.11	5.9	3.0	9.5	3.17	0.0	0.0	0.0	–
Medium	86.5	89.5	82.9	0.93	5.0	3.9	6.6	1.69	1.7	1.3	2.3	1.72
High	86.9	88.9	84.8	0.95	5.8	6.3	5.2	0.81	2.9	2.2	3.6	1.59
All groups	**86.8**	**89.0**	**84.4**	**0.95**	**5.4**	**4.8**	**6.1**	**1.28**	**2.1**	**1.6**	**2.7**	**1.71**

TABLE A8.10
Proportion of Population Completing Middle and Matriculation Levels and Gender Disparity by Population Group in Rural Punjab

Population group	Middle level (aged 15+)				Matriculation level (aged 17+)			
	Total	Male	Female	F/M	Total	Male	Female	F/M
Household income								
Up to 20,000	9.8	13.4	6.3	0.47	9.2	11.9	6.4	0.54
20,001–40,000	14.8	18.5	10.5	0.57	15.3	20.5	9.2	0.45
40,001–62,000	11.7	12.5	10.7	0.86	19.2	23.3	14.4	0.62
62,001–86,000	16.9	19.3	14.1	0.73	20.2	24.6	14.9	0.61
Above 86,000	14.3	16.5	11.9	0.72	25.6	33.9	16.3	0.48
Landholding								
Landless wage earner	6.9	10.1	3.4	0.34	5.1	8.0	1.7	0.22
Marginal	13.2	16.5	9.5	0.58	17.0	20.7	12.7	0.61
Small	14.0	17.6	9.8	0.56	18.2	24.0	11.3	0.47
Medium	12.3	14.4	9.8	0.68	15.7	19.7	11.1	0.57
Large	15.1	16.7	13.2	0.79	19.5	25.3	12.9	0.51
Landless others	14.9	18.0	11.6	0.64	18.2	23.7	12.5	0.53
All land owners	13.6	16.3	10.4	0.64	17.5	22.3	12.0	0.54
All land non-owners	12.0	15.1	8.7	0.57	13.6	17.9	8.8	0.49
Occupation								
Agriculture	13.9	17.3	10.1	0.58	15.6	19.8	10.8	0.54
Salaried+prof.+s.empl.	13.3	14.1	12.5	0.88	25.0	32.1	17.1	0.53
Wage earners	7.0	10.3	3.3	0.32	5.2	8.1	1.8	0.23
All others	15.6	19.5	11.4	0.59	15.4	20.1	10.3	0.51
Caste								
SCs	9.4	13.0	5.6	0.43	7.4	11.9	2.3	0.19
Religion								
Hindus	14.9	18.4	11.2	0.61	16.4	22.0	10.1	0.46
Other minorities	12.4	15.3	9.1	0.60	15.8	20.0	11.0	0.55
Household size								
Up to 4	11.6	15.2	7.5	0.49	14.8	19.6	9.3	0.47
5–7	11.9	14.4	9.1	0.64	15.9	20.9	10.5	0.50
8 and above	15.1	18.3	11.5	0.63	15.5	19.5	11.0	0.57
Poverty line								
Lower segment below	8.5	12.6	4.7	0.37	7.6	10.7	4.5	0.42
Upper segment below	9.6	11.8	7.5	0.64	5.9	7.5	4.2	0.56
Lower segment above	14.4	17.6	10.9	0.62	15.8	20.3	10.9	0.54
Upper segment above	13.2	15.4	10.6	0.68	23.8	30.4	15.9	0.52
Adult literacy								
Female literate	6.8	0.0	11.0	0.00	4.1	0.0	7.1	0.00
Male literate	11.7	19.2	0.0	0.00	10.7	17.9	0.0	0.00
Both literate	17.2	19.3	15.1	0.78	22.8	28.2	17.1	0.61
Village development								
Low	11.0	10.9	11.2	1.03	10.9	12.2	9.7	0.80
Medium	12.3	16.1	8.0	0.50	14.4	18.7	9.7	0.52
High	13.7	15.9	11.2	0.70	17.5	23.0	11.3	0.49
All groups	**12.8**	**15.7**	**9.5**	**0.61**	**15.6**	**20.2**	**10.4**	**0.51**

TABLE A8.11
Percentage Distribution of Students (aged 6–14 years) and Gender Disparity by Type of School by Population Group in Rural Punjab

Population group	Govt schools				Govt-aided schools				Private schools			
	Total	Male	Female	F/M	Total	Male	Female	F/M	Total	Male	Female	F/M
Household income												
Up to 20,000	87.3	84.7	90.4	1.07	0.9	1.2	0.5	0.41	11.5	13.6	9.1	0.67
20,001–40,000	80.1	79.1	81.4	1.03	0.1	0.1	0.2	1.27	19.3	20.8	17.4	0.84
40,001–62,000	68.5	62.7	76.8	1.23	7.5	9.9	4.0	0.40	23.9	27.4	19.0	0.69
62,001–86,000	68.4	65.3	72.7	1.11	0.6	1.1	0.0	0.00	30.2	32.4	27.3	0.84
Above 86,000	59.2	53.4	65.4	1.23	2.5	4.8	0.0	0.00	38.3	41.8	34.6	0.83
Landholding												
Landless wage earner	91.4	89.1	94.3	1.06	0.0	0.0	0.0	–	8.6	10.9	5.7	0.52
Marginal	75.2	70.4	80.4	1.14	2.7	5.3	0.0	0.00	22.1	24.4	19.6	0.81
Small	78.6	74.0	82.5	1.11	0.2	0.4	0.0	0.00	20.1	25.6	15.4	0.60
Medium	73.3	67.9	81.1	1.19	0.7	0.8	0.5	0.57	25.9	31.2	18.1	0.58
Large	63.5	61.2	66.3	1.08	2.8	5.0	0.0	0.00	33.2	32.7	33.7	1.03
Landless others	78.5	76.8	80.8	1.05	2.4	2.7	1.9	0.68	18.8	19.9	17.3	0.87
All land owners	73.1	68.5	78.3	1.14	1.6	3.0	0.1	0.03	24.8	28.3	20.9	0.74
All land non-owners	83.1	81.2	85.7	1.06	1.5	1.8	1.2	0.67	15.1	16.7	13.1	0.78
Occupation												
Agriculture	75.9	72.1	80.3	1.11	1.1	2.0	0.1	0.05	22.4	25.6	18.8	0.73
Salaried+prof.+s.empl.	71.4	67.1	76.7	1.14	4.0	5.0	2.8	0.55	24.1	26.9	20.5	0.76
Wage earners	91.3	88.7	94.6	1.07	0.0	0.0	0.0	–	8.7	11.3	5.4	0.48
All others	79.2	79.3	79.1	1.00	1.1	2.0	0.0	0.00	19.7	18.7	20.9	1.12
Caste												
SCs	88.1	83.3	95.2	1.14	0.0	0.0	0.0	–	11.8	16.7	4.5	0.27
Religion												
Hindus	76.5	73.1	81.0	1.11	0.5	0.9	0.0	0.00	23.0	26.0	18.9	0.73
Household size												
Up to 4	61.0	61.3	60.3	0.98	6.0	7.5	3.2	0.43	33.1	31.2	36.5	1.17
5–7	81.9	78.5	86.2	1.10	1.6	2.2	0.7	0.32	16.1	19.0	12.6	0.67
8 and above	76.6	74.5	78.9	1.06	0.3	0.5	0.0	0.00	22.9	24.6	21.0	0.85
Poverty line												
Lower segment below	92.6	90.0	95.0	1.06	0.6	1.3	0.0	0.00	6.8	8.7	5.0	0.58
Upper segment below	88.8	86.0	92.4	1.08	0.5	0.0	1.1	-	10.7	14.0	6.5	0.46
Lower segment above	75.0	73.5	76.8	1.04	1.2	2.1	0.1	0.05	23.1	23.7	22.4	0.94
Upper segment above	65.6	60.1	72.8	1.21	4.2	5.8	2.2	0.37	30.2	34.1	25.1	0.74
Adult literacy												
None literate	87.5	81.3	94.3	1.16	0.0	0.0	0.0	–	12.5	18.7	5.7	0.31
Female literate	82.1	78.2	87.4	1.12	0.0	0.0	0.0	–	17.9	21.8	12.6	0.58
Male literate	83.8	80.5	88.0	1.09	0.9	1.6	0.0	0.00	15.3	17.9	12.0	0.67
Both literate	72.5	71.2	74.1	1.04	2.7	3.7	1.3	0.35	24.2	24.4	24.0	0.98
Village development												
Low	75.7	64.7	90.9	1.40	0.0	0.0	0.0	–	24.1	35.3	8.7	0.25
Medium	81.8	77.3	87.8	1.14	0.1	0.2	0.0	0.00	18.1	22.4	12.2	0.54
High	75.0	75.3	74.8	0.99	3.6	5.5	1.5	0.27	20.6	18.4	23.1	1.25
All groups	**78.6**	**75.7**	**82.2**	**1.09**	**1.6**	**2.3**	**0.7**	**0.29**	**19.5**	**21.8**	**16.8**	**0.77**

TABLE A8.12

Percentage Distribution of Household Annual Expenditure on Schooling (6–14 years) in Government Schools and Gender Disparity by Population Group in Rural Punjab

(Annual expenditure in rupees)

Population group	Govt schools						
	Fees	Books	Coaching	Transpt	BL	Total	#St/Rhhd
Household income							
Up to 20,000							
Person	13.9	79.3	5.6	1.2	0.0	819	1.9
Gender disparity	1.22	1.06	0.34	0.00	0.00	0.89	0.91
20,001–40,000							
Person	14.4	78.1	5.0	2.5	0.0	985	1.9
Gender disparity	1.01	1.05	0.33	1.42	0.00	0.65	0.81
40,001–62,000							
Person	20.2	76.4	3.1	0.3	0.0	881	1.6
Gender disparity	0.56	1.12	2.95	0.00	0.00	1.03	0.88
62,001–86,000							
Person	21.4	67.4	5.8	5.4	0.0	998	1.8
Gender disparity	0.91	1.16	1.09	0.03	0.00	0.73	0.81
Above 86,000							
Person	18.9	64.4	9.3	7.3	0.0	1,137	2.0
Gender disparity	1.14	0.96	1.08	0.94	0.00	1.07	1.15
Landholding							
Landless wage earner							
Person	17.7	80.5	1.4	0.4	0.0	586	1.9
Gender disparity	1.47	0.95	0.08	0.00	0.00	0.66	0.81
Marginal							
Person	13.1	81.0	5.8	0.0	0.0	936	1.8
Gender disparity	1.06	1.08	0.27	0.00	0.00	1.31	1.08
Small							
Person	20.4	72.7	1.6	5.4	0.0	1,243	2.2
Gender disparity	0.74	1.08	2.06	0.88	0.00	1.13	1.30
Medium							
Person	16.4	70.0	3.4	10.2	0.0	1,071	1.9
Gender disparity	1.13	1.08	0.90	0.48	0.00	0.95	0.81
Large							
Person	21.6	68.2	10.0	0.2	0.0	972	1.8
Gender disparity	0.66	1.01	2.13	1.65	0.00	0.73	0.87
Landless others							
Person	13.1	77.7	8.0	1.3	0.0	957	1.8
Gender disparity	1.08	1.10	0.42	0.00	0.00	0.67	0.79
All land owners							
Person	17.6	73.6	4.8	4.0	0.0	1,049	1.9
Gender disparity	0.84	1.08	0.85	0.60	0.00	1.04	1.02
All land non-owners							
Person	14.3	78.5	6.2	1.0	0.0	815	1.9
Gender disparity	1.20	1.05	0.40	0.00	0.00	0.67	0.80
Occupation							
Agriculture							
Person	18.2	72.6	4.9	4.3	0.0	1,078	2.0
Gender disparity	0.82	1.10	0.77	0.65	0.00	0.97	0.96
Salaried+prof.+s.empl.							
Person	14.3	78.3	5.8	1.6	0.0	979	1.8
Gender disparity	1.25	1.07	0.31	0.00	0.00	0.83	0.91
Wage earners							
Person	17.1	80.1	2.5	0.4	0.0	588	1.9
Gender disparity	1.51	0.95	0.37	0.00	0.00	0.66	0.83
All others							
Person	10.8	79.0	9.7	0.5	0.0	907	1.8
Gender disparity	0.83	1.10	0.62	0.00	0.00	0.66	0.78

(Contd.)

TABLE A8.12 (contd.)

Population group	Govt schools						
	Fees	Books	Coaching	Transpt	BL	Total	#St/Rhhd
Caste							
SCs							
Person	10.4	89.0	0.6	0.0	0.0	644	1.8
Gender disparity	1.24	0.99	0.00	0.00	0.00	0.58	0.78
Religion							
Hindus							
Person	13.0	80.7	6.3	0.0	0.0	884	1.9
Gender disparity	1.02	1.03	0.62	0.00	0.00	0.78	0.84
Other minorities							
Person	16.9	74.3	5.4	3.3	0.0	951	1.9
Gender disparity	0.99	1.08	0.52	0.50	0.00	0.86	0.95
Household size							
Up to 4							
Person	12.9	73.3	13.8	0.0	0.0	591	1.3
Gender disparity	1.55	1.13	0.19	0.00	0.00	0.51	0.53
5–7							
Person	13.5	77.1	5.8	3.7	0.0	912	1.9
Gender disparity	0.98	1.07	0.64	0.51	0.00	0.85	0.89
8 and above							
Person	21.9	74.7	3.3	0.1	0.0	1,027	2.1
Gender disparity	1.01	1.02	0.70	0.30	0.00	0.84	0.97
Poverty line							
Lower segment below							
Person	19.5	78.2	2.3	0.0	0.0	688	2.0
Gender disparity	1.47	0.94	0.29	0.00	0.00	0.94	1.10
Upper segment below							
Person	13.4	80.7	3.7	2.1	0.0	1,006	2.1
Gender disparity	0.93	1.13	0.11	0.00	0.00	0.73	0.83
Lower segment above							
Person	14.7	76.5	7.1	1.7	0.0	937	1.8
Gender disparity	0.84	1.08	0.59	1.11	0.00	0.79	0.82
Upper segment above							
Person	19.3	68.2	6.1	6.4	0.0	957	1.8
Gender disparity	1.11	1.03	1.12	0.46	0.00	1.00	0.94
Adult literacy							
None literate							
Person	14.6	76.1	3.8	5.4	0.0	590	1.9
Gender disparity	1.43	0.98	0.35	1.03	0.00	0.84	1.06
Female literate							
Person	22.0	75.8	2.3	0.0	0.0	841	2.2
Gender disparity	0.61	1.14	1.50	0.00	0.00	0.93	0.80
Male literate							
Person	15.2	76.4	4.4	4.1	0.0	732	1.7
Gender disparity	1.27	1.04	0.02	1.18	0.00	0.71	0.88
Both literate							
Person	15.7	76.2	6.7	1.4	0.0	1,172	1.9
Gender disparity	0.94	1.08	0.72	0.01	0.00	0.85	0.83
Village development							
Low							
Person	8.9	67.0	1.3	22.8	0.0	1,254	2.0
Gender disparity	1.02	1.11	2.14	0.69	0.00	0.91	1.02
Medium							
Person	15.3	80.7	2.8	1.1	0.0	812	1.8
Gender disparity	1.05	1.02	0.95	0.02	0.00	0.83	0.84
High							
Person	17.8	72.7	9.5	0.1	0.0	1,000	1.9
Gender disparity	0.99	1.10	0.44	0.00	0.00	0.80	0.92
All groups							
Person	15.9	76.2	5.5	2.4	0.0	911	1.9
Gender disparity	1.01	1.06	0.56	0.52	0.00	0.83	0.88

Notes: BL: Boarding and lodging; #St/Rhhd: Number of students per rural household.

TABLE A8.13

Percentage Distribution of Household Annual Expenditure on Schooling (6–14 years) in Private Schools and Gender Disparity by Population Group in Rural Punjab

(Annual expenditure in rupees)

Population group	Private schools						
	Fees	Books	Coaching	Transpt	BL	Total	#St/Rhhd
Household income							
Up to 20,000							
Person	45.7	51.0	3.2	0.0	0.0	1330	1.3
Gender disparity	0.78	1.12	4.19	0.00	0.00	0.53	0.57
20,001–40,000							
Person	43.7	47.2	6.2	2.8	0.0	2202	1.4
Gender disparity	1.01	1.05	1.31	0.00	0.00	0.58	0.66
40,001–62,000							
Person	35.9	48.6	9.4	6.2	0.1	2008	1.3
Gender disparity	0.80	0.81	10.79	0.91	0.00	0.66	0.50
62,001–86,000							
Person	32.9	52.3	5.2	9.6	0.0	3385	1.6
Gender disparity	0.98	1.05	0.12	1.66	0.00	0.64	0.61
Above 86,000							
Person	43.0	52.7	1.1	3.3	0.0	2333	1.8
Gender disparity	1.02	1.02	7.66	0.21	0.00	0.59	0.77
Landholding							
Landless wage earner							
Person	57.4	42.4	0.2	0.0	0.0	1305	1.4
Gender disparity	0.40	2.16	0.00	0.00	0.00	0.26	0.40
Marginal							
Person	37.0	48.6	8.6	5.9	0.0	1515	1.4
Gender disparity	0.68	1.73	0.13	0.55	0.00	0.59	0.76
Small							
Person	45.3	42.7	8.0	4.0	0.1	2665	1.5
Gender disparity	0.86	1.28	1.06	0.12	0.00	0.41	0.70
Medium							
Person	36.5	52.7	0.7	10.1	0.0	2153	1.5
Gender disparity	1.03	1.03	1.16	0.75	0.00	0.54	0.39
Large							
Person	38.5	53.6	6.8	1.1	0.0	2999	1.9
Gender disparity	1.02	0.74	13.26	1.31	0.00	0.64	0.82
Landless others							
Person	40.5	51.9	4.0	3.7	0.0	2028	1.3
Gender disparity	1.09	0.85	2.94	1.23	0.00	0.76	0.65
All land owners							
Person	39.4	49.7	6.0	4.9	0.0	2279	1.6
Gender disparity	0.90	1.08	1.53	0.59	0.00	0.54	0.66
All land non-owners							
Person	42.7	50.7	3.5	3.2	0.0	1891	1.3
Gender disparity	0.95	0.94	3.23	1.38	0.00	0.67	0.59
Occupation							
Agriculture							
Person	39.5	51.1	5.1	4.3	0.0	2357	1.6
Gender disparity	0.94	0.97	2.92	0.58	0.00	0.54	0.63
Salaried+prof.+s.empl.							
Person	40.2	51.2	4.5	4.1	0.0	2101	1.3
Gender disparity	1.01	0.91	2.23	1.19	0.00	0.82	0.61
Wage earners							
Person	57.4	42.3	0.3	0.0	0.0	1299	1.4
Gender disparity	0.40	2.13	0.00	0.00	0.00	0.24	0.37
All others							
Person	39.4	47.3	7.6	5.7	0.0	1850	1.6
Gender disparity	1.00	1.22	0.31	0.59	0.00	0.55	0.87

(Contd.)

TABLE A8.13 (contd.)

Population group	Private schools						
	Fees	Books	Coaching	Transpt	BL	Total	#St/Rhhd
Caste							
SCs							
Person	36.1	51.6	0.2	12.1	0.0	1371	1.1
Gender disparity	1.31	1.05	0.00	0.00	0.00	0.08	0.18
Religion							
Hindus							
Person	43.5	51.1	2.0	3.5	0.0	1702	1.5
Gender disparity	1.02	1.07	1.20	0.00	0.00	0.46	0.55
Other minorities							
Person	38.5	50.9	6.0	4.6	0.0	2260	1.4
Gender disparity	0.95	0.97	1.75	0.98	0.00	0.68	0.71
Household size							
Up to 4							
Person	51.0	42.8	6.2	0.0	0.0	1509	1.3
Gender disparity	0.69	1.23	3.89	0.00	0.00	0.54	0.63
5–7							
Person	39.8	52.5	1.8	5.9	0.0	2047	1.3
Gender disparity	0.90	1.06	2.29	0.87	0.00	0.57	0.54
8 and above							
Person	38.8	48.8	9.6	2.8	0.0	2547	1.8
Gender disparity	1.10	0.90	1.37	0.58	0.00	0.66	0.78
Poverty line							
Lower segment below							
Person	31.9	68.1	0.0	0.0	0.0	740	1.2
Gender disparity	0.32	1.50	0.00	0.00	0.00	0.58	0.60
Upper segment below							
Person	62.0	37.2	0.8	0.0	0.0	1301	1.4
Gender disparity	0.73	1.52	0.67	0.00	0.00	0.21	0.35
Lower segment above							
Person	38.9	49.6	8.3	3.1	0.0	2203	1.5
Gender disparity	1.03	0.99	1.50	0.18	0.00	0.69	0.74
Upper segment above							
Person	40.0	52.2	1.0	6.8	0.0	2500	1.4
Gender disparity	0.94	0.96	6.71	1.51	0.00	0.57	0.57
Adult literacy							
None literate							
Person	54.2	39.5	0.1	6.2	0.0	1126	1.2
Gender disparity	0.30	2.44	0.00	0.00	0.00	0.14	0.28
Female literate							
Person	39.5	59.8	0.6	0.0	0.0	2094	1.7
Gender disparity	1.20	0.89	0.00	0.00	0.00	0.26	0.41
Male literate							
Person	40.6	58.2	1.2	0.0	0.0	1864	1.6
Gender disparity	1.13	0.86	12.08	0.00	0.00	0.42	0.54
Both literate							
Person	39.5	48.9	6.5	5.1	0.0	2376	1.5
Gender disparity	0.96	1.02	1.43	0.75	0.00	0.75	0.78
Village development							
Low							
Person	47.5	44.7	0.1	7.6	0.0	1434	1.3
Gender disparity	0.40	1.89	0.00	0.00	0.00	0.06	0.18
Medium							
Person	43.9	50.5	3.3	2.3	0.0	2171	1.5
Gender disparity	0.97	0.98	2.33	0.54	0.00	0.38	0.40
High							
Person	36.4	50.4	7.4	5.7	0.0	2161	1.5
Gender disparity	1.02	1.01	1.11	0.72	0.00	1.11	1.16
All groups							
Person	40.8	50.1	4.9	4.2	0.0	2098	1.5
Gender disparity	0.93	1.02	1.84	0.79	0.00	0.60	0.63

Notes: BL: Boarding and lodging; #St/Rhhd: Number of students per rural household.

TABLE A8.14
Short-Juration and Major Morbidity Prevalence Rates and Gender Disparity by Population Group in Rural Punjab

Population group	Short-duration morbidity ('000 popn)				Major morbidity per lakh popn
	Diarr.	Cold and Cough	Fever	Total	
Household income					
Up to 20,000					
Person	15	95	36	143	6941
Gender disparity	1.23	1.08	1.57	1.25	1.26
20,001–40,000					
Person	17	110	40	167	6812
Gender disparity	0.59	1.07	1.29	1.08	1.12
40,001–62,000					
Person	21	103	30	152	6766
Gender disparity	1.48	1.19	1.03	1.21	1.36
62,001–86,000					
Person	12	95	41	148	7712
Gender disparity	2.53	0.99	0.68	0.96	1.47
Above 86,000					
Person	10	126	31	164	4505
Gender disparity	4.46	1.36	1.19	1.36	1.12
Landholding					
Landless wage earner					
Person	21	95	42	155	7554
Gender disparity	0.97	1.18	1.03	1.16	1.38
Marginal					
Person	13	127	36	171	6258
Gender disparity	0.30	1.03	1.23	1.02	1.14
Small					
Person	21	102	39	163	8204
Gender disparity	1.54	1.26	1.29	1.32	1.39
Medium					
Person	13	116	30	156	5179
Gender disparity	3.42	0.91	0.51	0.91	1.58
Large					
Person	11	104	41	153	3997
Gender disparity	5.58	1.75	0.86	1.49	0.80
Landless others					
Person	14	97	32	142	7096
Gender disparity	0.83	1.00	2.37	1.21	1.15
All land owners					
Person	15	112	36	161	6072
Gender disparity	1.53	1.16	0.96	1.15	1.26
All land non-owners					
Person	16	96	36	147	7272
Gender disparity	0.90	1.06	1.62	1.19	1.23
Occupation					
Agriculture					
Person	15	115	37	165	6005
Gender disparity	2.36	1.19	1.01	1.22	1.30
Salaried+prof.+s.empl.					
Person	13	101	37	150	7025
Gender disparity	0.46	0.90	2.05	1.07	0.93
Wage earners					
Person	21	94	41	154	7522
Gender disparity	0.85	1.25	0.98	1.16	1.32
All others					
Person	15	94	27	133	6944
Gender disparity	0.93	1.01	1.86	1.15	1.52

(Contd.)

Population group	Short-duration morbidity ('000 popn)				Major morbidity per lakh popn
	Diarr.	Cold and Cough	Fever	Total	
Caste					
SCs					
Person	18	72	42	125	6105
Gender disparity	0.72	1.26	1.01	1.22	0.60
Religion					
Hindus					
Person	18	91	28	131	4823
Gender disparity	1.58	0.99	1.28	1.16	1.21
Other minorities					
Person	15	109	38	162	7482
Gender disparity	0.97	1.16	1.19	1.16	1.23
Household size					
Up to 4					
Person	18	103	36	156	6808
Gender disparity	1.15	1.25	1.95	1.41	1.21
5–7					
Person	14	100	38	150	6809
Gender disparity	1.21	0.92	1.13	1.00	1.20
8 and above					
Person	18	112	33	159	6435
Gender disparity	1.08	1.39	1.20	1.35	1.36
Poverty line					
Lower segment below					
Person	15	113	35	159	7369
Gender disparity	1.12	1.17	1.20	1.22	1.40
Upper segment below					
Person	17	84	38	137	6202
Gender disparity	1.44	0.98	2.14	1.32	1.06
Lower segment above					
Person	18	106	37	158	6955
Gender disparity	0.85	1.12	1.15	1.11	1.15
Upper segment above					
Person	10	109	33	152	5996
Gender disparity	2.89	1.13	1.06	1.17	1.53
Adult literacy					
None literate					
Person	16	89	40	145	7880
Gender disparity	1.00	1.21	0.99	1.14	1.23
Female literate					
Person	10	102	42	149	7820
Gender disparity	1.00	1.74	2.07	1.93	1.13
Male literate					
Person	13	96	41	150	6635
Gender disparity	1.21	0.99	1.61	1.16	1.35
Both literate					
Person	17	113	32	159	6187
Gender disparity	1.04	1.09	1.15	1.13	1.24
Village development					
Low					
Person	12	104	4	121	7841
Gender disparity	0.62	2.29	0.20	1.83	1.71
Medium					
Person	19	101	33	148	6986
Gender disparity	1.35	1.02	1.00	1.08	1.34

(Contd.)

TABLE A8.14 (contd.)

Population group	Short-duration morbidity ('000 popn) Diarr.	Cold and Cough	Fever	Total	Major morbidity per lakh popn
High					
Person	12	109	44	165	6184
Gender disparity	0.94	1.12	1.54	1.21	1.09
Age (years)					
0–4					
Person	74	154	36	253	966
Gender disparity	1.17	0.73	0.88	0.88	0.85
5–14					
Person	8	117	34	156	1501
Gender disparity	0.67	0.85	1.21	0.93	0.22

(Contd.)

TABLE A8.14 (contd.)

Population group	Short-duration morbidity ('000 popn) Diarr.	Cold and Cough	Fever	Total	Major morbidity per lakh popn
15–34					
Person	8	98	31	137	3168
Gender disparity	1.43	1.51	1.22	1.44	1.55
35–59					
Person	6	83	43	131	12,826
Gender disparity	0.97	1.20	1.79	1.38	1.73
60 and above					
Person	9	80	45	134	25,502
Gender disparity	0.90	1.54	0.92	1.22	0.99
All groups					
Person	16	104	36	154	6692
Gender disparity	1.15	1.11	1.25	1.17	1.25

TABLE A8.15

Short-duration Morbidity Prevalence Rates and Gender Disparity by Age and Population Group in Rural Punjab

Population group	Short-duration morbidity ('000 popn) Age groups (completed years) 0–4	5–14	15–34	35–59	60+	All
Household income						
Up to 20,000						
Person	228	160	130	96	130	143
Gender disparity	0.94	1.02	1.33	1.91	1.78	1.25
20,001–40,000						
Person	246	147	167	141	160	167
Gender disparity	0.69	0.94	1.15	1.26	1.93	1.08
40,001–62,000						
Person	251	169	122	141	149	152
Gender disparity	1.00	1.04	1.60	1.28	0.51	1.21
62,001–86,000						
Person	328	158	109	148	62	148
Gender disparity	0.85	0.52	5.81	0.62	0.63	0.96
Above 86,000						
Person	340	151	122	177	111	164
Gender disparity	1.29	0.95	1.95	2.11	0.06	1.36
Landholding						
Landless wage earner						
Person	270	172	138	100	102	155
Gender disparity	0.76	1.11	1.25	2.06	1.27	1.16
Marginal						
Person	191	195	189	113	169	171
Gender disparity	0.61	0.82	1.30	0.88	1.77	1.02
Small						
Person	305	150	142	138	140	163
Gender disparity	0.62	1.67	2.00	1.42	0.89	1.32
Medium						
Person	284	161	91	156	209	156
Gender disparity	0.82	0.57	2.28	1.06	0.54	0.91
Large						
Person	250	148	124	181	88	153
Gender disparity	1.50	0.97	2.46	1.56	0.58	1.49
Landless others						
Person	228	134	135	124	124	142
Gender disparity	1.21	0.85	1.18	1.41	2.33	1.21

(Contd.)

Population group	Short-duration morbidity ('000 popn) Age groups (completed years) 0–4	5–14	15–34	35–59	60+	All
All land owners						
Person	259	164	139	146	151	161
Gender disparity	0.79	0.91	1.79	1.23	0.93	1.15
All land non-owners						
Person	247	148	136	115	116	147
Gender disparity	0.96	0.96	1.21	1.60	1.89	1.19
Occupation						
Agriculture						
Person	258	172	131	164	150	165
Gender disparity	0.86	0.92	2.02	1.29	1.08	1.22
Salaried+prof.+s.empl.						
Person	243	113	157	131	146	150
Gender disparity	0.99	0.62	1.30	1.14	1.34	1.07
Wage earners						
Person	262	171	140	95	108	154
Gender disparity	0.73	1.19	1.17	2.12	1.30	1.16
All others						
Person	234	147	126	87	104	133
Gender disparity	1.09	0.98	1.06	1.43	2.12	1.15
Caste						
SCs						
Person	235	122	84	113	113	125
Gender disparity	1.02	1.10	1.05	1.85	5.38	1.22
Religion						
Hindus						
Person	299	136	86	108	123	131
Gender disparity	1.12	1.02	0.97	1.70	1.82	1.16
Other minorities						
Person	240	161	154	141	141	162
Gender disparity	0.81	0.95	1.47	1.33	1.10	1.16
Household size						
Up to 4						
Person	213	148	169	116	137	156
Gender disparity	0.98	1.32	1.92	1.71	0.30	1.41

(Contd.)

TABLE A8.15 (contd.)

Population group	Short-duration morbidity ('000 popn) Age groups (completed years)					
	0–4	5–14	15–34	35–59	60+	All
5–7						
Person	261	165	133	107	135	150
Gender disparity	0.95	0.75	1.02	1.26	1.69	1.00
8 and above						
Person	261	145	127	177	132	159
Gender disparity	0.73	1.19	2.18	1.43	1.17	1.35
Poverty line						
Lower segment below						
Person	274	180	137	92	170	159
Gender disparity	0.66	0.91	2.12	1.44	1.55	1.22
Upper segment below						
Person	221	135	107	140	128	137
Gender disparity	0.99	1.59	1.26	1.65	1.50	1.32
Lower segment above						
Person	247	159	149	132	135	158
Gender disparity	0.86	0.96	1.11	1.33	1.78	1.11
Upper segment above						
Person	283	149	134	143	112	152
Gender disparity	1.10	0.63	2.39	1.31	0.20	1.17
Adult literacy						
None literate						
Person	213	180	134	95	105	145
Gender disparity	0.76	1.00	1.47	1.33	1.23	1.14

(Contd.)

TABLE A8.15 (contd.)

Population group	Short-duration morbidity ('000 popn) Age groups (completed years)					
	0–4	5–14	15–34	35–59	60+	All
Female literate						
Person	298	136	129	138	97	149
Gender disparity	1.30	2.40	2.17	3.33	1.26	1.93
Male literate						
Person	287	154	138	83	150	150
Gender disparity	0.87	0.89	1.46	1.59	1.55	1.16
Both literate						
Person	249	151	139	160	140	159
Gender disparity	0.91	0.84	1.38	1.25	1.10	1.13
Village development						
Low						
Person	255	145	105	55	139	121
Gender disparity	0.38	2.60	2.93	1.25	1.84	1.83
Medium						
Person	247	152	132	126	114	148
Gender disparity	0.98	0.85	1.21	1.36	0.85	1.08
High						
Person	260	163	147	148	157	165
Gender disparity	0.84	0.91	1.63	1.29	1.57	1.21
All Groups						
Person	253	156	137	131	134	154
Gender disparity	0.88	0.93	1.44	1.38	1.22	1.17

TABLE A8.16

Major Morbidity Prevalence Rates and Gender Disparity by Population Group in Rural Punjab

Population group	Major morbidity (per lakh popn) Age groups (completed years)					
	0–4	5–14	15–34	35–59	60+	All
Household income						
Up to 20,000						
Person	905	1543	2828	14,110	29,609	6941
Gender disparity	0.74	0.14	1.31	1.57	1.11	1.26
20,001–40,000						
Person	703	1895	4275	13,157	20,861	6812
Gender disparity	–	0.39	1.66	1.94	0.54	1.12
40,001–62,000						
Person	1351	2066	3139	9542	34,262	6766
Gender disparity	–	–	1.88	3.77	1.04	1.36
62,001–86,000						
Person	1547	396	2154	16,735	26,807	7712
Gender disparity	2.76	–	2.58	1.30	1.40	1.47
Above 86,000						
Person	1162	652	1996	9440	14,107	4505
Gender disparity	–	–	0.90	1.07	2.04	1.12
Landholding						
Landless wage earner						
Person	2019	1323	3877	17,724	24,701	7554
Gender disparity	1.27	0.23	1.67	1.78	1.13	1.38
Marginal						
Person	0	319	3635	13,704	17,750	6258
Gender disparity	1.27	–	1.85	1.23	0.73	1.14
Small						
Person	0	1843	3795	14,356	36,113	8204
Gender disparity	1.27	0.48	0.85	2.66	1.21	1.39

(Contd.)

Population group	Major morbidity (per lakh popn) Age groups (completed years)					
	0–4	5–14	15–34	35–59	60+	All
Medium						
Person	250	0	2,758	9096	26,683	5179
Gender disparity	–	0.48	9.68	2.38	0.90	1.58
Large						
Person	4214	927	1850	5674	12,018	3997
Gender disparity	0.36	1.20	1.15	0.56	1.34	0.80
Landless others						
Person	244	2792	2823	13,200	29,470	7096
Gender disparity	0.36	0.11	1.28	1.89	0.85	1.15
All land owners						
Person	849	769	3105	10,865	23,445	6072
Gender disparity	0.24	0.51	1.68	1.64	1.05	1.26
All land non-owners						
Person	1061	2243	3221	14,834	27,706	7272
Gender disparity	1.69	0.14	1.45	1.81	0.93	1.23
Occupation						
Agriculture						
Person	807	697	3403	9762	25,769	6005
Gender disparity	–	0.63	2.14	2.04	0.93	1.30
Salaried+prof.+s.empl.						
Person	0	2337	3494	12,589	23,752	7025
Gender disparity	–	0.13	1.17	1.31	0.73	0.93
Wage earners						
Person	1892	1281	3707	18,104	23,298	7522
Gender disparity	1.22	0.24	1.68	1.61	1.19	1.32

(Contd.)

TABLE A8.16 (contd.)

Population group	Major morbidity (per lakh popn) Age groups (completed years)					
	0–4	5–14	15–34	35–59	60+	All
All others						
Person	871	2973	1699	14,691	29,990	6944
Gender disparity	1.22	0.10	0.57	2.22	1.30	1.52
Caste						
SCs						
Person	0	2513	1888	13,033	32,250	6105
Gender disparity	1.22	–	0.18	1.15	0.52	0.60
Religion						
Hindus						
Person	0	1258	2060	10,339	19,593	4823
Gender disparity	0.74	0.00	2.05	1.54	0.63	1.21
Other minorities						
Person	1400	1647	3661	13,998	27,109	7482
Gender disparity	0.76	0.27	1.39	1.73	1.12	1.23
Household size						
Up to 4						
Person	2304	3166	3356	15,042	19,728	6808
Gender disparity	1.10	0.03	1.50	1.78	1.54	1.21
5–7						
Person	700	916	2915	13,386	27,682	6809
Gender disparity	1.62	0.44	1.43	1.54	0.89	1.20
8 and above						
Person	655	1625	3474	10,845	24,271	6435
Gender disparity	–	0.26	1.78	2.17	1.03	1.36
Poverty line						
Lower segment below						
Person	924	1359	3710	13,758	31,996	7369
Gender disparity	0.90	0.26	1.82	1.94	1.59	1.40
Upper segment below						
Person	988	993	2062	13,864	26,499	6202
Gender disparity	5.77	–	2.28	1.06	0.81	1.06

(Contd.)

TABLE A8.16 (contd.)

Population group	Major morbidity (per lakh popn) Age groups (completed years)					
	0–4	5–14	15–34	35–59	60+	All
Lower segment above						
Person	639	1899	3966	12,506	25,421	6955
Gender disparity	0.80	0.32	1.15	1.98	0.74	1.15
Upper segment above						
Person	1978	1084	1874	12,482	20,552	5996
Gender disparity	0.39	–	3.59	1.68	1.51	1.53
Adult literacy						
None literate						
Person	1490	1151	3371	18,911	27,852	7880
Gender disparity	0.81	0.27	1.27	1.33	1.43	1.23
Female literate						
Person	0	6056	1908	14,895	28,438	7820
Gender disparity	0.81	0.42	9.97	1.51	0.81	1.13
Male literate						
Person	1525	840	2876	13,636	26,963	6635
Gender disparity	1.65	–	1.37	2.10	0.83	1.35
Both literate						
Person	554	1448	3338	10,375	23,967	6187
Gender disparity	0.34	0.20	1.62	1.96	0.95	1.24
Village development						
Low						
Person	2859	1759	5054	12,857	33,478	7841
Gender disparity	0.34	0.41	0.93	2.33	1.02	1.71
Medium						
Person	810	1193	3012	12,899	29,903	6986
Gender disparity	1.06	0.20	2.15	1.68	1.04	1.34
High						
Person	930	1856	3117	12,721	19,790	6184
Gender disparity	0.24	0.21	1.21	1.74	0.93	1.09
All groups						
Person	966	1501	3168	12,826	25,502	6692
Gender disparity	0.85	0.22	1.55	1.73	0.99	1.25

TABLE A8.17

Per Person Household Expenditure for Treatment of Illness and Gender Disparity by Population Group in Rural Punjab

Population group	Cost of short illness		Cost of long illness			
	Fees and medicines	Proportion of total cost	Fees and medicines	Proportion of total cost	Per sick person	Per reporting
Household income						
Up to 20,000						
Person	156	0.97	121	0.73	1751	1906
Gender disparity	1.11	1.05	1.20	1.38	0.95	0.94
20,001–40,000						
Person	270	0.91	100	0.59	1477	1594
Gender disparity	0.75	1.06	1.16	1.71	1.04	1.02
40,001–62,000						
Person	245	0.92	125	0.90	1860	2072
Gender disparity	0.30	1.01	1.02	1.03	0.75	0.68
62,001–86,000						
Person	171	0.92	149	0.92	1942	2119
Gender disparity	0.81	1.01	0.96	0.93	0.65	0.62

(Contd.)

Population group	Cost of short illness		Cost of long illness			
	Fees and medicines	Proportion of total cost	Fees and medicines	Proportion of total cost	Per sick person	Per reporting
Above 86,000						
Person	142	0.86	78	0.84	1738	1771
Gender disparity	1.12	0.94	0.74	1.20	0.66	0.69
Landholding						
Landless wage earner						
Person	162	0.92	134	0.66	1780	1880
Gender disparity	0.76	1.01	1.16	1.30	0.84	0.87
Marginal						
Person	247	1.00	89	0.81	1432	1706
Gender disparity	0.99	1.10	1.16	1.47	1.02	0.98
Small						
Person	323	0.92	136	0.87	1669	1844
Gender disparity	0.94	1.07	1.19	1.05	0.86	0.86

(Contd.)

Table A8.17 (contd.)

Population group	Cost of short illness		Cost of long illness			
	Fees and medicines	Proportion of total cost	Fees and medicines	Proportion of total cost	Per sick person	Per reporting
Medium						
Person	183	0.86	137	0.92	2662	2700
Gender disparity	0.45	1.09	1.17	0.91	0.74	0.76
Large						
Person	154	0.91	70	0.83	1768	1876
Gender disparity	0.97	1.02	0.58	1.16	0.73	0.66
Landless others						
Person	183	0.92	105	0.63	1484	1611
Gender disparity	0.61	0.98	1.06	1.75	0.92	0.87
All land owners						
Person	233	0.93	111	0.87	1833	2015
Gender disparity	0.83	1.08	1.10	1.10	0.87	0.85
All land non-owners						
Person	175	0.92	116	0.64	1602	1720
Gender disparity	0.66	0.99	1.10	1.53	0.89	0.87
Occupation						
Agriculture						
Person	238	0.91	108	0.86	1813	1932
Gender disparity	0.87	1.05	0.95	1.11	0.73	0.73
Salaried+prof.+s.empl.						
Person	259	0.99	115	0.63	1642	1854
Gender disparity	0.54	1.10	1.01	1.83	1.09	0.99
Wage earners						
Person	159	0.92	130	0.66	1740	1852
Gender disparity	0.77	1.01	1.13	1.28	0.86	0.87
All others						
Person	107	0.87	104	0.73	1499	1653
Gender disparity	0.76	0.96	1.69	1.45	1.12	1.09
Caste						
SCs						
Person	268	0.95	130	0.81	2133	2208
Gender disparity	0.31	0.98	0.54	1.15	0.89	0.87
Religion						
Hindus						
Person	191	0.93	125	0.80	2593	2744
Gender disparity	0.56	0.96	1.03	1.22	0.85	0.91
Other minorities						
Person	211	0.93	110	0.70	1479	1620
Gender disparity	0.83	1.07	1.11	1.41	0.90	0.86
Household size						
Up to 4						
Person	223	0.90	95	0.39	1402	1684
Gender disparity	0.91	1.07	0.79	2.23	0.65	0.58
5–7						
Person	176	0.91	125	0.84	1837	1936
Gender disparity	0.65	1.02	1.06	1.08	0.89	0.89
8 and above						
Person	238	0.95	104	0.86	1631	1767
Gender disparity	0.82	1.05	1.37	1.11	1.01	0.97
Poverty line						
Lower segment below						
Person	180	0.98	118	0.74	1612	1708
Gender disparity	1.45	1.13	1.00	1.55	0.71	0.67
Upper segment below						
Person	146	0.93	119	0.62	1927	2110
Gender disparity	1.00	1.05	1.37	1.39	1.29	1.39
Lower segment above						
Person	242	0.91	108	0.72	1564	1705
Gender disparity	0.54	1.03	1.10	1.50	0.95	0.92
Upper segment above						
Person	172	0.91	118	0.87	1978	2144'
Gender disparity	1.03	0.97	1.01	0.93	0.66	0.65
Adult literacy						
None literate						
Person	159	0.93	136	0.68	1735	1876
Gender disparity	0.89	1.05	0.87	1.33	0.71	0.69
Female literate						
Person	125	0.89	153	0.89	1962	1971
Gender disparity	1.10	0.93	2.20	0.97	1.96	1.98
Male literate						
Person	163	0.90	95	0.76	1433	1607
Gender disparity	0.80	1.03	1.50	1.09	1.11	1.08
Both literate						
Person	243	0.93	110	0.73	1779	1923
Gender disparity	0.69	1.05	1.00	1.47	0.81	0.79
Village development						
Low						
Person	236	0.92	154	0.84	1971	1971
Gender disparity	0.70	0.99	3.11	1.20	1.82	1.82
Medium						
Person	206	0.94	123	0.69	1763	1930
Gender disparity	0.69	0.96	1.10	1.41	0.82	0.82
High						
Person	195	0.91	97	0.79	1,577	1,712
Gender disparity	0.85	1.16	0.92	1.24	0.84	0.80
Age (years)						
0–4						
Person	353	0.88	8	0.80	899	1,221
Gender disparity	0.30	0.97	1.19	1.16	1.40	1.10
5–14						
Person	140	0.92	14	0.71	953	1,050
Gender disparity	0.77	1.02	0.41	0.98	1.89	1.69
15–34						
Person	185	0.92	67	0.71	2122	2320
Gender disparity	1.09	1.02	1.36	1.41	0.88	0.82
35–59						
Person	224	0.97	218	0.65	1706	1869
Gender disparity	0.71	1.12	1.29	1.68	0.74	0.72
60 and above						
Person	167	0.93	420	0.90	1649	1737
Gender disparity	1.52	1.05	0.89	0.96	0.89	0.91
All groups						
Person	203	0.92	114	0.73	1703	1847
Gender disparity	0.75	1.04	1.10	1.34	0.88	0.86

(Contd.)

TABLE A8.18
Fertility Rate by Population Group in Rural Punjab

Population group	Crude birth rate per '000	TFR (15–49)	Average children ever born to ever married women			Crude death rate
			Boys	Girls	Total	
Household income						
Up to 20,000	24	3.5572	1.7	1.7	3.3	10
20,001–40,000	22	3.5256	1.6	1.5	3.1	11
40,001–62,000	21	2.3824	1.4	1.0	2.3	5
62,001–86,000	19	2.1844	1.3	1.1	2.3	9
Above 86,000	20	2.4758	1.5	1.1	2.6	2
Landholding						
Landless wage earner	29	4.3135	1.7	1.7	3.4	13
Marginal	20	2.7924	1.6	1.4	3.0	8
Small	20	2.8357	1.3	1.2	2.6	9
Medium	27	3.5383	1.6	1.2	2.7	4
Large	19	2.2837	1.3	1.0	2.4	4
Landless others	19	2.8235	1.7	1.5	3.1	9
All land owners	22	2.8084	1.5	1.2	2.7	6
All land non-owners	23	3.4084	1.7	1.6	3.2	11
Occupation						
Agriculture	23	2.9282	1.4	1.2	2.7	6
Salaried+prof.+s.empl.	18	2.7978	1.6	1.4	3.0	5
Wage earners	29	4.2680	1.7	1.7	3.4	13
All others	17	2.4640	1.7	1.5	3.2	14
Caste						
SCs	27	4.5297	1.7	1.6	3.3	9
Religion						
Hindus	20	2.9736	1.6	1.4	3.0	8
Other minorities	23	3.1111	1.5	1.4	2.9	9
Household size						
Up to 4	19	2.1949	1.1	0.9	2.0	18
5–7	19	3.0359	1.8	1.6	3.4	8
8 and above	29	4.0703	1.5	1.3	2.7	5
Poverty line						
Lower segment below	28	4.0679	1.7	1.8	3.5	11
Upper segment below	25	4.8674	1.9	1.9	3.8	6
Lower segment above	23	2.9385	1.5	1.3	2.8	10
Upper segment above	15	2.0701	1.4	1.0	2.4	5
Adult literacy						
None literate	27	4.9161	1.8	1.8	3.6	15
Female literate	9	1.7133	1.5	2.0	3.5	2
Male literate	22	4.0809	1.7	1.4	3.1	9
Both literate	22	2.5475	1.4	1.2	2.6	7
Village development						
Low	23	3.4573	1.6	1.6	3.2	17
Middle	22	3.1842	1.6	1.4	3.0	8
High	23	2.9054	1.5	1.4	2.8	9
All groups	**22**	**3.1006**	**1.6**	**1.4**	**3.0**	**9**

TABLE A8.19
Contraceptive Prevalence Rate for Ever Married Women by Population Group in Rural Punjab

Population group	Termination method % EMW	Vasectomy users % to all	Spacing method % EMW	Loop/CopT user % to all	% EMW using methods
Household income					
Up to 20,000	31.3	6.0	11.6	24.3	42.9
20,001–40,000	35.2	10.8	10.9	30.8	46.1
40,001–62,000	21.3	17.3	21.5	56.1	42.9
62,001–86,000	26.7	8.6	29.9	41.2	56.6
Above 86,000	27.6	1.8	19.1	54.6	46.7
Landholding					
Landless wage earner	31.0	7.8	6.6	9.5	37.6
Marginal	30.6	1.9	19.0	29.5	49.6
Small	25.8	16.4	19.3	41.4	45.1
Medium	27.0	10.2	20.1	60.0	47.0
Large	28.0	0.7	20.5	61.5	48.5
Landless others	33.0	11.0	14.2	30.3	47.3
All land owners	27.8	7.2	19.7	47.8	47.5
All land non-owners	32.3	9.8	11.2	25.6	43.5
Occupation					
Agriculture	28.6	6.8	18.8	53.4	47.4
Salaried+prof.+s.empl.	31.7	15.5	13.7	25.6	45.4
Wage earners	30.2	7.6	7.4	14.6	37.6
All others	31.8	5.6	19.1	28.0	50.8
Caste					
SCs	29.9	3.1	5.0	16.9	34.8
Religion					
Hindus	29.1	4.8	9.1	16.2	38.3
Other minorities	30.2	8.8	18.1	44.8	48.3
Household size					
Up to 4	16.3	9.8	13.4	33.7	29.7
5–7	38.5	8.8	12.6	32.2	51.0
8 and above	23.5	7.6	21.4	49.1	44.9
Poverty line					
Lower segment below	27.8	2.9	9.5	27.5	37.3
Upper segment below	39.5	3.1	12.7	33.8	52.1
Lower segment above	30.4	12.1	17.2	38.1	47.6
Upper segment above	24.8	8.6	16.9	50.0	41.8
Adult literacy					
None literate	37.2	2.9	4.6	38.5	41.8
Female literate	33.0	0.0	7.5	15.3	40.5
Male literate	30.7	7.2	11.5	37.5	42.3
Both literate	27.1	13.0	21.4	40.9	48.5
Village development					
Low	37.1	1.0	8.4	0.0	45.4
Middle	30.7	12.8	12.9	47.1	43.6
High	28.4	4.2	19.3	35.3	47.7
All groups	**30.1**	**8.6**	**15.4**	**39.6**	**45.5**

TABLE A8.20
Reasons for Non-adoption of Birth Control Measures by Population Group in Rural Punjab

(per cent)

Population group	Non-adoption	Reasons for not using birth control measures					
		Demand factors	Want son	Health factors	Supply factors	Household factors	Lack of knowledge
Household income							
Up to 20,000	57.5	29.8	5.0	8.5	1.0	10.5	38.2
20,001–40,000	50.2	27.6	3.8	13.2	0.0	6.9	43.6
40,001–62,000	58.6	36.3	5.7	5.1	0.2	5.7	36.1
62,001–86,000	50.2	23.7	1.8	7.1	0.0	8.9	41.3
Above 86,000	51.3	24.0	8.1	9.5	0.0	10.7	39.2
Landholding							
Landless wage earner	62.4	34.7	6.4	11.3	1.7	10.8	29.2
Marginal	50.4	30.1	1.6	10.0	0.3	6.8	45.6
Small	54.9	30.7	5.5	5.1	0.0	5.2	39.6
Medium	53.0	33.1	4.3	10.5	0.3	8.9	37.2
Large	51.5	27.6	6.7	7.0	0.0	5.6	36.3
Landless others	52.7	23.9	4.3	9.1	0.0	10.4	46.8
Land owners	52.5	30.5	4.5	8.1	0.2	6.6	39.8
Landless	56.5	28.5	5.2	10.0	0.7	10.5	39.2
Occupation							
Cultivators	52.6	29.0	4.2	8.6	0.2	6.9	40.1
Salaried+prof.+s.empl.	54.6	19.2	4.4	12.0	0.0	10.1	46.6
Wage earners	62.4	34.8	6.2	11.5	1.6	10.2	30.0
All others	49.2	36.8	5.4	2.4	0.0	9.3	43.5
Caste							
SCs	65.2	33.0	5.2	6.4	1.1	9.1	38.2
Religion							
Hindus	61.7	25.3	5.8	8.3	0.5	9.5	43.8
Other minorities	51.7	31.2	4.5	9.2	0.5	8.1	38.9
Household size							
Up to 4	70.3	40.0	3.7	5.7	0.0	10.2	34.9
5–7	49.0	24.0	5.6	10.0	0.8	9.5	44.0
8 and above	55.1	30.0	4.6	10.1	0.3	6.4	36.0
Poverty line							
Lower segment below	60.3	31.5	3.4	9.5	2.2	7.6	38.3
Upper segment below	50.6	19.1	7.6	10.7	0.3	10.5	45.4
Lower segment above	52.4	31.4	4.6	9.3	0.0	9.4	38.0
Upper segment above	57.6	29.7	5.1	7.5	0.0	6.9	40.2
Adult literacy							
None literate	58.2	31.4	5.7	13.2	1.4	8.5	34.4
Female literate	59.5	26.6	2.2	0.4	0.0	5.6	44.0
Male literate	57.7	24.7	5.4	8.5	0.0	13.0	42.3
Both literate	51.5	31.0	4.6	8.7	0.4	7.1	39.8
Village development							
Low	54.6	25.2	1.6	24.7	0.0	9.9	31.0
Medium	56.4	28.8	4.4	8.9	0.7	10.8	40.2
High	52.3	30.8	5.9	7.4	0.2	5.6	39.5
All groups	**54.5**	**29.4**	**4.9**	**9.1**	**0.5**	**8.7**	**39.5**

TABLE A8.21

Distribution of Ever Married Women Having Delivery in Previous Year by Population Group in Rural Punjab

Population group	EMW having delivery previous year	Post-natal care received	Attended by trained person	Place of delivery: Hospital	Place of delivery: CHC/PHC	Place of delivery: Home	EMW % Immunization
Household income							
Up to 20,000	15.1	30.8	67.0	11.1	7.5	81.3	70.6
20,001–40,000	14.6	40.0	79.0	11.3	5.6	83.1	81.1
40,001–62,000	15.0	53.1	68.8	25.7	0.9	73.4	76.3
62,001–86,000	12.0	22.5	70.9	22.5	13.3	64.2	90.6
Above 86,000	11.1	43.2	72.0	25.9	7.7	66.4	72.4
Landholding							
Landless wage earner	18.9	30.7	63.6	4.2	8.8	87.0	72.8
Marginal	13.1	43.4	88.1	16.6	0.0	83.4	76.0
Small	12.9	21.3	56.1	7.2	7.8	85.0	72.2
Medium	17.8	33.7	78.1	35.1	5.3	59.5	86.0
Large	10.9	57.7	62.5	21.9	11.1	67.0	68.8
Landless others	12.5	44.3	77.2	15.8	4.9	79.2	78.2
Land owners	13.7	37.2	72.1	21.0	5.7	73.3	76.9
Landless	15.0	37.6	70.5	10.1	6.8	83.1	75.6
Occupation							
Cultivators	14.3	41.4	72.7	22.0	5.3	72.7	79.7
Salaried+prof.+s.empl.	11.3	48.8	75.2	21.0	8.2	70.8	78.2
Wage earners	19.0	29.5	65.7	4.0	8.3	87.8	69.2
All others	12.2	26.8	73.7	9.5	3.0	87.5	76.9
Caste							
SCs	18.8	32.8	78.3	6.5	7.5	86.1	73.2
Religion							
Hindus	13.6	33.2	73.0	12.6	7.0	80.3	66.7
Other minorities	14.5	38.4	71.9	17.1	5.3	77.6	79.2
Household size							
Up to 4	11.5	15.7	68.3	6.8	19.3	73.9	77.9
5–7	12.4	40.4	73.4	10.4	3.9	85.7	75.5
8 and above	19.4	41.4	70.0	23.4	4.5	72.1	76.3
Poverty line							
Lower segment below	16.8	38.9	58.5	7.7	4.6	87.7	74.7
Upper segment below	18.9	32.7	68.1	14.5	5.0	80.5	68.9
Lower segment above	14.0	37.6	79.5	16.3	6.5	77.2	77.2
Upper segment above	10.0	41.0	66.5	23.6	9.4	66.9	82.9
Adult literacy							
None literate	17.2	18.0	70.0	7.6	7.6	84.8	65.1
Female literate	6.4	32.0	68.0	7.0	0.0	93.0	57.0
Male literate	14.9	28.1	70.7	12.7	8.4	78.9	70.7
Both literate	13.8	50.0	72.2	20.0	5.1	75.0	84.1
Village development							
Low	15.9	2.8	97.2	18.2	5.6	76.2	52.0
Middle	14.0	29.2	71.5	15.8	6.9	77.4	77.5
High	14.6	51.7	67.7	14.3	5.6	80.1	77.7
All groups	**14.3**	**37.4**	**71.3**	**15.3**	**6.3**	**78.5**	**76.2**

TABLE A8.22

Percentage of Children (aged 12–23 months) Immunized and Gender Disparity by Population Group in Rural Punjab

Population group	Percentage of children (12–23 months)				
	DPT 3 doses	Polio 3 doses	BCG 1 dose	Measles 1 dose	All 8 doses
Household income					
Up to 20,000					
Person	66.59	63.17	68.56	61.17	57.75
Gender disparity	0.71	0.71	0.78	0.74	0.79
20,001–40,000					
Person	76.25	73.37	82.01	70.41	64.65
Gender disparity	1.09	1.09	1.17	1.27	1.29
40,001–62,000					
Person	89.54	86.85	86.85	85.55	76.12
Gender disparity	1.21	1.13	1.28	1.16	1.25
62,001–86,000					
Person	68.63	64.33	64.33	64.33	60.03
Gender disparity	0.86	0.75	0.75	0.75	0.63
Above 86,000					
Person	71.47	71.47	62.22	59.54	50.30
Gender disparity	0.73	0.73	0.90	0.96	1.28
Landholding					
Landless wage earner					
Person	62.28	55.28	62.32	51.17	44.17
Gender disparity	0.66	0.65	0.79	0.75	0.85
Marginal					
Person	83.12	83.12	86.95	80.86	80.86
Gender disparity	1.24	1.24	1.15	1.20	1.20
Small					
Person	84.27	81.31	84.87	78.35	70.08
Gender disparity	0.75	0.67	0.99	0.71	0.71
Medium					
Person	85.39	85.39	85.39	75.88	75.88
Gender disparity	1.04	1.04	1.04	1.18	1.18
Large					
Person	54.64	54.64	50.19	51.98	40.79
Gender disparity	1.58	1.58	1.33	1.24	2.07
Landless others					
Person	76.09	73.93	79.21	76.09	70.81
Gender disparity	1.01	0.96	1.01	1.10	1.05
All land owners					
Person	78.55	77.68	78.72	73.07	68.46
Gender disparity	1.02	0.99	1.07	1.01	1.06
All land non-owners					
Person	68.72	63.98	70.20	62.79	56.59
Gender disparity	0.84	0.82	0.91	0.95	0.99
Occupation					
Agriculture					
Person	73.14	73.14	75.15	66.84	64.32
Gender disparity	0.93	0.93	0.94	0.92	0.98
Salaried+prof.+s.empl.					
Person	86.24	79.35	81.05	83.35	71.29
Gender disparity	1.00	0.82	1.12	1.07	0.98
Wage earners					
Person	64.04	57.37	64.08	53.45	46.77
Gender disparity	0.64	0.62	0.76	0.71	0.78
All others					
Person	79.49	79.49	84.36	81.92	77.05
Gender disparity	1.28	1.28	1.27	1.36	1.38
Caste					
SCs					
Person	67.26	67.26	80.76	61.08	56.62
Gender disparity	0.95	0.95	1.03	1.06	1.29
Religion					
Hindus					
Person	71.64	71.64	78.26	64.81	63.17
Gender disparity	1.01	1.01	1.10	1.06	1.23
Other minorities					
Person	74.06	71.35	73.04	68.43	62.70
Gender disparity	0.89	0.84	0.94	0.93	0.95
Household size					
Up to 4					
Person	64.03	59.29	70.96	53.78	49.04
Gender disparity	0.98	0.91	1.19	1.45	1.39
5–7					
Person	76.40	73.85	75.59	74.40	69.80
Gender disparity	0.96	0.95	1.07	0.88	0.96
8 and above					
Person	71.94	68.95	73.14	62.98	56.20
Gender disparity	0.85	0.81	0.82	1.04	1.06
Poverty line					
Lower segment below					
Person	58.40	55.03	64.23	51.64	46.35
Gender disparity	0.34	0.37	0.45	0.40	0.45
Upper segment below					
Person	68.14	63.58	68.14	59.48	54.91
Gender disparity	1.05	0.91	1.05	0.93	0.96
Lower segment above					
Person	79.52	77.07	80.34	74.31	68.99
Gender disparity	0.97	0.95	1.03	1.03	1.04
Upper segment above					
Person	78.05	75.52	73.50	74.99	67.91
Gender disparity	1.17	1.10	1.33	1.27	1.36
Adult literacy					
None literate					
Person	56.85	51.08	56.85	54.30	48.54
Gender disparity	0.77	0.76	0.77	0.68	0.77
Female literate					
Person	84.89	84.89	84.89	78.56	78.56
Gender disparity	1.06	1.06	1.06	1.17	1.17
Male literate					
Person	67.53	64.78	75.50	55.12	52.38
Gender disparity	0.78	0.75	0.89	0.99	0.95
Both literate					
Person	80.72	78.44	79.36	76.32	69.26
Gender disparity	1.01	0.99	1.09	1.08	1.14
Village development					
Low					
Person	95.07	85.21	95.07	90.14	80.28
Gender disparity	1.14	1.21	1.14	1.32	1.45
Medium					
Person	72.64	68.51	74.61	68.14	60.77
Gender disparity	1.02	0.98	1.11	1.02	1.08
High					
Person	72.21	72.21	70.98	63.94	62.71
Gender disparity	0.67	0.67	0.69	0.79	0.81
All groups					
Person	73.20	70.22	74.08	67.47	62.00
Gender disparity	0.91	0.88	0.97	0.96	1.00

(Contd.)

9 Village Level Study in Punjab: Baroohi and Buani

9.1 Introduction

This chapter is based on a qualitative study of two villages, Baroohi and Buani in Punjab, undertaken in the year 1994–5. The report presents a profile of the two districts, Hoshiarpur and Ludhiana, in which these villages are located and compares them with respect to education, health, and social security.

Village Baroohi is located in Hoshiarpur which is one of the most backward districts of Punjab; village Buani is located in Ludhiana, one of the most advanced districts of Punjab. Both villages are well connected with *pucca* or metalled roads to nearby towns and villages. Agriculture is the major occupation in these villages.

9.2 Baroohi Village

9.2.1 Location and Topography

Baroohi is located in Dasua *tehsil* of Hoshiarpur district. While the district headquarters are approximately 38 km away, the state capital of Chandigarh is 200 km away from the village. Its block development office lies within 20 km at Bhunga.

Well metalled roads connect this interior village via Manhata to the nearest town, Gardhiwala, which is 20 km away; while on the other side the road links up with Dholwaha, Haryana, and Hoshiarpur. Koe, the village commonly bracketed with Baroohi in this region as Koe–Baroohi, is 5 km away but is regularly visited by the villagers for their necessities. The nearest railway station is at Dasua. The frequency of the buses passing through the village is very poor.

The topography consists of forest-covered semi-hills, as also of numerous *nalas* that overflow the area. Prominent among the forest trees are the khartoum, sheesham, kikar, symbal, *jamun*, *amb*, *tun*, *coumble*, *rajain*, *dek*, and *keenu*. The common bushes of this area are the *garna*, *moloh*, *kangu*, *mandar*, *bagar* (*ban*), and *khatkane*.

The climate of the district is typical of the plains of north India. The summer months, from April to June, experience a maximum temperature of 38^{0}C while the winters from December to February are cold. Heavy rainfall in the monsoon months of July and August gives rise to a proliferation of seasonal nalas that disrupt daily life by flowing over the roads. As they are difficult to cross, the village remains cut off during this season.

The Soil Conservation Department has set up small-stoned check dams to control the soil erosion that inevitably follows in the wake of overflowing nalas. It has also undertaken non-profitable cultivation of sandy soil for this reason. Similarly, Thusi, a bigger dam with a length of about 35 km, protects the lower part of the village against soil erosion. It collects the water of all the nalas and diverts the overflow into river Beas. This serves two simultaneous objectives, one for providing irrigation facility for an 80-acre area and the other, for filling a pond for the use of cattle. Generally, the availability of water is inadequate in months other than the rainy season. At such times there is no water logging in the streets or within houses as almost all the streets here are pucca.

9.2.2 Land and Common Property Areas

The total geographical area of this village is 1285 acres. Of this 591 acres consist of individual cultivable land, approximately 200 acres is forest land, and about 460 acres is panchayat land.

This area may further be divided into 317 acres of hills and 145 acres under nalas. The Government of Punjab owns 197 acres of the village land while the Central Government owns 30 acres.

There are 225 heads of households owning land. This implies that in some families the land has been split without the family being separated. At the time of consolidation in 1971–2, the landholding genealogies were 31 with the following break up: 16 bahti, six brahmin, four rajput, three SC, one carpenter, and one jat. The brahmin and rajput households have shifted out of the village by selling their land. However, the same number of families of small businessmen have settled down in this village from outside. At the time of partition, 32 families migrated to Pakistan while only two or three families from Pakistan settled in the village. The geographic inhabited area of the village is growing, as many families have shifted near their farms in the last two or three decades.

Forest Area

Depletion of the common property forest area had been occurring for the last eight years. To reduce this environmental threat, the World Bank has put in place a multi-million scheme of plantation in the Kandi area. For about five years the whole area under forest was replanted and a strict vigil was kept by the Forest Department. Intrusions by cattle or by firewood collectors were strictly watched and the forest area was reclaimed during this period. The World Bank scheme further provided a maximum of employment to men, women, and children in these years. However, the scheme has become the focus of discontent as the cutting of trees was completely banned under panel code 4 and 5 without the permission of the Forest Department. This has resulted in tree felling in an underhand manner or by theft. The villagers would like to see the ban lifted, especially that on the felling of individual trees.

PANCHAYAT LAND

The second common property in this village is the land under the Panchayat. This land is leased out to one contractor every year who collects one-third as leased-out revenue produce from the individual farmers to whom this land has been further leased out.

ENCROACHMENT

Cultivators in Baroohi have occupied almost half of the Panchayat land illegally. They have also encroached upon the 30 acre of Central Government land which could not be auctioned because of a legal hurdle. Similarly, the Forest Department plantation under the World Bank scheme has been forcibly occupied with alleged official connivance. Other land belonging to the school, kabra (mohammedan cremation place), or shamlat (community land) has also been encroached by the villagers.

9.2.3 Population

According to the 1991 Census, the population growth rate of Hoshiarpur district was the lowest at 14.84 per cent with the highest sex ratio (946), and the highest percentage of Hindu population (59.43) in Baroohi. The castewise distribution of households in Baroohi is given in Table 9.1.

TABLE 9.1
Castewise Distribution of Households, Baroohi

Caste	Number
Bahti (agriculturist low caste)	114
Adharmi (SC)	31
Mistri	10
Rajput	7
Brahmin	3
Doomeney	2
Total	**167**

The above number is arrived at through mapping. The village school teachers in their survey of eligible children last year reported the total number of households as 167 with a population break-up of 401 males and 405 females. The total number of ration cards in the village is 168 while the population with respect to ration card consumer units is 1000. Another population count is provided by the United Nations Development Programme (UNDP) listing in 1993 which gives a figure of 160 households consisting of 828 persons. There are six Sikh families while some SCs also follow the Sikh traditions. About 32 Muslim families left for Pakistan in 1947. At present there are no Muslim or Christian families or any conversions in the village. The Hindus and Sikhs have a common culture and they celebrate each others' festivals.

BACKWARD AND SCHEDULED CASTES

There is no dominant caste in the village. The bahti, a backward caste is, however, the major caste in the village followed by the SCs. The Bahtis have some marginal agricultural land but are more backward than the SCs who are engaged in rope making (*ban*).

The SCs live in a separate hamlet, which is surrounded by forest on all sides. Proximity to the forest exposes their homes to the occasional forest fire, which burns their houses as well. As they are located at a distance from the road across a nala, they are isolated from the main village during the rains. For those who have set up houses near their fields the distance from the road and from sources of water and electricity poses a problem. Other caste houses are better located.

9.2.4 General Environment

Only 10 per cent of the village houses—that invariably belong to the service classes from all castes—have pucca walls, floor, and roof. Other houses are *kutcha* with a thatched roof (with congress grass). Both the kutcha and pucca houses have a similar pattern of two rooms, one kitchen, and a verandah facing an open courtyard. The cattle sheds are generally separate but a few houses use one of their living rooms as a cattle shed. A frequent sight is that of a badly damaged wall covered by a bushy fencing as the household cannot afford to raise it again. Grain and flour storage may alternate between mud and metallic drums or caved kilter plastered with mud inside. No one has a smokeless *chulla* and there is no gobar gas plant. Only two or three per cent houses are double storeyed.

The residents of the village are mainly Hindus though there are a few Sikh families as well. A profusion of temples testifies to the religious bent of mind of the inhabitants. Dotted on the landscape are various temples to Puranic deities and other saints such as: Shiva, Baba Balak Nath, Lakh Nath, Nau Gaja, Panch Peer, Baba Deet Singh, Sidh Charno, and Naga temple. Small temples also exist within a few houses. The SCs and backward castes worship the Panch Peers in temples that other castes do not visit. The language written and spoken in the village is Punjabi which, however, takes on a Himachali or Hindi accent as this district is adjacent to Himachal Pradesh.

9.2.5 Occupation

AGRICULTURE

Agriculture is the main occupation of the villagers. Almost all villagers except the SCs own some land. In the peak season, all the family members work in the fields. Though males constitute the main workers; during the lean agriculture period, the males take up wage labour while females and children work in their own fields. The landholding is small, so agricultural wage labour is negligible in the village. The villagers go out or else work in the village for the plantation in the forest and cutting trees. For such paid work also, generally the males go out but within the village some females also accompany the males. Children do not undertake paid labour.

The SCs mostly work in their own houses and make ban (Ropes). Most of them have small machinery for this. Both males and females work equally and children also help them. The living standard of SCs is better than that of the dominant caste households. A few men are engaged in service, and only two anganwadi workers are females. A few men are involved in *tokra* making, managing petty shops, etc. Almost all the males except SCs and brahmins, look for work outside the village and go wherever they get it.

CHILD LABOUR

Almost all children belonging to all castes help to supplement the family income, though there is no paid child labour except in the case of one SC child who is studying as well as working while staying with another family. After school hours, children are engaged in collecting firewood, leaves of medicinal importance, cattle grazing and sometimes agricultural operations during the peak period. At the age of 8–9 years both boys and girls start helping with such activities.

MIGRATION

A few brahmins and rajputs have moved out of the village as they found employment elsewhere. Despite occasional crop failures the villagers in general did not move out. There is no seasonal migration as the villagers do not migrate even if they do not get full employment for many months. By and large, the villagers find wage labour up to at least a sustainable level and are apprehensive of going out to distant places in search of gainful labour. Four families have leased in land in the nearby village and are engaged in cultivation while staying there temporarily for the last two or three years. They also own small pieces of land in this village. There is a known and constant influx of wage labour from outside into Punjab. But in the Kandi area this in-migration is completely missing. Even in the peak agricultural season there is no requirement of paid wage labour. As there is no such pressure, the effect on the wage rate is not much. The contractors do bargain the rates for cutting the trees, and the wage rates vary a little depending upon the distance from the village. Usually, tree cutting is carried out in the lean period.

For non-agricultural labour, the various departments of forest, irrigation and public health, PWD, etc. pay the rates fixed by the government or on the basis of job specification. The Panchayat also pays on the basis of job specification. Private contractors generally hire only males, but female labour when hired is paid a little lesser than the males.

There are about 25 males who have passed the matriculation exams, and except for three or four of them no one found employment. About half of the others have started working in their own fields and as wage labour, etc. The rest are idle and are vocal about their disappointment over educating the youngsters. Their problems are highlighted in the focus group discussion (FGD) held separately for them. No one from this village has ever held a job of any significant status. One person got an officer's rank in the army, but he never visited this village thereafter.

ANIMAL HUSBANDRY

Almost all the households have cattle. Mostly they keep *desi* buffaloes, while a few own desi cows and goats. About half of the landholding households keep bullocks, and others get the land ploughed by hired tractors. The tractors are hired from a nearby village as there is no tractor in this village.

The milk production is so meagre that no organized milk selling exists. The milk is sold to neighbours but even this is not common. Only in the lean months do the villagers make arrangements of sharing milk with each other. No one collects even a litre of milk for commercial purposes. The rate of milk in the internal exchange is around Rs 7 per litre.

For artificial insemination, the buffaloes are taken to a hospital in the nearby village. The villagers leave out common bulls (he buffalo, he bull, and he goat). The hospital staff rarely come to the village for cattle immunization and the villagers rarely bother to go to the hospital to get the cattle immunized.

GOVERNMENT/NGO SCHEMES

While there is no non-governmental organization (NGO) working in this village, various government schemes such as PDS, afforestation, arranging drinking and irrigation water, soil erosion control by putting check walls to control the path of nalas, construction of pucca streets under the Punjab Government's grant, Jawahar Rozgar Yojana (JRY), and ICDS are available in this village. Schemes such as the IRDP, Universal Immunization Programme (UIP), family welfare, and non-formal education are either unsuccessful or are just non-starters.

The PDS started last year from within the village and it distributes controlled items such as sugar, kerosene, and rice. Sugar is distributed in quantities varying from 350 gm to 385 gm per member, rice in amounts of 500 gm per member, and 5 litres of kerosene per ration card every month. Non-controlled items like pulses, soaps, and detergent powders are also sold occasionally. The owner of the PDS shop stated that he gets four to five kg less sugar in each bag from the distribution point, whereas he cannot give even 10 gm less to the public. So his profit, whatever it is, goes in this adjustment of sugar. The consumers, of course, complained about the quality and quantity of sugar.

Under the World Bank afforestation scheme, wage labour was abundant for the last five years. This scheme has at present been stopped. The strict vigilance of the forest department, which is a fallout of this scheme, has made the villagers unhappy as they find it a problem to obtain firewood as well as to graze their cattle.

Drinking water was made available to this village in 1985. Last year—with a small check wall on a perennial nala and with connected pipes—a minor irrigation facility was arranged for about 80 acres of land along with provision for filling a pond for cattle.

Check walls were erected last year along the path of the main nala so as to minimize soil erosion from the sides of the nala. Though an engineer might have assigned the various locations of the check walls, the village leaders were critical of these locations as they were not consulted. In the last five years, the Punjab Government has given grants worth Rs 4.50 lakhs for the construction of pucca streets (Table 9.2).

TABLE 9.2
Grants for Construction of Pucca Roads, Baroohi

Year	Grant (Rs)	JRY amount (Rs)
1989–90	36,375	7200
1990–1	–	4530
1991–2	21,875	1100
1992–3	171,875	5920
1993–4	145,500	7040
1994–5	74,250	3400
Total	**449,875**	**29,190**

Most of the streets that are constructed are pucca and work on the remaining streets is continuing. The JRY is another government-sponsored scheme, under which the village received Rs 29,190 between 1989 and 1995. The yearwise break up is given in Table 9.2. This money was spent on repairing the school building, repair and maintenance of wells and ponds, and minor work on the roads/streets.

Under the IRDP, loans were cleared for only a few cases, but since the last two to three years people have not sought these or even if they try they do not get the required sanction. They complained that a huge bribe is demanded to pass such loans. Therefore, interest in this scheme was low.

The Expanded Programme of Immunization (EPI) and family welfare schemes are also not very successful here. No one from the health department visits the village. Only the unlicensed private practitioners are frightened by the health department and in turn they persuade people to go in for family planning. If the villagers go to the Koe health centre, for EPI, either the staff or the drugs stock is not available. When they approach the district hospital, they are turned away on the ground that for EPI the villagers should approach Koe village only. Mostly the villagers get immunization done privately. Non-formal education, which was started with great enthusiasm, turned out to be a non-starter in this village. The administration did a perfect job of mapping and locating the uneducated in the age group of 15 to 45. They found about 75 such people in this village. Many small groups, separated into males and females, were formed. The educated youth were motivated to teach these groups. The study material was distributed, but when the rural rapid appraisal (RRA) team was in the village, it found very few people coming in one or two groups. About 10–12 persons could learn a bit, while the others have almost left. Many programmes are on at the district, tehsil, and block level and could create a wave for non-formal education, but there is no village-level motivation.

9.2.6 *Infrastructural Facilities*

TABLE 9.3
Amenities and Services, Baroohi

Amenities	Place	Distance (km)
Approach road	Up to village	0
Bus stop	In village	0
Railway station	Dasua	38
Post office	Koe	4
Community television	No	NA
Community radio	No	NA
Library reading room	No	NA
Electric street light	No	NA
Bank	Manhota	5
Co-operative credit society	No	–
Regulated market/mandi	Gardhiwala	18
Pharmacy/drug outlet	Gardhiwala	18
Sources of drinking water for both SC and others	(a) Dug well	NA
	(b) Piped water	NA
	(c) Baurrie	NA
	(d) Hand Pump	NA

Note: NA—Not available.

TABLE 9.4
Time Line, Baroohi

Mandis	Before 1950
Shops	Before 1950
Radio	1960
School	1965
Hand pump*	1975
Electricity@	1976
Piped water	1985
Metalled road	1985
Television	1986
Private bus	1987
Anganwadi	1987
Refrigerator, scooter	1989
Private doctor	1990
PDS#	1994

Notes: * In the school, not for public use; @ Harijan hamlet got electricity in 1995 and a portion of the village with about 30 houses still has no electric line; # PDS started in 1992 but had to be stopped due to the complaints from the consumers within a year.

SHOPS

In this village there are three shops which sell miscellaneous items. These are very small shops and keep grocery and other items of day-to-day needs. Two shops are run by a couple of retired people on a part-time basis and a third functions full time. The per day sale of each of these shops is about Rs 200 to Rs 300. Since the last one year, a balmiki from outside has opened a leather shop. He collects the skin of dead animals in the village by paying Rs 50 to Rs 150 to the owner for each animal.

CO-OPERATIVE CREDIT SOCIETIES

There is no co-operative credit society in the village. A multi-purpose co-operative society was established many years back, but stopped functioning after a few years. The villagers are unable to harmonize with each other and do not allow any scheme to function without interference.

DRINKING WATER

There are four sources of drinking water in the village, namely: dug wells, taps (piped water), hand pumps, and *baurrie*. The SC hamlet has a dug well. The second hamlet has dug wells and hand pumps. The third portion of the village has piped water, which is in short supply. A single water works station supplies water to eight villages. In this village there are eight water taps and there are regular fights for water. A few SC households are also using these taps. They complained that they are harassed on caste grounds. They are allowed to take water only after the others. The more outspoken women take advantage at the cost of others.

In peak summer, the problem of drinking water becomes even more acute with an increase in consumption requirements and a decrease in availability. Then these households have to collect water from a baurrie, which is 1–2 km away. The pond or nala water is used mostly for the cattle, and clothes are also washed in its streams. Personal hygiene is also affected by the shortage of water. Not only in the winters, but even in summers people cannot bathe daily and they wash clothes only after 3–7 days.

ANGANWADI

An anganwadi has been functioning in the Panchayat house for the last four years with one female worker and one female attendant. On an average, around 20 children come here daily. These children are collected by the attendant mainly from the upper part of the village. Women of the lower part, where the anganwadi exists do not send their children here. They complain that the workers do not care for the children and do not give nutrients properly. The SC hamlet is far off and they demand that the attendant should collect their children, but in the absence of this arrangement they do not send their children. The anganwadi does not get a regular supply of milk powder or other supplements. The toddlers at the anganwadi are very disciplined and recited poems heading the group in turn. There are three untrained dais in this village. Almost all the deliveries are handled by them using traditional methods. The cord is cut by scissors or any other tool available in the household. A sitting posture is usually adopted in case of a delivery which takes longer time.

9.2.7 Education

The government primary school at Baroohi has been in existence for the last 20 years. The government high school, however, is located at Koe where children go after completing primary school. There is no transport available so the students walk to school. The senior secondary school and college are at Gardhiwal (approximately 18 km away). The concept of private schooling is not known in this village as yet.

PRIMARY SCHOOL

Three teaching posts have been sanctioned for this school but for the last one year only two teachers are in service. According to these teachers, the school's total requirement is for five teachers. Both the teachers are matriculates with Junior Basic Training (JBT) and have teaching experiences of 32 and 20 years, respectively. The location of the school is along the roadside and in the upper part of the village. The primary school has a spacious lawn with a roadside boundary wall. This lawn is used mostly for holding classes except in the rainy season. The school has two spacious and pucca rooms constructed by the government in 1986. Due to leakage, the condition of these rooms is so bad that in the rainy season, when these rooms are required, they cannot be used. There are three other smaller rooms which are pucca but have thatched roofs. These were constructed by the Panchayat in 1991, as the school was earlier functioning in kutcha rooms. There is no electricity and its need is also not felt. In the rooms there are blackboards, but there are no portable blackboards for the classes held outside. There is a hand pump in the school since the last 20 years. This was the first hand pump in this village. There is one open air pucca stage in the lawns.

Two years ago the school was supplied with 35 mats, out of which only three are in usable condition now. The quality of the mats supplied was so bad that when the stock was reopened after the vacation, the mats were found tattered into bits and pieces. Bad quality mats were supplied to not only this school but all the schools of the block. Nobody dared to complain as they feared a transfer to further remote areas without achieving any positive results. Mostly, the children were found sitting on the ground—some on mats and the others on their wooden *fattas*. There were sufficient tables and chairs for the teachers. The number of students enrolled in September 1994 is as shown in Table 9.5.

Between September 1994 and February 1995, five students from Class I dropped out and one student from Class III shifted out from the school.

Children were admitted in Class I at a very grown up age which could be as old as 13 years of age. The teachers say that they continuously persuaded the parents to get these

TABLE 9.5

No. of Students Enrolled in Primary School, Baroohi

Class	All			SC			Backward		
	Total	M	F	Total	M	F	Total	M	F
I	33	19	14	9	6	3	22	12	10
II	28	11	17	6	4	2	21	7	14
III	26	14	12	5	2	3	20	11	9
IV	26	13	13	4	2	2	22	11	11
V	21	9	12	3	0	3	15	8	7
Total	**134**	**66**	**68**	**27**	**14**	**13**	**100**	**49**	**51**

grown up children admitted. The parents narrate a different story. They say that the teachers do not admit the children at an early age. However, the children of influential people get admitted at an early age. The teachers do not admit children in large numbers as the strength of the teachers is less and they cannot handle too many children. The teacher student ratio is 2:134 in five classes. The teachers agreed that it is very difficult for them to handle very young children in such large numbers. The second reason for their refusal to admit is that some parents bring their children after October when half of the syllabus has been covered and teachers cannot make up for the time lost.

There are problems of non-enrolment, late enrolment, and drop-outs. The problem of non-enrolment exists because parents cannot afford the cost or they argue that the benefits of education are not substantial. Late enrolment occurs becuase parents take the help of their children to take care of their siblings. This is also the reason for some of the drop-outs. The other reason for drop-outs is attitude of the parents towards education. The village population estimates, and a list of eligible students is prepared every year (Tables 9.6 and 9.7).

9.2.8 Social Issues—Customs and Practices

Being located in the interior the village is less exposed to outside influences. The villagers do not go to far off places nor do people from outside visit this village. Social links such as marriage are also within the district or are alliances with people in the adjoining districts of Ropar, Jallandhar, and Gurdaspur in Punjab and Hamirpur in Himachal Pradesh. Most marriage alliances are with nearby villages. Inter-caste marriages are not prevalent, though some inter-religious (between Hindus and Sikhs) marriages can be seen. Both brother and sister can be married in the same village. There are some cases of exchange marriages also, for example, the brother marrying his sister's sister-in-law. In one household, an old

TABLE 9.6

Eligibility List Prepared by Teachers, Baroohi

Year	Population			Eligibility 6–7 years			Admitted 6–7 years		
	M	F	T	M	F	T	M	F	T
1991–2	405	376	781	11	12	23	11	12	13
1992–3	397	400	797	10	11	21	10	11	21
1993–4	402	401	803	9	15	24	9	15	24
1994–5	386	383	869	11	12	23	11	12	23
1995–6	401	405	806	11	7	18	*	*	*

Note: * To be admitted in April 1995.

TABLE 9.7

List of Drop-outs, Baroohi

Year	Class										Re-admitted
	I		II		III		IV		V		
	M	F	M	F	M	F	M	F	M	F	
1991–2	4	1	–	–	1*	0	–	–	–	–	All
1992–3	5	2	–	–	–	–	3@	1#	–	–	All
1993–4	2	3	–	–	–	–	–	–	–	–	All
1994–5	3	2	–	–	–	–	–	–	–	–	To be admitted last year

Notes: * Uninterested, used to sit by the way to school; @ (a) Weak in education (b) Bad home environment # Girl was ill with chicken pox.

lady married three of her sons and daughter in her parental village. Child marriages are not prevalent. The marriageable age for males and females is about 22–6 and 18–24, respectively. Usually, the marriage party consists of 30 to 40 males, though recently, some females have also started accompanying the males. The villagers serve food to the community one day before the marriage ceremony. The expenses incurred for marrying either a boy or a girl vary from Rs 6000 to Rs 60,000. Among the general caste the highest expense is around Rs 100,000. The highest expense for SCs is around Rs 25,000. There has been no dowry problem recently.

The village has never witnessed any caste or religious conflict. At the height of extremist activities, some outside miscreants tried to create disturbance within the village. In one instance outsiders came and wanted to construct a Gurudwara, but the local people did not like the outsiders and succeeded in getting rid of them. In another incident, a few nihangs ran away with the village he-goats. The villagers followed and intercepted them at a nearby village. An armed fight was averted when the nihangs, feeling insecure being less in number, left the goats and ran away. The SCs are settled in a separate cluster, though there are a few SCs who recently settled along with other castes. There were conflicts for fetching water from the taps due to the shortage of water supply. The SC women allege that they are discriminated against by the upper caste women. But it is apparent that 'might is right' at the taps. The weaker women of the other castes also suffer.

At the time of birth of a male child, sweets and drinks are served, and a loudspeaker is installed in the house. Some people organize a ceremony called *Chhati*, when they call their relatives and friends. The pandits perform *poojas*. The SCs have no culture of poojas.

After a death in any family, the relatives and friends console the bereaved for about ten days and then a death ceremony (*Kirya Karam*) is performed. For the SCs, the granthis from the gurudwara, and for other castes, the pandit performs these ceremonies. No other ceremony such as *Janew*, *Minarche*, etc. is performed.

Purdah (*ghungat*) is still observed, but the women in purdah can talk to anyone. Except for brahmins, all castes go in for widow remarriage. There is no case of dowry death, suicide or deaths due to other unnatural causes. There are a few cases of women dying at the time of delivery or after a few days due to delivery-related problems (maternal mortality). Some women are known to have died due to abortion performed by quacks.

Sex between unmarried children is not common, but a few cases have been reported. There is no case of polygamy or polyandry. Though the preference for a male child is strong, female child negligence or infanticide does not exist. No one knows about the pregnancy test for sex determination.

The culture of the joint family is changing with more and more sons setting up their families separately after marriage. Due to this two-thirds of the families are nuclear.

There is no shortage of firewood, therefore, smokeless chulas and gobar gas have not been introduced in this village. One family was observed using an LPG stove.

The men wear kurta pyjamas as a rule, with the exception of some young people who wear pants and shirts. The women wear *salwar-kameej* and *dupatta*. Girls wear frocks up to 7–8 years of age and then start wearing salwaar-kameej.

FOOD AND LIQUOR CONSUMPTION

All castes except the brahmins are non-vegetarian, though non-vegetarian food is cooked rarely. People consume three meals a day. No family sells milk. Whatever little milk is produced from desi cattle is not sufficient even for own consumption. All the villagers get an adequate supply of grains but fruits, vegetables, and pulses are eaten in quantities that are much less than these required. Almost all the males smoke. Most of them drink liquor casually, but one-fourth of them have a regular drinking habit. There are 2–3 instances of males selling their property for drinks. Females do not drink or smoke. No family has a toilet in their house. The nalas or the jungle are used as a substitute for toilets.

FAIRS AND FESTIVALS

Deepawali

A large number of festivals and fairs are celebrated in this village. The most important of these being the Hindu Deepawali. All other castes and communities celebrate Deepawali. They usually light oil lamps in their houses and at other important places. Children celebrate by burning crackers. There is no community get-together. The villagers associate Deepawali with Lord Rama, though in Sikh history this festival is also associated with a Sikh Guru's release from prison.

Dussehra

All communities celebrate this festival. The effigies of Ravana, etc. are burnt in a nearby village, where a fair is organized every year. The villagers celebrate this festival in the Hindu tradition.

Lohri

This is also another traditional Hindu festival celebrated by all castes. Families with newly-weds or a new-born male child during the last year, celebrate this festival with more festivity.

Baishakhi

This festival is associated with the harvesting of wheat and other *rabi* crops. This day is considered an auspicious start to harvesting the crop. All farmers initiate the harvesting and gather at the temple to thank the deity. People attend fairs in the nearby villages. For the Sikhs, this day is of special importance as on this day the Sikh religion was founded.

Rakshabandhan

This Hindu festival of tying a thread on the brother's wrist is also celebrated individually by all castes. The brothers in return gift some item or money to the sister.

Holi
The festival of colours is not celebrated with much vigour in this village. Only young children play with colours. Women and men generally do not play, but people are generally in a festive mood and some young men drink. Other festivals of Muslims and Sikhs are not celebrated by any community, though some Sikh auspicious days are celebrated by individuals.

POLITICAL CONSCIOUSNESS

The villagers are strongly anti-establishment as they feel that any government that comes to power does not bother about their area. Neither senior officials, nor village-level workers such as the patwari, or the Panchayat secretary visit the village. Other functionaries like the gram sewak, who serves about 35 Panchayats, and the multiple health worker (MHW) have also neglected this area. Except at the time of elections, no leader visits this place. Even for canvassing, the contestants send their supporters. There is no political leader from this village and the people do not strongly favour any particular political party.

BLOCK DEVELOPMENT OFFICIALS/PANCHAYAT SECRETARY

Panchayat Secretary
The Panchayat secretary of this village has 22 Panchayats under him. The work load can be estimated from this. He visits this village on the 14th and 29th of every month for about two hours each day. He writes all Panchayat resolutions and income expenditure during this stay along with attending to any matter discussed by the villagers. Though his headquarters are at Koe, he cannot be located there. Apart from visiting 22 Panchayats, many days are spent in meetings at the block office, ministerial duty, etc.

Gram sewak
That there is one gram sewak present in this village was denied by everybody at the Panchayat meeting as nobody had seen him, or heard about him. The Panchayat secretary, however, maintained that the gram sewak had 35 Panchayats under his charge so he may not have found time to visit this village. When this grievance was brought to the notice of the DC Hoshiarpur, namely that the village-level Government functionaries were not available for the villagers, the DC stated that they had other work. The above officials who are supposed to be living with the villagers are useless for the village needs if they are not available.

The patwari is the other village-level worker under the tehsil. He has two Gram Panchayats in his charge, Koe and Baroohi. His head office is not located in any of these villages, but at Gardhiwala.

The forest guard is the only government official who stays in this village. The villagers aired a lot of resentment against the forest department, which does not allow anyone to cut wood, and if someone is found doing so, heavy bribes are charged to avoid official action.

9.2.9 Summary of Focus Group Discussions

Four FGDs were held to ascertain the status of developments in the areas of education, health and social security. The details of the participants in these focus groups are as follows.

CURRENTLY MARRIED YOUNG MALES

Six of the participants had more than primary level of education, one SC was illiterate while another had passed the fourth standard. The participants belonged to the SC (4) and backward caste (4). Three of them had marginal land. Five of them came from nuclear families. The occupations of the participants were rope making (2), wage labour with or without cattle care and cultivation (4), self-employed in shop (1) and flour mill owner (1). The wives of all the participants were involved in household work, with two of them sharing the burden of cattle care also. The wife of one of the participants had died 15 days prior to the discussion due to an abortion which was poorly handled by the so-called doctors operating in the village. The number of children ranged from one to four. Out of 25 live births reported by the participants, all were alive.

MARRIED WOMEN WITH CHILDREN LESS THAN 5 YEARS AS WELL AS SCHOOL-GOING CHILDREN FROM THE UPPER PART OF THE VILLAGE

The participants were SCs (4) and other (6), all in the age group 22–30 years. Their education and qualification were as follows: illiterate (2), literate (3), and above primary school level (5). Only four of them had a small piece of cultivable land. Four of them belonged to a joint family. The occupation of all the participants were cattle care and household work; three of them were also helping in cultivation. The number of live births to these participants varied from one to five. Out of the 33 live births to these women, all were alive.

MARRIED WOMEN WITH CHILDREN LESS THAN FIVE YEARS AS WELL AS SCHOOL-GOING CHILDREN

The participants in this group were backward caste (8) and SC (3) residing in the lower part of the village. The age group was 25–35 years. Four of them were educated up to the primary level or above and others were illiterate. None of them owned land in their own or in their spouse's name and nine had nuclear families. Almost all the women worked in the household and also looked after the cattle. Their spouses were involved in: wage labour (7), service (2), retired (1), and unemployed (1). The number of live births and living children varied from 0 to 6; out of 40 live births to these participants only one female died. The woman whose daughter died was 25 years old and had no other issue. The rest had at least one male child. Except one woman, all the others had at least one female child also.

ELDERLY WOMEN AGED 60 YEARS AND ABOVE

In this FGD for elderly women the age of the elderly participants was between 60 and 90 years, and they belonged to SC (4), and backward caste (10). All of them were illiterate, and nine were widows. The number of living children were between four and seven. All women had living male as well as female children, except one who did not have a daughter. But half of them were not staying with their children or daughters-in-law. Seven of them were engaged in cattle care, with or without household work, five were doing only household work, and two were unable to do any work because of extreme old age and disability. None of them reported having weak eyesight. Other diseases found were: paralysis (1), arm–leg pain (4), breathing problem (1), and only one of them did not have any problem.

EDUCATION

A Government Primary School has been functioning in the village since 1967. To attend high school, the students have to go to Koe (5 km away) on foot. In the rainy season, schooling is a problem because of the nalas which overflow on the roads. Education beyond high school is difficult because of long distances and lack of proper transport facilities.

The response from all three groups was in favour of the benefits of education. They believed that education enables one to keep proper accounts, improves the status of the family, empowers one to earn better from labour and work, improves marriage prospects for both boys and girls, and helps in bringing up the next generation in a better way.

All women felt that educated people would get better employment and would provide old age support to their parents. One of the women reported that the educated will also be able to cultivate their fields better.

The SC men and women thought that educated people could travel easily, perform better in self-employment, read and write letters and newspapers and would in general, be more intelligent and smart.

The upper caste male added that an educated person could fight for his rights better, could decide his priorities, could keep pace with the changing world, and could interact better with the officials.

Four of them felt that if an educated person does not get a job, he may not take interest in wage labour, and instead do small jobs at the household level. The others did not support these disadvantages. All the participants reported financial constraint as a major reason for dropping out as parents could not always arrange for books, uniforms, etc. when required. The second common reason was the child being weak in studies. One of the educated participants in the women's group pointed out that parents often send their children to graze cattle in their school-going years. After some time the child starts enjoying the freedom of grazing and does not get time and also loses interest in studies. Parents say the child's brain could not absorb studies.

The men's group listed the reasons for drop-out as illiteracy of parents, baby sitting (due to small gaps between siblings), distance to school, too few children so that the pretext of age and teacher's beating is given for dropping out. It was found out from records and from discussions with the teachers that about 10 to 15 per cent children in Class I drop out due to the discouragement of their teachers and are re-admitted in the following year.

A few women listed watching television and quarrels with other children as the reasons for dropping out. One of the women felt that it is a tense experience to send the child to school in addition to which the child would not help with the household chores. Grown up girls are not sent out of the village for high school education. Barring a few intelligent students, others could be forced by parents to withdraw from school. There are no caste conflicts in the schools. Children are admitted in the Class I as late as eleven years of age. Primary school admission is a problem due to the small number of teachers available. There is no problem of non-enrolment.

All the participants reported that parents generally do not disturb the children during their studies and motivate them to do homework given by the teachers. Although, a separate study space is generally not available in the houses, the students find their own suitable place. The students are involved in only small jobs such as buying pulses, serving drinking water, etc. Boys start doing some household work at the age of 12 to 15 years, while girls start as early as 8 to 9 years.

The drop-outs from the school occur only after primary school. After dropping out the boys roam around idly. The girls started some household work such as cattle care, cooking, cleaning, stitching, etc. The reasons for absenteeism of students were problems in the family, attending a marriage or other functions, etc. On these occasions generally, the elder child or the person who could attend the house better was asked to manage the house. There was no gender bias. Incomplete homework was also a reason for being absent.

All participants expressed as basic needs: a proper sitting arrangement, first aid box, repair of buildings, supply of fans, etc. A few knew that SC children could get free books, scholarships, etc. but there was no awareness of a mid-day meal scheme.

The anganwadi has been working since 1987 in the lower part of the village. The anganwadi worker collects children from one side of the village only and the SCs feel neglected. No one was aware that aid to pregnant and nursing mothers was to be supplied by the anganwadi. The anganwadi worker reported receiving foodgrains but she said no one came to collect these. Only a few children were collected daily, but on days when some official came for a visit, a larger number of children were collected. Most of the time the main worker remains absent as she is married outside the village.

HEALTH

Only one unqualified private practitioner is available in the village. He started practising in this village and has done so for the last five years. He keeps both Ayurvedic and Allopathic medicines. He has kept a BP checking apparatus and a stethoscope. Sometimes he prescribes costly medicines, which are usually neglected by the patients. He belongs to village Koe which is about 4 km from here. About 8 to 10 patients are attended by him daily, although the number varies from 5 to 15. Patients from a nearby villages also come to him. The type of diseases attended to by him are cold, cough, diarrhoea, indigestion, stomach ache, pneumonia, malaria, worms, typhoid, joint pain, low BP, eye flu, etc. However, other illnesses such as leucorrhoea, backache, and asthma; minor accidents, and snake bites, etc. are also treated. He refers the cases that need specialised care to senior doctors in Hoshiarpur. Patients generally come after a period of 4 to 5 days of illness, after trying home remedies, and once they recover a bit they stop the medication. In an emergency, patients from his village call him at night. His total earning is reported to be around Rs 5000, out of which half the payment is on credit. Medicines are purchased by him twice a month.

The dispensary at Koe has one doctor, a nurse and a multiple health worker (MHW). These health workers and the required drugs are however, not available most of the times. The only public health facility is the PHC at Gardhiwal or the district hospital at Hoshiarpur for preventive and curative purposes.

There are no flush toilets in any of the households. Everybody goes around the nalas for defecation and afterwards they wash their hands with ash or mud, using soap only rarely. There are no proper bathrooms which provide privacy. Women take a bath in a temporary shed made with cots, etc. Their personal hygiene also suffers due to shortage of water. In areas where water is freely available in summers, people take a bath daily or on alternate days. In winters, bathing after 3 to 6 days is common. Clothes are changed as and when they look dirty or start smelling.

Sources of drinking water are hand pump, well, tap water, and baurrie. At different locations, different sources of water are available. The SCs take well water. The upper part of the village had the advantage of a hand pump, well and baurrie, but the lower part only had tap water and a baurrie was used when tap water was not available. It was believed that the quality of water from all sources is good. Boiled water is consumed only during illness on the advice of the doctor.

The causes of illness reported were eating previous day's left over food, weakness, excess work, lack of cleanliness in the house, poor personal hygiene, and mental tension. One of the women remarked that fear of their husbands' anger creates tension and leads to illness. Some believed that fate, supernatural power, misdeeds of the last birth, evil eye, and evil spirit were the causes of illness.

A seasonal effect on disease was also reported by most, with a higher prevalence in the rainy season. The common diseases reported were cold, cough, asthma, TB, weak eyesight/eye flu, malaria, typhoid, fever, dysentery, headache, stomach ache and joint pain, paralysis, polio, etc.

Women-specific diseases were leucorrhoea and prolapsed uterus. The males did not know about women-specific diseases. All agreed that women were more prone to illness. The communicable diseases recognized were cold, cough, and eye problems which were spread by sharing food and clothes with an infected person. The dietary precautions were not followed during illness, though most of them were aware of these. A premature birth or still birth were attributed to the weak constitution of the mother.

The causes of infant deaths were seen as premature birth, lack of proper diet and rest to the pregnant woman, lack of other antenatal care, lack of proper feed to the infant, and not seeking medical help during the child's illness.

During pregnancy almost all women reduce their diet because of digestion problems but some do believe that if a woman is weak she may not be able to bear a heavy child, causing maternal mortality. Even after delivery only a few can afford a rich diet, otherwise a normal diet is given. Women work till the last day of delivery and resume working 13 days after delivery. In some households, where there was no one to help, women even started working after 2–3 days. During pregnancy no health check-ups were done. The dai only came when the labour pain started. The mother-in-law and other elderly women usually pray in case some problem develops rather than seek medical help. Perhaps, medical help in any case is almost out of their reach. The dai does not bring any kit and the cord is cut with a blade or scissors provided by the household. The dai attends to the mother and child for 13 days. Rarely had any delivery taken place outside the village in the cities. The dai charges Rs 100 to Rs 500 per delivery.

The villagers believed that if a pregnant women worked during an eclipse or did not get immunized, it could cause a deformity in the child. Antenatal care was negligible. Immunization and iron and folic acid tablets were taken by only a few. After delivery the woman usually changed her clothes after 13 days but now this practice is changing. During delivery an old sheet is used and the child is also wrapped in old clothes for 13 days.

During and after an illness, there was no concept of rest. Initially, either some home remedies were tried or no treatment was taken for 3–4 days. If money is available, then treatment is sought from a local doctor and if this does not cure, private doctors in the cities are visited. All participants stated that they prefer allopathic remedy.

The non-availability of medicine, non-availability of doctors at the proper time and behaviour of the staff were stated as some of the reasons for not visiting the public health facility. Most agreed that educating the mother reduces the chances of illness in children as she would keep the house clean and tidy. She would also know when to seek treatment and administer doses.

Women were empowered in terms of cash flow decisions for buying small items and seeking medical help for the child. If they did not have money, they could even borrow. Only the employed men had bank accounts while none of the women had one.

SOCIAL SECURITY

No one had any kind of savings or ornaments. Minor help could be taken from the neighbours. However, no major help could be sought as every one leads a hand to mouth existence. Thus, dependence on ones' savings and community help was ruled out. One old woman said that even land is not a form of security, as they could not cultivate it themselves and it was less productive. All considered their sons as an old age security and felt that though daughters would serve and care during illness, they could not be of any help financially. Rarely did any daughter extend financial help or any sons-in-law allow them to do so. Everybody considered old women a burden, though the grandchildren talked nicely to them. The old women enjoyed their daughters' visits. Conflicts within the family occur due to poverty, financial constraints, drinking habit of men, children's education and other children-related issues. Women have to be the first to surrender in such conflicts. If women do not stop arguing, they are beaten by the men. One of the women remarked that all conflicts are solved in the night before sleeping. The grown up children and parents sometimes help to ease tension.

9.2.10 Morbidity Awareness (Free Listing)

A morbidity schedule on free listing of illness was canvassed in this village from 20 married women in the reproductive age group. The age groups were 25 to 35 years (14) and 36 to 45 years (6). The education level of twelve SC women is as follows: below primary (3), primary (1), and illiterate (8). Bahti (cultivating caste) women have educational levels of primary (1) and illiterate (4). Two carpenter (OBC) caste women had a primary level of education. The sole rajput woman was illiterate.

First, the women were asked, without probing, to name the illnesses prevalent in this village. When they exhausted the list then probes like seasonal variations, age variations (childhood, old age and women-specific diseases) were tried to get an exhaustive list of possible diseases. These diseases are of the recent past, that is, last two to four years. In some cases, the responses of the respondent remained focussed around the illness experienced in their households, by relatives or in the neighbourhood, since the young women did not move around frequently in the village.

None of the diseases were common to all the women. The highest reported diseases were cold–cough (70 per cent), and fever without any symptom (65 per cent), leucorrhoea (65 per cent), body and joint pain (45 per cent), malaria (45 per cent), and low BP (30 per cent). The other diseases reported by 20 per cent of the women were excessive menses and dizziness. Apart from these, various other illnesses were reported by 5 per cent to 15 per cent of the women. Chronic and acute illnesses were reported in same numbers.

One of the SC women, aged 27 years remarked, 'illness was less in last few years because of draught conditions; where water is more illness is more'. An illiterate, bahti woman, aged 25 years said that she started suffering from leucorrhoea seven days after her first child was born. Out of the 12 SC women interviewed, 8 were suffering from white discharge which started: after marriage (3), after first child (2), and after a number of childbirths (3). Apart from these free listings, the interviewer talked to 15 other SC women and 11 of them were found to be suffering from leucorrhoea. This illness is highly prevalent in women, and some of them had a prolapsed uterus also. The symptoms and causes of most of the diseases were reported correctly. Some of the respondents could not identify the causes of some of the illnesses. Of course, some did report very unrealistic causes of diseases, such as deteriorated malaria becomes typhoid, jaundice due to eating clay; white discharge due to drinking excess tea, due to dirt and filth in and around houses; leucorrhoea due to cattle near the kitchen: and malaria due to heat, etc.

TABLE 9.8

Prevalence Rate of Illness, Baroohi

(*N* = 20)

Local name	Standard name	No.	Percentage
Sardi jukam	Cough, cold	14	70
Bukhar	Fever without other symptoms	13	65
Safed pani	Leucorrhoea	13	65
Badan dard, Jor dard	Body pain, joint pain	9	45
Malaria	Malaria	9	45
Ghat BP	Low BP	6	30
More bleeding	Excess menses	4	20
Chakkar ana	Dizziness	4	20
Ankh dard	Eye infection	3	15
Tatian lagna	Diarrhoea	3	15
Pneumonia	Pneumonia	3	15
Bhar padna	Prolapsed uterus	3	15
Ulti	Vomiting	3	15
Kamar dard	Back ache	3	15
Dama	Asthama	2	10
Kaleji da dard	Liver problem	2	10
Typhoid	Typhoid	1	5
Peelia	Jaundice	1	5
Bacha hone	Delivery problem	1	5
Peshab rukna	Urination problem	1	5
Gillarr	Goitre	1	5
Bacha na hona	Sterility	1	5
Daura	Fits	1	5
Dant dard	Tooth ache	1	5
Gathia	Arthritis	1	5
Sir dard	Headache	1	5
Phora phinsi	Skin problem	1	5

9.3 Buani Village

9.3.1 General Background

Village Buani is located in district Ludhiana, which is one of the most advanced districts of Punjab. It was dominated by cultivating families for four decades, until the canals passing the village on its three sides, raised the water level to such an extent that cultivation had to be stopped. As a result, new and diversified occupations such as truck driving, dairy farming, teaching, small-scale manufacturing, etc. came into existence. Villagers started giving importance to education, in a desire to get white-collar jobs. Buani can be considered as a developed village with all the modern facilities.

9.3.2 Infrastructural facilities

AMENITIES AND SERVICES

The various amenities and services available to the people of Buani and their accessibility is being listed in Table 9.9.

TABLE 9.9
Amenities and Services, Buani

Amenities	Place	Distance (km)
Approach road	Up to village	0
Bus stop	In the village	0
Railway station	Doraha	6
Post office	In the village	0
Community TV	–	–
Community radio	–	–
Library/reading room	–	–
Street lights	–	–
Bank	Doraha	6
Co-operative credit society	In the village	0
Regulated grain market/mandi	Doraha	6
Pharmacy/drug outlet	Doraha	6
Services of drinking water for SCs and others	–	0
Handpump and pipe water just started in the village	–	–

SHOPS

There is no chemist shop in the village. To get prescribed medicines the people go to Doraha. There are, however, ten grocery shops in the village, of which three are located in the SC area. Items of daily needs are available here. Two or three shops which had been operating for a long time, have been closed due to a financial crunch because of giving too much credit.

COOPERATIVE CREDIT SOCIETIES,
LOCAL MONEY LENDERS, ETC.

In emergencies, people borrow within the village. If a large amount is needed, it is borrowed on interest at the rate of

TABLE 9.10
Time Line, Buani

Grocery shop, Gurudwara general, Flour mill	1900
Primary school	1905
Plague	1921
Hand pump	1935
Wine shop, transport	1942
Pucca street, plague	1952
Agricultural cooperative	1953
Transistor, radio, tractor	1954
Scooter, motor cycle	1955
Kila bandi (partial consolidation)	1956
Water logging problem (maximum)	1957
Water logging drain constructed	1972
Electricity, SS Industry, the harijan cooperative farming society, land allotted 25 acres to 35 households	1960
Tube well, post office	1962
TV, transport	1963
Ration depot (PDS)	1964
Pucca road, middle school, tidi dal	1965
Refrigerator	1968
Bus service	1978
Organization to send persons abroad	1979
Purdah vanished, cooler, high school pucca building, ANM	1980
Veterinary hospital, milk dairy	1983
Shed for cremation ground	1984
Harijan Gurudwara	1986
Floods, all village street made pucca	1988
Kerosene oil depot	1993

10 per cent per annum There are 5–6 such households, which give loans on interest. Though, there is no co-operative credit society *per se* the following three co-operative societies fulfil this function in the village. These are:

(1) Janta Sudhar Co-operative (Co-operative Agriculture Services Societies Ltd—CASS Ltd)
(2) Harijan Co-operative Society
(3) Flour Mill Co-operative Society

CASS Ltd

This is the first co-operative society of the village. It was registered on 5 May 1953. The building was constructed in 1966–7 on a one bigha area plot. Earlier, it was functioning from a private house in the village. It has a staff of three workers, one secretary, one salesman, one peon. The President of the society is from Buani. In an executive body of seven members, there are three members from Buani and four from Bhattal. Elections for these posts are held after every five years. Members of this society are from Buani as well as Bhattal and add up to a total of 596 members, with 492 members from Buani. The registration fee is Rs 5 and one can hold a maximum share of Rs 2450. Out of 596, 197 are agricultural members and 399 are short-term members who can avail a loan up to ten times the amount of their share. An agricultural loan can be taken up to Rs 24,500. A small farmer (with land less than 7.5 kila) can take a loan up to 20 times the amount of his share. All agricultural share holders (97) have taken a loan. They can obtain fertilizers, pesticides, and weedicides from the society. There are no short-term members since 1990 as they have not returned the loans taken earlier. The defaulters are 110 agriculture members and 132 short-term members. The rate of interest is 12 per cent and 15 per cent per annum.

Harijan Co-operative Society

This society has been in existence since consolidation (1955). It purchased land at a cost of Rs 30,000 which was contributed by all its members. This society could not function successfully and now remains only on paper. Practically, the land is divided among all the members. A few have even sold off their share of the land, while the rest cultivate their shares individually. The society members cultivated the land jointly for a period of 10–15 years but without any substantial return as the land was not good being situated near a canal, 'Dadi sati', where there is a lot of water logging. Land revenue is collected even now from the new owners. No specific reason for the division of the land came to light.

Flour Mill Co-operative Society

This flour mill co-operative was started in 1961, with an amount of Rs 15,000. There are ten members and all of them coincidentally are jat land-holders. There are two members each from three families and one each from four families. So far, there has never been any conflict among the members. The *Jamindars* (jats) established this co-operative when water logging started affecting the income of the village. The staff consists of one secretary and one worker. Profit is divided bi-monthly and on an average, one member gets Rs 250 per month. Besides the flour mill, there is one speller and one small rice shelter. This flour mill is located on the boundary road of the village towards Landha village near a bus stop. In area it is one bigha which is taken on lease at a rent of Rs 1400 annum. A part of the land is cultivated. The maintenance expenses are taken from the profit.

On a daily basis five to seven quintals of wheat come to the mill. The rate is 30 paise per kg for wheat and paddy has been available only for the last six months. Earlier the rate was 25 paise only, and *makka* is at a rate of 50 paise per kg. Another small flour mill was set up in a nearby village but it failed. The flour mill operators complain about the erratic supply of electricity on account of which they are unable to expand their work further.

DRINKING WATER

The only source of drinking water is the hand pump. There are 5–6 wells in the village but these are not used for drinking water. Each house, irrespective of caste, has its own hand pump from which the water is consumed as it is. Due to excessive water logging, the ground water level is high. The villagers reported that the hand pump water tastes bad in the rainy season. The high level of ground water could be seen in one of the wells near the pond. It was seen that the water level in the well was almost the same as that of the pond even in the month of December.

A water tank belonging to the water supply department has been erected in the village. Pipes to carry water from this tank were laid in the street. Taps are provided at a few places but the supply is not efficient as the supply pipes are made of PVC, and at some places the joints have started leaking, disrupting the water supply. In the rainy season, when the chances of an epidemic outbreak are higher, people drink the same water without boiling.

PUBLIC DISTRIBUTION SYSTEM

Under the PDS, 400 ration cards are issued. The items sold are kerosene oil, levy sugar, control rate cloth, soap, detergent, tea, etc. Kerosene oil is distributed once a month. Sugar is given at the rate of 380 gm per head. Supply is usually regular but sometimes when it is short, many people are deprived of their share. Also many times, the quality of sugar is not good, especially that of the imported sugar. Kerosene oil distributed is 10 litres per ration card. The announcement regarding the arrival of supply is made on the Gurudwara loudspeaker. People complain about the shortage in supply of Di-ammonia Phosphate and ration card items. Also, the soil treating and water-testing department of the laboratory is not helpful.

9.3.3 Education

There are two government-run schools in this village, a primary school and a high school.

PRIMARY SCHOOL

This school is located in the general caste area, in the centre of the village. Though the primary school has been functioning since 1905, the construction of the building was started in 1950 with only two rooms being fully complete in 1980. At present, there are 5–6 rooms with verandahs in front, and a green courtyard covered fully from all sides. Each room has a ceiling fan donated by the Panchayat. There are no mats for children. They bring their own mats from home as the wooden planks supplied by the school are inadequate for all the children. These planks have also been donated by the villagers.

Recently, an electric water motor was installed in the school with some financial help from the villagers. For this Rs 1000 was contributed by the co-operative milk dairy, Rs 2500 by local industries, and Rs 300 by the teachers. It has been seen that the Panchayat as well as the general public is very co-operative in promoting any kind of community project being developed in the village.

The sanctioned number of posts for teachers is five of which only two posts are filled. A teacher for Class III has been arranged by collecting Rs 10 from each student in addition to Rs 50 given by the school. This teacher is a 10 + 2 standard local girl and parents are giving this fee voluntarily. The other two posts are lying vacant, and hence one teacher has to manage two classes. While there is a proper toilet for the teachers, that for the students is only a five feet wall covering with no proper door on drainage facility. For latrine, children go to the open fields after taking permission from the teachers. The teacher's toilet is not accessible to the children.

There is no Class IV employee for sweeping or swabbing. Students are asked to do this job by the teachers but the children as well as their parents refused. Instead, they agreed to pay 0.50 paise each for sweeper's wages, who now does this job. Even the electricity bill is shared by the children by paying 0.50 paise each. There are no indoor or outdoor games available. Children participate only in sports such as running, etc.

There is no mid-day meal scheme operating in the school. Only the SC girls get free books without binding. To encourage enrolment of SC girls, they are given Re 1 per day for attending the school. The amount is paid on a monthly basis. This scheme has proved instrumental in improving the enrolment and retention of SC girls. Out of this money, the girls get their uniform stitched. The enrolment of SC children is shown in Table 9.11.

TABLE 9.11
Scheduled Caste Children Enrolled in Primary School, Buani

Class	Total no. of SC children	Boys	Girls
I	24	14	10
II	17	9	8
III	12	7	5
IV	13	8	5
V	19	11	8
Total	**85**	**49**	**36**

A survey for identifying eligible children has not been carried out since the last few years. Teachers obtain such information from the students. The retention rate may be studied from Table 9.12.

TABLE 9.12
Retention Rate in Primary School, Buani

	1993–4	1992–3	1991–2	1989–90
Total	43	42	79	43
Pass	29	40	79	35
Fail	14	2	–	8

The standard of education is reasonable. Some of the observations were that though Hindi is a subject in Classes III and IV, the children could not speak this language. Junior classes learn tables by rote. The monitor who handles the class in the teacher's absence is selected on the basis of his/her calibre only. In a few classes, even SC children are monitors. Children of all castes intermingle and sit freely in one classroom. A few children were observed calling each other by caste names (example, '*Dekho ji eh chamar nahi hatda*'). Boys and girls play together. The segregation starts from Class IV onwards.

Students are asked by the teachers to purchase 'help' books to simplify the prescribed texts and the use of such books was very common among children. The sale of such books is arranged by the teachers in the school campus.

Many children have an additional tuition at home. One of the school teachers takes tuition classes after school hours at a rate of Rs 50 per child per month. The children did not report any persuasion from the teachers for this purpose.

Corporal punishment exists as a disciplinary measure in the school, and neither the children nor their parents mind it. Conversation with the children led to the conclusion that from the very beginning their mind is conditioned to accept that elders have a right to punish them if they commit any mistake. The parents view this measure as a means of mending the child's ways. Despite the physical punishment the rapport of teachers (except mathematics lady teacher) with the students was observed to be cordial.

The teachers felt that the block officer is not at all co-operative. He is reported to be a drunkard who demands money to expedite work. Whenever the Head teacher goes to his office to collect the salary of the staff, or for any other official work he has to bribe him. Also, sometimes teachers have been asked to forcibly sell red cross tickets, etc. which they find very difficult. The block officer has also ignored the teachers' request for mats.

HIGH SCHOOL

The high school came into existence in 1980 and it is located on the outskirts of the residential area, towards the SC houses. It has a big building with a very big playground constructed at a cost of Rs 4 lakh in 1980 and has a total of 10–12 rooms. The building was built solely with the contribution of the villagers, it is also well maintained and whitewashed by contributions from the villagers who feel proud of their collective effort. In all the rooms, a pucca blackboard, and complete and well-maintained furniture (desks) is provided. There is a ceiling fan in each class room which is airy with proper lighting. There is a separate room for the clerk, a room for the Principal's office, two rooms that serve as staff rooms, one big room for the science laboratory, one kitchen and a library. The science laboratory as well as the library are not used frequently. The apparatus in the laboratory has rusted while library books are locked up in a cupboard. No child is reported to have ever used the laboratory or the library.

There are four hand pumps for drinking water at the school. The electric motor had to be disconnected on account of non-payment of the high amounts of electricity bills. The physical infrastructure is satisfactory. The total staff strength is 14. Out of these, there are four post-graduate teachers while the others are graduate trained teachers. There are six female teachers and eight male teachers: two science teachers (one medical, one non-medical); two maths teachers; four social studies teachers, one Hindi teacher and one physics teacher. As the medium of instruction is Punjabi, the social studies teacher who is an MA in Punjabi has been taking the Punjabi language classes also. The staff strength was completed in late 1994 only. Earlier there was a shortfall of three teachers and hence the children had to contribute to pay the government teacher's salary. The post for a Punjabi language teacher has not been sanctioned, though an application has been submitted to the Education Department. The post of Head Master had been lying vacant from December 1991 to October 1994. One peon, one chowkidar and one sweeper are posted.

TABLE 9.13

Teacher–Student Ratio, High School, Buani

Class	Students
VI	55
VII	58
VIII	37+42=79 (in two sections)
IX	41
X	34

The reason for a declining trend in the retention rate in the higher classes is the parent's lack of interest in the child's education. The principal of the school stated that most of the parents could not tell the real name by which their child was enrolled in the school. In government schools, people send their children mainly because of low fees, etc. Girls have beneficiaries in this situation. Fees for children from a family (general or SC) whose income is greater than Rs 1000 is Rs 6 per month, while no fee is charged from those children whose family income is less than Rs 1000. For classes VI to VIII the fee is Rs 3.75 per month with an admission fee of Rs 6. Everybody pays the fee regularly and in time. The SC children get free textbooks. Tuition fee is free on an income basis only. Scholarship worth Rs 19 per month is paid usually after the month of September. The grant has to be received from the treasury at Khanna. Uniform is prescribed for the students. Girls wear suits and boys wear trousers and shirts.

The school is equipped with all the teaching aids but these have hardly been used. No indoor games are available in the school and the few generally played are kho-kho, kabaddi, and athletics. These games being cheaper are commonly played and the school has produced district-level teams in kho-kho and kabaddi. Except for kho-kho, all the other games are played by boys only. In the playground, a stadium has been built and this is used for holding the annual sports festival of the village, where many outside teams are invited to participate. These sports are held with a gap of 10–15 days after the famous 'Kila Raipur Sports'—the mini Olympics of India.

Though there are a large number SC students there is no representative from the SC households in the ineffective parent teacher association (PTA). The level of education imparted by the school is far from satisfactory. Discussions with the principal revealed that the main reasons for this were the insufficient number of teachers and the absence of a head master. This led to the undisciplined atmosphere in the school. In the last four years, a large number of girls have been withdrawn from the school. Noticeable and sizeable conflicts have occurred on the campus with students lobbying with two different groups of teachers. Male teachers could be seen drunk in the school hours, while the boys idled their time and teased the girls in their classes. The classes were not held regularly as the teachers were not regular. Overall, the situation was really bad and this fact was endorsed by the villagers. At present, there are some improvements in the educational standard in the school and female enrolment is also expected to improve.

No class or caste bias is apparent either in the teachers' behaviour or among the children who mingle freely. There is no fixed sitting arrangement in the classrooms. Corporal punishment is accepted by students, parents, and teachers. Each class has one monitor who is an intelligent student. About 50 children from the better-off families go to a public school at Doraha in a van, the attraction being English as the medium of instruction, a better standard of education, and better discipline. After Class X, students mostly join the Rara Sahib Co-ed. College, though very few girls take up college studies. A fear that their girls may become spoilt with an exposure to the outside world deters the parents from sending girls to college. Also, they do not like their grown up daughters travelling in crowded buses and becoming the target of boys' teasing.

Salaries, or any grant from the government has to be collected by the school authority from the treasury office at Khanna, where they often face harassment at the hands of the treasury officers. While salary collection is not a problem; for arrears or other allowances, the full amount cannot be received without paying a bribe to the clerks.

Discussion with the teachers and the principal led to some conclusions and recommendations, which are as follows:

1. Education should be job oriented.
2. The examination system being faulty, needs to be improved.
3. Parents do not realize the value of internal exams.
4. Teachers should do self-evaluation every year.
5. The headmaster should be given powers to pull up or to encourage teacher for poor or good performance, respectively.

DROP-OUT

Non-enrolment and drop-outs do not exist—there has been 100 per cent enrolment for the last five years and no child has dropped out before primary level and very rarely has any child dropped out at the matriculation stage.

9.3.4 Health

SUB-CENTRE

A Sub-centre has been functioning in the village since 1980. The staff consists of one auxiliary nurse midwife (ANM) and one MHW. The villages attached to the sub-centre are Landha, Landha Khurd, Roul, Bhattal, Deep Nagar, Canal Colony, and Buani. As per its Health Survey in 1994, the eligible target population for immunization was 150 and there were 115 expecting mothers in the village. Buani's achievement is 103 immunizations out of 150 and 80 out of 115 for prenatal care. Prophylasis (vitamin A) is given to the children after nine months and subsequently with a six-month gap. Expecting women are given folic acid tablets. A BCG injection is given to a child between one month and 10 years of age. The ANM prescribes 'Ashoka Arisht' for irregular periods, 'Coormin' for worms, Crowne amplicilin capsules for cold and cough for adults.

Tetanus Toxoids (TT) vaccination is administered to expecting mothers in two doses. The first is given in the fifth month and the other in ninth month. If the second child is due within a gap of two and a half years then only one TT dose is given to the expectant woman. No case of bitot spot has been noticed for the last 15 years. The ANM pays home visits and undertakes post-natal care. Her limited and outdated knowledge may prove harmful, especially in successfully achieving the ultimate goal of EPI.

The centre is equipped with a weighing machine (ordinary) foot-scale and has an adequate supply of oral rehydration solution (ORS). Nirodh is supplied without any guidance. The condom packets are kept in a basket and are collected shyly by the males (30–5 years) on their own. There is no interaction at all on this issue (family planning) between the ANM and the males of the village. The only interaction that the ANM has is with the eligible women. Women come to the centre for intra-uterine device (IUD), sterilizations, pills, etc. No case of male sterilization exists in the village. According to the ANM, people here use abortion as a means of family planning. Amniocentesis (sex detection test) is used very frequently by the people. As the female foetus is aborted, no case of infanticide is noticed. People prefer to detect the sex of the foetus early and abort. Private clinics charge Rs 550 to Rs 1000 per test after the fourth month of pregnancy. The miscarriage rate is two to three per cent.

The other health functionary at the sub-centre is the MHW. Since 1988 he has been responsible for the Malaria Eradication Programme. The villages under the jurisdiction of the MHW are Buani, Landha and Landha-Khurd, Raul, Bhattal. He has distributed his week days as three days for Buani, two for Landha, one each for Roul and Bhattal. While his headquarters are at Buani which he visits twice a month for collecting samples for malaria, there is no record of his visits however. Villagers reported that he rarely visited each and every household. The sample collected by him is given for testing at Payal and only the positive results are reported back. Patients are then given chloroquine tablets. The prescription given by the MHW is one tablet to a child of 1–4 years; 2 tablets a day for child of 4–8 years, 3 tablets to child of 8–12 years, 4 tablets a day to patients in the age group of 12 years and above. The number of patients recorded and tested for malaria is listed in Table 9.14.

TABLE 9.14
Malaria Patients, Buani

Year	No. of malaria positive patients
1988	15
1989	10
1990	5
1991	5
1992	3

Note: For the years 1993 and onwards, no malaria case has been reported.

The positive results are obtained after four days and thus treatment starts on the fifth day. The MHW suggested that laboratories should be closer to the sub-centre, and if possible in the same village where the sub-centre is located.

Except for AIDS training, both the ANM and the MHW have not attended any other training programme. About AIDS too, they have acquired only limited knowledge. No effort is made to create awareness among villagers about this fatal disease. Surprisingly, even after the training, the MHW did not know about HIV or MMR. Further, he was using ordinary big stitching needles for taking blood samples of patients. These needles were kept in a small box and were not even sterilized.

ANGANWADI

There is no anganwadi in the village, but people feel the need of setting up one as the requirement for this exists.

DAI

There is no dai in the village. Many cases are attended to by the ANM. For delivery cases, she charges between Rs 300 to Rs 400 per case. Mostly, people use the services of dais brought from the nearby village of Landha or Bhattal. People express a lot of confidence in these dais who have probably been trained, but their delivery kits are rarely used.

PRIVATE PRACTITIONERS

There are two private practitioners in the village. A third one belongs to this village but practices in Raul and other nearby villages. Dr Lachhman Das who belongs to this village has been practicing from his shop cum residence for about 47 years. He has, therefore, witnessed many developments in the village. He is an active Congress worker and has contested assembly elections. He has been in politics since 1944 and was a freedom fighter. In 1985, he contested elections against the Chief Minister and won. Now he is affiliated with V. P. Singh (Janata Dal).

He was trained under Faqir Chand, registered medical practitioner (RMP) at Doraha and thereafter worked in Dayanand Hospital for 4–5 years, before he started practising in this village. He practices both Allopathic and Ayurvedic systems of medicines. The list of various diseases attended to by him is a long one. The general ones are flu, malaria, diarrhoea, dysentery, typhoid, cholera, vomiting, weakness, low and high blood pressure, eye and ear problems, gall bladder stone, gastroenteritis, joint pain, tooth problem. Cases reported of malaria, typhoid, cholera, high BP are few. Children are afflicted with the following illnesses: tonsils, cough, loose motions, fever, weak liver, acute malnutrition. Old people suffer from cold–cough, urine problems, stones, headaches, high and low blood pressure, ear infections, etc. Women have diseases like excess bleeding, leucorrhoea, uterus swelling, anaemia, cancer, apart from many cases of abortion and miscarriage which he does not handle. Sexual diseases that are prevalent are mainly early discharge in case of men; no AIDS/STD case is reported. According to him there is no case of bitot spot or water-borne disease, while worms and jaundice are very rare. A great number of illnesses spread in the months of August–September, that is, the rainy season.

Patients from nearby villages also come in large numbers, such that 50–60 patients are attended to by him daily. He also gives medicine on credit to the poor. Villagers come to him mainly for treatment. Only for illnesses which he cannot treat, are the patients taken outside for treatment. He is said to have a very good reputation among villagers. He pays home visits when required. For delivery cases, he gives a labour pain injection, only if needed. If vaccinations like measles, whooping cough, etc. are unavailable in the dispensary, people go to Doraha, Ludhiana. He also keeps such injections in his refrigerator and is known to have given a glucose drip for two serious cases. For diagnosis, he does not use laboratory tests but diagnoses the illness from the symptoms. For example, jaundice is diagnosed from the pale colour of urine, eyes, etc. flu from throat pain, white patch on tongue, etc; He has attended to a large number of cases of acute malnutrition (5–7 women patients with nails pressed down). According to him, a large number (10–15 per cent) of women are anaemic.

The other doctor, S. Hoshiar Singh belongs to some other village and commutes daily to Buani. Having been an apprentice with an MBBS doctor, he has been practicing in the village for the last one and a half years. The illnesses attended to by him are loose motions, vomiting, fever. In winters, more cases of cough and cold are reported. Infants suffer from cough and loose motions while old people suffer mainly from chronic cough. He does not know much about the prevalence of women's illnesses, as his patients are mainly men. He treats about 30–40 patients everyday in his clinic which is open from 9 A.M. to 5 P.M. After that he practices in his own village.

According to him, there are no water-borne diseases in the village. Malaria and typhoid are reported in summer. Cases of cuts and wounds of violence also come to him. No child patient has ever come to him directly from the school. His patients are mostly SCs. He does not treat skin diseases but refers all such cases to a skin specialist. He also pays home visits. He does not subscribe to any medical journal to update his knowledge. Whenever he cannot diagnose and treat, he consults senior doctors outside.

The third doctor is a young SC boy. He is under matriculate. Like the others he has worked under a doctor and got to know about medicines. He cycles to other nearby villages and practices there. No one from this village ever goes to him because he does not stay here, so he is not known to many. He has claimed to have treated patients with sexually transmitted diseases (STD), fever, cold, cough, etc. This may imply that there may be STD cases in this village but they go to other places for treatment for the sake of secrecy.

9.3.5 Population

Table 9.15 shows that the maximum number of households is of jats. Jats of gotra jhaj are the predominant caste in the village. Apart from being in a majority, the other factors making them powerful are their land holding and economic position. Jat households, even without agricultural land are economically well-off. This is because of their successful adoption of the transport business.

TABLE 9.15
Castewise Household Population, Buani

Caste	No. of households
Jat	114
Carpenter	34
Brahmin	23
Nai	24
Harijan	76
Balmiki	12
Goldsmith	5
Ghumar	5
Jheevar	6
Darji (Cheemba)	3
Muslim	2
Total	**304**

Another predominant caste group is that of carpenters on account of their hold on the village economy. All households of carpenters run industries in the village and earn a good income. The other castes include brahmin, nai, harijan, balmiki, goldsmith, ghumar, jheevar, darzi and two households of Muslims.

Except in the harijan area, all other houses are intermixed. The SC area, locally known as Vehrra, comprises all the households of castes such as harijans, balmikis and ghumars. The SC area is at one side of the village but it adjoins the residential area inhabited by the other caste people. Despite their separate location, there is not much untouchability. Untouchability in fact has recently taken the form of class difference.

At the time of partition, there were quite a large number of Muslim households. Even at that time, no conflict occurred in the village. A number of Muslim families left for Pakistan peacefully. They were given due protection by other villagers. During the period of terrorist activities, Hindus were helped and protected by the Sikhs. Not even a single Hindu family was troubled at that time. Till now, there has not been a single case of caste conflict.

There are two households of Muslims (as shown in the table) belonging to two brothers living in adjoining houses. At the time of partition their father did not leave the country. Their occupation is mainly agriculture. Over a period of time, these families have adopted a largely Hindu—Sikh culture and left many customs of the Muslim religion. The women are not fussy about wearing burkhas or about other Mohammedan customs such as observing purdah while talking to outside men. One girl is studying in college at Rara Sahib. A Muslim woman in her fifties revealed that no one in her house knew how to read the Quran. They had adopted the life style of the Hindus and Sikhs amidst whom they live.

During the decade of terrorist activities no one really got converted to any other religion. The brahmins were not found to be very rigid in this village. Young boys sport beards, while in some houses, they keep the Sikh Gurus' photographs. Till today, no communal clash has occurred.

9.3.6 Social Issues—Customs and Practices

FOOD HABITS

People cook meals three times a day. Wheat is consumed in summers and makka is used in addition to wheat in winters. Mostly, people of all castes are vegetarian and eat pulses and vegetables. Rice is consumed occasionally, on some function or festival. Women are total vegetarians while men eat non-vegetarian food outside their houses, very rarely preparing a non-vegetarian dish at home; at functions such as marriages, the men eat meat. Eggs are consumed at home. The diet is good and each household gets sufficient food. In winters, the quality of food improves because along with saag (leafy vegetables), butter milk, ghee and milk are also available in the house.

DRINKING HABIT

A large majority (nearly 75 per cent) of the adult male population drinks. This habit is more prevalent among the local industrialists who are carpenters by caste while the SCs too do not lag behind. No one makes liquor at home, drink being usually bought at the local wine shop, which sells on an average Rs 7000 worth of liquor per day, the rate of a full bottle being Rs 65. The shop is open from 12 noon to 10 P.M. It was earlier near the village boundary road but after the constant persuasion of the villagers, the shop was shifted outside the village near the canal. Men drink by the side of the canal in the evenings, when it is usually a very crowded place. The practice of drinking at home is not observed as the women object to it.

Drinks serve as a means of giving men kicks as well as entertainment. At marriages it is expected that drinks will be served. No one is aware of detoxication centres. Four or five persons tried to get rid of this addiction by taking treatment from private medical practioners, but two of them started drinking again.

The extent of this addiction leads to frequent conflicts within the family. In such cases, women suffer the most. In many households, the problem is so grave that the conflicts have led to separation even after 15–20 years of marriage. The villagers are not happy about the existence of a wine shop and would like to see it shifted to a far off place. This may not eliminate the addiction but will definitely reduce the habit.

Women do not drink or smoke. Smoking is not common even among men. Other addictions like drugs are taken mostly by SCs who work as labourers. These are *pheni*, *jarda*, *doda* (local names). One such addict went to the extreme limit of selling his household items for buying his jarda. The family is now in acute poverty.

COOKING CHULLAH

About 50 per cent of the households have cooking gas. They bring the refill cylinder from Daroha on their own two-wheeler scooters. Cooking gas is used as a supplementary means for cooking. All the households have an open local chullah, mostly in the courtyard. A small boundary wall is made around the chullah to convert the place into an open kitchen. Every household has a kitchen and a chullah. This chullah is seldom used except in the rainy season or acute winter mornings and nights. This kitchen is otherwise used for keeping utensils.

The fuels for the chullah consist of cow dung cakes and sometimes the dry by-product of sugarcane. Since each and every household has cattle, there is no scarcity of fuel. The households who have a better financial status and are educated, use cooking gas. The smokeless chullah is not in use in any household as women find it extremely time consuming. They do not grumble about the smoke damaging their eyes, but prefer open kitchens as these are less harmful. There is one gobar gas plant in the village in a jat household which is, however, non-functional. The household does not know where to lodge a complaint to get it repaired. There is scope for a community gobar gas plant.

TYPE OF DRESS

Men wear pants and shirts. At home they wear kurta pyjamas. The cloth is generally of good quality. The younger generation wears shirts and pants at home also and always likes to be well dressed. Women wear salwar kameej only, the cloth being generally expensive and synthetic. The younger generation especially wears bright colours and likes shining cloth, cotton clothes being seen as below their status. Among children of five to six years of age, the girls wear frocks after which they are made to wear suits. From 13–14 years onwards, they have to wear a dupatta also. Boys wear pants and shirts from a very young age of 6–7 years, very few children come to primary school in frocks and shorts.

The impact of urbanization is apparent from the lifestyle of the villagers. Young married women wear make-up even at home and even for going to the toilets, out in the fields. Marriage customs among the various castes include cross-cousin marriages while marriages within the village are not seen in Buani. Usually marriages are settled in Punjab—usually within adjoining districts, and within caste and religion only. The custom of giving a heavy dowry is prevalent—furniture, beds, suits, ornaments—are all given to the girl. The marriageable age of girls is 20 to 25 years and that for the boys it is a couple of years more.

9.3.7 Summary of Focus Group Discussions

Four focus group discussions were held inside the Panchayat bhawan. They comprised two discussions for women in the reproductive age group, one for elderly women above 60 years of age and one for men belonging to different castes.

Of the two FGDs held for women in the reproductive age group, the women participants of the first group represented many castes such as: jat (3), brahmin (2), mohammedan (1), barber (1), ghumar (1), and jhewar (2). The age group was 25–40 years old. The educational status was matriculate (4), primary level (3), and illiterate (3). The number of children varied from one to seven; four of the participants having two sons each and three other participants having only daughters. Except two, all were living in a joint family and all were doing only household work. Four of them have agricultural land. The involvement of the participants was generally good, though two were shy and reticent.

In the FGD held exclusively for SC women in the reproductive age group, the participants were in the age group 24–35 years. Their qualifications were: BEd (1), matriculate (1), above primary (4), below primary (1), and illiterate (3). There were three participants with one male child, and seven with two male children. Except one, all had female children also ranging from one to five. Four of them belonged to nuclear families and all of them were involved only in household work. The rating for both these FGDs was very satisfactory, all the women were present with good participation and involvement.

The age group in the FGD for men was 24–35 years and one of the participants was unmarried. Others who were married had children between one to five. Six of them had at least one male child. Out of the 23 children born to their wives, all were alive. Three participants came from joint families. Their occupations included: wage labour (4), self-employed mechanical works (2), carpenter (1), cycle repair (1), other service (1). No one had land and all were healthy.

The FGD for elderly women had ten participants in the age group of 55–90 years. Six of them were widows. All were illiterate. The total number of surviving children were 38 and half of them were sons. The number of surviving children varied from two to seven with at least one son. Only one SC balmiki woman was living alone with her husband, all others were with their sons or along with their husbands if alive. The caste structure of the group was brahmin (1), tailor (1), barber (1), ghumar (1), jat (1), carpenter (1), and SC (4), which covers almost all the major castes. One SC balmiki woman was employed in sweeping other's houses, while the rest of the women were involved in petty household jobs such as baby sitting, utensil cleaning, etc. One jat woman owned marginal land. The elderly participants were very vocal about the need for pension and hoped that the research team would initiate some action to meet this need.

EDUCATION

Most of the participants expressed the view that education is helpful in making a child economically independent; it also improves interaction with the outside world because it enables reading of newspapers and transport sign boards as well as writing letters. The general caste women also stated that an educated child could guide the illiterate parents and would provide better old age support. The SC group felt that education would be useful in maintaining accounts and in civilizing villagers and making them good citizens. Educated girls could also get some employment (according to the SC women), and would be able to tackle emergencies in a better way (according to general caste women).

In acquiring education, girls enjoy equal status till matriculation after which they cannot continue further, as they are generally not allowed to go out of the village. Also they have to be trained in household activities before marriage. Only the men's FGD group was vocal about the disadvantages of education. They stated that if those who are educated do not get employed as per their qualifications, then it is a wastage of time and money.

There is no problem of non-enrolment and there are no drop-outs up to the primary level. Rarely has anybody dropped out from high school, because of weakness in studies. Educated parents help their children in studies while private coaching (tution) is common in this village. The children who drop out (if any) roam around or participate in the family activities. The old women remarked that in their childhood, girls were not allowed to go to school, and it is due to this lack of educaion that they face problems in travelling or talking to outsiders. The old women are not consulted regarding the education of their grandchildren. Once it is decided to withdraw a child, the child has no say and happily accepts the decision.

While SC children are entitled to free uniform, scholarship, and textbooks along with a fee concession, the women FGD participants stated that these concessions are not given most of the times. It was also felt that poor children from other castes should also get such concessions.

After coming from school, both boys and girls help in household activity. Girls are involved more in sweeping, swabbing, and fodder collection, etc. The boys help in minor shopping in the village itself. The standard of education in private schools in the nearby town is considered to be much better and many parents, who can afford it, send their children to these schools. In the village primary school, there is a lack of sitting material such as mats, etc. Most of the participants complained about the non-availability of toilets for students in both the schools. They also felt that a larger number of teachers is also needed to ensure good education. With the joining of the new head master, there is a tremendous positive change in the environment and discipline of the school. Children miss school only if they are sick or sometimes when they do not want to study. Students generally do not share their school problems with parents. Some participants expressed the need to set up a college in the village.

HEALTH

The sub-centre in the village does not actively help in the implementation of EPI, FP, and other government programmes like malaria eradication, etc. The centre does not keep curative medicines. A government medical dispensary in the nearby village or other higher government facilities are rarely visited for curative medicines. An experienced RMP functions in this village. For minor ailments or at the initial stage of any illness, patients consult this RMP, but if they are not cured they go to the private facilities in the town, about 7 km away.

Due to bad sanitation, diseases spread to a great extent in this village especially in the rainy season, when water logging occurs all around and water enters the houses. Most of the women could not see that the quality of water affects illness, but the men's group pointed out that with the ground water level being so high, the drainage water seepage comes directly in to the hand pumps. Sometimes green algae comes out in the hand pump water. This spreads water-borne diseases while stagnant water all around the village spreads malaria. The participants of men's group said that unsafe drinking water gives rise to stomach problems, liver diseases, and cholera/vomiting, etc. The women's group also agreed that loose motions, and vomiting are extremely common in this village but they have never thought of the cause of these. Nobody drinks boiled water unless recommended by the doctor.

Consuming uncovered food or overeating creates health problems. Men showed a greater awareness of communicable diseases. They reported such diseases as chicken pox, cholera, cold, asthma, and skin problems. Some of the women named skin problems as an example of communicable diseases, which spread by sitting close to the infected person.

To keep the children healthy, there should be cleanliness in the house, care about their personal hygiene, timely and proper immunization, and provision of a good diet. Generally, dietary precautions during illness as advised by the doctor are observed. Boiled water is given with salt and elaichi and solid diet is reduced during diarrhoea. The sub-centre distributes ORS packets during the incidence of diarrhoea. Pregnant women and children get immunized and consume multi-vitamins. Mother's milk is considered good for the child.

The spread of diseases was reported to be the effect of bad sanitation and hygiene. Women believe in the influence of the evil eye (nazar), while some of them believe that the misdeeds of the previous birth cause illness. The SC women's group participants thought that illness occurs due to weakness, seasonal variations, and poor diet. The men's group recognized the possibility of tension affecting sleep and in turn creating health problems. The cause of chronic diseases such as cancer and TB was linked to smoking and drinking habits of men by the general caste women.

For all types of illnesses, people take Allopathic medicines only. One of the SC women with a large number of children said, 'because of many deliveries I got the disease of white discharge, which got cured with treatment'. The women-specific diseases mentioned in this group were excess menses, white discharge, prolapsed uterus, stomach problem (navel adjustment) and sinking heart due to low BP. Treatment for such diseases is sought only in a few serious cases from the private practitioners in the town.

The SC women could not ascertain the causes of infant deaths and foetal mortality, but the general caste women linked these deaths with pneumonia, cold, lack of proper care, pregnant women not getting immunization or neglecting to take other prenatal care. Women are more prone to sickness especially after deliveries performed by the available untrained dais. The deliveries take place mainly in the village with the help of these dais. Some call the ANM who charges Rs 300 to Rs 400 for normal deliveries and for difficult deliveries they go to the private health facility in the nearest town. Those who can digest food, increase their diet during pregnancy.

While rest is prescribed to children during illness, adults do not take any rest themselves. No differential treatment is given to males and females for medication. Due to the rush and crowding in public hospitals, the villagers do not frequently visit these. Educated women are able to prevent the sickness of children. Either of the parents who is at home and finds out that the child is sick gets the medicine.

SOCIAL SECURITY

Women are empowered to cash flow, in fact the whole income remains with them. They can spend it on medication and small personal needs without asking anybody. Women do keep some money separately for emergency. Many men, women, and children have savings accounts. The male participants remarked, 'we do not worry about our future, but we worry about our children's future; so we save money for their needs'. Even the women or elderly participants were not worried about their future. They were sure that their sons would fulfil their financial needs and that their daughters would nurse them during illness. In households that lose their main earning member, the women earn by working in others' houses: cattle care, sweeping, stitching, etc. In spite of the good financial status of the residents most of them expected the government to provide free medication and old age pension. A consensus existed on having two to three children with a clear preference for a son. There is no adultery. However, due to many transporters in the population, the truck drivers are exposed to the risk of AIDS and STDs. This was a cause of concern in the male focus group.

Intra-family conflicts do occur due to the drinking habits of men, some occur on financial matters, or on account of the character of the partner. Also when either of the partners disregards the other the result is heated argument. In such conflicts generally the women give in. Only sometimes the male partner surrenders. Such conflicts are solved within the family but sometimes with the help of women's parents. Inter-family conflicts do not take place.

GENERAL IRRITANTS AND SUGGESTIONS

A need for a trained dai was felt by the women. The other needs mentioned were: place for garbage disposal, funds for septic-type toilets, measures to control the rainy season water entering the houses, generation of employment opportunity, specially for women by introducing small-scale industry, regular power supply, etc. Need is also felt for a gobar gas plant for the village and a college. There should be a play ground for the children. The women wanted a balwadi for the young children.

9.3.8 Free Listing of Illnesses

A morbidity schedule on free listing of illness was made from interviews with 20 married women. The age groups of the women were: 20 to 35 years (13), 36 to 45 years (5), and 46 to 63 years (2). The women represented different castes such as scheduled caste (8), jat (6), brahmin (1), ghumhar (2), carpenter (2) and barber (1). Their educational level was as follows: illiterate (7), primary (7), middle (3) and matriculate or above (3). The women interviewed were from different parts of this compact village with a very high level of interaction between them. The women were well aware of the morbidity in and around the village. They were asked to recall the recent morbidity pattern, that is, illnesses in the last two to four years. Once they exhausted the list without probe, some probes like seasonality, gender, age (children, old age and women-specific disease with emphasis on reproductive morbidity) were used to facilitate the responses. In this village, the reporting of disease was high. The most commonly reported illnesses were cold–cough (95 per cent), fever without other symptoms (80 per cent), stomach problems (50 per cent), and malaria, measles/chicken pox, low BP (40 per cent each). These women reported many chronic diseases. Asthma was quite (35 per cent) prevalent. As there is a lot of water logging, malaria is widespread. Women-specific diseases were menses problems (25 per cent), leucorrhoea (25 per cent) and prolapsed uterus (10 per cent). A good number of women reported skin problems, joint pain, typhoid, eye problem, etc. The percentage and number of illnesses listed are given in Table 9.16.

Most of them identified some causes for the prevailing diseases. The causes reported were for measles/chicken pox as an after-effect of fever, typhoid or malaria, menses problem due to a swelling in the uterus; white discharge as an effect of IUD or due to prolapsed uterus. Fever due to sun stroke or after immunization; asthma by giving unsuitable injections; cold–cough due to temperature variations; malaria from mosquito bite; back pain as an after-effect of sterilization; typhoid because of seasonal variations; diarrhoea due to extreme summer or winter; scabies due to wearing synthetic dresses or dryness in the rainy season.

9.3.9 Re-checking of Schedules

The net sown area of the village was shown as 113 acres more than the correct figure. Gross cropped area and gross irrigated area is the same (2526 acre) as reported, but the gross cropped area was reported to be 40 acres more. Total geographical area of the village was under-reported (60 acres). In this village there is no ST family. The total number of students enrolled under the STs are actually OBCs. A government dispensary with a trained doctor was reported to be operating since the last 15 years in this village, but in reality there is a sub-centre with an ANM and a malaria eradication worker. A government dispensary with a trained doctor is located in the adjoining village 3 km away. The village has the facility of a PHC (17 km) and a FWC as well as a pharmacy (7 km). A government scheme of employment under JRY was available and the water supply installation was in progress. Apart from this, the rest of the village schedule was correct.

In this village, the Department of Public Water Works had started the installation of pipelines. At the time of survey, pipeline connections throughout the village were almost complete. Test distribution of water had been carried out. Actual water supply was not restored. Thus, so far the source of drinking water is the hand pump in all seasons. The source of water being listed as piped taps was wrongly written at the time of schedule canvassing. Three households own one buffalo each and there is a cow in a fourth household, which were not reported earlier. Three households do not own tubewells contrary to the reporting. The household income was underreported by Rs 3000, Rs 10,800 and Rs 8000 in three households. Purchased wheat, rice, sugar and edible oils were reported less in three households while wheat and other cereals purchased were reported as more in one household. Wage rate and number of days worked during last year was reported less for one member of a household. The morbidity schedules (female schedules) were canvassed correctly.

TABLE 9.16
Prevalence Rate of Illness, Buani

(*N* = 20)

Local name	Standard name	No.	Percentage
Najla, jukam, gala	Cold, cough, sore throat	19	95
Bukhar	Fever without other symptoms	16	80
Diarrhoea, dysentery, vomiting, worms, etc.	Stomach problems	10	50
Malaria	Malaria	8	40
Khasra, mata	Measles, chicken pox	8	40
Feeling low, chakar ana	Low BP	8	40
Dama	Asthma	7	35
Khaj khujli, phora phinsi	Skin problem, scabies, boils	6	30
Joron da dard	Joint pain	6	30
Typhoid	Typhoid	6	30
Ankh dard, motia	Eye flu, cataract	6	30
Pairra, excess menses	Menses problems	5	25
Safed pani	Leucorrhoea	5	25
Dil di bimari, blood pressure	Heart trouble, high BP	5	25
Jarh wala phora	Cancer	3	15
Kan da dard	Ear pain	3	15
Sir sard	Headache	3	15
Daura	Fits (shivering hands, stiff neck)	3	15
Polio	Polio	3	15
Kamar dard	Back ache	2	10
Bhar padna	Prolapsed uterus	2	10
Bava seer	Piles	1	5
Dant dard	Tooth ache	1	5
Peelia	Jaundice	1	5
Adhrang	Paralysis	1	5
TB	TB	1	5
Appendicitis	Appendicitis	1	5
Chhati dard	Chest pain	1	5
Sugar	Diabetes	1	5

UTTAR PRADESH

The relative backwardness of Uttar Pradesh as compared to that in many other states of India persists in levels of living, health-care facilities, education, and demographic parameters. With a population that has increased with a decadal difference of 25.48 per cent during 1981–91, it makes it difficult to provide even the basic necessities such as food, shelter, and clothing to the common person. The incidence of poverty in the state is very high with the average percentage of population below the poverty line being higher than the national average. According to a report of the NCAER more than half of the population belongs to the lowest income group while only 4 per cent belongs to the highest income group.

The land distribution is highly skewed among the rural households with 3 per cent households owning large landholdings while 13 per cent being landless. Uttar Pradesh also has a dismal literacy rate of only 57.36 per cent, much lower than the national average. There is also a very wide inter-district variation in the literacy rates. The overall enrolment rate in the state is 58.50 per cent with the rate varying widely across districts and between the sexes. There is an urgent need to improve facilities provided in the health sector. There is a widespread inter-district variation in the distribution and the number of hospitals, Primary Health Centres, and doctors.

Social evil like child marriage is also prevalent in the state with more than 10 girls out of 100 in the age-group of 10–14 years getting married. This has an adverse effect on not only health, but also on education. Uttar Pradesh needs urgent government intervention for its overall development.

10 Secondary Data Report for Uttar Pradesh

10.1 Profile of the State

Under the British administration, the provinces of Agra and Oudh were combined into the United Province of Agra and Oudh. The name was shortened to United Provinces in 1935. After Independence, in 1950, United Provinces was renamed as Uttar Pradesh, and it became a state in the Indian Union. The state is bounded by Tibet and Nepal in the north, Himachal Pradesh in the north-west, Haryana in the west, Rajasthan in the south-west, Madhya Pradesh in the south, and Bihar in the east.

In 1999, a separate state of Uttaranchal was created out of the state of Uttar Pradesh. Uttaranchal consists of 13 districts and has a population of 8,479,562 (provisional) comprising 4,316,401 males and 4,163,161 females, according to the 2001 Census. Populationwise, it ranks twentieth among states and union territories, and areawise, it stands at the eighteenth place with a total area of 53,483 sq. km. The population density in the state is 159 persons per sq. km. The variables considered in this report are not available separately for Uttaranchal, as well as for the newly created districts of Uttar Pradesh. Hence, the study pertains to Uttar Pradesh when Uttaranchal was not a separate state.

Uttar Pradesh, the most populous state of India, has a total population of 13.91 crore, which constitutes 16.44 per cent of India's total population. It has a population density of 473 persons per sq. km. Its total geographical area is 2.94 lakh sq. km. A little more than 21 per cent of the total population belongs to the Scheduled Castes (SCs) whereas the Scheduled Tribe (ST) population is only 0.2 per cent of the state population. As compared to this, about 16 per cent of India's total population is SC. The number of females per thousand males is 882 in the state as compared to 929 for the country as a whole. The literates constitute 57.4 per cent of the state population, while the literacy rate in India (excluding Jammu and Kashmir) is 65.4 per cent according to 2001 Census. Among the major states, Uttar Pradesh ranks fourteenth in per capita income and number of beds in hospitals (see Box 10.1). The female literacy rate, at 25.3 per cent, is much lower than that for India, which is 39.3 per cent. During 1981–91, the state population grew by 22.9 per cent as against the 22.7 per cent decadal growth of India's population. The state is divided into 63 districts. The area and population of all the districts may be obtained from the 1991 Census.

About 20 per cent of the state's population is urban, while about 26 per cent of India's population is urban. Uttar Pradesh ranks twelfth in the share of urban population to the total population (see Box 10.1). The rural population of this state lives in 1.13 lakh villages (1981 Census). About 74 per cent of these villages have a population size below 1000 persons. In other words, most of the rural people are settled in small-sized villages, scattered over the land area of 2.94 lakh sq. km.

The preponderance of the rural population makes the state economy primarily agrarian. Agriculture contributes about 43 per cent of the state domestic product (SDP) and employs a majority of the labour force. The occupational distribution of the total main workers in the state shows that 72.2 per cent of them are cultivators and agricultural labourers. A little more than 82 per cent of the main workers in the rural areas of the state are engaged in agriculture—61 per cent as cultivators and 21 per cent as agricultural labourers.

Agricultural land is obviously the basic source of output, income, and employment for the rural population. The distribution of land is highly skewed. The Agricultural Landholdings Census of 1990–1 shows that the number of holdings with size less than 1 ha constitutes about 74 per cent of the total number of holdings in the state, while the corresponding figure is 58 per cent for India as a whole. Data collected by the National Sample Survey Organization (NSSO) in its 37th round show that the concentration ratio of land ownership among the rural households is 0.64, indicating no change in the ratio calculated on the basis of data from the 8th round of the NSS. The proportion of landless labour households, though it has declined over time, is still about 5 per cent (NSS 37th round) in the state.

Given the size and distribution of agricultural land, the agricultural sector of the state produces nearly one-fifth of India's total foodgrains; about 37 per cent of wheat and 13 per cent of rice. The state produces about 46 per cent of the sugarcane output in the country, despite lower yield rates than some other states such as Punjab, Haryana, Andhra Pradesh, Karnataka, and Maharashtra.

There are about 7.5 lakh artisans in the state. Hand-knitted woollen carpets of Varanasi and Mirzapur, *chikan* of Lucknow,

BOX 10.1
Profile of Uttar Pradesh

Item	Unit	Year	Uttar Pradesh		Highest		Lowest		India
			Rank	Actual	State	Actual	State	Actual	Actual
CMIE index	No.	1995	11	112	Punjab	171.9	Bihar	91.3	100
HDI indicators (Pal and Pant)		1993	13	0.530	Punjab	0.793	Bihar	0.503	1
(Shiva Kumar)		1991	15	0.292	Kerala	0.651	UP	0.292	1
(Tilak)		1991	15	0.110	Kerala	0.775	UP	0.110	1
PCY (at 1980–1 prices)	Rs	1992–3	14	1591	Punjab	3730	Bihar	1142	2226
Urban population	%	1991	12	19.89	Maharashtra	38.7	HP	8.70	25.73
Literacy	per '000	2001	14	573.6	Kerala	909	Bihar	475	654
Life expectancy	Years	1986–90	15	53.4	Kerala	69.5	MP	53.0	57.7
Electrified dwellings	%	1988–9	13	8.9	HP	83.9	Bihar	4.5	26.9
Annual PC consumption of electricity	kWh	1991	13	186	Punjab	703	Assam	96	299
Road length	per '000 sq. km	1991	7	692	Kerala	3567	MP	321	621
No. of beds in hospitals	'0000	1993	14	32.7	Kerala	255.0	MP	26.3	68.3
No. of dispensaries	'0000	1990	10	1.3	Gujarat	15.2	MP	0.4	3.4
Regd. med. practitioners	'0000	1992	9	24.7	Tamil Nadu	82.9	UP	24.7	28.9
Agriculture									
Cereals (per capita)	kg.	1993–4	3	238.2	Punjab	1016.3	Kerala	32.0	193.7
Pulses (per capita)	kg.	1993–4	5	17.2	MP	48.8	Kerala	0.6	15.0
Total oil seeds	kg.	1993–4	10	10.6	MP	66.5	Kerala	0.4	24.6
Sugarcane (per capita)	kg.	1993–4	1	724.4	UP	724.4	HP	4.9	260.3
Potato (per capita)	kg.	1993–4	2	53.2	West Bengal	73.0	AP	0.1	20.7
Milk availability (per capita per day)	ml	1991	7	180	Punjab	672	Assam	0.05	218
Manufacturing									
Share in net value added from manufacturing	%	1993	4	9.1	Maharashtra	22.8	Punjab	4.1	100
Regd. working factories	%	1993	12	2.9	Bihar	20.8	HP	0.6	100
Share in employment of regd. working factories	%	1993	6	6.7	Maharashtra	14.7	HP	0.6	100

Note: PCY: per capita income.

Sources: CMIE Index 1995, District Profile, Centre for Monitoring Indian Economy; *Statistical Abstract*, 1992, CSO, Government of India.

terracotta of Gorakhpur, wood carving of Saharanpur, and brass wares of Moradabad have excelled in their craftsmanship. Uttar Pradesh has a contribution of about 75 per cent in the total exports of woollen carpets from the country.

There has been considerable development in the field of agriculture with respect to cropping pattern, irrigation, and mechanization. Uttar Pradesh occupies third position in per capita production of total cereals, fifth position in total pulses and first position in sugarcane production (see Box 10.1). The total area in the state under more than one crop and the extent of net irrigated area constitute about 21 per cent of India's total area under more than one crop and the total net irrigated area. However, there is wide spatial disparity in the level of agricultural development across the districts and regions in the state. The average yield of the principal crops in the state remains low.

The industrial base of the state is not as developed as that in some states like Maharashtra, Tamil Nadu, West Bengal, and Gujarat. The total number of working joint stock companies in the state constitutes only 5 per cent of India's total number of such companies and the amount of fixed capital. The share of the state in the total production of most of the industrial commodities is meagre, except in that of vegetable oils and sugar.

In fact, Uttar Pradesh is one of the backward states of India, whether in terms of per capita agricultural income per capita industrial income. In 1989–90, the SDP per capita (at 1980–1 prices) was Rs 1572 as against Rs 2169 for all India. The gross value of agricultural produce (at current prices) per capita was only Rs 1257 in 1988–9, and industrial output per capita was Rs 1091 in 1987–8. The number of workers in registered factories per lakh population was only 568 in 1987–8.

Poverty and unemployment are the two major human aspects of development whose magnitude reflect the final outcome of growth as well as the development efforts undertaken by the state since the inception of planning. The NSS data-based estimate of poverty (Agarwal et al. 1993) shows that in 1983–4 a little more than 45 per cent of the state's population was below the poverty line as compared to 39.4 per cent of India's population. The incidence of rural poverty was about 47 per cent in the state, while it was 40.2 per cent in the country as a whole. About 20 per cent of the total poor in the country belong to Uttar Pradesh, and a little more than 20 per cent of India's total rural poor belong to this state. The estimates of the 43rd round of the NSS (1987–8) show that 7.3 lakh labour force in Uttar Pradesh is unemployed (according to the usual status concept). The unemployment rate by daily status is 3.4 per cent in the state as against 6.1 per cent for India as a whole. This means that, according to daily status, about 94.23 lakh person days are unemployed. The category of unemployment by daily status also includes seasonal unemployment and underemployment.

The characteristics of employment also expose, to an extent, the latent nature of employment as well as underemployment, which have a certain bearing on poverty. *Sarvekshana* (1991) shows that most of the employed labour force, whether in rural or urban areas, is self-employed. A little more than 76 per cent of the workers by usual status are self-employed in agriculture, about 10 per cent of the total employed are regular wage earners, and about 25 per cent of them are casual workers in the agricultural sector of the state economy. Of the total workers by usual status in the non-agricultural sector, about 30 per cent are regular wage earners, 56 per cent are self-employed, and about 15 per cent are casual workers. Thus, about 71 per cent of the workers are self-employed and another 10 per cent are casual workers. Only 6.68 per cent of the workers are employed in registered working factories (see Box 10.1). The data indicate that there is a high degree of self-employment, casualization of the work force (that is, underemployment), and the existence of a small-sized regular wage employment sector, owing to the underdevelopment of the non-agricultural sector in the state.

The 43rd round of NSS (1987–8) shows that Uttar Pradesh shares about 9 per cent of the total unemployment (by daily status) in the country. The share of educated unemployment in the total unemployment of the state by usual status is 47.4 per cent as against about 40 per cent for India as a whole. The share of female unemployment is only 20 per cent in the state, while it is 33 per cent for India. The share of rural areas in the total unemployment is 76 per cent in the state, as against about 69 per cent for India. Thus it is clear that unemployment is widespread in rural areas and there is a high incidence of educated unemployment.

The CMIE index of development for the state is 72 for the year 1993. There are wide inter-district variations ranging from 38 for Chamoli to 155 for Kanpur Nagar. Kanpur is the most industrialized district in the state. The estimated coefficient of variation (CV) is 57 per cent, which shows very high inter-district variation in socio-economic development (see Map 10.1).

Thus, widespread poverty and a large un-employed and underemployed labour force in the agriculture-dominated state economy present a poor picture of the social and human aspects of development, despite there having been some perceptible growth and development, specially in the agricultural sector. The human development index (HDI) for the Indian states computed by both Shiva Kumar (1991) and Tilak (1991) places Uttar Pradesh at the bottom of the 15 major states, while the HDI computed by Pal and Pant (1993) ranks Uttar Pradesh thirteenth among the 15 major states.

10.2 Literacy and Primary Education

Education has been viewed as one of the major factors that act as a catalyst in bringing about economic, social, cultural, and technological changes in a society. Article 45 of the Constitution of India envisages that education shall be free, compulsory, and universal for children up to the age of 14 years. This goal, which was initially sought to be achieved by 1960, is still eluding the nation because of a number of constraints.

This section does not cover all the aspects of education. It is confined to formal education and, in particular, to primary education. It presents and analyses data on levels of literacy, enrolment rates, drop-out rates and mean years of schooling for various districts and population groups in Uttar Pradesh. It also looks at a few other parameters such as teacher–student ratio and geographical proximity of primary schools, and their influence on the achieved levels of literacy.

10.2.1 Factors Influencing Literacy and Primary Education

To become literate and to achieve other milestones in formal education it is necessary to get enrolled in a school and not discontinue before achieving the desired standard. Enrolment and drop-out rates are, therefore, likely to influence literacy (and other educational achievements). An analysis of these variables would be useful in the formulation of policies to achieve higher levels of literacy (and other achievements in formal education). However, it is difficult to get reliable data on these variables.

Enrolment ratios are obtained as the ratio of the recorded number of students in primary classes and the number of children in the relevant age group (6 to 11 years) estimated from census data.

The children in the age group 6–11 years do not constitute a proper universe of primary school-going children. The recorded number of students in the primary section includes

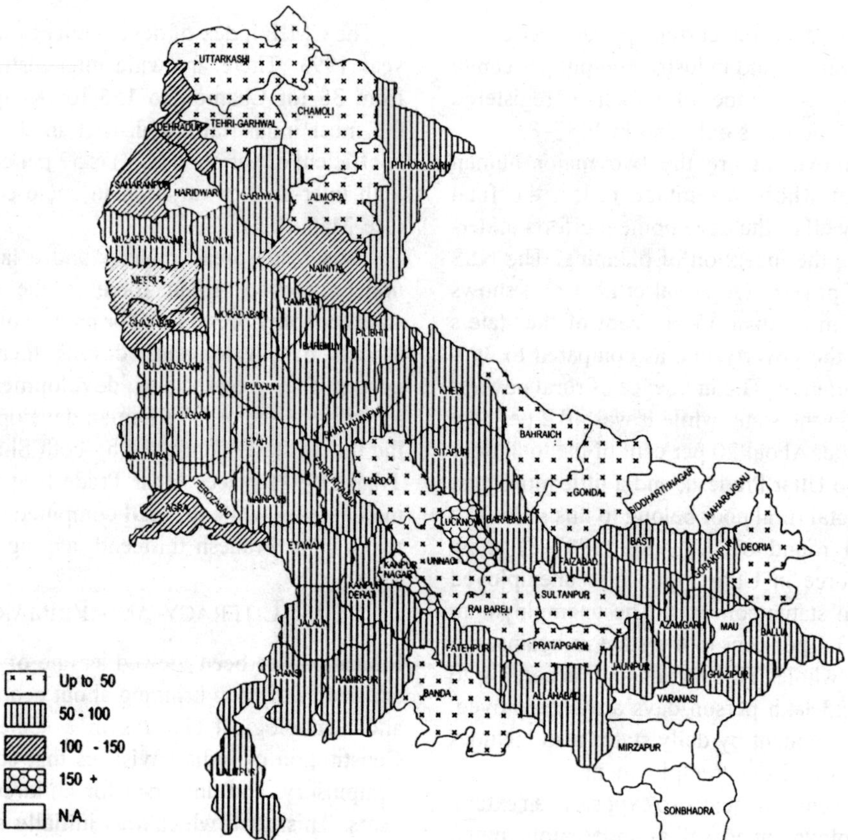

MAP 10.1: **Levels of Economic Development in Uttar Pradesh**

many who are not in this age group. Consequently, enrolment ratios estimated and published by the government departments turn out to be gross overestimates. Enrolment ratios crossing 100 per cent are a common observation in many states, including Uttar Pradesh. The reasons for this are: (i) enrolment earlier than age 6, especially among the urban elite; (ii) students above the age of 11 years also enrol in primary classes, particularly in rural areas; and (iii) fictitious enrolment (to receive the material incentives offered).

The reliability of estimated drop-out rates is no better. The methodology adopted for estimating drop-outs is based on certain assumptions. For example, it assumes that all students enrol only in Class I and either continue or drop out. The reality is, however, known to be different, Many children take admission in classes other than Class I. Consequently, drop-out rates available from secondary sources are underestimated to the extent that in many cases the estimates turn out to be negative. This is more apparent in states such as Kerala.

10.2.2 Gross Enrolment Rate

Enrolment rates for boys and girls across the 56 districts of Uttar Pradesh are displayed in Tables 10.E1 and 10.E2 for urban and rural areas respectively. These data, obtained from the Directorate of Basic Education, Uttar Pradesh, relate to 1991. Data for a more recent year could not be obtained.

The overall enrolment rate in the state is 58.50 per cent—almost every second child never goes to school. This rate is much lower among girls (50.48 per cent) than among boys (64.64 per cent). The recorded level of enrolment in primary school is worse than the level that prevails in many other states.

The enrolment rate varies widely across districts from a low of 38.41 per cent in Etah to 150.86 per cent in Garhwal. Enrolment among girls ranges between 32.29 per cent in Moradabad and 147.57 per cent in Garhwal. Enrolment among boys is the highest in Pithoragarh (178.72 per cent) and the lowest in Etah (27.93 per cent).

The enrolment rate is high (more than 80 per cent) in 10 districts. These are Chamoli (141.11 per cent), Tehri Garhwal (106.50 per cent), Garhwal (150.86 per cent), Pithoragarh (143.35 per cent), Almora (128.69 per cent), Etawah (80.24 per cent), Kanpur (89.65 per cent), Jhansi (83.33 per cent), Lalitpur (91.32 per cent), and Fatehpur (80.80 per cent).

It is low (less than 50 per cent) in 8 districts. These are Bijnor (46.60 per cent), Moradabad (45.12 per cent), Rampur (49.09 per cent), Ghaziabad (40.27 per cent), Etah (38.41 per cent), Lucknow (46.28 per cent), Gorakhpur (47.72 per cent), and Varanasi (47.52 per cent).

Enrolment among girls is lower than that among boys in almost all the districts. Total enrolment rate is higher in urban areas (68.03 per cent) than in rural areas (56.51

per cent). In urban Uttar Pradesh, girls have a marginally higher rate of enrolment (69.41 per cent) than boys (66.85 per cent) (Table 10.E1). In rural areas (Table 10.E2), however, boys (64.21 per cent) maintain their lead over girls (46.22 per cent).

10.2.3 Drop-out Rates

Tables 10.E1 and 10.E2 also present drop-out rates for urban and rural areas, respectively across the districts of Uttar Pradesh. The drop-out rate in the state is quite high at 45.02 per cent. Every second child enrolled fails to continue till the completion of primary education. The drop-out rate is marginally higher among girls (46.25 per cent) than among boys (44.44 per cent). In some districts, more than 70 per cent of the girls enrolled discontinue their studies before completing primary level. These are Moradabad (74.59 per cent), Shahjahanpur (74.18 per cent), Lalitpur (79.51 per cent), and Basti (71.71 per cent). In as many as 15 districts, more than 50 per cent of the boys enrolled drop out of school before completing primary education. In the case of girls the number of such districts is much larger at 20. The lowest drop-out rate among girls is 10.65 per cent in Lucknow, followed by Pratapgarh (14.81 per cent) and Nainital (20.17 per cent). Among boys the lowest drop-out rate is in Nainital (6.45 per cent) and the highest is in Ghaziabad (77.37 per cent). Drop-out rate is higher in urban areas than in rural areas.

Despite the provision of free and compulsory education to all children up to the age of 14 years in the Indian Constitution, the goal of universalization of elementary education has not been achieved, even after more than 50 years of Independence. There are three aspects of the universalization of elementary education: (i) universal enrolment; (ii) universal retention; and (iii) universal achievement. These aspects address certain questions. Are all children in the age group of 6–11 years enrolled in school? If enrolled, do they complete the desired level of education? If yes, do they complete it within the scheduled time and do they acquire quality education?

10.2.4 Mean Years of Schooling

The parameter of mean years of schooling, reflects whether all the children in the age group of 6–11 years are exposed to primary schooling in the state. The primary level of education consists of classes I–V, spanning a period of five years. A child requires a minimum of five years of time to complete primary education. Ideally, the mean years of schooling for the children in the age group of 6–11 years should be five years. Table 10.E3 presents the estimates of mean years of schooling for boys and girls across the districts of Uttar Pradesh. The mean years of schooling at the primary level in the state is 3.66 years—3.5 years for girls and 3.74 years for boys. This means that in Uttar Pradesh, on an average, a child in the age group of 6–11 years (who is enrolled in school) spends less than four years as against the expected five years of schooling. Mean years of schooling is high (more than four years) in Garhwal (4.17), Nainital (4.52), Rampur (4.11), Pilibhit (4.05), Sitapur (4.04), Unnao (4.15), Rae Bareli (4.25), Etawah (4.13), Kanpur (4.20), Hamirpur (4.48), Fatehpur (4.34), Pratapgarh (4.24), and Gonda (4.09).

The highest mean years of schooling for boys, observed in Nainital (4.59 years), is almost twice the lowest mean years of schooling, observed in Allahabad (2.36) and Moradabad (2.39). For girls, mean years of schooling is the highest in Lucknow (4.93) and the lowest in Moradabad (2.29). In many districts, girls are exposed to a longer duration of primary schooling than boys, for example Tehri Garhwal, Ghaziabad, Lucknow, Azamgarh, Sitapur, etc.

10.2.5 Teacher–Student Ratio

Qualitative changes in classroom practice will occur only when a good rapport is established between teacher and students. Overcrowded classes and single-teacher schools prevent the teachers from devoting enough time to their students. This widens the gap between teachers and students. The average teacher–student ratio in the districts at the primary level of education is, thus, a useful indicator having a bearing on the quality of education. Table 10.E3 presents these ratios across the districts in Uttar Pradesh (see Map 10.2).

The average teacher–student ratio for the state as a whole is 1 : 56 at the primary level. It is high in Rampur (72.0), Mainpuri (72.4), Sitapur (72.2), and Fatehpur (70.7). The ratio is low in Uttarkashi (24.6), Dehradun (32.6), Saharanpur (30.6) and Etah (38.4).

According to the Kothari Commission Report (1966), the teacher–student ratio should be around 1 : 40 at the primary level of education. If this ratio is considered as a norm, Table 10.E3 presents a near dismal picture. In as many as 52 out of 56 districts, the ratio exceeds the recommended norm. Even if the norm is relaxed and taken to be 50 students per teacher, only 14 districts are seen to conform to this. Many of the districts need more teachers in the primary schools.

10.2.6 Geographical Proximity of Primary Schools

The first step towards achieving the constitutional goal of universal elementary education is to ensure that a school with adequate infrastructure facilities is available within walking distance to all the school-going children. The Education Commission (1964–6) recommended that 'a primary school be made available within one mile from the home of every child and within the reach of every child' (Vol. II, 1970, para 7.14).

At the national level, approximately 95 per cent of the population has a primary school within the radius of 1 km. (Challenge of Education, A Policy Perspective 1986). The National Policy on Education (1986) also observes that more than 90 per cent of rural habitations now have schooling facilities within the radius of 1 km (ibid., p. 2). In Uttar Pradesh, only 61,811 out of 111,975 villages have a primary school within the village. Another 19,475 villages have a school within 1 km. Thus, about 72.59 per cent of the villages have a primary school within walking distance for children. Children in more than 5 per cent of the villages (6296 out of

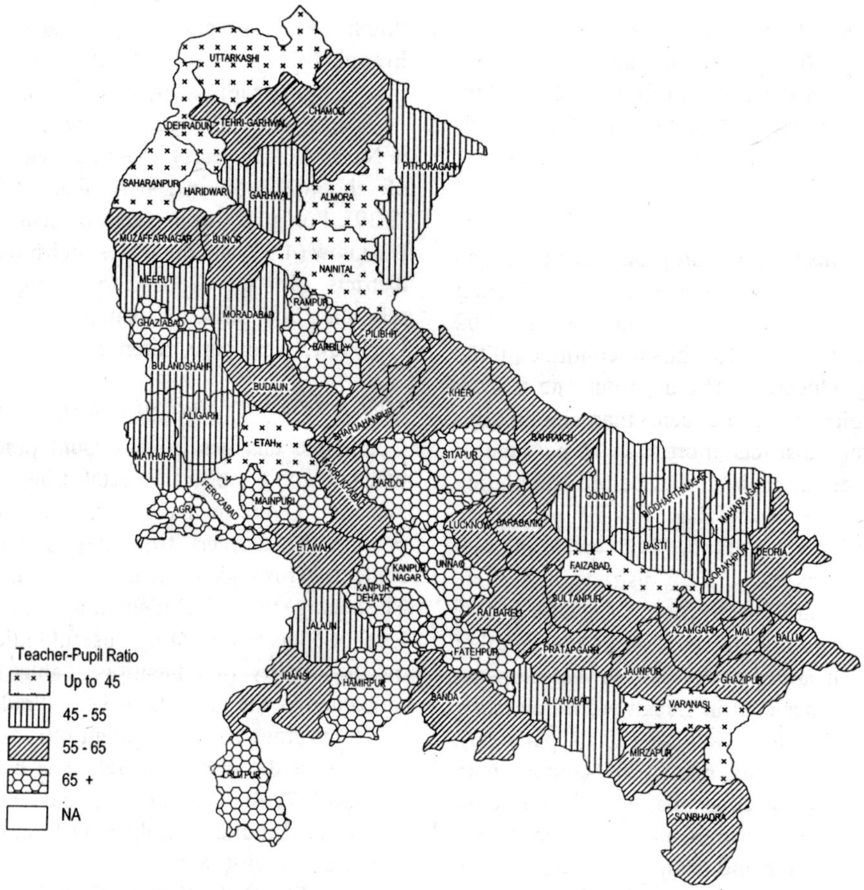

MAP 10.2: **Availability of Teachers in Uttar Pradesh**

111,975) have to walk a distance of more than 3 km to receive primary education, which by any standard is a very deplorable situation. The districtwise details are presented in Table 10.E4 (also see Map 10.3).

The existence of a primary school within the village or nearby is a prerequisite for the children to be able to attend school. Most of the states have succeeded in providing primary schools to children right inside the village or within their walking distance. The state of Uttar Pradesh is still far away from this goal. Many of the districts need more primary schools within the villages.

It can be observed (Tables 10.E3 to 10.E5) that the most literate districts are not those with the best schooling facilities. Districts such as Barabanki, Gonda, and Bahraich performed low in terms of literacy, enrolment, and discontinuance despite having good schooling facilities.

Table 10.1 contains data on employment in agriculture—as cultivators and agricultural labourers—along with enrolment and drop-out rates for some districts of Uttar Pradesh. It can be seen that many districts with high employment in agriculture have recorded high drop-out rate and low enrolment.

Increased number of schools and their geographical proximity, though necessary, are not sufficient to raise enrolment, reduce discontinuance and increase literacy. The problem, perhaps, should be approached from different angles, such as: (i) improvement of quality of teaching and other infrastructure in schools; (ii) change in curriculum, working hours, and vacation to make these compatible with the time disposition pattern and agricultural season in rural areas; and (iii) consideration of other population group specific socio-economic factors that influence enrolment and discontinuance.

10.2.7 Effective Literacy Rate

Literacy rate is one of the major indicators of human development. Table 10.E5 presents data obtained from the 1991 and 2001 Censuses on effective literacy rate in Uttar Pradesh and its districts. The overall literacy in the state was 41.60 per cent in 1991—55.73 per cent among males and 25.31 per cent among females. The state ranks quite low in terms of literacy among the states and union territories. Within the state, in 1991, Dehradun had the highest level of literacy (69.50 per cent) while Budaun (24.64) and Bahraich (24.39 per cent) had the lowest. In 48 out of 63 districts, illiterates are in a majority. However, in 2001 the literacy rate of undivided Uttar Pradesh (not considering districts of Uttaranchal separately) has gone up very rapidly in all the districts, irrespective of sex (see Map 10.3).

In 1991, in rural areas female literacy was extremely low in Moradabad (9.71 per cent), Rampur (8.06 per cent), Budaun (8.11 per cent), Bareilly (9.65 per cent), Bahraich (7.89

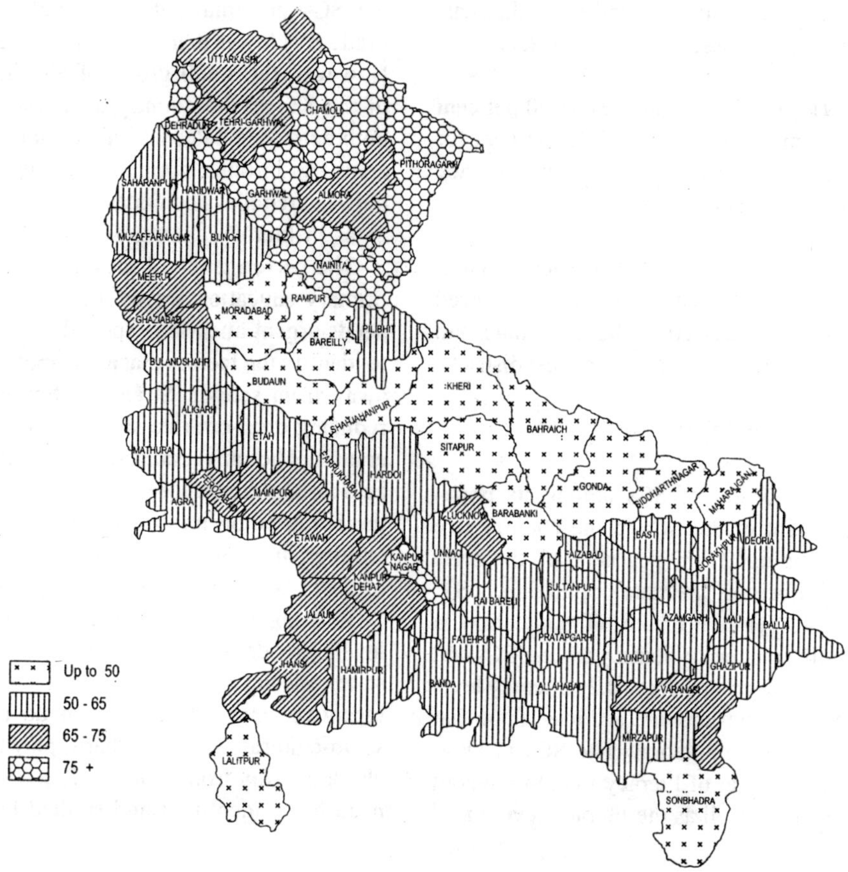

MAP 10.3: **Total Literacy in Uttar Pradesh (2001)**

TABLE 10.1
Employment in Agriculture, Enrolment, and Drop-out Rates in Select Districts of Uttar Pradesh, 1991

Districts	Per cent of main workers engaged in cultivation	Enrolment rate		Drop-out rate	
		Boys	Girls	Boys	Girls
Siddarthnagar	90.78	68.33	35.37	60.58	71.71
Maharajganj	88.98	60.36	33.31	21.07	41.72
Gonda	87.99	91.68	38.70	37.49	65.33
Bahraich	87.84	70.32	42.72	46.75	63.68
Kheri	87.34	72.85	58.42	47.66	59.34
Banda	85.78	70.52	53.43	42.98	65.81
Basti	85.53	68.33	35.37	60.58	71.71
Hardoi	85.34	82.90	60.67	46.38	48.35
Budaun	84.94	65.27	45.49	49.68	51.90
Sitapur	84.11	82.46	51.06	26.52	24.83
Garhwal	64.20*	153.81	147.57	21.49	30.36
Mathura	64.28	61.57	40.61	35.64	58.86
Bijnor	66.10	50.26	41.34	47.89	47.50
Mirzapur	66.28	74.61	48.04	29.57	47.17
Moradabad	67.43	55.73	32.29	65.39	74.59
Bareilly	67.52	88.36	61.85	51.23	58.19
Bulandshahr	67.69	82.20	41.60	42.61	48.77
Muzzafarnagar	67.94	62.93	51.51	44.03	42.58
Rampur	72.61	57.63	38.91	27.96	41.93
Allahabad	69.20	68.71	39.14	59.72	53.35

Note: * Including Basti.

Sources: Census of India 1991; Directorate of Basic Education, Uttar Pradesh.

per cent), and Gonda (9.66 per cent). In another 27 districts, rural female literacy had not crossed 20 per cent (see Map 10.4).

In urban areas in 1991, the literacy rate was 61.00 per cent for the state (69.98 per cent for males and 50.38 per cent for females). Kanpur Nagar recorded the highest urban literacy rate of 72.11 per cent—79.38 per cent for males and 63.06 per cent for females.

One important feature of this profile of literacy in Uttar Pradesh (as also in many other states) is the pronounced disparity between urban and rural areas, both in male and female literacy level. This pattern is similar across the districts.

10.2.8 Literacy among Scheduled Castes and Scheduled Tribes

The state has a large proportion of SCs among its population. About 21.18 per cent of the SCs in the country live in Uttar Pradesh, constituting 21.05 per cent of the state population. Only 0.21 per cent of the state population is ST, and constitutes about 0.42 per cent of the ST population in the country. A comparative picture of literacy among SCs and STs in Uttar Pradesh is displayed in Table 10.2. Literacy level among the SCs and STs in the country is lower than that among other segments of the population. The SCs in Uttar Pradesh have a much lower level of literacy than the overall level of literacy in the state as well as the literacy level of all the SCs in India. Literacy level among the STs in Uttar Pradesh is lower than the overall level of literacy in the state. However, the small group of STs in Uttar Pradesh is ahead of the STs in the country as a whole in terms of literacy—both among females and males and in rural as well as urban areas. As in other population groups, there is wide disparity between females and males as well as between rural and urban areas in literacy among SCs and STs in Uttar Pradesh.

The performance of the state in the levels of literacy and primary education leaves much to be desired. This problem needs urgent attention. Special studies should be undertaken to identify the factors that are responsible for keeping children away from school. Strategies for increasing enrolment and reducing drop-out rate should take these factors into consideration. The universalization of primary education seems to be a distant dream for the state. The current emphasis should, therefore, be on improvement in enrolment and retention of children in schools. An increase in the number of schools and teachers is necessary to ensure physical access to schools.

It is apparent that the rural literacy and female literacy levels are dragging down the average performance of the state. Special attention in terms of motivation, access, and incentives is needed. Widespread poverty in the state and socio-cultural factors, perhaps, play their roles in keeping the children away from schools. These factors and their interplay need to be identified and studied by competent scholars so

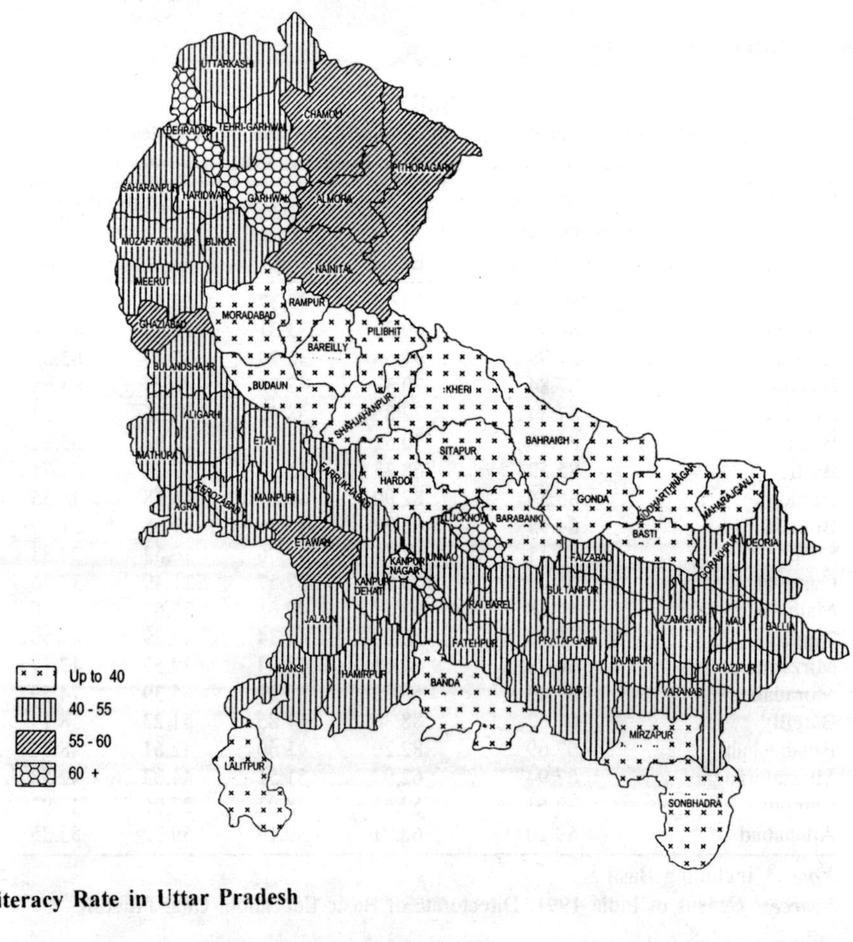

MAP 10.4: **Female Literacy Rate in Uttar Pradesh**

TABLE 10.2
Literacy among Scheduled Castes and Scheduled Tribes in Uttar Pradesh and India, 1991

Population group	All areas			Rural			Urban		
	Total	Male	Female	Total	Male	Female	Total	Male	Female
All in India	52.21	64.13	39.29	44.69	57.87	30.62	73.08	81.09	64.05
SCs in India	37.41	49.91	23.76	33.25	45.95	19.46	55.11	66.60	42.29
SCs in UP	26.85	40.80	10.69	24.76	38.87	8.47	42.30	54.79	27.36
STs in India	29.60	40.65	18.19	27.38	38.45	16.02	56.60	66.56	45.66
STs in UP	35.70	49.95	19.86	33.81	48.20	17.94	64.34	74.91	51.06
All in UP	41.60	55.73	25.31	36.66	52.05	19.02	61.00	69.98	50.38

Source: Census of India, 1991.

that future action plans can be formulated to improve the situation.

10.3 Health-care Facilities

The health status of the population is an important aspect of well-being. Good health is necessary for effective participation in economic and social activities and helps in achieving higher levels of human development. The available health-care facilities have a bearing on the achieved health status as measured by various indicators An assessment of the adequacy of these facilities in terms of the number of hospitals, dispensaries, doctors, and other medical staff is relevant in the context of human development.

The Eighth Plan envisaged providing health-care facilities to all by the end of the plan period. Accordingly, a three-tier integrated health-care system was evolved in the states. A network of community health centres (CHCs), primary health centres (PHCs), and sub-centres has been built up in rural areas to provide an easy access to health-care facilities. The physical targets fixed for rural areas are: (i) one sub-centre for 5000 persons in the plains and 3000 persons in the hilly and tribal areas; and (ii) one PHC for 30,000 persons in the plains and 20,000 persons in hilly and tribal areas. In urban areas the public health-care system consists of hospitals, dispensaries and health posts.

10.3.1 Hospitals, Dispensaries, and Health Posts

There are 1103 hospitals in the state. Of these, 876 are government hospitals and 227 are privately managed, and their distribution is quite uneven at the district level. Some of the districts like Garhwal, Pithoragarh, and Almora have a larger number of hospitals while Unnao, Budaun, and Aligarh have fewer hospitals in relation to population. There are 423 dispensaries in the urban areas of the state—379 managed by government agencies and another 44 which are privately managed. Their distribution across the districts is quite uneven in terms of numbers as well as in relation to the population of the districts.

The number of hospitals and dispensaries, even when seen in relation to the size of the population, does not really reflect the type and quality of services available. Hospitals and dispensaries are of different sizes. They also differ substantially in terms of the facilities that they provide. A proper assessment of the health-care services in these hospitals and dispensaries cannot be made in the absence of detailed information about their relative size and the facilities available.

10.3.2 Sub-centres, Public Health Centres, and Community Health Centres

Data presented in Table 10.H1 indicate that there are 20,153 sub-centres—a little over 18 sub-centres per lakh population in rural Uttar Pradesh. The state has 3.28 PHCs and 0.21 CHCs per lakh population in rural areas. The number of these facilities is close to the norm specified when the state as a whole is considered.

Among the districts, Garhwal tops the list with 37.08 sub-centres per lakh population and Bijnor occupies the lowest position with 11.04 sub-centres per lakh population. The number of sub-centres in most of the districts is only marginally below the norm of 20 sub-centres per lakh population. Deficiency is acute in Bijnor (11.04), Maharajganj (12.24), and Sonbhadra (12.14) districts (see Map 10.5).

There are 3652 PHCs in the state. Jhansi has the largest number (5.56) of PHCs per lakh population followed by Jalaun (5.26) and Banda (5.24). These figures are above the specified norm. Dehradun has the least number (0.78) of PHCs per lakh population. The district, however, is well served by sub-centres. Among the 62 districts, 20 have already reached the norm while another 15 are close to the norm with more than 3 PHCs per lakh population. As many as eight districts have fewer than 2 PHCs per lakh population and need more of these.

The state has 228 CHCs for its 11 crore rural population, implying about 0.21 CHCs per lakh population. Chamoli has the largest number (0.73) of CHCs per lakh rural population. Other districts with a larger number of CHCs per lakh rural population are Uttarkashi (0.45), Tehri Garhwal (0.40), Dehradun (0.40), Pithoragarh (0.39), and Almora (0.39). The districts most deficient in this regard are Barabanki (0.09), Faizabad (0.08), Varanasi (0.09), and Sonbhadra (0.11). The distribution of CHCs across districts seems to be very uneven and calls for corrective measures.

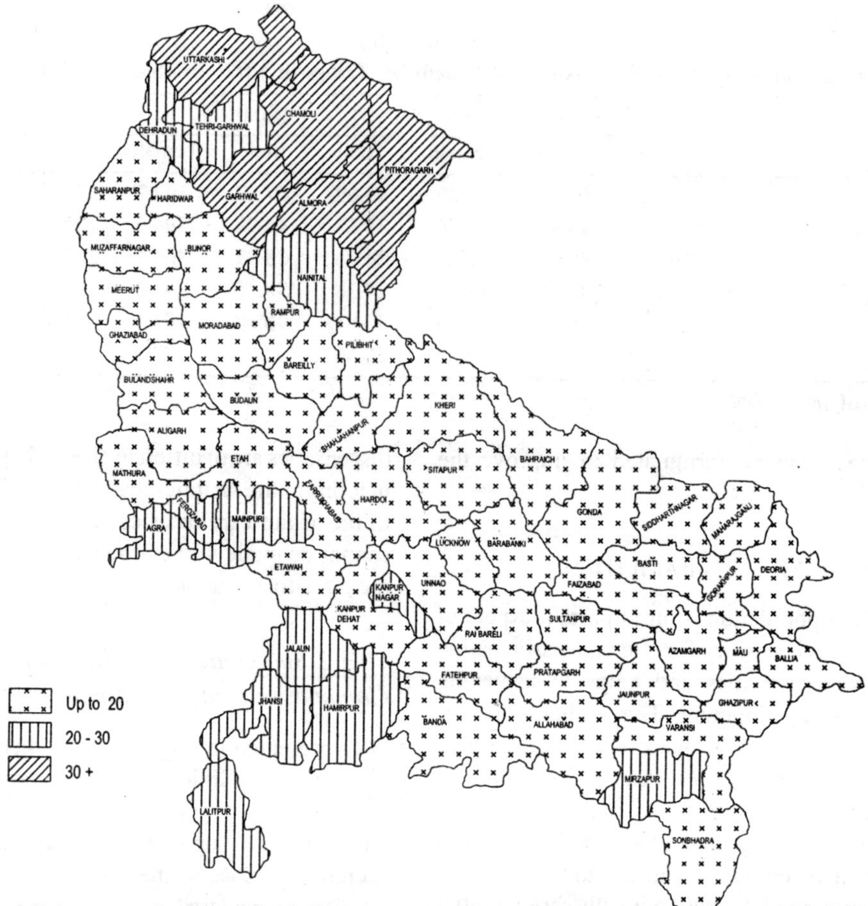

MAP 10.5: **Availability of Sub-centres in Uttar Pradesh**

10.3.3 Doctors and Paramedical Staff

There are 4857 doctors in position in various government hospitals and dispensaries in rural Uttar Pradesh in contrast to the 6757 posts sanctioned. This implies that there are about 4.4 doctors per lakh population (Table 10.H1). Uttarkashi has the largest number (26.07) of doctors per lakh rural population. Other districts with a high doctor–population ratio are Chamoli (18.10), Tehri Garhwal (19.19), Dehradun (22.34), Garhwal (19.96), and Nainital (18.22). Districts with a low doctor–population ratio include Aligarh (2.95), Pilibhit (2.58) Kanpur Dehat (2.08), Bahraich (2.20), Gonda (2.45), Siddharthnagar (1.46), Maharajganj (2.45), and Sonbhadra (2.58). An assessment of the adequacy of doctors cannot be made in the absence of any information about the number of private practitioners across the districts.

Table 10.H1 also furnishes information about family welfare centres (FWCs) in urban Uttar Pradesh. There are 4113 FWCs for 27.6 million urban population of the state, that is about 14.90 FWCs per lakh population. The districts of Uttarkashi (28.97), Chamoli (34.53), Tehri Garhwal (27.26), Garhwal (35.72), Pithoragarh (37.99), and Almora (33.64) are better served by FWCs than other districts. The district of Kanpur Nagar is most deficient in this regard. It has only 89 FWCs for 20 lakh urban population. In the absence of any information about privately managed health-care services, it is not possible to make any assessment of adequacy or otherwise of the existing facilities.

There are 6945 doctors available in Uttar Pradesh of which 2088 are in urban areas and 4857 are in rural areas. There are 3646 staff nurses in the state. The distribution of doctors and staff nurses across the districts is shown in Table 10.H2. Due to deficiency of data, it is not possible to present any analysis relating to the number of other permanent staff.

The partial information on the available health-care facilities has been analysed here in terms of quantity. Information about the quality of services offered by these institutions, an aspect that is no less important, could not be gathered and analysed here.

10.4 Some Demographic Parameters

The composition of the population in terms of age, sex, place of residence, and economic activities has a bearing on the prospects development and is, therefore, of interest in the context of human development. It is also relevant for chalking out plans to provide facilities of education, health care, drinking water, sanitation, housing, old age security and the like.

This section presents data on these demographic parameters which have a bearing on aspects of human development and looks into the variations in these across districts and across population groups. An attempt is also made to locate the factors that lead to these variations in the hope that the findings will be useful in improving the current level of achievements and reducing the disparities among the population groups.

10.4.1 Population Density

Population density, defined as the number of persons living per sq. km, is one of the important indices of population concentration. According to the 1991 Census, the population density of Uttar Pradesh is 473 against the national average of 273. The state ranks fourth in terms of population density after West Bengal (767), Kerala (749), and Bihar (497). The population density is, however, not uniform across the districts (Table 10.H3). Kanpur Nagar is the most densely populated district with 2271 persons per sq. km. Other densely populated districts are Meerut (882), Ghaziabad (1044), Lucknow (1093), Deoria (815), Mau (844), Varanasi (955), and Basti (734). The district of Uttarkashi is the most thinly populated with a density of only 30, followed by Chamoli (50), Pithoragarh (64), Lalitpur (149), and Sonbhadra (158).

The population density in urban areas is much higher at 5553 persons per sq. km than in rural areas at 385 only. The districts of Meerut (604), Ghaziabad (596), Kanpur Nagar (502), Pratapgarh (567), Allahabad (542), Barabanki (505), Faizabad (594), Sultanpuri (555), Maharajganj (557), Basti (700), Deoria (770), Mau (727), Azamgarh (701), Jaunpur (749), Ballia (648), Ghazipur (669), and Varanasi (719) have higher density in rural areas. On the other hand, the rural areas of Uttarkashi (28), Chamoli (46), Pithoragarh (59) and Sonbhadra (138) are sparsely populated.

Urban Agra has a population density of 28,541, which is the highest, followed by Allahabad (15,868), Budaun (12,977), Muzaffarnagar (11,791) Hardwar (11,538), and Lucknow (10,305). The districts of Chamol, (610) and Tehri Garhwal (590) have low population densities in urban areas.

10.4.2 Sex Ratio

Measured as the number of females per thousand males, the sex ratio in Uttar Pradesh is 879. This is marginally lower than the corresponding figure (927) for the country. The sex ratio is not uniform across the districts. The sex ratio in the districts of Chamoli (1003), Tehri Garhwal (1058), Garhwal (1060), Almora (1087), and Azamgarh (1007) are favourable to females largely due to a higher proportion of females in rural areas. Male selective migration from the rural areas of these districts is one of the factors behind this. In addition to these, there are a few more districts that have sex ratios favourable to females in rural areas, making the overall sex ratio close to 1000. These include Pithoragarh (985) and Jaunpur (994). In as many as 30 out of 62 districts in the state, there is a higher proportion of females in the rural population than in the urban population (Table 10.H3).

10.4.3 Scheduled Castes and Scheduled Tribes

There are about 29.3 million SCs in the state who constitute about 21 per cent of the total population of the state (Table 10.H3). The rural population has a higher proportion of SCs in all the districts. In the state as a whole, SCs constitute about 23 per cent of the population in rural areas In urban areas, they comprise about 12.5 per cent of the population. The SC population is fairly widely distributed across the districts, the proportion varying between 42.50 per cent in Sonbhadra and 12.99 per cent in Rampur (see Map 10.6).

The tribal population constitutes only 0.21 per cent of the state population. The tribals are largely concentrated in Chamoli (2.26 per cent), Dehradun (8.20 per cent), Pithoragarh (3.23 per cent), Nainital (5.84 per cent), and Kheri (1.19 per cent).

10.4.4 Level of Urbanization

The level of urbanization in Uttar Pradesh is marginally lower than the national average. The proportion of urban population is 19.84 per cent in the state, as compared to about 26 per cent in the country. The urban population of 27.6 million in Uttar Pradesh consists of 14.8 million males and 12.8 million females. There are pockets of high urbanization such as Kanpur Nagar (84.21 per cent), Lucknow (62.66 per cent), Dehradun (50.26 per cent), Ghaziabad (46.16 per cent), Agra (40.39 per cent), and Meerut (36.73 per cent). On the other hand, districts such as Tehri Garhwal (5.67 per cent), Almora (5.20 per cent), Kanpur Dehat (5.71 per cent), Pithoragarh (5.52 per cent), Siddharthnagar (3.48 per cent), Maharajganj (4.95 per cent), and Basti (6.42 per cent) have very low levels of urbanization (see Map 10.7).

10.4.5 Economic Activities

Of the 139 million population in the state, about 44 million participate in gainful economic activities—41 million as main workers and another 3 million as marginal workers. They constitute, respectively, about 29.73 per cent and 2.47 per cent of the total population. The work participation rate is higher in rural than in urban areas, for both main and marginal workers. In urban areas, 26.56 per cent are main workers and 0.57 per cent are marginal workers, while in rural areas they constitute 30.52 per cent and 2.94 per cent, respectively, of the population (Tables 10.H4 and 10.H5).

The participation as main workers is higher among males (49.31 per cent) than among females (7.45 per cent). The proportion of marginal workers is, however, larger among females (4.87 per cent) than among males (0.36 per cent). This is also true for urban and rural areas taken separately. The proportion of main workers among males varies between a narrow range of 56.40 per cent in Bahraich and 40.67 per cent in Garhwal. The variation in the proportion of main workers among females is much wider—between 1.10 per cent in Mainpuri and 45.00 per cent in Uttarkashi. As many as 25 out of 62 districts have a proportion of main workers among females less than 5 per cent while another 19 districts have this proportion between 5 per cent and 10 per cent. This exceeds 20 per cent in only seven districts. The participation as marginal workers is very low among males. Only in 8 out

TABLE 10.3
Some Demographic Parameters of Uttar Pradesh and the Neighbouring States, 1991

States	Persons living per sq. km	Females per thousand males	Per cent of SCs in population	Per cent of STs in population	Per cent of population living in urban areas
Uttar Pradesh	473	879	21.05	0.21	19.84
Madhya Pradesh	179	931	14.55	23.27	23.18
Bihar	497	911	14.55	7.66	13.14
Haryana	372	865	19.75	–	24.63
Himachal Pradesh	93	976	25.34	4.22	8.69
Rajasthan	129	910	17.29	12.44	22.88
India	273	927	16.48	8.08	25.71

Source: Census of India, 1991.

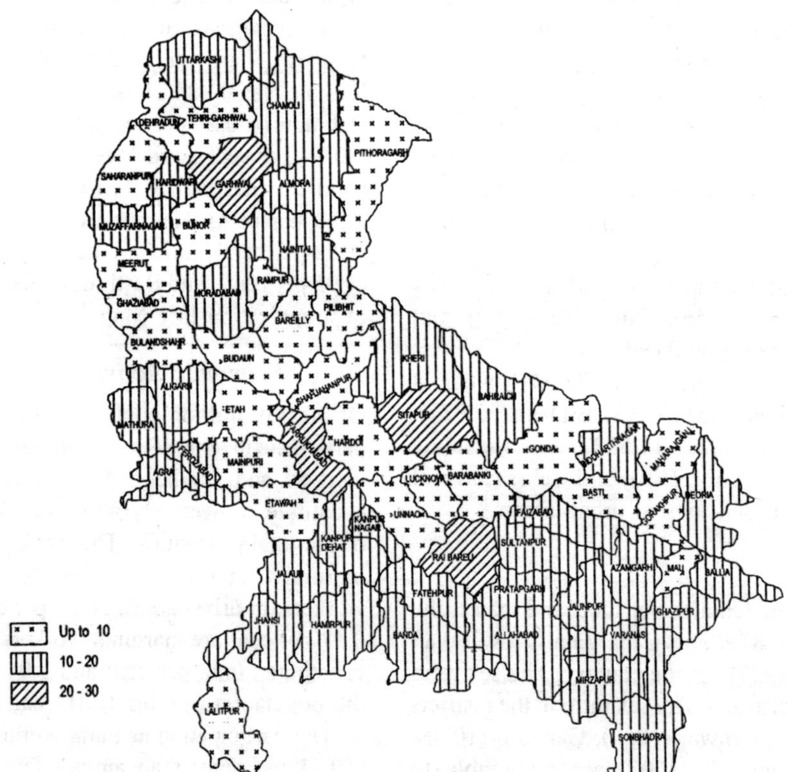

MAP 10.6: **Percentage of SCs and STs to Total Population in Uttar Pradesh**

of 62 districts is this proportion higher than 1 per cent, the highest being 2.51 per cent in Almora. Among females, this proportion is much higher. Lalitpur has the highest proportion of marginal workers among females at 19.16 per cent, followed by Banda (14.73 per cent), Hamirpur (14.21 per cent), Garhwal (13.34), and Pithoragarh (12.97 per cent). As many as eight districts have this proportion higher than 10 per cent. Participation as marginal workers is lower in urban areas, both among males and females, than in rural areas. The pattern between males and females is, however, similar for urban and rural areas taken separately.

Among main workers, about 72.21 per cent are engaged in agriculture—53.27 per cent as cultivators and another 18.94 per cent as agricultural labourers. Some districts like Uttarkashi (77.55 per cent), Chamoli (73.10 per cent), Tehri Garhwal (77.98 per cent), Pithoragarh (73.46 per cent), Almora (76.49 per cent), Budaun (73.47 per cent), Kheri (73.55 per cent), Sitapur (72.48 per cent), Hardoi (73.83 per cent), Bahraich

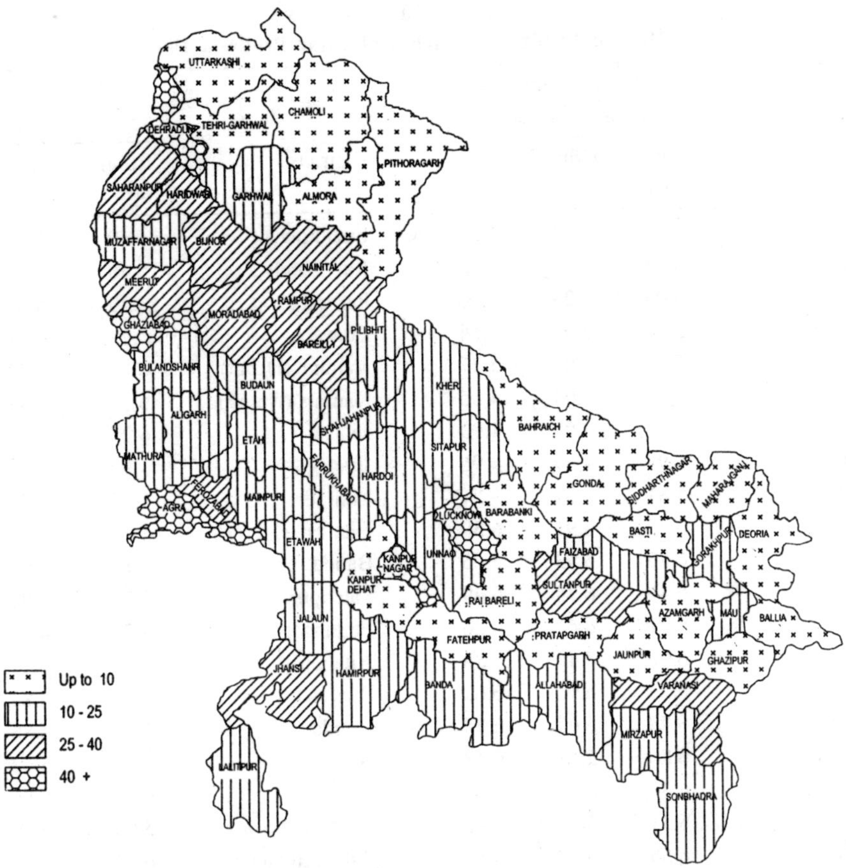

MAP 10.7: **Percentage of Urban Population to Total Population in Uttar Pradesh**

(72.91 per cent), Gonda (71.74 per cent), and Siddharthnagar (70.83 per cent) have a higher proportion of cultivators among main workers The urbanized districts of Dehradun (22.43 per cent), Meerut (32.61 per cent), Ghaziabad (25.89 per cent), Agra (36.19 per cent), Lucknow (29.73 per cent), and Kanpur Nagar (10.41 per cent) have a much lower proportion of cultivators among main workers. In the state as a whole, the proportion of cultivators among females (48.18 per cent) is only marginally lower than that among males (53.94 per cent). Across the districts, this proportion among females exceeds that among males in eight districts, and in many others the two proportions are close to each other. The rural areas of many of these districts (Chamoli, Tehri Garhwal, Garhwal, Pithoragarh, Almora) have a higher proportion of females in their population.

Although the proportion of female cultivators among female main workers is quite high, their proportion among total cultivators (male and female) as also the absolute number is, perhaps, not larger. This is because females are fewer in number and the proportion of main workers among them is lower. In six districts, the proportion of cultivators among female main workers exceeds 95 per cent; the lowest figure is for Kanpur Nagar at 10.23 per cent. The pattern is more or less similar for urban and rural areas separately.

The proportion of agricultural labourers among female main workers is higher than that among male main workers in many districts. The proportion is quite high in Kanpur Dehat (51.38 per cent), Hamirpur (58.45 per cent), Gorakhpur (60.18 per cent), Ballia (67.42 per cent), Ghazipur (50.84 per cent), Mirzapur (62.83 per cent), and Sonbhadra (53.07 per cent). These districts have a lower proportion of cultivators among female main workers.

The participation rate in household industries among females is higher than that among males in almost all the districts. Females participate in household industries in quite large proportions in the urban areas of Bijnor, Moradabad, Sitapur, Barabanki, Basti, Mau, Azamgarh, and Varanasi.

10.4.6 Household Size and Dependency Ratio

The average household size in Uttar Pradesh increased to 6.22 in 1991 from 5.77 in 1981. This increase is similar in urban and rural areas. The size of urban households increased from 5.89 in 1981 to 6.34 in 1991 while that in rural areas increased to 6.19 in 1991 from 5.75 in 1981. Households in urban Uttar Pradesh continue to be larger than those in rural areas in many districts and for the state as a whole. There is a wide variation in household size across the districts as well as between rural and urban areas within a district. The smallest household size is seen in the urban areas of Tehri Garhwal (3.94) while the largest size is in urban Mau (8.20).

The age composition of a population is of interest for a

TABLE 10.4
Household Size in Districts of Uttar Pradesh, 1991

Districts	Average size of household 1991			Districts	Average size of household 1991		
	Rural areas	Urban areas	All areas		Rural areas	Urban areas	All areas
Uttar Pradesh	6.19	6.34	6.22	Lucknow	5.49	5.72	5.63
Uttarkashi	5.33	4.16	5.22	Rae Bareli	5.40	5.83	5.44
Chamoli	5.04	4.25	4.96	Farrukhabad	6.29	6.66	6.36
Tehri Garhwal	5.24	3.94	5.14	Etawah	6.23	6.52	6.27
Dehradun	5.73	5.05	5.37	Kanpur (Dehat)	6.01	6.23	6.02
Garhwal	4.84	4.94	4.85	Kanpur (Nagar)	6.15	5.75	5.81
Pithoragarh	5.01	4.08	4.93	Jalaun	6.27	6.58	6.34
Almora	4.99	4.59	4.96	Jhansi	5.97	6.15	6.04
Nainital	5.81	5.51	5.71	Lalitpur	5.64	5.94	5.68
Bijnor	6.37	6.91	6.50	Hamirpur	5.87	5.82	5.86
Moradabad	6.55	6.93	6.65	Banda	6.13	6.07	6.12
Rampur	6.40	6.74	6.49	Fatehpur	5.70	6.01	5.73
Saharanpur	6.21	6.41	6.26	Pratapgarh	5.75	6.49	5.79
Hardwar	6.06	5.46	5.86	Allahabad	6.15	6.34	6.19
Muzaffarnagar	6.53	6.92	6.62	Bahraich	5.65	6.84	5.72
Meerut	6.78	6.67	6.74	Gonda	5.96	6.86	6.02
Ghaziabad	6.86	5.54	6.18	Barabanki	5.40	6.62	5.50
Bulandshahr	6.46	6.91	6.55	Faizabad	6.18	6.81	6.25
Aligarh	6.31	6.82	6.43	Sultanpur	5.90	6.40	5.92
Mathura	6.55	6.40	6.52	Siddharthnagar	6.04	6.11	6.04
Agra	6.61	6.46	6.55	Maharajganj	6.02	6.30	6.03
Ferozabad	6.45	6.76	6.53	Basti	6.28	6.74	6.31
Etah	6.21	6.61	6.27	Gorakhpur	6.40	6.63	6.44
Mainpuri	6.44	6.43	6.44	Deoria	6.51	7.10	6.55
Budaun	6.12	6.66	6.21	Mau	6.99	8.20	7.17
Bareilly	6.47	6.47	6.47	Azamgarh	6.97	7.84	7.03
Pilibhit	6.28	6.46	6.31	Jaunpur	6.88	7.15	6.90
Shahjahanpur	5.88	6.24	5.95	Ballia	7.20	7.68	7.25
Kheri	5.97	6.26	6.00	Ghazipur	6.79	7.64	6.84
Sitapur	5.73	6.44	5.80	Varanasi	7.42	7.43	7.42
Hardoi	5.81	6.66	5.90	Mirzapur	6.66	7.09	6.72
Unnao	5.56	5.94	5.61	Sonbhadra	5.62	4.66	5.47

Source: Census of India, 1991

number of reasons. The relative number of children below the age of 15 years, that of those in the working age of 15–59 years, and that of the old, aged above 60 years, are of special interest. These numbers determine their capacity to work, the proportion of persons to be supported economically (who cannot work and those to be brought up with care), and also the future growth pattern of the population. The parameters of total dependency ratio (TDR) and old age dependency ratio (OADR), as defined in Section 1.4.6, capture these aspects of the population.

These ratios have been computed from the 1981 Census data. Table 10.H6 shows the dependency ratios separately for the male and female population across the districts in Uttar Pradesh. The dependency ratio is lower among the female population in the state as a whole and in a majority of the districts. The gender gap is wider in the more urbanized districts, for example, Dehradun and Lucknow. The urbanized districts also have a somewhat lower dependency ratio. Urbanization attracts migrants at young ages, many of whom return to their rural homes after retirement from working life. This tends to lower the dependency ratio in urban areas, and also in the more urbanized districts. Such migrations are, perhaps, largely among males, making the gender gap wider in urban areas and the urbanized districts.

The total dependency ratio in the state as a whole is 942 per thousand—956 among males and 926 among females. It is higher in rural (972) than in urban areas (817). This is also the case for rural and urban areas across the districts.

The old age dependency ratio is much lower at 133 in the state. It is lower among females (128) than among males (138). This, perhaps, is due to a higher expectation of life among males in the state. The old age dependency ratio is higher in rural (141) than in urban areas (99). This is true for both males and females. Migration to urban areas at a young age and return to the rural home after retirement from working life might be one of the possible reasons.

10.5 Growth of Population

The population in Uttar Pradesh grew to 139 million in 1991 from 111 million in 1981, implying a decadal variation of 25.48 per cent. This is practically the same as the variation (25.49 per cent) observed during the previous decade, 1971–81. Both these growth rates are higher than those for the country. Among the neighbouring states, Madhya Pradesh showed a rise in the growth rate of population while in the other states it declined. Table 10.5 displays the rates of growth of population for Uttar Pradesh and the neighbouring states.

TABLE 10.5
Growth of Population in Uttar Pradesh and the Neighbouring States

State	Decadal variation (per cent)		Per cent of country's population
	1971–81	1981–91	in 1991
Uttar Pradesh	25.49	25.48	16.44
Madhya Pradesh	25.27	26.84	7.82
Bihar	24.06	23.54	10.21
Haryana	28.75	27.41	1.95
Himachal Pradesh	23.71	20.79	0.61
Rajasthan	32.97	28.44	5.20
India	25.00	23.52	100.00

Sources: Census of India, 1981, 1991.

A number of social and demographic factors have a bearing on the realized rate of fertility and growth of population.

The number of females in the reproductive age group, 15–44 years (the potential mothers), the proportion among them who are married and are, therefore, exposed to the risk of child-bearing, as well as their age at marriage have a direct influence on the fertility and the growth of population. Table 10.H7 presents data on the number of females in the age group 15–44 years, the percentage of married females in different age groups, and their mean age at marriage for all the districts of Uttar Pradesh by place of residence at the time of the 1981 Census.

It is observed from Table 10.H11 that the crude birth rate (CBR) decreased from 39.4 per thousand population to 37.3 during the period 1981 to 1991. The highest negative change is observed in Kanpur district (32.39 per cent) over the decades, followed by Garhwal (25.7) and Tehri Garhwal (21.6). All the districts show negative changes, except Varanasi and Mirzapur.

The prevailing mortality rate among children is known to influence the reproductive behaviour of couples and thus has a bearing on the realized fertility and growth of population. Moreover, child mortality rates, being sensitive to the available health-care facilities, are also important indicators of the well-being of the population.

Factors like the proportion of girls who are away from school also influence the realized fertility rate. A girl who is not enrolled in school or has dropped out early is likely to be married off early, thus contributing to an early onset of fertility.

The realized fertility rate also depends, to a large extent, on the level of knowledge among couples about the need for and the means of ensuring a small family by an appropriate choice of age at marriage and the efficient use of available contraceptive methods. It is easier to spread this knowledge among educated couples.

The couple protection rate (CPR) decreased from 35.5 per cent in 1991 to 33.7 per cent in 1992. Out of 62 reporting districts, 20 districts showed positive changes in the couple protection rate in Uttar Pradesh (see Table 10.H11). It is also observed that there are wide inter-district variations in the couple protection rate (see Map 10.8).

A study of the above mentioned factors and the ways of influencing them would be useful in the formulation and implementation of policies aimed at reducing the growth of population.

10.5.1 Almost Universal Marriage

Out of 520 lakh females in the state in 1981, about 238 lakh were in the age group 15–44 years. About 209 lakh, forming 88 per cent of the females in this age group, were married. This proportion is much higher than the corresponding figure, 80.48 per cent, for the country (excluding Assam). The mean age at marriage in the state is around 16.2 years. The mean age at marriage is lower in rural areas at 16.0 years than in urban areas at 17.4 years. The proportion of married females in the age group 15–19 years is 60.66 per cent in the state, ranging between 24.04 per cent in Dehradun and 86.43 per cent in Sultanpur. The peak child-bearing age is 20–4 years, and in this age group nearly 93.51 per cent of the females are married, the figure ranging between 73.89 per cent in Dehradun and 97.87 per cent in Sultanpur. In rural areas, the proportion of married females in this prime child- bearing age group is higher than that in urban areas in almost all the districts. Marriage is almost universal in Uttar Pradesh—seven out of ten girls are married before the age of 24 years.

10.5.2 Wide Prevalence of Child Marriage

About 11.38 per cent of the girls in the age group 10–14 years are married, indicating wide prevalence of child marriage in the state. In as many as 11 districts, the proportion exceeds

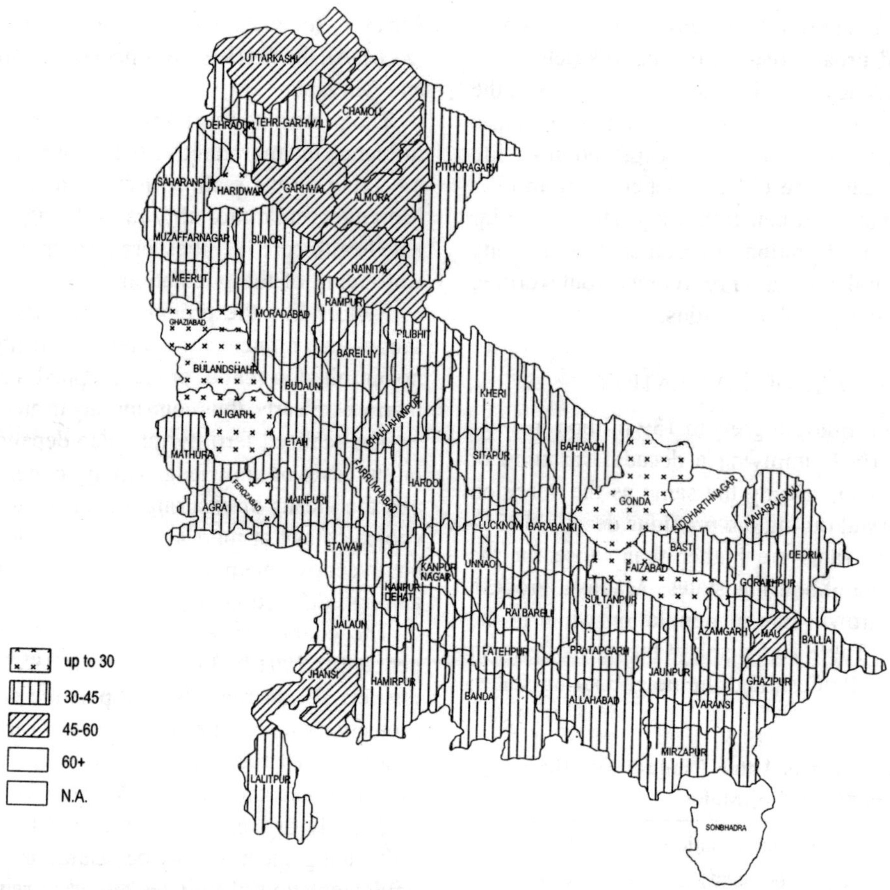

MAP 10.8: **Couple Protection Rate in Uttar Pradesh**

20 per cent. It is alarmingly high in Faizabad (37.41 per cent), Sultanpur (39.93 per cent), Basti (38.87 per cent), and Azamgarh (30.00 per cent). However, the proportion is not as high in all the districts. It falls short of 10 per cent in 37 out of 56 districts, and in 29 of these it is below 5 per cent. Some of the districts like Garhwal (1.74 per cent), Bijnor (0.80 per cent), Nainital (1.91 per cent), Moradabad (1.87 per cent), and Kanpur (1.68 per cent) have a low incidence of child marriage. This pattern is reflected in the mean age at marriage across the districts.

10.5.3 Low Age at Marriage

Across districts, the mean age at marriage ranges between 14.5 years in Lalitpur and 17.9 years in Bijnor. In rural areas, it ranges between 14.4 years in Lalitpur and 17.8 years in Bijnor. In urban areas, it is higher in almost all the districts and ranges between 15.6 years in Lalitpur and 18.5 years in Moradabad, Rampur, and Saharanpur.

The proportion of child marriages in the state is quite high. More than 10 girls out of 100 in the age group 10–14 years are married. This proportion is much higher than the corresponding national average of 6.23 per cent. The mean age at marriage is also quite low at 15.5 years, as compared to the national average of 17.3 years and that in the neighbouring states. However, the variation in the mean age at marriage across the districts is quite wide in Uttar Pradesh.

10.5.4 Death Rate and Child Mortality

The expectation of life at birth in Uttar Pradesh is 49.6 years for females, which is shorter than that for males at 52.3 years. In terms of expectation of life, Uttar Pradesh ranks low among the major states. The state experiences a death rate of around 10.1 per thousand persons, which is equal to the national average. These estimates are presented in Table 10.7. A large proportion of these deaths, in Uttar Pradesh as well as in other states, occurs in childhood. A scrutiny of the mortality conditions of children would, therefore, be of interest. Infant mortality rate (IMR) data indicate that as many as 98 deaths occur in childhood out of one thousand live births in the state. The corresponding figure (79) for the nation is much lower. The neighbouring states of Haryana (75) and Bihar (73) have much lower levels of IMR. However, Madhya Pradesh has an IMR of 104, which is much higher than that in Uttar Pradesh.

Estimates of IMR from Sample Registration Survey (SRS) data, though more reliable, are available only for the nation and the major states. The small sample size does not permit estimation at a lower level of disaggregation.

Four standard estimates of child mortality, viz., q(1), q(2), q(3), and q(5), obtained from data collected in the 1981 and 1991 Censuses, have, therefore, been used here to assess the relative positions of the districts and other population groups in the state. The estimate q(i) represents the expected number

TABLE 10.6

Mean Age at Marriage, Female Literacy Rate, and Percentage of SCs for Rural Areas, Percentage of Urban Population, and Percentage of Married Girls in 10–14 Age in Uttar Pradesh and the Neighbouring States

States	Mean age at marriage in rural areas (years)	Rural female literacy (per cent)	Per cent of scheduled castes in rural areas	Per cent of pop. living in urban areas	Per cent of married girls in age group 10–14 years
Uttar Pradesh	16.0	19.02	21.05	19.84	11.38
Madhya Pradesh	15.3	19.73	14.18	23.18	13.11
Himachal Pradesh	NA	49.79	25.99	8.68	1.49
Haryana	16.5	32.51	21.56	24.63	6.93
Bihar	15.9	17.95	15.25	13.14	10.37
Rajasthan	15.5	11.59	17.98	22.88	18.33
India	17.3	30.62	16.48	25.71	6.23

Note: NA—Not available.

Source: Census of India, 1981, 1991.

TABLE 10.7

Some Indicators of Health Status in Uttar Pradesh and the Neighbouring States

States	Crude birth rate (per '000 persons) 1992	Crude death rate (per '000 persons) 1992	Infant mortality rate (per '000 live births) 1992	Life expectancy at birth (1981–8)	
				Male (years)	Female (years)
Uttar Pradesh	36.3	10.1	98	52.3	49.6
Madhya Pradesh	34.9	12.9	104	50.6	51.8
Bihar	32.3	10.9	73	54.9	52.3
Haryana	32.0	8.7	75	61.5	59.5
Himachal Pradesh	28.1	8.8	–	58.5	62.9
Rajasthan	34.9	10.5	90	53.5	54.3
India	29.2	10.1	79	55.9	55.9

Sources: Census Atlas, National Volume I, 1991, Office of the Registrar General and Census Commissioner, New Delhi; *Statistical Abstract*, CSO, Govt. of India.

of deaths out of one thousand live births before reaching age i years.

For the state as a whole, the child mortality estimates q(1), q(2), q(3), and q(5) were 130, 152, 168, and 190 per thousand live births in 1981. These are much higher than the corresponding figures of 115, 123, 132, and 152 for the country. Uttar Pradesh ranks low in terms of child mortality among the major states (see Map 10.9). However, in 1991 the child mortality rate has reduced remarkably in all the districts of the states (Table 10.H8).

10.5.5 Urban–Rural Disparity

There is wide urban–rural disparity in each of the mortality rates. As the age of the child advances, the urban–rural disparity measured by these ratios seems to remain stable. This pattern is similar in most of the districts.

TABLE 10.8

Urban–Rural and Gender Disparity in Child Mortality Rates in Uttar Pradesh

Population group	Child mortality rates			
	q(1)	q(2)	q(3)	q(5)
Uttar Pradesh	130	152	168	190
Rural areas	139	165	183	204
Urban areas	81	91	101	116
Males	131	146	157	174
Females	128	159	181	208
India	115	123	132	152

Sources: Census of India 1981, Occasional Paper No. 5 of 1988.

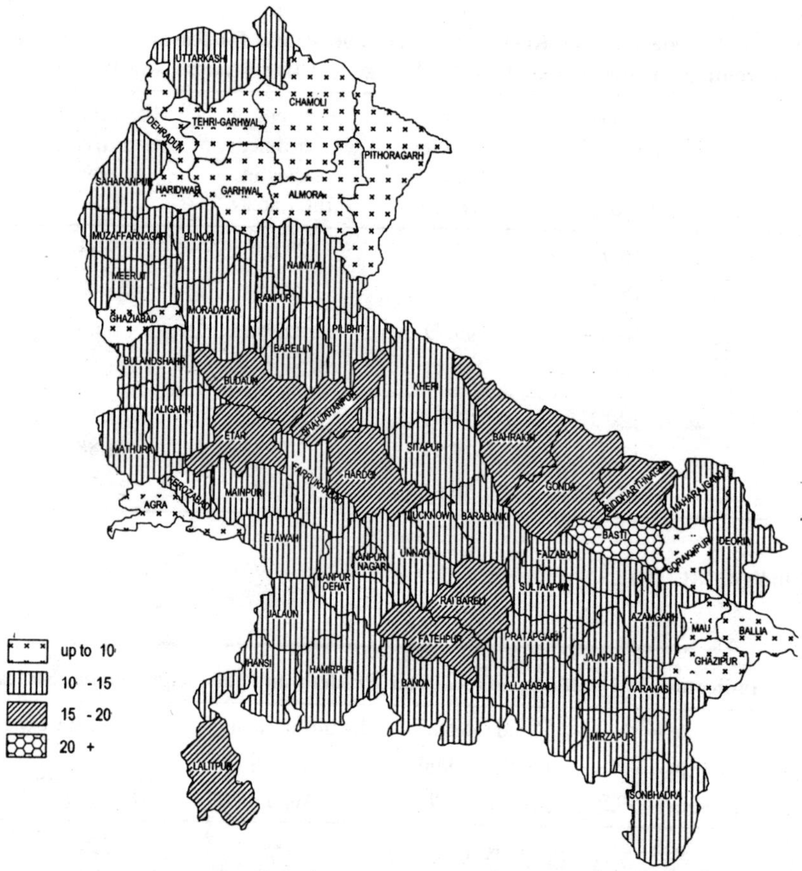

MAP 10.9: **Percentage of Children Who Died within Age of 5 years in Uttar Pradesh**

10.5.6 Gender Disparity

In the state as a whole, the chance of a girl child dying (0.128) is marginally lower than that of a boy child (0.130) till age of 1 year. However, by the age of 5 years the girl child is exposed to a higher risk of mortality than the boy child. The picture is more or less similar in rural and urban areas of the state. The scenario is similar across the districts. In some districts the chance of mortality among girls is less up to the age of 2 years. Beyond 2 years of age, the girl child is exposed to a higher risk of mortality.

10.5.7 Child Mortality and the Mother

The capabilities and handicaps of mothers determine, to a large extent, the health and mortality conditions to which children are exposed. The estimates of child mortality derived from data collected in the 1991 Census indicate that child mortality decreases with a rise in the education of the mother. These data also indicate that mortality is high among the children whose mothers work as agricultural labourers and other manual workers in rural areas. This has been observed in all the states.

Spreading education among mothers and future mothers, improving the working environment of female workers and raising the level of the general health-care facilities will go a long way in reducing child mortality. In the currently prevailing work environment, these mothers are unable to take adequate care of their children. Their children, deprived of maternal care, are exposed to a higher risk of morbidity and death.

10.5.8 Fertility Indices

There are variations in the realized rates of fertility across districts and across population groups, which is a consequence of the variation in the factors determining fertility.

The standardized indices that are used to measure the fertility levels of a population include general fertility rate (GFR), general marital fertility rate (GMFR), total fertility rate (TFR), and total marital fertility rate (TMFR) (see Section 1.5.3 for the definitions of these indices).

The religion that one follows has a close relation to one's culture and lifestyle, which in turn have a bearing on mortality and fertility rates. Table 10.H9 provides data on unadjusted fertility rates by religion for the state as a whole. Muslims (144) and Buddhists (136) experience a slightly higher GFR than the state average of 130. Similarly the GMFRs for Muslims (169), Sikhs (151), and Buddhists (158) are higher than the state average of 146. The TFR for the state is 4.3. Christians have the lowest TFR (2.1), while Sikhs and Buddhists have a TFR of 3.6 and 4.4, respectively. Hindus have a lower TFR (4.2) than Muslims (4.8). The TMFR is 5.4 among Muslims as compared to 4.6 among Hindus. Muslims seem to have a slightly higher fertility rate than the other segments of the population.

Fertility rates among all these communities vary across rural and urban areas. The TFR in urban Uttar Pradesh (3.9) is much lower than that in rural Uttar Pradesh (4.4). The other indices also indicate a similar pattern.

The adjusted fertility indices for all districts are presented in Table 10.H10. Taking the TFR as the index for comparison, it is seen that in 1981 Rampur had the highest value at 7.2, while Uttarkashi had the lowest value at 4.6. Other districts with a high value of TFR were Bijnor (6.9), Moradabad (6.8), Bulandshahr (6.6), Budaun (6.7), and Hardoi (6.6). The districts with low TFRs included Dehradun (4.7), Pithoragarh (4.7), and Almora (4.9). In 1991 the districts with high TFRs included Gonda (6.4), Pilibhit and Bijnor (6.3), and Fatehpur (6.1), and those with low TFRs were Dehradun (4.0), Chamoli and Pithoragarh (4.1), and Jhansi and Garhwal (4.3).

Adjusted fertility estimates are not available for rural and urban areas separately. Unadjusted fertility estimates available for rural and urban areas for the year 1981 from the Census are unreliable, but general observations can be made. As in the other states, fertility rates in urban Uttar Pradesh, measured by these indices, are lower than those in rural areas. Various methods of ensuring a small family, such as higher age at marriage and modern contraceptive methods, are widely adopted by the urban population. Other socio-cultural factors also seem to play their roles. The relative position of Uttar Pradesh with respect to other states in terms of various fertility indices is shown in Table 10.9.

10.6 Material Well-being

An adequate level of income and wealth would indicate the feasibility of leading a decent life and, therefore, of achieving a higher level of human development. A lower level of these would, of course, lead to the non-fulfilment of many of these aspirations and, thus, correspond to a lower level of human development. An analysis of the level of income earned and assets held, and also the distribution of these among the members of the community, would reveal an important aspect of human development.

10.6.1 Income and Consumption

The per capita income of the state in 1990–1 at current prices was Rs 3521 which is much lower than Rs 4963 for the country as a whole. Among the neighbouring states Haryana (Rs 7503) has substantially higher per capita income. The per capita income in Rajasthan (Rs 4191), Himachal Pradesh (Rs 4910), and Madhya Pradesh (Rs 4058) is higher while that in Bihar (Rs 2649) is lower than that of Uttar Pradesh. The state ranks quite low among major states in terms of per capita income (Table 10.10).

This average picture, however, does not reveal the disparity in income among the population. Data on income at the household level would be needed to assess the level of inequality and the incidence and intensity of poverty in the state. Unfortunately, such data are not available for any recent year. The National Council of Applied Economic Research (NCAER) collected data on household income in some of its occasional surveys; the latest one pertaining to the year 1993–4.

The NSS, in its various rounds, collects data on consumer expenditure. These are compiled and published in a grouped form—persons per thousand and average expenditure in various monthly per capita consumer expenditure (MPCE) classes. In the absence of similar data on income, data from the NSS pertaining to the year 1987–8 have been utilized to assess the extent of inequality and poverty in the state. One opinion is that since consumer expenditure is influenced by income in the past as well as income prospect in the foreseeable future it gives a better representation of welfare. So, its use is more appropriate.

Rural Uttar Pradesh was behind 26 states and union territories in terms of consumer expenditure in 1987–8, while urban Uttar Pradesh was behind 25 states and union territories. The per capita consumer expenditure in the state was Rs 217.07 in urban areas and Rs 148.59 in rural areas. The corresponding

TABLE 10.9
Adjusted Fertility Indices in Uttar Pradesh and the Neighbouring States

States	1981				1991			
	GFR	GMFR	TFR	TMFR	GFR	GMFR	TFR	TMFR
Uttar Pradesh	179	201	5.9	6.5	172	200	5.6	6.3
Madhya Pradesh	167	192	5.3	5.0	161	188	4.9	5.7
Bihar	160	182	5.2	5.7	163	186	5.3	5.9
Haryana	170	204	4.5	6.1	145	172	4.3	5.2
Rajasthan	185	209	6.1	6.5	162	184	5.1	5.6
India	152	189	4.9	5.9	138	173	4.3	5.5

Sources: Census of India, 1981, Fertility in India, An Analysis of 1981 Census Data, Occasional Paper No. 13 of 1988; District-level Estimates of Fertility and Child Mortality for 1991 and their Interrelations with other Variables, Occasional Paper No. 1 of 1997, Registrar General, India.

TABLE 10.10
Per Capita Income, Consumer Expenditure and Incidence of Poverty in Select States

	Per capita income (Rs) at 1990–1 price (Rs)	Average monthly consumer expenditure (Rs) in 1993–4		Estimated Gini coefficient in 1993–4			Population below the poverty line (per cent)
		Rural	Urban	Rural	Urban	1993–4	1999–2000
Uttar Pradesh	3521	273.83	388.97	0.2782	0.3230	40.85	31.15
Madhya Pradesh	4058	252.01	408.06	0.2774	0.3267	42.52	37.43
Bihar	2649	218.30	353.03	0.2239	0.3070	54.96	42.60
Haryana	7503	385.01	473.92	0.3007	0.2162	25.05	8.74
Himachal Pradesh	4910	350.63	746.93	0.2762	0.4345	28.44	7.63
Rajasthan	4191	322.39	424.73	0.2599	0.2904	27.41	15.28
India	4963	281.40	458.04	0.2816	0.3399	35.97	26.10

Sources: Levels and patterns of consumer expenditure 50th round (July 1993–June 1994), Department of Statistics, Government of India, 1996; The report of the expert group on estimation of proportion and number of the poor, Planning Commission, 1997 and 2002.

figures for the country were Rs 249.93 for urban and Rs 155.75 for rural areas. Thus, the state was lagging behind the country, though it was not very far behind. Measured in terms of the Gini coefficient, the distribution of consumer expenditure was more egalitarian in urban as well as in rural Uttar Pradesh, compared to that in the country as a whole. Within Uttar Pradesh, the distribution in rural areas was more egalitarian.

The proportion of persons below the poverty line in 1987–8 was quite high at 41.46 per cent in the state, much above the country's average of 38.86 per cent. Punjab had the second lowest incidence of poverty at 13.20 per cent, followed by Himachal Pradesh (15.45 per cent), in that year. Other states with a high incidence of poverty were Bihar (52.13 per cent), Orissa (55.58 per cent) and Madhya Pradesh (43.07 per cent).

The consumer expenditure increased to Rs 273.83 in 1993–4 from a low level of Rs 148.59 in 1987–8 in rural areas of Uttar Pradesh. It increased to Rs 388.97 in 1993–4 from Rs 217.07 in 1987–8 in urban areas. However, the proportion of persons below the poverty line remained as high as 40.85 per cent in 1993–4, which is much higher than the national average of 35.97 per cent. But in 1999–2000, the proportion of population below the poverty line has decreased to 31 per cent though still higher than the national average (see Table 10.10).

The percentage of population below the specified poverty line is a measure of the incidence of poverty—how many are poor. Sen (1976) devised a measure of the intensity of poverty—how poor are the poor.

10.6.2 Distribution of Landholdings

The current level of income and consumption reveals one aspect of material welfare. Consumer durables and productive assets held by households would reveal another. Disaggregated data on these aspects are not available in detail. However, a majority of the workers in rural areas are engaged in agriculture, and land is the major productive asset. The distribution of operational holdings would, therefore, reflect poverty and affluence in rural areas. The data on income and landholdings collected in the 32nd round of the NSS, when tabulated and analysed, indicated close correspondence between the size of the landholdings and rural poverty.

Some data on landholdings were collected in the Fifth Agricultural Census (1990–1). A study of the data reveals the following.

1. The number of operational holdings in the state is estimated at 200.7 lakh in 1990–1 as compared to 109.9 lakh in 1985–6, thereby showing an increase of 5.7 per cent during this five-year period.

2. The area operated also shows an increase of 1.9 per cent from 176.5 lakh hectares in 1985–6 to 179.9 lakh hectares in 1990–1.

3. The average size of a holding in the state declined from 0.93 hectares in 1985–6 to 0.90 hectares in 1990–1.

4. There is an increase in the number and area of operational holdings in the marginal and small categories during the period 1985–6 to 1990–1. The number and area for the marginal category increased by 7.5 per cent and 13.2 per cent and those for small category by 5.2 per cent and 6.7 per cent, respectively.

5. There has been a substantial fall in the number (–18.1 per cent) and area (–18.3 per cent) of operational holdings in the large category (measuring 10 hectares and above), during the period between the two agricultural censuses.

6. The marginal holdings, accounting for about 73.8 per cent of the total holdings in the state, have a share of only 31.4 per cent in the total area operated in 1990–1. On the other hand, large holdings, which accounted for only 0.2 per cent of the total number of holdings, covered 3.9 per cent of the total area operated in the state.

7. The districtwise results indicate that Deoria had the largest number of holdings for all social groups and Uttarkashi the lowest. The average size of a holding for all social groups varied between 0.48 hectares in Jaunpur and 1.96 hectares in Lalitpur.

8. The SC and ST population had shares of 16.4 per cent and 0.2 per cent in the total number of holdings in the state in 1990–1 and their shares in the area operated were 10.5 per cent and 0.3 per cent respectively.

9. The average size of a holding for SCs and STs was 0.57 hectares and 1.77 hectares respectively in 1990–1 as compared to 0.60 hectares and 1.72 hectares in 1985–6.

10. The largest number of holdings of SCs was located in Sitapur district and the lowest in Chamoli. The largest concentration of holdings of STs was in Nainital and the lowest in Pilibhit in 1990–1.

11. The average size of a holding for SCs varied from 10.21 hectares in Varanasi district to 1.73 hectares in Lalitpur district and that for STs from 0.32 hectares in Uttarkashi to 3.04 hectares in Kheri district in 1990–1.

10.7 Concluding Remarks

Uttar Pradesh is the largest state in the Indian Union where 16.44 per cent of the country's population lives. Almost every sixth Indian lives in Uttar Pradesh. The state has remained backward in most aspects of human development. The basically agrarian economy of the state has failed to prosper due to the lack of advancement of technology and the consequent low yield rate for most of the crops cultivated. The industrial base of the state is also not developed.

Uttar Pradesh is one of the most backward states in terms of literacy. The literacy rate is 41.6 per cent for the state and only 19.02 per cent are literate among the females in rural areas. However, these averages may not be very representative when there is a wide inter-district disparity. The co-efficient of variation (CV) (determines the extent of variation in per cent of average) is very high. It is observed that the CV is 47.4 per cent for literacy among rural females (see Table 10.11).

The CV is 30.4 per cent for total literacy. This implies that in some districts the literacy rate among males in urban areas is very high which reduces, to some extent, the overall disparity.

Government efforts for improving female literacy have not yielded much result in some districts such as Rampur, Budaun, Bahraich, and Maharajganj where the rate is only 8 per cent among rural females.

The teacher–student ratio is one of the indicators that reflect the quality of education. The average teacher–student ratio is 57 students per teacher, indicating the acute shortage of teachers. However, the CV is 20 per cent, which implies that the distribution of teachers among the districts is not very highly skewed.

The CMIE index of development shows a wide inter-district disparity, ranging from 43 for Chamoli to 185 for Kanpur Nagar. Kanpur is the most industrially advanced district of the state. At the other extreme is Chamoli, which is the least industrialized district. The CV is 47 per cent, which shows a very high inter-district disparity in socio-economic development.

The district averages for doctors per lakh population, child mortality at the age of 5 and agricultural labour may again not be very representative. It seems that there are wide inter-district disparities. The CV is as high as 46 per cent, 42 per cent and 48 per cent for doctors per lakh population, child mortality and agricultural labour, respectively. However, the CV is 28 per cent in the case of distribution of sub-centres among the districts of Uttar Pradesh.

The per capita income in the state is one of the lowest among the major states. In terms of per capita consumption, the state lags behind 25 (out of 31) states and union territories. The distribution of consumer expenditure is more egalitarian than that in the country. Perhaps, most of the people are poor in the state. According to the officially released estimates, 41.46 per cent of the population in the state was below the poverty line in 1987–8. The state gets a low score in material well-being.

The birth rate, death rate and IMR are quite high, and life expectancy is low. The population in the state is growing at a rate faster than that in many other states. The poor performance in the health sector brings a low score for the state.

Despite some ancient seats of learning in the state, the average level (quality and quantity) of education in the state is low. In terms of literacy, the state ranks as low as 27 among 31 states and union territories. Female literacy in rural areas of the state is yet to cross 20 per cent; in a large number

TABLE 10.11

Average, Standard Deviation and Co-efficient of Variation of HDI Indicators in Uttar Pradesh

	Total literacy rate	Female literacy rate	Teacher–student rate	CMIE index of development	Doctors per lakh popn	Agri-cultural labourers	Child mortality	Sub-centres per lakh population
Avg	41.6	20.1	56.7	63.8	77.1	17.7	165.4	20.1
SD	12.6	9.5	11.3	36.2	35.4	8.5	69.1	5.6
CV	30.4	47.4	19.9	56.7	45.9	47.9	41.7	28.0

Avg—Average; SD—Standard Deviation; CV—Co-efficient of variation of districts it is less than 10 per cent. The prevalence of child marriage and low age at marriage still keep a large number of girls away from school. Apart from keeping female literacy low, they also contribute to an early onset of fertility. Girls who are away from school are married off early.

The state requires improvements in the facilities for education, including schools. Only 70 per cent of the villages in the state are equipped with a primary school while many other states have succeeded in providing primary schools to the children within their habitation.

Being backward in almost all the dimensions of human development, the state of Uttar Pradesh has been rightly ranked low by various scholars (see Box 10.1) in terms of aggregate scores for human development. Concerted efforts are needed to improve the deplorable situation. Uttar Pradesh being the largest state, the overall development of the country largely depends on its development. The performance of Uttar Pradesh in human development thus assumes special significance.

TABLE 10.E1

Districtwise Primary School Enrolment and Drop-out Rates (Boys, Girls & Total) for Urban Uttar Pradesh, 1991

State/district	Enrolment rates						Drop-out rates								
	Total no. of eligible children for enrolment (6–11 years)			Enrolment rate (per cent)			No. of children enrolled in class I in 1984			No. of children enrolled in class V in 1984			Drop-out rate (per cent)		
	Boys	Girls	Total	Boys	Girls	Total	Boys	Girls	Total	Boys	Girls	Total	Boys	Girls	Total
Uttar Pradesh	**2,364,372**	**2,018,237**	**4,382,609**	**66.85**	**69.41**	**68.03**	**414,982**	**241,389**	**656,371**	**194,266**	**131,091**	**325,357**	**53.19**	**44.86**	**50.13**
Uttarkashi	1300	1192	2492	93.62	91.11	92.42	357	200	557	197	171	368	44.82	14.50	33.93
Chamoli	2653	2299	4952	151.64	169.12	159.75	714	2879	3593	342	316	658	52.10	89.02	81.69
Tehri Garhwal	1574	1395	2969	144.47	161.72	152.58	533	333	866	236	243	479	55.72	27.03	44.69
Dehradun	39,404	31,792	71,196	65.30	73.00	68.74	4613	3975	8588	3867	3050	6917	16.17	23.27	19.46
Garhwal	3749	3344	7093	135.08	145.72	140.10	1095	1051	2146	836	919	1755	23.65	12.56	18.22
Pithoragarh	2133	1890	4023	218.24	162.28	191.95	1130	664	1794	456	351	807	59.65	47.14	55.02
Almora	3650	3232	6,882	180.49	171.6	176.32	875	719	1594	640	690	1330	26.86	4.03	16.56
Nainital	43,417	21,960	65,377	68.99	47.86	61.89	4550	3469	8019	3999	2780	6779	12.11	19.86	15.46
Bijnor	105,937	48,754	154,691	38.95	80.52	52.05	10,320	5628	15,948	4079	2694	6773	60.47	52.13	57.53
Moradabad	101,053	92,141	193,194	71.46	68.70	70.14	22,085	10,336	32,421	9328	4343	13,671	57.76	57.98	57.83
Rampur	34,877	32,647	67,524	59.52	97.85	78.05	3300	2086	5386	2504	1556	4060	24.12	25.41	24.62
Saharanpur	72,523	65,586	138,109	66.43	88.86	77.08	14,877	9920	24,797	7338	5592	12,930	50.68	43.63	47.86
Muzaffarnagar	70,726	57,998	128,724	44.91	94.41	67.22	9751	6312	16,063	5890	4143	10,033	39.60	34.36	37.54
Meerut	111,355	96,145	207,500	51.24	63.46	56.90	15,343	9170	24,513	8805	4891	13,696	42.61	46.66	44.13
Ghaziabad	108,869	89,982	198,851	40.65	33.28	37.32	14,806	6632	21,438	3355	3962	7317	77.34	40.26	65.87
Bulandshahr	53,911	46,652	100,563	59.61	51.85	56.01	9337	4952	14,289	4503	2360	6863	51.77	52.34	51.97
Aligarh	80,519	66,063	146,582	62.52	43.78	54.08	15,609	12,258	27,867	3710	2532	6242	76.23	79.34	77.60
Mathura	41,111	35,154	76,265	57.22	55.13	56.26	5906	4651	10,557	2963	2210	5173	49.83	52.48	51.00
Agra	128,941	112,943	241,884	97.84	49.30	75.18	15,534	10,154	25,688	8436	5265	13,701	45.69	48.15	46.66
Etah	38,281	32,220	70,501	31.19	81.24	54.06	7931	1174	9105	3145	1066	4211	60.35	9.20	53.75
Mainpuri	17,148	15,371	32,519	78.29	33.88	57.30	4057	1926	5983	1159	844	2003	71.43	56.18	66.52
Budaun	40,979	34,784	75,763	84.34	76.91	80.93	7102	5025	12,127	4187	3077	7264	41.04	38.77	40.10
Bareilly	81,969	77,731	159,700	76.17	92.27	84.0	12,153	7503	19,656	5837	3609	9,446	51.97	51.90	51.94
Pilibhit	21,679	18,899	40,578	52.81	85.99	68.27	2053	1283	3336	1204	1022	2226	41.35	20.34	33.27
Shahjahanpur	37,962	30,785	62,747	59.41	63.95	61.45	5335	3215	8550	1500	1272	2772	71.88	60.44	67.58
Kheri	22,783	18,719	41,502	58.39	77.09	66.82	3866	2527	6393	1500	1187	2687	61.20	53.03	57.97
Sitapur	32,750	29,999	62,749	91.13	93.39	92.21	5902	3348	9250	3512	2523	6035	40.49	24.64	34.76
Hardoi	27,603	24,690	52,293	86.62	82.72	84.78	5752	3039	8791	2641	1740	4381	54.09	42.74	50.16
Unnao	27,163	27,170	54,333	83.03	66.66	74.85	3328	2259	5587	2748	1529	4277	17.43	32.32	23.45
Lucknow	105,191	99,571	204,762	53.14	63.31	58.09	11,247	5484	16,731	7763	4725	12,488	30.98	13.84	25.36

(Contd.)

TABLE 10.E1 (contd.)

Districtwise Primary School Enrolment and Drop-out Rates (Boys, Girls & Total) for Urban Uttar Pradesh

State/district	Enrolment rates						Drop-out rates								
	Total no. of eligible children for enrolment (6–11 years)			Enrolment rate (per cent)			No. of children enrolled in class I in 1984			No. of children enrolled in class V in 1984			Drop-out rate (per cent)		
	Boys	Girls	Total	Boys	Girls	Total	Boys	Girls	Total	Boys	Girls	Total	Boys	Girls	Total
Rae Bareli	18,690	15,470	34,160	74.22	84.39	78.83	3579	2053	5632	2256	1409	3665	36.97	31.37	34.93
Farrukhabad	42,784	36,311	79,095	44.47	61.62	52.34	6695	4451	11,146	3990	2843	6833	40.40	36.13	38.70
Etawah	30,235	22,996	53,231	68.99	83.68	75.34	5324	2543	7867	1872	1572	3444	64.84	38.18	56.22
Kanpur	149,983	131,119	281,102	94.76	89.93	92.50	31,517	24,794	56,311	20,683	15,774	36,457	34.38	36.38	35.26
Jalaun	27,948	21,928	49,876	59.71	72.25	65.23	5128	3150	8278	2877	1813	4690	43.90	42.44	43.34
Jhansi	47,834	43,948	91,782	97.22	91.80	94.63	16,154	11,112	27,266	5641	4057	9698	65.08	63.49	64.43
Lalitpur	8780	7646	16,426	117.84	169.72	141.99	3210	2262	5472	807	577	1384	74.86	74.49	74.71
Hamirpur	24,791	22,810	47,601	85.87	88.75	87.25	2870	1380	4250	1669	1098	2767	41.85	20.43	34.89
Banda	21,121	23,897	45,018	91.00	76.43	83.27	5172	3624	8796	2708	1631	4339	47.64	54.99	50.67
Fatehpur	14,815	14,652	29,467	97.12	72.90	85.08	3102	2014	5116	1665	1155	2820	46.32	42.65	44.88
Pratapgarh	10,304	8529	18,833	39.90	46.72	42.99	1421	1577	2998	1198	1165	2363	15.69	26.13	21.18
Allahabad	71,855	64,941	136,796	42.83	41.40	42.15	30,703	9292	39,995	3823	3852	7675	87.55	58.54	80.81
Bahraich	20,077	16,837	36,914	83.33	80.04	81.83	2990	1394	4384	1522	871	2393	49.10	37.52	45.42
Gonda	21,446	17,511	38,957	88.14	96.90	92.08	3870	3081	6951	2149	1418	3567	44.47	53.98	48.68
Barabanki	19,953	16,604	36,557	91.14	75.89	84.22	4371	1952	6323	1764	1001	2765	59.64	48.72	56.27
Faizabad	28,418	26,182	54,600	35.83	31.17	33.59	3688	2120	5808	2127	1170	3297	42.33	44.81	43.23
Sultanpur	10,447	8909	19,356	43.04	42.26	42.68	2060	1349	3409	717	304	1021	65.19	77.46	70.05
Basti	15,789	14,493	30,282	83.41	65.30	74.74	4411	1775	6186	2012	585	2597	54.39	67.04	58.02
Gorakhpur	47,104	41,706	88,810	37.61	65.42	50.67	6941	5111	12,052	5456	2781	8237	21.39	45.59	31.65
Deoria	28,578	25,199	53,777	86.19	74.37	80.65	3627	2072	5699	2882	1677	4559	20.54	19.06	20.00
Azamgarh	40,335	36,128	76,463	47.46	39.12	43.52	3816	1727	5543	2106	1190	3296	44.81	31.09	40.54
Jaunpur	21,889	16,320	38,209	84.73	68.17	77.66	3909	1488	5397	1705	1157	2862	56.38	22.24	46.97
Ballia	19,138	18,396	37,534	91.48	67.15	79.55	3597	2379	5976	1992	1450	3442	44.62	39.05	42.40
Ghazipur	17,061	14,841	31,902	87.66	85.74	86.77	4351	2297	6648	2318	1321	3639	46.72	42.49	45.26
Varansi	115,038	104,626	219,664	64.64	64.09	64.38	27,257	11,048	38,305	7969	6225	14,194	70.76	43.65	62.94
Mirzapur	28.749	26,130	54,879	91.69	77.59	84.97	5758	4172	9930	3686	2333	6019	35.98	44.08	39.39

Sources: 1. Census of India, 1981 and 1991.
2. Directorate of Basic Education, Uttar Pradesh, Allahabad.

TABLE 10.E2

Districtwise Primary School Enrolment and Drop-out Rates (Boys, Girls & Total) for Rural Uttar Pradesh, 1991

State/district	Enrolment rates						Drop-out rates								
	Total no. of eligible children for enrolment (6–11 years)			Enrolment rate (per cent)			No. of children enrolled in class I in 1984			No. of children enrolled in class V in 1984			Drop-out rate (per cent)		
	Boys	Girls	Total	Boys	Girls	Total	Boys	Girls	Total	Boys	Girls	Total	Boys	Girls	Total
Uttar Pradesh	**11,986,339**	**8,968,179**	**20,954,518**	**64.21**	**46.22**	**56.51**	**1,697,738**	**751,934**	**2,449,672**	**979,543**	**400,866**	**1,380,409**	**42.30**	**46.69**	**43.65**
Uttarkashi	16,876	16,447	33,323	77.74	46.70	62.42	2959	1801	4760	1973	706	2679	33.32	60.80	43.72
Chamoli	31,429	30,813	62,242	158.74	120.13	139.63	8328	5706	14,034	4861	4270	9131	41.63	25.17	34.94
Tehri Garhwal	43,202	42,579	85,781	128.36	81.12	104.91	13,430	4801	18,231	6315	2843	9158	52.98	40.78	49.77
Dehradun	42,148	38,512	80,660	67.88	66.37	67.16	9270	5365	14,635	4178	3406	7584	54.93	36.51	48.18
Garhwal	44,244	39,739	83,983	155.40	147.72	151.77	10,226	9346	19,572	8052	6321	14,373	21.26	32.37	26.56
Pithoragarh	39,539	38,280	77,819	176.59	103.91	140.84	10,175	6599	16,774	6450	3508	9958	36.61	46.84	40.63
Almora	59,368	61,512	120,880	150.36	102.45	125.98	13,939	12,377	26,316	10,296	7128	17,424	26.14	42.41	33.79
Nainital	88,341	81,528	169,869	76.43	66.87	71.84	10,626	7113	17,739	10,198	5668	15,866	4.030	20.31	10.56
Bijnor	181,724	151,864	333,588	56.85	28.77	44.07	23,144	9886	33,030	13,360	5451	18,811	42.27	44.86	43.05
Moradabad	313,036	250,188	563,224	50.66	18.88	36.54	66,220	22,549	88,769	21,236	4012	25,248	67.93	82.21	71.56
Rampur	120,065	97,185	217,250	57.08	19.11	40.09	10,956	3871	14,827	7766	1903	9669	29.12	50.84	34.79
Saharanpur	166,226	168,772	334,998	78.76	31.70	55.05	44,251	21,492	65,743	17,922	7166	25,088	59.50	66.66	61.84
Muzaffarnagar	228,321	186,006	414,327	68.51	38.13	54.87	29,824	13,468	43,292	16261	7215	23,476	45.48	46.43	45.77
Meerut	219,238	176,457	395,695	64.12	34.45	50.89	30,649	14,415	45,064	23,167	8137	31,304	24.41	43.55	30.53
Ghaziabad	147,438	119,504	266,942	46.13	37.96	42.48	22,946	9241	32,187	5189	4127	9316	77.39	55.34	71.06
Bulandshahr	175,956	189,017	364,973	89.23	39.07	63.25	30,513	12,685	43,198	18,368	6675	25,043	39.80	47.38	42.03
Aligarh	271,997	216,059	488,056	59.72	37.77	50.00	35,369	8504	43,873	19,729	7366	27095	44.22	13.38	38.24
Mathura	163,328	127,205	290,533	62.66	36.60	51.25	18,477	10,231	28,708	12,729	3912	16641	31.11	61.76	42.03
Agra	248,213	228,517	476,730	70.80	40.51	56.28	26,794	13,812	40,606	17,715	5950	23,665	33.88	56.92	41.72
Etah	213,443	158,936	372,379	27.35	46.32	35.45	41,698	16,831	58,529	15,044	5285	20,329	63.92	68.60	65.27
Mainpuri	187,110	143,564	330,674	84.81	73.71	79.99	43,173	18,287	61,460	16,611	8763	25,374	61.52	52.08	58.71
Budaun	210,224	159,357	369,584	61.55	38.64	51.67	30,878	12,595	43,473	14,925	5399	20324	51.66	57.13	53.25
Bareilly	193,371	156,381	349,752	62.64	49.84	56.92	26,987	8873	35,860	13,252	3237	16,489	50.89	63.52	54.02
Pilibhit	101,950	85,918	187,868	63.24	34.17	49.95	11,221	4597	15,818	7645	3271	10,916	31.87	28.84	30.99
Shahjahanpur	147,324	121,889	269,213	84.43	52.08	69.78	29,535	13,316	42,851	9901	2996	12,897	66.48	77.50	69.9
Kheri	202,394	161,304	363,698	74.47	56.26	66.39	26,358	12,575	38,933	14318	4953	19,271	45.68	60.61	50.5
Sitapur	231,233	191,541	422,774	81.24	43.90	64.32	31,007	11,925	42,932	23,607	8957	32,564	23.87	24.89	24.15
Hardoi	220,833	180,704	401,537	82.43	57.66	71.28	36,630	14,120	50,750	20,084	7122	27,206	45.17	49.56	46.39
Unnao	179,670	156,183	335,853	76.04	54.75	66.14	24,402	12,749	37,151	14,265	6920	21,185	41.54	45.72	42.98
Lucknow	113,404	101,260	214,664	40.22	29.19	35.01	20,213	5825	26,038	12,158	4380	16,538	39.85	24.81	36.49

(Contd.)

TABLE 10.E2 (contd.)

Districtwise Primary School Enrolment and Drop-out Rates (Boys, Girls & Total) for Rural Uttar Pradesh, 1991

State/district	Enrolment rates						Drop-out rates								
	Total no. of eligible children for enrolment (6–11 years)			Enrolment rate (per cent)			No. of children enrolled in class I in 1984			No. of children enrolled in class V in 1984			Drop-out rate (per cent)		
	Boys	Girls	Total	Boys	Girls	Total	Boys	Girls	Total	Boys	Girls	Total	Boys	Girls	Total
Rae Bareli	185,633	165,551	351,184	89.79	59.74	75.62	28,954	12,729	41,683	21,591	8473	30,064	25.43	33.44	27.87
Farrukhabad	201,666	163,195	364,861	78.57	55.25	68.14	30,982	17,302	48,284	21702	11,279	32981	29.95	34.81	31.69
Etawah	174,014	144,445	318,459	86.51	74.50	81.06	25,083	13,370	38,453	18,436	10,807	29,243	26.50	19.17	23.95
Kanpur	232,986	200,605	433,591	79.13	62.24	71.32	25,009	18,154	43,163	22,861	14,684	37,545	8.59	19.11	13.02
Jalaun	91,268	74,222	165,490	64.38	50.26	58.05	15,402	8129	23,531	10363	5721	16,084	32.72	29.62	31.65
Jhansi	80,826	67,202	148,028	92.82	56.47	76.32	14,633	7648	22,281	7959	3218	11,177	45.61	57.92	49.84
Lalitpur	61,631	47,266	108,897	97.81	65.26	83.68	12,373	5072	17,445	3005	926	3931	75.71	81.74	77.47
Hamirpur	118,826	95,058	213,884	79.83	53.18	67.98	13,633	5355	18,988	9894	4061	13,955	27.43	24.16	26.51
Banda	164,783	138,053	302,836	67.90	49.44	59.48	21,767	12,575	34,342	12,653	3907	16,560	41.87	68.93	51.78
Fatehpur	161,193	140,366	301,559	92.85	66.06	80.38	21,711	11,606	33,317	16,939	8160	25,099	21.98	29.69	24.67
Pratapgarh	188,460	167,402	355,862	89.85	54.43	73.19	31,082	12,397	43,479	23,041	9887	32,928	25.87	20.25	24.27
Allahabad	322,408	316,873	639,281	74.47	38.68	56.73	65,756	24,203	89,959	35,030	11,773	46,803	46.73	51.36	47.97
Bahraich	226,966	182,216	409,182	69.17	39.27	55.85	30,834	9205	40,039	16,488	2979	19,467	46.53	67.64	51.38
Gonda	193,777	239,178	432,955	92.07	34.44	60.23	30,650	15,936	46,586	19,431	5137	24,568	36.60	67.76	47.26
Barabanki	202,719	163,607	366,326	78.47	53.33	67.24	37,941	12,592	50,533	16,918	6996	23,914	55.41	44.44	52.68
Faizabad	236,831	200,834	437,665	62.57	55.08	59.13	53,761	28,785	82,546	30,999	15,864	46,863	42.34	44.89	43.23
Sultanpur	206,263	181,247	387,510	91.38	70.55	81.64	51,591	25,524	77,115	23,514	10,748	34,262	54.42	57.89	55.57
Basti	384,055	330,330	714,385	67.71	34.06	52.15	105,599	27,235	132,834	41,354	7623	48,977	60.84	72.01	63.13
Gorakhpur	403,100	353,213	756,313	63.02	29.52	47.37	49,212	18,582	67,794	38,864	11,028	49,892	21.03	40.65	26.41
Deoria	395,460	350,582	746,042	66.45	38.19	53.17	50,674	20,351	71,025	30,326	12,149	42475	40.15	40.30	40.20
Azamgarh	337,706	305,553	643,259	84.45	53.92	69.95	55,995	20,820	76,815	36,966	15,503	52,469	33.98	25.54	31.69
Jaunpur	284,924	246,950	531,874	76.55	60.13	68.92	51,309	24,396	75,705	36,360	15,375	51,735	29.14	36.98	31.66
Ballia	191,951	166,737	358,688	80.29	64.94	73.16	29,283	19,651	48,934	19,218	12,384	31602	34.37	36.98	35.42
Ghazipur	207,539	190,411	397,950	79.94	57.08	69.00	37,086	19,332	56,418	24,601	11,914	36,515	33.66	38.37	35.28
Varansi	350,849	290,764	641,613	50.17	31.57	41.74	40,428	22,462	62,890	34,217	16,184	50,401	15.36	27.95	19.86
Mirzapur	194,857	179,138	373,995	72.09	43.73	58.50	26,792	13,568	40,360	19,238	7039	26,277	28.19	48.12	34.89

Sources: 1. Census of India, 1981 & 1991.
2. Directorate of Basic Education, Uttar Pradesh, Allahabad.

TABLE 10.E3

Districtwise Mean Years of Schooling at Primary Level and Teacher–Student Ratio, 1983–4 to 1989–90

State/district	Mean years of schooling			Teacher–student ratio
	Boys	Girls	Total	
Uttar Pradesh	**3.74**	**3.50**	**3.66**	**55.9**
Uttarkashi	3.63	2.88	3.35	24.6
Chamoli	3.45	3.14	3.30	56.6
Tehri Garhwal	2.87	3.53	3.05	56.7
Dehradun	3.45	3.96	3.66	32.6
Garhwal	4.28	4.06	4.17	48.3
Pithoragarh	3.46	3.53	3.49	48.7
Almora	4.05	3.76	3.91	44.8
Nainital	4.59	4.42	4.52	43.3
Bijnor	3.29	3.37	3.31	60.6
Moradabad	2.39	2.29	2.37	50.8
Rampur	4.27	3.73	4.11	72.0
Saharanpur	2.85	2.43	2.70	30.6
Muzaffarnagar	3.18	3.08	3.15	55.5
Meerut	3.48	3.31	3.42	48.6
Ghaziabad	2.71	3.47	2.94	66.2
Bulandshahr	3.55	3.27	3.46	54.9
Aligarh	3.00	3.32	3.09	54.6
Mathura	4.30	3.13	3.85	49.8
Agra	4.13	3.60	3.94	69.7
Etah	2.42	2.70	2.50	38.4
Mainpuri	2.82	3.44	3.01	72.4
Budaun	3.55	3.34	3.48	58.8
Bareilly	3.39	3.37	3.38	68.5
Pilibhit	4.01	4.13	4.05	56.3
Shahjahanpur	2.85	2.65	2.78	61.2
Kheri	3.93	3.51	3.79	64.7
Sitapur	3.95	4.25	4.04	72.2
Hardoi	3.76	3.82	3.78	67.3
Unnao	4.23	4.01	4.15	62.5
Lucknow	3.42	4.93	3.82	50.6
Rae Bareli	4.26	4.22	4.25	61.6
Farrukhabad	3.90	3.84	3.88	58.7
Etawah	4.00	4.37	4.13	59.3
Kanpur	4.37	3.97	4.20	69.3
Jalaun	3.84	4.05	3.91	50.5
Jhansi	2.92	2.54	2.78	59.1
Lalitpur	2.65	2.45	2.59	89.6
Hamirpur	4.41	4.66	4.48	65.8
Banda	3.66	2.85	3.36	59.7
Fatehpur	4.44	4.16	4.34	70.7
Pratapgarh	4.21	4.34	4.24	62.7
Allahabad	2.36	2.88	2.50	45.2
Bahraich	3.82	3.80	3.82	55.6
Gonda	4.55	3.24	4.09	51.6
Barabanki	3.16	3.93	3.36	58.6
Faizabad	3.42	3.15	3.33	41.4
Sultanpur	2.49	2.84	2.60	60.5
Basti	2.43	2.98	2.54	51.6
Gorakhpur	4.26	3.91	3.93	53.1
Deoria	3.92	4.04	3.96	63.9
Azamgarh	3.81	4.28	3.94	58.3
Jaunpur	3.84	3.73	3.81	64.3
Ballia	4.04	3.74	3.92	58.5
Ghazipur	3.75	3.77	3.76	64.1
Varansi	3.74	3.77	3.75	42.8
Mirzapur	3.98	3.44	3.79	56.8

Source: Directorate of Basic Education, Uttar Pradesh, Allahabad.

TABLE 10.E4
Districtwise Distribution of Villages by Distance from School, 1991

State/district	Total number of villages	Number of villages with primary school				
		Within village	Between 0 and 1 km	Between 1 and 3 km	Between 3 and 5 km	Beyond 5 km
Uttar Pradesh	**111,975**	**61,811**	**19,475**	**24,393**	**4958**	**1338**
	(100)	**(55.20)**	**(17.39)**	**(21.78)**	**(4.34)**	**(1.19)**
Uttarkashi	657	454	90	99	13	1
	(100)	(69.10)	(13.70)	(15.07)	(1.98)	(0.15)
Chamoli	1503	815	330	351	7	0
	(100)	(54.22)	(21.96)	(23.35)	(0.47)	–
Tehri Garhwal	1938	1013	599	326	0	0
	(100)	(52.27)	(30.91)	(16.82)	–	–
Dehradun	722	495	84	101	27	15
	(100)	(68.56)	(11.63)	(13.99)	(3.74)	(2.08)
Garhwal	3229	1315	1001	853	60	0
	(100)	(40.72)	(31.00)	(26.42)	(1.86)	–
Pithoragarh	2160	886	427	675	172	0
	(100)	(41.02)	(19.77)	(31.25)	(7.96)	–
Almora	3003	1414	748	827	13	1
	(100)	(47.09)	(24.91)	(27.54)	(0.43)	(0.03)
Nainital	1734	997	322	400	15	0
	(100)	(57.50)	(18.57)	(23.07)	(0.86)	–
Bijnor	2127	855	403	662	155	52
	(100)	(40.20)	(18.95)	(31.12)	(7.29)	(2.44)
Moradabad	2467	1595	354	478	38	2
	(100)	(64.65)	(14.35)	(19.38)	(1.54)	(0.08)
Rampur	1092	527	172	322	52	19
	(100)	(48.26)	(15.75)	(29.49)	(4.76)	(1.74)
Saharanpur	1260	716	223	282	34	5
	(100)	(56.83)	(17.70)	(22.38)	(2.70)	(0.40)
Hardwar	490	306	50	116	18	0
	(100)	(62.45)	(10.20)	(23.67)	(3.67)	–
Muzaffarnagar	881	680	52	62	87	0
	(100)	(77.19)	(5.90)	(7.04)	(9.88)	–
Meerut	882	763	47	58	11	3
	(100)	(86.51)	(5.33)	(6.58)	(1.25)	(0.34)
Ghaziabad	704	556	34	59	49	6
	(100)	(78.98)	(4.83)	(8.38)	(6.96)	(0.85)
Bulandshahr	1362	933	163	216	50	0
	(100)	(68.50)	(11.97)	(15.86)	(3.67)	–
Aligarh	1704	1156	185	267	96	0
	(100)	(67.84)	(10.86)	(15.67)	(5.63)	–
Mathura	867	676	55	106	16	14
	(100)	(77.97)	(6.34)	(12.23)	(1.85)	(1.61)
Agra	905	707	63	109	19	7
	(100)	(77.95)	(6.96)	(12.04)	(2.10)	(0.77)
Firozabad	797	542	52	150	52	1
	(100)	(68.01)	(6.52)	(18.82)	(6.52)	(0.13)
Etah	1509	1040	150	188	94	37
	(100)	(68.92)	(9.94)	(12.46)	(6.23)	(2.45)
Mainpuri	820	567	90	113	47	3
	(100)	(69.15)	(10.98)	(13.78)	(5.73)	(0.37)

(Contd.)

TABLE 10.E4 (contd.)

Districtwise Distribution of Villages by Distance from School, 1991

State/district	Total number of villages	Number of villages with primary school				
		Within village	Between 0 and 1 km	Between 1 and 3 km	Between 3 and 5 km	Beyond 5 km
Budaun	1772 (100)	1167 (65.86)	172 (9.71)	369 (20.82)	61 (3.44)	3 (0.17)
Bareilly	1851 (100)	1147 (61.97)	168 (9.08)	380 (20.53)	147 (7.94)	9 (0.49)
Pilibhit	1180 (100)	580 (49.15)	158 (13.39)	308 (26.10)	109 (9.24)	25 (2.12)
Shahjahanpur	2124 (100)	1064 (50.09)	161 (7.58)	603 (28.39)	180 (8.47)	116 (5.46)
Kheri	1687 (100)	1158 (68.64)	165 (9.78)	258 (15.29)	95 (5.63)	11 (0.65)
Sitapur	2315 (100)	1532 (66.18)	303 (13.09)	332 (14.34)	101 (4.36)	47 (2.03)
Hardoi	1881 (100)	1567 (83.31)	101 (5.37)	132 (7.02)	76 (4.04)	5 (0.27)
Unnao	1682 (100)	1274 (75.74)	126 (7.49)	232 (13.79)	31 (1.84)	19 (1.13)
Lucknow	822 (100)	647 (78.71)	84 (10.22)	84 (10.22)	5 (0.61)	2 (0.24)
Rae Bareli	1715 (100)	1015 (59.18)	419 (24.43)	276 (16.09)	5 (0.29)	0 –
Farrukhabad	1567 (100)	939 (59.92)	215 (13.72)	315 (20.10)	93 (5.93)	5 (0.32)
Etawah	1462 (100)	937 (64.09)	151 (10.33)	255 (17.44)	65 (4.45)	54 (3.69)
Kanpur Dehat	1624 (100)	1268 (78.08)	185 (11.39)	144 (8.87)	27 (1.66)	0 –
Kanpur Nagar	261 (100)	179 (68.58)	20 (7.66)	50 (19.16)	9 (3.45)	3 (1.15)
Jalaun	939 (100)	705 (75.08)	47 (5.01)	136 (14.48)	51 (5.53)	0 –
Jhansi	759 (100)	616 (81.16)	17 (2.24)	81 (10.67)	31 (4.08)	14 (1.84)
Lalitpur	683 (100)	470 (68.81)	42 (6.15)	103 (15.08)	41 (6.00)	27 (3.95)
Hamirpur	917 (100)	795 (86.70)	29 (3.16)	59 (6.43)	28 (3.05)	6 (0.65)
Banda	1203 (100)	866 (71.99)	95 (7.90)	159 (13.22)	81 (6.73)	2 (0.17)
Fatehpur	1349 (100)	929 (68.87)	64 (4.74)	294 (21.79)	62 (4.60)	0 –
Pratapgarh	2185 (100)	1090 (49.89)	821 (37.57)	274 (12.54)	0 –	0 –
Allahabad	3524 (100)	1691 (47.99)	571 (16.20)	591 (16.77)	470 (13.34)	201 (5.70)
Bahraich	1878 (100)	1449 (77.16)	204 (10.86)	200 (10.65)	20 (1.06)	5 (0.27)
Gonda	2805 (100)	1858 (66.24)	288 (10.27)	421 (15.01)	134 (4.78)	104 (3.71)

(Contd.)

TABLE 10.E4 (contd.)

Districtwise Distribution of Villages by Distance from School, 1991

State/district	Total number of villages	Number of villages with primary school				
		Within village	Between 0 and 1 km	Between 1 and 3 km	Between 3 and 5 km	Beyond 5 km
Barabanki	2043 (100)	1491 (72.98)	182 (8.91)	279 (13.66)	55 (2.69)	36 (1.76)
Faizabad	2644 (100)	1274 (48.18)	662 (25.04)	625 (23.64)	74 (2.80)	9 (0.34)
Sultanpur	2488 (100)	1524 (61.25)	435 (17.48)	391 (15.72)	130 (5.23)	8 (0.32)
Siddarthnagar	2431 (100)	761 (31.30)	428 (17.61)	907 (37.31)	232 (9.54)	103 (4.24)
Maharajganj	1187 (100)	525 (44.23)	285 (24.01)	286 (24.09)	70 (5.90)	21 (1.77)
Basti	4487 (100)	1187 (26.45)	760 (16.94)	2058 (45.87)	419 (9.34)	63 (1.40)
Gorakhpur	2860 (100)	1170 (40.91)	880 (30.77)	810 (28.32)	0 –	0 –
Deoria	3538 (100)	2013 (56.90)	688 (19.45)	797 (22.53)	30 (0.85)	10 (0.28)
Mau	1427 (100)	631 (44.22)	347 (24.32)	301 (21.09)	128 (8.97)	20 (1.40)
Azamgarh	3661 (100)	1187 (32.42)	873 (23.85)	1261 (34.44)	278 (7.59)	62 (1.69)
Jaunpur	3245 (100)	1300 (40.06)	840 (25.89)	920 (28.35)	174 (5.36)	11 (0.34)
Ballia	1767 (100)	889 (50.31)	561 (31.75)	287 (16.24)	27 (1.53)	3 (0.17)
Ghazipur	2523 (100)	916 (36.31)	598 (23.70)	905 (35.87)	102 (4.04)	2 (0.08)
Varansi	3657 (100)	1490 (40.74)	1,173 (32.08)	974 (26.83)	20 (0.55)	0 –
Mirzapur	1698 (100)	905 (53.30)	181 (10.66)	397 (23.38)	107 (6.30)	108 (6.36)
Sonbhadra	1321 (100)	597 (45.19)	282 (21.35)	319 (24.15)	65 (4.92)	58 (4.39)

Note: Figures in parentheses represent percentages.

Source: Directorate of Economics and Statistics, Uttar Pradesh, Lucknow.

TABLE 10.E5

Districtwise Effective Literacy Rates by Place of Residence and Sex, 1991 and 2001

State/district	Rural areas			Urban areas			All areas			All areas 2001		
	Male	Female	Total	Male	Female	Total	Male	Female	Total	Male	Female	Total
Uttar Pradesh	**52.05**	**19.02**	**36.66**	**69.98**	**50.38**	**61.00**	**55.73**	**25.31**	**41.60**	**70.23**	**42.98**	**57.36**
Uttarkashi	66.76	20.66	44.50	89.60	67.62	80.93	68.74	23.57	47.23	84.52	47.48	66.58
Chamoli	80.99	38.35	58.95	89.46	67.60	81.42	82.01	40.37	61.08	89.89	63.00	76.23
Tehri Garhwal	70.96	24.79	46.46	84.86	65.92	78.41	72.10	26.41	48.38	85.62	49.76	67.04
Dehradun	68.27	44.39	57.34	86.96	73.71	81.04	77.95	59.26	69.50	85.87	71.22	71.22
Garhwal	83.12	47.08	63.85	78.80	72.09	76.11	82.46	49.44	65.35	91.47	66.14	77.99
Pithoragarh	78.35	35.69	56.88	90.83	75.69	84.32	79.44	38.37	59.01	90.57	63.14	76.48
Almora	78.95	37.31	56.63	90.85	80.04	86.37	79.96	39.60	58.66	90.15	61.43	74.53
Nainital	65.59	37.55	52.55	72.44	55.09	64.62	67.88	43.19	56.52	87.39	70.98	79.60
Bijnor	52.18	22.50	38.56	53.70	38.03	46.38	52.56	26.47	40.53	70.18	47.28	59.37
Moradabad	36.51	9.71	24.39	55.02	39.76	47.94	41.65	18.34	31.03	56.66	33.32	45.74
Rampur	28.30	8.06	19.17	49.01	34.01	41.98	33.79	15.31	25.37	48.62	27.87	38.95
Saharanpur	49.32	19.89	35.96	66.83	50.93	59.49	53.85	28.10	42.11	72.26	51.42	62.61
Hardwar	50.50	21.74	37.43	78.45	62.76	71.34	59.51	34.93	48.35	75.06	52.60	64.60
Muzaffarnagar	54.52	24.14	40.65	63.16	43.96	54.20	56.63	29.12	44.00	73.11	48.63	61.68
Meerut	62.02	27.60	46.44	68.65	48.75	59.43	64.47	35.62	51.30	76.31	54.12	65.96
Ghaziabad	64.85	27.75	48.15	72.97	51.44	63.28	68.64	38.81	55.22	81.04	59.12	70.89
Bulandshahr	61.38	20.08	42.56	64.18	39.83	52.82	61.96	24.30	44.71	75.55	42.82	60.19
Aligarh	58.30	20.39	41.22	65.82	46.41	56.85	60.19	27.17	45.21	73.22	43.88	59.70
Mathura	60.49	15.62	40.82	69.32	45.40	58.32	62.55	23.04	45.03	77.60	43.77	62.21
Agra	59.07	17.64	40.71	68.96	48.92	59.77	63.09	30.83	48.58	79.32	48.15	64.97
Firozabad	57.47	23.13	42.13	66.10	47.64	57.63	59.76	29.85	46.30	77.81	53.02	66.53
Etah	52.07	18.28	37.08	64.40	44.71	55.26	54.09	22.91	40.15	69.13	40.65	56.15
Mainpuri	62.76	29.51	47.87	74.27	55.11	65.37	64.26	33.05	50.21	78.27	52.67	66.51
Budaun	30.54	8.11	20.75	50.63	33.34	42.62	33.96	12.82	24.64	49.85	25.53	38.83
Bareilly	36.62	9.65	24.67	57.09	39.22	48.84	43.33	19.85	32.78	59.12	35.13	47.99
Pilibhit	41.03	11.87	27.90	59.01	39.86	50.22	44.37	17.22	32:10	63.82	35.84	50.87
Shahjahanpur	38.57	12.28	27.15	59.03	40.92	50.63	42.68	18.59	32.07	60.53	34.68	48.79
Kheri	37.78	12.50	26.48	64.09	47.29	56.39	40.58	16.35	29.71	–	–	–
Sitapur	40.19	12.73	27.98	64.64	46.35	56.28	43.10	16.90	31.41	61.02	35.08	49.12
Hardoi	47.56	16.34	33.82	64.13	44.09	54.87	49.45	19.75	36.30	65.08	37.62	52.64
Unnao	49.15	19.87	35.64	67.35	47.14	57.97	51.63	23.62	38.70	67.62	42.40	55.72
Lucknow	48.60	19.05	35.15	76.77	62.38	70.12	66.51	46.88	57.49	76.63	61.22	69.39
Rae Bareli	51.41	18.22	35.40	71.44	50.13	61.59	53.30	21.01	37.78	69.03	40.44	55.06
Farrukhabad	58.14	28.20	44.79	65.50	47.72	57.27	59.48	31.97	47.13	72.40	50.35	62.27
Etawah	64.73	34.65	51.28	74.39	57.02	66.35	66.24	38.34	53.69	81.15	57.49	70.75
Kanpur Dehat	62.54	34.96	50.09	68.58	51.56	60.79	62.88	35.92	50.71	76.84	54.49	66.59
Kanpur Nagar	61.55	34.83	49.56	79.38	63.06	72.11	76.73	58.82	68.75	82.08	72.50	77.63
Jalaun	63.59	26.13	46.91	75.50	50.27	64.02	66.21	31.60	50.72	79.14	50.66	66.14
Jhansi	59.05	19.61	41.09	78.56	54.56	67.39	66.76	33.76	51.60	80.11	51.21	66.69
Lalitpur	39.79	10.47	26.41	78.37	52.22	66.10	45.22	16.62	32.12	64.45	33.25	49.93
Hamirpur	51.86	16.35	35.83	70.67	41.98	57.58	55.13	20.88	39.64	72.76	40.65	58.10
Banda	48.26	12.21	32.01	72.78	44.46	60.05	51.50	16.44	35.70	69.89	37.10	54.84
Fatehpur	58.55	24.87	42.87	71.63	48.70	61.05	59.88	27.25	44.69	73.07	44.62	59.74
Pratapgarh	59.20	18.88	38.97	77.33	49.55	64.46	60.29	20.48	40.40	74.61	42.63	58.67
Allahabad	53.42	13.87	34.96	78.47	58.76	69.69	59.14	23.45	42.66	77.13	46.61	62.89
Bahraich	33.51	7.89	22.01	60.26	43.14	52.36	35.57	10.73	24.39	46.32	23.27	35.79

(Contd.)

TABLE 10.E5 (contd.)

Districtwise Effective Literacy Rates by Place of Residence and Sex, 1991 and 2001

State/district	Rural areas			Urban areas			All areas			All areas 2001		
	Male	Female	Total	Male	Female	Total	Male	Female	Total	Male	Female	Total
Gonda	37.56	9.66	24.67	70.17	48.71	60.29	40.00	12.58	27.34	56.28	21.58	34.71
Barabanki	41.51	12.96	28.53	57.79	38.68	48.87	43.00	15.41	30.42	60.12	35.64	48.71
Faizabad	53.06	19.46	36.84	72.58	50.61	62.57	55.49	22.97	39.90	70.73	43.35	57.48
Sultanpur	54.15	19.40	37.32	79.64	53.07	67.55	55.36	20.84	38.69	71.85	41.81	56.90
Siddharthnagar	39.94	10.91	26.13	67.40	38.18	53.84	40.91	11.84	27.09	58.68	28.35	43.97
Maharajganj	44.20	8.68	27.35	72.70	41.04	58.06	45.67	10.28	28.90	65.40	28.64	47.72
Basti	50.19	15.78	33.74	72.17	48.46	61.34	51.68	17.82	35.54	68.16	39.00	54.28
Gorakhpur	56.09	17.23	37.25	78.52	56.74	68.59	60.61	24.49	43.30	76.70	44.48	60.96
Deoria	53.72	16.53	35.30	74.09	47.77	61.85	55.34	18.75	37.30	76.31	43.56	59.84
Mau	56.85	23.56	40.26	71.82	49.88	61.29	59.44	27.86	43.80	78.97	52.86	64.86
Azamgarh	55.06	20.85	37.68	68.94	47.76	58.91	56.13	22.67	39.22	70.50	42.44	56.15
Jaunpur	61.37	20.59	40.79	73.00	47.98	61.22	62.24	22.39	42.22	77.16	43.53	59.98
Ballia	59.44	23.76	41.99	72.22	48.16	60.88	60.76	26.13	43.89	73.15	43.92	58.88
Ghazipur	60.05	22.33	41.46	78.36	51.01	65.56	61.48	24.38	43.27	75.45	44.39	60.06
Varanasi	60.94	20.94	41.95	72.92	50.13	62.52	64.37	28.87	47.70	73.66	48.59	67.09
Mirzapur	52.22	18.55	36.54	69.84	45.49	58.67	54.75	22.32	39.68	70.51	39.89	56.10
Sonbhadra	41.12	12.49	27.92	84.08	60.20	74.08	47.56	18.65	34.40	63.79	34.26	49.96

Sources: Census of India, 1991 and 2001.

TABLE 10.H1

Districtwise Number of Sub-centres, PHCs, CHCs, and Doctors per lakh Rural Population and Urban Family Welfare Centres per lakh Population for Allopathy System, 1992

State/district	Total rural population	Sub-centres		PHC		CHC		Doctors per lakh population	Urban FWCs per lakh population
		Number	Per lakh population	Number	Per lakh population	Number	Per lakh population		
Uttar Pradesh	**111,506,372**	**20,153**	**18.08**	**3652**	**3.28**	**228**	**0.21**	**4.36**	**14.90**
Uttarkashi	222,448	69	31.02	4	1.80	1	0.45	26.07	28.97
Chamoli	414,331	133	32.10	9	2.17	3	0.73	18.10	34.53
Tehri Garhwal	547,258	159	29.05	10	1.83	2	0.40	19.19	27.36
Dehradun	510,199	139	27.24	4	0.78	2	0.40	22.34	15.71
Garhwal	601,353	223	37.08	15	2.49	2	0.34	19.96	35.72
Pithoragarh	524,295	179	34.14	11	2.10	2	0.39	14.88	37.99
Almora	783,110	254	32.43	14	1.79	3	0.39	11.88	33.64
Nainital	1,037,210	287	27.67	12	1.16	3	0.29	18.22	22.07
Bijnor	1,839,169	203	11.04	53	2.88	3	0.17	3.21	15.44
Moradabad	2,981,566	485	16.27	85	2.85	7	0.24	3.68	13.69
Rampur	1,109,425	170	15.32	34	3.06	2	0.18	3.79	14.77
Saharanpur	1,719,377	293	17.04	70	4.07	5	0.29	3.37	15.43
Hardwar	776,346	139	17.90	24	3.09	2	0.26	5.93	14.65
Muzaffarnagar	2,143,313	362	16.89	70	3.27	5	0.24	4.20	13.01
Meerut	2,171,355	410	18.88	72	3.32	4	0.19	5.89	15.04
Ghaziabad	1,455,673	278	19.10	47	3.23	4	0.28	5.91	12.82
Bulandshahr	2,257,064	390	17.28	64	2.84	3	0.14	3.28	16.19
Aligarh	2,467,484	388	15.72	72	2.92	5	0.21	2.95	13.88
Mathura	1,475,935	261	17.68	51	3.46	4	0.28	5.08	14.50
Agra	1,639,935	393	23.96	57	3.48	2	0.13	5.06	13.23
Firozabad	1,125,494	234	20.79	32	2.84	1	0.09	4.80	15.95

(Contd.)

TABLE 10.H1 (contd.)

Districtwise Number of Sub-centres, PHCs, CHCs, and Doctors per lakh Rural Population and Urban Family Welfare Centres per lakh Population for Allopathy System, 1992

State/district	Total rural population	Sub-centres		PHC		CHC		Doctors per lakh population	Urban FWCs per lakh population
		Number	Per lakh population	Number	Per lakh population	Number	Per lakh population		
Etah	1,869,740	326	17.44	63	3.37	4	0.22	4.81	15.46
Mainpuri	1,142,856	336	29.40	47	4.11	3	0.27	3.68	37.96
Budaun	2,017,033	341	16.91	68	3.37	3	0.15	4.56	16.00
Bareilly	1,905,151	355	18.63	68	3.57	2	0.11	4.72	13.45
Pilibhit	1,046,247	182	17.40	31	2.96	3	0.29	2.58	14.78
Shahjahanpur	1,574,764	301	19.11	49	3.11	3	0.19	3.47	15.51
Kheri	2,161,259	387	17.91	60	2.78	1	0.05	3.01	17.06
Sitapur	2,513,341	437	17.39	81	3.22	6	0.24	3.70	16.59
Hardoi	2,424,471	423	17.45	70	2.89	1	0.05	4.25	17.05
Unnao	1,901,099	344	18.09	59	3.10	3	0.16	4.05	17.71
Lucknow	1,031,577	204	19.78	35	3.39	2	0.20	7.95	10.28
Rae Bareli	2,112,898	379	17.94	65	3.08	3	0.15	4.83	18.10
Farrukhabad	1,985,645	363	18.28	50	2.52	4	0.21	3.47	16.50
Etawah	1,790,954	323	18.04	65	3.63	3	0.17	3.96	15.58
Kanpur Dehat	2,016,274	356	17.66	66	3.27	4	0.20	2.08	18.03
Kanpur Nagar	381,154	81	21.25	11	2.89	1	0.27	0	4.37
Jalaun	950,180	230	24.21	50	5.26	3	0.32	5.79	21.92
Jhansi	863,342	251	29.07	48	5.56	3	0.35	7.76	18.72
Lalitpur	646,495	180	27.84	31	4.80	2	0.31	4.80	26.53
Hamirpur	1,211,846	305	25.17	60	4.95	3	0.25	5.20	25.13
Banda	1,622,718	322	19.84	85	5.24	4	0.25	6.04	17.96
Fatehpur	1,711,228	309	18.06	64	3.74	3	0.18	0	18.62
Pratapgarh	2,088,599	360	17.24	65	3.11	6	0.29	4.07	18.02
Allahabad	3,898,948	594	15.23	100	2.56	10	0.26	3.67	13.01
Bahraich	2,546,844	445	17.47	55	2.16	5	0.20	2.20	19.36
Gonda	3,308,349	528	15.96	102	3.08	5	0.16	2.45	15.87
Barabanki	2,197,820	377	17.15	72	3.28	2	0.09	5.05	18.23
Faizabad	2,631,261	401	15.24	80	3.04	2	0.08	3.69	16.42
Sultanpur	2,444,802	394	16.12	73	2.99	7	0.29	3.44	17.52
Siddarthnagar	1,648,377	284	17.23	29	1.76	5	0.31	1.46	20.17
Maharajganj	1,593,461	195	12.24	23	1.44	3	0.19	2.45	19.30
Basti	2,562,696	434	16.94	118	4.60	8	0.32	0	17.06
Gorakhpur	2,490,726	470	18.87	83	3.33	5	0.20	2.77	17.73
Deoria	4,113,897	672	16.33	38	0.92	10	0.25	2.53	17.78
Mau	1,201,787	218	18.14	57	4.74	5	0.42	3.99	17.21
Azamgarh	2,928,166	475	16.22	87	2.97	8	0.28	3.65	16.84
Jaunpur	2,993,297	478	15.97	86	2.87	8	0.27	3.51	17.62
Ballia	2,038,186	383	18.79	67	3.29	7	0.35	4.37	17.40
Ghazipur	2,238,315	402	17.96	67	2.99	4	0.18	5.09	17.39
Varansi	3,538,334	616	17.41	112	3.17	10	0.09	4.35	15.35
Mirzapur	1,428,499	390	27.30	53	3.71	5	0.35	7.63	17.49
Sonbhadra	930,958	113	12.14	33	3.54	1	0.11	2.58	17.35

Source: Directorate of Health and Family Welfare, Uttar Pradesh, Lucknow.

TABLE 10.H2
Districtwise Number of Doctors and Nurses, 1992

State/district	Doctors			Staff nurses
	Urban areas	Rural areas	All areas	All areas
Uttar Pradesh	**2088**	**4857**	**6945**	**3646**
Uttarkashi	19	58	77	36
Chamoli	24	75	99	52
Tehri Garhwal	30	105	135	22
Dehradun	27	114	141	72
Garhwal	36	120	156	46
Pithoragarh	21	78	99	36
Almora	44	93	137	44
Nainital	47	189	236	110
Bijnor	35	59	94	35
Moradabad	49	110	159	70
Rampur	34	42	76	42
Saharanpur	42	58	100	70
Hardwar	13	46	59	33
Muzaffarnagar	41	90	131	43
Meerut	46	128	174	134
Ghaziabad	32	86	118	36
Bulandshahr	30	74	104	48
Aligarh	28	64	92	43
Mathura	37	75	112	27
Agra	45	83	128	190
Firozabad	13	54	67	29
Etah	34	90	124	23
Mainpuri	32	42	74	32
Budaun	23	92	115	75
Bareilly	32	90	122	66
Pilibhit	22	27	49	30
Shahjahanpur	24	54	78	56
Kheri	33	65	98	51
Sitapur	45	93	138	60
Hardoi	41	103	144	17
Unnao	36	77	113	37
Lucknow	124	82	206	376
Rae Bareli	52	102	154	84
Farrukhabad	38	69	107	43
Etawah	31	71	102	31
Kanpur Dehat	13	42	55	12
Kanpur Nagar	50	0	50	185
Jalaun	35	55	90	40
Jhansi	40	67	107	131
Lalitpur	30	31	61	28
Hamirpur	34	63	97	24
Banda	35	98	133	27
Fatehpur	22	0	22	24
Pratapgarh	25	85	110	59
Allahabad	44	143	187	89
Bahraich	37	56	93	58
Gonda	25	81	106	39
Barabanki	23	111	134	63
Faizabad	30	97	127	36
Sultanpur	24	84	108	76
Siddarthnagar	13	24	37	5
Maharajganj	16	39	55	1

(Contd.)

TABLE 10.H2 (contd.)
Districtwise Number of Doctors and Nurses, 1992

State/district	Doctors			Staff nurses
	Urban areas	Rural areas	All areas	All areas
Basti	21	0	21	60
Gorakhpur	49	69	118	89
Deoria	24	104	128	49
Mau	24	48	72	35
Azamgarh	33	107	140	35
Jaunpur	41	105	146	49
Ballia	25	89	114	48
Ghazipur	35	114	149	36
Varansi	44	154	198	115
Mirzapur	23	109	132	29
Sonbhadra	13	24	37	5

Source: Directorate of Health and Family Welfare, Uttar Pradesh, Lucknow.

TABLE 10.H3
Districtwise Population Density, Sex Ratio, Percentage of Urban Population and Scheduled Caste and Tribe Population, and CMIE Index, 1991

State/district	Rural areas				Urban areas				All areas				Percentage of urban popln.	CMIE index
	Populn. density	Sex ratio	Percentage of SCs	Percentage of STs	Populn. density	Sex ratio	Percentage of SCs	Percentage of STs	Populn. density	Sex ratio	Percentage of SCs	Percentage of STs		
Uttar Pradesh	**385**	**884**	**23.16**	**0.24**	**5553**	**860**	**12.51**	**0.06**	**473**	**879**	**21.05**	**0.21**	**19.84**	**72**
Uttarkashi	28	939	23.54	1.01	1005	683	12.97	0.35	30	918	22.78	0.96	7.20	47
Chamoli	46	1049	17.58	1.92	610	624	16.61	5.76	50	1003	17.49	2.26	8.91	38
Tehri Garhwal	125	1098	14.44	0.10	590	563	10.25	0.20	131	1058	14.2	0.11	5.67	40
Dehradun	174	861	15.15	15.88	4974	826	11.67	0.60	332	843	13.40	8.20	50.26	142
Garhwal	112	1119	13.91	0.23	1180	705	10.62	0.18	125	1060	13.52	0.22	11.89	51
Pithoragarh	59	1004	20.83	2.89	1960	783	15.67	7.53	64	985	20.45	3.23	7.44	55
Almora	145	1116	22.44	0.26	7868	736	15.95	1.30	155	1087	22.02	0.33	5.20	46
Nainital	155	883	18.02	8.49	5543	842	11.22	0.39	227	870	15.80	5.84	32.64	132
Bijnor	418	865	25.13	0.10	3883	890	7.33	0.00	538	871	20.67	0.08	25.07	92
Moradabad	514	842	19.13	0.01	9079	879	8.32	0.02	691	852	16.14	0.01	27.65	85
Rampur	482	846	16.10	0.00	6234	893	4.22	0.01	635	858	12.99	0.00	26.14	84
Saharanpur	474	846	26.81	0.00	9636	868	9.92	0.03	626	851	22.50	0.01	25.54	118
Hardwar	331	849	26.46	0.26	11,538	841	10.71	0.01	476	846	21.58	0.18	30.96	–
Muzaffarnagar	521	852	15.66	0.00	11,791	883	9.07	0.00	681	860	14.04	0.00	24.60	70
Meerut	604	839	18.14	0.00	4436	874	14.08	0.01	882	852	16.64	0.00	36.73	112
Ghaziabad	596	832	19.16	0.00	8423	831	16.40	0.01	1044	832	17.89	0.01	46.16	146
Bulandshahr	534	850	23.21	0.00	4827	880	13.52	0.01	655	856	21.20	0.00	21.56	75
Aligarh	510	834	24.80	0.00	6431	867	17.67	0.01	657	842	23.01	0.00	25.14	72
Mathura	393	803	21.95	0.00	5132	860	14.68	0.03	507	816	20.23	0.01	23.57	71
Agra	411	815	21.99	0.01	28,541	857	24.99	0.01	683	832	23.20	0.01	40.39	105
Firozabad	559	822	19.99	0.01	1177	861	17.31	0.01	649	832	19.28	0.01	26.58	–
Etah	425	815	18.02	0.00	7704	873	13.84	0.00	505	824	17.32	0.00	16.72	57
Mainpuri	422	827	19.81	0.00	3234	878	15.89	0.01	477	833	19.29	0.00	13.21	81
Budaun	393	796	18.62	0.00	12,977	877	11.36	0.00	474	810	17.34	0.00	17.62	57
Bareilly	497	822	15.43	0.01	4389	875	7.00	0.02	688	839	12.66	0.02	32.79	76
Pilibhit	302	850	17.80	0.13	8062	870	8.12	0.01	367	853	16.01	0.10	18.15	96
Shahjahanpur	347	800	20.27	0.01	11,411	880	9.42	0.05	434	816	18.02	0.02	20.76	76
Kheri	283	839	28.98	1.32	5633	863	9.50	0.11	315	842	26.90	1.19	10.66	76
Sitapur	443	829	35.23	0.01	4657	860	10.18	0.01	497	833	32.22	0.01	12.04	51
Hardoi	409	812	34.37	0.00	5306	869	10.31	0.00	459	818	31.55	0.00	11.74	50
Unnao	422	872	32.98	0.12	5532	880	15.04	0.05	483	873	30.54	0.11	13.60	47

(Contd.)

TABLE 10.H3 (contd.)

Districtwise Population Density, Sex Ratio, Percentage of Urban Population and Scheduled Caste and Tribe Population, and CMIE Index, 1991

State/district	Rural areas				Urban areas				All areas				Percentage of urban popln.	CMIE index
	Populn. density	Sex ratio	Percentage of SCs	Percentage of STs	Populn. density	Sex ratio	Percentage of SCs	Percentage of STs	Populn. density	Sex ratio	Percentage of SCs	Percentage of STs		
Lucknow	437	857	40.68	0.02	10,305	871	10.67	0.05	1093	866	21.88	0.04	62.66	152
Rae Bareli	466	936	31.24	0.07	2868	877	15.91	0.03	504	931	29.86	0.06	9.04	47
Farrukhabad	471	827	18.54	0.01	7416	872	13.43	0.13	571	835	17.59	0.03	18.63	78
Etawah	420	824	26.86	0.00	6284	870	15.20	0.01	491	831	25.03	0.00	15.71	57
Kanpur Dehat	397	842	25.74	0.03	3225	862	15.80	0.02	418	843	25.17	0.03	5.71	82
Kanpur Nagar	502	838	25.84	0.07	6674	822	11.24	0.04	2271	824	13.54	0.04	84.21	155
Jalaun	211	823	28.86	0.00	4463	849	22.03	0.00	267	829	27.35	0.00	22.08	62
Jhansi	177	852	32.12	0.01	3940	880	23.75	0.02	285	863	28.8	0.01	39.61	73
Lalitpur	129	859	26.90	0.05	5139	888	14.26	0.01	149	863	25.12	0.05	14.05	57
Hamirpur	170	839	25.73	0.00	5127	853	20.90	0.00	205	841	24.89	0.00	17.22	65
Banda	214	843	24.20	0.00	5245	831	16.76	0.00	244	841	23.25	0.00	12.86	49
Fatehpur	420	882	25.76	0.02	2256	874	15.22	0.00	457	882	24.72	0.02	9.90	51
Pratapgarh	567	993	22.12	0.00	3684	880	10.66	0.01	595	987	21.49	0.00	5.52	42
Allahabad	542	889	27.49	0.05	15,868	821	12.93	0.02	678	875	24.46	0.04	20.77	62
Bahraich	372	838	17.36	0.37	6934	874	5.85	0.01	402	841	16.46	0.34	7.85	41
Gonda	454	874	16.32	0.46	4364	866	6.18	0.02	486	873	15.57	0.43	7.41	44
Barabanki	505	855	28.92	0.01	4735	888	8.40	0.00	550	858	27.02	0.01	9.28	53
Faizabad	594	933	24.97	0.00	3995	853	9.39	0.00	660	924	23.15	0.00	11.66	54
Sultanpur	555	938	22.93	0.01	3592	848	10.00	0.00	557	934	22.36	0.01	25.95	47
Siddharthnagar	476	914	16.91	0.00	2000	879	10.50	0.00	489	913	16.69	0.00	3.48	–
Maharajganj	557	911	19.70	0.16	2369	880	13.65	0.17	569	909	19.40	0.16	4.95	–
Basti	700	920	21.68	0.01	2427	859	13.76	0.00	734	916	21.17	0.01	6.42	59
Gorakhpur	408	940	24.16	0.01	3624	857	12.85	0.04	489	924	22.04	0.02	22.02	75
Deoria	770	974	16.09	0.01	3244	884	8.79	0.00	815	967	15.55	0.01	7.35	50
Mau	727	982	24.99	0.00	5128	932	7.65	0.00	844	974	22.06	0.00	16.88	–
Azamgarh	701	1015	26.62	0.01	4180	912	12.45	0.01	745	1007	25.61	0.01	7.16	59
Jaunpur	749	1001	22.68	0.00	5533	899	9.58	0.00	796	994	21.78	0.00	6.89	51
Ballia	648	951	15.39	0.01	5104	904	8.28	0.00	709	946	14.69	0.01	9.91	51
Ghazipur	669	963	21.38	0.02	5586	895	10.41	0.04	716	957	20.57	0.02	7.38	51
Varanasi	719	909	21.38	0.00	7768	861	9.48	0.01	955	896	18.14	0.00	27.20	91
Mirzapur	320	886	27.94	0.00	4195	866	13.51	0.00	366	883	25.95	0.00	13.80	–
Sonbhadra	138	880	47.23	0.01	4156	753	11.93	0.02	158	862	42.50	0.01	13.40	–

Sources: Census of India, 1991; CMIE Index, 1993, District Profile, Centre for Monitoring Indian Econmomy.

TABLE 10.H4

Districtwise Workers in Urban Areas (Main and Marginal) as Percentage to Urban Population, Workers in Household Industry for Urban Areas as Percentage to Total Urban Main Workers, 1991

State/district	Main workers			Marginal workers			Workers in HH industry		
	Male	Female	Total	Male	Female	Total	Male	Female	Total
Uttar Pradesh	**46.19**	**3.75**	**26.56**	**0.18**	**1.03**	**0.57**	**4.64**	**13.77**	**5.24**
Uttarkashi	49.86	11.82	34.42	1.31	2.16	1.66	1.49	0.72	1.38
Chamoli	54.24	17.56	40.15	0.33	1.45	0.76	0.47	8.11	1.75
Tehri Garhwal	57.58	7.49	39.53	0.70	1.97	1.16	0.07	0.23	0.08
Dehradun	49.66	6.12	29.96	0.14	0.35	0.23	0.50	1.95	0.63
Garhwal	52.18	6.34	33.23	0.15	1.23	0.60	0.19	1.36	0.29
Pithoragarh	45.65	11.10	30.48	0.46	4.04	2.03	1.23	11.79	2.92
Almora	53.06	10.87	35.18	1.92	6.79	3.98	0.80	1.54	0.90
Nainital	48.87	4.04	28.38	0.37	1.06	0.68	1.15	4.69	1.38
Bijnor	47.03	2.10	25.88	0.11	0.72	0.40	3.52	22.26	4.24
Moradabad	47.65	3.31	26.91	0.08	0.99	0.50	6.06	24.60	7.12

(Contd.)

TABLE 10.H4 (contd.)

Districtwise Workers in Urban Areas (Main and Marginal) as Percentage to Urban Population, Workers in Household Industry for Urban Areas as Percentage to Total Urban Main Workers, 1991

State/district	Main workers			Marginal workers			Workers in HH industry		
	Male	Female	Total	Male	Female	Total	Male	Female	Total
Rampur	49.80	3.40	27.91	0.21	1.13	0.64	3.34	16.82	4.12
Saharanpur	48.24	2.38	26.93	0.08	0.33	0.20	1.33	6.23	1.53
Hardwar	47.30	3.70	27.38	0.08	0.53	0.29	0.85	6.56	1.20
Muzaffarnagar	48.09	3.39	27.12	0.16	1.67	0.87	2.74	7.15	3.00
Meerut	47.70	3.18	26.94	0.16	1.19	0.64	4.94	9.49	5.19
Ghaziabad	47.61	3.40	27.55	0.77	3.08	1.82	1.57	2.96	1.65
Bulandshahr	45.91	2.51	25.60	0.25	1.52	0.84	2.77	9.58	3.09
Aligarh	45.26	3.08	25.67	0.16	1.30	0.69	4.82	11.89	5.21
Mathura	45.84	3.21	26.13	0.14	1.05	0.56	4.10	7.84	4.32
Agra	47.75	2.82	27.02	0.15	0.70	0.40	6.10	14.67	6.52
Firozabad	46.51	2.57	26.19	0.07	0.27	0.16	1.76	7.54	2.03
Etah	45.74	2.49	25.58	0.26	2.47	1.29	3.29	19.39	4.02
Mainpuri	44.57	2.03	24.69	0.08	0.16	0.12	1.24	3.27	1.32
Budaun	48.35	2.11	26.74	0.12	1.06	0.56	1.67	9.92	1.97
Bareilly	47.81	2.27	26.56	0.13	0.33	0.22	2.85	7.84	3.05
Pilibhit	47.81	2.49	26.73	0.15	1.08	0.58	1.97	12.49	2.42
Shahjahanpur	47.88	2.10	26.45	0.14	0.32	0.22	4.24	13.04	4.57
Kheri	48.52	2.50	27.21	0.01	0.07	0.04	1.68	3.62	1.76
Sitapur	47.05	3.15	26.75	0.13	0.55	0.32	7.77	21.72	8.53
Hardoi	47.45	2.90	26.74	0.07	0.38	0.22	4.72	13.08	5.14
Unnao	47.21	3.30	26.66	0.17	1.48	0.78	2.69	8.39	3.02
Lucknow	45.50	4.84	26.57	0.13	0.23	0.17	2.75	3.43	2.80
Rae Bareli	45.38	3.93	26.01	0.20	1.66	0.88	1.71	4.95	1.94
Farrukhabad	47.65	5.87	28.19	0.10	1.15	0.59	2.05	8.44	2.67
Etawah	45.25	2.58	25.39	0.05	0.13	0.08	3.90	15.59	4.46
Kanpur Dehat	46.87	3.24	26.67	0.02	0.12	0.07	1.28	6.11	1.55
Kanpur Nagar	44.95	2.55	25.82	0.00	0.00	0.00	0.60	1.67	0.65
Jalaun	45.15	3.25	25.91	0.09	0.76	0.40	2.18	8.04	2.52
Jhansi	43.98	5.76	26.09	0.32	1.84	1.03	4.22	15.69	5.41
Lalitpur	44.86	5.90	26.53	0.13	2.15	1.08	2.07	10.44	2.95
Hamirpur	46.04	6.50	27.84	0.31	4.73	2.35	2.61	5.94	2.97
Banda	46.03	6.27	27.99	0.21	3.81	1.85	2.43	5.77	2.77
Fatehpur	45.77	4.34	26.45	0.13	1.16	0.61	2.58	5.12	2.78
Pratapgarh	43.71	4.71	25.45	0.10	1.49	0.75	2.93	6.32	3.22
Allahabad	42.21	4.79	25.34	0.21	0.95	0.54	4.36	14.63	5.24
Bahraich	47.18	3.29	26.72	0.38	1.82	1.05	2.76	7.60	3.04
Gonda	44.71	3.51	25.59	0.17	0.72	0.42	1.79	4.33	1.95
Barabanki	48.23	6.10	28.41	0.12	0.93	0.50	11.39	39.21	14.20
Faizabad	46.54	4.33	27.11	0.03	0.51	0.25	7.83	10.88	8.06
Sultanpur	44.58	4.51	26.19	0.16	1.71	0.87	3.99	8.21	4.32
Siddharthnagar	46.56	3.13	26.24	0.16	3.83	1.88	2.98	3.33	3.00
Maharajganj	45.81	4.71	26.57	0.16	2.05	1.04	3.56	3.72	3.57
Basti	42.85	4.68	25.21	0.69	3.20	1.85	8.90	21.88	10.02
Gorakhpur	41.15	3.73	23.88	0.08	0.17	0.12	3.03	9.85	3.52
Deoria	42.18	3.62	24.09	0.24	1.01	0.60	4.65	4.97	4.67
Mau	42.50	11.38	27.49	0.19	2.08	1.10	48.33	76.35	53.92
Azamgarh	42.41	6.43	25.25	0.27	1.56	0.89	26.47	59.62	30.50
Jaunpur	41.20	3.81	23.49	0.07	0.67	0.35	4.45	15.23	5.28
Ballia	41.24	4.33	23.71	0.15	0.50	0.31	2.58	3.63	2.67
Ghazipur	39.84	4.18	23.00	0.09	0.89	0.46	4.62	12.15	5.26
Varanasi	45.12	4.75	26.44	0.12	0.91	0.49	21.19	34.59	22.30
Mirzapur	46.03	4.95	26.96	0.35	2.01	1.12	9.12	15.78	9.68
Sonbhadra	47.26	2.82	28.17	0.11	0.28	0.18	0.54	2.35	0.62

Source: Census of India, 1991.

TABLE 10.H5

Districtwise Rural Population, Workers (Main and Marginal) as Percentage to Rural Population, Cultivators, Agricultural Labourers, and Workers in Household Industry for Rural Areas as Percentage to Total Main Workers, 1991

State/district	Total population			Main workers			Marginal workers			Cultivators			Agricultural labourers			Workers in HH industry		
	Male	Female	Total	Male	Female	Total	Male	Female	Total	Male	Female	Total	Male	Female	Total	Male	Female	Total
Uttar Pradesh	**59,197,138**	**52,309,234**	**111,506,372**	**50.10**	**8.36**	**30.52**	**0.41**	**5.81**	**2.94**	**64.52**	**52.77**	**63.01**	**18.94**	**38.61**	**21.47**	**1.71**	**2.43**	**1.80**
Uttarkashi	114,723	107,725	222,448	50.77	47.16	49.02	1.29	4.34	2.77	67.23	96.79	81.00	1.88	0.80	1.37	0.92	0.40	0.68
Chamoli	202,168	212,163	414,331	43.62	41.46	42.52	1.46	8.32	4.97	60.14	96.56	78.32	1.19	0.41	0.80	0.99	1.22	1.11
Tehri Garhwal	260,889	286,369	547,258	41.82	37.58	39.60	1.44	10.13	5.98	66.84	98.17	82.40	1.54	0.39	0.97	0.58	0.05	0.32
Dehradun	274,112	236,087	510,199	51.69	15.43	34.91	1.03	7.51	4.02	33.56	68.79	40.77	16.68	14.11	16.15	1.11	0.83	1.05
Garhwal	283,753	317,600	601,353	38.74	25.48	31.74	1.57	14.62	8.46	52.37	95.92	70.84	2.47	1.39	2.01	0.79	0.17	0.53
Pithoragarh	261,674	262,621	524,295	45.51	38.27	41.88	2.21	13.60	7.92	61.17	96.30	77.25	1.07	0.43	0.78	1.67	1.40	1.55
Almora	370,074	413,036	783,110	40.92	40.24	40.56	2.56	11.10	7.06	62.40	97.60	80.82	1.32	0.64	0.96	1.23	0.22	0.70
Nainital	550,781	486,429	1,037,210	50.68	15.72	34.28	3.44	15.10	8.91	50.45	73.99	55.51	22.74	18.86	21.91	0.78	0.72	0.77
Bijnor	986,099	853,070	1,839,169	50.71	2.12	28.17	0.18	1.70	0.89	44.70	27.68	44.10	34.89	27.40	34.63	3.10	21.32	3.73
Moradabad	1,618,396	1,363,170	2,981,566	50.99	2.01	28.60	0.13	2.60	1.26	68.75	57.16	68.38	17.62	16.35	17.58	1.48	9.55	1.74
Rampur	600,967	508,458	1,109,425	53.32	1.96	29.78	0.36	4.11	2.08	73.11	36.69	72.02	17.03	37.45	17.65	0.72	6.78	0.90
Saharanpur	931,608	787,769	1,719,377	52.61	2.47	29.64	0.12	1.72	0.85	41.70	18.28	40.80	37.86	51.96	38.40	1.39	5.77	1.55
Hardwar	419,974	356,372	776,346	52.50	2.57	29.58	0.12	1.47	0.74	39.82	18.20	38.96	35.87	42.88	36.15	1.79	6.71	1.99
Muzaffarnagar	1,157,388	985,925	2,143,313	52.00	6.10	30.88	0.47	8.66	4.23	45.77	30.75	44.40	32.92	49.59	34.44	1.38	3.21	1.54
Meerut	1,180,533	990,822	2,171,355	50.11	4.38	29.24	0.63	5.80	2.99	46.48	36.85	45.82	27.35	39.17	28.16	1.72	3.80	1.86
Ghaziabad	794,425	661,248	1,455,673	47.48	2.29	26.95	0.65	8.09	4.03	44.80	32.80	44.33	21.42	34.97	21.94	1.26	2.54	1.31
Bulandshahr	1,220,244	1,036,820	2,257,064	47.34	2.79	26.87	0.40	5.54	2.76	54.96	47.04	54.58	24.26	32.50	24.65	1.35	3.59	1.46
Aligarh	1,345,184	1,122,300	2,467,484	48.77	3.01	27.96	0.42	6.53	3.20	52.46	44.62	52.08	27.80	33.86	28.10	1.55	5.20	1.73
Mathura	818,745	657,190	1,475,935	48.48	3.27	28.35	0.14	3.33	1.56	55.97	51.24	55.73	22.27	30.76	22.71	1.66	4.21	1.79
Agra	903,464	736,471	1,639,935	48.74	1.85	27.69	0.15	1.86	0.91	58.37	39.72	57.81	16.70	28.47	17.05	2.05	8.35	2.24
Firozabad	617,887	507,607	1,125,494	49.12	1.18	27.50	0.06	0.51	0.26	58.69	40.49	58.34	18.85	24.58	18.96	0.75	5.50	0.84
Etah	1,030,210	839,530	1,869,740	51.52	1.57	29.09	0.45	5.11	2.54	74.37	58.17	73.98	14.64	19.00	14.75	0.79	7.05	0.95
Mainpuri	625,572	517,284	1,142,856	49.83	0.96	27.71	0.05	0.87	0.42	75.72	51.32	75.34	12.15	19.08	12.26	0.60	5.73	0.68
Budaun	1,122,951	894,082	2,017,033	55.20	1.46	31.38	0.12	2.41	1.14	83.11	59.82	82.63	10.24	19.06	10.42	0.38	4.07	0.46
Bareilly	1,045,462	859,680	1,905,151	53.47	0.96	29.78	0.11	1.08	0.55	72.36	39.90	71.89	16.20	26.07	16.34	0.75	5.59	0.82
Pilibhit	565,685	480,562	1,046,247	53.04	1.65	29.43	0.14	3.04	1.48	73.09	36.99	72.16	17.77	40.32	18.35	0.49	4.55	0.59
Shahjahanpur	874,870	699,894	1,574,764	56.89	1.16	32.12	0.06	0.59	0.30	77.43	45.45	76.92	15.10	34.48	15.41	0.61	2.68	0.65
Kheri	1,175,010	986,249	2,161,259	56.20	2.34	31.62	0.09	1.79	0.87	80.33	47.37	79.22	12.95	42.84	13.96	0.59	2.18	0.64
Sitapur	1,374,119	1,139,222	2,513,341	56.14	2.91	32.01	0.10	1.74	0.84	80.36	55.16	79.32	11.30	31.61	12.13	1.43	3.95	1.54
Hardoi	1,338,200	1,086,271	2,424,471	54.85	2.98	31.61	0.11	2.37	1.12	81.02	57.51	80.03	10.68	26.35	11.34	0.77	4.21	0.92
Unnao	1,015,650	885,449	1,901,099	53.34	6.38	31.47	0.24	6.23	3.03	77.21	60.61	75.64	11.16	31.67	13.10	0.85	1.32	0.89
Lucknow	555,548	476,029	1,031,577	53.20	7.70	32.20	0.23	4.41	2.16	68.06	52.09	66.30	14.09	33.29	16.21	0.92	2.91	1.14

(Contd.)

TABLE 10.H5 (contd.)

Districtwise Rural Population, Workers (Main and Marginal) as Percentage to Rural Population, Cultivators, Agricultural Labourers, and Workers in Household Industry for Rural Areas as Percentage to Total Main Workers, 1991

State/district	Total population			Main workers			Marginal workers			Cultivators			Agricultural labourers			Workers in HH industry		
	Male	Female	Total	Male	Female	Total	Male	Female	Total	Male	Female	Total	Male	Female	Total	Male	Female	Total
Rae Bareli	1,091.313	1,021,585	2,112,898	51.05	11.75	32.05	0.50	7.99	4.12	67.40	46.75	63.74	17.18	45.81	22.26	1.02	1.30	1.07
Farrukhabad	1,086.732	898,913	1,985,645	51.76	2.14	29.30	0.08	1.30	0.64	76.55	22.30	74.76	12.75	17.90	12.92	0.64	18.30	1.22
Etawah	981 821	809,133	1,790,954	49.40	1.39	27.71	0.01	0.18	0.09	68.12	34.29	67.35	18.32	42.99	18.88	0.63	2.83	0.68
Kanpur Dehat	1,094.700	921,574	2,016,274	50.19	4.38	29.25	0.04	0.42	0.21	64.17	37.76	62.36	21.17	52.42	23.31	0.48	0.79	0.50
Kanpur Nagar	207,379	173,775	381,154	51.53	4.51	30.09	0.01	0.09	0.04	50.98	34.83	49.88	25.40	50.70	27.13	0.36	1.10	0.41
Jalaun	521,282	428,898	950,180	50.12	7.10	30.70	0.36	10.61	4.99	66.99	42.90	64.47	23.08	52.56	26.16	0.64	0.87	0.66
Jhansi	466,226	397,116	863,342	50.93	11.52	32.80	0.75	14.95	7.28	68.78	47.18	65.29	16.16	44.39	20.72	2.17	3.59	2.40
Lalitpur	347,791	298,704	646,495	53.83	10.33	33.74	0.50	21.99	10.42	80.25	62.49	77.73	7.83	30.77	11.08	1.14	1.93	1.25
Hamirpur	659,024	552,822	1,211,846	52.06	13.34	34.39	0.56	16.22	7.71	60.55	34.44	55.93	27.15	60.26	33.01	1.81	1.38	1.73
Banda	880,464	742,254	1,622,718	52.18	19.39	37.18	0.95	16.33	7.99	66.52	55.98	64.00	23.68	41.06	27.83	1.44	1.16	1.38
Fatehpur	909,040	802,188	1,711,228	51.08	12.18	32.84	0.47	10.65	5.25	62.00	47.62	59.50	22.26	45.84	26.36	1.66	2.13	1.74
Pratapgarh	1,047,806	1,040,793	2,088,599	45.50	12.95	29.28	0.35	5.50	2.91	66.84	51.78	63.52	16.40	42.56	22.16	1.88	1.71	1.84
Allahabad	2,063,534	1,835,414	3,898,948	47.74	16.81	33.18	0.29	5.39	2.69	53.43	43.35	51.02	24.84	47.24	30.19	2.86	4.17	3.18
Bahraich	1,385,499	1,161,345	2,546,844	57.18	5.28	33.51	0.50	13.00	6.20	79.07	50.83	77.04	13.08	43.65	15.28	0.41	0.78	0.44
Gonda	1,765,719	1,542,630	3,308,349	54.92	9.26	33.63	0.36	8.13	3.98	77.95	58.72	75.48	13.64	37.89	16.76	0.42	0.35	0.41
Barabanki	1,185,225	1,013,033	2,198,258	55.93	9.27	34.43	0.21	3.59	1.77	74.98	51.19	72.02	13.05	38.52	16.21	1.84	4.26	2.14
Faizabad	1,360,961	1,270,300	2,631,261	49.53	9.40	30.16	0.21	4.10	2.09	67.35	43.88	63.82	18.72	48.49	23.20	1.15	1.75	1.24
Sultanpur	1,261,650	1,183,152	2,444,802	48.78	9.14	29.59	0.29	4.57	2.36	64.28	40.51	60.73	22.18	49.99	26.33	1.55	2.96	1.76
Siddharthnagar	861,313	787,064	1,648,377	52.27	11.64	32.87	0.34	8.31	4.15r	75.30	57.51	72.29	16.57	38.25	20.23	0.80	1.44	0.91
Maharajganj	833,946	759,515	1,593,461	51.92	15.31	34.47	0.38	8.72	4.36	66.48	49.55	62.90	23.07	48.01	28.35	0.78	0.34	0.69
Basti	1,335,022	1,227,674	2,562,696	49.60	8.53	29.92	0.40	6.63	3.38	72.50	49.41	69.35	15.88	44.34	19.77	1.41	1.89	1.47
Gorakhpur	1,283,514	1,207,112	2,490,726	45.03	9.47	27.80	0.32	3.81	2.01	51.78	29.86	48.16	28.69	63.87	34.50	1.22	1.44	1.26
Deoria	2,084,433	2,029,464	4,113,897	45.95	9.15	27.80	0.69	7.20	3.90	65.11	45.34	61.90	19.61	49.50	24.46	1.01	1.04	1.01
Mau	606,213	595,574	1,201,787	44.48	11.03	27.90	1.44	11.16	6.26	61.01	41.49	57.18	17.46	45.64	22.98	4.47	6.39	4.85
Azamgarh	1,453,543	1,474,623	2,928,166	43.95	8.63	26.16	0.66	7.36	4.03	67.55	47.64	64.24	15.53	44.05	20.26	2.53	3.11	2.62
Jaunpur	1,495,530	1,497,667	2,993,297	42.78	8.46	25.61	0.34	4.93	2.64	67.87	58.75	66.37	11.18	30.77	14.42	1.67	2.14	1.74
Ballia	1,044,536	993,550	2,038,186	43.56	9.64	27.03	0.33	3.02	1.64	50.00	23.70	45.42	31.47	68.46	37.91	0.84	1.31	0.93
Ghazipur	1,140,500	1,097,815	2,238,315	44.05	9.96	27.33	0.27	4.47	2.33	59.46	40.38	56.04	21.88	52.01	27.27	0.96	1.45	1.05
Varanasi	1,853,248	1,685,086	3,538,334	46.43	11.33	29.71	0.48	7.13	3.65	43.65	37.35	42.51	18.38	49.67	24.06	13.07	6.93	11.96
Mirzapur	757,310	671,189	1,428,499	49.17	14.77	33.01	0.53	6.62	3.39	43.40	26.58	39.87	25.45	65.06	33.78	9.48	3.28	8.17
Sonbhadra	495,199	435,759	930,958	53.82	23.75	39.75	0.65	8.44	4.30	55.88	43.30	52.36	24.39	53.79	32.62	1.64	0.56	1.34

Source: Census of India, 1991.

TABLE 10.H6

Average Size of Household and Total Dependency Ratio by Sex and Place of Residence, 1981

State/district	All areas							Rural areas							Urban areas						
	Average size of household	Total dependency ratio			Old age dependency ratio			Average size of household	Total dependency ratio			Old age dependency ratio			Average size of household	Total dependency ratio			Old age dependency ratio		
		Total	Male	Female	Total	Male	Female		Total	Male	Female	Total	Male	Female		Total	Male	Female	Total	Male	Female
Uttar Pradesh	**5.77**	**942**	**956**	**926**	**133**	**138**	**128**	**5.89**	**972**	**1002**	**939**	**141**	**149**	**134**	**5.75**	**817**	**773**	**872**	**99**	**98**	**100**
Uttarkashi	5.01	732	681	795	122	118	127	3.94	748	706	795	127	125	130	5.11	540	449	730	60	50	81
Chamoli	4.70	856	936	785	128	135	122	4.04	881	1000	784	135	148	124	4.76	604	507	797	61	53	78
Tehri Garhwal	5.06	938	1035	856	146	157	138	3.63	953	857	1075	149	129	175	5.15	469	364	706	65	62	72
Dehradun	5.33	729	679	795	107	111	101	5.01	826	787	876	120	130	107	5.66	638	582	715	94	88	96
Garhwal	4.86	985	1110	884	152	183	139	4.52	1108	1228	1014	174	201	153	4.90	632	529	810	73	67	82
Pithoragarh	4.92	878	938	822	134	148	120	3.89	912	1010	827	140	161	121	4.99	603	523	730	77	65	94
Almora	5.00	941	1044	854	148	170	130	4.39	973	1118	860	154	182	133	5.05	562	454	762	77	72	84
Nainital	5.68	901	842	977	105	108	101	5.44	943	891	1009	114	120	106	5.78	800	727	897	84	82	86
Bijnor	5.98	1035	1052	1016	141	154	127	6.38	1048	1069	1024	144	158	128	5.85	999	1004	993	133	143	121
Moradabad	5.90	1029	1044	1012	133	144	120	6.47	1069	1095	1038	142	154	128	5.71	930	915	947	110	117	102
Rampur	5.99	1025	1021	1031	133	142	122	6.30	1015	966	1083	132	135	127	5.89	870	840	905	111	112	109
Saharanpur	5.73	943	952	933	130	145	111	5.73	992	1022	957	138	157	115	5.73	824	788	870	110	117	102
Muzaffarnagar	5.99	972	990	951	129	147	109	6.31	994	1021	962	135	155	112	5.91	867	888	916	110	120	99
Meerut	6.06	941	939	943	133	146	119	5.75	996	1012	978	146	162	127	6.22	830	796	872	109	113	103
Ghaziabad	6.42	920	918	923	115	122	107	5.49	993	1023	958	133	147	118	7.03	795	845	859	85	83	87
Bulandshahr	6.10	1023	1065	975	147	158	134	6.47	1038	1090	981	152	166	137	6.02	961	968	953	86	128	119
Aligarh	5.91	966	985	944	134	140	128	6.00	998	1025	966	143	150	135	5.88	868	861	876	107	108	107
Mathura	6.05	942	952	930	124	239	119	5.75	1185	1425	946	138	159	117	6.14	827	791	872	122	119	127
Agra	6.18	889	888	889	103	105	101	6.29	971	993	945	117	121	112	6.11	768	736	808	83	82	85
Etah	5.78	953	970	933	134	137	131	6.03	931	982	936	138	141	135	5.73	911	903	921	111	112	110
Mainpuri	5.87	920	941	896	124	129	119	5.98	934	963	900	127	133	120	5.86	819	782	865	144	98	106
Budaun	5.66	956	946	969	146	139	154	6.01	946	926	970	150	141	161	5.59	950	939	963	123	123	122
Bareilly	5.95	967	944	997	129	127	130	6.05	1027	1014	1043	142	142	143	5.91	835	788	893	95	96	102
Pilibhit	5.74	969	935	1012	124	123	125	5.88	989	951	1036	131	128	135	5.71	896	854	848	105	102	108
Shahjahanpur	5.43	906	875	946	129	128	130	5.71	914	885	952	137	136	138	5.37	874	834	923	96	95	97
Kheri	5.53	923	898	955	133	133	124	5.95	941	906	960	137	137	137	5.48	847	161	904	95	90	102
Sitapur	4.99	930	921	940	151	152	149	6.36	942	939	946	156	158	154	4.87	826	774	891	105	100	111
Hardoi	5.27	920	912	930	128	128	129	5.93	926	920	933	131	131	131	5.20	877	849	910	106	104	109
Unnao	5.36	920	918	923	132	132	131	5.65	929	933	924	136	138	134	5.32	935	813	910	104	95	111

(Contd.)

TABLE 10.H6 (contd.)

Average Size of Household and Total Dependency Ratio by Sex and Place of Residence, 1981

State/district	All areas							Rural areas							Urban areas						
	Average size of household	Total dependency ratio			Old age dependency ratio			Average size of household	Total dependency ratio			Old age dependency ratio			Average size of household	Total dependency ratio			Old age dependency ratio		
		Total	Male	Female	Total	Male	Female		Total	Male	Female	Total	Male	Female		Total	Male	Female	Total	Male	Female
Lucknow	5.37	766	727	815	104	102	106	5.53	894	879	913	134	133	134	5.20	664	611	733	80	78	83
Rae Bareli	4.89	928	961	832	147	152	142	5.66	939	981	896	152	158	146	4.84	799	744	867	91	87	96
Farrukhabad	5.90	994	926	1082	118	118	118	6.02	952	950	954	118	122	113	5.88	848	811	894	96	95	98
Etawah	5.57	948	936	931	119	127	110	5.82	967	990	939	122	131	110	5.52	848	817	884	105	104	106
Kanpur	5.53	819	771	881	101	102	98	5.38	945	925	970	127	133	120	5.67	692	624	786	74	73	75
Jalaun	6.00	883	880	886	116	117	115	6.12	899	907	895	120	123	118	5.97	814	782	855	98	94	103
Jhansi	5.72	885	845	897	116	108	126	5.96	916	922	909	127	121	134	5.58	837	803	877	100	87	115
Lalitpur	5.23	907	907	905	120	115	126	5.51	913	916	910	122	117	128	5.18	865	851	881	108	101	116
Hamirpur	5.65	936	1049	911	134	137	131	5.61	951	983	916	140	143	135	5.66	863	841	888	108	105	113
Banda	5.86	971	936	979	125	129	120	5.75	989	986	993	127	131	121	5.88	843	812	883	110	111	108
Fatehpur	5.37	950	950	949	129	135	123	5.17	958	961	955	133	139	125	5.40	867	848	895	96	97	96
Pratapgarh	5.48	993	1106	891	157	174	142	5.87	999	1123	889	159	178	143	5.46	888	851	933	116	111	123
Allahabad	5.80	920	921	919	115	119	110	5.80	857	780	900	116	116	115	5.80	723	661	805	87	83	92
Bahraich	5.15	906	906	906	136	135	137	6.02	906	908	903	138	137	139	5.09	911	896	946	106	103	110
Gonda	5.30	893	917	865	142	143	141	5.68	894	925	861	154	146	143	5.27	875	827	934	111	106	116
Barabanki	5.15	888	886	889	150	153	148	6.05	885	888	882	153	156	151	5.07	920	874	976	118	119	116
Faizabad	5.73	925	963	884	151	156	145	6.04	939	990	887	155	161	148	5.70	1104	1454	865	163	227	119
Sultanpur	5.58	957	1045	873	152	163	142	5.78	1073	1058	1,090	163	166	160	5.57	808	756	873	89	89	89
Basti	5.72	936	970	900	152	157	146	6.10	939	979	899	154	160	148	5.70	885	821	965	110	101	120
Gorakhpur	5.91	943	974	911	141	144	138	6.21	965	1009	820	148	153	143	6.56	750	685	834	85	80	90
Deoria	6.33	1021	1071	971	144	151	137	6.37	1025	1086	968	146	154	137	6.33	951	901	1011	118	111	128
Azamgarh	6.66	1060	1179	954	160	180	142	7.10	1073	1209	955	166	148	146	6.62	940	938	942	105	109	100
Jaunpur	6.37	1037	1157	929	150	166	135	6.64	1045	1180	927	153	171	137	6.35	935	900	977	105	101	109
Ballia	6.84	985	1081	955	158	168	149	6.94	1019	1085	958	156	163	150	6.83	902	881	926	128	121	135
Ghazipur	6.94	1023	1105	945	161	171	147	6.87	1034	1130	946	165	182	149	6.95	901	869	938	124	123	126
Varansi	6.65	937	939	933	126	128	123	6.42	979	711	940	136	142	130	6.74	829	762	914	101	98	105
Mirzapur	5.81	955	940	970	122	124	120	5.45	971	970	972	128	132	124	5.86	853	775	962	83	76	92

Source: Census of India, 1981.

TABLE 10.H7

Number of Females in the Age Group 15–44 years, Percentage of Married Females in Different Age Groups, and Mean Age at Marriage, 1981

State/district	All areas	Urban areas						Rural areas					
	Mean age at marriage	Number of females in age group	Percentage of married females in the age group				Mean age at marriage	Number of females in age group	Percentage of married females in the age group				Mean age at marriage
	(years)	15–44	10–14	15–19	20–4	15–44	(years)	15–44	10–14	15–19	20–4	15–44	(years)
Uttar Pradesh	**16.20**	**4,386,389**	**2.85**	**34.00**	**79.29**	77.74	**17.40**	**19,385,877**	**13.32**	**67.80**	**97.04**	**90.91**	**16.00**
Uttarkashi	17.00	2458	1.92	30.28	86.00	79.92	18.00	40,867	4.75	57.01	94.88	87.01	16.90
Chamoli	16.40	5780	2.69	31.04	85.48	76.71	16.90	86,036	4.75	50.38	95.30	83.93	16.40
Tehri Garhwal	16.80	4088	1.28	21.22	78.44	73.77	18.00	117,935	2.68	53.07	96.40	98.75	16.70
Dehradun	17.70	86,419	0.68	14.84	63.81	78.35	18.40	84,010	5.24	33.28	85.30	89.35	17.10
Garhwal	16.80	12,899	1.58	18.70	72.02	72.06	17.60	140,207	1.75	35.40	93.47	78.97	16.80
Pithoragarh	16.10	5963	1.05	19.41	65.26	67.65	17.10	113,516	4.25	56.66	92.88	84.37	16.10
Almora	16.10	9506	0.23	15.45	54.95	62.22	17.50	176,189	2.67	51.29	94.49	83.62	16.10
Nainital	17.00	68,177	0.77	23.08	72.58	69.61	17.60	169,166	2.34	42.51	89.72	82.19	16.80
Bijnor	17.90	100,746	0.63	22.78	24.38	63.58	18.30	290,026	0.85	32.11	94.15	82.62	17.80
Moradabad	17.40	181,858	0.68	22.53	74.47	72.81	18.50	453,124	2.35	50.88	96.81	85.91	17.10
Rampur	17.40	69,412	0.43	16.41	61.02	65.23	18.50	165,942	2.97	51.64	94.15	87.39	17.10
Saharanpur	17.60	156,809	1.51	22.10	73.15	74.06	18.50	399,463	3.26	46.27	95.66	85.77	17.30
Muzaffarnagar	17.10	106,591	1.97	31.65	82.25	77.59	17.70	364,421	3.57	47.34	95.30	85.30	16.90
Meerut	17.10	189,826	1.98	27.20	77.26	75.15	17.70	381,207	2.24	45.21	95.34	85.23	16.90
Ghaziabad	16.90	138,221	1.65	31.18	82.35	79.71	16.70	247,067	2.88	48.77	95.77	85.80	16.60
Bulandshahr	16.80	97,254	2.24	33.57	83.86	78.56	17.30	383,400	2.44	47.22	96.47	85.95	16.70
Aligarh	16.70	130,402	1.45	31.85	78.41	77.00	17.40	394,799	2.43	52.16	96.99	87.47	16.50
Mathura	16.50	70,455	2.92	40.84	84.46	81.62	16.80	244,830	4.62	58.85	98.03	89.09	16.50
Agra	16.60	250,612	1.99	32.45	78.15	75.61	17.30	356,347	3.56	60.31	97.80	90.08	16.20
Etah	16.40	62,037	1.72	39.55	85.38	80.74	17.00	317,437	3.48	61.87	97.51	89.74	16.30
Mainpuri	16.10	42,663	1.93	39.58	84.86	80.25	16.80	320,564	3.23	64.20	97.74	90.04	16.00
Budaun	16.50	66,644	1.32	33.82	83.00	78.89	17.60	327,114	6.21	69.68	97.45	91.27	16.30
Bareilly	16.80	144,759	1.04	27.61	74.57	74.58	17.90	309,326	5.85	68.50	97.58	91.54	16.40
Pilibhit	16.70	35,061	2.01	29.79	78.37	77.02	18.00	167,904	6.94	65.54	96.37	91.06	16.40
Shahjahanpur	16.40	68,986	1.77	12.90	80.38	78.78	17.20	262,845	8.23	75.32	97.03	92.61	16.20
Kheri	16.80	40,975	2.23	38.97	85.92	82.38	17.40	361,823	5.99	67.66	95.94	91.45	16.70
Sitapur	16.40	52,874	2.59	37.24	80.36	78.80	17.40	429,511	6.97	69.90	97.19	91.84	16.40
Hardoi	16.50	53,797	2.25	41.46	86.93	81.67	17.40	412,879	4.61	69.66	97.54	91.49	16.40
Unnao	16.60	47,449	3.08	36.48	85.99	80.59	17.10	342,605	4.83	53.69	95.58	87.68	16.50

(Contd.)

TABLE 10.H7 (contd.)

Number of Females in the Age Group 15–44 years, Percentage of Married Females in Different Age Groups, and Mean Age at Marriage, 1981

State/district	All areas	Urban areas						Rural areas					
	Mean age at marriage (years)	Number of females in age group 15–44	Percentage of married females in the age group 10–14	15–19	20–4	15–44	Mean age at marriage (years)	Number of females in age group 15–44	Percentage of married females in the age group 10–14	15–19	20–4	15–44	Mean age at marriage (years)
Lucknow	17.20	253,872	1.77	24.62	68.02	72.10	18.00	202,680	6.96	60.52	94.61	89.30	16.40
Rae Bareli	15.70	31,339	5.59	45.43	83.63	81.89	17.20	390,366	22.15	72.15	96.96	91.53	15.60
Farrukhabad	16.30	68,437	3.66	59.46	94.55	80.69	16.90	332,359	4.01	64.06	96.61	89.97	16.20
Etawah	15.80	56,818	1.86	38.92	85.43	79.68	15.70	303,557	3.51	64.24	97.49	89.77	16.40
Kanpur	17.00	395,606	1.46	28.62	77.95	98.50	17.50	411,534	1.84	48.28	95.57	86.05	16.50
Jalaun	15.60	43,250	2.84	47.26	90.59	83.86	16.70	164,843	6.87	75.99	98.45	92.77	15.30
Jhansi	15.30	96,831	4.69	49.31	82.39	80.41	16.10	148,322	11.71	81.76	98.74	94.08	14.90
Lalitpur	14.50	16,823	10.34	54.87	88.81	84.62	15.60	103,929	29.17	89.24	98.82	95.69	14.40
Hamirpur	15.20	43,101	8.43	56.75	90.51	86.01	15.80	208,019	13.82	80.06	98.29	93.53	15.10
Banda	15.80	39,007	6.39	52.50	88.30	84.78	16.60	278,936	15.17	81.83	98.55	94.13	15.70
Fatehpur	16.70	31,406	1.95	34.85	83.85	79.60	17.40	303,131	2.83	52.50	94.97	86.92	16.60
Pratapgarh	14.80	19,433	10.11	59.70	90.94	86.80	16.80	396,404	26.53	83.02	98.16	94.14	14.80
Allahabad	16.50	174,744	2.10	27.63	73.36	74.95	18.00	656,862	8.46	71.60	97.39	91.92	16.10
Bahraich	15.80	33,788	4.00	45.39	85.57	82.80	17.10	434,705	20.23	78.60	97.71	93.93	15.80
Gonda	15.40	44,150	8.30	48.37	87.58	84.83	17.10	580,657	29.39	83.34	97.97	94.37	15.30
Barabanki	15.90	37,174	4.82	40.76	85.81	81.24	17.50	386,852	22.59	76.83	96.66	92.50	15.80
Faizabad	15.10	56,559	8.14	41.42	82.72	80.69	16.80	478,647	41.01	85.15	98.00	94.55	14.90
Sultanpur	14.90	14,856	10.23	46.16	80.71	81.93	16.50	455,061	41.04	87.84	98.52	94.98	14.80
Basti	15.00	35,947	14.28	55.37	89.72	86.97	16.30	755,534	40.15	83.25	98.09	94.75	14.90
Gorakhpur	15.20	91,015	5.75	37.32	78.04	78.52	16.90	754,807	28.06	83.62	98.40	94.77	15.00
Deoria	16.10	48,066	6.93	54.03	92.61	87.38	17.00	723,617	13.23	73.93	97.65	92.71	16.00
Azamgarh	15.20	72,054	8.64	50.86	88.88	83.81	17.10	736,985	32.21	81.86	97.93	94.00	15.00
Jaunpur	15.20	36,188	5.79	53.14	89.79	85.46	16.60	544,836	22.55	84.30	98.49	94.44	15.10
Ballia	16.10	38,955	6.90	49.99	91.91	85.10	17.00	394,976	12.43	71.53	97.37	91.49	16.00
Gazipur	15.90	33,645	7.13	52.94	87.97	84.68	16.80	403,230	17.75	76.39	97.63	92.61	15.90
Varanasi	15.80	215,707	5.01	50.18	83.54	82.54	17.10	594,868	19.49	84.85	98.56	94.72	15.30
Mirzapur	15.50	54,897	6.45	59.78	90.16	88.22	16.40	379,600	16.00	80.96	98.18	93.96	15.40

Source: Census of India, 1981, Part VI-A, Series 23.

TABLE 10.H8

Districtwise Child Mortality Estimates for All Areas, 1991

State/district	q(1)			q(2)			q(3)			q(5)		
	Male	Female	Total	Male	Female	Total	Male	Female	Total	Male	Female	Total
Uttar Pradesh	**98**	**104**	**99**	**117**	**118**	**117**	**122**	**121**	**122**	**135**	**132**	**134**
Uttar Pradesh (1981)	131	128	130	146	159	152	157	181	168	174	208	190
Uttarkashi	94	86	96	98	98	98	114	117	116	142	142	142
Chamoli	71	61	65	76	64	74	82	79	80	84	80	82
Tehri Garhwal	67	74	69	79	77	78	83	83	83	89	104	93
Dehradun	55	51	53	74	57	67	79	61	73	81	69	76
Garhwal	67	71	69	81	79	80	88	83	86	91	89	90
Pithoragarh	79	72	76	100	83	91	109	87	94	114	94	99
Almora	37	42	40	70	73	71	71	75	72	86	81	84
Nainital	83	74	80	93	103	99	99	107	104	110	111	111
Bijnor	109	91	99	104	105	105	113	112	113	117	121	120
Moradabad	101	75	89	102	89	98	112	125	119	121	139	125
Rampur	84	134	101	109	143	126	116	147	132	124	150	137
Saharanpur	66	55	61	89	89	89	94	93	94	101	107	104
Hardwar	74	77	76	86	86	84	83	87	87	86	105	98
Muzaffarnagar	78	116	88	102	123	112	116	131	121	124	140	129
Meerut	47	55	51	78	86	81	97	89	94	107	91	104
Ghaziabad	63	64	64	66	69	68	72	70	71	74	71	73
Bulandshahr	72	102	98	84	110	105	96	112	109	101	121	117
Aligarh	98	114	104	100	123	111	107	135	120	115	143	126
Mathura	61	73	67	80	90	85	87	111	98	93	132	111
Agra	53	65	58	64	81	74	69	92	79	74	106	89
Etah	118	147	131	131	167	144	137	172	151	146	179	161
Mainpuri	94	110	99	99	123	106	113	130	121	121	152	128
Budaun	149	141	146	156	162	159	161	179	164	168	192	171
Bareilly	109	118	112	114	127	118	123	135	127	130	147	139
Pilibhit	100	127	123	117	136	127	122	139	127	131	144	137
Shahjahanpur	118	141	129	140	156	149	145	171	158	156	176	164
Kheri	89	71	85	106	97	102	114	115	115	132	121	129
Sitapur	123	97	111	122	126	125	127	139	129	134	150	137
Hardoi	140	121	131	158	144	151	169	180	163	178	199	184
Unnao	95	99	97	122	131	129	133	143	137	139	156	144
Lucknow	82	85	84	86	89	88	91	96	94	104	102	103
Rae Bareli	104	109	107	134	143	142	150	152	152	159	168	163
Farrukhabad	62	84	78	109	118	112	117	123	119	126	135	132
Etawah	81	87	85	110	130	120	125	139	134	137	154	144
Kanpur	77	74	71	87	89	88	95	105	100	107	115	111
Jalaun	79	94	83	111	126	118	117	131	127	124	153	132
Jhansi	98	111	105	102	114	106	108	122	115	117	134	126
Lalitpur	87	118	103	132	143	136	139	162	142	141	176	158
Hamirpur	100	111	105	116	133	124	127	149	137	132	172	148
Banda	113	102	107	118	112	115	124	134	127	135	158	141
Fatehpur	127	99	106	138	129	134	145	151	147	149	176	162
Pratapgarh	117	105	111	121	134	124	126	138	131	136	159	147
Allahabad	111	108	109	123	136	129	127	140	133	131	157	143
Bahraich	112	148	138	150	159	155	159	175	163	162	189	169
Gonda	114	138	130	121	154	136	127	167	146	135	180	157
Barabanki	78	106	98	101	119	110	112	127	119	121	136	127

(Contd.)

TABLE 10.H8

Districtwise Child Mortality Estimates for All Areas, 1991

State/district	q(1)			q(2)			q(3)			q(5)		
	Male	Female	Total	Male	Female	Total	Male	Female	Total	Male	Female	Total
Faizabad	88	79	82	89	91	90	96	99	98	105	116	110
Sultanpur	96	96	96	111	146	128	114	158	135	123	164	143
Basti	131	141	135	169	174	172	189	195	191	207	202	205
Gorakhpur	63	59	61	77	82	80	82	90	85	91	103	96
Beoria	89	93	91	92	124	106	97	121	109	105	129	116
Azamgarh	97	87	92	104	116	107	111	124	117	120	131	127
Jaunpur	77	88	82	94	102	99	99	114	106	114	134	124
Ballia	36	41	38	43	52	46	48	56	50	58	64	61
Ghazipur	51	68	63	67	76	72	71	79	76	75	83	79
Varanasi	70	83	76	86	104	90	98	114	104	107	112	112
Mirzapur	84	84	84	96	104	100	114	141	124	124	153	132

Source: District Level Estimates of Fertility and Child Mortality for 1991 and their Inter-Relations with other Variables, Occasional Paper No. 1 of 1997, Registrar-General, India.

TABLE 10.H9

State-level Religionwise Fertility Indices by Place of Residence

Religious community	All areas				Rural areas				Urban areas			
	GFR	GMFR	TFR	TMFR	GFR	GMFR	TFR	TMFR	GFR	GMFR	TFR	TMFR
All religions	**130**	**146**	**4.3**	**4.7**	**132**	**148**	**4.4**	**4.8**	**125**	**140**	**3.9**	**4.3**
Hindus	127	142	4.2	4.6	129	144	4.3	4.7	116	130	3.7	4.0
Muslims	144	169	4.8	5.4	145	169	4.9	5.5	143	168	4.7	5.3
Christians	69	117	2.1	3.7	91	154	2.7	4.8	61	104	1.9	3.3
Sikhs	106	151	3.6	4.8	121	173	4.1	5.4	79	112	2.9	3.8
Jains	95	136	2.9	3.9	108	155	3.3	4.4	92	132	2.8	3.8
Buddhists	136	158	4.4	5.1	145	169	4.7	5.4	93	108	3.3	3.8

Source: Child Mortality Estimate of India, Census of India, 1981, Occasional Paper No. 5 of 1988.

TABLE 10.H10

Districtwise Adjusted Fertility Indices, 1981 and 1991

State/district	1981				1991			
	GFR	GMFR	TFR	TMFR	GFR	GMFR	TFR	TMFR
Uttar Pradesh	**179**	**201**	**5.9**	**6.5**	**172**	**200**	**5.6**	**6.3**
Uttarkashi	143	167	4.6	5.1	152	187	4.7	5.6
Chamoli	152	183	5.0	5.6	127	162	4.1	5.0
Tehri Garhwal	165	195	5.7	6.2	151	190	4.8	5.7
Dehradun	147	197	4.7	6.0	128	179	4.0	5.8
Garhwal	152	193	5.3	5.9	128	176	4.3	5.5
Pithoragarh	141	170	4.7	5.3	133	165	4.1	5.1
Almora	145	177	4.9	5.5	138	177	4.5	5.6
Nainital	183	229	5.9	7.0	171	219	5.4	7.0
Bijnor	207	253	6.9	8.0	191	243	6.3	7.6
Moradabad	204	246	6.8	7.7	168	207	5.5	6.5
Rampur	211	259	7.2	8.3	178	225	5.9	7.1
Saharanpur	183	220	6.1	6.8	174	216	5.5	6.7
Hardwar	183	220	6.1	6.8	169	214	5.4	6.8
Muzaffarnagar	182	216	6.2	6.8	178	220	5.8	6.9

(Contd.)

TABLE 10.H110 (contd.)

Districtwise Adjusted Fertility Indices, 1981 and 1991

District	1981				1991			
	GFR	GMFR	TFR	TMFR	GFR	GMFR	TFR	TMFR
Meerut	188	226	6.2	7.0	157	196	5.1	6.2
Ghaziabad	188	223	6.1	6.9	140	171	4.5	5.4
Bulandshahr	194	229	6.6	7.3	178	216	5.9	6.9
Aligarh	193	217	6.5	7.2	173	211	5.7	6.7
Mathura	188	214	6.3	6.8	181	210	5.7	6.5
Agra	189	225	6.3	7.0	155	186	4.9	5.8
Etah	190	213	6.4	6.9	186	218	6.0	6.8
Mainpuri	183	206	6.2	6.6	180	207	5.8	6.6
Budaun	200	224	6.7	7.3	194	223	6.3	7.0
Bareilly	193	224	6.4	7.2	181	221	5.8	7.0
Pilibhit	192	215	6.3	6.8	194	225	6.3	7.2
Shahjahanpur	194	217	6.5	7.1	166	191	5.5	6.1
Kheri	177	197	5.9	6.3	153	175	5.1	5.7
Sitapur	183	203	6.2	6.6	157	177	5.1	5.6
Hardoi	199	221	6.6	7.2	159	189	5.1	5.9
Unnao	173	199	5.8	6.4	174	206	5.7	6.6
Lucknow	156	195	5.2	6.1	139	179	4.4	5.8
Rae Bareli	178	196	6.0	6.4	180	207	6.0	6.6
Farrukhabad	187	212	6.2	6.8	164	193	5.4	6.1
Etawah	180	204	6.0	6.5	157	181	5.1	5.6
Kanpur	169	205	5.5	6.4	123	167	3.9	6.7
Jalaun	173	189	5.6	6.0	158	176	4.9	5.5
Jhansi	173	194	5.6	6.1	145	166	4.3	5.0
Lalitpur	195	208	6.5	6.8	179	192	5.6	5.9
Hamirpur	178	193	5.8	6.2	156	172	4.9	5.3
Banda	187	201	6.1	6.6	183	201	5.8	6.2
Fatehpur	174	201	5.9	6.5	186	219	6.1	7.0
Pratapgarh	167	179	5.8	5.9	171	191	5.6	6.1
Allahabad	176	199	5.8	6.4	181	208	5.8	6.6
Bahraich	177	190	5.9	6.1	168	185	5.6	6.0
Gonda	175	189	5.8	6.1	193	212	6.4	6.8
Barabanki	160	175	5.3	5.8	153	172	5.2	5.6
Faizabad	161	175	5.4	5.6	164	181	5.4	5.8
Sultanpur	172	184	5.8	6.1	177	192	5.8	6.2
Basti	182	194	6.0	6.3	164	175	5.5	6.0
Gorakhpur	175	189	5.8	6.1	160	180	5.3	5.8
Deoria	175	190	5.8	6.1	177	200	5.8	6.4
Azamgarh	171	184	5.8	6.1	176	194	5.8	6.2
Jaunpur	177	190	5.9	6.2	168	184	5.6	5.9
Ballia	149	163	5.0	5.3	155	175	5.0	5.6
Ghazipur	162	177	5.3	5.7	155	174	5.2	5.6
Varansi	167	183	5.4	5.7	160	179	5.1	5.6
Mirzapur	170	183	5.6	5.9	189	207	6.0	6.4

Sources: Child Mortality Estimate of India. Census of India, 1981, Occasional paper No. 5 of 1988. District Level Estimates of Fertility and Child Mortality for 1991 and their Inter-Relations with other Variables, Occasional Paper No. 1 of 1997, Registrar-General, India.

TABLE 10.H11

Districtwise Crude Birth Rate (1981 and 1991) and Changes over the Decade

State/district	CBR 1981 (adj.)	CBR 1991	Change in CBR	CPR due to all methods		Inc. (+)/ dec. (–) in CPR col (5–6)
				CPR 1992	CPR 1991	
Uttar Pradesh	**39.42**	**37.3**	**–5.38**	**33.7**	**35.5**	**–1.8**
Agra	41.07	36.6	–10.88	41.3	40.4	0.9
Aligarh	40.56	38.3	–5.57	27.4	29.8	–2.4
Allahabad	39.69	37.5	–5.52	34.2	34.3	–0.1
Almora	36.11	30.4	–15.81	50.6	48.0	2.6
Azamgarh	40.20	38.1	–5.22	33.8	35.0	–1.2
Budaun	41.06	39.7	–3.31	33.6	35.0	–1.4
Bahraich	38.61	36.9	–4.43	34.5	35.1	–0.6
Ballia	34.09	33.8	–0.85	33.6	35.4	–1.8
Banda	39.85	36.0	–9.66	36.6	38.6	–2.0
Barabanki	35.39	34.3	–3.08	37.0	38.7	–1.7
Bareilly	39.80	38.2	–4.02	30.3	31.1	–0.8
Basti	41.29	39.0	–5.55	43.6	46.6	–3.0
Bijnor	42.93	38.4	–10.55	34.3	36.2	–1.9
Bulandshahr	40.59	36.7	–9.57	28.8	33.2	–4.4
Chamoli	38.83	32.6	–16.09	50.4	47.0	3.4
Dehradun	33.70	27.6	–18.10	42.2	39.6	2.5
Deoria	39.97	38.6	–3.43	35.3	36.1	–0.8
Etah	39.67	38.2	–3.71	33.7	34.1	–0.5
Etawah	37.94	35.2	–7.22	33.8	34.8	–1.0
Faizabad	37.30	35.3	–5.34	24.4	25.5	–1.1
Farrukhabad	39.49	36.4	–7.82	35.6	36.7	–1.1
Fatehpur	37.99	35.6	–6.29	39.0	40.9	–1.9
Garhwal	36.86	27.4	–25.66	47.3	44.2	3.1
Ghaziabad	40.50	37.2	–8.15	29.9	29.8	0.1
Ghazipur	37.69	37.6	–0.24	35.1	35.7	–0.6
Gonda	39.69	37.9	–4.51	29.8	31.3	–1.5
Gorakhpur	40.41	36.9	–8.69	44.7	46.7	–2.1
Hamirpur	37.98	35.9	–5.48	44.8	44.4	0.4
Hardoi	42.16	36.7	–12.96	34.8	35.6	–0.8
Jalaun	37.35	34.6	–7.36	40.1	39.2	0.9
Jaunpur	41.83	39.3	–6.05	35.7	35.9	–0.2
Jhansi	38.11	34.4	–9.73	48.6	45.0	3.6
Kanpur	37.27	25.2	–32.39	36.0	NE	–
Kheri	38.09	34.7	–8.90	36.7	38.4	–1.7
Lalitpur	42.31	40.2	–4.99	43.8	43.4	0.4
Lucknow	36.36	30.4	–16.39	37.2	37.3	–0.1
Mainpuri	39.42	36.9	–6.63	43.0	44.7	–1.7
Mathura	38.80	37.8	–2.58	30.2	31.8	–1.6
Meerut	39.74	35.1	–11.42	37.3	38.8	–1.5
Mirzapur	37.30	39.7	6.42	45.3	44.3	1.0
Moradabad	42.47	40.3	–5.11	32.4	34.9	–2.5
Muzaffarnagar	38.67	36.0	–6.90	34.0	34.9	–0.9
Nainital	39.43	33.8	–14.28	40.2	38.8	1.4
Pilibhit	39.89	39.7	–0.48	32.3	33.1	–0.8
Pithoragarh	34.99	30.7	–12.26	56.8	56.5	0.3
Pratapgarh	40.15	36.8	–8.34	39.4	37.7	1.7

(Contd.)

TABLE 10.H11 (contd.)
Districtwise Crude Birth Rate (1981 and 1991) and Changes over the Decade

State/district	CBR 1981 (adj.)	CBR 1991	Change in CBR	CPR due to all methods: CPR 1992	CPR 1991	Inc. (+)/ dec. (–) in CPR col (5–6)
Rae Bareli	40.92	37.3	–8.85	35.4	37.7	–2.3
Rampur	43.62	40.4	–7.38	38.0	39.8	–1.8
Saharanpur	39.24	36.1	–8.00	36.7	39.5	–2.8
Shahjahanpur	40.11	36.7	–9.25	33.1	30.4	2.7
Sitapur	39.43	35.6	–9.71	33.4	34.9	–1.5
Sultanpur	40.87	36.9	–9.41	30.6	32.7	–2.1
Tehri Garhwal	41.18	32.3	–21.56	43.1	40.0	3.1
Unnao	38.01	34.7	–8.71	39.1	40.4	–1.3
Uttarkashi	33.48	32.8	–2.03	47.8	48.7	–1.0
Varanasi	37.65	38.1	1.20	33.1	33.9	–0.8

Note: CPR is couple protection rate.

Sources: Sample Registration System, Estimate of Birth rate and Death rate, 1995, Government of India; Analytical Review of Couple Protection Rates (1991–2) Evaluation and Intelligence Division. Department of Family Welfare, Government of India, New Delhi.

TABLE 10.P1
Per Thousand Distribution of Persons over MPCE Classes and Average Monthly Consumer Expenditure Per Person in Uttar Pradesh

Rural			Urban		
Monthly per capita expenditure class (MCPE) (Rs)	Persons per thousand	Average expenditure per month (Rs)	Monthly per capita expenditure class (MCPE) (Rs)	Persons per thousand	Average expenditure per month (Rs)
0–90	52	55.73	0–65	83	75.92
90–110	84	73.13	65–80	102	100.17
110–35	121	87.80	80–95	145	121.99
135–60	132	102.45	95–110	130	147.45
160–85	115	117.54	110–25	88	172.48
185–215	91	132.31	125–40	83	200.28
215–55	100	149.60	140–60	114	234.30
255–310	79	170.01	160–80	92	278.53
310–85	87	196.72	180–215	71	344.55
385–520	76	243.21	215–80	48	441.10
520–700	42	320.30	280–385	26	606.58
700 +	21	590.50	385 +	18	1008.30
All classes	**1000**	**148.59**		**1000**	**217.07**

Source: Sarvekshana, Vol. XV, No. 1, July–September, 1991, Issue No. 48.

TABLE 10.P2

Distribution of Number of Operational Holdings and Area Operated for All Social Groups in Uttar Pradesh, 1985–6 and 1990–1 and Average Size of Holdings for All Groups, SCs and STs (1990–1)

Size class	Number ('000)		Percentage variation in 1990–1 over 1985–6	Area ('000 hectares)		Percentage variation in 1990–1 over 1985–6	Size per holding (in ha)		
	1985–6	1990–1		1985–6	1990–1		All groups	SCs	STs
Marginal	**137,818**	**143,193**	**7.5**	**49,933**	**56,534**	**13.2**	**0.4**	**0.34**	**0.35**
Below 0.02 ha	4091	5103	24.8	60	75	25	0.0	0.02	0.01
0.02–0.5	93,945	99,510	5.9	22,114	25,486	15.2	0.3	0.24	0.23
0.5–1.0	39,783	43,580	9.5	27,759	30,974	11.6	0.7	0.68	0.69
Small 1.0–2.0	**29,643**	**31,185**	**5.2**	**41,149**	**43,907**	**6.7**	**1.4**	**1.34**	**1.43**
Semi-medium	**15,817**	**15,425**	**–2.5**	**43,131**	**42,058**	**–2.5**	**2.7**	**2.63**	**2.06**
2.0–3.0	10,825	10,595	–2.1	26,053	25,558	–1.9	2.4	2.36	2.45
3.0–4.0	4990	4838	–3.2	17,078	16,499	–3.4	3.4	3.39	3.46
Medium	**6021**	**5485**	**–8.9**	**33,774**	**30,420**	**–9.9**	**5.6**	**5.31**	**5.86**
4.0–5.0	2685	2,577	–4.0	11,907	11,411	–4.2	4.4	4.41	4.47
5.0–7.5	2515	2,197	–12.6	14,971	13,085	–12.6	6.0	5.88	6.01
7.5–10.0	828	710	–13.4	6896	5924	–14.1	8.3	8.36	8.44
Large	**553**	**452**	**–18.1**	**8495**	**6938**	**–18.3**	**15.3**	**13.93**	**12.68**
10.0–20.0	489	401	–17.9	6233	5864	–18.8	12.6	12.71	12.19
> 20.0 ha	63	51	–19.5	2261	1874	–17.1	36.7	33.30	24.5
All sizes	**189,852**	**200,740**	**5.7**	**176,482**	**179,857**	**1.9**	**0.9**	**0.57**	**1.77**

Source: Agricultural Census, 1990–1, Ministry of Agriculture, Agricultural Census Division.

11 Survey Report for Uttar Pradesh

The units of observation and analysis of this study are rural households. The total number of households selected in the sample was 4251 (of which 215 were non-response), spread over 217 villages and 23 districts in the state.

TABLE 11.1
Allocation of Sample Households in Various Strata

	Stratum	Occupation	Selected sample households
1	Households containing at least one pregnant woman		290
2	Households containing at least one child aged less than 12 months but no pregnant women		594
3	Muslim	Marginal farmer	170
4	Muslim	Small farmer	114
5	Muslim	Large farmer	46
6	Muslim	Agricultural labourer	149
7	Muslim	Other	289
8	Scheduled castes	Marginal farmer	244
9	Scheduled castes	Small farmer	155
10	Scheduled castes	Large farmer	30
11	Scheduled castes	Agricultural labourer	313
12	Scheduled castes	Other	253
13	Others	Marginal farmer	382
14	Others	Small farmer	372
15	Others	Large farmer	249
16	Others	Agricultural labourer	295
17	Others	Other	306
		Total	4251

11.1 Major Findings

The survey has collected a number of indicators in the areas of: (a) income and material well-being; (b) education; and (c) health-care facilities for rural Uttar Pradesh. However, in this report, only a few selected variables have been considered, such as (i) household and per capita income, (ii) poverty line groups, (iii) asset ownership, (iv) literacy rate, (v) net enrolment rate, (vi) expenditure on morbidity, (vii) immunization, (viii) CBR, and (viii) crude death rate (CDR). An evaluation of the intra-group and inter-group differentials of these indicators is attempted in this section, along with an analysis of the gender disparities in the access to education and health-care facilities.

11.1.1 Household and Per Capita Income

Table A11.1 presents the per capita household income and percentage of households belonging to different population groups. About 4 per cent of the households belong to the high-income group of Rs 62,001–86,000 and about 4 per cent to the group of Rs 86,000 and above. On the other hand, 55 per cent of households belong to the low-income group of up to Rs 20,000. The mean per capita income of the group Rs 86,000 and above is estimated to be Rs 14,889, which is about eight times more than the per capita income of the lowest income group.

About 3 per cent households own large landholdings but about 13 per cent are landless. About 46 and 18 per cent are marginal and small farmers respectively. As expected, the per capita income of large landholding groups is about Rs 10,571, which is six times the income of landless wage earners. The per capita income of the salaried earner, professional and self-employed group is Rs 5271, which is the highest among the occupation groups. This income is marginally less than the income of the small landholding group (Rs 5424).

The highest per capita income of Rs 4235 is observed for Hindus and the lowest is Rs 3025 for SCs in the social groups. The per capita income of Muslims is Rs 3826, which is marginally less than that of Hindus.

Household sizes of both 5–7 and 8 and above have similar incomes of Rs 4100. A similar distribution is observed in village development groups. The per capita income of different village development groups is close to the mean income of the state at Rs 1485. A high per capita income of Rs 5712 is observed for the both literate group. This income is one and a half times the income of the none literate household group. An equal income distribution is observed between female literate and male literate groups of households.

Very high intra-group income differentials are observed among the poverty line groups. The per capita income is only Rs 985 of those belonging to the lower segment below the poverty line group and a very high per capita income of

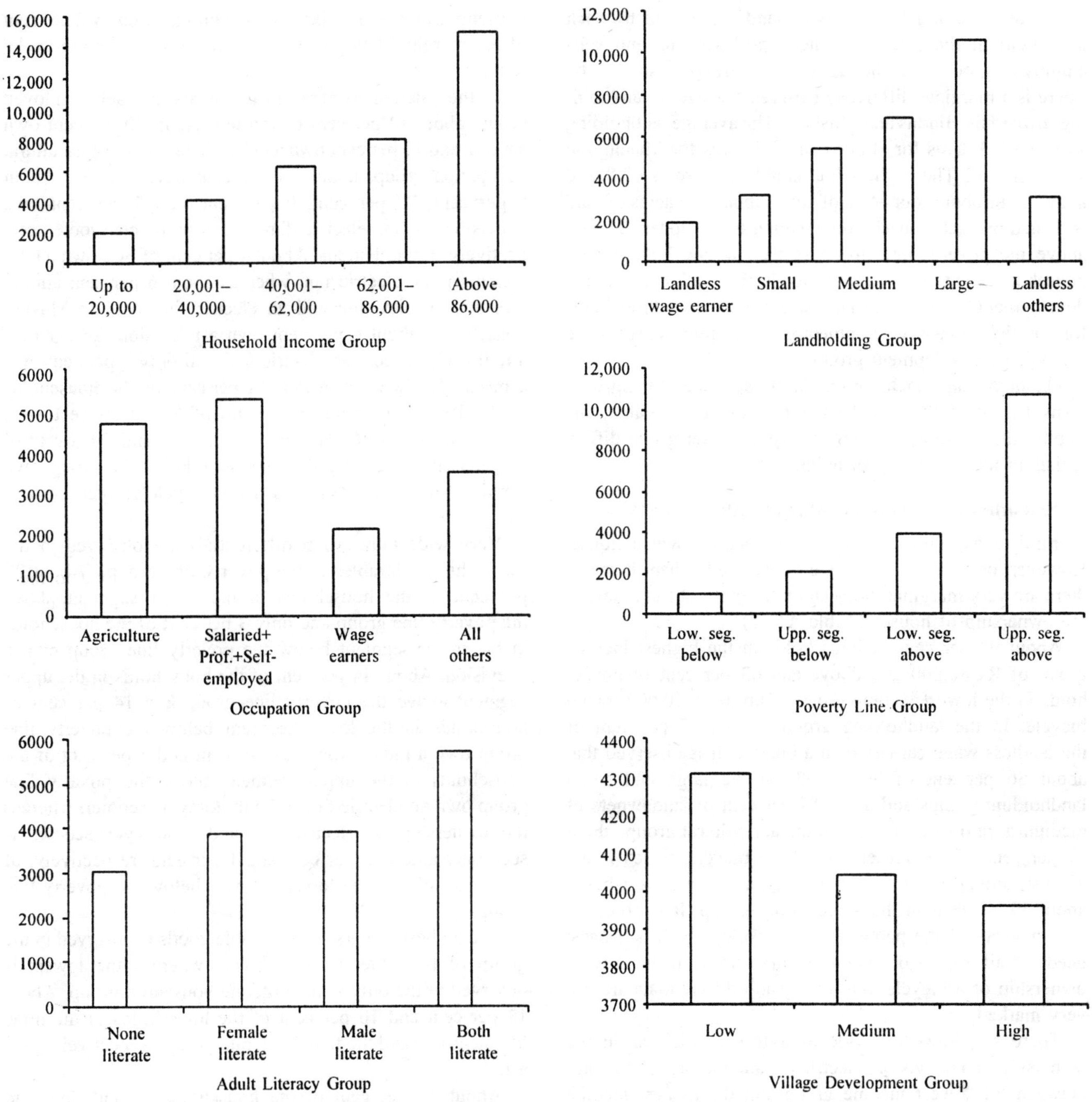

FIGURE 11.1: **Per Capita Income by Population Group (in Rupees per annum)**

Rs 10,715 is observed for those who are categorized in the upper segment above the poverty line group.

The intra-group income differentials are very high in household income, landholding and poverty line categories. The inter-group differential is also remarkably high. The source-wise income distribution is presented in Tables A11.2 and A11.3)

11.1.2 Ownership of Assets

OWNERSHIP OF LAND AND ANIMALS

The most valuable assets for the rural people are land and animals, and they contribute to the household income in many ways. The highest income group household owns about 12 acres whereas the lowest income group households own only about one acre of land (see Table A11.4). Very high intra-group differentials are observed in the ownership of land across the household income groups. However, a fair distribution is observed in the ownership of livestock, like draught and milch animals, in the household income groups.

The marginal farmers own about one acre of land, while large farmers own about 25 acres. On an average, each landholding household owns two draught animals. However, the ownership of milch animals ranges from one for landless wage earners to three for large landholding group.

About three and four acres of land are owned by each household in the salaried earners, professionals and self-employed group and the agricultural group, respectively. There is a marginal difference between the size of landholdings owned by Hindus and Muslims. The average landholding sizes are 3.3 acres for Hindus and 3.5 acres for Muslims in social groups. The highest household size group of 8 and above owns about four acres of land. About five acres of land is owned by each household belonging to the upper segment above the poverty line group as well as the both literate household group. A fair distribution is observed in the village development groups. The land size ranges from three acres for the high village development group to four acres for the low village development group.

On an average, each household, irrespective of the group, owns two draught animals and two milch animals. This implies that there are no intra-group and inter-group differentials in the ownership of animals.

OWNERSHIP OF HOUSEHOLD AND DURABLE ASSETS

In rural areas, almost all groups of people own a house. However, only 18 per cent have a separate kitchen. It seems there are very marginal intra- and inter-group differentials in the ownership of houses (Table A11.5).

About 93 per cent of households in the highest income group of Rs 86,000 and above and 63 per cent of households in the lowest income group of up to Rs 20,000 own a bicycle. In the landholding groups, about 55 per cent of the landless wage earners own a bicycle. It is observed that about 86 per cent of households in the large and small landholding groups and about 87 per cent of landowners of medium size own a bicycle. In the agricultural group, about 77 per cent of the households own a bicycle, which is the highest among all the occupation groups, the lowest being about 59 per cent in the wage earner group. It is observed that majority of the people buy a bicycle, which is a basic need for all groups of people in rural areas. In the case of ownership of a bicycle, the intra-group differentials are not very marked.

There are, however, wide intra-group variations in the ownership of a television, electric fan and motorcycle/scooter between the lowest income group and the highest income group. The ownership of television ranges from 3 per cent for the lowest income group households to about 37 per cent for the highest income group households. However, the ownership of radio ranges from 17 per cent for the households in the lowest income group to 65 per cent for the households in the highest income group.

About 5 per cent of the households in the marginal landholding group and 34 per cent of the households in the large landholding group own a television. The ownership of an electric fan ranges from 3 per cent for landless wage earners to about 27 per cent for the large landholding group. However, relatively large numbers of people own a radio in the landholding groups. About 20 per cent of the households in the large landholding group and only 2 per cent of the marginal landholding households own a motorcycle/scooter.

In the salaried earners, professionals and self-employed group, about 14 per cent own a television, 40 per cent own a radio, and 17 per cent own an electric fan. In the agricultural occupation group, about 30 per cent have a radio. About 9 per cent, 27 per cent, 9 per cent, and 3 per cent own television, radio, electric fan and motorcycle/scooter respectively among Hindus. About 4 per cent of SCs own a television and an electric fan, whereas about 6 per cent among STs own a television and an electric fan. Among Muslim households, about 6 per cent own a television, 26 per cent a radio, 13 per cent an electric fan, and only 3 per cent own a motorcycle/scooter. About 14 per cent of the households in the large household size group of 8 and above own a television. About 36 per cent, 16 per cent, and 5 per cent of the households among this big household size group own a radio, an electric fan, and a motorcycle/scooter, respectively.

Very wide intra-group differentials are observed in the ownership of durables in the poverty line groups. About 20 per cent of the households in the upper segment above the poverty line group and only 3 per cent of the households in the lower segment below the poverty line group own a television. About 44 per cent of the households in the upper segment above the poverty line group and 14 per cent of households in the lower segment below the poverty line group own a radio. About 22 per cent and 7 per cent of the households in the upper segment above the poverty line group own an electric fan and a motorcycle/scooter, whereas the ownership of electric fan and motorcycle/scooter is seen only among 5 per cent and 1 per cent, respectively, of the households in the lower segment below the poverty line group.

The highest ownership of durable goods is observed in the group of both literate households, whereas the lowest is observed in the only female literate household group. About 13 per cent and 10 per cent of the households in the none literate group and the female literate group, respectively, own a radio.

About 25 per cent of the households in both low and high village development groups own a radio. A fair and equal distribution is observed among the village development groups. In the high village development group, about 17 per cent own a television, 19 per cent own an electric fan, and 5 per cent own a motorcycle/scooter

The ownership of durable goods reflects the standard of living as well as the material well-being of the rural people. It is observed that the intra-group differentials are very high in the ownership of durable goods. However, the differential is relatively less between the groups. The ownership of such goods is largely determined by the income of the people belonging to different groups. As income varies within the group, the ownership of durable goods also varies.

11.1.3 Literacy Rate

The literacy rate is about 37 per cent in the lowest income group whereas it is 74 per cent in the highest income group. In the lowest income group, the literacy rate among males and females is 52 per cent and 19 per cent, respectively. On the other hand, in the highest income group, the literacy rate is about 90 per cent for males and 57 per cent for females. A very high gender disparity exists in the lowest income group. This disparity, however, decreases continuously from the lowest to the highest income groups (see Table A11.7).

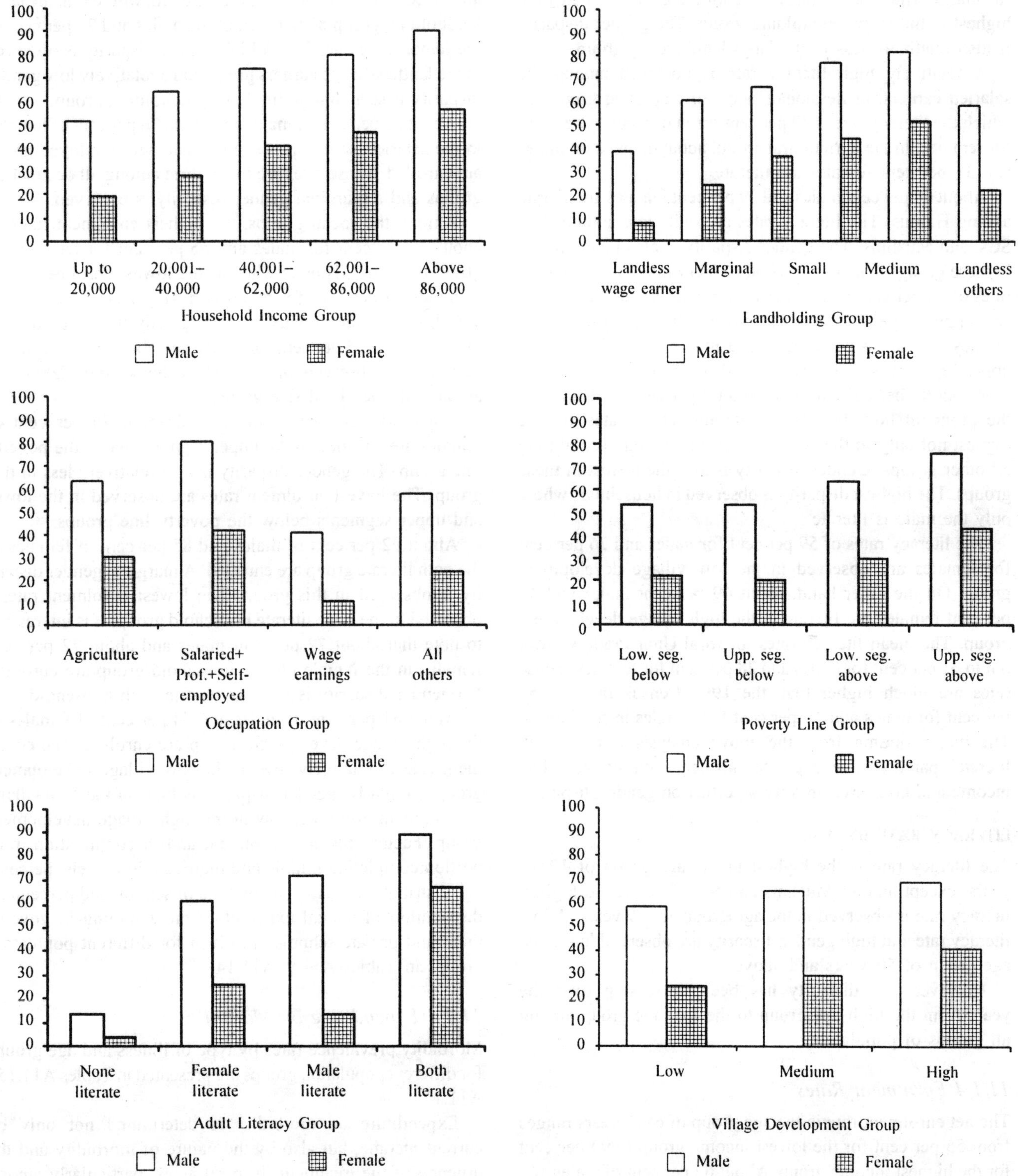

FIGURE 11.2: **Male–Female Literacy Rate by Population Group (percentage)**

A similar distribution is observed in the landholding groups. The lowest literacy rate of about 24 per cent is observed for landless wage earners and the highest, about 69 per cent, is observed among large landowners. The highest gender disparity is observed among the landless wage earners with literacy rates of 7 per cent for females and 38 per cent for males. The literacy rates for both males and females are highest in the large landholding group. The gender disparity is also relatively less in the large landholding group.

A relatively high literacy rate is observed among the salaried earners, professionals and self-employed group for which the literacy rate is 80 per cent for males and 41 per cent for females. In the agricultural group, about 63 per cent males and 31 per cent females are literate.

About 64 per cent males and 29 per cent females are literate among Hindus. The literacy rates are quite low among STs, SCs, and Muslims. The gender disparity is also much higher in these groups than among Hindus. Very low female literacy rates of 22 per cent and 20 per cent are observed in the lower and upper segment below the poverty line groups. A high literacy rate of 76 per cent among males is observed in the upper segment above the poverty line group.

About 90 per cent of males and 67 per cent of females in the group of both literate are literate. These rates are the highest not only in the adult literacy groups but also among all other groups. Gender disparity is also the lowest in these groups. The highest disparity is observed in households where only the male is literate.

The literacy rates of 59 per cent for males and 26 per cent for females are observed in the low village development group. On the other hand, about 69 per cent males and 41 per cent females are literate in the high village development group. The mean literacy rates for rural Uttar Pradesh work out to 62 per cent for males and 28 per cent for females. These rates are much higher than the 1991 Census rates of 52 per cent for males and 19 per cent for females in rural areas. The major finding from the above analysis is that 'both literate' parents have a greater influence on literacy than income and also have an adverse effect on gender disparity.

LITERACY RATE BY AGE

The literacy rate is the highest in the age group of 10–14 years, except among Muslims and STs. The second highest literacy rate is observed in the age group 15–19 years. A low literacy rate and high gender disparity are observed in the old age group of 50 years and above.

However, the disparity has been decreasing over the years from the high age group to the low age group among all groups of population.

11.1.4 Enrolment Rates

The net enrolment rate in the age group of 6–14 years ranges from 55 per cent for the lowest income group to 90 per cent for the highest income group. About 67 per cent of males and 40 per cent of females in the lowest income group of up to Rs 20,000 are enrolled. The gender disparity is also very high. Very high enrolment rates of 91 per cent among males and 89 per cent among females are observed in the highest income group of Rs 86,000 and above. In this income group the gender disparity is negligible (see Table A11.8).

In the landless wage earners groups, 53 per cent of the males and 26 per cent of the females are enrolled, whereas in the large landholding group 87 per cent of the males and 75 per cent of the females are enrolled. A high gender disparity is observed in the landless wage earners group and a relatively low gender disparity is seen among the large landholding group.

About 85 per cent of males and about 76 per cent of females in the salaried earner, professional and self-employed group are enrolled. These rates are the highest among all occupation groups and a marginal gender disparity is observed.

Among the social groups, the highest enrolment rates of about 76 per cent for males and 55 per cent for females are observed among Hindus whereas the lowest enrolment rates of about 56 per cent for males and 41 per cent for females are observed among Muslims. Marginally higher enrolment rates of about 75 per cent for males and about 59 per cent for females are observed in the highest household size group among all household size groups.

About 85 per cent of males and about 76 per cent of females are enrolled in the upper segment above the poverty line group. The gender disparity is also relatively less in this group. The lowest enrolment rates are observed in the lower and upper segments below the poverty line groups.

About 92 per cent of males and 85 per cent of females in the both literate group are enrolled. A marginal gender disparity is observed in this group. The lowest enrolment rate is observed in the none literate household group. It is interesting to note that about 72 per cent males and about 72 per cent females in the female literate household group are enrolled. No gender disparity is seen to exist in such households.

About 81 per cent of males and 64 per cent of females in the high village development group are enrolled. The enrolment rate is relatively low in the low village development group. Similarly, gender disparity is high in the low village development group but low in the high village development group. Factors for non-enrolment and discontinuation, proportion completing middle and matriculation levels, percentage distribution of students by type of school, and percentage distribution of annual expenditure on schooling in government and private schools are given for different population groups in Tables A11.9–A11.14.

11.1.5 Expenditure on Morbidity

Morbidity prevalence rates by type of illness and age groups for different population groups are presented in Tables A11.15–A11.17.

Expenditure on morbidity is determined not only by current income, but also by the nature of morbidity and the urgency of the treatment. In rural areas, particularly among the low income population groups, even valuable assets such

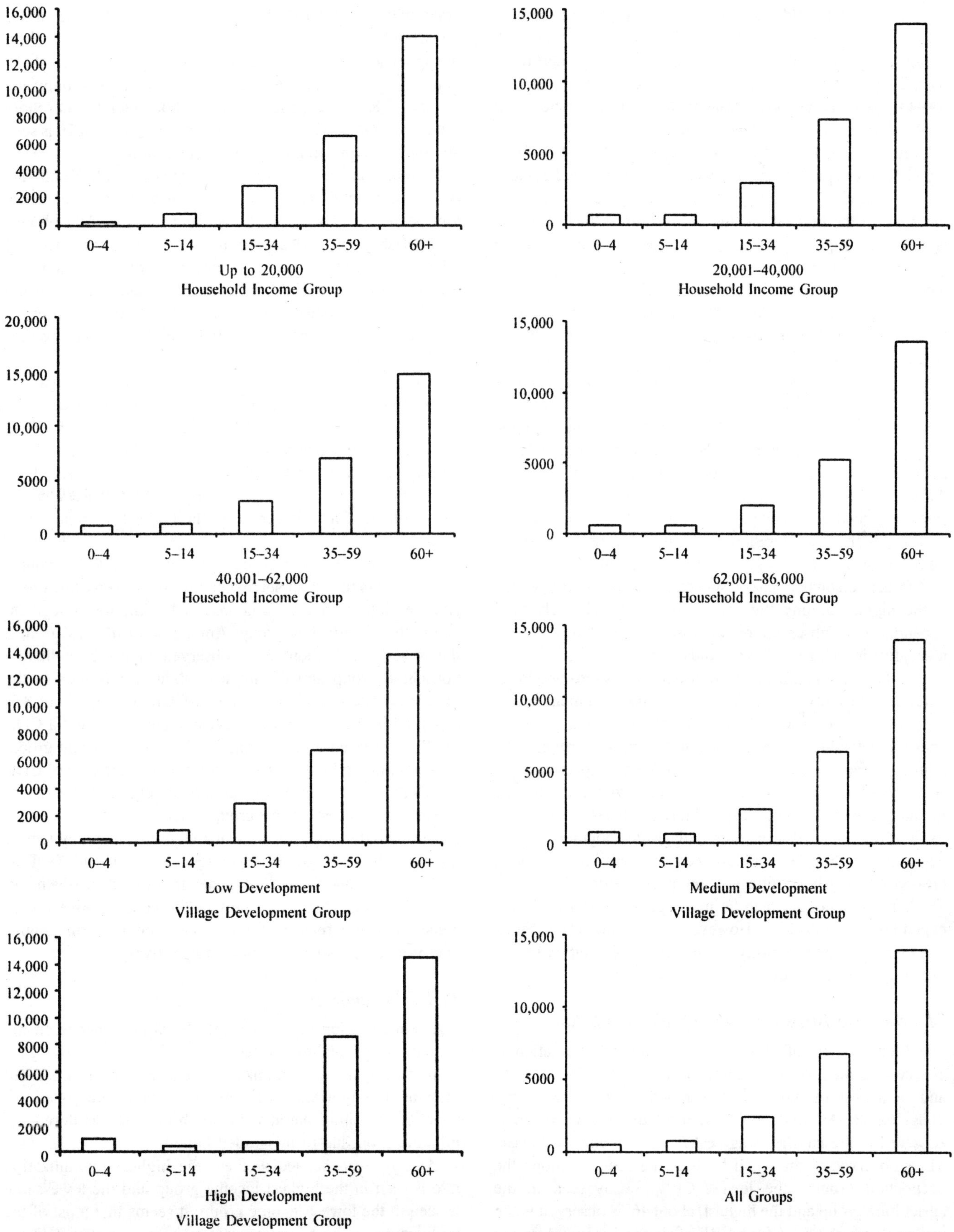

FIG. 11.3: **Major Morbidity Prevalence Rate by Age and Population Group (per lakh population)**

as animals, land, gold, etc. are sold to meet these expenses. On an average, Rs 118 is spent per person per year on short duration morbidity like diarrhoea, cold and cough, and fever by the lowest income group of up to Rs 20,000, whereas Rs 94 is spent per person per year by the highest income group of Rs 86,000 and above (see Table A11.18).

However, the highest expenditure on long-duration morbidity such as epilepsy, hypertension, diabetes, heart disease, mental disease, tuberculosis (TB), leprosy, and cancer is incurred by the highest income group. Intra-group variation is not very high as far as expenditure on long-duration morbidity is concerned: it ranges from Rs 1785 for the lowest income group to Rs 2214 for the highest income group.

The highest expenditure on short-duration morbidity is Rs 172 among the landless others and the lowest is Rs 98 among small landowners. Similarly, for long-duration morbidity among landholding groups the lowest expenditure of Rs 1527 is observed among the landless others and the highest of about Rs 1891 is incurred by the landless wage earners.

The highest expenditure on short-duration as well as long-duration morbidity in occupation groups is observed among the salaried, professional and self-employed group. A very small marginal difference is observed in the expenditure on both short- and long-duration morbidity, between the agricultural and wage earners groups. On an average, SCs spend Rs 135 per person per year on short duration morbidity, which is the highest among the social groups. A relatively high expenditure is observed on both short- and long-duration morbidity in large size households.

Similarly, the highest expenditure on both short- and long-duration morbidity is observed in the upper segment below the poverty line group. A majority of this group probably consists of landless wage earners and marginal farmers. The highest expenditure of Rs 150 and Rs 3865, respectively, on short- and long-duration morbidity is observed in the female literate group. The highest expenditure on short-term morbidity is observed in the medium village development group, while the highest expenditure on long-term morbidity is observed in the high village development group.

There does not seem to be much gender disparity in the expenditure on morbidity. However, the expenditure on short- and long-duration morbidity among females is slightly higher than that among males.

11.1.6 Crude Birth Rate and Crude Death Rate

The highest CBR of about 42 per thousand population is observed in the medium income group of Rs 40,001–62,000 and the lowest, of about 32, is observed in the income group of Rs 62,001–86,000. Similarly, the highest CBR of 46 is observed in the landless wage earners group and the lowest, 31, is observed in the small landholding group. Among the occupation groups, the lowest CBR, 33, is seen in the agriculture group and the highest, about 46, is observed in the wage earners groups. A high CBR of about 41 is found among SCs as well as Muslims, and the lowest, about 37, is observed among Hindus. A CBR of about 42 is observed in the largest household size group. A CBR of about 41 is observed in both the upper segment below the poverty line group as well as the none literate group. Among the adult literacy groups the lowest CBR, 33, is observed in the both literate household group (see Table A11.19). The lowest CBR of about 29 is seen among the high village development group.

Among the income groups, the lowest crude death rate (CDR) of about 6 per thousand population is observed in the highest income group of Rs 86,000 and above, and the highest CDR of about 13 is observed in the lowest income group of up to Rs 20,000. Similarly, among landholding groups, the lowest CDR of 7 is observed in the large landholding group and the highest, about 12 per thousand population, is observed for both landless others and medium landholding groups (see Table A11.19).

A CDR of only about 7 is observed for the salaried earner, professional and self-employed group among the occupation groups whereas the highest CDR of about 14 is observed for the wage earners group. The CDR ranges from 9 for STs as well as Muslims to 11 for both SCs and Hindus. A very high CDR of about 17 is observed in the smallest household size and the lowest, 8, is observed in the highest household size group.

Among poverty line groups, the lowest CDR of about 9 is observed in the upper segment above the poverty line group and the highest, about 12, is observed in the lower segment below the poverty line group. Among adult literacy groups, the lowest CDR about 6, is observed in the both literate household group and the highest, about 18, is seen in the female literate household group. A CDR of only about 8 is observed in the high village development group and a CDR of 12 is observed in the medium village development group.

The intra- and inter-group differentials in the case of CDR are also not very high. However, a relatively high CDR is observed in the lowest income group, wage earners group, smallest household size group, none literate group, and only female literate household group. In these households, the CDR is probably high due to a lack of money for immediate treatment.

Tables 11.20 and 11.21 present the contraceptive prevalence rates and reasons for non-adoption of birth control measures by population groups, respectively.

11.1.7 Immunization

The immunization of mother and the child depends on the availability of health-care facilities in rural areas. The government organizes immunization camps in rural areas but these are highly irregular. Even if such camps are organized, most of the time, parents do not bring their children for immunization due to misguided beliefs.

Among ever-married women, the highest immunization rate is seen in the highest income group and the lowest rate is seen in the lowest income group. It seems that most of the mothers do not go for immunization before or after delivery (see Table A11.22).

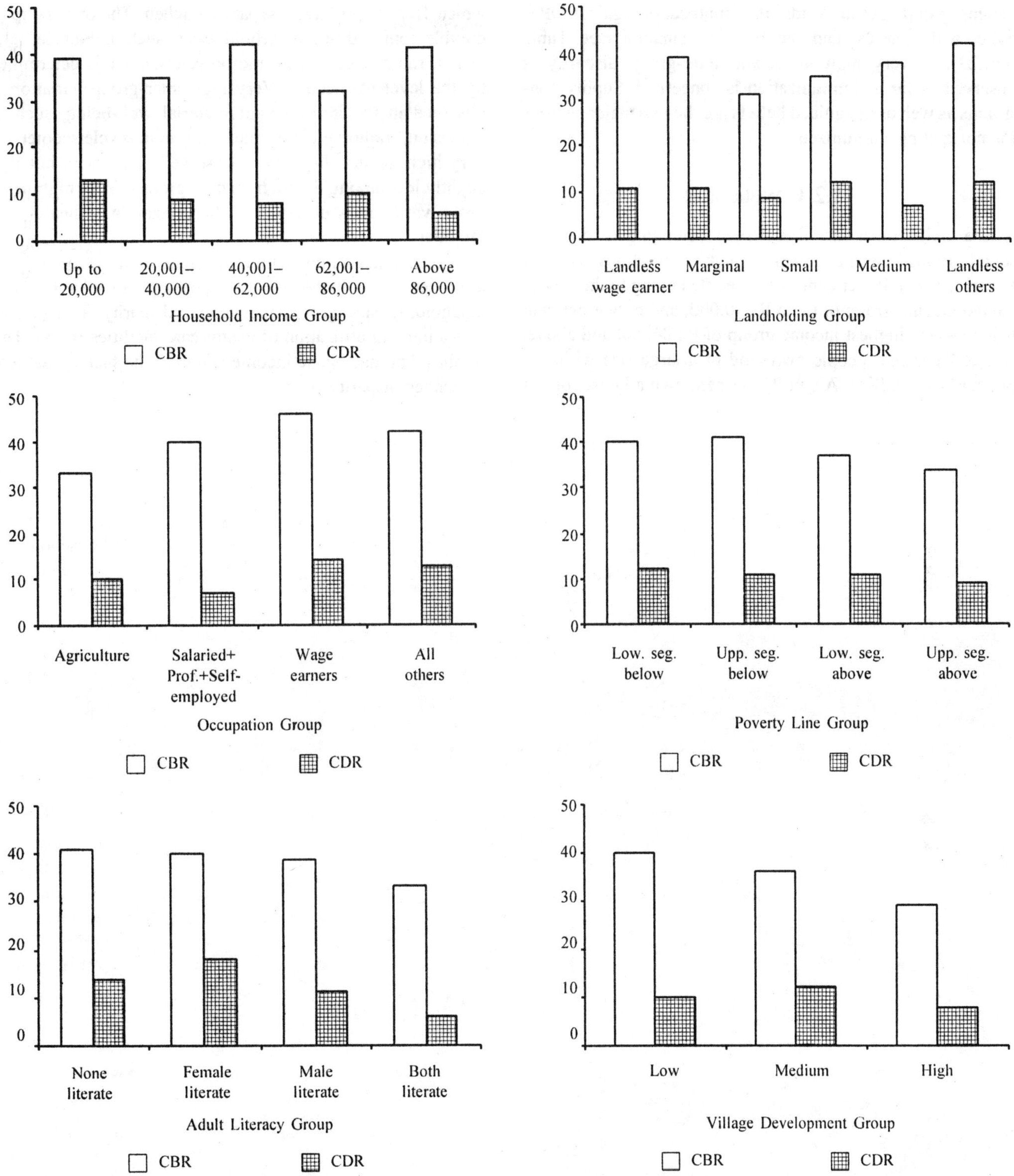

FIGURE 11.4: **Crude Birth Rate and Crude Death Rate by Population Group (per thousand population)**

Among landholding groups, about 64 per cent of mothers belonging to the large landholding group and only about 37 per cent of those belonging to the landless group are immunized. Very wide intra-group differentials are observed in the landholding groups. A very high immunization rate, about 71 per cent, is observed among high village development group. For all other groups, the immunization rate ranges from 33 per cent for the lower segment below the poverty line group to 56 per cent for the both literate group. The immunization rate is exceptionally low among STs, at only about 9 per cent.

Immunization pattern among children in the age group of 12–23 months shows that children belonging to the higher income groups get all kinds of immunization against DPT, polio, and measles, and the BCG vaccination (see Table A11.23). A very high intra- and inter-group disparity is observed as far as immunization is concerned. Supply constraints as well as misguided beliefs are the two major reasons for not getting immunized.

11.2 Conclusion

It is a well-known fact that people belonging to different social groups live in different economic conditions. In Uttar Pradesh, about 55 per cent of the people belong to the lowest annual income group of up to Rs 20,000, and only 4 per cent belong to the highest income group of Rs 86,000 and above. About 3 per cent people own land of a large size while 24 per cent are landless. About 98 per cent own a house, out of which 18 per cent have a separate kitchen. The ownership of durable commodities/household assets such as bicycle, television, radio, electric fan, motorcycle/scooter is determined by the level of income. Very high inter-group variation is observed in the indicators of material well-being, such as television, radio, electric fan, and motorcycle/scooter. A very high gender disparity is observed in literacy, but it is slightly less among the high income groups. Very high inter-group variation is observed in the utilization of health-care facilities.

It seems that immunization of mother and that of children are concomitant. In the high income group, as well as the large landholding size group, the gender disparity in accessing education and utilization of health-care facilities is less. This implies that inadequate income is one of the factors that lead to gender disparity.

TABLE A11.1
Levels of Income and Distribution of Households by Population Group in Rural Uttar Pradesh

Population group	No. of sample households	% estmtd households	Household size	Income (Rs per year) Per household	Per capita
Household income					
Up to 20,000	2215	54.9	5.4	10,701	1966
20,001–40,000	1109	27.2	6.9	28,336	4079
40,001–62,000	411	10.4	7.8	49,349	6305
62,001–86,000	157	3.9	8.9	71,896	8054
Above 86,000	144	3.6	9.7	144,419	14,889
Landholding					
Landless wage earner	482	11.7	5.3	10,118	1921
Marginal	1749	46.1	6.1	19,399	3163
Small	762	18.3	6.9	37,633	5424
Medium	331	8.0	8.0	55,527	6924
Large	124	3.1	8.9	94,051	10,571
Landless others	588	12.7	5.9	18,214	3085
All land owners	2966	75.6	6.6	30,739	4627
All land non-owners	1070	24.4	5.6	14,337	2561
Occupation					
Agriculture	1,937	48.4	6.3	29,710	4700
Salaried+prof.+s.empl.	626	16.4	7.5	39,339	5271
Wage earners	742	18.3	5.5	11,564	2097
All others	731	17.0	6.5	22,413	3457
Caste					
STs	74	2.0	6.5	21,370	3292
SCs	1154	27.0	5.7	17,259	3025
Religion					
Hindus	3218	87.4	6.3	27,079	4235
Muslims	808	12.4	6.3	24,298	3826
Household size					
Up to 4	1078	25.7	3.1	15,381	4906
5–7	1857	46.3	5.9	24,255	4108
8 and above	1101	28.0	10.2	41,207	4055
Poverty line					
Lower segment below	702	18.8	6.7	6,557	985
Upper segment below	834	20.6	6.7	13,646	2033
Lower segment above	1665	40.2	6.4	25,141	3929
Upper segment above	835	20.3	5.8	61,990	10,715
Adult literacy					
None literate	1387	32.4	5.0	15,238	3021
Female literate	50	1.3	5.4	20,646	3850
Male literate	1738	43.7	6.6	25,824	3904
Both literate	861	22.6	7.9	45,358	5712
Village development					
Low	2390	58.4	6.3	26,908	4304
Medium	1323	33.9	6.6	26,797	4040
High	323	7.6	6.3	25,111	3958
All groups	**4036**	**100.0**	**6.4**	**26,733**	**4185**

TABLE A11.2
Sourcewise Percentage Distribution of Household Income by Population Group in Rural Uttar Pradesh

Population group	Percentage distribution w.r.t. total household income											
	Agr.+alld act.	Artisan/ ind. work	Petty trd. sm. bus.	Or. trd. bus.	Salaried empl.	Qualified prof.	Rent/int./ dividend	Agr. wage	Non-agr. wage	Other sources	All sources	Actual value
Household income												
Up to 20,000	47.2	11.0	5.7	0.7	9.2	0.2	0.5	10.0	14.2	1.4	100	10,701
20,001–40,000	52.9	8.4	4.2	2.9	20.6	0.6	0.5	1.9	6.3	1.6	100	28,336
40,001–62,000	57.6	5.2	2.5	2.3	25.9	0.3	0.5	0.4	2.8	2.4	100	49,349
62,001–86,000	60.0	5.1	1.1	2.9	26.6	0.3	0.3	0.4	0.9	2.3	100	71,896
Above 86,000	59.6	3.2	0.3	4.0	30.1	1.0	0.2	0.0	0.7	0.9	100	144,419
Landholding												
Landless wage earner	3.2	2.2	1.0	0.2	1.7	0.0	0.0	27.9	61.5	2.3	100	10,118
Marginal	45.7	8.8	3.7	2.7	26.1	0.5	0.3	3.8	6.7	1.7	100	19,399
Small	66.2	2.6	1.1	3.1	22.5	0.2	0.4	0.6	1.3	2.0	100	37,633
Medium	76.5	2.2	0.2	2.0	16.4	0.7	0.2	0.3	0.7	0.8	100	55,527
Large	83.5	2.3	0.6	0.1	11.9	0.3	0.1	0.0	0.1	1.1	100	94,051
Landless others	2.1	31.1	16.5	5.7	33.9	1.3	2.2	1.6	3.4	2.2	100	18,214
All land owners	62.5	4.8	1.9	2.3	21.4	0.4	0.3	1.7	3.1	1.5	100	30,739
All land non-owners	2.5	21.3	11.2	3.8	23.0	0.8	1.4	10.5	23.0	2.3	100	14,337
Occupation												
Agriculture	86.2	2.5	0.8	0.3	6.1	0.4	0.2	1.3	1.5	0.8	100	29,710
Salaried+prof.+s.empl.	20.7	0.6	0.7	0.1	75.1	1.1	0.2	0.3	0.6	0.5	100	39,339
Wage earners	13.4	1.8	1.0	0.5	1.2	0.0	0.0	24.2	56.3	1.6	100	11,564
All others	15.6	37.9	16.9	16.1	1.0	0.2	1.7	1.3	2.3	6.9	100	22,413
Caste												
STs	56.6	4.3	2.2	5.1	19.1	0.0	0.0	4.5	7.5	0.7	100	21,370
SCs	45.9	8.9	3.0	0.9	16.7	0.6	0.5	9.4	12.2	1.9	100	17,259
Religion												
Hindus	55.8	6.0	2.8	2.4	22.3	0.5	0.4	2.8	5.5	1.5	100	27,078
Muslims	44.8	14.7	5.5	3.4	16.5	0.5	0.5	3.4	7.7	2.8	100	24,298
Household size												
Up to 4	59.1	7.8	3.0	1.0	12.8	0.1	1.0	5.3	8.1	1.8	100	15,381
5–7	56.8	7.0	3.3	2.0	19.1	0.6	0.3	3.4	6.3	1.2	100	24,255
8 and above	51.0	6.7	2.9	3.6	27.0	0.5	0.3	1.5	4.3	2.0	100	41,207
Poverty line												
Lower segment below	49.0	10.0	4.0	0.0	5.0	0.2	0.5	14.2	16.2	1.1	100	6557
Upper segment below	43.7	11.3	6.3	2.5	9.4	0.2	0.0	9.5	15.6	1.6	100	13,646
Lower segment above	49.7	8.8	4.5	2.2	22.2	0.5	0.6	2.9	6.7	1.9	100	25,141
Upper segment above	61.6	4.3	1.1	3.1	25.5	0.6	0.4	0.2	1.7	1.5	100	61,990
Adult literacy												
None literate	54.0	10.9	3.6	0.4	5.5	0.0	0.7	9.2	13.6	2.1	100	15,238
Female literate	56.6	15.0	3.9	4.4	10.1	0.0	0.0	7.0	3.1	0.0	100	20,646
Male literate	52.6	9.0	3.6	2.0	21.2	0.6	0.4	2.4	6.6	1.6	100	25,824
Both literate	57.1	2.7	2.2	4.1	30.1	0.6	0.4	0.2	1.0	1.5	100	45,358
Village development												
Low	56.8	7.1	2.2	1.9	21.6	0.4	0.4	2.9	4.8	1.9	100	26,908
Medium	52.2	7.1	4.1	3.5	21.6	0.6	0.6	2.8	6.4	1.2	100	26,797
High	48.7	5.9	5.2	3.5	21.6	0.4	0.2	2.8	10.0	1.6	100	25,111
All groups	**54.6**	**7.0**	**3.1**	**2.5**	**21.6**	**0.5**	**0.4**	**2.9**	**5.7**	**1.6**	**100**	–
Actual value	**18,643**	**13,667**	**12,362**	**31,859**	**27,682**	**19,901**	**9121**	**4071**	**8189**	**12,264**	–	**26,733**

TABLE A11.3

Average (per reporting household) Wage Income and its Share in Total Income by Population Group in Rural Uttar Pradesh

Population group	Agricultural wage		Non-agr. wage		All wages		Wage as per cent of total income			Per cent of households getting 50% income from wages
	Average wage	Per cent of rep. hhs	Average wage	Per cent of rep. hhs	Average wage	Per cent of rep. hhs	Agr. wage	Non-agr. wage	All wage	
Household income										
Up to 20,000	3465	27.9	5563	24.9	5495	42.8	9.0	12.9	22.0	28.5
20,001–40,000	4663	10.6	10,810	14.9	10,178	20.7	1.7	5.7	7.4	7.1
40,001–62,000	4829	3.8	17,790	7.2	15,828	9.2	0.4	2.6	3.0	2.2
62,001–86,000	6506	4.0	27,533	2.2	16,981	5.2	0.4	0.9	1.2	1.4
Above 86,000	2700	1.1	33,539	2.8	24,992	3.8	0.0	0.6	0.7	0.6
Landholding										
Landless wage earner	4169	61.6	7886	71.7	8,221	100.0	25.4	55.9	81.3	98.8
Marginal	3468	19.5	6903	17.0	5968	31.0	3.5	6.1	9.5	13.2
Small	3959	5.3	9208	4.9	7586	8.7	0.6	1.2	1.8	1.0
Medium	6393	2.0	13,301	2.7	11,262	4.3	0.2	0.7	0.9	1.1
Large	2800	0.6	4954	1.8	4438	2.4	0.0	0.1	0.1	0.6
Landless others	2365	11.4	5720	9.9	4388	19.0	1.5	3.1	4.6	0.0
All land owners	3560	13.4	7274	11.9	6232	21.6	1.6	2.8	4.4	8.4
All land non-owners	3866	35.4	7603	39.5	7563	57.8	9.6	20.9	30.5	47.3
Occupation										
Agriculture	3050	11.4	5470	7.2	4468	16.6	1.2	1.3	2.5	0.0
Salaried+prof.+s.empl.	1975	5.6	4658	4.6	3754	8.7	0.3	0.5	0.8	0.0
Wage earners	4333	58.8	8263	71.7	8469	100.0	22.0	51.2	73.2	98.1
All others	2722	9.8	6141	7.7	4627	16.0	1.2	2.1	3.3	0.0
Caste										
STs	2775	31.8	4970	29.2	5688	41.0	4.1	6.8	10.9	28.2
Cs	3660	40.3	6127	31.2	6019	56.3	8.6	11.1	19.6	33.8
Religion										
Hindus	3593	19.2	7322	18.4	6722	30.3	2.5	5.0	7.5	17.7
Muslims	4619	16.5	8211	20.7	7748	31.7	3.1	7.0	10.1	19.9
Household size										
Up to 4	3105	24.0	5597	20.2	5130	36.6	4.8	7.4	12.2	23.8
5–7	3720	20.1	7,201	19.3	6743	31.7	3.1	5.7	8.8	19.5
8 and above	4741	11.9	10,037	16.2	9625	22.7	1.4	3.9	5.3	9.9
Poverty line										
Lower segment below	2576	32.8	3625	26.7	3780	47.9	12.9	14.7	27.6	36.8
Upper segment below	4161	28.2	6955	27.9	6951	44.8	8.6	14.2	22.8	28.6
Lower segment above	4358	15.2	9293	16.5	8465	25.9	2.6	6.1	8.7	11.0
Upper segment above	4039	3.5	15,287	6.1	12,559	8.6	0.2	1.5	1.7	3.1
Adult literacy										
None literate	3666	34.7	6,696	28.1	6178	51.0	8.4	12.3	20.7	31.8
Female literate	6051	21.6	5,583	10.3	7194	26.2	6.3	2.8	9.1	19.5
Male literate	3726	15.1	8,299	18.6	7793	27.1	2.2	6.0	8.2	15.0
Both literate	3074	3.1	7,513	5.6	6752	7.7	0.2	0.9	1.1	3.5
Village development										
Low	3688	19.5	7,278	16.1	6382	29.6	2.7	4.4	7.0	16.0
Medium	3747	18.0	7,213	21.7	7035	31.8	2.5	5.8	8.3	20.3
High	3597	17.7	9,158	24.9	9424	31.0	2.5	9.1	11.6	21.7
All groups	**3701**	**18.8**	**7,444**	**18.6**	**6,850**	**30.4**	**2.6**	**5.2**	**7.8**	**17.9**

TABLE A11.4
Land and Livestock Owned by Households by Population Group in Rural Uttar Pradesh

Population group	Landholdings			Draught animals			Milch animals		
	Per cent of rep. hhs	Average rep. hh	Average all groups	Per cent of rep. hhs	Average rep. hh	Average all groups	Per cent of rep. hhs	Average rep. hh	Average all groups hh
Household income									
Up to 20,000	64.6	1.9	1.2	24.9	2.0	0.5	55.1	1.7	0.9
20,001–40,000	84.8	3.4	2.9	35.2	1.9	0.7	72.2	1.9	1.4
40,001–62,000	93.8	4.5	4.2	42.5	2.3	1.0	80.6	2.1	1.7
62,001–86,000	95.6	5.9	5.7	47.0	2.2	1.0	86.4	2.2	1.9
Above 86,000	99.3	11.8	11.7	41.2	2.1	0.9	89.6	2.7	2.4
Landholding									
Landless wage earner	–	–	–	4.2	1.7	0.1	43.9	1.3	0.6
Marginal	100.0	1.1	1.1	34.8	2.0	0.7	65.7	1.7	1.1
Small	100.0	3.6	3.6	42.1	1.9	0.8	81.0	2.0	1.6
Medium	100.0	7.1	7.1	52.8	2.3	1.2	87.1	2.2	1.9
Large	100.0	25.0	25.0	57.9	2.6	1.5	91.4	3.3	3.0
Landless others	–	–	–	5.6	1.6	0.1	37.4	1.6	0.6
All land owners	100.0	3.4	3.4	39.4	2.0	0.8	72.7	2.0	1.4
All land non-owners	–	–	–	4.9	1.6	0.1	40.5	1.4	0.6
Occupation									
Agriculture	99.3	4.1	4.1	45.8	2.0	0.9	76.4	2.1	1.6
Salaried+prof.+s.empl.	77.2	2.9	2.2	28.1	2.1	0.6	68.6	1.8	1.3
Wage earners	36.0	0.7	0.3	11.7	2.2	0.3	48.6	1.5	0.7
All others	49.0	1.6	0.8	12.5	1.7	0.2	46.0	1.5	0.7
Caste									
STs	72.0	3.0	2.2	44.5	1.7	0.8	65.1	1.8	1.2
SCs	63.3	1.9	1.2	25.4	2.0	0.5	56.2	1.7	1.0
Religion									
Hindus	77.7	3.3	2.6	32.5	2.1	0.7	67.4	1.9	1.3
Muslims	60.8	3.5	2.1	20.0	1.8	0.4	46.7	1.7	0.8
Household size									
Up to 4	67.6	2.1	1.4	20.7	2.2	0.5	50.4	1.7	0.9
5–7	75.2	3.4	2.6	30.3	2.0	0.6	66.6	1.8	1.2
8 and above	83.4	4.2	3.5	41.6	2.0	0.8	75.3	2.1	1.6
Poverty line									
Lower segment below	61.5	1.6	1.0	27.9	1.9	0.5	55.7	1.7	0.9
Upper segment below	68.2	1.8	1.2	27.2	1.9	0.5	60.8	1.7	1.0
Lower segment above	77.6	3.3	2.6	31.5	2.0	0.6	65.4	1.9	1.2
Upper segment above	92.2	5.7	5.2	36.7	2.2	0.8	76.3	2.1	1.6
Adult literacy									
None literate	64.0	2.3	1.4	23.1	2.1	0.5	53.5	1.8	1.0
Female literate	75.1	2.0	1.5	11.3	1.9	0.2	55.3	1.5	0.8
Male literate	76.7	2.9	2.2	34.9	2.0	0.7	67.6	1.8	1.2
Both literate	90.1	5.3	4.8	35.8	2.1	0.8	76.4	2.1	1.6
Village development									
Low	79.2	3.7	2.9	34.2	2.1	0.7	66.3	2.0	1.3
Medium	73.2	2.7	2.0	26.8	2.0	0.5	62.0	1.7	1.1
High	58.8	3.2	1.9	25.3	1.7	0.4	66.8	1.7	1.1
All groups	**75.6**	**3.4**	**2.5**	**31.0**	**2.0**	**0.6**	**64.9**	**1.9**	**1.2**

TABLE A11.5
Amenities Available in House by Population Group in Rural Uttar Pradesh

Population group	Percentage of households having					
	Kutcha house	Separate kitchen	Electric connection	Protected water	Piped water	Toilet
Household income						
Up to 20,000	68.9	12.7	14.4	67.3	14.5	8.6
20,001–40,000	51.5	19.3	20.4	71.3	14.9	11.2
40,001–62,000	40.4	30.4	30.6	74.3	14.7	14.8
62,001–86,000	30.1	37.5	42.1	76.7	13.6	20.0
Above 86,000	23.8	36.4	50.6	81.7	17.0	16.3
Landholding						
Landless wage earner	79.0	7.9	10.1	69.7	13.0	8.8
Marginal	59.8	16.1	15.4	67.3	14.5	8.3
Small	47.7	23.5	24.5	74.1	15.1	10.4
Medium	41.1	33.2	34.5	74.4	14.0	19.4
Large	35.3	39.6	40.6	77.5	17.6	13.8
Landless others	64.0	12.5	25.8	69.5	15.9	15.2
All land owners	53.9	20.7	20.7	70.1	14.7	10.2
All land non-owners	71.2	10.3	18.3	69.6	14.5	12.1
Occupation						
Agriculture	56.6	19.7	19.1	71.9	14.5	10.2
Salaried+prof.+s.empl.	40.8	26.9	32.5	64.1	15.5	11.6
Wage earners	75.4	10.3	8.8	69.2	12.8	8.4
All others	60.2	13.8	23.1	71.2	16.5	13.3
Caste						
STs	70.4	13.8	13.4	78.3	17.2	9.5
SCs	68.8	11.0	12.4	68.4	12.0	4.9
Religion						
Hindus	57.8	17.7	20.0	68.1	14.6	7.5
Muslims	61.0	20.0	20.0	83.1	14.9	33.3
Household size						
Up to 4	66.7	12.5	12.9	67.2	14.7	8.4
5–7	58.2	18.2	19.4	69.6	15.3	10.5
8 and above	50.2	23.2	27.8	73.2	13.7	12.9
Poverty line						
Lower segment below	71.4	12.6	16.0	60.8	14.8	7.0
Upper segment below	68.3	13.2	14.1	70.0	14.1	9.0
Lower segment above	55.9	17.7	19.2	72.3	14.5	11.4
Upper segment above	39.7	29.3	31.8	74.1	15.3	14.2
Adult literacy						
None literate	77.2	7.2	9.1	68.8	12.4	9.3
Female literate	56.1	18.8	17.7	75.4	10.5	7.7
Male literate	55.9	16.7	16.8	68.7	13.4	8.7
Both literate	35.1	36.7	42.5	73.9	20.5	16.7
Village development						
Low	64.3	15.1	16.0	66.2	10.7	8.2
Medium	49.8	20.5	22.0	74.2	18.5	11.4
High	46.8	31.1	42.8	80.2	28.0	26.2
All groups	**58.1**	**18.1**	**20.1**	**70.0**	**14.7**	**10.7**

TABLE A11.6

Consumption of Foodgrains and Utilization of PDS by Population Group in Rural Uttar Pradesh

Population group	Annual household income (Rs)	Annual per capita income (Rs)	Per capita consumption of foodgrains (kg/month)	Percentage of households using PDS	Quantity of cereals (kg) bought from PDS (per hh/month)	Per cent requirement of cereals met from PDS
Household income						
Up to 20,000	10,701	1966	15.1	5.8	28.0	20.1
20,001–40,000	28,336	4079	14.9	5.0	42.2	30.8
40,001–62,000	49,349	6305	15.6	5.0	43.8	46.2
62,001–86,000	71,896	8054	15.2	2.3	16.2	21.2
Above 86,000	144,419	14,889	15.3	1.7	51.8	13.1
Landholding						
Landless wage earner	10,118	1921	14.2	2.1	41.8	13.2
Marginal	19,399	3163	15.2	8.4	29.1	24.6
Small	37,633	5424	15.8	2.3	48.3	31.6
Medium	55,527	6924	15.5	3.1	79.3	43.9
Large	94,051	10,571	15.9	3.4	9.9	6.4
Landless others	18,214	3085	14.0	2.7	31.7	21.3
All land owners	30,739	4627	15.4	6.1	33.1	26.3
All land non-owners	14,337	2561	14.1	2.4	35.9	16.4
Occupation						
Agriculture	29,710	4700	15.9	2.9	35.4	20.5
Salaried+prof.+s.empl.	39,339	5271	14.4	13.4	34.5	40.8
Wage earners	11,564	2097	14.6	5.3	27.1	18.5
All others	22,413	3457	14.4	3.9	34.8	16.1
Caste						
STs	21,370	3292	14.4	10.3	12.9	12.9
SCs	17,259	3025	14.7	5.7	33.1	22.6
Religion						
Hindus	27,078	4235	15.3	5.9	33.7	25.3
Muslims	24,298	3826	14.3	0.5	7.3	2.0
Household Size						
Up to 4	15,381	4906	17.4	5.9	24.1	32.4
5–7	24,255	4108	15.4	6.4	33.8	27.1
8 and above	41,207	4055	14.2	2.6	51.3	16.4
Poverty line						
Lower segment below	6,557	985	14.9	6.1	30.0	18.2
Upper segment below	13,646	2033	14.5	4.7	31.4	17.8
Lower segment above	25,141	3929	15.1	5.7	33.5	29.3
Upper segment above	61,990	10,715	16.4	3.8	40.5	37.4
Adult literacy						
None literate	15,238	3021	15.2	2.9	19.1	10.6
Female literate	20,646	3850	15.6	6.8	12.1	25.3
Male literate	25,824	3904	15.1	5.0	33.1	22.8
Both literate	45,358	5712	15.2	9.0	41.2	37.2
Village development						
Low	26,908	4304	15.2	5.1	33.6	22.4
Medium	26,797	4040	15.2	5.1	31.0	25.1
High	25,111	3958	14.6	6.7	40.1	40.4
All groups	**26,733**	**4185**	**15.2**	**5.2**	**33.4**	**24.5**

TABLE A11.7
Literacy Rate (per cent) and Gender Disparity by Population Group in Rural Uttar Pradesh

Population group	Literacy rate (aged 7 and above)			
	Total	Male	Female	F/M
Household income				
Up to 20,000	36.7	51.7	19.3	0.37
20,001–40,000	48.0	64.0	28.1	0.44
40,001–62,000	58.9	73.6	40.8	0.55
62,001–86,000	64.8	79.8	46.4	0.58
Above 86,000	74.0	89.9	56.5	0.63
Landholding				
Landless wage earner	24.4	38.2	7.4	0.20
Marginal	43.7	60.1	24.5	0.41
Small	52.9	66.8	36.2	0.54
Medium	62.2	77.0	44.6	0.58
Large	68.8	82.2	51.8	0.63
Landless others	42.2	58.8	21.8	0.37
All land owners	49.9	65.4	31.6	0.48
All land non-owners	34.2	49.5	15.4	0.31
Occupation				
Agriculture	48.5	63.3	30.6	0.48
Salaried+prof.+s.empl.	62.4	80.3	41.1	0.51
Wage earners	26.8	40.3	10.2	0.25
All others	41.5	57.2	23.5	0.41
Caste				
STs	33.6	46.5	16.0	0.34
SCs	32.4	48.1	13.7	0.29
Religion				
Hindus	48.2	64.0	29.3	0.46
Muslims	35.0	47.1	20.2	0.43
Household size				
Up to 4	32.0	46.5	14.4	0.31
5–7	46.0	61.0	27.3	0.45
8 and above	51.8	67.9	33.3	0.49
Poverty line				
Lower segment below	38.2	53.1	21.5	0.41
Upper segment below	37.9	52.9	20.1	0.38
Lower segment above	48.0	63.8	29.1	0.46
Upper segment above	61.5	76.2	42.9	0.56
Adult literacy				
None literate	9.6	13.9	4.3	0.31
Female literate	47.2	61.7	26.2	0.42
Male literate	46.3	71.9	13.6	0.19
Both literate	78.8	89.5	67.2	0.75
Village development				
Low	43.9	59.0	25.6	0.43
Medium	49.2	65.5	29.9	0.46
High	55.9	69.1	40.9	0.59
All groups	**46.7**	**62.0**	**28.3**	**0.46**

TABLE A11.8

Ever Enrolment, Discontinuation, and Non-attendance Rates for Children (aged 6–14 years) by Population Group in Rural Uttar Pradesh

(per cent)

Population group	Ever enrolment rate				Discontinuation rate				Non-attendance rate			
	Total	Male	Female	F/M	Total	Male	Female	F/M	Total	Male	Female	F/M
Household income												
Up to 20,000	54.7	66.6	40.3	0.61	4.4	3.9	5.3	1.38	6.5	5.9	7.6	1.29
20,001–40,000	67.7	75.1	58.3	0.78	4.9	3.5	7.1	2.04	6.2	7.7	3.8	0.49
40,001–62,000	75.5	83.1	66.0	0.79	3.1	1.7	5.4	3.10	7.9	5.9	11.2	1.90
62,001–86,000	81.0	85.7	75.3	0.88	3.0	3.8	1.8	0.48	3.9	5.0	2.6	0.52
Above 86,000	89.7	91.0	88.7	0.97	3.4	1.2	5.2	4.54	10.8	14.3	7.6	0.54
Landholding												
Landless wage earner	41.3	52.9	25.7	0.48	5.1	5.3	4.4	0.84	9.5	10.6	6.5	0.61
Marginal	63.3	74.2	50.5	0.68	4.7	3.9	6.1	1.56	4.7	4.1	5.7	1.39
Small	72.4	78.3	65.5	0.84	3.6	1.5	6.5	4.26	7.9	8.5	7.0	0.83
Medium	75.6	80.6	69.7	0.86	3.4	2.3	4.8	2.07	7.2	5.4	9.8	1.83
Large	81.6	87.2	75.1	0.86	2.4	1.3	3.9	3.03	12.5	17.6	5.5	0.31
Landless others	57.9	68.2	44.1	0.65	4.5	4.6	4.1	0.88	7.9	8.9	5.7	0.64
All land owners	68.1	76.7	58.0	0.76	4.1	2.9	5.9	2.00	6.4	6.2	6.7	1.07
All land non-owners	50.5	61.4	35.9	0.58	4.7	4.9	4.2	0.86	8.5	9.6	6.0	0.62
Occupation												
Agriculture	66.2	75.3	55.2	0.73	4.3	2.7	6.8	2.47	8.0	8.0	8.0	1.00
Salaried+prof.+s.empl.	80.9	85.1	75.6	0.89	2.6	2.3	3.0	1.27	4.5	4.8	4.1	0.84
Wage earners	44.8	57.3	29.1	0.51	5.6	5.0	7.1	1.41	6.2	6.9	4.5	0.65
All others	59.4	69.5	47.5	0.68	5.1	4.9	5.4	1.11	6.5	6.0	7.3	1.20
Caste												
STs	53.6	60.6	41.3	0.68	3.9	3.9	3.9	1.02	3.3	4.6	0.0	0.00
SCs	53.3	66.0	36.7	0.56	4.3	4.7	3.3	0.70	4.5	4.9	3.5	0.72
Religion												
Hindus	66.4	75.8	55.0	0.73	3.8	3.1	5.1	1.65	6.5	6.6	6.2	0.94
Muslims	49.7	56.4	41.4	0.73	7.0	5.2	10.0	1.92	9.2	9.0	9.6	1.07
Household size												
Up to 4	66.1	71.9	56.1	0.78	4.3	2.5	8.2	3.28	8.9	9.1	8.5	0.94
5–7	60.9	71.5	47.2	0.66	3.8	3.1	5.3	1.73	6.9	6.1	8.6	1.40
8 and above	67.3	75.3	58.6	0.78	4.5	3.7	5.6	1.52	6.3	7.3	4.9	0.68
Poverty line												
Lower segment below	54.4	65.6	42.0	0.64	4.0	3.6	4.6	1.27	5.7	5.8	5.6	0.97
Upper segment below	55.0	65.7	40.9	0.62	5.5	5.4	5.8	1.06	6.8	5.9	8.6	1.44
Lower segment above	68.7	77.3	58.1	0.75	4.2	2.5	6.8	2.68	6.3	6.7	5.6	0.83
Upper segment above	80.8	84.7	76.1	0.90	3.0	2.2	4.0	1.86	8.7	9.4	7.8	0.83
Adult literacy												
None literate	36.7	48.9	19.9	0.41	4.4	4.3	4.6	1.08	10.1	9.6	11.7	1.21
Female literate	71.8	72.0	71.7	1.00	2.5	0.0	4.7	–	3.6	0.0	6.8	–
Male literate	66.8	78.4	52.5	0.67	4.7	4.1	5.8	1.43	5.5	6.1	4.4	0.72
Both literate	88.5	92.3	84.5	0.92	3.5	1.5	5.7	3.71	7.1	6.6	7.6	1.17
Village development												
Low	60.5	69.5	49.4	0.71	4.0	2.9	5.8	2.03	6.8	6.8	6.9	1.01
Medium	68.3	77.4	57.3	0.74	4.4	3.5	5.9	1.69	6.3	6.5	6.1	0.94
High	72.7	81.3	63.6	0.78	4.4	5.2	3.2	0.61	8.3	9.3	6.9	0.74
All groups	**64.2**	**73.2**	**53.4**	**0.73**	**4.2**	**3.3**	**5.6**	**1.70**	**6.8**	**6.9**	**6.6**	**0.96**

TABLE A11.9

Factors for Non-enrolment (per cent) of Children (aged 6–14 years) and Gender Disparity by Population Group in Rural Uttar Pradesh

Population group	Suppply factors	Demand factors	Interest factors	Customs factors
Household income				
Up to 20,000				
Person	12.7	50.1	54.3	13.1
Gender disparity	1.17	1.09	0.99	1.70
20,001–40,000				
Person	8.0	37.7	58.0	11.3
Gender disparity	0.71	1.18	1.15	2.90
40,001–62,000				
Person	12.7	27.3	60.0	19.3
Gender disparity	0.80	0.66	1.00	2.89
62,001–86,000				
Person	27.6	36.2	54.8	8.0
Gender disparity	2.20	0.68	0.87	0.60
Above 86,000				
Person	7.9	23.7	44.2	3.6
Gender disparity	–	1.61	1.25	–
Landholding				
Landless wage earner				
Person	13.4	59.3	56.2	13.3
Gender disparity	1.18	1.00	1.04	2.34
Marginal				
Person	9.8	40.6	57.0	12.9
Gender disparity	1.07	1.13	1.01	1.60
Small				
Person	14.8	39.6	56.4	11.9
Gender disparity	1.09	1.23	0.97	3.85
Medium				
Person	22.4	35.1	51.9	20.1
Gender disparity	1.17	0.84	1.00	1.20
Large				
Person	12.6	25.9	53.5	15.3
Gender disparity	0.44	1.48	1.35	–
Landless others				
Person	8.0	50.6	51.7	9.5
Gender disparity	1.46	1.12	1.12	2.70
All land owners				
Person	12.2	39.4	56.3	13.4
Gender disparity	1.03	1.13	1.01	1.84
All land non-owners				
Person	10.8	55.2	54.1	11.5
Gender disparity	1.25	1.04	1.07	2.45
Occupation				
Agriculture				
Person	14.6	39.6	58.7	15.0
Gender disparity	0.99	1.20	0.96	1.92
Salaried+prof.+s.empl.				
Person	5.2	25.0	56.5	6.4
Gender disparity	1.53	1.44	1.28	1.34
Wage earners				
Person	12.3	55.1	52.2	14.5
Gender disparity	1.06	0.93	0.93	2.19
All others				
Person	8.0	50.6	52.4	9.0
Gender disparity	1.55	1.04	1.24	2.26
Caste				
STs				
Person	6.5	52.4	59.7	22.7
Gender disparity	1.50	0.57	1.22	3.27
SCs				
Person	12.2	49.3	59.4	12.6
Gender disparity	1.06	1.00	1.01	1.69
Religion				
Hindus				
Person	11.0	44.6	55.8	12.5
Gender disparity	1.06	1.04	1.06	2.30
Muslims				
Person	15.4	42.4	54.9	14.5
Gender disparity	1.32	1.24	0.90	1.41
Household size				
Up to 4				
Person	8.9	47.6	59.9	14.2
Gender disparity	1.37	1.33	0.83	1.74
5–7				
Person	12.4	46.6	56.3	13.4
Gender disparity	0.77	1.05	0.98	1.91
8 and above				
Person	11.5	40.9	54.2	12.0
Gender disparity	1.77	1.09	1.14	2.27
Poverty line				
Lower segment below				
Person	13.0	53.0	50.9	13.7
Gender disparity	0.89	1.06	1.01	1.78
Upper segment below				
Person	11.0	47.0	56.2	12.3
Gender disparity	1.67	1.03	0.97	1.55
Lower segment above				
Person	10.8	36.3	57.5	12.8
Gender disparity	0.92	1.19	1.11	2.90
Upper segment above				
Person	14.4	37.5	61.8	11.7
Gender disparity	1.25	0.95	1.02	1.97
Adult literacy				
None literate				
Person	12.7	51.7	56.2	14.0
Gender disparity	0.89	1.09	1.01	1.41
Female literate				
Person	19.9	38.7	75.8	6.4
Gender disparity	1.61	1.55	0.94	–
Male literate				
Person	11.3	38.8	56.7	12.2
Gender disparity	1.72	1.09	1.02	4.73
Both literate				
Person	7.6	29.3	44.2	10.1
Gender disparity	0.66	1.84	1.47	2.03
Village development				
Low				
Person	14.2	44.0	57.1	12.2
Gender disparity	1.01	1.18	1.01	1.72
Medium				
Person	7.1	45.3	51.9	13.3
Gender disparity	1.64	0.88	1.07	2.67
High				
Person	11.3	40.8	60.7	17.5
Gender disparity	1.33	1.30	1.00	2.19
All groups				
Person	11.8	44.2	55.6	12.8
Gender disparity	1.10	1.08	1.03	2.01

(Contd.)

TABLE A11.10

Factors for Discontinuation (per cent) of Children (aged 6–14 years) and Gender Disparity by Population Group in Rural Uttar Pradesh

Population group	Suppply factors	Demand factors	Interest factors	Customs factors
Household income				
Up to 20,000				
Person	23.1	76.3	76.3	56.8
Gender disparity	3.87	0.82	0.82	0.85
20,001–40,000				
Person	23.1	62.9	62.9	46.8
Gender disparity	1.30	0.64	0.64	0.87
40,001–62,000				
Person	40.3	44.6	44.6	56.3
Gender disparity	1.56	0.85	0.85	0.85
62,001–86,000				
Person	15.7	68.4	68.4	52.4
Gender disparity	6.54	0.81	0.81	0.37
Above 86,000				
Person	22.6	4.9	4.9	54.8
Gender disparity	–	–	–	0.46
Landholding				
Landless wage earner				
Person	25.2	89.7	89.7	36.9
Gender disparity	1.37	0.91	0.91	1.44
Marginal				
Person	17.4	66.2	66.2	49.3
Gender disparity	1.86	0.63	0.63	0.64
Small				
Person	28.4	54.2	54.2	51.1
Gender disparity	1.85	0.75	0.75	0.76
Medium				
Person	51.0	39.3	39.3	69.5
Gender disparity	5.44	1.34	1.34	1.05
Large				
Person	66.4	33.6	33.6	69.4
Gender disparity	1.68	0.44	0.44	1.38
Landless others				
Person	15.8	77.8	77.8	63.1
Gender disparity	2.96	0.79	0.79	0.81
All land owners				
Person	25.8	59.0	59.0	52.9
Gender disparity	2.48	0.67	0.67	0.78
All land non-owners				
Person	19.5	82.5	82.5	52.8
Gender disparity	1.96	0.83	0.83	0.99
Occupation				
Agriculture				
Person	31.8	57.4	57.4	55.0
Gender disparity	2.01	0.74	0.74	0.88
Salaried+prof.+s.empl.				
Person	19.5	56.6	56.6	43.4
Gender disparity	–	0.56	0.56	0.65
Wage earners				
Person	15.6	71.2	71.2	47.0
Gender disparity	0.55	0.80	0.80	1.07
All others				
Person	16.6	78.4	78.4	58.5
Gender disparity	2.25	0.58	0.58	0.56
Caste				
STs				
Person	28.2	58.9	58.9	100.0
Gender disparity	–	2.34	2.34	1.00

(Contd.)

Population group	Suppply factors	Demand factors	Interest factors	Customs factors
SCs				
Person	28.2	74.3	74.3	49.5
Gender disparity	1.35	0.40	0.40	1.13
Religion				
Hindus				
Person	25.9	64.5	64.5	55.7
Gender disparity	2.82	0.67	0.67	0.87
Muslims				
Person	19.0	61.0	61.0	38.0
Gender disparity	1.00	0.68	0.68	0.51
Household size				
Up to 4				
Person	46.1	69.4	69.4	40.4
Gender disparity	4.06	0.62	0.62	1.50
5–7				
Person	30.6	62.0	62.0	60.8
Gender disparity	2.18	0.62	0.62	0.74
8 and above				
Person	17.0	64.1	64.1	48.2
Gender disparity	2.46	0.70	0.70	0.87
Poverty line				
Lower segment below				
Person	11.4	71.1	71.1	67.7
Gender disparity	1.62	0.81	0.81	0.76
Upper segment below				
Person	21.6	85.5	85.5	45.8
Gender disparity	7.93	0.84	0.84	0.84
Lower segment above				
Person	29.6	56.2	56.2	46.6
Gender disparity	1.29	0.77	0.77	0.70
Upper segment above				
Person	31.6	34.7	34.7	66.2
Gender disparity	2.20	0.21	0.21	1.14
Adult literacy				
None literate				
Person	25.4	79.9	79.9	52.9
Gender disparity	1.07	0.67	0.67	1.09
Female literate				
Person	–	–	–	66.7
Gender disparity	–	–	–	–
Male literate				
Person	21.6	64.9	64.9	58.4
Gender disparity	2.59	0.77	0.77	0.94
Both literate				
Person	30.2	53.9	53.9	42.2
Gender disparity	11.88	0.59	0.59	0.58
Village development				
Low				
Person	30.5	68.1	68.1	50.7
Gender disparity	2.39	0.74	0.74	0.99
Medium				
Person	15.7	57.7	57.7	49.9
Gender disparity	2.75	0.50	0.50	0.67
High				
Person	30.9	64.7	64.7	78.6
Gender disparity	2.06	1.06	1.06	0.89
All groups				
Person	24.6	63.6	63.6	52.9
Gender disparity	2.38	0.66	0.66	0.81

TABLE A11.11
Proportion of Population Completing Middle and Matriculation Levels and Gender Disparity by Population Group in Rural Uttar Pradesh

Population group	Middle level (aged 15+)				Matriculation level (aged 17+)			
	Total	Male	Female	F/M	Total	Male	Female	F/M
Household income								
Up to 20,000	9.9	15.8	3.3	0.21	4.6	7.7	1.1	0.14
20,001–40,000	13.7	19.9	6.0	0.30	6.7	10.5	2.1	0.20
40,001–62,000	15.1	18.9	10.5	0.56	9.9	14.6	4.4	0.30
62,001–86,000	14.0	18.2	8.8	0.48	11.7	19.3	2.8	0.14
Above 86,000	16.1	18.6	13.1	0.70	13.8	18.2	8.6	0.47
Landholding								
Landless wage earner	6.5	11.2	1.0	0.09	1.8	3.2	0.2	0.06
Marginal	11.6	18.1	4.1	0.22	5.8	9.3	1.9	0.20
Small	14.3	19.0	8.6	0.46	8.9	13.7	3.3	0.24
Medium	15.6	18.8	11.7	0.62	10.4	15.8	3.9	0.25
Large	18.1	20.8	14.7	0.71	12.5	17.7	6.2	0.35
Landless others	10.9	17.5	3.1	0.18	5.6	9.5	1.2	0.13
All land owners	13.2	18.6	6.8	0.37	7.6	11.8	2.7	0.23
All land non-owners	8.9	14.6	2.2	0.15	3.9	6.6	0.7	0.11
Occupation								
Agriculture	13.2	18.5	6.9	0.38	7.3	11.4	2.6	0.22
Salaried+prof.+s.empl.	15.2	20.7	8.8	0.42	10.5	15.9	4.1	0.26
Wage earners	7.3	12.4	1.1	0.09	2.0	3.4	0.2	0.07
All others	11.0	17.3	3.7	0.22	5.7	9.5	1.6	0.17
Caste								
STs	7.4	13.0	0.7	0.05	2.2	4.1	0.0	0.00
SCs	8.8	14.8	1.8	0.12	3.8	6.4	0.8	0.13
Religion								
Hindus	12.9	18.5	6.3	0.34	7.4	11.5	2.6	0.22
Muslims	8.0	12.7	2.3	0.18	2.9	5.0	0.6	0.12
Household size								
Up to 4	8.6	13.8	2.6	0.19	4.5	6.8	1.9	0.28
5–7	12.6	18.3	5.7	0.31	6.5	10.4	2.0	0.19
8 and above	13.5	18.8	7.3	0.39	8.1	12.6	2.8	0.22
Poverty line								
Lower segment below	10.5	16.0	4.5	0.28	4.4	7.7	0.9	0.11
Upper segment below	10.0	16.1	3.1	0.20	4.6	7.3	1.5	0.20
Lower segment above	12.9	18.7	6.0	0.32	7.3	11.8	2.0	0.17
Upper segment above	15.0	19.1	9.8	0.51	10.4	14.5	5.2	0.36
Adult literacy								
None literate								
Female literate	7.7	0.0	13.0	0.00	3.3	0.0	6.1	0.00
Male literate	13.9	24.5	0.0	0.00	6.5	11.8	0.0	0.00
Both literate	20.0	21.7	18.2	0.84	13.3	18.5	7.6	0.41
Village development								
Low	11.5	16.9	5.0	0.30	6.6	10.3	2.1	0.21
Medlum	13.3	19.3	6.5	0.34	7.4	11.7	2.6	0.22
High	14.2	18.2	9.5	0.52	6.5	9.6	2.8	0.30
All groups	**12.3**	**17.8**	**5.9**	**0.33**	**6.9**	**10.8**	**2.3**	**0.22**

TABLE A11.12
Percentage Distribution of Students (aged 6–14 years) and Gender Disparity by Type of School by Population Group in Rural Uttar Pradesh

Population group	Govt schools				Govt-aided schools				Private schools			
	Total	Male	Female	F/M	Total	Male	Female	F/M	Total	Male	Female	F/M
Household income												
Up to 20,000	60.5	59.3	62.8	1.06	14.8	15.1	14.2	0.94	24.6	25.5	22.9	0.90
20,001–40,000	54.7	53.5	56.7	1.06	18.3	18.6	17.9	0.96	27.0	27.9	25.5	0.91
40,001–62,000	53.7	50.7	58.7	1.16	17.6	19.6	14.3	0.73	28.5	29.7	26.4	0.89
62,001–86,000	57.0	63.1	48.9	0.78	14.2	7.4	23.2	3.12	28.8	29.5	27.9	0.95
Above 86,000	43.5	47.2	40.3	0.85	18.3	16.7	19.7	1.18	38.1	36.1	40.0	1.11
Landholding												
Landless wage earner	61.5	58.1	70.9	1.22	16.4	17.7	12.6	0.71	22.1	24.1	16.5	0.68
Marginal	56.3	54.5	59.5	1.09	16.3	16.9	15.3	0.91	27.3	28.4	25.2	0.89
Small	57.6	57.7	57.5	1.00	15.3	13.8	17.5	1.27	27.1	28.5	25.0	0.87
Medium	59.2	61.6	55.7	0.90	15.9	15.3	16.8	1.10	24.6	23.0	26.9	1.17
Large	48.1	49.4	46.3	0.94	17.0	17.9	15.7	0.88	34.9	32.7	38.0	1.16
Landless others	51.3	54.0	45.8	0.85	19.9	18.7	22.5	1.20	28.8	27.3	31.7	1.16
All land owners	56.5	56.0	57.4	1.03	16.0	15.9	16.2	1.02	27.4	28.0	26.3	0.94
All land non-owners	55.0	55.6	53.8	0.97	18.6	18.3	19.3	1.05	26.3	26.1	26.9	1.03
Occupation												
Agriculture	59.3	58.8	60.3	1.03	15.3	15.5	14.9	0.96	25.3	25.6	24.8	0.97
Salaried+prof.+s.empl.	50.9	51.4	50.1	0.98	18.6	18.1	19.3	1.07	30.4	30.6	30.3	0.99
Wage earners	57.3	54.9	63.4	1.16	15.6	15.6	15.6	1.00	27.1	29.5	21.0	0.71
All others	53.9	53.9	53.9	1.00	17.8	17.4	18.3	1.05	28.3	28.6	27.7	0.97
Caste												
STs	75.3	72.7	81.8	1.12	2.6	3.6	0.0	0.00	22.2	23.7	18.2	0.77
SCs	64.9	63.5	68.1	1.07	17.5	17.9	16.6	0.93	17.4	18.3	15.3	0.84
Religion												
Hindus	58.5	57.7	59.8	1.04	16.5	16.5	16.6	1.01	24.9	25.8	23.5	0.91
Muslims	36.4	39.6	30.5	0.77	16.4	15.9	17.3	1.08	47.1	44.3	52.2	1.18
Household size												
Up to 4	57.5	56.3	60.4	1.07	15.9	16.6	14.5	0.88	26.1	26.5	25.1	0.95
5–7	58.9	58.0	60.7	1.05	15.9	16.4	14.8	0.90	25.2	25.6	24.5	0.96
8 and above	53.7	53.6	53.8	1.00	17.1	16.4	18.2	1.11	29.1	30.0	27.9	0.93
Poverty line												
Lower segment below	60.9	59.9	62.5	1.04	13.7	14.0	13.3	0.96	25.2	25.9	24.2	0.93
Upper segment below	56.4	56.2	57.0	1.02	16.3	15.8	17.2	1.09	27.3	28.0	25.8	0.92
Lower segment above	56.5	56.0	57.4	1.02	17.8	17.3	18.8	1.09	25.6	26.7	23.6	0.88
Upper segment above	51.1	51.1	51.2	1.00	16.4	17.7	14.8	0.84	32.4	31.3	34.0	1.09
Adult literacy												
None literate	58.6	57.8	61.1	1.06	13.6	14.9	9.1	0.61	27.6	26.9	29.8	1.11
Female literate	67.7	57.7	76.7	1.33	7.5	5.5	9.3	1.69	24.9	36.8	14.0	0.38
Male literate	57.3	56.2	59.4	1.06	16.7	17.1	15.9	0.93	26.0	26.6	24.7	0.93
Both literate	53.3	54.1	52.4	0.97	17.8	16.5	19.4	1.18	28.7	29.4	28.0	0.95
Village development												
Low	58.8	59.1	58.3	0.99	12.8	13.1	12.3	0.94	28.2	27.7	29.2	1.06
Medium	56.5	54.4	60.1	1.10	17.6	18.2	16.5	0.90	25.9	27.3	23.5	0.86
High	38.9	40.3	36.9	0.92	34.7	30.7	40.1	1.31	26.4	29.0	23.0	0.79
All groups	**56.3**	**55.9**	**56.9**	**1.02**	**16.5**	**16.4**	**16.6**	**1.01**	**27.2**	**27.6**	**26.4**	**0.96**

TABLE A11.13

Percentage Distribution of Household Annual Expenditure on Schooling (6–14 years) in Government Schools and Gender Disparity by Population Group in Rural Uttar Pradesh

(Annual expenditure in rupees)

Population group	Govt schools						
	Fees	Books	Coaching	Transpt	BL	Total	#St/Rhhd
Household income							
Up to 20,000							
Person	21.0	76.3	2.0	0.7	0.0	430	1.6
Gender disparity	1.14	1.01	0.19	0.00	0.00	0.49	0.52
20,001–40,000							
Person	17.0	78.1	3.8	1.0	0.1	532	1.7
Gender disparity	1.00	1.06	0.44	0.05	0.00	0.65	0.62
40,001–62,000							
Person	17.7	81.2	1.1	0.0	0.0	518	2.0
Gender disparity	1.02	1.02	0.00	0.00	0.00	0.76	0.70
62,001–86,000							
Person	22.0	77.7	0.3	0.0	0.0	616	2.1
Gender disparity	1.09	0.97	0.00	0.00	0.00	0.70	0.58
Above 86,000							
Person	24.7	69.9	5.1	0.2	0.0	659	2.1
Gender disparity	1.03	1.04	0.43	0.00	0.00	0.85	0.96
Landholding							
Landless wage earner							
Person	20.4	78.7	0.9	0.0	0.0	351	1.5
Gender disparity	1.13	0.96	2.42	0.00	0.00	0.49	0.45
Marginal							
Person	21.0	77.0	1.8	0.2	0.0	485	1.7
Gender disparity	0.98	1.03	0.44	0.18	0.00	0.66	0.61
Small							
Person	18.6	78.9	1.3	1.2	0.0	513	1.8
Gender disparity	1.20	0.99	0.40	0.00	0.00	0.61	0.68
Medium							
Person	18.2	77.2	2.4	1.8	0.4	584	2.1
Gender disparity	0.91	1.08	0.87	0.00	0.00	0.65	0.63
Large							
Person	18.1	74.7	6.5	0.7	0.0	741	2.0
Gender disparity	1.49	0.96	0.47	0.82	0.00	0.61	0.68
Landless others							
Person	17.7	74.5	7.7	0.1	0.0	416	1.5
Gender disparity	1.12	1.12	0.00	0.00	0.00	0.38	0.41
All land owners							
Person	19.8	77.4	2.1	0.7	0.1	518	1.8
Gender disparity	1.05	1.02	0.49	0.06	0.00	0.64	0.64
All land non-owners							
Person	18.7	76.0	5.2	0.1	0.0	389	1.5
Gender disparity	1.13	1.06	0.09	0.00	0.00	0.42	0.43
Occupation							
Agriculture							
Person	19.0	77.2	2.5	1.2	0.1	493	1.8
Gender disparity	1.19	1.00	0.51	0.08	0.00	0.53	0.60
Salaried+prof.+s.empl.							
Person	19.1	76.9	3.9	0.0	0.0	615	1.9
Gender disparity	0.84	1.12	0.17	0.00	0.00	0.83	0.69
Wage earners							
Person	22.6	76.9	0.5	0.0	0.0	384	1.4
Gender disparity	1.12	0.96	2.65	0.00	0.00	0.45	0.46
All others							
Person	20.3	77.7	1.9	0.1	0.0	433	1.7
Gender disparity	1.07	1.01	0.18	0.00	0.00	0.68	0.58
Caste							
STs							
Person	15.6	83.4	1.0	0.0	0.0	623	2.5

(Contd.)

TABLE A11.13 (contd.)

Population group	Govt schools						
	Fees	Books	Coaching	Transpt	BL	Total	#St/Rhhd
Gender disparity	1.10	1.00	0.00	0.00	0.00	0.43	0.44
SCs							
Person	19.5	77.8	1.8	0.8	0.0	385	1.6
Gender disparity	1.38	0.93	0.92	0.00	0.00	0.45	0.46
Religion							
Hindus							
Person	19.7	77.0	2.6	0.6	0.1	493	1.7
Gender disparity	1.07	1.02	0.36	0.07	0.00	0.61	0.61
Muslims							
Person	17.5	79.5	2.0	1.1	0.0	496	1.6
Gender disparity	0.90	1.07	0.26	0.00	0.00	0.49	0.43
Household size							
Up to 4							
Person	17.1	80.2	0.6	2.1	0.0	408	1.3
Gender disparity	0.91	1.08	0.00	0.00	0.00	0.71	0.46
5–7							
Person	18.5	77.9	3.0	0.6	0.0	465	1.6
Gender disparity	1.07	1.01	0.55	0.07	0.00	0.51	0.52
8 and above							
Person	21.2	75.9	2.4	0.4	0.1	548	2.1
Gender disparity	1.07	1.03	0.21	0.11	0.00	0.71	0.71
Poverty line							
Lower segment below							
Person	22.6	75.0	2.2	0.2	0.0	425	1.7
Gender disparity	1.13	1.01	0.13	0.00	0.00	0.62	0.60
Upper segment below							
Person	18.7	79.3	1.2	0.8	0.0	494	1.7
Gender disparity	1.18	0.98	0.53	0.00	0.00	0.46	0.48
Lower segment above							
Person	19.5	77.0	2.7	0.7	0.1	480	1.8
Gender disparity	1.04	1.03	0.41	0.07	0.00	0.58	0.60
Upper segment above							
Person	18.2	77.2	3.9	0.7	0.0	595	1.7
Gender disparity	0.98	1.07	0.30	0.12	0.00	0.79	0.75
Adult literacy							
None literate							
Person	18.4	79.8	1.8	0.0	0.0	373	1.5
Gender disparity	1.13	0.98	0.70	0.00	0.00	0.28	0.31
Female literate							
Person	19.0	81.0	0.0	0.0	0.0	747	1.6
Gender disparity	0.53	1.19	0.00	0.00	0.00	2.35	1.46
Male literate							
Person	20.1	75.5	3.4	0.9	0.1	457	1.7
Gender disparity	1.08	1.05	0.18	0.07	0.00	0.53	0.57
Both literate							
Person	19.5	77.8	2.0	0.6	0.0	607	1.9
Gender disparity	1.08	1.00	0.72	0.05	0.00	0.80	0.81
Village development							
Low							
Person	18.0	79.2	2.2	0.6	0.1	475	1.7
Gender disparity	1.07	1.00	0.75	0.16	0.00	0.52	0.55
Medium							
Person	23.0	73.4	2.9	0.6	0.0	487	1.8
Gender disparity	1.06	1.06	0.08	0.00	0.00	0.73	0.65
High							
Person	15.0	80.6	3.4	1.0	0.0	691	1.7
Gender disparity	0.82	1.10	0.38	0.00	0.00	0.66	0.68
All groups							
Person	19.6	77.2	2.6	0.6	0.0	492	1.7
Gender disparity	1.07	1.03	0.35	0.07	0.00	0.60	0.60

Notes: BL: Boarding and lodging; #St/Rhhd: Number of students per rural household.

TABLE A11.14

Percentage Distribution of Household Annual Expenditure on Schooling (6–14 years) in Private Schools and Gender Disparity by Population Group in Rural Uttar Pradesh

Population group	Private schools						
	Fees	Books	Coaching	Transpt	BL	Total	#St/Rhhd
Household income							
Up to 20,000							
Person	34.9	58.6	4.1	0.2	2.2	589	1.4
Gender disparity	0.93	0.88	2.33	0.16	49.34	0.45	0.44
20,001–40,000							
Person	30.0	57.6	11.2	0.8	0.3	790	1.7
Gender disparity	1.02	1.17	0.30	2.19	0.56	0.48	0.54
40,001–62,000							
Person	30.8	50.9	8.8	4.4	5.2	1,094	1.6
Gender disparity	0.96	0.83	0.47	0.98	36.14	0.41	0.54
62,001–86,000							
Person	34.0	60.9	3.1	2.0	0.0	1,153	1.9
Gender disparity	0.85	1.00	2.34	3.08	0.00	0.43	0.71
Above 86,000							
Person	28.0	52.3	10.9	5.4	3.5	1,726	2.0
Gender disparity	1.22	1.36	0.30	0.77	0.00	1.16	1.25
Landholding							
Landless wage earner							
Person	37.9	60.7	1.4	0.0	0.0	542	1.3
Gender disparity	1.04	1.00	0.00	0.00	0.00	0.27	0.25
Marginal							
Person	30.4	59.8	7.5	0.3	1.9	709	1.6
Gender disparity	1.09	0.90	0.82	2.82	13.55	0.47	0.50
Small							
Person	33.3	53.9	8.3	1.7	2.7	944	1.6
Gender disparity	1.04	1.14	0.54	0.85	0.00	0.43	0.59
Medium							
Person	29.7	46.6	11.9	5.5	6.3	1,294	1.7
Gender disparity	0.77	1.13	0.31	0.68	0.00	0.69	0.82
Large							
Person	32.7	60.2	4.0	3.1	0.0	1,583	2.2
Gender disparity	0.88	1.04	0.84	2.02	0.00	1.03	0.85
Landless others							
Person	30.9	55.2	8.9	5.0	0.0	707	1.5
Gender disparity	0.91	1.12	0.56	1.32	0.00	0.60	0.56
All land owners							
Person	31.4	55.8	8.2	1.9	2.7	900	1.7
Gender disparity	0.98	1.01	0.57	1.18	3.86	0.54	0.58
All land non-owners							
Person	32.9	56.7	6.8	3.6	0.0	651	1.4
Gender disparity	0.91	1.07	0.63	1.61	0.00	0.49	0.45
Occupation							
Agriculture							
Person	33.3	56.8	8.8	1.0	0.2	859	1.6
Gender disparity	1.02	1.13	0.20	4.93	0.62	0.48	0.57
Salaried+prof.+s.empl.							
Person	28.0	52.2	11.0	5.6	3.1	1,071	1.8
Gender disparity	0.99	0.87	1.16	0.69	0.00	0.71	0.70
Wage earners							
Person	38.0	60.5	0.7	0.0	0.7	528	1.4
Gender disparity	0.91	1.05	0.00	0.00	3.78	0.26	0.28
All others							
Person	30.2	58.5	3.0	0.2	8.1	765	1.6
Gender disparity	0.97	1.04	0.00	0.00	1.56	0.55	0.56
Caste							
STs							
Person	35.4	64.6	0.0	0.0	0.0	460	1.3
Gender disparity	1.32	0.85	0.00	0.00	0.00	0.54	0.30

(Contd.)

TABLE A11.14 (contd.)

Population group	Private schools						
	Fees	Books	Coaching	Transpt	BL	Total	#St/Rhhd
SCs							
Person	34.0	62.9	2.0	1.1	0.0	588	1.4
Gender disparity	1.16	0.86	1.45	14.01	0.00	0.39	0.36
Religion							
Hindus							
Person	31.4	55.2	8.6	2.3	2.5	926	1.6
Gender disparity	0.97	1.00	0.61	1.45	4.53	0.51	0.54
Muslims							
Person	33.0	62.5	2.5	1.2	0.7	501	1.6
Gender disparity	1.02	1.08	0.33	0.04	0.00	0.72	0.66
Household size							
Up to 4							
Person	30.6	60.7	5.1	1.4	2.2	535	1.2
Gender disparity	1.24	0.87	0.41	21.57	0.93	0.32	0.41
5–7							
Person	31.7	56.7	9.6	0.6	1.4	717	1.4
Gender disparity	1.08	1.01	0.29	1.46	0.00	0.39	0.48
8 and above							
Person	31.6	55.0	7.1	3.4	3.0	1,061	1.9
Gender disparity	0.89	1.04	0.88	0.92	2.16	0.68	0.66
Poverty line							
Lower segment below							
Person	32.5	60.5	7.0	0.0	0.0	598	1.6
Gender disparity	0.94	0.90	3.13	0.00	0.00	0.60	0.54
Upper segment below							
Person	36.8	60.5	1.8	0.3	0.7	587	1.6
Gender disparity	0.91	1.09	0.47	0.15	0.50	0.54	0.43
Lower segment above							
Person	30.1	53.5	10.1	2.5	3.8	883	1.6
Gender disparity	0.91	0.92	0.48	1.27	0.95	0.42	0.51
Upper segment above							
Person	31.0	55.5	8.1	3.4	2.0	1,219	1.6
Gender disparity	1.07	1.13	0.39	1.29	0.00	0.67	0.81
Adult literacy							
None literate							
Person	38.2	59.3	1.3	0.1	1.1	532	1.4
Gender disparity	1.10	0.97	0.00	0.00	1.00	0.28	0.33
Female literate							
Person	43.5	56.5	0.0	0.0	0.0	504	1.2
Gender disparity	1.24	0.84	0.00	0.00	0.00	0.66	0.42
Male literate							
Person	32.7	55.9	8.2	1.7	1.5	711	1.6
Gender disparity	1.03	1.02	0.29	1.45	0.00	0.45	0.50
Both literate							
Person	29.0	55.3	9.4	3.1	3.3	1,219	1.7
Gender disparity	0.95	1.04	0.71	1.01	2.19	0.68	0.79
Village development							
Low							
Person	30.9	54.0	10.3	1.1	3.6	757	1.7
Gender disparity	0.95	0.97	0.52	2.62	16.44	0.59	0.59
Medium							
Person	32.2	56.0	6.6	3.8	1.4	991	1.6
Gender disparity	1.00	1.06	0.73	1.14	0.00	0.46	0.51
High							
Person	31.8	65.9	1.8	0.4	0.0	855	1.5
Gender disparity	1.01	1.05	0.00	0.00	0.00	0.60	0.59
All groups							
Person	31.6	56.0	8.0	2.2	2.3	852	1.6
Gender disparity	0.97	1.02	0.58	1.26	3.92	0.53	0.56

Notes: BL: Boarding and lodging; #St/Rhhd: Number of students per rural household.

TABLE A11.15

Short-duration and Major Morbidity Prevalence Rates and Gender Disparity by Population Group in Rural Uttar Pradesh

Population group	Short-duration morbidity ('000 popn) Diarr.	Cold and Cough	Fever	Total	Major morbidity per lakh popn
Household income					
Up to 20,000					
Person	31	50	28	99	3317
Gender disparity	0.92	0.82	1.15	0.97	1.18
20,001–40,000					
Person	37	55	26	103	3774
Gender disparity	0.98	0.89	1.34	1.08	1.26
40,001–62,000					
Person	25	51	22	90	3835
Gender disparity	0.80	0.77	1.11	0.90	1.09
62,001–86,000					
Person	30	45	25	90	3156
Gender disparity	0.92	0.77	2.65	1.17	1.27
Above 86,000					
Person	20	37	19	72	3573
Gender disparity	1.25	1.00	3.00	1.43	1.42
Landholding					
Landless wage earner					
Person	29	39	23	88	3060
Gender disparity	1.22	0.84	1.42	1.14	0.82
Marginal					
Person	32	52	27	99	3400
Gender disparity	0.96	0.86	1.24	1.00	1.37
Small					
Person	30	53	24	95	3559
Gender disparity	0.87	0.76	1.26	0.96	1.08
Medium					
Person	30	46	23	88	3685
Gender disparity	1.03	0.81	1.45	1.09	1.36
Large					
Person	17	40	31	82	4354
Gender disparity	0.75	0.89	2.70	1.36	1.09
Landless others					
Person	35	60	30	112	3862
Gender disparity	0.78	0.88	1.06	0.99	1.18
All land owners					
Person	31	51	26	96	3529
Gender disparity	0.94	0.83	1.33	1.02	1.27
All land non-owners					
Person	32	51	27	101	3501
Gender disparity	0.94	0.87	1.19	1.05	1.03
Occupation					
Agriculture					
Person	32	53	25	97	3437
Gender disparity	0.84	0.79	1.33	0.98	1.24
Salaried+prof.+s.empl.					
Person	31	53	30	104	3347
Gender disparity	1.18	0.84	1.30	1.10	1.22
Wage earners					
Person	30	43	24	90	3808
Gender disparity	1.14	0.90	1.44	1.10	1.07
All others					
Person	28	51	26	96	3698
Gender disparity	0.80	0.96	1.11	1.00	1.28

(Contd.)

Population group	Short-duration morbidity ('000 popn) Diarr.	Cold and Cough	Fever	Total	Major morbidity per lakh popn
Caste					
STs					
Person	32	28	50	109	4290
Gender disparity	1.16	0.51	0.68	0.78	1.65
SCs					
Person	41	53	28	107	3199
Gender disparity	0.77	0.74	1.30	0.92	1.36
Religion					
Hindus					
Person	30	51	26	96	3415
Gender disparity	0.93	0.82	1.29	1.00	1.21
Muslims					
Person	36	53	24	101	4297
Gender disparity	1.01	1.02	1.35	1.15	1.22
Household size					
Up to 4					
Person	36	54	26	102	3494
Gender disparity	0.76	0.54	1.99	0.93	1.02
5–7					
Person	34	53	29	103	3597
Gender disparity	0.92	0.88	1.08	0.98	1.22
8 and above					
Person	27	47	24	90	3460
Gender disparity	1.03	0.92	1.42	1.10	1.26
Poverty line					
Lower segment below					
Person	25	40	27	84	3268
Gender disparity	1.41	0.90	1.33	1.17	0.98
Upper segment below					
Person	35	57	27	105	3763
Gender disparity	0.88	0.84	1.03	0.94	1.32
Lower segment above					
Person	32	52	28	100	3410
Gender disparity	0.88	0.91	1.42	1.08	1.25
Upper segment above					
Person	31	53	22	95	3761
Gender disparity	0.83	0.66	1.38	0.89	1.26
Adult literacy					
None literate					
Person	37	58	23	101	3692
Gender disparity	0.87	0.73	1.26	0.95	1.12
Female literate					
Person	52	67	27	137	2321
Gender disparity	1.13	0.82	1.53	1.05	1.46
Male literate					
Person	32	52	26	98	3432
Gender disparity	0.99	0.93	1.16	1.03	1.35
Both literate					
Person	24	42	29	90	3563
Gender disparity	0.91	0.82	1.55	1.09	1.10
Village development					
Low					
Person	31	51	23	94	3619
Gender disparity	0.85	0.89	1.48	1.06	1.28

(Contd.)

TABLE A11.15 (contd.)

Population group	Short-duration morbidity ('000 popn)				Major morbidity per lakh popn
	Diarr.	Cold and Cough	Fever	Total	
Medium					
Person	31	50	28	97	3407
Gender disparity	1.01	0.76	1.14	0.95	1.10
High					
Person	29	51	40	118	3338
Gender disparity	1.45	0.88	1.13	1.08	1.28
Age groups (years)					
0–4					
Person	97	92	43	215	483
Gender disparity	1.10	0.69	1.12	0.94	0.85
5–14					
Person	18	46	36	97	774
Gender disparity	1.31	1.07	1.15	1.10	0.81
15–34					
Person	15	27	17	53	2489
Gender disparity	0.91	0.84	1.41	1.11	2.39
35–59					
Person	28	52	16	78	6733
Gender disparity	0.50	0.72	1.83	0.92	1.26
60 and above					
Person	45	89	25	132	14,009
Gender disparity	0.73	0.91	1.51	0.97	0.82
All groups					
Person	31	51	26	97	3523
Gender disparity	0.94	0.84	1.30	1.02	1.21

TABLE A11.16

Short-duration Morbidity Prevalence Rates and Gender Disparity by Age and Population Group in Rural Uttar Pradesh

Population group	Short-duration morbidity ('000 popn) Age groups (completed years)					
	0–4	5–14	15–34	35–59	60+	All
Household income						
Up to 20,000						
Person	216	96	57	76	145	99
Gender disparity	0.86	1.07	1.06	0.92	0.90	0.97
20,001–40,000						
Person	227	111	50	81	140	103
Gender disparity	1.02	1.24	1.16	0.83	0.96	1.08
40,001–62,000						
Person	194	90	52	76	107	90
Gender disparity	1.22	0.82	0.75	0.87	0.62	0.90
62,001–86,000						
Person	225	70	45	101	85	90
Gender disparity	0.59	1.37	1.73	1.07	5.12	1.17
Above 86,000						
Person	182	66	40	63	93	72
Gender disparity	1.08	0.99	2.67	1.55	1.78	1.43
Landholding						
Landless wage earner						
Person	199	79	53	60	155	88
Gender disparity	1.03	1.01	1.91	0.97	0.88	1.14
Marginal						
Person	219	100	46	87	134	99
Gender disparity	0.98	1.09	1.04	0.82	1.04	1.00
Small						
Person	215	91	60	70	134	95
Gender disparity	1.03	1.11	0.74	0.86	0.91	0.96
Medium						
Person	223	85	47	71	88	88
Gender disparity	0.78	1.88	1.14	1.14	0.33	1.09
Large						
Person	168	85	44	78	104	82
Gender disparity	0.69	0.54	4.21	2.29	4.31	1.36
Landless others						
Person	224	124	73	77	160	112
Gender disparity	0.79	1.00	1.20	0.97	0.88	0.99
All land owners						
Person	216	95	50	81	126	96
Gender disparity	0.95	1.13	1.01	0.91	0.99	1.02
All land non-owners						
Person	212	104	64	69	158	101
Gender disparity	0.90	1.00	1.44	0.98	0.88	1.05
Occupation						
Agriculture						
Person	221	93	51	81	138	97
Gender disparity	0.93	1.14	0.88	0.84	0.96	0.98
Salaried+prof.+s.empl.						
Person	228	114	54	77	141	104
Gender disparity	1.02	1.00	1.22	1.23	1.00	1.10
Wage earners						
Person	196	86	50	75	119	90
Gender disparity	0.97	1.17	1.78	0.79	0.86	1.10
All others						
Person	203	99	60	76	114	96
Gender disparity	0.82	1.07	1.16	0.98	1.09	1.00
Caste						
STs						
Person	292	90	77	84	78	109
Gender disparity	0.93	0.36	0.62	0.83	3.58	0.78
SCs						
Person	227	109	56	88	150	107
Gender disparity	0.89	1.03	1.09	0.70	0.78	0.92
Religion						
Hindus						
Person	213	95	53	79	133	96
Gender disparity	0.90	1.08	1.10	0.92	0.98	1.00
Muslims						
Person	226	109	50	72	125	101
Gender disparity	1.19	1.25	1.25	0.83	0.81	1.15
Household size						
Up to 4						
Person	229	98	54	85	143	102
Gender disparity	0.87	1.13	1.37	0.72	0.40	0.93

(Contd.)

TABLE A11.16 (contd.)

Population group	Short-duration morbidity ('000 popn) Age groups (completed years)					
	0–4	5–14	15–34	35–59	60+	All
5–7						
Person	215	109	60	79	137	103
Gender disparity	0.98	1.07	0.84	0.91	0.97	0.98
8 and above						
Person	211	85	45	76	124	90
Gender disparity	0.92	1.12	1.46	1.00	1.20	1.10
Poverty line						
Lower segment below						
Person	194	77	47	60	134	84
Gender disparity	0.84	1.61	1.46	0.96	1.11	1.17
Upper segment below						
Person	221	99	61	96	124	105
Gender disparity	0.90	0.97	0.94	0.92	0.91	0.94
Lower segment above						
Person	225	109	53	70	135	100
Gender disparity	1.09	1.18	1.16	0.85	0.92	1.08
Upper segment above						
Person	210	89	47	93	131	95
Gender disparity	0.77	0.78	0.94	1.02	0.99	0.89
Adult literacy						
None literate						
Person	226	96	52	85	152	101
Gender disparity	0.96	0.93	1.21	0.84	0.76	0.95

(Contd.)

TABLE A11.16 (contd.)

Population group	Short-duration morbidity ('000 popn) Age groups (completed years)					
	0–4	5–14	15–34	35–59	60+	All
Female literate						
Person	297	139	36	157	255	137
Gender disparity	1.83	1.56	0.35	0.64	0.68	1.05
Male literate						
Person	213	101	56	77	124	98
Gender disparity	1.02	1.13	0.94	0.86	0.99	1.03
Both literate						
Person	204	90	49	70	124	90
Gender disparity	0.76	1.22	1.42	1.17	1.22	1.09
Village development						
Low						
Person	206	90	51	84	118	94
Gender disparity	0.91	1.10	1.32	1.00	0.96	1.06
Medium						
Person	208	100	51	73	154	97
Gender disparity	0.95	1.12	0.81	0.74	0.98	0.95
High						
Person	313	132	72	56	119	118
Gender disparity	1.05	1.05	1.17	1.17	0.93	1.08
All groups						
Person	215	97	53	78	132	97
Gender disparity	0.94	1.10	1.11	0.92	0.97	1.02

TABLE A11.17

Major Morbidity Prevalence Rates and Gender Disparity by Population Group in Rural Uttar Pradesh

Population group	Major morbidity (per lakh popn) Age groups (completed years)					
	0–4	5–14	15–34	35–59	60+	All
Household income						
Up to 20,000						
Person	279	836	2004	6639	14,007	3317
Gender disparity	0.12	0.94	2.48	1.40	0.71	1.18
20,001–40,000						
Person	754	633	2920	7421	14,026	3774
Gender disparity	1.98	0.80	1.88	1.26	0.93	1.26
40,001-62,000						
Person	754	944	2946	6914	14,741	3835
Gender disparity	0.40	0.55	2.19	1.12	0.91	1.09
62,001–86,000						
Person	562	559	2044	5292	13,633	3156
Gender disparity	0.40	–	9.30	0.66	1.23	1.27
Above 86,000						
Person	0	848	3679	4901	12,828	3573
Gender disparity	0.40	1.77	3.69	1.26	0.63	1.42
Landholding						
Landless wage earner						
Person	441	714	970	7701	15,041	3060
Gender disparity	0.40	0.38	0.78	1.13	0.39	0.82
Marginal						
Person	272	648	2663	6390	13,538	3400
Gender disparity	1.01	0.73	2.74	1.59	0.81	1.37
Small						
Person	358	661	2843	6210	14,736	3559
Gender disparity	1.65	0.78	1.70	1.12	0.75	1.08

(Contd.)

Population group	Major morbidity (per lakh popn) Age groups (completed years)					
	0–4	5–14	15–34	35–59	60+	All
Medium						
Person	1847	1102	1668	7682	11.807	3685
Gender disparity	0.20	1.77	5.71	1.29	0.97	1.36
Large						
Person	0	1318	3473	7971	13,461	4354
Gender disparity	0.20	2.35	1.07	1.20	0.98	1.09
Landless others						
Person	596	1015	2789	6880	16,340	3862
Gender disparity	1.37	0.46	4.19	0.78	1.09	1.18
All land owners						
Person	472	745	2634	6594	13,600	3529
Gender disparity	0.57	0.98	2.33	1.39	0.82	1.27
All land non-owners						
Person	521	879	1963	7239	15,818	3501
Gender disparity	3.22	0.43	2.72	0.93	0.78	1.03
Occupation						
Agriculture						
Person	601	841	2369	6197	13,542	3437
Gender disparity	0.90	1.20	1.91	1.47	0.83	1.24
Salaried+prof.+s.empl.						
Person	484	631	2798	6866	10,535	3347
Gender disparity	0.77	0.59	3.89	1.03	0.59	1.22
Wage earners						
Person	279	583	2239	8938	15,005	3808
Gender disparity	0.77	0.84	2.55	0.97	0.74	1.07

(Contd.)

TABLE A11.17 (contd.)

Population group	Major morbidity (per lakh popn) Age groups (completed years)					
	0–4	5–14	15–34	35–59	60+	All
All others						
Person	363	917	2708	6097	18,389	3698
Gender disparity	–	0.32	2.36	1.51	1.03	1.28
Caste						
STs						
Person	0	0	2902	6983	22,534	4290
Gender disparity	–	0.32	4.10	1.33	1.90	1.65
SCs						
Person	140	283	2228	7071	13,233	3199
Gender disparity	–	1.77	2.48	1.41	0.85	1.36
Religion						
Hindus						
Person	443	768	2517	6484	13,035	3415
Gender disparity	0.33	0.15	1.13	0.76	0.68	0.70
Muslims						
Person	745	824	2351	8652	21,092	4297
Gender disparity	2.58	0.26	2.64	1.42	0.93	1.22
Household size						
Up to 4						
Person	0	1116	2027	7102	16,487	3494
Gender disparity	2.58	0.57	1.84	1.29	0.69	1.02
5–7						
Person	546	762	2399	7017	14,561	3597
Gender disparity	0.22	0.87	2.74	1.23	0.86	1.22
8 and above						
Person	562	681	2707	6373	12,872	3460
Gender disparity	2.49	0.89	2.26	1.29	0.81	1.26
Poverty line						
Lower segment below						
Person	397	805	2061	6300	13,624	3268
Gender disparity	–	0.94	1.18	1.32	0.71	0.98
Upper segment below						
Person	653	1093	2520	7085	15,025	3763
Gender disparity	0.76	1.08	2.81	1.23	1.01	1.32
Lower segment above						
Person	394	693	2483	6725	12,864	3410
Gender disparity	5.10	0.40	2.80	1.29	0.81	1.25
Upper segment above						
Person	573	529	2930	6784	15,722	3761
Gender disparity	0.38	2.08	2.76	1.21	0.73	1.26
Adult literacy						
None literate						
Person	320	787	1872	8394	15,121	3692
Gender disparity	0.17	0.61	1.81	1.34	0.80	1.12
Female literate						
Person	0	928	3518	1679	9,769	2321
Gender disparity	0.17	–	1.28	1.34	0.99	1.46
Male literate						
Person	363	728	2703	6429	13,160	3432
Gender disparity	5.10	0.92	2.33	1.41	0.83	1.35
Both literate						
Person	857	835	2683	5934	14,526	3563
Gender disparity	0.45	0.90	3.17	0.94	0.82	1.10
Village development						
Low						
Person	271	930	2822	6755	13,908	3619
Gender disparity	0.58	1.09	2.27	1.28	0.90	1.28
Medium						
Person	726	608	2343	6308	14,069	3407
Gender disparity	0.82	0.45	2.46	1.13	0.78	1.10
High						
Person	973	366	720	8528	14,477	3338
Gender disparity	1.98	–	21.39	1.71	0.51	1.28
All groups						
Person	483	774	2489	6733	14,009	3523
Gender disparity	0.85	0.81	2.39	1.26	0.82	1.21

(Contd.)

TABLE A11.18

Per Person Household Expenditure on Treatment of Illness and Gender Disparity by Population Group in Rural Uttar Pradesh

Population group	Cost of short illness		Cost of long illness			
	Fees and medicines	Proportion of total cost	Fees and medicines	Proportion of total cost	Per sick person	Per reporting
Household income						
Up to 20,000						
Person	118	0.81	59	0.64	1785	1937
Gender disparity	0.86	1.11	1.12	1.18	0.95	0.93
20,001–40,000						
Person	123	0.75	65	0.72	1731	1832
Gender disparity	1.15	1.20	0.98	0.97	0.78	0.78
40,001–62,000						
Person	122	0.76	63	0.73	1659	1848
Gender disparity	0.65	1.15	1.05	0.93	0.96	0.92
62,001–86,000						
Person	272	1.14	57	0.79	1811	2090
Gender disparity	1.52	1.00	1.20	1.10	0.95	0.99
Above 86,000						
Person	94	0.78	79	0.68	2214	2253
Gender disparity	2.69	0.93	1.44	1.00	1.02	1.05
Landholding						
Landless wage earner						
Person	103	0.79	57	0.69	1891	2013
Gender disparity	0.95	1.09	0.78	1.45	0.95	0.88
Marginal						
Person	134	0.81	62	0.72	1839	1965
Gender disparity	0.79	1.16	1.26	1.04	0.92	0.89
Small						
Person	98	0.76	62	0.66	1760	1887
Gender disparity	1.12	1.11	0.94	1.32	0.87	0.90

(Contd.)

Table A11.18 (contd.)

Population group	Cost of short illness		Cost of long illness			
	Fees and medicines	Proportion of total cost	Fees and medicines	Proportion of total cost	Per sick person	Per reporting
Medium						
Person	133	1.01	66	0.71	1797	2104
Gender disparity	2.24	1.29	1.76	1.03	1.30	1.27
Large						
Person	115	0.77	74	0.64	1704	1727
Gender disparity	2.92	1.03	0.74	0.70	0.68	0.66
Landless others						
Person	172	0.80	58	0.60	1527	1680
Gender disparity	0.85	0.98	0.80	0.74	0.67	0.70
All land owners						
Person	124	0.82	63	0.70	1804	1945
Gender disparity	1.04	1.17	1.18	1.08	0.93	0.92
All land non-owners						
Person	141	0.80	58	0.63	1670	1814
Gender disparity	0.89	1.02	0.79	0.96	0.77	0.76
Occupation						
Agriculture						
Person	116	0.81	58	0.67	1688	1831
Gender disparity	1.41	1.28	1.12	1.17	0.90	0.93
Salaried+prof.+s.empl.						
Person	151	0.86	64	0.64	1937	2137
Gender disparity	0.92	0.94	1.10	0.77	0.91	0.86
Wage earners						
Person	118	0.79	65	0.75	1719	1858
Gender disparity	0.67	1.07	1.23	1.31	1.15	1.04
All others						
Person	142	0.78	69	0.73	1892	1977
Gender disparity	0.69	1.09	0.93	1.02	0.72	0.74
Caste						
STs						
Person	107	0.80	57	0.61	1343	1390
Gender disparity	0.59	0.81	0.81	1.35	0.49	0.52
SCs						
Person	135	0.82	45	0.68	1421	1549
Gender disparity	0.67	1.08	1.42	1.24	1.04	1.04
Religion						
Hindus						
Person	127	0.81	60	0.69	1758	1904
Gender disparity	1.03	1.13	1.12	1.01	0.92	0.91
Muslims						
Person	131	0.80	81	0.67	1896	1991
Gender disparity	0.85	1.13	0.98	1.36	0.81	0.79
Household size						
Up to 4						
Person	122	0.86	48	0.72	1391	1538
Gender disparity	0.84	1.03	0.76	0.99	0.74	0.74
5–7						
Person	117	0.77	56	0.65	1562	1713
Gender disparity	1.14	1.15	1.02	1.07	0.83	0.85
8 and above						
Person	139	0.84	72	0.71	2098	2216
Gender disparity	0.95	1.16	1.23	1.07	0.98	0.94

(Contd.)

Table A11.18 (contd.)

Population group	Cost of short illness		Cost of long illness			
	Fees and medicines	Proportion of total cost	Fees and medicines	Proportion of total cost	Per sick person	Per reporting
Poverty line						
Lower segment below						
Person	80	0.87	55	0.62	1703	1855
Gender disparity	1.13	1.29	0.96	1.41	0.98	0.99
Upper segment below						
Person	162	0.77	78	0.66	2074	2193
Gender disparity	0.63	1.07	1.36	0.96	1.04	0.98
Lower segment above						
Person	132	0.81	59	0.72	1730	1862
Gender disparity	1.42	1.24	0.94	0.99	0.75	0.74
Upper segment above						
Person	125	0.84	59	0.74	1582	1748
Gender disparity	0.83	0.91	1.23	1.07	0.97	1.02
Adult literacy						
None literate						
Person	107	0.80	61	0.71	1668	1813
Gender disparity	1.02	1.17	1.11	1.16	0.99	0.93
Female literate						
Person	150	0.77	89	0.86	3865	3865
Gender disparity	0.58	1.08	0.98	0.84	0.67	0.67
Male literate						
Person	145	0.83	58	0.65	1691	1822
Gender disparity	1.11	1.12	1.17	1.09	0.87	0.87
Both literate						
Person	116	0.79	69	0.71	1957	2110
Gender disparity	0.84	1.12	0.98	0.97	0.89	0.91
Village development						
Low						
Person	117	0.83	63	0.68	1748	1863
Gender disparity	1.18	1.05	1.05	1.07	0.82	0.83
Medium						
Person	145	0.79	59	0.74	1748	1930
Gender disparity	0.87	1.25	1.15	1.16	1.05	1.00
High						
Person	121	0.84	71	0.57	2128	2302
Gender disparity	0.70	1.09	1.20	0.80	0.94	0.95
Age groups (years)						
0–4						
Person	214	0.85	7	0.73	1492	1926
Gender disparity	0.75	1.03	1.56	1.36	1.84	1.98
5–14						
Person	139	0.96	21	0.61	2785	2880
Gender disparity	1.01	1.09	0.89	0.65	1.09	1.19
15–34						
Person	68	0.77	45	0.71	1839	1998
Gender disparity	1.56	1.24	1.88	1.05	0.78	0.85
35–59						
Person	120	0.77	111	0.64	1652	1752
Gender disparity	0.84	1.07	1.27	1.30	1.01	0.97
60 and above						
Person	199	0.61	240	0.78	1715	1895
Gender disparity	1.18	1.44	0.62	1.00	0.76	0.73
All groups						
Person	127	0.81	62	0.69	1775	1917
Gender disparity	1.01	1.13	1.09	1.06	0.90	0.89

TABLE A11.19
Fertility Rate by Population Group in Rural Uttar Pradesh

Population group	Crude birth rate per '000	Crude death rate per '000	TFR (15–49)	Average children ever born to ever married women		
				Boys	Girls	Total
Household income						
Up to 20,000	39	13	6.1091	1.7	1.5	3.2
20,001–40,000	35	9	5.5246	1.8	1.4	3.2
40,001–62,000	42	8	6.4667	1.6	1.3	2.9
62,001–86,000	32	10	4.4498	1.6	1.3	3.0
Above 86,000	41	6	6.1830	1.4	1.4	2.8
Landholding						
Landless wage earner	46	11	6.9516	1.8	1.5	3.3
Marginal	39	11	5.9656	1.6	1.5	3.1
Small	31	9	4.9684	1.6	1.4	3.0
Medium	35	12	5.3422	1.6	1.4	3.0
Large	38	7	5.8553	1.7	1.4	3.0
Landless others	42	12	6.8428	1.9	1.5	3.5
All land owners	36	10	5.6147	1.6	1.4	3.1
All land non-owners	44	12	6.8966	1.9	1.5	3.4
Occupation						
Agriculture	33	10	5.1799	1.7	1.4	3.1
Salaried+prof.+s.empl.	40	7	6.0573	1.7	1.4	3.0
Wage earners	46	14	7.1238	1.7	1.5	3.2
All others	42	13	6.6065	1.7	1.5	3.3
Caste						
STs	40	9	6.2476	2.0	1.4	3.4
SCs	41	11	6.0680	1.7	1.5	3.2
Religion						
Hindus	37	11	5.7451	1.6	1.4	3.1
Muslims	41	9	7.0169	1.9	1.6	3.5
Household size						
Up to 4	34	17	3.8603	1.1	0.8	1.9
5–7	35	11	5.8515	1.8	1.6	3.4
8 and above	42	8	6.6983	1.7	1.6	3.3
Poverty line						
Lower segment below	40	12	6.2721	1.8	1.7	3.6
Upper segment below	41	11	6.6682	1.8	1.5	3.3
Lower segment above	37	11	5.5539	1.6	1.4	3.0
Upper segment above	34	9	5.3187	1.5	1.2	2.8
Adult literacy						
None literate	41	14	6.4678	1.8	1.5	3.3
Female literate	40	18	7.5876	1.6	2.0	3.6
Male literate	39	11	6.4761	1.7	1.4	3.2
Both literate	33	6	4.5910	1.5	1.4	2.9
Village development						
Low	40	10	6.1947	1.7	1.4	3.1
Middle	36	12	5.6698	1.7	1.5	3.1
High	29	8	4.7035	1.8	1.6	3.4
All groups	**38**	**11**	**5.8903**	**1.7**	**1.5**	**3.1**

TABLE A11.20
Contraceptive Prevalence Rate for Ever Married Women by Population Group in Rural Uttar Pradesh

Population group	Termination method % EMW	Vasectomy users % to all	Spacing method % EMW	Loop/CopT user % to all	% EMW using methods
Household income					
Up to 20,000	13.0	9.6	7.2	24.4	20.1
20,001–40,000	14.7	10.6	8.8	26.1	23.5
40,001–62,000	15.0	9.5	9.3	26.6	24.3
62,001–86,000	13.6	7.1	11.1	16.1	24.7
Above 86,000	12.1	5.0	15.7	36.0	27.9
Landholding					
Landless wage earner	11.2	9.1	6.6	25.6	17.8
Marginal	14.2	12.5	7.3	21.7	21.6
Small	13.7	5.6	9.5	31.7	23.2
Medium	14.7	7.9	11.6	28.0	26.3
Large	16.4	14.5	15.3	34.3	31.8
Landless others	12.0	3.0	8.7	20.3	20.7
All land owners	14.3	10.4	8.8	26.6	23.1
All land non-owners	11.6	5.7	7.8	22.4	19.4
Occupation					
Agriculture	14.3	8.5	10.0	29.1	24.4
Salaried+prof.+s.empl.	16.8	15.4	8.1	22.8	24.9
Wage earners	11.5	8.6	6.6	22.9	18.0
All others	10.6	3.4	7.1	19.6	17.7
Caste					
STs	19.7	0.0	3.2	45.9	22.9
SCs	11.6	11.0	8.9	15.0	20.5
Religion					
Hindus	14.9	9.5	8.2	24.6	23.0
Muslims	4.9	9.9	11.6	30.9	16.4
Household size					
Up to 4	5.9	5.4	7.1	23.1	13.1
5–7	17.7	11.2	8.7	27.2	26.4
8 and above	12.6	7.9	9.1	25.2	21.7
Poverty line					
Lower segment below	14.4	10.6	5.6	17.1	20.1
Upper segment below	13.0	8.1	7.0	23.6	20.0
Lower segment above	13.7	9.1	9.9	28.1	23.6
Upper segment above	13.9	10.8	10.5	27.5	24.4
Adult literacy					
None literate	9.1	7.7	8.6	32.0	17.7
Female literate	19.6	17.1	6.1	54.6	25.7
Male literate	13.8	6.2	7.5	17.5	21.3
Both literate	17.5	14.2	10.5	30.0	28.0
Village development					
Low	12.7	8.8	8.4	27.6	21.1
Middle	15.1	10.4	8.7	23.4	23.8
High	15.4	9.9	9.5	23.2	24.9
All groups	**13.7**	**9.5**	**8.6**	**25.8**	**22.3**

TABLE A11.21
Reasons for Non-adoption of Birth Control Measures by Population Group in Rural Uttar Pradesh

(per cent)

Population group	Non-adoption	Reasons for not using birth control measures: Demand factors	Want son	Health factors	Supply factors	Household factors	Lack of knowledge
Household income							
Up to 20,000	79.3	37.4	17.0	13.2	1.1	10.6	20.3
20,001–40,000	76.8	39.0	13.9	12.1	1.9	14.4	18.5
40,001–62,000	76.6	40.7	10.8	11.0	0.5	11.3	18.9
62,001–86,000	74.4	37.3	12.7	13.5	1.0	8.4	20.0
Above 86,000	69.9	31.5	18.2	9.5	0.7	12.6	25.0
Landholding							
Landless wage earner	82.2	43.4	13.5	10.4	1.2	18.2	18.8
Marginal	78.4	37.5	16.8	12.5	1.0	9.4	19.9
Small	76.8	38.5	13.3	13.5	1.9	10.6	21.3
Medium	73.7	35.1	16.7	13.3	1.5	11.6	18.4
Large	68.2	34.5	11.7	12.8	0.0	6.8	25.9
Landless others	79.3	37.7	13.9	12.4	1.5	18.3	17.3
Land owners	76.9	37.3	15.7	12.8	1.2	9.8	20.3
Landless	80.6	40.4	13.7	11.5	1.4	18.3	18.0
Occupation							
Cultivators	75.6	35.3	15.5	15.1	1.5	10.2	21.6
Salaried+prof.+s.empl.	75.1	40.8	15.3	9.6	1.4	8.2	20.5
Wage earners	82.0	41.2	14.2	11.8	1.3	14.9	18.4
All others	82.3	38.9	15.4	9.6	0.5	16.2	15.9
Caste							
STs	77.1	42.2	5.5	19.0	2.1	5.3	30.6
SCs	79.5	38.7	17.0	16.2	1.6	5.6	20.7
Religion							
Hindus	77.0	39.0	16.4	13.1	1.4	6.7	20.8
Muslims	83.6	31.1	6.8	8.7	0.2	47.4	12.4
Household size							
Up to 4	86.9	45.1	19.0	11.3	1.0	4.9	17.8
5–7	73.6	33.9	14.7	16.7	1.7	12.0	21.0
8 and above	78.3	39.0	14.2	9.1	1.0	14.2	19.5
Poverty line							
Lower segment below	79.2	37.4	15.3	11.4	1.2	12.3	20.5
Upper segment below	79.9	38.5	18.6	11.5	0.9	11.4	19.8
Lower segment above	75.8	39.1	13.5	13.4	1.6	12.4	19.3
Upper segment above	76.9	35.2	14.2	13.6	0.9	9.7	20.2
Adult literacy							
None literate	82.3	35.2	16.9	17.1	1.7	12.7	18.2
Female literate	74.3	20.3	7.2	18.9	0.0	17.5	26.6
Male literate	78.7	40.2	14.3	10.5	1.4	11.0	20.6
Both literate	72.0	37.7	15.5	11.0	0.6	11.5	19.9
Village development							
Low	78.9	37.9	14.7	12.8	1.0	10.2	21.2
Medium	76.2	38.9	16.0	13.1	1.6	11.9	17.2
High	75.1	33.9	16.1	7.4	1.8	23.8	21.2
All groups	**77.7**	**38.0**	**15.2**	**12.5**	**1.3**	**11.7**	**19.8**

TABLE A11.22

Distribution of Ever Married Women Having Delivery in Previous Year by Population Group in Rural Uttar Pradesh

Population group	EMW having delivery previous year	Post-natal care received	Attended by trained person	Place of delivery: Hospital	CHC/PHC	Home	Immunization %
Household income							
Up to 20,000	22.2	13.1	28.5	4.4	4.7	90.7	38.8
20,001–40,000	20.0	21.9	31.4	10.6	6.4	81.4	47.2
40,001–62,000	22.6	12.4	28.9	6.2	7.5	86.4	41.4
62,001–86,000	20.9	26.6	30.9	16.2	8.8	75.0	40.7
Above 86,000	23.4	24.0	52.5	35.4	11.8	52.8	58.1
Landholding							
Landless wage earner	25.5	18.2	28.2	2.8	6.6	90.6	44.8
Marginal	22.0	15.7	28.6	7.8	5.2	86.7	40.8
Small	17.8	15.4	30.1	9.1	5.4	84.0	46.7
Medium	19.9	27.0	39.1	14.9	8.8	74.6	40.1
Large	21.7	11.1	38.3	12.0	21.0	67.0	63.6
Landless others	24.4	12.9	30.6	6.6	2.0	91.4	37.3
Land owners	20.7	16.8	30.8	9.2	6.6	83.5	43.2
Land less	24.9	15.4	29.5	4.8	4.2	91.0	40.8
Occupation							
Cultivators	19.0	14.5	29.9	8.1	7.1	83.9	44.5
Salaried+prof.+s.empl.	22.2	22.6	34.7	15.9	5.7	77.7	45.8
Wage earners	25.7	18.6	25.1	3.0	5.6	91.4	40.2
All others	24.0	12.0	32.6	5.1	4.2	90.6	37.8
Caste							
STs	22.3	0.0	34.0	13.4	0.0	86.6	8.7
SCs	22.2	16.2	28.0	5.5	2.7	91.4	45.1
Religion							
Hindus	21.1	17.0	30.4	8.3	6.7	84.4	42.7
Muslims	25.7	12.9	30.1	6.9	1.5	91.5	41.9
Household size							
Up to 4	15.8	13.7	31.7	9.8	6.7	83.5	45.4
5–7	20.1	15.7	28.5	6.7	4.5	87.9	42.1
8 and above	25.2	17.7	31.7	8.9	7	83.7	42.4
Poverty line							
Lower segment below	23.7	11.2	24.0	2.7	5.5	91.2	32.8
Upper segment below	23.0	18.7	31.1	6	4.4	89.2	42.8
Lower segment above	20.4	16.2	29.7	8.7	5.7	85.2	46.0
Upper segment above	19.7	21.7	41.6	19.2	10.4	69.8	46.9
Adult literacy							
None literate	23.2	12.6	27.0	3.1	5.3	91.6	36.8
Female literate	23.5	14.2	14.2	14.2	14.2	71.6	49.1
Male literate	22.6	14.0	28.3	7.7	3.3	88.6	39.0
Both literate	18.5	25.6	39.2	14.4	11.6	72.7	56.1
Village development							
Low	22.3	14.8	32.0	7.8	7.0	84.6	41.4
Middle	21.0	14.9	25.4	8.5	4.4	86.6	40.0
High	18.4	41.9	43.4	8.8	5.1	86.0	71.3
All groups	**21.6**	**16.4**	**30.4**	**8.1**	**6.0**	**85.4**	**42.6**

TABLE A11.23

Percentage of Children (aged 12–23 months) Immunized and Gender Disparity by Population Group in Rural Uttar Pradesh

Population group	Percentage of children (12–23 months)				
	DPT 3 doses	Polio 3 doses	BCG 1 dose	Measles 1 dose	All 8 doses
Household income					
Up to 20,000					
Person	47.47	49.59	58.15	45.79	37.70
Gender disparity	0.97	0.96	1.05	0.94	0.93
20,001–40,000					
Person	52.55	53.88	61.73	51.41	43.72
Gender disparity	0.86	0.87	0.80	0.75	0.86
40,001–62,000					
Person	55.92	55.98	64.10	50.03	41.90
Gender disparity	0.90	0.90	0.99	0.98	0.99
62,001–86,000					
Person	56.02	57.08	62.57	42.47	40.59
Gender disparity	1.14	1.19	1.31	1.37	1.26
Above 86,000					
Person	73.28	76.43	81.50	71.64	63.42
Gender disparity	0.98	0.91	1.04	1.12	1.05
Landholding					
Landless wage earner					
Person	40.40	40.71	55.59	40.14	30.24
Gender disparity	0.79	0.70	0.81	0.76	0.86
Marginal					
Person	51.88	55.20	60.64	49.17	43.45
Gender disparity	0.95	0.95	1.05	0.95	0.91
Small					
Person	51.94	53.44	65.31	51.28	43.09
Gender disparity	0.97	0.88	0.87	0.84	0.99
Medium					
Person	51.15	54.55	62.65	46.38	37.27
Gender disparity	0.94	0.96	1.05	0.99	0.93
Large					
Person	70.43	70.43	70.43	49.17	49.17
Gender disparity	1.09	1.09	1.09	1.11	1.11
Landless others					
Person	56.11	52.69	59.06	55.25	42.55
Gender disparity	0.97	1.08	1.02	1.00	1.12
All land owners					
Person	52.66	55.36	62.53	49.38	42.88
Gender disparity	0.95	0.94	1.00	0.92	0.93
All land non-owners					
Person	48.49	46.88	57.38	47.92	36.58
Gender disparity	0.88	0.90	0.91	0.89	1.00
Occupation					
Agriculture					
Person	51.50	54.51	62.81	47.02	40.05
Gender disparity	0.89	0.88	0.97	0.92	0.88
Salaried+prof.+s.empl.					
Person	59.42	60.85	65.94	57.21	48.57
Gender disparity	1.03	1.07	1.00	0.93	1.03
Wage earners					
Person	41.91	41.23	53.63	40.20	32.66
Gender disparity	0.92	0.81	0.95	0.83	0.85
All others					
Person	53.62	54.44	60.37	54.15	45.52
Gender disparity	0.99	1.02	1.00	0.97	1.11
Caste					
STs					
Person	34.41	34.41	24.39	10.48	10.48
Gender disparity	0.57	0.57	0.00	0.00	0.00
SCs					
Person	45.66	45.69	56.58	44.79	35.53
Gender disparity	0.99	0.95	0.99	0.87	0.93
Religion					
Hindus					
Person	52.38	54.13	61.55	49.46	42.20
Gender disparity	0.93	0.93	0.97	0.91	0.93
Muslims					
Person	46.38	47.40	58.99	45.67	35.22
Gender disparity	1.04	1.03	1.05	0.97	1.15
Household size					
Upto 4					
Person	53.32	57.05	67.23	54.14	45.94
Gender disparity	0.81	0.79	0.90	0.79	0.85
5–7					
Person	52.35	53.12	61.56	51.82	42.07
Gender disparity	1.08	1.09	1.06	1.02	1.12
8 and above					
Person	50.46	52.28	59.18	44.92	39.26
Gender disparity	0.86	0.86	0.94	0.88	0.85
Poverty line					
Lower segment below					
Person	40.53	39.46	48.14	35.52	27.89
Gender disparity	0.98	1.00	1.10	0.89	0.84
Upper segment below					
Person	49.52	53.55	60.84	48.43	41.78
Gender disparity	0.90	0.88	0.94	0.93	0.94
Lower segment above					
Person	54.65	56.03	64.38	52.79	44.79
Gender disparity	0.94	0.93	0.94	0.85	0.92
Upper segment above					
Person	61.69	64.12	71.28	58.13	49.62
Gender disparity	1.00	1.03	1.07	1.15	1.22
Adult literacy					
None literate					
Person	44.41	44.90	54.51	44.60	36.26
Gender disparity	0.85	0.77	0.88	0.83	0.84
Female literate					
Person	58.23	69.09	73.96	47.85	47.85
Gender disparity	1.15	1.62	1.40	1.71	1.71
Male literate					
Person	48.65	50.10	59.08	45.61	36.85
Gender disparity	0.93	0.91	0.95	0.85	0.88
Both literate					
Person	66.40	69.33	73.51	61.39	56.04
Gender disparity	1.02	1.09	1.09	1.07	1.10
Village development					
Low					
Person	50.23	51.58	59.84	47.08	39.58
Gender disparity	0.94	0.94	1.02	0.95	0.99
Medium					
Person	53.32	56.14	62.02	50.48	43.66
Gender disparity	0.95	0.96	0.93	0.88	0.90
High					
Person	57.55	55.20	73.50	62.93	47.41
Gender disparity	0.90	0.80	0.93	0.89	0.89
All groups					
Person	51.63	53.28	61.26	49.02	41.33
Gender disparity	0.94	0.93	0.98	0.92	0.95

(Contd.)

12 Village Level Study in Uttar Pradesh: Nathupur

12.1 Introduction

Village Nathupur selected for this qualitative study is situated in the district of Varanasi in Uttar Pradesh. Varanasi is located on the banks of the Ganges, and is an ancient seat of learning. It acquired this name as it is bounded by the Varuna stream in the north and the Asi river in the south. It is a multi-religious and sacred land where Hinduism, Buddhism, and Jainism have flourished. Sarnath, where the Buddha preached his first sermon after attaining inner peace and enlightenment, is about 12 km away. At Sarnath, Emperor Ashoka built a hundred-feet high Dharma Rajika Stupa. The lions on the stupa are the national emblem of India. Varanasi is significant not only as a pilgrimage spot, it is also of considerable archaeological and historical interest for the visitors, as many rulers over the centuries ruled kingdoms that were located here.

Vibhuti Narain Singh was the last king to rule a kingdom at Varanasi. Allahabad is situated to the west of Varanasi, Jaunpur to the north-west, Ghazipur to the north-east, Mirzapur to the south, and Shahabad (Bihar) to the east. The climate of the district is almost of the sub-tropical monsoon type. The river front, Kashi Vishwanath Temple, Sarnath, Durga Temple, Tulsi Manas Mandir, Bharat Mata Mandir, Ramnagar Fort, Alamgir Mosque, Gyanvyapi Mosque, Bhairav Mandir, and Banaras Hindu University are some of the prominent places here. The district has been a centre of education and learning, particularly in the Indian systems of medicine. It is famous for its handicrafts, artistic goods, silk saris, and carpets. It is also famous for manufacturing diesel locomotives.

12.2 Nathupur Village

12.2.1 Location

Village Nathupur is located about 13 km away from Varanasi and can be approached by a metalled road. It lies in the development block, Kashi Vidyapeeth, which is at a distance of 4 km from tehsil Varanasi and is situated close to the Diesel Locomotive Works (DLW). The village has its nearest post office located at Bhulanpur, 1 km away. The lokhpal, kanugo, tehsildar, and sub-divisional magistrate are all stationed at Varanasi. The village comes under the jurisdiction of police station Rohinia which is on the GT road, at a distance of 3 km. Nathupur is surrounded by Marauli in the north, Shivadaspur in the north-east, Bhulanpur in the west, and Ghoghulpur (Jalatipatti) in the south.

The village has an extreme climate. In summer, from March to June, the mercury rises to 47°C. From mid-June to August is the rainy season, and the village gets water-logged as no proper drainage facility exists especially in the yadava and harijan bastis. The winter months are chilly and extend from September to February.

12.2.2 Historical Background

At present the village is spread over 74 hectares of land with its socio-economic life deeply influenced by the DLW set up in its vicinity. In the earlier decades, however, Nathupur was identified with the term 'kurmis bahal' as it was dominated by the kurmis, a backward caste. The ancestral occupation of the landowning kurmis, who claimed to be kurmbansi rajputs or kurm kshatriyas, was cultivation. Other castes, such as the lohars, rajbhar, and harijans, were wage earners dependent on the kurmis—who were held in high esteem by the villagers. In 1956, the government purchased land from the kurmis at Rs 1000 per bigha. The villagers had no option as they were not allowed to sell land to anybody other than the government. Almost all the kurmis sold their land to the government and thereafter took up jobs in the DLW, which were linked to the sale of land. This changed the social complexion of the village.

12.2.3 Caste Composition of Households

The village broadly consists of seven bastis, namely, kurmis (4), harijans (1), rajbhars (1), and nai bastis (1). There are 253 households comprising kurmis, rajbhars, vishwakarmas, yadavas, harijan chamars, brahmans, thakurs, guptas, and telis.

The brahmans, thakurs, and vaishyas are the upper castes, while the backward castes include the kurmis, rajbhars, yadavs, and vishwakarmas. Harijans are at the bottom of the hierarchy. In the village, the backward castes are the dominant castes. Statuswise, the salaried class is at the top followed by petty shopkeepers, agricultural labourers, and masons. Beedi- and *mala*-making are considered as inferior activities.

Most of the kurmi caste families are no longer land owners or cultivators, and have taken up service as their occupation. Harijans, who constitute 13 per cent of the households, are SCs. Their predominant occupation is *rajgiri* (construction labour) though it is not their traditional occupation. A few harijan households are engaged in selling vegetables. Bhars (rajbhars) form 12 per cent of the total households of this village. They are also engaged in service like the kurmis. A few families are engaged in petty shopkeeping. Among the economically-backward vishwa-karmas, 12 lohar households are engaged in their traditional occupation as blacksmiths. A few are in service jobs. The yadavas who settled in the village many years ago, constitute about 4 per cent of the households. They are primarily engaged in milk trading. They sell milk in the nearby DLW colony. The village also has brahmin, sunar, and gupta households.

12.2.4 Demographic Profile

Using coloured chalk sticks and a variety of seeds, an exercise of social mapping was undertaken with the participation of villagers in order to generate a few household variables. Nine variables were generated: households owning land, *kutcha* households, service as major occupation, number of aged members (above 60 years), widows, physically disabled persons, major illnesses, caste, and income ranking (see Table 12.1).

TABLE 12.1
Household Variables, Nathupur

Caste	No. of house-holds	Land-owning households	Service as major occupation	No. of kutcha houses
1. Kurmis	121	43	30	1
2. Rajbhars	31	2	7	7
3. Harijans	34	–	26	1
4. Viswakarmas	12	–	5	2
5. Yadavs	11	–	6	1
6. Others	46	20	20	–

It is clear that the kurmis are of the dominant caste, accounting for nearly 50 per cent of the households, followed by others (those who have come either from Bihar or UP to work in the DLW). Harijans account for only 13 per cent of the households. Seventeen per cent of the households own cultivable land and almost all of these belong to the kurmi caste, except two households who are rajbhars. All others are landless.

Thrity-seven per cent of the households are engaged in service as the principal occupation. Out of these, more than three-fourths households belong to the kurmis, harijans, and other castes. Seventy-six per cent of the harijan households and 25 per cent of the kurmi households are engaged in service. Most of the houses in Nathupur are *pucca* and only 12 houses are kutcha.

TABLE 12.2
Variables, Nathupur

Caste	Persons aged > 60 years	Widows	Major illnesses (no.)	Physically handi-capped
1. Kurmis	36	17	4	5
2. Rajbhars	10	4	4	–
3. Harijans	–	–	–	–
4. Viswakarmas	2	3	–	2
5. Yadavs	2	2	–	–
6. Others	2	1	–	2
All	**52**	**27**	**8**	9

Table 12.2 shows that every fourth household has at least one aged person (above 60 years). There are 27 widows and nine physically handicapped persons. Eight cases of major illness were reported. Income stratification was done by the villagers themselves, using their own perceptions. The distribution is presented in Table 12.3.

TABLE 12.3
Income Stratification, Nathupur

Caste	Low	Medium	High
1. Kurmis	5	99	7
2. Rajbhars	10	21	–
3. Harijans	5	29	–
4. Vishwakarmas	2	10	–
5. Yadavs	1	10	–
6. Others	2	41	3
All	**25**	**210**	**10**

It can be seen that 210 households are classified in the middle income category, whereas 25 and 10 households figure in the low and high income groups, respectively.

About 12 houses have mud walls and 233 houses have pucca roofs made with bricks. Kutcha houses have a sloping *khaprail* roof. Crop-waste roofs are absent. The houses of well-to-do families have built-in toilets. Forty latrines were built under the Jawahar Rozgar Yojana (JRY) but they are non-functional. Most of them have either no roof or are filled with stones and waste material. The majority of the population defecates in the open fields. The houses of nai basti are generally cleaner because the migrants working in the DLW live there.

Inter-caste interaction is limited. There is a clear-cut social division in the village between the harijans (SC) and the backward castes. There is a further subdivision within the backward castes, that is, between the kurmis and the rajbhars. Another visible division is seen between the natives and the in-migrants (consisting of families from Bihar) who migrated to the village and joined the DLW.

All castes have been ranked in terms of education, health, social well-being, and occupation (Table 12.4).

TABLE 12.4
Ranking Matrix for Nathupur

Caste	Education	Health	Social well-being	Occupation
1. Kurmis	1	2	1	Service, petty shop, cultivation
2. Harijans	5	5	5	Construction labour, vegetable selling, service
3. Rajbhars	2	4	2	Service, masonry
4. Yadavs	4	1	3	Milk selling
5. Vishwakarmas	3	3	4	Service, blacksmith work
6. Others (thakurs, sunars, guptas, telis, and brahmans)	2	2	2	Service, small business

Note: Based on the matrix of different groups.

MIGRATION

The village has witnessed in-migration as well as out-migration. People who had sold their land migrated to either Varanasi or Jaunpur, while outsiders who took up work with the DLW preferred to take up residence in the village on account of its proximity to the DLW and the cheap accommodation that it offered.

12.2.5 General Environment

The village has rural as well as urban communities, as some of those employed in the DLW are people from urban areas who have migrated to the village. The population is almost wholly Hindu except for one Muslim. There are no Sikhs, Christians, Jains, or Buddhists.

TYPE OF HOUSES

More than 80 per cent of the villagers live in pucca houses, and about 20 per cent live in kutcha houses. Many houses which appear to be pucca from the outside do not have pucca floors. Some villagers mentioned that they preferred to construct an extra room instead of plastering the floor of already constructed rooms. They prefer to have more rooms as these are required for storing grains, keeping cattle, etc. A few households clean their kutcha floors monthly. Most of the pucca houses are whitewashed every year. This shows that the villagers keep their houses clean.

The women folk in the village spend most of their time in the kitchen. The pucca houses have a separate kitchen whereas kutcha houses have no separate kitchen. A large majority of the households use dung-cakes as fuel. The affluent sections use LPG cylinders. As a result of the widespread use of dung-cakes as fuel, most of the women reported having breathing problems.

12.2.6 Infrastructure

ELECTRICITY

The village was electrified in 1987. Nearly 90 per cent of the households have an electric connection, however, the supply is erratic. Due to the short supply of electricity, villagers find it difficult to install tube wells and electric utility items. Electricity charges are fixed at Rs 28 per month.

The nearest post office is in Bhulanpur PAC 34 which is 4 km away. However, most of the villagers use the postal services at the DLW post office. A telephone is available in a medical shop. To avail of STD services, the villagers go near the railway line (DLW), which is 100 yards away. There is no bank and the villagers use the banking services of the DLW branch of State Bank of India and Bank of Baroda.

SHOPS

The village has its own market where commodities of daily use are available. A large number of shops are on the main road. These include grocery shops, chemist shop, tailoring shop, tea stalls, pan stalls, egg sellers, vegetable vendors, coal shop, etc. For special functions and ceremonies, the villagers go either to the DLW market or to Varanasi for wholesale or fancy goods. There is a public distribution system (PDS) shop which distributes only kerosene oil. People do not have ration cards.

EDUCATION

The village had one primary school named Gyan Bharati which was established in 1970 in a rented building. In 1990, the enrolment was 178 students (112 boys and 66 girls). According to the villagers, the school was closed after the teachers created some trouble. For middle and high school facilities the students go to the DLW colony.

SANITARY FACILITIES

Sanitation and hygiene within the village includes three elements: liquid waste disposal, solid waste disposal, and drainage.

Toilet facilities are available in a limited number of households. The functional latrines have been constructed by individual initiative and expense, mostly by those belonging to the salaried class. Nearly 40 latrines were constructed under the JRY but they do not have proper roofs, or side walls and the villagers do not use them. It is observed that even though the villagers are interested in the construction of latrines, village politics is the cause for their non-functioning. In harijan and yadav bastis no sanitary arrangements are available. In the absence of proper facilities, defecation in the open is very common among these castes. The nearby fallow land is used for this purpose.

WATER SUPPLY

Open wells and hand pumps are the two sources of water in the village. There are 25 open wells but hardly a quarter of these cater to the villagers' needs. Further, the number of pumps is also very limited. Out of total nine hand pumps, two are sanctioned under the legislative quota, while the remaining seven are under the JRY. It is observed that without the proper-functioning hand pumps, the latrine facilities are of no use. An important aspect is the location or placement of these hand pumps. At present, all seven public hand pumps are installed in areas where people close to the former *pradhan* live. As they do not allow anybody to draw water from the hand pumps, these are used as private amenities. The harijan basti has only one hand pump. It is very difficult for the harijans to draw water from a single source but the higher castes do not allow them to draw water from their water sources.

During summer, the open wells dry up, and it is difficult to obtain water. The yadav basti suffers the most because the residents need large quantities of water for their animals. When the open wells dry up they have to fetch water from the DLW colony which is nearly one km away. As their main source of income is selling of milk, the lack of water affects their livelihood. The pradhan had selected a site here for the installation of hand pumps keeping in view his election prospects. Women prefer hand pumps to open wells, because the time saved can be devoted to other household work. They also consider pumps as a comparatively safe source of water.

There is a scarcity of water for bathing. The water level has gone down to nearly 60 feet. It takes at least five minutes to draw up a single bucket of water. Cooking, washing, and meeting the requirements of animals have a higher priority. Bathing is not a regular practice in the village, especially among the harijans, yadavas, and others in the non-salaried class.

12.2.7 Health Care

In village Nathupur most of the people prefer the allopathic treatment given by private medical practitioners. Traditional medicine comes next on their scale of importance. The villagers follow the traditional system of medical care for stomach upset, sun stroke, and dog bite. For other illnesses, modern medical care is sought. There are approximately ten registered medical practitioners (RMPs) who charge Rs 50–80 per visit—an amount that an average villager cannot afford.

The general tendency among the villagers, especially the women, is to ignore diseases in early stages. The reasons for this are ignorance, illiteracy, poverty, and non-availability of proper health-care facilities at the village level.

INCIDENCE OF DISEASES

During the pre-independence period, diseases such as plague, smallpox, and malaria were major killers. The morbidity patterns show a preponderance of malaria and stomach diseases. Absence of any public medical care facilities in the village has made the villagers dependent on expensive private medical care. Gastro-intestinal diseases were reported by the largest number of people, followed by respiratory diseases such as cold, cough, fever, TB, and asthma. Among adult males, cancer, TB, and unspecified fever are more common while among children, pneumonia and diarrhoea are prevalent. Three cases of dog bite were also reported in the village.

12.2.8 Social Issues: Customs and Practices

FOOD AND DRINK

A majority of the people in the village are vegetarian. There are restrictions on the cooking of meat, egg, fish, etc. in the common kitchen. Rice, wheat, and dal are consumed in almost every household. However, those who are poor, such as the lohar caste, eat only mahuwa as they are unable to afford wheat or rice. Most of the people consume two meals a day. Puri and vegetables are cooked in every household on main festivals and marriages. *Arhar* pulse and vegetables such as *ninua*, *pattal*, *kathal*, potato, *karaila*, and onion are commonly used.

Consumption of alcohol is very common among all the communities. There is a government shop and the daily wage earners usually go there. The main fuel resource in the village is cow dung cakes but the salaried class uses cooking gas.

MARRIAGE AND FAMILY

Marriages are arranged by negotiations and all the communities practise monogamy. There is not even a single case of polygamy, polyandry, or consanguineous marriage in the village. Only the kurmis and rajbhars follow the practice of giving dowry. Recently, a newly-married *bahu* aged 18 years tried to run away as her kurmi family in-laws harassed her for not bringing the anticipated dowry.

The village has a few nuclear families. The villagers follow the practice of male inheritance and succession. After the death of father, the property is inherited by sons.

Authority in the family generally lies with the eldest male member. In the salaried households, financial authority is delegated to the eldest female member. The eldest son takes all decisions concerning the household purchases.

The language spoken in the village is Bhojpuri which is akin to Hindi. All the communities speak the same language. Verbal as well as non-verbal modes of greeting are followed. Elders say 'namaskar', younger people touch the feet of elders, and young boys shake hands.

LOTTERY AND GAMBLING

On the main road a lottery centre is located, where a large number of villagers try their luck. Some villagers spend up to 50 per cent of their daily wages on either lottery or gambling in the hope of getting rich overnight. The lottery addicts purchase single-digit lottery tickets every morning and wait anxiously for the results to be declared. Frequently, they forego their wages too. Gradually, children too are influenced by the lottery mania and gambling. They steal money from their houses and purchase lottery tickets while others sit under a tree and gamble. Gambling and lottery permeate the atmosphere of the village.

FESTIVALS

Ganga Dussehra: This festival is celebrated with much gaiety and fervour in the months of May and June. Most of the villagers go to Varanasi to take a dip in the Ganges; they believe that the river washes away all their sins.

Dussehra: This is celebrated by almost all castes.

OTHER ACTIVITIES

Jai Hind Club is a sports club and its members (village youth) regularly play football in the nearby DLW ground. In recent years, they have achieved recognition of such stature that five or six players have played for the district at the state level and have won trophies. Two or three have represented India at international games (in Korea, at the junior level).

Whenever there are any social gatherings in the village such as in marriages/death, the club members bring rations, cook, erect tents, invite villagers, serve food, and maintain peace. All the villagers are full of praise for this club.

WOMEN'S STATUS

Women's role in paid economic activities is limited to beedi-making, mala-making, and selling vegetables. A few women work as maids in the nearby colony. Women are generally involved in the watch and ward work, cooking, looking after children, cleaning, fetching water, purchasing rations, washing clothes, etc. Among the kurmi and harijan families, the women contribute to the family income. However, the status of women is low in most of the communities.

12.2.9 Occupations

A few households, mainly kurmis, are engaged in cultivation. Yadavas are engaged in animal husbandry. There is a pond where fishing is done. The village has many unskilled labourers, from the kurmi, rajbhar, and harijan castes, who go to Varanasi as masons. A few skilled labourers, such as carpenters, blacksmiths, etc., are also present. Business and petty shop-keeping are prominent occupations.

12.2.10 Summary of Focus Group Discussions

The main objective of the focus group discussions (FGDs) was to document the perceptions of various groups about the utility of education, utilization of health-care services, and savings behaviour in the village. For this purpose it was decided to form six focus groups: (i) women with children up to 5 years of age; (ii) women with children of school-going age; (iii) women belonging to SC (harijan) category; (iv) elderly women (above 60 years); (v) widows; and (vi) men whose wives are less than 35 years of age.

WOMEN WITH CHILDREN UP TO 5 YEARS OF AGE

In this group, the average age of the ten participants was 25 years and the number of children was 25. One of the participants had completed BA, one intermediate, and one had education only up to the primary level. All others were illiterate. The group represented the four major castes of the village, namely, kurmi, rajbhar, vishwakarma, and harijan. All of them lived either in a joint or nuclear family and the age at marriage was 20 years. Fifty per cent owned land either in their own name or in the name of their spouse. Seven of the participants were bahus of the village with infants less than 12-month old. The discussion was conducted in a peaceful atmosphere with minimum disturbance. The inferences drawn and the judgements made are on the basis of detailed questions regarding health, education, and social well-being.

The participants seemed to be ignorant about health care. During pregnancy, almost everybody continues to do household work such as drawing water, looking after children, cooking food, and other chores. After delivery they are allowed to rest for 15–20 days. Their special diet is ghee and milk. Their appetite is considerably reduced during pregnancy as they believe that food eaten in large quantities is not good for the child. A dominant view reported in the discussion was that the women limit their food intake in the gestation period as they fear that the child would be overgrown. Older women recommend light food such as *lauki* and dal while certain items are restricted, for example, meat, jackfruit, brinjal, and sweet potato. All participants are ignorant about iron and folic acid tablets. However, four or five women had consumed vitamin A tablets. This clearly reflects their ignorance about maternal care.

Most of them had delivered their first child at their *sasural*. The concept of first delivery at mother's home is not practised in the village. Those with one child or a sufficient number of children stayed at their husbands' house. Women are not allowed to consult any doctor before, during, or after pregnancy, mainly because there are no lady doctors. They consult the doctor only if there are any complications like temperature, etc. As regards pregnancy management and the attitude towards child care, both are neglected. There were also a few cases of miscarriage. These were due to pressure of work on the expectant mother, in addition to deficiency of essential nutrients in the food. Women also reported that their children are very thin at the time of birth. The high IMR may be attributed to the observed negligence during pregnancy.

Women do not care much about the management of antenatal care. They establish no rapport with the medical personnel during the delivery time. With no specific preference regarding doctors, they consult any available doctors if home remedies prove to be ineffective.

WOMEN WITH SCHOOL-GOING CHILDREN

The discussion with mothers of children who were of school-going age had nine participants. Caste-wise they represented the harijan, kushvaha, kurmi, and viswakarma castes. The average age of the participants was 41 years. One of them was a teacher while another could read and write. The rest were illiterate. Each had some land. All of them stayed in either joint or nuclear families. Two were employed—one as a teacher and the other had a *pan* shop. The remaining were all housewives. All these women were well-off in the context of the village except the one whose husband ran a trolley. The average family size was five with female children predominating.

As regards education, all women were in favour of educating their children. Kurmi women opined that education improves the status of the younger generation whereas the harijan women emphasised the link between education and employment. Kushwah and vishwakarma women said that education is necessary for a happy life, looking after their children, and coping with calamities. Harijan women reported a lack of resources for children's education. The illiterate, regretted not going to school, and wanted their children to go to school. All women said that society does not encourage or motivate the children. They are willing to reduce their regular expenditure if quality education is made available, irrespective of distance.

As regards health, they opined that the cause of illness is dirt. If surroundings are clean, nobody gets infected. Whenever anybody is ill, diet is given as prescribed by doctor. They use home remedies for minor illnesses, like *panna* for heat stroke and *phan ki* for stomach upset and loss of appetite. Major illnesses such as cancer, TB, leprosy, and polio are considered incurable.

The participants in the discussion felt that it is not very difficult for a couple to save money if both of them earn. Everybody faces calamities. Some amount can always be kept at home, say, for medical treatment. They realize the importance of savings. The teacher and educated woman commented that imparting education to children is also a saving.

WOMEN BELONGING TO SCHEDULED CASTE (HARIJAN) CATEGORY

This discussion, in which eight women participated, was conducted in the harijan basti itself as the women preferred to be comfortable in their own surroundings. Their average age was 24 years, and on an average the families had four children. Fifty per cent of them could write while the remaining were illiterate. All belonged to joint families and only one had her own land. One woman washed dishes in the DLW colony, others were housewives. Their husbands were engaged in occupations such as cycle repairing, vegetable selling, masonry, or tailoring, or were working as mechanics. Earlier, the harijans used to work in traditional occupations but at the time of discussion none of them were engaged in these.

The village as a whole lacks educational facilities. Otherwise the women are willing to send their children to school. They cannot afford education in private schools, while government schools hardly benefit anyone except the government employees. Distance too is a hindrance. People consider education as an accumulation of academic knowledge which helps them in getting better *rojgar*.

As regards hygiene, women drink even uncovered water. They do not see any linkage between water and illness. They eat fresh food and the leftover is disposed. Surroundings are unhygienic. The drains are open and mosquitoes freely breed here. Common diseases are cough, cold, dysentery, and vomiting.

Proper immunization facilities are not available for mothers or children. They regret not going to school. They felt that if they had been literate, they could have worked somewhere to supplement their husbands' incomes.

ELDERLY WOMEN (ABOVE 60 YEARS)

Twelve women participated in the FGD and their average age was 62 years. They belonged to various castes. Most of these women look after their children and are involved in household chores such as drawing water, etc. One woman reported doing nothing. All the women stay with their families, except two who stay with their daugher-in-law and son, separately. There is a distinction in the economic status of these women. Seven of them belonged to relatively well-off families, while the remaining could be considered as poor. The women categorized as well-off were well dressed, had gold jewellery in the form of large earrings, a nose ring, and chain. They had a certain air of pride and superiority. The women categorized as poor, lacked such possessions and the manner of superiority. There were only two women who had had any formal primary education. These women could read and write with understanding. Amongst ailments, weak eyesight and hearing ability, and joint pain were reported the most.

WIDOWS

Ten widows, with an average age of 57, participated in the discussion. None of them could read or write. Four of them were engaged in some occupations like washing dishes, roasting grains, and selling vegetables and dung cakes. Almost every widow was suffering from some ailment such as pain in the joints, chest or stomach. One of them was staying independently, and one with her children. Two were staying with their daughters-in-law while the others with their sons. One lived in a rented house whereas the others had their own accommodation. The participation was satisfactory. Each woman contributed her best. Detailed questions relating to their status in the family, savings, health problems, daily routine, perception about life, etc. were asked.

Almost all women agreed that their status in the family and society had declined after the demise of their husbands. Working widows said that if their husbands had been alive they would not have allowed them to work. However, circumstances were forcing them to sell dung cakes and vegetables. They felt the need for savings but said that in selling dung cakes, vegetables and grains, savings are a distant dream.

MEN WITH WIVES LESS THAN 35 YEARS OF AGE

In the discussion, eight persons with an average age of 38 years participated. Castewise they represented the patel, vishwakarma, kurmi, bhardwaj, and harijan communities. Almost all the participants could read and write. Except for two, the rest were landless. Only two belonged to nuclear familes. As the poorest member was engaged in cycle repairing, it can be inferred that the group is relatively well-off within the village context. Overall, the FGD was conducted in a congenial atmosphere.

As regards savings, they reported that the people have invested in Peerless (akin to LIC), and operate post office accounts and have provident fund (PF) accounts. They are exposed to modern instruments of saving. Though savings are not substantial, they do make saving strategies.

On the whole, the participants reported that the families in the village have a large size. An average family has 6 or 7 members. Their prosperity is because of the sons. They consider children as a good security. They stated that sons as well as daughters should be equally educated, and keep a portion of their savings for education. All of them agreed that education is not just to get jobs.

12.2.11 Findings of Focus Group Discussions

EDUCATION

The educational level of women as well as men was in conformity with the general trend in eastern UP. Most of the women cannot read or write though a few were graduates and working as teachers. The literacy level was higher among men.

The village is backward in terms of its education level. The only primary school, Gyan Bharti, has been shut down and at present there are no schools in the village. The children of the DLW employees receive education in DLW schools but for others, access to educational facilities is severely limited due to the large distance.

Although educational facilities are not available within the village, most of the women participants prefer to educate their children. Kurmi women felt that education helped to improve an individual's status; harijan women emphasized the link between education and employment. Kushwah and vishwakarma women took a broader perspective of the usefulness of education in living a happy life, in being able to look after children in a better way, and in increasing their coping abilities for the ups and downs in life. Illiterate mothers regretted not going to school as they felt that if they were literate they could have supplemented the household income. They are willing to sacrifice their personal needs, if required, to educate their children. Elderly, illiterate women have not educated their children and do not give it too much importance as they see it as very expensive. Widows in the groups believed that the educated unemployed are better than the uneducated employed as education develops a child's mind and provides them with job opportunities.

Men in the FGD considered education in terms of some sort of value addition and agreed that this does not ensure employment. However, they are not prepared to divert funds to educate girls. As the men value education, they have greater expectations from their children.

Many students drop out before completing elementary education because of addiction to lottery, gambling, and alcohol. The reason for dropping out among the harijans is poverty and among the yadavs it is the scarcity of water that does not allow them to send their children to school. Further, because of distance, access to education is limited.

Although educational facilities are not available within the village, most of the women prefer to educate their children. The response of all women, irrespective of caste, age, etc. are on similar lines. Moreover, as they value education, they have more expectations from their children. They consider education as a means of getting recognition in the society, though it does not guarantee jobs. There are no high returns from education in their view.

HEALTH

Concepts of health and health practices differed among the literate and illiterate participants in the FGDs. The illiterate were largely tradition-bound, particularly the yadavs and harijans. A majority of the women participants had poor knowledge of contraceptive methods, ante/post natal management, diet during pregnancy or other illnesses, need for supplementary food for the child, immunization dosage or schedules, child birth weight or development indicators, awareness of causes of diseases, and hygienic practices.

Women in the reproductive age group with infants or children up to five years of age expressed ignorance of the importance of iron and folic acid tablets during pregnancy. They observed a traditional diet of lauki and dal, avoiding meat, jackfruit, brinjal, and potato as they considered them to be sticky items that would retard the growth of the embryo by sticking to it. Further they feared eating during pregnancy as the child might overgrow. Thus, they deprive themselves of the extra intake of nutrients required during this period. The low birth weight and infant mortality reported by them could be linked to the low maternal diet intake.

Domiciliary births are dominant, the pattern being traditional child birth at home with an untrained *dai* in attendance. The participants stated that there were no medical or paramedical staff visits or lady doctors available for consultation.

The women are ignorant of most contraceptive methods other than sterilization by surgery. They are afraid of this method because they felt that they would get weak and are thus, hesitant to take this step. They are aware of the free distribution of *Nirodh* but say that it is not available to them, perhaps because of their low status. They are unaware of *Mala D*. They want to limit the size of their families because they cannot cope with the expenses and difficulties caused by having too many children.

However, some felt that family planning would result in weakness and therefore, did not practice it. Husbands too discouraged it. Harijan women were not in favour of family planning, rejecting it totally.

A majority of the males are alcoholic and are least conscious about their health. Male participants associated dysentery and TB with blood and were ignorant of the test for malaria. As dog bites are common in the village, the participants were aware of modern as well as ayurvedic treatment for the same. Some women advised 'looking' inside seven wells to treat dog bites.

Drinking water is kept uncovered in harijan households, because they do not see any linkage between contamination and disease. Similarly, the drains are uncovered facilitating the breeding of mosquitoes. Unhygienic surroundings and scarcity of water are major problems, especially in yadav and harijan bastis. Dung is commonly seen lying in heaps adjacent to houses. This can be a breeding ground for mosquitoes and other insects that spread a number of diseases. Lanes are kutcha in the basti. Dust pollution is a major problem. During the rainy season the problem of transportation and water pollution also become quite acute. Water from the railway line overflows the kutcha street making it muddy. This also leads to the breeding of mosquites and a foul smell pervades the air.

SOCIAL SECURITY/SAVINGS

Fifty women participated in five of the six FGDs. Apart from a couple of teachers, most of the women were illiterate housewives. Representing different castes, they belonged to the poorer sections of the community. The status of women is generally low, with little or no autonomy inside or outside the household. In paid economic activity they participate in beedi- or mala-making or selling vegetables. Ownership of land was rare among all the participants, whether male or female.

In the discussions, social security was largely seen as that provided by savings or by children in old age. Elderly women unanimously stated that children provide the best security as compared to land, cash, or gold. They also felt that possession of money gives status. Widows recognized the need for savings but were not able to put apart anything from lowly-paid economic activities as dung cake or vegetable selling. Though there is a pension scheme in the village, the women do not receive the one hundred rupees pension regularly. Educated women save in the banks as do working couples.

The importance of savings for security was clearly communicated. While savings in physical assets are rare, savings in financial assets are visible. Housewives with school-going children or infants put away in hiding, whatever meagre amount is possible, for use in emergency or sickness. This is mostly without the knowledge of their alcoholic or unemployed husbands. Male participants of the FGDs had invested in Peerless and operated other modern instruments of savings like PF and post office accounts.

The participants said that they need money for constructing houses, daughter's marriage, treatment, and other calamities. Voluntary savings in financial assets are found to be limited whereas compulsory savings are dominant. Savings (not voluntary but forced) are the highest in the salaried class. In order to meet emergencies in the household, women save some money as liquid cash in the house itself. This is done voluntarily.

The percentage of voluntary savings is the highest in households that have literates—irrespective of family size and caste. Savings in the form of financial assets are maximum among the salaried class, who are employed in DLW. The various forms of saving are listed in Table 12.5.

TABLE 12.5
Form of Savings in Nathupur

Occupation	Form of saving
1. Wage earner	Voluntary—liquid cash
2. Salaried	Forced—cash
3. Petty shopkeeper	Voluntary—cash+assets
4. Others	Voluntary—assets

People belonging to the dominant salaried class are better employed with better wages and job security, they eat nutritious food, have good living conditions, and also possess a social network. Wage earners, self-employed, petty shopkeepers and others get low wages, are underemployed, malnourished, indebted, and involved in social conflicts. The major part of their income is spent on less nutritious food items and very little is left to meet other non-food requirements. Households in the lower income group—due to high illiteracy, higher proportion of dependents, and meagre source of income—have very little savings. Contrary to this, households in the high income groups, irrespective of caste, have more savings on account of high literacy and more earning hands.

12.2.12 Free Listing of Illnesses

Health is a very important element in the well-being of an individual. Knowledge and awareness of health is crucial for the utilization of health facilities. Free listing of the names of illnesses as given by the women indicates their awareness of diseases and terminology. Questions were asked about the symptoms of the diseases they were familiar with. The vocabulary reflects both the knowledge and incidence of diseases in the village. Table 12.6 reflects the various illnesses listed by the villagers.

Twenty women, representing a homogeneous population, were separately asked about their knowledge of illnesses. They were in the age group of 20 to 55 years. The average age was 38 years. They represented kurmis (7), lohars (3), harijans (4), rajbhars (1), yadavs (2), sonars (1), and telis (2); only four of them were literate up to Class eighth.

The younger women did not disclose much due to fear or shyness in spite of continuous probing. The older women freely disclosed all types of illnesses. It was also found that women who are literate have more knowledge about illnesses, their symptoms, and causes as compared to those who are illiterate.

TABLE 12.6
Free Listing of Illnesses

S. No.	Illness	Frequency	Symptoms	Causes
1.	Fever	16	Shivering, rise in body temperature, headache, dizziness, vomiting, laziness, diarrhoea, cough, rashes, reddish eye, pain in body	Mosquito bite, exposure to sun, dirt, wrong bathing hours, hot/cold, do not know
2.	Cholera	12	Vomiting, diarrhoea, indigestion, weakness, excess thirst, dysentry, excess sweating, feverishness	Stale food, contaminated water, dehydration, overeating, food poisoning, indigestion, do not know
3.	Cancer	8	Boil is palpable, delayed healing of wound, yellowish skin, boil in stomach, blood becomes water, loss of appetite, weakness, pain	Some infections, do not know
4.	Jaundice	7	Continuous fever, yellowish colour, weakness, pain in body, loss of appetite, drowsiness	Contaminated water, eating excess sweets, deficiency of blood, excess spices
5.	Irregular menses	7	Menses irregular, headache, pain, weakness, loss of appetite, vomiting, excess bleeding, swelling in uterus	Deficiency, excess blood, deformity in uterus, do not know
6.	Gastric/ Indigestion	7	Pain in joints, pain in stomach, gas, headache, fear, uneasiness, swelling, diarrhoea	Abortion, excess fat, lifting of heavy load, swelling of veins, oily food, spices, do not know
7.	Heart problem	7	Pain in chest, uneasiness, heart beats fast, blood from gums, excess sweat, anxiety, swelling of veins	Worry, tension, unbalanced diet, excess fat, shock
8.	Pneumonia	6	Rise in body temperature, faster breath, dryness on face, dry veins, vomiting, contortion of limbs	Excessive bath, hot/cold, high body temperature, excess heat, improper feeding practices
9.	Polio	6	Limbs become dumb, fever prolonged	Wrong medication, do not know
10.	Respiratory problem	6	Faster breath, cough, feverish, weakness, laziness, loss of energy	Weakness, pressure of work, hot/cold
11.	Tuberculosis	6	Infection in lungs, dryness, blood in cough	Infection, do not know
12.	Cold/Cough	6	Running nose, cough, sneezing, feverish, body ache	Excess bath
13.	Vomiting	4	Diarrhoea	Overeating
14.	Rabies	3	Barking of patient, pain, madness, possible death	Dog bite, flow of poison in blood
15.	Rheumatic pain	5	Insomnia, pain in joints, difficult movements, laziness, exhaustion	Weakness, hereditary, post-caesarian effect

(Contd.)

TABLE 12.6 (contd.)

Free Listing of Illnesses

S. No.	Illness	Frequency	Symptoms	Causes
16.	Rashes	4	Uneasiness	Do not know
17.	Stomach ache	2	Pain in stomach, movement of baby felt in the womb.	Gas formation, possible tumour
18.	Headache	2	Ache in forehead and eyes, dizziness, drowsiness	Excess exposure to sun, worry, anxiety, weakness, pressure of work
19.	Diarrhoea	2	Vomiting, diarrhoea, stomach pain, contaminated feeding, dehydration	Contaminated water, excess spices
20.	Backache/Body-ache	2	Pain in joints and waist, exhaustion	After delivery, after operation, worry
21.	Abortion	2	Excess bleeding, weakness, excessive tiredness	Do not know
22.	Worms	2	Yellowish eye, dizziness, dryness	Mud, contaminated water
23.	Diarrhoea	2	Excess motions, body pain, stomach ache	Spicy food, overeating
24.	Filaria	2	Swelling and pain in legs, reddish legs	Do not know
25.	Diabetes	2	Loss of appetite, difficulty in urination, yellowish urine	Excess sugar
26.	Plague	2	Swelling, pox	Mice
27.	Sterilization	1	Giddiness, laziness, loss of appetite	Family planning operation
28.	White discharge	1	Whitish discharge, weakness	Do not know
29.	Dysentry	1	Continuous motions	Stale food, contaminated water, flies
30.	Piles	1	Boil at a particular place	Spicy food and hot items
31.	Rashes (Chicken pox)	1	Reddish dots all over the body	Infection, supernatural
32.	Abnormal delivery	1	Too much pain, difficult oozing of the matter.	Narrow passage
33.	Anaerobic	1	Weakness, headache, deficiency of blood, pain in stomach	Mud, hereditary
34.	Premature delivery	1	Yellowing, dry and underweight body	Tuberculosis
35.	Still birth	1	No movement of the baby inside the womb	Deficiency of nutritious food
36.	Paralysis		A portion of the body becomes still	No proper circulation of blood, smoking, drinking
37.	Miscarriage	1	No movement of baby inside the womb	Spicy food, excess heat inside the womb
38.	Reddening of scalp	1	Reddish spots under hair	Do not know

(Contd.)

TABLE 12.6 (contd.)
Free Listing of Illnesses

S. No.	Illness	Frequency	Symptoms	Causes
39.	Eye disorder	1	Excess exposure to sunlight, hot/cold	Swelling of eyes, excess flow of matter
40.	Snake bite	1	Weakness, dizziness, bitter marks	Snake bite
41.	Mental disorder	1	Adamant, vulgar talk or giddiness	Weakness of mind, anger, ghost
42.	Leprosy	1	Whitening of skin, deformation of limbs	On its own, do not know
43.	Goitre	1	Swelling in neck	Do not know
44.	Blood pressure (BP)	1	Headache, pain in eyes, dizziness, weakness, swelling of body	Worry
45.	Tetanus	1	Wound	Open wound, flies sit over it
46.	Dryness	1	Discomfort, pain in eyes, steady gaze	Do not know
47.	Skin disorder	1	Whitish patches and spots	Infection
48.	Infertility	1	Childless	Defect in the reproductive organ.